A First Language

A First Language   *The Early Stages*

Roger Brown

Harvard University Press   Cambridge, Massachusetts

© Copyright 1973 by the President and Fellows of Harvard College
All rights reserved
Fifth Printing, 1976
Library of Congress Catalog Card Number 72–95455
ISBN 0–674–30325–3 (cloth)
ISBN 0–674–30326–1 (paper)
Printed in the United States of America

This book is affectionately dedicated to Esther Sorocka

Preface

A difficulty with writing a book using research, like this one, is that it consumes time; and research activity (happily, if you take the long view) does not wait upon the completion of one's book. If you are ever to finish at all you have to pick a date when the evidence will be arbitrarily considered all "in" and the date you pick must necessarily be well in advance of the ultimate date of publication. The greater the research vitality of the field the greater the risk that your work will be, in some respects, "out of date" by the time it appears in print. That risk is presently rather large in the study of first-language development. I think it important, therefore, to give the chronology of the writing of the several parts of this work so that readers may keep track of the evidence that could have been taken into account and the evidence that could not have been taken into account.

A draft of Stage I was written first in the summer and fall of 1969. Of the work available to me then, several were of particular importance in shaping the overall direction of the argument: Lois Bloom's thesis not yet published as a book; I. M. Schlesinger's paper taking a semantic approach to early speech in a pre-publication draft; the not-yet-published reports by Beatrice and Allen Gardner of their success in teaching something of the American Sign Language to the chimpanzee Washoe; the (1968) article by Charles Fillmore on case grammar, and Melissa Bowerman's thesis data on the acquisition of Finnish together with her working-paper critique of pivot grammar. These works, in conjunction, persuaded me that taking account of semantics as well as grammar, the approach to data I have called the method of rich interpretation, was the fruitful line to pursue with child speech. By the summer of 1971 much new data was available on Stage I, especially the naturalistic studies of languages unrelated to English coming mostly from Berkeley and largely inspired by Dan Slobin, but also experimental data by Gleitman, Shipley, and Alloway, Peter and Jill de Villiers, and others. These later developments broadened the scope of generalizations one could make about the constructional meanings expressed in Stage I and considerably complicated what it was necessary to say about word order as the first syntactic device. I felt it necessary in the summer of 1971 to write a quite thorough-going revision of Stage I. I did not, for sheer limitations of time and vitality, update my descriptions of case grammar and other strictly linguistic research for which I apologize.

In the summer of 1971 I also wrote the Introduction to the book which attempts an overview of English grammar and the meanings encoded by grammar together with a very inexpert comparison with Japanese. This led rather naturally to a discussion of my views, as of that summer, as to whether the two "linguistic" chimps, the Gardners' Washoe and David Premack's Sarah, might reasonably be said to have acquired the essentials of language. The Introduction closes with a description of our own longitudinal research project involving the children Adam, Eve, and Sarah, a description that is really propaedeutic to Stage I and Stage II.

Stage II was originally written in the spring and summer of 1970. New research relevant to this stage has not since accumulated in great quantity, largely because most new investigations are still concerned with Stage I. Consequently I undertook in December of 1971 and January of 1972 only minor revisions of Stage II. The chapter of Conclusions was written at the same time, and the book essentially completed in this period.

I hope I have made all my intellectual debts clear by citation throughout the book, but there are a few people whose help seems to me to go well beyond that of the ordinary citation. I think, in particular, of Ursula Bellugi (now Bellugi-Klima), Colin Fraser, and Courtney Cazden who were with the project from the start, collected the data, and did the transcriptions for, respectively, Adam, Eve, and Sarah. The regularities that appear in these data owe much to the great care they exercised in their work, and the ideas about these regularities owe much to their thinking. I think, also, of researchers who have done dissertations directly using our longitudinal data or on problems related to these data: Jean Berko (now Berko-Gleason) did her famous experiments on morphology even before the longitudinal project started; Ursula Bellugi-Klima exhaustively analyzed the development of negation; Courtney Cazden did the only controlled experiment I know on the interpolation of "expansions," and her later work on inflections forms an important part of the Stage II data; Richard Cromer did a path-breaking study of semantic development, the evolution of time concepts; Melissa Bowerman did a deeply searching study of the acquisition of Finnish with comparisons to other languages; Donald Olivier did a brilliant computer-simulation study of the problem of segmentation learning; Michael Maratsos made a study, full of highly ingenious experimental methods, of the child's understanding and use of definite and nondefinite articles. I am grateful to them all and proud to have been associated with them.

Many other young scientists were in contact with our work in its early stages and have gone on to become major contributors to the field. I think particularly of David McNeill and Dan Slobin. In Stage I, I seem to disagree with McNeill more than with anyone else but that certainly does not mean that I am unappreciative of his great talents and of the interest he has brought to developmental psycholinguistics (which he, incidentally, christened as such) by his ability to conceive of bold and fascinating generalizations. Dan Slobin, by initiating with such Berkeley colleagues as Susan Ervin-Tripp and John Gumperz, the field study of exotic languages has to my mind enormously increased the power and interest of our work.

Among linguists I am obviously much in debt to Noam Chomsky for his brilliant descriptions of English structure. This is a rather embarrassing debt since I believe he would say now, as he has said in the past, that there is little chance of learning anything of significance from the mere "flux" of language performance. I, obviously, think he is wrong about this and am, personally, much more interested in the data of performance than I am in speculation about not very well specified innate language acquisition devices. Among younger linguists William Labov shares my interest in performance, and my many citations to his work make evident the considerable intellectual debt I owe to his published works. In addition, he did the enormously generous thing of reading both Stage I and Stage II, and writing to me two long letters of detailed comment. I have used and acknowledged many of these comments but, obviously, Mr. Labov is not accountable for my selective reactions and understandings. I am also grateful to Mr. Michael Maratsos for giving me written comments on both Stage I and Stage II and to Mr. I. M. Schlesinger for doing the same for Stage I. In all cases these gentlemen read the first drafts of the stages rather than the revision published here. Charles Fillmore, intending no contribution to child language, in his initial (1968) paper on case grammar considerably influenced my thinking. His own thinking has gone on evolving, and I can only plead limitations of time for not pursuing it through its later evolution. Edward Klima, among transformational linguists, has been more patient than anyone else in explaining things to me and has shown more interest than anyone else in the evidence of child speech.

The discussion of Japanese in the Introduction is practically guaranteed to include some foolish statements on my part since even my book-derived knowledge of the language is slight. I did ask Glen Baxter and Aki Shimizu of the Harvard Yenching Institute to look only at my transliterated Japanese sentences and point out the more horrendous mistakes. They were so kind as to do so. I did not feel that I could ask them to review the general remarks in the text about the Japanese language.

The research reported in this book done by myself, my associates, and my students has been largely supported by Public Health Service Research Grants MH-7088 (The Child's Acquisition of Grammar) from the National Institute of Mental Health in the years 1962–1966 and by Grant 5 R01 HD02908 (Studies of Linguistic Control in Childhood) from the National Institute of Child Health and Human Development in 1967–1972. My gratitude for the generosity and flexibility with which these grants have been administered is great. Esther Sorocka has been executive secretary to the project from the start, and no one has made a greater contribution to it. Unless, of course, it is Adam, Eve, and Sarah themselves and their ever-gracious, ever-welcoming parents.

Having been a psychologist for about 20 years I have lived through a number of promising and lively research traditions. Sadly enough many of these have left no important trace in the form of new knowledge. Developmental psycholinguistics is today a lively and promising research field. It is my deepest wish for it that it will leave behind a clear increment to psychological knowledge.

Contents

Tables

Figures

I hafta pee-pee just to pass the time away.

—Eve

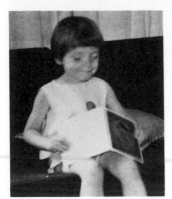

Eve

Adam

Sarah

An Unbuttoned Introduction

Unbuttoned, only in the rather limited sense that I will eschew all formal linguistic notation. I must do so because I want to attempt something quite audacious, a kind of overview, or general plan, of the design of English with respect to sentence construction and the meanings carried by constructions. This overview is in five parts ordered in what I believe to be the order of development in children of the knowledge in question and corresponding to Stages I through V which are the chapter headings of this volume (I and II) and its planned successor (III, IV, and V). This overview of the design of a language in developmental order may apply not only to English but, allowing for differences of detail, to all languages. The description is indebted to a great many linguists but it is not fully consistent with the views of any of them, and it is so informal as to outrage the loosest of them.

This is a work about sentence construction and sentence understanding, and that is certainly not all there is to the acquisition of a first language; it completely excludes pronunciation and the growth of vocabulary. The five aspects to be described do not even exhaust processes of sentence construction. What they are is a set of major processes, existing in every language I have ever read about and accounting for much of the power that language brings to our species. They are, furthermore, processes whose development in childhood it has proved possible to chart with some success.

Why begin with a loose characterization of kinds of knowledge that will later be characterized more exactly and with qualifications that are needed? Partly because we are here dealing with grammar, and for that subject a certain amount of consciousness-raising is necessary. Among the problems of psychology, grammar belongs with perception rather than with the likes of aggression-control or attitude-change, simply because the first two are only problems occasionally and for some people, whereas the latter two evidently are often-occurring problems for everyone. Grammar and perception work just fine most of the time for most people whereas aggression-control and attitude-change are not processes we are very good at.

Of course linguistic processes, in general, tend to be invisible. The mind's eye seeks the meaning and notices the medium as little as the physical eye notices its own aqueous humor. This work is concerned with the meanings of construction forms as well as with the linguistic means for expressing these meanings. One might expect consciousness-raising to be a necessary preliminary only for the mechanisms and not for the meanings, but I think that is not quite right. Construction meanings are more often out of awareness than are the meanings of content words. They are furthermore generally subtle and, though ubiquitous, hard to characterize in explicit terms.

Still there is no doubt that the means of expression — grammar — is more difficult to see than the meanings expressed. For that reason I will set down not only English examples of grammatical forms but also examples from Japanese, a historically independent language (except for the lexical borrowings of recent years) which, in instance after instance, uses some means of expression quite different from the English. When all examples are given in a single language, and that one the familiar native language, it is particularly difficult to separate sense from form. Even setting aside the elaborate stylistic variation in Japanese (Inoue, 1969, says that there are four distinct styles), we shall still expose ourselves to countless differences of both form and meaning. And yet I think that you will end by feeling as I do, that the two are obviously species of a single genus, their variation almost trifling by comparison with their enormous common denominator as languages. Which does not mean that it should be easy for us to speak Japanese, something I cannot do at all.

Following our survey of the five aspects of construction we will briefly review the accomplishments of two chimpanzees, Washoe and Sarah, who have, in recent years, accomplished more in a linguistic way than any nonhuman primate before them. With the overview behind us we will not, I think, feel disposed to say that even these chimpanzees have mastered language.

I do not deceive myself into thinking that any effort at consciousness-raising will make grammar interesting to everyone nor even to very many. It is an odd interest, dependent, I suspect, on some rather kinky gene which, fortunately for our species, is not very widely distributed in the population.

The five aspects of sentence construction correspond with the five stages that comprise the body of this book and its projected companion. Toward the end of the Introduction we shall have a description of the longitudinal research project, our study of the preschool years of three children, Adam, Eve, and Sarah, which comprises the core empirical work in the books. We shall have, in addition, a description of the strategies of exposition used in the writing of the stages and the efforts that have been made to utilize data beyond our own.

The Introduction to my book, *Words and Things* (1958), begins: "A child of eleven or twelve, who some years before had been seen completely naked in the Caune Woods seeking acorns and roots to eat, was met in the same place toward the end of September 1797 by three sportsmen who seized him as he was climbing a tree to escape from their pursuit." This is the opening sentence of the first report of Dr. Jean-Marc-Gaspard Itard on his efforts to teach a first language to the Wild Boy of Aveyron, a report that has recently served as the basis for a beautiful film by François Truffaut with the title "The Wild Child." Dr. Itard's efforts are fascinating because he attempted by means of fully deliberate training procedures to accomplish a small part of what almost every child seems effortlessly to accomplish in his preschool years. This is an accomplishment so astounding that one naturally looks everywhere for some insight into its operation. For *Words and Things* I studied Dr. Itard's reports. For the present work I did something rather more quixotic. I enrolled one summer in a Berlitz "total immersion" course in Japanese, a language of which I knew nothing at all.

The Berlitz total immersion experience has a few things in common with the experience of the preschool child learning a first language. In the first place you work at it most of your waking hours from 8:30 A.M. until about 5:00 P.M. In the second place it is entirely in the one-to-one conversational mode; no words are ever written down. This means, among other things, that you must recognize words by sound only and find word boundaries and stems (the segmentation problem) without the aid of the spacing that print provides. In the third place, of course, the Berlitz method makes no use of the native language but is entirely carried on in the new language. My skilled and charming teacher began with the words: "How do you do? That's the last English we will use." And it was, for this teacher. However, later on I had a less experienced teacher who, wanting to demonstrate creditable progress for the Berlitz supervisor roaming the halls, would sometimes ask me questions in loud Japanese and then prompt my answers with whispered English translations.

Working only in the new language can be a great strain on both teacher and student. Sometimes I think it really does lead to experiences akin to those of the preliterate child but often, surely not. After the first lesson in which various things on a desk were named, I realized that I did not know whether *hon,* for instance, meant *book* or *pad* or *magazine* or even *cover*, since the constrasts that would separate out *book* as the intended meaning had not been used. And of course children have that problem of isolating the defining (though generally not explicitly known or expressible) properties of referents.

In addition, one makes errors of segmentation like those children sometimes make. Hearing again and again the question *Kore wa nan desu ka?* (What is this?) but never seeing it printed I conceived of *korewa* as a single word; it is spoken without pause. Some lessons later I learned that *wa* is a particle, an unchanging uninflected form, that marks the noun it follows as the topic of the sentence. Interestingly enough I did not, at once, reanalyze my word *korewa* and such others as *sorewa* and *arewa* into noun and particle forms. I did not do that until I started to hear such object forms as *kore o* and *sore o* and *are o* in which *o* marks the direct object. Then the truth dawned on me, and the words almost audibly cracked into *kore, sore,* and *are,* three demonstratives which took *wa* in the nominative form and *o* in the objective. How beautifully consistent! Children learning English as their native language also sometimes mistake often repeated forms like *What's this?* or *it's* or *Put it* for single words. We shall see in the latter part of Stage II what it is in their speech that makes their segmentation errors discoverable by us.

But the insistence on avoiding the first language sometimes seems to lead to a great waste of time and to problems children, for some reason, seem not to have. One long morning my teacher tried to put across three verbs, *kimasu, yukimasu,* and *kaerimasu,* with the aid of paper and pencil drawings of pathways and persons and loci, and by much moving of herself and of me — uncomprehendingly passive as a patient in a hospital. But I could not grasp the concepts. I feel Mr. Berlitz would have suffered no great dishonor if she had said to me that the concepts in question sometimes go by the names *come, go,* and *return*.

For one golden week I had the same skilled and lovely teacher, and we progressed apace with much positive transference on my part. Then Berlitz started switching its schedules, and I had some lessons with two new teachers. It was a most painful weaning. I forgot words, I stuttered, my appetite fell off. When I think about it afterwards I believe the primary problem was that my first teacher had perfect knowledge of what I knew and did not know, and so her language drills moved by small steps introducing only one new thing at any given time. And so I seldom failed. My new teachers, not having the same knowledge of where I was at, at a given point, often introduced too many things at once, and whole sentences would be incomprehensible to me.

I am sorry to admit it but my performance with the new teachers was a better predictor of my ultimate performance in the real world than was the highly accomplished rattling off of everything up to the counterfactual conditional that I managed with my first teacher. On the day I finished my course (two weeks was all I allotted) I was met outside the Berlitz door by a Japanese friend. He, thinking to give me as an easy start, asked in Japanese: "Where is your car?" I was completely floored and could make nothing of the sentence except that it called for a reply. I realized then that my peak accomplishments had been narrowly adapted to a drill procedure in which almost all of a sentence was so well practiced as not to need to be processed deeply at all, leaving all my attention free to focus on some single new element and get that right. A sentence, however simple, drawn from the total construction potential of a language is a very different thing from the same sentence well prepared for by a pyramid of practice.

All this is so you will know that, with respect to Japanese, I am a Wild Boy still, and the notes I will make about Japanese grammar are drawn from books (Inoue, 1969; Jorden, 1963; Niwa and Miyako, 1969; Shirato, 1962; Yamagiwa, 1942) and likely to be wrong in some detail or other since the books never capture all that the accomplished speaker knows, and this reader never captures all the author meant. Inoue (1969) has attempted an explicit transformational grammar of a substantial portion of Japanese, and her work has been especially valuable to me. It is necessary to note, however, that she derives the more polite and respectful styles in Japanese by transformation from strings underlying the "standard familiar style." Most of the other books give sentence examples (in one or another form of romanized spelling, of course) in the polite style used between strangers, and so Inoue's examples differ stylistically from the others.

Five Aspects of Sentence Construction

As I have said the five aspects of construction described here correspond with the principal topics of Stages I–V. What is later described fully and formally is here only illustrated and in an informal way.

Relations or Roles within the Simple Sentence

Consider this sentence: *Mr. Smith cut the rope with a knife.* It includes three noun phrases: *Mr. Smith; the rope;* and *a knife.* These three noun phrases have distinct semantic roles in the sentence or one might say distinct semantic relations with the verb *cut.* Mr. Smith causes or performs the action, a role I will here call "agent." A knife plays a part in the action; it is used by the agent and so plays a role I will call "instrument." The rope, finally, is that object which suffers a change of state as a result of the action taken, a role I will here call "patient."

It is most important to distinguish agent, patient, and instrument and the other intrasentence roles I will characterize from two grammatical notions with which they are easily confused. Agent, patient, and instrument are semantic notions and have been so defined. They are all of them noun phrases which is a certain kind of major category or unit in a sentence. A unit must be a noun or noun phrase in order to function in the roles or relations we are describing, but the role played by the particular noun phrase varies with the particular sentence. In other sentences *Mr. Smith* might play such other roles as patient *(They drowned Mr. Smith),* experiencer *(Mr. Smith wanted a drink),* or beneficiary *(Mr. Smith owns a Rolls-Royce).* The possibilities for *the rope* and *a knife* are less general but certainly the former can be an instrument *(They hanged him with a rope)* and the latter a patient *(He broke the knife).*

The categorical unit called noun phrase is less likely to be confused with semantic relations than are such *grammatical* relations as subject and direct object. This is because the latter are themselves relational or configurational concepts, and they are major syntactic means of *expressing* the semantic relations. Less abstract than subject and object, though related to them in English, are the simple linear positions of the noun phrases in question. Expressed in relation to the verb we can say that these are, in the sentence *Mr. Smith cut the rope with a knife,* respectively: preverbal *(Mr. Smith)*; immediately postverbal *(the rope)*; and second postverbal *(with a knife).*

The difference in degree of abstraction between a notion like subject and surface linear order may be best illustrated by introducing the passive-voice approximate paraphrase of our sentence. It is: *The rope was cut by Mr. Smith with a knife. The rope* and *Mr. Smith* have interchanged surface positions but remain, respectively, object and subject in what Noam Chomsky (1965) calls the "deep structure" of the sentence. A syntactic subject is defined by Chomsky in configurational terms as the noun phrase directly dominated by the symbol "sentence" and the direct object as the noun phrase dominated by the node labeled "verb phrase." By these definitions *Mr. Smith* is the deep subject of the sentence and *the rope* object in both the active and passive voice even though their linear positions change in the surface sentence.

Linear position is a major syntactic aspect of English often signaling the semantic role of a noun phrase. It seems, furthermore, to be the first aspect of syntax to which children are sensitive. While linear position is closely related to syntactic relations like subject and object it should be recognized that these latter more abstract notions need not necessarily be invoked until the variety of sentence forms reaches a level that justifies them.

Several writers have recently attempted to define the semantics of the basic sentence relations: Schlesinger (1971) among psychologists; Fillmore (1968) and Chafe (1970) among linguists. There are certain differences of opinion among them, and none claims to have identified the correct and full list of semantic roles noun phrases may play. In Table 1 I have made a list of major types, definitions, and examples; a list that is closer to the treatment of Chafe than of any of the other authors largely because I have read him most recently.

Table 1.   Some semantic roles played by noun phrases in simple sentences

Role	Definition	Examples
Agent	Someone or something which causes or instigates an action or process. Usually animate but not always, an agent must be perceived to have its own motivating force.	*Harriet* sang. *The men* laughed. *The wind* ripped the curtains.
Patient	Someone or something either in a given state or suffering a change of state.	*The wood* is dry. He cut *the wood*.
Experiencer	Someone having a given experience or mental disposition.	*Tom* saw the snake. *Tom* wanted a drink.
Beneficiary	Someone who profits from a state or process, including possession.	*Mary* has a convertible. This is *Mary's* car. Tom bought *Mary* a car.
Instrument	Something that plays a role in bringing about a process or action but which is not the instigator; it is used by an agent.	Tom opened the door with *a key*. Tom used *his knife* to open the box.
Location	The place or locus of a state, action, or process.	The spoon is in *the drawer*. Tom sat in *the chair*.
Complement	The verb names an action that brings something into existence. The complement, on a more or less specific level, completes the verb. This use of the word "complement" is not, incidentally, its most common use in linguistics.	Mary sang *a song*. John played *checkers*.

Source: Adapted from Chafe, 1970.

The noun phrases which play the roles of Table 1 are ultimately simple when they are single nouns. In fact, however, noun phrases of any degree of complexity may play these roles, and the whole noun phrases themselves may contain other noun phrases in one role or another. In fact, as is well known, many linguists hold that the list of possible sentences of a language is infinitely long just because the phrase structure rule rewriting noun phrase is a recursive rule which rewrites the noun phrase symbol as a determiner and a noun together with, optionally, a sentence.

Let me illustrate the kind of complexity that is possible. The sentence in Table 1: *Tom sat in the chair* might be *Tom sat in Mary's chair.* In this latter case the noun phrase *Mary's chair* functions as a whole, as a location but it is made up of a beneficiary *(Mary)* and a patient *(chair).* The first unfoldings of maximally simple roles into roles having internal role structure is one of the most fascinating developments of Stage I speech. Let us have a more extreme example, very far beyond Stage I competence. The entire sentence, *Mr. Smith cut the rope with a knife,* becomes a nominalization in: *That Mr. Smith cut the rope with a knife surprised John.* In this case the nominalization, which has an internal structure involving an agent, patient, and instrument, functions as a patient with John as experiencer. We shall return to these complicated forms when we discuss the embedding of one simple sentence within another.

How might our sample sentence about Mr. Smith be expressed in Japanese? The most ordinary form would be: *Sumisu-san wa nao o naifu de kirimashita.* Of course the spelling is romanized, and the words *Sumisu* and *naifu* do not result from a remarkable independent convergence of English and Japanese but are rather English words assimilated to the Japanese syllabic system; there are now very many such in Japanese. The Japanese sentence, like the English, has three nouns playing three semantic roles: *Sumisu* is *Smith* the agent; *nao* is *rope* the patient; *nafu* is knife the instrument. The suffix *-san* is a respectful address form something like *Mr.,* and *kirimashita* is a polite past tense form of *cut.*

The first point of interest is the difference of linear order among the noun phrases. In English we have subject-verb-object-prepositional phrase or agent-action-patient-instrument. In Japanese we have subject-object-instrument-verb or, semantically, agent-patient-instrument-action. The order subject-object-verb is simply the most usual in Japanese. Other possibilities exist and are used, as we shall see, for expressive purposes. English is much more rigid about linear order, and order is a more reliable index of semantic role than it is in Japanese. One thing I remember most clearly about my Japanese lessons is that the switch from English subject-verb-object order to Japanese subject-object-verb order caused me no trouble at all. I venture to say that I almost never made a mistake in this dimension. There is, I suspect, something very simple and automatic for human beings about the linearization of speech units. The results of Stage I suggest as much. This might not apply to orders seldom or never found in languages

(Greenberg, 1963) such as one placing the object before the subject.

We have three words left over in our Japanese sentence, and they are the interesting ones: *wa, o,* and *de.* All these are unchanging uninflected words called particles or postpositions, of which Japanese makes lavish use. Their use is not limited to the marking of semantic relations (they are also used to mark interrogation, conjunction, and so on), but they are primarily used for the intrasentence relations. As markers of semantic relations they follow the noun phrase they mark, and they are more reliable markers of such relations in Japanese than is linear order, precisely because order is often varied for expressive purposes.

The particle *wa* which follows *Sumisu-san* is usually said to mark the grammatical "topic" of a sentence and to be best translated by the words "as for." The topic of a sentence might be an agent, an experiencer, a patient, even a location. The particle marking the grammatical subject is usually said to be *ga.* In fact *wa* and *ga* contrast with one another as grammatical subjects in a very complex way. When the subject is already known, already a topic of conversation, what Chafe calls "old information" *wa* is likely to be used. For "new information," for information of special interest *ga* is used. For example, in answering the Japanese equivalent of a *who* or *what* question one would always use *ga* to mark the subject because the question asks for specification of just that constituent of the sentence, the subject. Where a speaker of English would place emphatic stress and pitch on a subject to indicate that it was *Sumisu-san,* who cut the rope and not *Tanaka-san,* the Japanese would mark the agent with *ga* rather than with *wa.* As Inoue (1969) shows, however, there is much more than semantic emphasis to the contrast between *wa* and *ga.*

The particle *o* following *nao* or *rope* marks what is grammatically the object and semantically the patient. The particle *de* marks in our sentence what is semantically the instrument. This is not the only use of *de* which has also a location function as in *I bought it in Kyoto: Kyōto de kaimashita.*

The Japanese sentence we have looked at is not the only one that might be used as an approximate equivalent of *Mr. Smith cut the rope with a knife.* If we wanted to give special emphasis to the patient *rope* we would say: *Nao o naifu de Sumisu-san ga kirimashita* (patient-instrument-agent). If we wanted to emphasize the instrument we might say: *Naifu de nao o Sumisu-san ga kirimashita* (instrument-patient-agent). The shift for the agent from *wa* to *ga* results in these cases from a special order rule rather than a matter of emphasis. What should be apparent from these examples, and this is the only important point, is that the particles *wa* or *ga, o,* and *de* are more reliable or trustworthy indicators of semantic role than is linear order in Japanese. In English, linear order is a much more reliable cue to semantic role though prepositions (by contrast with Japanese postpositions) like *by* (passive-voice subject) and *with* (for instrument and other roles) are also important cues or signals of semantic role.

There are other particles in Japanese that mark semantic roles. Thus *Tanaka-san no hon* means roughly *Mr. Tanaka's book.* The particle *no* marks possessives but has also other functions which overlap with those of the genitive generally in English. Thus *Amerika no tabako* means *American cigarettes* and *ashita no shimbun* means *tomorrow's newspapers.*

The particle *ni* is often used as a location marker roughly equivalent to *in* or *on.* There are other location particles resembling in semantic such English prepositions as *from, to,* and so on. The particles *wa* and *ga* generally mark the topic or subject, we have seen, and the Japanese subject, like the English subject, may play such roles as agent, patient, experiencer, and beneficiary. Which role the subject is in may normally be learned from the meaning of the particular verb. In Japanese, as in English, the noun phrase may expand into a structure having any amount of internal role complexity. One might, for instance say, not only, *hon ni (in the book)* but *watakushi no hon ni (in my book).*

In summary, one kind of meaning that languages express is that of the semantic role of the noun phrase which may, alternatively, be described as the semantic relation between a noun phrase and a verb. We shall see, in Stage I, that it is quite uncertain which semantic relations have psychologically functional reality. How finely roles ought to be defined is unsettled; ultimately each role is a little different depending on the verb involved. That truth does not obscure the fact that a limited set of general roles such as those set down in Table 1 seems to occur in all known languages.

Comparing unrelated languages we can see differences in the grammatical devices used to express semantic relations. Japanese relies heavily on postpositions or particles; English relies heavily on linear order and on prepositions. Having said that, it is necessary to point out that there are a number of tidy propositions that are simply not true. It is not the case, within one language, that each general semantic relation stands in a distinct one-to-one relation with some particular expressive device. It is not the case that a particular class of expressive device (for example, particles in Japanese) is used only and always to express semantic relations. Comparing languages it is not the case that semantically related expressive devices (for example, *ni* in Japanese and *in* in English) bundle together just the same set of semantic distinctions. I sometimes regret this untidiness, as a student of language seeking order, but remind myself that languages were not designed by anyone but are, rather, products of extended biological and cultural evolution. What we may be sure of is that they are as tidy as they need to be to serve the purposes of human communication.

Modulations of Meaning within the Simple Sentence

In English modulations of meaning are such as the inflection of the noun for plural number and of the verb for tense and aspect; the provision of the copula *be* and of definite and nondefinite articles to mark a referent as specific or nonspecific

and of particular prepositions like *in* and *on* to further specify locations
suggested by word order alone. In Stage II there is an extended discussion of the
differences between basic semantic relations and modulations of meaning.
The terms "basic" and "modulations" suggest, of course, that the latter is somehow
less fundamental than the former, almost a kind of "trimming." While the
Stage II discussion considers many possible justifications for this distinction there
is one that, though rough, seems more fundamental than any other. One easily
conceives of meanings for naming words (nouns, verbs, and adjectives) in the
absence of any modulation but one does not easily conceive of number, past tense,
progressive aspect, referent specificity, and the like, in abstraction from any
thing, person, action, state, or quality.

The modulations studied in Stage II are not an exhaustive list for English.
One might, for instance, have included auxiliary verbs like *can* and *must,* and
semi-auxiliaries like *wanna* and *gonna,* since these are inconceivable except
in connection with some main verb naming a state, process, or action. The selection
was not arbitrarily made but was restricted by a criterion of acquisition to be
discussed in Stage II. In brief we could only select forms for which it is possible
to identify contexts in which the form is obligatory. We wanted to use, as a criterion,
occurrence in 90 percent or better of obligatory contexts in six consecutive
sampling hours. As it turned out the 14 morphemes modulating meaning that we
were able to study in English are all phonetically minimal forms; monosyllables
or less and almost never receive heavy stress. The expressive devices used in other
languages for modulating meanings need not have this surface property. One
property we suspect they will have, however, is membership in small morpheme
classes which do not readily admit new members — unlike noun, verb, and
adjective classes. One property that our grammatical morphemes expressing
modulations of meaning *may* have also in other languages is a slow relatively
long-drawn out development requiring even several years to reach criterion. From
Stage I they are almost entirely missing; in Stage II they begin, but even by Stage V
some have not reached criterion. There are a number of possible reasons for this.
The modulations are, in some intuitive sense, less essential than basic names
and relations. In English at least the forms of expression in most cases vary with
phonetic and grammatical properties of other words; they exist in multiple
linguistically contingent forms (allomorphs).

The problem of commensurability between languages is tremendous for the
modulations, and it is a problem we have only begun to explore. Ultimately
the differences may be of great value for identifying the determinants of acquisition,
but that remains to be determined.

I am not able to make a point-for-point comparison between English and
Japanese but we can sample the kinds of differences for which developmental
psycholinguists must be prepared. Plural number is not expressed on Japanese
nouns: *hon* may equally well be *book* or *books.* Indeed, except in a very few

circumstances, plurality is not expressed at all. Articles, definite or nondefinite, simply do not exist in Japanese. Their utilization in English is so delicate a matter that one rarely finds them used quite correctly by a Japanese who has learned English as an adult. In Stage II a hypothesis is put forward in explanation of the Japanese ability to manage very nicely without the recurrent expression of specificity and nonspecificity of reference.

The modulating concepts themselves must not be expected to be identical from language to language. Where English has one main copula, the several allomorphs of *be,* Japanese has three morphemes and three meanings. There is an equational denotative copula as when one says *Hon desu (It is a book).* There is a copula that signals *existence* in some location and, when the object is inanimate, that copula is *arimasu;* thus *Soko ni hon ga arimasu* says *There is a book there.* Existence of an animate being is expressed with still another copula *imasu;* thus *Soko ni kodomo ga imasu* says *There is a child there.*

There are similarities between the languages as well as differences. All three of the Japanese copulas are clearly distinct grammatically from main verbs, even as our copula is a form unto itself. Japanese does have a past and a future as well as a progressive and a perfective. The differences in means of expression are of course very great, the number of regular conjugations, the number of irregular forms, and the mechanisms themselves. Japanese has verb forms expressing incipient action and intentional action which remind us semantically of the English *gonna, wanna,* though the means are different. The dimensions of semantic modulation clearly vary from language to language but not in an unlimited way.

Modalities of the Simple Sentence

We have until now considered major semantic relations and modulations within a simple sentence that has been by implication also declarative and affirmative. But the remarkable and powerful fact is that all such sentences can be mapped, as wholes, into other sentence modalities, and that these others seem to be the same set in all languages: *yes-no* interrogatives; constituent interrogatives, imperatives and negatives.

Yes-No Questions

Consider the sentence we used to illustrate noun phrase roles: *Mr. Smith cut the rope with a knife.* Corresponding to this sentence is a *yes-no* interrogative that leaves all the relations and modulations intact: *Did Mr. Smith cut the rope with a knife?* To which the answer is either Yes, which assents to the proposition, or *No,* which dissents from it. From the point of view of syntactic expression this English question is a particularly complicated one. The general rule is to interchange the relative positions of sentence subject and first auxiliary verb, which is marked for tense, in mapping declaratives into interrogatives. In the present example there was no auxiliary verb in the declarative, and in this circumstance the auxiliary *do* is supplied and marked for tense as *did*. Japanese also maps this and every declarative into the *yes-no* interrogative, but by using a different syntactic means, in fact a particle *ka*. There is no permutation of order; instead *ka* is simply placed at the end of the sentence: *Sumisu-san wa nao o naifu de kirimashita ka?*

There are several variants on the usual *yes-no* question which are identical in sense in English and Japanese but vary in means of expression. Ordinarily in both languages the interrogative has a rising intonation, accompanied by final *ka* in Japanese and by a permutation of order in English. It is, in some circumstances, possible to use a declarative intonation in both languages letting the syntax express the question. In informal usage the syntactic expression may be omitted and the rising intonation alone left to carry the question: *Mr. Smith cut the rope with a knife? (Sumisu-san ga nao o naifu de kirimashita?)*

Finally there are tag questions or requests for confirmation of the declarative proposition to which they are appended. In English these are complex constructions involving negation, interrogation, and deletion; thus: *You're learning, aren't you?* or *Mr. Smith cut the rope, didn't he?* Japanese requests for confirmation are much simpler. Like *nicht wahr?* in German or *n'est-ce pas* in French, they are fixed forms not contingent on the grammar of the declarative sentence to which they are appended. In fact the simple particle *ne* at the end does the job. When the basic declarative is negative, and a negative answer is expected, English uses an affirmative tag; thus: *He doesn't understand, does he?* The Japanese way to accomplish the same purpose is similar, although the tag remains the same, thus: *Wakarimasen ne (He doesn't understand, does he?)* In fact, of course English also has some simple and uncontingent tags used occasionally by adults and exclusively by very young children: *He understands, right?*

Questions Requesting that a Constituent Be Specified

To my way of thinking this is one of the most elegant and powerful sets of rules in all languages. For English these questions have come to be called *wh-* questions because in all cases but one the critical words involved start with that pair of letters: *who, whose, what, where, when, why, how.* In effect, in English, questions of this type correspond with individual declarative sentences in which there is one unknown, or *x* element, corresponding to some major grammatical constituent. It is as if the questioner were to say: "I know all about this sentence except for one point, and on this point I should like specific information." The form of the word plus the remainder of the sentence indicate clearly what kind of point is in doubt.

Table 2 lists many, though not all the *wh-* possibilities in English. In order to illustrate so many I have had to use a rather uncommonly elaborate sentence, and so that "new boy" will make sense you might imagine the question being asked

Table 2. Questions requesting specification of a constituent

Constituent	Presumed State of Knowledge of Speaker	Question Requesting Specification of a Constituent
Subject nominal	*X* will read *Ivanhoe* slowly in the library this evening.	Who will read *Ivanhoe* slowly in the library this evening?
Object nominal	The new boy will read *X* slowly in the library this evening.	What will the new boy read slowly in the library this evening?
Predicate	The new boy will *X* slowly in the library this evening.	What will the new boy do slowly in the library this evening?
Locative adverbial	The new boy will read *Ivanhoe* slowly *X* this evening.	Where will the new boy read *Ivanhoe* slowly this evening?
Time adverbial	The new boy will read *Ivanhoe* slowly in the library *X*.	When will the new boy read *Ivanhoe* slowly in the library?
Manner adverbial	The new boy will read *Ivanhoe X* in the library this evening.	How will the new boy read *Ivanhoe* in the library this evening?
Attributive nominal	*X* boy will read *Ivanhoe* slowly in the library this evening.	Which boy will read *Ivanhoe* slowly in the library this evening?

in an English public school. The first column names the grammatical constituent of which the speaker is presumed to be ignorant. The second column places an *x* in the linear position within the declarative sentence of the constituent for which specification is requested. The third column lists the normal respective *wh-* questions. In English one usually responds to such questions with just the information requested since the rest of the sentence may be said to be understood.

In all the *wh-* questions the *wh-* word is placed first in the sentence. For subject nominals and attributive nominals that is the natural position; for all the others it is not, and there is the effect of movement to the front from the natural position of the constituent. This movement however, is only one of two changes. Except again for the subject nominal and attributive nominal you will notice that the linear positions of the sentence subject and the auxiliary have been interchanged. This interchange is, with complete generality, identical with that required for the full *yes-no* question. *Wh-* questions are not, however, spoken with rising intonation usually but with normal declarative intonation.

While the *wh-* word specifically requests a particular grammatical constituent and may be answered by that constituent alone the constituents themselves in conjunction with other words in the sentence, especially the verb, indicate what semantic role is to be specified. Thus *who* in Table 2 asks for an agent, since something is to be done by someone. The same word *who* might ask for an experiencer, as in *Who wants Ivanhoe,* or in other sentences a patient or beneficiary. The rest of the sentence together with the interrogative form makes clear the role to be specified. *What will the new boy read?* asks for a patient; *Where will he read?*

for a location; and so on. The attributive, predicate, and manner adverbial involve other matters. In considerable degree, however, we see that *wh-* questions stand in an interesting relation to the intra-sentence semantic relations which English-speaking children express in Stage I. The *wh-* form is of course a much more abstract one than any particular noun phrase, and its placement involves both movement to the beginning of the sentence (preposing) and subject-auxiliary interchange.

One would not call the Japanese words which request specification of a constituent *wh-* forms, since none of them contain those letters; *"d* questions" would be nearer the mark. For *dare* is *who,* and *doko* is *where,* and *dono* is *which; doshite* is *why, nan,* or its allomorph *nani,* is *what,* and *itsu* is *when.* The system is a fascinating variant on the one we know for English. When no subject is expressed, and that is the usual case for the Japanese, the interrogative word is preposed. Thus:

Dare desu ka?	*Who is [it]?*
Nan desu ka?	*What is [it]?*
Dare no desu ka?	*Whose is [it]?*
Doko ni imasu ka?	*Where is [it]?*
Itsu desu ka?	*When is [it]?*
Dōshite desu ka?	*Why is [it]?*
Dono hito desu ka?	*Which person is [it]?*

In all the above examples notice that there is the final interrogative *ka.* The bracketed [it] represents a form needed for adequate English translation but not actually present in the Japanese sentence. It is interesting also that, while preposing occurs as in English, there can be no interchange of subject and auxiliary since in sentences like these there is no subject. However, the interrogative particle *ka,* which is something like the functional equivalent of the interrogative interchange of English does appear.

What happens when there is some person, action, or thing of interest about which the question is asked? Most usually the interrogative form is not placed first but gives way to the topic of interest marked with the particle *wa.* Thus:

Kono hito wa dare desu ka?	*Who is this?*
Kore wa nan desu ka?	*What is this?*

In these sentences *this* is identified as topic and the question word takes second place. Likewise:

Kabuki wa dō deshita ka? How was the Kabuki?
Kabuki e wa dare to i ikimashita ka? With whom did you go to the Kabuki?

Finally here are examples from Inoue (1969) which appear as abstract strings, not pronounceable as such, underlying sentences in the standard intimate style. We have first a *yes-no* question and then a question requesting specification of a constituent.

> *Titi wa koo kak was ta ka?* (Literally, *As for father in this way wrote* [*he*]*?*)
> *Tita wa doo kak was ta ka?* (Literally, *As for father, in what way, wrote* [*he*]*?*)

The bracketed *he* has no equivalent in the Japanese sentences. The first sentence would probably be pronounced: *Chichi wa kō kaita ka?* and the second: *Chichi wa dō kaita ka?*

Yamagiwa (1942) summarizes usual word order in such cases by saying: "In an interrogative sentence the person, action, or thing about which the question is asked is placed first and followed by *wa,* the interrogative pronoun comes next, the verb or inflected suffix *(desu* or *da)* next and the particle *ka* last" (p. 41). The interrogative word then is not always preposed but may move to second position with preposing of a topic. It is not, however, interchanged with an auxiliary verb.

The particle *ka* may be replaced by rising intonation. Responses to *d* interrogatives may be whole sentences or they may be truncated though not in exactly the manner of English responses. Indefinite forms like our *something, someone, somewhere,* and *sometime,* which name noun phrase roles in a general way without requesting specification are expressed in Japanese by the elegant means of appending the particle *ka* to the respective *d* word, thus: *nani ka* is *something; dare ka, someone; doko ka, somewhere; itsu ka, sometime.*

With the system of requests for constituent specification the feeling is especially strong, I think, that the semantic or communicational need is a human constant. The means of expression, the syntax, varies between the languages but the variation is limited, and *wh-* questions and *d* questions give the impression of rule systems almost accidentally a bit askew even though there is no known historical tie between them.

Negatives

It is possible to categorize the meanings of negative sentences in any number of ways. Several authors (Bloom, 1970; McNeill and McNeill, 1968) have presented evidence that there is some order to the emergence of negative meanings in child speech and not only an order of syntactic means. (See Bellugi, in press, for a detailed treatment of the emergence of English negative syntax.) Bloom distinguishes three primary meanings: nonexistence, rejection, and denial. Nonexistence of some referent may be expressed in adult English by such forms as: *There isn't any soap* or *There is no more noise.* Such sentences are ordinarily used when a referent has recently been present or might reasonably have been expected to be present. Rejection of a referent is expressible in such sentences as *I don't want any lunch* or

No more soup, and is likely to be coupled with pushing away or turning away from a present referent. Bloom includes under this heading refusals to comply with a request or command such as are expressed in *I won't go,* but one might of course make a separate semantic category of refusal. Finally there is the negative sentence that denies the truth of some proposition: *It isn't raining out; Columbus did not land on Plymouth Rock;* and so on. In all these cases it is worth noting that negative speech is tuned to propositions which somebody or other is thought to have grounds for believing to be true. It may be oneself as when one yells from the shower where there ought to be soap, "There's no soap"; or it may be another who has asserted or given cause for us to think he believes something requiring correction as when we say, "It's not raining now." One does not negate what no one is thought to have any reason to believe at a given time.

McNeill and McNeill (1968) discussing the development of negative expression in two Japanese children make distinctions corresponding with Bloom's nonexistence, rejection, and denial, but they also find it useful to distinguish two dimensions she does not. One of these, called "internal-external," distinguishes between negations based on what might be called internal evidence (for example, *I don't want any lunch*) and negations based on external or public evidence (for example, *The lamp didn't break*). The other dimension the McNeills call "entailment-nonentailment." The idea here is that one may make a negative statement like *No, that's an apple not a pear,* which not only denies one proposition but explicitly asserts the truth of an alternative proposition. Alternatively one may simply deny the truth of one proposition *(No, that's not a pear)* without asserting the truth of any of the indefinitely numerous alternative propositions that might be true but are certainly not entailed. Clearly one can express these semantic dimensions in English as easily as in Japanese. In Stage III we will discuss the evidence that there is an order of emergence to the semantics of negation. If there is such an order it is important to make the distinctions, but obviously those mentioned here do not exhaust the semantic categories of negation that one might make and which it may ultimately prove important for the student of development to make.

The full syntax of English negation (see Klima, 1964) is extremely complex involving the interjection *no,* the indefinites *nothing* and *anything,* and so on. But the most general rule, surely, is that which maps affirmative sentences into negative counterparts by interpolating the word *not* or its contraction *n't* after the first auxiliary of the verb. This is that very same auxiliary that is interchanged in linear position with the subject to produce *yes-no* questions. And, in both cases, when there is no actual auxiliary present in the declarative affirmative form the word *do* is introduced and carries the tense of the sentence. So we have such negatives as *He isn't calling, I can't swim, I don't ski, I won't fly,* and so on.

I have found no account of the syntax of negation in Japanese comparable in scope and explicitness with that Klima has given us for English, but I suspect an account of the whole would be equally complicated. We shall say only enough here to indicate that the expressive means, while it is as systematic as English is, of course, different. Even the words *iie,* which is very close to English *no,* and *hai,* which is very close to *yes,* are not exactly the same in usage as their English counterparts. *Hai* means *What you just said is right,* and *iie* means *What you just said is wrong* but the forms are not part of polite usage. In response to affirmative questions like *Are you going?* the Japanese and English forms are equivalent; one says, in effect, *What you just said* (that you are going) *is correct,* and the other says, *It is incorrect.* But, with negative questions, the English and Japanese forms diverge. If the question is, in English, *Aren't you going?* it presupposes an affirmative answer, and *yes* means *I am going* or, in effect, *what you presuppose is correct but what you said* (that you aren't going) *is not correct.* The answer *no,* in English, agrees with what the speaker has said (that you aren't going) but disagrees with the speaker's presupposition. For negative questions Japanese responses confirm or deny what has been said, not what we English speakers presuppose. Thus *hai* in answer to *Aren't you going?* means: *What you said is correct, I am not going. Iie* means: *What you said is incorrect; I am going.* The semantic possibilities are just the same in English and Japanese, and they are divided between just two forms of response. The languages use them in the same way with affirmative questions but in opposite ways with negative questions.

The primary means of negation in Japanese, corresponding to the insertion of *not* in English, is an inflection *-masen* on the verb stem (in the polite style). If Mr. Smith, in our illustrative sentence does not cut the rope, one would say in Japanese: *Sumisu-san wa nao o naifu de kirimasen.* To make the verb past as well as negative one would say: *kirimasen deshita.* To take another example: *I don't understand* might be *Watakushi wa wakarimasen,* though the subject would usually be omitted. The copula *desu* is, as usual, a bit different; the negative is *de wa arimasen* (or such alternates as *ja arimasen* or *de arimasen*). Thus, *This isn't a book* might be: *Hon de wa arimasen.* Probably it is needless to say that there are countless complications: more than one regular verb conjugation, several levels of politeness, adjective endings peculiar to negative statements, and so on. But in general *-masen* on the verb stem is about as sure a sign of negation in Japanese as is *not* in English.

Imperatives

Katz and Postal (1964) suggest that the meaning of the imperative is, roughly, "the speaker requests (asks, demands, insists, etc.) that" (p. 76). In English the imperative is informally expressed by using no subject at all but beginning with the uninflected verbs (for example, *Pass the salt*), which may be softened with *please.* Imperatives have an "understood" subject *you* (singular or plural) and no other subject. When a straight imperative fails to inspire action it may be intensified, especially by mothers and fathers of small children, by making the subject explicit: "You eat your peas." In situations of formal authority and minimum politesse, as in the armed forces, one may even get "You will fall in, at once." Indeed some transformational linguists have argued that the imperative is derived from underlying strings having *you will,* with deletion being usual. Partly on the ground that *will you?* is the proper tag question for a subject-less imperative: *Pass the salt, will you?* There are arguments against this derivation but I do not want to go into them here.

In adult English a great variety of forms not imperative in syntax have been recruited to the use of the imperative sense. The declarative: *I wonder if you can reach the salt* may have an imperative sense as may such an interrogative as: *Could you reach the salt?* All these forms are designed to soften the tone of the verbal effort to elicit an action from another. With very few facts to go on I will still guess that such softening of the imperative occurs in all languages.

As it happens English imperatives, though clearly common in the speech even of Stage I children, are impossible to identify on purely linguistic grounds. This is because the Stage I child, like the adult Japanese, very often produces subjectless sentences which are intended as declaratives or interrogatives. Development of imperative syntax in child English is a matter of, in the first place, narrowing down the subjectless sentence to exclusively imperative uses and, in the second place, the addition of softeners like "Please" or "Would you."

The Japanese show an especially great concern with softening the imperative. There is an actual imperative inflection of the verb (as there is not in English) consisting of *-o* or *-e,* according to the conjugation class of the verb. But imperatives like *Tabero! (Eat!)* or *Matte! (Wait!)* are limited to abrupt, rough speech used by men to intimates or inferiors. The variety of more polite variants is very great and, as in English, employs forms which are not syntactic imperatives at all. One very common form uses a gerund of the verb marked by *-te* or *-de* as inflection in conjunction with the word *kudasai,* which is probably best translated as "if you please." Thus, *Katte, kudasai* would mean *Please buy* and *Matte, kudasai, Please wait.* There are very many other possibilities translating most readily into such English forms as *I would like.* Probably one cannot express in Japanese the imperative of such verbs as *need* or *like* or *want* any more than one can in English, since these are states that seem founded in the realities of human psychology. I have not, however, seen any discussion of the matter with respect to Japanese.

Embedding of One Sentence within Another

There are a great many forms such sentences can take in English. In general one looks for evidence of more than one subject and predicate but because of various deletion rules these are often difficult to recognize. Here I will mention only three varieties of embedding, the varieties selected because they are among the first to appear in child speech and because they relate interestingly to aspects of sentence construction already described.

Object Noun Phrase Complements

With a certain class of transitive verbs, including *think, know, guess, tell, hope,* and *mean,* one may have in place of a simple object noun an intact simple sentence in the role of the noun. The following examples are from Adam, Eve, and Sarah.

> *I hope I don't hurt it.*
> *I think it's the wrong way.*
> *I mean that's a* D.
> *You think I can do it?*

These embeddings are perhaps the easiest of all to recognize because the embedded sentence appears exactly as it would if it stood alone as an independent simple sentence. In other types of embedding the embedded sentence looks quite unlike a simple sentence that can stand alone. For instance, in *It annoys the neighbors for John to play the bugle,* one may not at once recognize the sentence *John plays the bugle* because of the "complementizer," as it is called (Rosenbaum, 1967) "for . . . to." For the sentences we have listed above there is also a complementizer *that,* which may optionally precede the subject of the embedded sentence. As it happens the children did not use it.

In our listing in Table 1 of basic semantic roles played by simple noun phrases we included the role Chafe (1970) calls "complement" to deal with such cases as *Mary sang a song* and *John played checkers.* Chafe uses "complement" to name a noun phrase that completes the meaning of a verb on a more or less specific level. I think it reasonable to suggest that verbs like *think, know, tell, hope,* and *mean* are "completable" in just this same way but by propositions rather than by the names of the objects. This class of object noun phrase complements, with or without *that,* seems to play the same role as Chafe's complement noun phrase; it specifies the sense of a verb, but with a full proposition rather than with a simple noun.

I would not leave the impression that these few remarks exhaust the complex subject of noun phrase complements (see Rosenbaum, 1967). There are several varieties of complementizer used with different verb classes. In addition the complement may serve as a subject rather than an object as in: *That John called early annoyed Bill.* In this subject role we do not find them in early child speech.

Indirect or Embedded Wh- *Questions*

Indirect or embedded *wh-* questions are interestingly related both to the semantic roles of Table 1 and the *wh-* questions in the interrogative modality. Table 3 lists a set of examples including two sentences actually produced by the children of our study. Table 3 also lists the semantic role each embedded or constituent sentence seems to play in the embedding or matrix sentence. Thus the first embedded sentence is agent of *fix;* the second, patient of *fixed;* the third, experiencer of *recognize;* the fourth, beneficiary of *gave;* the fifth, instrument of *opened;* the sixth, location of *are;* the seventh, time of *I can lift;* the eighth, complement of *sang.* Only time is an addition to the list of Table 1.

Table 3.   Some indirect (or embedded) *wh-* questions and the semantic roles they fill

Semantic Role	Sentence
Agent	Whoever broke this must fix it.
Patient	He fixed what he could.
Experiencer	Whoever killed her recognizes this weapon.
Beneficiary	They gave money to whomever they met.
Instrument	Whatever Tom opened the box with was sharp.
Location	Know where my games are?[a]
Time	When I get big I can lift you up.[a]
Complement	Mary sang what I like to hear.

[a]Sentences produced by children in our study.

How is the semantic of the embedded sentences of Table 3 to be distinguished from that of the relations of Table 1 and such questions as appear in Table 2? The new sentences are not in the interrogative modality even though they use *wh-* words. The sentences do not request specification of a particular grammatical constituent or semantic role. In fact the role is specified in the sentence as it stands but by proposition not by name. In the first sentence it is as if one were to say: "I do not know the identity of the agent who *must fix it* but I know something about that agent: he is the person who broke it." In the case of instrument it is as if one were to say: "I do not know the name of the instrument Tom used in opening the box but I can tell you one thing about it; it was sharp." As I see these sentences then, they are semantically like simple sentences involving single nouns in various semantic roles with the difference that the person or thing is specified by a proposition rather than by name.

The syntax of the embedded *wh-* sentence differs from that of the *wh-* question in one obvious respect. The interchange in position between subject and first member of the auxiliary which helps mark the interrogative does not occur. Thus it is not *Where are my games?* but . . . *where my games are* and not *What do I like to hear?* but . . . *what I like to hear.*

Relative Clauses

In the object noun phrase complement a simple sentence as a whole plays the role of object *(I think I can do it).* In such sentences there is no one noun that one can think of as the essential object (such as *I* in the illustration) that is merely modified by the remainder. In the indirect questions a *wh-* word plays the object role or some other semantic role such as agent or location *(I see what you mean; I know where he is)* but the *wh-* word is not like a content noun which in itself actually specifies some distinct object, person, or place; the *wh-* word is empty save for the role it marks. In the embedded question, however, there is a further proposition which modifies the *wh-* word, telling us something more specific about it: *I know where he is.* Relative clauses may be contrasted with the two kinds of embeddings just discussed in that they do occur with an ordinary noun that is playing some major semantic role, the clause itself adds additional information about the noun. The following may not at first seem to conform to the description I have given of relative clauses because of certain optional deletions, replacements, and word order changes which are briefly described in the paragraph that follows. Asterisked examples were obtained from children.

> *The man who came to dinner stayed a week.*
> *The argument the dean made surprised the students.*
> *I am disturbed by the tale you tell.*
> **Now where's a pencil I can use?*
> **That a box that they put it in.*

In all the above sentences and generally in sentences containing single relative clauses, there are two propositions made about the same noun phrase. This is not obvious because relative pronouns *(who, which, whom, that)* may replace a noun phrase or, in certain circumstances, both noun phrase and relative pronoun may be omitted. Indeed, when a relative pronoun subject precedes a present tense of *be,* the *be* form may also be omitted.

The common underlying structure of the sentences will be much clearer if we present them in full in a form that was fully grammatical in English from about the sixteenth to the eighteenth century.

> *The man, which man came to dinner, stayed a week.*
> *The argument, which argument the dean made, surprised the students.*
> *I am disturbed by the tale, which tale you tell.*
> *Now where's a pencil, which pencil I can use?*
> *That a box, which box they put it in.*

The semantic roles of the nouns in the matrix sentence vary: *man* seems to be an agent; *argument* a complement, and so on. The relative clause itself, however, seems always simply to function as an attributive (a possible addition to the roles of Table 1). It is a proposition that modifies a noun in the matrix sentence.

"Nonrestrictive" relative clauses, as they are called, are intended to have an effect rather like that of a full compound sentence in which two independent statements are made about one subject. To use an example from Jacobs and Rosenbaum (1968): *Professors like music and professors are idealistic* means the same thing as the nonrestrictive relative *Professors, who like music, are idealistic.* The restrictive relative clause, on the other hand, is intended to delimit its reference and to say that the major proposition (the matrix sentence) is true only for that subclass which satisfies *both* attributes. In written English commas are not used with restrictive clauses: *Professors who like music are idealistic.* This says that just those professors who like music are idealistic. In speech, pauses may mark the nonrestrictive relative clause and the absence of pauses the restrictive, or it may just be hard to tell what the speaker intends. The difference is a profound one, however, for the embedded restrictive clause, not being an independent proposition, cannot properly stand on its own. The nonrestrictive relative clause comes much closer to the compound or coordinated sentence.

It is clear that one can, in Japanese, form the equivalents of the three kinds of embeddings described for English, though detailed and explicit rules are not available in the English sources that I am able to use. The verb *omoimasu* meaning *believe* or *think* together with the formal quotative particle *to* takes simple sentences as object complements. In English, of course, one says *I think (that)* . . . followed by some intact proposition. In Japanese the complement or proposition comes first and *to omoimasu* at the end. Here are some examples:

> *Tanaka-san wa byōki da to omoimasu. (I think Mr. Tanaka is*
> *sick* or, more literally, *Mr. Tanaka is sick, so I think.)*
> *Raigetsu kaeru to omoimasu. (I think you will come back next*
> *month* or, more literally, *Next month you will come back,*
> *so I think.)*
> *Anata wa Kobe e irasshata to omoimashita. (I thought you*
> *had left for Kobe* or, more literally, *You, for Kobe had*
> *left, so I thought.)*

Indirect questions seem to serve in Japanese all the semantic roles they fill in English. The question word is used as in direct questions but certain changes occur in the verb. Here are some examples:

> Direct Question: *Dare desu ka? (Who is he?)*
> Indirect Question: *Dare ka wasuremashita. (I forgot who he is.)*
> Direct Question: *Doko e ikimasu ka? (Where are you going?)*
> Indirect Question: *Doko e iku ka shirimasen. (I don't know*
> *where you are going.)*

The semantic functions are close to those of English, perhaps identical, but the syntax is, of course, different.

The grammar of noun-modifying embedded clauses (which might alternatively be called relative clauses) has been worked out in some explicit detail by Inoue (1969). In illustration let us start with the following simple sentence in the form of an abstract string underlying the standard intimate form:

Kare ga hon o kak ta. (He wrote a book or, more literally, *He book wrote.)*

The sentence would be realized in speech as: *Kare ga hon o kaita.* The string might be made into a relative clause modifying *he* and suitable for embedding in a matrix sentence by placing the noun to be modified at the end in the following manner:

Hon o kak ta kare ga . . . (He, who wrote a book, or, more literally, *Book wrote he . . .)*

This string, in turn, would be pronounced: *Hon o kaita, kare ga . . .*

The other noun in the orginal string, *book,* might alternatively be made the noun to which the rest of the sentence is affixed as a modifier or relative clause. The process is the same: the noun to be modified is moved to final position. Thus:

Kare ga kak ta hon . . . (The book [*that*] *he wrote* or, more literally,
The he wrote book. . .)

This string would be pronounced: *Kare ga kaita hon.* In either of these forms the sentence is prepared to be embedded in sentences saying something additional about either, respectively, *he (who wrote a book)* or *the book (that he wrote).* The relative clause is a kind of sentence attributive or modifier of a noun as it is in English but the Japanese syntax is quite unlike the English in detail.

Embedding, in general, is from the syntactic point of view any process which makes one sentence into a grammatical constituent of another sentence, whether the constituent be subject, object, verb complement, some sort of adverbial, adjectival, or whatever. From a semantic point of view embedding may be regarded as any process that places a proposition in a particular semantic role within another proposition whether that role be agent, patient, experiencer, beneficiary, instrument, location, or whatever. Embedding may be distinguished from our fifth construction process, coordination, which also combines simple sentences, in that coordinated sentences are not assigned constituent or semantic roles one within another but are related in other ways. Our examples of embedding have almost all been of the simplest kind; cases in which just one sentence is embedded in just one other sentence. In adult speech and writing, and even in the later preschool years of childhood it is common to find embeddings of much greater complexity involving three, four, five, and even more simple sentences. From the point of view of transformational linguistics the possible complexity of embedding (and also of coordination) is not simply very large but infinite. It is infinite because it is thought to derive ultimately from a recursive pair of rules, rules that can be applied one after the other to each other's output, with no necessary termination. The rule that rewrites the symbol for "sentence" includes a noun phrase, and the rule that rewrites the noun phrase includes, optionally, a sentence. The evident limitations on the actual complexity of human linguistic performance are, from this point of view, the result of strictly psychological rather than linguistic limitations. The point is arguable and has been much argued but it will not be argued by me until there are more facts to go on.

Coordination of Simple Sentences and Propositional Relations

Coordination of simple sentences is a fascinating and immensely powerful process. At a first level, however, it is difficult to see any point to it, let alone power. One may in English take any two or more sentences and link them conjunctively with *and*. Some early examples from the children in our study follow.

> *You snap and he comes.*
> *We went up in Foxboro and there were slides.*
> *I did this and I did that.*
> *And the dog back in and the dog back out.*
> *No, you have some and I have some.*

Each sentence is complete and could stand alone; nothing at all obvious is accomplished semantically by coordinating them with *and*.

In all the full coordinations we have heard children speak and in most, if not all, we have heard from adults, there is some kind of continuity of thought in the coordinated sentences. If they were not coordinated we would find it natural to hear first one and then the other. But semantic continuity, though usual in performance, seems not to be a necessary condition of grammaticality. To quote a nice example from Jacobs and Rosenbaum (1968) "Galileo scanned the skies and adolescents scorned the schools." I agree with the authors that this is an unexpected but not an ungrammatical sentence. Though I would not guarantee that all linguists, let alone literate laymen, would agree.

When two (or more) simple sentences have a stretch in common as well as a stretch that differs it becomes possible to cut out some redundancy in the process of coordination. Suppose the sentences were:

> *Mary sang.*
> *Mary danced.*

The identical element, *Mary,* which is a noun phrase in the syntactic role of subject and the semantic role of agent need not be repeated. Instead one can delete one appearance of the identical element and link the nonidentical stretches with *and,* producing *Mary sang and* danced. Suppose, alternatively that the simple sentences were:

> *Mary sang.*
> *John sang.*

Now it is the subjects which are different and must be joined by *and*. The verbs are identical, and one may be deleted. The result:

Mary and John sang.

It turns out that partial identity and partial difference is the essential precondition for coordinating independent sentences, but there are major conditions on these differences and identities. Not all will qualify for coordination. Much of what we know, for sure, about these conditions was put down by Chomsky in 1957, though Jacobs and Rosenbaum made significant additions in 1968. The clearer facts for one common sort of coordination are summarized in the general formula at the bottom of Table 4.

Table 4. A general rule of coordination with examples

Constituents Coordinated	Identical Strings	Sentence
Subject	Predicate	John and Mary walked to the store.
Predicate	Subject	John went to the store and bought some gum.
Direct objects	Subject and verb	John bought some gum and a book.
Subject and verb[a]	Direct object	John bought and Mary chewed some gum.[b]
Locative adverbials	Subject, verb, and object	John bought gum in the grocery and in the delicatessen.
Time adverbials	Subject, verb, and object	John bought gum in the morning and at night.
Manner adverbials	Subject, verb, and object	John chose a flavor quickly and confidently.

[a]Not a constituent.
[b]Ungrammatical sentence.

General formula: $\begin{array}{c} z + x + w \\ z + y + w \end{array} \Rightarrow z + x$ and $y + w$

Where: 1. Either z or w may be null.
2. X and y are constituents of the same type.
3. X and y play the same syntactic (or semantic) roles in their respective sentences.

The symbols $Z, X, Y,$ and W simply stand for stretches of undefined length in two sentences. Initial identities are marked Z and final identities $W;$ the parts that differ and could be joined with *and* are X and Y. The formula includes both an initial identity *(Z)* and a final identity *(W)* because both are possible but, in fact, only one or the other is a necessary condition for coordination.

There are two conditions on the $X's$ and $Y's$ that may be coordinated, and they amount to a requirement that they be structurally identical though lexically distinct.

In the first place X and Y must be constituents or "natural parts" of their respective sentences and, furthermore, constituents of the same type. Both must be noun phrases or verb phrases or locative adverbials or whatever. Table 4 lists a set of examples that meet this condition. For a pair of sentences that do not meet this condition consider the following:

[The boy will have] [been running]
[The boy will have] [the ball]

The initial bracketed stretches might seem to be Z segments in Chomsky's formula since they are superficially identical and the final stretches, the X and Y of the formula, since they are lexically distinct. However, in this case X and Y are not structurally matched; Y (the ball) is a constituent, a direct object, but X is not a constituent at all but simply an arbitrary chunk of the verb phrase. In addition the initial Z segments are not truly identical, since *have* in the first sentence is an auxiliary whereas it is a main verb in the second. If we coordinate these sentences we get: *The boy will have been running and the ball* which is clearly ungrammatical.

The second constraint on X and Y is that they not only be constituents of the same type but constituents playing the same syntactic role in their respective sentences. Both must be subjects or predicates or direct objects or in some other syntactic role. Table 4 lists a set of cases in which this condition also is satisfied. There is some question whether it is really syntactic roles that must be matched rather than semantic roles. Fillmore (1968) has rather flatly asserted that the latter is the really essential condition (though he uses the term "case" for what I have called "semantic role"). In fact it is not easy to think of sentences which separate syntactic role from semantic role and meet the other conditions for coordination. One such case seems to be the pair:

[John] [opened the door]
[The key] [opened the door]

Both *John* and *the key* are syntactic subjects but *John* is an agent and *the key* an instrument. The coordination *John and the key opened the door* definitely seems ill-formed to me and seems to support the view that it is semantic roles which must be matched. But it will take more than a single pair to settle this issue. It is likely to take some years of linguistic work.

A word about the third sentence in Table 4, the single ungrammatical sentence. It is included to show that when the identical stretches meet the conditions that are intended to be imposed on the nonidentical stretches to be coordinated (same kind of constituent in the same role) that does not suffice to make fully grammatical coordination possible. With the nonidentical stretches to be coordinated, not structurally matched as in the example, the resultant sentence is ungrammatical.

The fact that coordination with deletion is constrained by the structural considerations listed at the bottom of Table 4 is of great importance to the student of language development. A child who can freely construct well-formed coordinations with deletions across a range of types must have developed knowledge of sentence constituents, of constituent types, and of syntactic or semantic role. All this knowledge is also required for simple sentences but coordination goes beyond simple sentences in the size of the linguistic unit to be planned and in the necessity to recognize identical and nonidentical but structurally matched stretches. No doubt it is because coordination with deletion presupposes the knowledge required for simple sentences, and in addition the knowledge specific to coordination, that coordinations appear later in development than simple sentences for children learning English and, conceivably, all languages.

Though it may not be obvious, the conjunction *and* has, as logicians know, a definite meaning. Strawson (1952) expresses the meaning of the related logical symbol in the following way. Where p and q stand for propositions and $p.q$ stands for *p and q* then the conditions in which $p.q$ is true and the conditions in which it is false are as follows:

p	q	$p.q.$
True	True	True
False	True	False
True	False	False
False	False	False

In short $p.q$ is true only if p and q are, respectively, both true. Insofar as *and* corresponds to the logical symbol for conjunctions, and it seems to correspond closely, it has a definite meaning and a meaning of great importance.

Strawson's simple truth table for $p.q$ provides an excellent opportunity to suggest one of the ways in which grammar relates to logic. The p and q of propositional logic may have any degree of complexity. Grammar, especially the rules of embedding and coordination, provide the apparatus by which p and q can be built up into indefinitely complex structures without changing the conditions of truth and falsity of the propositions involved. Consider, for instance, the example $p.q$. This may at the simplest level be something like "Mary sings and Mary dances." At a next level it might be: "Mary's singing pleases Tom and Mary's dancing annoys him." At a still higher level of complexity $p.q$ might be: "The fact that Mary's singing pleases Tom was news to Jim and the fact that Mary's dancing annoys Tom was news to Sam." Both p and q have increased greatly in complexity in the above examples and yet the overall truth conditions for $p.q$ remain the same. Of course the conditions for ascertaining the truth of p and q, respectively, have also grown more complex. It seems reasonable to suggest that without the recursive resources of language it might not be possible to reason at all about propositions of such complexity.

In general I mean to suggest that a major function of language in thought, though one totally undemonstrated by experiment, may be the power it provides to expand the *p* and *q* of propositional logic without changing truth values.

Besides the conjunctive *and,* which seems to be the first coordination to appear in child speech, there are of course many others: the disjunctive *or,* as in *John will drive or Mary will drive;* the causal forms, *because* and others as in *The car stopped because it was out of gas;* the conditional forms, *if . . . then,* and others; the forms of succession in time, *and then* and others; the contrastive forms like *but, nevertheless, although,* and so on.

The contrastive coordinators like *but* are particularly interesting because of what they reveal of individual and cultural beliefs. In general, *p but q* is used when *q* is not a proposition which one would have been led to expect to be true on the basis of the truth of *p.* In fact, one would expect, on the basis of *p, not-q* to be true. To take a seasonal example, "They predicted fine weather but it was cloudy and cold." Of course, *p* does not imply *not-q* in a strictly logical sense, in sentences like this. At least it does not do so unless we are so mad as to believe some such suppressed premise as: "Predictions of the weather bureau always come true." Probably the most reasonable way to interpret *but* is as a signal that some usual expectation set up by *p* is about to be explicitly disconfirmed. The fascinating thing is the kinds of expectations that people hold. Besides all the reasonable kinds that might reflect actual empirical trends, there are such as:

> *Mary was beautiful but poor.*
> *Mary was poor but bright.*
> *Mary was plain but rich.*

Indeed it seems to be a general rule, at least in the American use of *but,* that when two attributes are to be assigned the same person or thing one uses *but* unless both are undesirable or both desirable. Any good-bad crossover seems to elicit *but.* Which is certainly not a simple reflection of the way the world goes. It is, as I have argued elsewhere (Brown, 1965), more like an expression of the nonlogical principles of cognitive dissonance or imbalance.

Children learning English start with *and* and *and then,* but they soon start using *but, because, so,* and many others, in certain restricted semantic circumstances. The full developmental story of the understanding of the coordinating forms seems to extend as far as early adolescence.

Inoue (1969) has made quite a detailed study of the rules of coordination underlying Japanese sentences. The meanings of the connectives or conjunctions seem to run about the same range as those in English; there being forms equivalent to *and, but, if, therefore,* etc. Coordination of full sentences is straight-forward enough with the connective appearing between the two coordinated sentences. What is particularly interesting is Inoue's treatment of coordinations with deletion.

Except for differences in the order of constituents, special rules affecting *wa* and *ga* and a few other minor matters, the basic formula is so far as I can see identical with that of English. When two sentences are in part identical and in part distinct, the identical stretch appears just once, and the differing stretches may be joined with a conjunctive provided that they are constituents of the same type playing the same syntactic (or semantic) roles in their respective sentences.

It is striking to see a few examples. In Inoue's representation these are strings underlying sentences in the standard intimate style. I will omit the pronounceable versions of all the strings that follow, merely noting that they differ considerably from the underlying string, but they are not needed to expose the principles of coordination. The bracketing and literal translations are my own.

> 1a. [*Seitotati ga kono hon o*] [*kari ta*].
>   [*The students this book*] [*borrowed*].
> 1b. [*Seitotati ga kono hon o*] [*yom ta*].
>   [*The students this book*] [*read*].

Coordination: *Seitotati wa kono hon o kari te yom ta.*
              The students this book borrowed and read.
Notice that *te* is *and;* that *Seitotati ga* becomes *Seitotati wa.*

> 2a. [*Koko no ryoori wa*] [*yasu i*].
>   [*This place's food*] [*is inexpensive*].
> 2b. [*Koko no ryoori wa*] [*oisi i*].
>   [*This place's food*] [*is delicious*].

Coordination: [*Koko no ryoori wa*] [*yasu kute oisi i*].
             [*This place's food*] [*is inexpensive and delicious*].
Notice that *te (and)* is contained in *kute,* a required morphophonemic change here.

In both the above examples the coordinated constituents are verb phrases; in the first action verbs in the past and in the second case predicate adjectives. So coordination occurs here and in the rest of Inoue's examples for units that are constituents, constituents of the same type, and constituents fulfilling the same roles in their respective sentences. The identical stretches in the first case, since they include both subject and object, would not be linearly continuous in English but would lie on either side of the verb. That would not, of course, prevent a completely parallel coordination, which would be: *The students borrowed and read the book.* The general formula at the bottom of Table 4, you may recall, provides for identical stretches on either side of a nonidentical but structurally matched stretch. In the second example for the identical stretch I chose the rather clumsy words *This place's food* because it brings out the similarity between the English genitive *'s* inflection and particle *no* in Japanese and the fact that both in English and Japanese we can have a noun phrase as subject in this sentence. However, a more colloquial translation would be: *The food here is inexpensive and delicious.*

If Inoue's rules for coordinations with deletion are correct then there is a really strong resemblance here in syntax and not only in meaning between the English and the Japanese cases. In the absence of much knowledge of other languages I will guess that the basic syntax of coordination is the same in all languages. If so we may expect to find simple sentences developmentally well in advance of coordinations with deletion, even when length in words is not different. We may expect it because the coordinations involve structural knowledge essential to simple sentences but going beyond it.

In summary five major processes of sentence construction have been described in both semantic and syntactic terms, and with examples from both English and Japanese. They are:

1. Semantic roles such as agent, patient, instrument, locative, etc., in simple sentences expressed by linear order, syntactic relations, prepositions or postpositions.

2. Semantic modulations such as number, specificity, tense, aspect, mood, etc., expressed by inflections or free forms belonging to small closed classes.

3. Modalities of the simple sentence: *yes-no* interrogation, request for specification of a constituent, negation, imperative.

4. Embedding of one simple sentence as a grammatical constituent or in a semantic role in another including all the roles of 1, all the constituents which one may ask to be specified in 3.

5. Coordination of full sentences or of partially identical and partially distinct (but structurally matched) sentences with deletion of one representation of the identical stretches. The coordinated sentences appear with connector words that approximate in meaning to relations of propositional logic.

I suggest that these five processes constitute the core of English sentence construction and, with some allowance for variation in syntax and meaning, of language generally. While we have the whole plan more or less in mind it is opportune to review the accomplishments of Washoe and Sarah, the two nonhuman primates whose linguistic successes have surprised us all and to ask whether these successes add up to the attainment of language.

Linguistic Apes

The teachers of Washoe and Sarah, when they began their experiments, can have felt no lack of Cassandras. Noam Chomsky, in *Language and Mind* (1968) had written: "It is quite natural to expect that a concern for language will remain central to the study of human nature, as it has been in the past. Anyone concerned with the study of human nature and human capacities must somehow come to grips with the fact that all normal humans acquire language, whereas acquisition of even its barest rudiments is quite beyond the capacities of an otherwise intelligent ape." (p. 59). Eric Lenneberg, in *New Directions in the Study of Language* (1964) writes: "There is no evidence that any nonhuman form has the capacity to acquire even the most primitive stages of language development" (p. 67). I have always suspected that confident pronouncements like these must have helped motivate Allen and Beatrice Gardner and David Premack to show that two female chimpanzees, Washoe and Sarah, had the capacity for at least the rudiments, and maybe much more.

When Chomsky and Lenneberg wrote the statements quoted above these statements correctly summarized the outcome of research efforts to teach chimpanzees to talk. There had been five major efforts of this sort (Kellogg, 1968) but two were especially well known. The Winthrop Kelloggs (1933), about 40 years ago, raised Gua, a female chimpanzee, at home and as a child, and they compared her progress with that of their own child, Donald. Gua gave some evidence of "understanding" utterances; at any rate, she responded distinctively and appropriately to about 70, but then dogs do the same on a smaller scale. Gua did not speak at all. However, Viki, another famous home-raised chimp, also a female, learned to make four sounds that were recognizable approximations to English words. Viki was given intensive training by her foster parents, Keith and Cathy Hayes (1951), but the four word-like sounds seemed to mark the upper limit of her productive linguistic capacity. So Chomsky and Lenneberg had the evidence on their side when they wrote, but since then we have had reports of the progress of Washoe (Gardner and Gardner, 1969, 1971) and of Sarah (Premack, 1970a, 1970b, 1971).

In most ways the two contemporary experiments are unlike. Allen and Beatrice Gardner, of the University of Nevada (Washoe is named for Washoe County, Nevada) have had their chimpanzee since she was about one year old in 1966. As of this writing (June 1971) she is about six years old and not yet sexually mature. They have attempted to teach Washoe the American Sign Language (ASL), a system which is believed to have most of the properties common to human languages generally (McCall, 1965). While not raised in quite the same way as a child (Washoe spent the nights in her own 2½ room trailer in the Gardners' back yard) she spent each day in their large fenced yard or in their house, and there was almost always at least one person interacting with her by means of the American Sign Language (ASL). The Gardners used every sort of explicit training method to get her to produce signs including demonstration, operant shaping, and "putting through" or molding her hands. They also simply chatted with her as one does with a small child during the routines of feeding, bathing, playing, toileting, and so on. The method was essentially the naturalistic one used with well-tended children: language was steadily beamed at her. At four years Washoe was making semantically appropriate use of 85 different signs and producing strings or sequences, which may or may not be sentences, up to 5 signs long. Some of the strings are novel; her own creations. The ASL functioned between Washoe and her trainers as a genuine medium of communication. She did not simply respond to the initiative of her trainers but she herself constantly initiated communication. The number of signs she produced at supper time, for instance, came to average about 150. Her accomplishments were tested experimentally as well as being recorded in diaries.

David Premack's approach has been quite different. Sarah is a mature caged female who has not been in continual interaction with human beings. Premack has constructed experimental paradigms which are intended to preserve the essence of universal features of linguistic structure or function. He has paradigms of reference, of *yes-no* and *wh-* questions and negatives, of bracketing or subwhole organization within the predicate; paradigms even of the copula, the plural, the conjunction *and,* of quantifier words (*all, none,* etc.), of class terms for color, shape, and size, and of the conditional (*if . . . then).*

Premack has characteristically "shaped" Sarah toward a terminal accomplishment by the Skinnerian method of successive approximation in which small steps in the direction of the desired performance are rewarded — usually with food. So far these seem to be a set of independent language games not necessarily integrated into a single system. The words in these games are plastic tokens varying in size, shape, color, and texture which will adhere to a magnetized slate. Sentences are written in the vertical. The games do not seem to have taken on autonomous interest for Sarah. If the tokens are left in her cage she does not apparently use them to initiate communication, but then Premack's paradigms often involve logical relations and other content probably not very relevant to Sarah's desires.

Both procedures — the semi-naturalistic and experimental paradigmatic — offer rich opportunities for drawing the wrong conclusions. But the opportunities come at rather different points. I think we are lucky to have both going at once, and there is some chance of getting the truth before we are through.

Neither Premack nor the Gardners have made a full conclusive report on their respective researches; they expect such reports to be made as books. It is necessary to say, then, what evidence is available to me as of this writing in June 1971. In April 1970 the Neurosciences Research Program in Brookline, Massachusetts, held a two-day conference on the subject "Are Apes Capable of Languages?" under the chairmanship of Detlev Ploog of the Max Planck Institute in Munich (Ploog and Melnechuk, 1971). I met Premack there and listened with fascination to his account of his experiments, and joined in the discussion of them. Premack has published three accounts of his work (1970a, 1970b, 1971). In 1970–71 he was Visiting Professor of Psychology at Harvard, and I had the opportunity to hear him describe his work to a group of psychologists and logicians and several chances to ask him questions about it.

Allen and Beatrice Gardner, early in their study, sent out periodic summaries in diary form to psychologists who they thought might be interested, and I was lucky enough to be on their list. My interest was really not seriously engaged until the fifth summary (1968). On the first page of that report I read that in April 1967, the tenth month of the project, Washoe, then between 18 and 24 months old, began to use signs in combination (Gardner and Gardner, 1971). Combinations suggest syntactic construction, and that is a capacity we had all thought exclusively human.

In the spring of 1969 we persuaded the Gardners themselves to pay us a visit at Harvard for two days showing films of Washoe, and discussing her achievements with the group here studying the development of language in children. The Gardners made an early report of their work in *Science* in 1969, and a fuller report, including comparisons with early child speech, "Two-Way Communication with an Infant Chimpanzee" (1971), which reports on the first 36 months of their attempt to teach the ASL to Washoe. The Gardners and I have also exchanged letters and phone calls, and I have sent them data on the children in our study for the purpose of comparison with Washoe.

The Gardners and I met most recently by accident; in early January, 1971, walking up Nob Hill in San Francisco. They were on a short holiday, and gave me the sad news that the home-raised period of Washoe's training had just come to an end. A mature chimpanzee is a strong animal that can easily kill a man, and Washoe had become dangerous to new graduate student assistants, without whom the training schedule could not be maintained. Consequently it had become necessary to send Washoe to a Primate Station where an effort would be made to continue the experiment. As you may imagine with an animal so nearly human as a chimpanzee, daily contact over several years creates strong ties of affection. I had the sad impression, as I talked with the Gardners, that they felt something like the parents of a child who has had to be sent away because of the eruption of unaccountable unmanageable behavior.

The question of the Neurosciences Conference "Are Apes Capable of Language?" cannot actually be answered on any neurological grounds, and the behavioral evidence from Washoe and Sarah really has given the question a different aspect. One might better ask: "Have these chimps demonstrated a capacity for language?" The question cannot be approached at all without taking some position on the nature of language and the reason for asking the question. I see four different approaches, at the moment, and they are as follows:

The definition of language begins with the notion that any language will be or will have been the major medium of communication in some human social group, the members of which are not afflicted with any major sensory or motor impairment. This makes the various sign languages of the world borderline cases (since they are used by human but deaf groups) whose status as language requires demonstration. Languages, then, are such things as English, German, Samoan, Finnish, Latin, Japanese, and so on. But this is only a set of instances, a kind of list.

The process of definition can advance by attempting to formulate the universal characteristics of language. While no one has all the necessary data, there have been attempts to do this job by Greenberg, 1963, Hockett, 1960, Altmann, 1967, and others. Altmann's list, an expansion of Hockett's earlier one, is especially interesting because a continual comparison is made with the communication systems of animals. It is a very long list that includes vocal production, aural reception, semanticity, arbitrary denotation, productivity or openness, the possibility of displacement in time and space of the message from its denotation, duality (or the use of a small number of meaningless elements, vowels and consonants or distinctive features, to build up a very large number of meaningful elements, words or morphemes) the possibility of prevarication or saying what is untrue, and many more. With some such list one can operationalize the question "Have Sarah and Washoe shown a capacity for language?" into the question whether they have demonstrated all the capacities on the list. The question in this form has an unequivocal answer, and the answer is no.

   Sarah and Washoe are disbarred from full linguistic participation by the very first requirement: vocal production and aural reception. In both chimpanzees the linguistic performance is manual rather than vocal, signs with the hands for Washoe and the manipulation and placement of plastic tokens for Sarah. But it is precisely this divorcement of vocalization from certain other properties of human language which we take to be a major virtue of the contemporary studies. We think it accounts for the fact that Washoe and Sarah have accomplished so much more on the production side than did Viki or Gua or any other antecedent. There is good reason to believe that the production of vowels and consonants and prosodic features is, simply as a motor performance, something to which chimpanzees are not well adapted. The chimpanzee articulatory apparatus is quite different from the human, and chimpanzees do not make many speechlike sounds either spontaneously or imitatively. Both the Gardners and Premack seem to have thought that previous experiments in the linguistic-chimpanzee tradition might have failed not because of an incapacity that was essentially linguistic but because of a motoric ineptitude that was only incidentally linguistic. And I think we must all agree that vocal production cannot be the essence of linguistic capacity, since writing systems are certainly languages, and sign systems used by human communicators very likely are.

   The introduction of a distinction between essential and incidental linguistic attributes of course raises the further question; From what point of view or on what ground do you make the distinction? One possibility is to define as essential only those attributes which are unique to language, attributes not found in any other system of thought or behavior. This seems to me to be the position taken by Noam Chomsky in 1967 in a conference on "Brain Mechanisms Underlying Speech and Language." He takes the position that properties like syntactic organization, purposiveness, and informativeness which might be shared by human language and by some animal communication systems are shared by far too many systems besides these. Walking, for instance, is purposive, has a kind of syntactic organization, and can be informative. The speed of walking can tell us how interested the walker is in reaching his goal, and we could formulate that information as a proposition. The essential properties in Chomsky's view are two: the fact that human language by means of constructional processes determines a set of sound-meaning correspondences which have an infinite range; the presumed necessity of a distinction between the surface structure of a sentence which determines how it is spoken and the deep structure of a sentence that determines its semantic interpretation. If these two are the "barest rudiments" of language, which Chomsky said in his 1968 statement are "quite beyond the capacities of an otherwise intelligent ape" then there is every reason to suppose that he does not find his views threatened by the achievements of either Washoe or Sarah. Neither one has shown control of an infinite set of sound-meaning correspondences, and for neither one has it been shown that a surface-structure/deep-structure distinction must be made. In this sense of language, as in the first, the answer is clearly negative to the question whether Washoe or Sarah has demonstrated linguistic capacity.

In various ways Chomsky's position on this question is unsatisfying. The properties defined as essential are abstract structural properties inferred from judgments that some but perhaps not all speakers of English can make, and these structural properties are expressed in a certain formal notation. They are a long way from behavior either human or animal. Even among linguists there is controversy over the proper form of notation and the necessity of postulating syntactic deep structure. Experiments with educated adults have not provided clear demonstration of these capacities. For example, Blumenthal (1966) and Stolz (1967) have shown that, even with unlimited time and with paper and pencil to compensate for memory limitations, most college students are not able to understand sentences, having three relative clauses that are self-embedded, for example, *The nurse that the cook that the maid met saw heard the butler*. Furthermore, almost all subjects call recursive sentences of this sort "ungrammatical" though they are not supposed to be so by Chomsky's theory. In fact infinite self-embedding is in theory grammatical. Chomsky's "essentials" will certainly keep the animals "out," but what is the use of that if it is not clear that we ourselves are "in"?

Chomsky's "barest rudiments" have the further interesting property that, allowing ourselves to draw structural conclusions from the data of spontaneous speech, children are not clearly producing what must be called language in Stages I, II, and III. Not until Stages IV and V with the appearance of embeddings and coordinations do we have much reason to suppose that the child has represented in his brain an infinite set of sound-meaning correspondences. This conclusion about child speech is not necessarily the wrong conclusion; it is just novel. What goes before "language" in development is only linguistic by courtesy of its continuity with a system which in fully elaborated form is indeed a language.

There is a third approach one can take to the definition of language, alternative alike to the listing of all universal properties and the listing of only the unique properties. This third approach focuses on an evolutionary question: "Why is the mode of life of the human species radically unlike that of any other animal species?" The mode of life of a species, manifesting such a diversity of modes as ours, can be unlike all others only in a very abstract way. And so it is. Human life differs from other animal life in the comparative importance of cultural evolution as opposed to biological evolution. Cultural evolution, or change that occurs because of transmitted information, from person to person and generation to generation, is vastly more important for us than for any other species. Indeed the amount of cultural transmission, whether of knowledge, customs, art, superstitions, or technology that occurs in species other than man is triflingly small. In man it is immense and is thought to be primarily responsible for the great diversity of life modes within one species. Cultural evolution is much faster than biological. Compare the time it took to evolve amphibians and then earth-dwelling animals by means of natural selection with the time it has taken man to invent the means to live on or under the sea, high in the air, and now outside the earth's atmosphere. From this evolutionary point of view, which seems the interesting one to take in comparing man with Washoe and Sarah or any other animals, the more relevant properties of language would be those that make possible the differences between the human and the nonhuman modes of life.

There are two kinds of function we might have in mind in looking for evolutionarily significant linguistic properties. We might concentrate on primarily cognitive, not essentially social functions, if we knew what language had done for human thought, and, could select out as more important properties those that have most increased the power of thought. Unfortunately we know next to nothing about what language has done for thought, and cannot even be sure that language has importantly affected the power of thought.

Probably the best established strictly linguistic aid to cognition is the use of names in covert rehearsal as a technique for extending short-term memory (see Flavell, 1970). For example, a child asked to remember certain members of a large array of varied objects may be able to say the names over to himself when the objects are concealed, and then use the rehearsed names to pick out the originally designated set when the full array is once again exposed. Children seem to learn to use language in this way, and it is a useful technology of cognition but a comparatively slight one. It did not get us to the moon. Possibly very much more important reasoning processes are dependent on sentence construction, and especially the powerful processes of embedding and coordination, but no one has even attempted to determine whether this is true. So we are simply too ignorant of the role of language in thought to select out, on this basis, some properties as more vital to our way of life than others.

Our ignorance of the cognitive uses of language leaves the communicative social function as the possible one to look at if we are interested in the evolutionary importance of language. Here matters are more out in the open and correspondingly clearer. It is evident that every human being knows very much more, whether true or false, folly or superstition, than he could possibly have learned from his own direct experience, and that he has learned a great deal of it by means of linguistic transmission. Language obviously makes experience cumulative and enables members of a community to learn what other members know without having had all the experiences of the others. With the permanency that writing gives, this process of accumulation stretches across the centuries and becomes vast indeed. We spend a great deal of our time, all our lives, learning through language what others have come to know in some other way. Of the universal properties of language, which ones seem most important from this point of view?

I would say semanticity or meaningfulness, without which nothing else would matter. But some kinds and degrees of semanticity are available to many animal species (the honey bee is probably the most famous case). What has not seemed to be present in any other species is the ability to communicate by compositional or syntactic means a range of sound-meaning correspondences which, whether infinitely large or not, is at any rate incalculably large. Chomsky is certainly right in saying that, except for routine greetings and things of that sort, almost every sentence we hear is new to us. New in our lifetime, often new in the whole history of the language. That immense scope, the productivity or openness of language, achieved through the kinds of construction processes described in the first section of this Introduction, has seemed uniquely human and uniquely powerful from an evolutionary point of view, since it means that any kind of information whatsoever can be encoded and transmitted. As a third important property I would add "displacement," the possibility of transmitting information from another time and place, the independence sentences have of their nonlinguistic setting. For if we were limited to the emission of sentences somehow triggered by present circumstances then the receiver of the sentence could learn from those present circumstances rather than from the sentence, and the accumulation of experiences across individuals and generations would not occur. From the evolutionary point of view, then, these three: semanticity, productivity, and displacement seem to me important in a way that oral-aural transmission, duality of structure, and the like do not. One can imagine cultural evolution displacing biological evolution as a mechanism of change in the absence of many attributes of language but not, I think, without semanticity, productivity, and displacement. Which is not to say that the other attributes of human language have no value for the human species, they all seem to have advantages of one sort or another, but they seem less essential.

The five processes of sentence construction described in this introduction as a developmentally ordered general design of English and, perhaps, all languages may be regarded as an expansion of the attribute called "productivity." The mechanisms for expressing semantic roles and modulation of meaning, the modalities of simple sentences, embedding and coordination are a core particularization of the meaning of productivity. With these in mind we can look at the achievements of Washoe and Sarah and see how close they come to language. We will consider first Washoe and her achievements with the ASL.

Washoe's Accomplishments

The American Sign Language exists in two forms. There is a finger-spelling form in which a sign is provided for each letter of the alphabet, and one simply spells

English in the air. This is not the form in which Washoe has been trained. In the second form signs are directly semantic and do not work through English. Some signs are iconic, the form suggests the sense. To make the sign for flower the fingers are drawn together in a tulip shape and presented to the nostrils as if sniffing. Other signs are entirely arbitrary. Elizabeth McCall (1965) has provided evidence that ASL is indeed a language, since it admits of the formation of most of the sentence types of English. If her description is correct it follows a grammar distinguishable from English and yet very close to English. In particular in McCall's description the sequential order of content words naming agents, actions, objects, attributes, and the like generally conforms to English order.

There is a great deal of evidence that Washoe's 85 signs are understood by her. Some of this evidence is experimental and well-controlled (Gardner and Gardner, 1971). In two drill sessions a day she has been required to name either real objects, or pictures of objects, or three-dimensional miniatures of objects. In a typical sort of series there would be three exemplars of each of 30 objects. Most of the exemplars would be entirely new instances belonging, however, to familiar categories. The order of presentation would be prepared by one experimenter, by shuffling a deck of cards, for instance, and placing them face down. A second experimenter would pick them up without looking at them, show each to Washoe, record her first response, and only then check to see if it was correct. Washoe has typically gotten 50 to 55 correct out of 99. If she were simply producing the signs involved at random she would be expected to get two or three correct. Her errors typically fall into semantic clusters: one article of grooming is confused with another; one food with another; one animal with another.

Of course the strings she creates are the really exciting thing, since they suggest a degree of semantic and syntactic productivity. These strings are very much like the first sentences of children. As Stage I will, in due course, disclose, the first sentences of children for the most part express the semantic role or relations we have called agent, experiencer, beneficiary, patient, location, and so on. There are several additions that need to be made to the list of Table 1, and Stage I is not monolithic; the complexity of the relations and roles expressed increases during the Stage. With these qualifications it is fair to say that Stage I speech centers on the major semantic roles and, in English at least, on sentence intonation contour and word order as the syntactic mechanisms expressing them. Modulations and modalities are either totally missing or only present in a primitive germinal form. Embedding and coordination are absent. About 75 percent of all utterances from all the Stage I children studied by any investigator involving any language known to me are classifiable as expressions of a small set of semantic roles or relations.

In their most recent paper, written after their discussion with our group here, the Gardners (1971) have made a classification of 294 different two-sign combinations produced by Washoe between April 1967 and June 1969 using, with slight modifications, our Stage I categories (as listed in Brown, 1970). They find that

228 or 78 percent of the combinations fit the categories they used. This result suggests that Washoe by the age of four years was performing much in the manner of a Stage I child, a stage that is attained by the children on record somewhere between 16 months and 27 months. The fact that Washoe, who was exposed to ASL all day long much as a child is exposed to his first language, with the addition of a certain amount of deliberate training which may or may not have been important, should settle first on the same sorts of constructions as children do is a striking one. Even the difference in age of attainment, favoring as it does the human primate, seems to make sense.

There is a difference between Washoe's Stage I strings and those of Stage I children to which I attached much importance in a paper called "The First Sentences of Child and Chimpanzee" (1970). In their fifth and sixth diary summaries the Gardners had noted that, for Washoe, the signs in a combination tended eventually to occur in all possible orders with no evident changes of meaning correlated with the changes of order. For children learning English this is definitely not the case. With a few exceptions and complications, to be discussed in Stage I, children speaking English use words in just that order appropriate to the semantic relations which the referent circumstances suggest that the child intends to express. This difference of attention to word order is potentially of great significance.

Bloom (1970) and Schlesinger (1971) before me, and I in 1970, have argued that "appropriate" word order is the prime aspect of the child's early sentences that justifies our attributing to him the intention to communicate certain semantic roles or relations. It is primarily word order that enables us to argue that the child learning English in his first multi-word utterances is not simply naming in succession various features of a complex referent situation but rather is expressing a certain structure among these features. The fact that a child typically says *Cat bite* when a cat is the agent and *Bite cat* when the cat is a patient (and perhaps a dog the agent) is an important one. If Washoe freely alternates the equivalents of *Cat bite* and *Bite cat* regardless of the cat's semantic role then what is there to show that she intends more than a kind of sequence of names?

In the 1970 paper I argued, however, that the problem of Washoe's semantic intentions should be considered still open. For many reasons. In the first place the Gardners had not then, and still have not, reported frequency data for appropriate and inappropriate orders. The possibility exists that Washoe has shown a "preference" for appropriate orders. In the second place I argued in 1970 that while appropriate order can be used as *evidence* for the intention to express semantic relations, the lack of such order does not establish the *absence* of such intentions. It does not do so because appropriate word order is not strictly *necessary* for purposes of communication for either the Stage I child or the Stage I chimpanzee. This is because most of these sequences are produced concurrently with a referent situation which would ordinarily admit of only one sensible interpretation whether the order was right or wrong.

To the above qualifications the 1970 paper added important information, supplied by Allen Gardner, suggesting that Washoe's sign sequences were not simply signs in succession but constructions planned as wholes. Before one can make a grammatical analysis of child speech it must be "segmented" into utterances which mark off just those words that are in construction with one another. Segmentation on this level proves to be very easily done with children for the reason that when they begin to make multi-word combinations they already control several of the prosodic patterns (of stress and pitch) which adults use to mark off sentences. One easily hears declarative, interrogative, and emphatic patterns in early child speech. An adult who uses ASL also has devices for marking off sentences (Stokoe et al., 1965). One of these is to keep the hands in the signing space until a sentence is finished, and only then allowing the hand to fall into a position of repose. Washoe also typically has marked construction segments by keeping her hands in the signing area until the end, only then letting them fall into loose fists or bringing them to rest on some nearby surface or on her own body.

Since the 1970 paper appeared, several other considerations have come forward which argue that Washoe may well have relational semantic intentions even though she does not regularly use appropriate word order. In the first place there is the fact that children operate on an acoustic input whereas Washoe operates on a visual input. It is possible that sequencing of auditory input is just easier than sequencing of visual input. The really essential control case is a study of a human child learning ASL as his first language. This will tell us whether appropriate order is as reliable with the deaf child as with the hearing child. Ursula Bellugi-Klima has such a study in progress now, and we shall eventually learn the answer to this important question. Her experience has already shown what we all might have guessed, that correction of the child's sequences by the parent is not so easy with Sign as with speech since the parents' hands are often otherwise occupied. Probably, then, the Gardners did not often correct Washoe's inappropriate orders. In addition, Premack has clearly shown that another chimpanzee, Sarah, can use symbol order (vertical) with semantic distinctiveness when the trainer makes his rewards contingent on correct order.

There are, finally, several other considerations which, taken together, seem to me to throw the weight of present evidence in favor of the view that Washoe has been expressing semantic relations like those of the Stage I child. In the first place, as we shall see in Stage I, it has very recently been shown that when children are exposed to a language which, unlike English, does not use rigid sequential orders for certain meanings and also use certain order contrasts to signal contrasts of meaning then the children do not, always on their own, match particular orders to particular relational meanings. And even among children exposed to English there is now one on record who, briefly to be sure, did not use referent order in Stage I. We do not know as yet just how realiably the Gardners modeled their sign sequences on English word order though the probability is that they did so more

reliably than do deaf adults who are fluent in sign. In any event the absence
from Washoe's data of reliably appropriate sign order seems a less crucial piece of
negative evidence than it did in 1970. At the present time I am inclined to assign
some positive weight to the fact that 78 percent of her two-sign constructions,
identified as constructions by Washoe's own "segmenting" behavior, were identifiable
by the Gardners as expressive of just about the set of relations regularly found in
Stage I child speech. There are, after all, many conceivable combinations of two
signs which, in context, could not easily be given one of the basic relational
interpretations. Even in child speech at Stage I, when it is viewed with the perspective
made available by studies of languages of varied types, it is the use of intonation
contours to mark word sequences as in construction, rather than word order that is
the single universal syntactic device of Stage I. And it is ultimately the relational
interpretability of these constructions, heard in context, that justifies attributing
relational semantic intentions to the child. So, as matters now stand, and Stage I will
show that this is the case, the evidence that Washoe has Stage I language is about
the same as it is for children.

Of course it is the Gardners who will be able to make the best judgment about
Washoe's early sign sequences, since only they have all the data and the daily direct
experience with Washoe. If Washoe has a Stage I competence this is not enough
to conclude that she has language in the sense either of all its universal properties or
of just its unique properties. It does, however, seem to be enough of a linguistic
capacity to have supported a considerable degree of cultural evolution. And so we
are left with the question: Why has not the chimpanzee species used this capacity to
transmit information and so build on the experience of past generations? I would
not rule out the possibility that chimpanzees in fact make more use of a linguistic
capacity than has generally been supposed. I say this because early work on
chimpanzee communication concentrated on vocalization, and that may not be where
the highest capacities appear. Studies of movement and gesture may change
the picture.

It is important to remember finally that the Gardners have not reported on the
period beyond the first 36 months and that Washoe is still in training. Stage I
knowledge may not be the limit of her linguistic capacities. Premack's results, of
course, suggest that the limits of chimpanzee capacity are far beyond anything in
Stage I.

Sarah's Accomplishments

The list of Sarah's accomplishments is certainly impressive. In the 1971 *Science*
article Premack describes paradigms for: reference, sentence, *yes-no* interrogatives,
wh- interrogatives, negatives, metalinguistic utterance (for example, *name* of);
the class concepts of color, shape, and size; compound or coordinated sentences,
the copula, pluralization, the quantifiers *all, none, one, several;* the logical

connective *if . . . then* or ⊃. While Premack does not, of course, organize these paradigms as I have done there seems to be at least one from all five aspects of sentence construction.

Several things strike me as odd about Sarah's achievements; odd simply in the sense of not fitting easily into my framework of ideas. She seems to do about as well on one problem as on another (generally correct about 70–80 percent of the time) in spite of what I, at least, think of as great differences of complexity among the problems with judgments of relative complexity being based partly on developmental order of acquisition, but more importantly on orderings for complexity implicit in their grammar or semantics. As David Premack has said to me, there is no reason to suppose that children at home get anything like optimal training in language. That is true enough. The second aspect of complexity, the way in which one construction involves more knowledge than another, is less easily explained away, but it is possible that the sequence of training procedures was such as to build from the less complex to the more complex.

A second slightly odd feature is the failure of Sarah to take up her token language as a medium of communication. She is always the respondent who solves problems when the experimenter sets them. She has almost never initiated communication. When the tokens have been left in her cage she has either ignored them or, once or twice, repeated some recent exercise. In this respect Sarah is quite unlike Washoe and, of course, unlike human children. Washoe constantly uses Sign to initiate interaction to get what she wants, to comment on events. Premack is inclined to think that Sarah's more passive role is simply a consequence of the training procedures which have not developed the initiating role. An interest in initiating communication does not appear on any list of linguistic universals I know of, but when it is absent we notice how unhuman the performance is. Somewhere here, perhaps, lies the answer to the question of why, if chimpanzees have so much linguistic capacity, they do not, in the wild state, make more use of it.

Aside from these two minor oddities there are really two major questions about the paradigmatic demonstrations themselves. One is well known in psychology by the name of the "clever Hans problem" (Pfungst, 1911). The other, and a more complex one, I shall call the "pigeon ping-pong problem."

Hans, you may know, was a horse who at his cleverest seemed to be able to do arithmetic. His trainer, Herr von Osten, would pose a problem in addition or multiplication, for instance, and Hans would tap one forefoot until he had tapped that number of times which corresponded with the answer, at which point Hans would stop. It was at length discovered that Hans could not do his sums correctly when none of the humans present knew the answers to the problems posed. The explanation proved to be that when Hans performed correctly it was because his questioner, von Osten or anyone else, assumed a kind of expectant posture until the right number of hoofbeats had sounded, and then by unwitting postural relaxation gave Hans the cue he needed to stop him. Wearing blinders or with an uninformed interrogator Hans turned out to have no knowledge at all of arithmetic.

In Sarah's case, the possibility (which Premack, 1971, calls the "Clever Gretel problem") must be considered that her several trainers all of whom in the major experiments knew the answers to the problems they posed may have unintentionally signaled the correct choices to Sarah. There are many ways this can happen; one that we have learned to watch for with small children is binocular fixation. The experimenter looks at the object to be selected and the child looks not at the objects presented but at the experimenter's face. When I saw a slide of Sarah and her trainer working almost cheek by jowel in front of the magnetized board holding the tokens I felt that the Clever Hans possibility had to be taken seriously with these experiments. Premack has done some experiments (1971) designed to check on the possibility but we cannot evaluate these until we have reviewed the nature of his paradigms.

About ten years ago, in the laboratory of B. F. Skinner (1962), pigeons were, by a clever training procedure, brought to play something that looked very like a game of table tennis. They did not, however, keep score or develop strategies for misleading one another. One might say that their performance was, in certain superficial ways, like that of humans playing a game of ping-pong but in other ways, which we think of as belonging to the essence of the game, the pigeon performance was not ping-pong. The pigeon ping-pong problem is a completely general one for experimental paradigms. The question always arises whether the paradigm preserves the essential properties of the process it is intended to represent. And, for each of Sarah's linguistic accomplishments the question must be asked. Has she really shown comprehension of the sentence, of the copula, of the conditional, and so on? As with the Clever Hans problem we cannot raise the issues until we have a look at several of the paradigms.

One of Sarah's more impressive performances was to demonstrate seeming comprehension of an imperative compound sentence involving deletion of a matched subject and verb with coordination of the direct object and locative. In prior training the tokens for fruits, containers, and so on had been linked with their referents by a kind of exchange process. In the sequence leading up to the compound sentence Premack began with the constituent sentences listed as (1) and (2) in Table 5. In looking at the table, which summarizes successive steps in the procedure, it is important to remember that not English words but tokens were used. There is something mesmerizing for the native speaker about the sight of the words which makes it easy for us to attribute all the linguistic knowledge we bring to such strings to the performance with tokens. Maybe we will be justified in doing that when the evidence is reviewed but we do not want to do it automatically. The simple sentences were at first presented side by side in all possible pairs with reward being made contingent on the correct double response. Then all possible pairs were arranged one above another in the equivalent of full coordinations without deletion (3). Then in (4) the subject *Sarah* was deleted once and finally in (5) both subject and verb were deleted once. The result is a compound imperative with deletion; the absence of a conjunction like *and* is of no importance (and was used in others of Premack's paradigms). The deletions caused Sarah no trouble; she continued to perform correctly between 75 and 80 percent of the time. Finally transfer tests were made involving substitutions for the verb or the object and locative nouns. And Sarah's performance was unimpaired.

Table 5.   Successive problems in the paradigm for comprehension of a compound sentence with deletions

1	2	3	4	5
Sarah	Sarah	Sarah	Sarah	Sarah
insert	insert	insert	insert	insert
banana	apple	banana	banana	banana
dish	pail	pail	pail	pail
		Sarah	insert	apple
		insert	apple	dish
		apple	dish	
		dish		

Source: Adapted from Premack, 1970 b.

Consider next the paradigms for *yes-no* and *wh-* questions. These involve both real objects (key, pencil, etc.), represented in Table 6 by words not in italics, as well as tokens *(same, not same, yes, no),* represented in Table 6 by italicized words. The paradigm relies, as Premack stresses, on the fact that the chimpanzee readily recognizes many of the objects we recognize and will very readily "match to sample," or put together two that are alike. Tokens for *same* and *different* (or *not same*) were then introduced. Sarah would be given two objects (for example, two keys or one key and one pencil) and reward was made contingent on her choosing the correct token from the two offered: *same; not same.*

The stage was now set for a simple sort of *wh-* question. The essence of this kind of question is to ask for the specification of a particular unspecified constituent; the *wh-* word form in English indicates what kind of constituent is in question. Premack used a token for *?* to serve this function, and simply placed it between two objects which were either the same or different. Sarah was then to replace the question mark with the token correctly specifying the relation between the objects, and she was offered the two alternatives: *same* and *not same.* The *wh-* question of the experiment (ii in Table 6) is then made up of a combination of real objects and a token. It is a kind of functional equivalent to such an English sentence as: "*A* is what to *B*?" or, more usually, "What is the relation between *A* and *B*?" Premack also put the *wh-* question in another form approximating to: "What is *A* not the same as?" with objects being offered as alternatives.

Table 6.   Major steps in paradigms of *wh-* and *yes-no* questions

	Materials
Real objects	key, pencil
Tokens	*same, not same*
	yes, no
	?
	Procedures
Display	key key; key pencil
Alternatives	*same, not same*
Display	key *?* key; key *?* pencil
Alternatives	*same, not same*
Translation	*What is relation between key and key?*
Display	*?* key *same* key; *?* key *same* pencil
Alternatives	*yes, no*
Translation	*Is key same as key?*

Source: Adapted from Premack, 1970 b.

From the paradigm of the *wh-* question it is possible to develop a paradigm of the *yes-no* question. Premack clearly traces the connection by showing that what was necessary was to ask whether a certain named relation was true or not. This he did, after certain training preliminaries, by placing the *?* token at the start of the string and the relational forms, *same* or *not same,* between matched or unmatched objects. The alternatives were, of course, *yes* or *no* with, as always, reward contingent on the right choice. This part-object, part-token question might be paraphrased in English as: "Is key the same as key?" The *yes-no* question can be put in four different forms using these materials, and Premack tested for transfer from some forms to others rather than for different relations and objects. Sarah made some mistakes but still was significantly successful.

In describing these few paradigms I have not included each atomic step in the procedure because the account is long enough as it is. It is to be understood that the general technique was always the same: to set up three-term contingencies in which reward (some well-liked food) depended upon emission of the right response in the presence of the right stimulus complex with the stimulus patterns getting progressively more complicated. As these paradigms show, great ingenuity and considerable insight into the nature of language went into Premack's part of this work, and the paradigms described here are not even the most impressive in these respects.

With reference to just the paradigms described let us ask first the ping-pong question. Are these linguistic performances or do they only look like linguistic performances? Evidently Sarah has made certain responses which were appropriate to all the problems presented. The question is whether the range of problems and responses is near enough to the range available to humans to justify attributing to Sarah the linguistic capacities Premack has attributed to her. In fact, it is not at all difficult to think of things humans can do with coordination, *yes-no,* and *wh-*questions, which Sarah has not been shown to be able to do. But whether she has done *enough* is not really possible to say. What she has done, if it can be replicated, seems to me a very valuable empirical input to the general problem that engages us all: What essentially is language and how can it be learned? The differences between Sarah's performance across all the paradigms and the human performance in the real case that seem to me most likely to be important are two: possible dependence of terminal accomplishments on specific atomic preliminary programs; a great difference in systematic scope of performance.

In general Sarah's paradigms seem to function as a set of independent carefully programmed language games. She has almost never (Premack tells me there have been a couple of exceptions) had sessions in which she received several sorts of sentences and never apparently sessions in which any one of all the kinds of sentences she presumably understands might be presented. I am, of course, reminded of my two weeks of Japanese at Berlitz. I, like Sarah, had a very ingenious teacher who programmed her lessons in an almost Skinnerian way. But I learned, to my chagrin, that my knowledge was very narrowly adapted to just that kind of situation. Processing a sentence which comes to you as simply one from among the infinite possibilities of a language seems to be a very different matter from processing that sentence when it arrives as the crowning problem in a pyramid of training which has made one familiar with most of the components involved and put them in a state of readiness. Sarah may be as narrowly adapted to Tokenese as I was to Japanese. But fluent speakers of a language are not thus narrowly adapted. The difference is an important one, potentially quite revealing about how sentence processing is done. But it is in any case, at present, a difference.

Between the human and the chimpanzee there are vast differences of scope at the level of lexicon or vocabulary. For instance, in such compound sentences as *Sarah insert banana pail apple dish* Premack has tested for transfer to several different fruits and containers and at least one other verb *(withdraw).* Obviously humans can handle an enormous variety of subjects, action verbs, objects, and locations, and there is a comparable great difference of lexical scope between each paradigm and the human accomplishment it models. However, Premack accepts this and has deliberately set out to test grammatical operations keeping vocabulary at a minimum, since the size of the lexicon, which varies widely among humans anyway and grows slowly in childhood, seems less important than grammatical capacity. Presumably the lexicon size could, if one took the time, be made large enough to be immensely useful to a chimpanzee, providing the grammatical potential is there. I think this is a very reasonable view, and it is not really the limitation of lexical scope that I want to call attention to.

I think the limitation in systematic grammatical scope is likely to be more important. Our review of five aspects of sentence construction puts us in a position to appreciate the magnitude of that difference. Consider the compound sentence

Sarah insert banana pail apple dish, and let it for the moment be a declarative rather than an imperative. How is that English sentence related to other English sentences for adult human speakers? It has of course well-defined negative, imperative, and interrogative counterparts. The negative is not limited to some other small family of sentences, and the interrogative to still another. Furthermore, the relationship across modalities is completely general and completely systematic. Not just the sentence cited but any affirmative declarative whatever can be mapped into all the other modalities and by means of just the same abstract transformations in the case of each particular modality. This is not to say that we necessarily use the transformations as formulated in linguistics when we speak and understand but only that the system is there and must somehow be used. Furthermore, adult speakers can rapidly construct negative, imperative, declarative, and interrogative counterparts that are completely determinate if asked to do so and can do it for just about any sentence.

As another example consider the *wh-* question, which in Premack's paradigms is limited to the same-different relation. Human speakers can take a sentence like *Sarah insert banana pail apple dish* and construct a *wh-* question asking for specification of any major grammatical constituent (or semantic role) in that sentence: *Who inserts . . . ?; What does Sarah insert in the pail . . . ?; What does Sarah do? Where does Sarah insert the apple?;* and so on. Furthermore, these questions are constructible in accordance, though not necessarily by means of, rules which are completely general on an abstract level.

Consider the process of coordinating and deleting. The same sort of difference of scope and systematicity exists. Coordination may occur for any constituents providing they are of the same type and play the same syntactic (or semantic) role and that the sentence remainders are identical. It is the remainder that is deletable on one occurrence, of course. This is an order of systematic generality immeasurably beyond that demonstrated in Premack's compound sentence paradigm.

I could continue to exemplify differences of systematic scope. Do they matter, however? Certainly they matter in terms of the power of the system. But they may also matter in terms of how the operations in question are actually performed even where the scope of examples is small. I should be surprised if they did not.

Some psychologists interested in Premack's work are of the opinion that it has more to do with Sarah's ability to perform logical operations than grammatical operations, but I do not see that this is so. True enough Premack has studied aspects of comprehension of terms from both predicate logic (the quantifiers) and propositional logic (the $\supset$ relation). However, I think these do not take us very far into logic. I would like to indicate the kind of experiment that would take us further. In the work on quantifiers Sarah was trained on what might be called the referential senses of *all, none, one,* and *several.* In effect she was required to distinguish cases like "All crackers are round" from cases like "None (or no) crackers are round." But these quantifiers have inferential meanings as well as referential, and it is the inferential senses that figure in logic. Suppose Sarah is taught "No x is y," can she infer that "No y is x?" If she is taught that "All x is y," will she know that the inference "All y is x" is not valid? Not easy experiments to design, I am afraid, but I think they are the kinds of thing required if logical capacities are to be tested.

What about the Clever Hans (or Gretel) possibility? This is a problem that affects the meaning of the obtained data, and not just the representativeness of the paradigms. In his *Science* article (1971) Premack describes a series of production and comprehension experiments that he did after the principal experiments to check out this possibility. He introduced a new trainer who did not know the token language and so did not know which answer was correct in any given problem. The tokens were set in one-to-one correspondence with numerals for him, and so he was given problems to set Sarah in numerical code and reported her responses, by microphone, as numbers. Premack writes of the problems: "Familiar materials were used since the question was whether or not she could respond to old words when the cues were strictly linguistic". (p. 821). This statement does not make clear whether only the tokens and problem types were familiar or whether the actual individual problems were. Some at least were, since the examples cited include *Give Sarah X* (where *X* was a nut, candy, or fruit) and *Red ? apple* (with *color of* the answer), and these are problems that were used in earlier training sessions. In addition to tasks like the two described, Sarah was given comprehension problems of the type *Sarah take blue,* with three colored cards available and problems involving the conditional sign ⊃.

In several dimensions Sarah's performance deteriorated in these "blind" circumstances. For instance, the verticality of her sentences suffered. Instead of placing tokens more or less under one another as had been her mature practice, she tended to let the tokens sprawl across the board in a way she had done early in training. As to the performance level it fell below her usual standard, fell to 70 percent or less, but Premack concludes, it remained well above chance. Premack concludes that these tests with a trainer ignorant of the token language . . . "infirm the hypothesis that her performance was based mainly on non-linguistic cues" (p. 821).

There are several minor quarrels one might have with this conclusion. For instance, the trainer did not remain totally ignorant of the token language but began to learn it. However, Premack says (1971) that his partial knowledge was not such as could account for Sarah's success.

There is, to my thinking, one major objection which does not permit confident exclusion of the Clever Hans alternative. The fact that at least some and conceivably all the problems were familiar ones. It is true enough that Sarah's ability to supply "color of" as the token required by the question "Red ? apple" when the trainer does not know the answer shows that she has come to be able to respond to the pattern of tokens alone and is not dependent on extra-linguistic cues from the trainer. That is the way it is now, but was it so in the original training? Suppose that some substantial number of the configurations presented were familiar ones. Might she not originally have learned the correct answer from nonlinguistic cues emitted by knowledgeable trainers but then at length committed to memory the tokens that would bring reward in the presence of this or that problem configuration. Probably even Hans could have learned certain routine responses to repeated and familiar questions; cases where he was not dependent on the trainer's cues. With the chimpanzee, and with no counting involved, the possibility seems much greater. I do not feel that the Clever Hans controls Premack has reported definitively rule out the possibility of trainer cues in the original learning and so am not certain that the data mean what Premack takes them to mean.

The Study of Adam, Eve, and Sarah

In the fall of 1962[1] Ursula Bellugi, Colin Fraser, and I began a longitudinal study of the development of English as a first language in the preschool years of two children, whom we have called Adam and Eve. A third child, whom we call Sarah, joined the company somewhat later. The children were selected from some thirty who were initially considered. Adam, Eve, and Sarah were selected primarily because they were all just beginning to speak multi-word utterances, had highly intelligible speech, and were highly voluble which meant we would not have to sit around forever to get usefully large transcriptions. And because the investigators undertaking primary responsibility for each child (Ursula Bellugi for Adam; Colin Fraser for Eve; Gloria Cooper for Sarah at first, and later Courtney Cazden) felt comfortable with the child and the parents.

All the children were only children at the start of the study. Adam is the son of a minister who lived at first in Cambridge and later in Boston. Eve is the daughter of a man who was at the time a graduate student at Harvard and who lived in Cambridge. Sarah is the daughter of a man who worked as a clerk, at the start of the study, and their home was in Cambridge. The parents of Adam both had college degrees; Eve's father had a college degree and her mother a high school degree; the parents of Sarah both had high school degrees.

The principal data of the study are transcriptions of the spontaneous speech of the child and his mother (occasionally the father and others) in conversation at home. For each child we have at least two hours of transcription for every month, but within these limits the schedules have varied somewhat. For Adam and Eve a

1. The first five years of this work were supported by Public Health Service Grant MH-7088 from the National Institute of Mental Health, and the second five years by Grant HD-02908 from the National Institute of Child Health and Development. We are deeply grateful for the generosity of this support and the intelligent flexibility with which both grants have been administered. Miss Esther Sorocka has been executive secretary to the project from the beginning, and her importance to the success it has had is very great. The parents of Adam, Eve, and Sarah, and the three children themselves by their unfailing, welcoming friendliness made the whole project possible.

two-hour visit every second week was the basic schedule. For Sarah it was one half-hour each week. These are minimum schedules; when interesting things seemed to be happening fast much more speech was recorded. We found that the visits required two persons, the main investigator and one assistant (Richard Cromer, Gordon Finley, Courtney Cazden, and Melissa Bowerman have all served as assistants). One member of the team devoted himself to a written transcription, on the scene, of the speech of the child and mother (and any others) together with notes about important actions and objects of attention. The other took on the role of playmate for the child and also tended the tape recorder. All conversations were taped. In the case of Adam and Eve the microphone was in a fixed position, and all concerned simply tried to keep interaction within the microphone's range. For Sarah we required a record of higher fidelity because her records were to be phonetically transcribed in a narrow notation including prosodic and paralinguistic expressive features. Accordingly we sewed a microphone into a garment she was always asked to wear, and her speech was transmitted wirelessly to the tape. The final transcriptions, which constitute the primary data of the project, were made by the investigator principally responsible for each child working from the tape recording in conjunction with the on-the-spot transcription to make a single best record. These were made as soon after the visit as possible. Our experience is that transcription from tape of the speech of children at an early age, even when it is relatively intelligible child speech, needs the assistance of memory of the scene and a written record made on the scene.

The transcriptions of Adam and Sarah are simply at the morphemic level, that is, if a meaningful element was sounded well enough to be recognized, it was recorded in normal English spelling with no effort being made to render the particularities of the child's pronunciation. However, the transcribers, Ursula Bellugi and Colin Fraser, took great pains over grammatically significant and phonetically minimal features like inflections, prepositions, articles, and contracted auxiliaries. It is a tribute to their immense care, I know, that the data described in Stage II are so remarkably orderly. Gloria Cooper and Melissa Bowerman did the phonetic transcriptions for Sarah. These have been of considerable value for checking on points where one worried whether the transcriptions of Adam and Eve were accurate. They have always proved to be so, on their own level. Sarah's transcriptions have not been used as yet for a study of the development of phonology but would be valuable for that purpose. Anyone planning to undertake a phonetic record must be warned that it is an immense labor.

During the first year of the project a group of students of the psychology of language met each week to discuss the state of the children's construction process as of that date. The regular participants were: Jean Berko Gleason, Ursula Bellugi (now Bellugi-Klima), Colin Fraser, Samuel Anderson, David McNeill, Dan Slobin, Courtney Cazden, Richard Cromer, and Gordon Finley. We had wonderfully stimulating, light-hearted discussions. Anyone in developmental psycholinguistics looking over the membership of this seminar will realize how bounteous that year was. In the seminar small experiments or near-experiments were often suggested and then tried by the main investigators. The results were sometimes useful but never conclusive; the difficulties of experimentation on language with small children are considerable, and we put the transcription schedule first.

At the end of the first year the project suffered the kind of blow to which longitudinal studies are liable: Eve's family had to move to Nova Scotia, and our 20 two-hour transcriptions were all we would be able to obtain from her. We continued taking data from Adam and Sarah for another four years. But as it happened the fact of Eve's withdrawal has shaped my role in the project even until the present time. I decided to concentrate on just the developmental period for which we had data from all three children. As it happened Eve's speech developed so much more rapidly than that of Adam and Sarah that 10 months of her transcriptions equalled about 20 months for Adam and Sarah.

Long before the end of the first year the children got way ahead of the seminar. Their records were far too rich to be analyzed in a two-hour session. It became clear that a fine-grained analysis was a big job and had to be undertaken by one person. Even then only a fraction of the data could be examined. Still I was determined to make the effort because I had not set out to create an immense archive that no one would ever use.

It is sensible to ask and we were often asked, "Why not code the sentences for grammatically significant features and put them on a computer so that studies could readily be made by anyone?" My answer always was that I was continually discovering new kinds of information that could be mined from a transcription of conversation and never felt that I knew what the full coding should be. This was certainly the case and indeed it can be said that in the entire decade since 1962 investigators have continued to hit upon new ways of inferring grammatical and semantic knowledge or competence from free conversation. But, for myself, I must, in candor, add that there was also a factor of research style. I have little patience with prolonged "tooling up" for research. I always want to get started. A better scientist would probably have done more planning and used the computer. He can do so today, in any case, with considerable confidence that he knows what to code.

Our three children were not at the same chronological age when we began our study; Eve was 18 months; Adam and Sarah were 27 months. We had not equated for age because we knew, from much earlier work, that children acquire language at widely varying rates. We had rather equated them from the length of their utterances, both the mean length (MLU) and the upper bound or longest utterance. The mean length of utterance (MLU) is an excellent simple index of grammatical development because almost every new kind of knowledge increases length: the number of semantic roles expressed in a sentence, the addition of obligatory morphemes, coding modulations of meaning, the addition of negative forms and auxiliaries used in interrogative and negative modalities, and, of course,

Table 7.   Rules for calculating mean length of utterance and upper bound

1. Start with the second page of the transcription unless that page involves a recitation of some kind. In this latter case start with the first recitation-free stretch. Count the first 100 utterances satisfying the following rules.

2. Only fully transcribed utterances are used; none with blanks. Portions of utterances, entered in parentheses to indicate doubtful transcription, are used.

3. Include all exact utterance repetitions (marked with a plus sign in records). Stuttering is marked as repeated efforts at a single word; count the word once in the most complete form produced. In the few cases where a word is produced for emphasis or the like (*no, no, no*) count each occurrence.

4. Do not count such fillers as *mm* or *oh*, but do count *no, yeah,* and *hi*.

5. All compound words (two or more free morphemes), proper names, and ritualized reduplications count as single words. Examples: *birthday, rackety-boom, choo-choo, quack-quack, night-night, pocketbook, see saw*. Justification is that no evidence that the constituent morphemes function as such for these children.

6. Count as one morpheme all irregular pasts of the verb (*got, did, went, saw*). Justification is that there is no evidence that the child relates these to present forms.

7. Count as one morpheme all diminutives (*doggie, mommie*) because these children at least do not seem to use the suffix productively. Diminutives are the standard forms used by the child.

8. Count as separate morphemes all auxiliaries (*is, have, will, can, must, would*). Also all catenatives: *gonna, wanna, hafta*. These latter counted as single morphemes rather than as *going to* or *want to* because evidence is that they function so for the children. Count as separate morphemes all inflections, for example, possessive {s}, plural {s}, third person singular {s}, regular past {d}, progressive {iŋ}.

9. The range count follows the above rules but is always calculated for the total transcription rather than for 100 utterances.

embedding and coordinating. All alike have the common effect on the surface form of the sentence of increasing length (especially if measured in morphemes, which includes bound forms like inflections rather than words). By the time the child reaches Stage V, however, he is able to make constructions of such great variety that *what* he happens to say and the MLU of a sample begin to depend more on the character of the interaction than on what the child knows, and so the index loses its value as an indicator of grammatical knowledge.

Table 7 presents a copy of the rules we used in calculating mean length of utterances (MLU) and upper bound or longest utterance for a transcription. These rules take account of things we learned about child speech in the first year of the study, for example, the fact that compound words are not analyzed as such and the fact that the irregular pasts that occur early are not used with semantic consistency or contrasted with present forms. Still no claim can be made that these are just the right rules. They have, however, served all of us well as a simple way of making one child's data comparable with another's, one project with another, and in limited degree, development in one language comparable with development in another.

When I say that the indices have served us well I mean simply that two children matched for MLU are much more likely to have speech that is, on internal grounds, at the same level of constructional complexity than are two children of the same chronological age. We know that we are going to run into serious inconsistencies and uncertainties with some foreign languages, and these are discussed in Stage I. However, the MLU may be effectively redefined or we may find some other, almost equally simple index, preferable. In any case we are getting beyond the point where a single index is vital because we are accumulating knowledge about the acquisition order of general construction types and their meanings, and it is the order of knowledge we really care about.

I calculated the MLU's and upper bounds for all sample transcriptions for all children. The results when MLU is plotted against chronological age for just the period in which Eve participated in the study appear as Figure 1. The values rise quite consistently with age, for Eve most amazingly so. It was almost impossible to fail to find an increment every time two weeks had elapsed. As I remember it the one downward jog came on a day when Eve had a cold. This stretch of development, common to the three children, is what I undertook to analyze in some detail — a good many years ago.

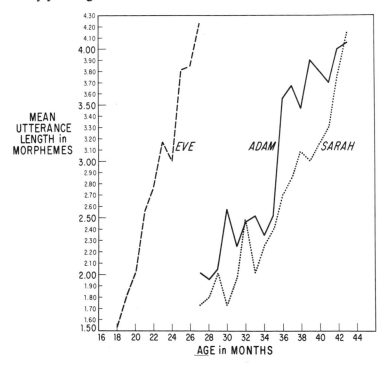

Figure 1. Mean utterance length and chronological age for three children

How to proceed? There was far too much data in even this interval to be
exhaustively analyzed. I decided to divide the total shared developmental stretch at
five points as nearly as possible equidistant from one another in terms both of MLU
and upper bound (UB) and draw 713 consecutive complete utterances from each
child at each point for detailed linguistic analysis. The odd number, 713, was
an accidental consequence of the size of the transcriptions from which the first
samples were drawn.

Table 8. Target values and approximations attained for mean length of
utterance and upper bounds

| Stage | Target Value | | Approximation Attained | |
	MLU	Upper Bound	Maximum Distance from MLU	Maximum Distance from Upper Bound
I	1.75	5	.31	2
II	2.25	7	.05	1
III	2.75	9	.25	1
IV	3.50	11	.20	1
V	4.00	13	.06	1.67

Table 8 describes my target values which for MLU begin at 1.75 and end at
4.00 with increments of 0.50 (except for III to IV). The upper bounds begin at 5.0
and proceed by increments of 2.0 to 13.0. Of course I could not hit these targets
exactly for the samples of varying size from each child. And so Table 8 also describes
the widest departures from the target values that the data ever forced me to accept.
These are never very great.

Figure 2 is just like Figure 1 except that the Roman numerals I–V and
corresponding horizontal lines mark the points at which fifteen 713 utterance
samples were taken. These were my preliminary Stages I to V. Then the work of
analysis began. I decided to press for an explicit generative grammar for each
sample but, because I knew any such grammar would have to remain indeterminate
at countless points, I undertook also to write extensive annotations describing
alternative formulations, gaps in the evidence, and so forth. Of course the data of
performance have long ago been pronounced (Chomsky, 1964) an inadequate
base for a grammar that attempts to represent competence or knowledge. I agree that
it always is but I venture to say that not many people know how much can be
milked from mere performance in the case of small children — especially
conversational performance in which you can track relations between sentences.
I have found the process of grammar writing a continual discovery of new things to
look at, new aspects of the data that could tell me something about the knowledge
in the minds of these three children.

Why write admittedly indeterminate grammars? Simply because the requirement
to be fully explicit and develop rules that will really derive the sentences you have
obtained forces a kind of intense examination and continuing re-examination of the

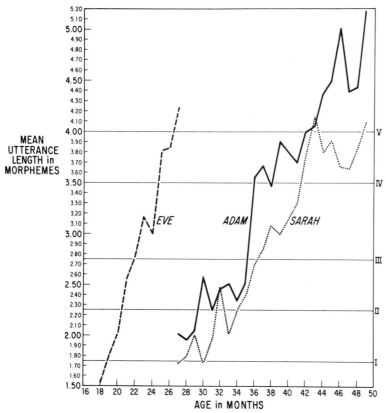

Figure 2.   Mean utterance length and age in three children

data, and so is a good way to get to know it very well. The 15 annotated grammars took something like two months each to do, with the time longer in the later stages. I suppose they are mostly 50 pages or more long. In the years that this took, linguistic theory, of course, went on changing in response to intuition and logical arguments, and when I saw the point of a change I also shifted my procedure and formal notation. In the end I was left with 15 weighty manuscripts which not more than half-a-dozen people in the world have the *knowledge,* the *patience,* and the *interest* to read; nay, not so many as half a dozen.

In the process I formed a conception of great commonality among these unacquainted children and of a remarkably invariant order in the kinds of things they said. I learned that there were some points on which the data were simply too thin to support any sort of generalization; for example, the order of adverbs. I also formed a conception of the kinds of things about which something might reasonably be said, and these are the five constructional processes described in the beginning of the chapter. The 15 grammars I now regard as a protracted preliminary exploration, not boring to me because of the puzzle properties each one develops.

One can stand a lot of sorting and resorting when it is done with hypotheses in mind which make the outcomes exciting. I am personally reluctant to hand this process over to a computer. About two years ago I started to write a new set of Stages I–V, but sticking this time to the kinds of things about which something can be said and hoping to make myself clear to more than half-a-dozen readers.

It remains only to answer a question that was put to me, with some asperity, a few years ago after a talk about child language: "What is this work about really?" It is not about the way the child's mind in fact processes sentences in speaking and understanding. I do not know how that is done. It is about knowledge; knowledge concerning grammar and the meanings coded by grammar. Knowledge inferred, of course, from performance, from sentences spoken, the settings in which they are spoken, and from signs of comprehension or incomprehension of sentences spoken by others. The book primarily presents evidence that knowledge of the kind described develops in an approximately invariant form in all children, though at different rates. There is also evidence that the primary determinants of the order are the relative semantic and grammatical complexity of constructions rather than their frequency or the way in which parents react to them. I believe that this knowledge must somehow be utilized in actual sentence processing, in speaking and under-standing, but cannot say how. I hope the volumes will help to establish reasonably firm generalizations about the unfolding of construction knowledge in children, generalizations on which theory can build.

The Expository Plan of this Work

The plan is not quite the same for any two stages but there are several things that are constant throughout.

1. The stages are not known to be true stages in Piaget's sense; that is they may not be qualitative changes of organization forced on the investigator by the data themselves. The original equidistant samples based on MLU were simply a device for sampling the data; a discontinuous sampling imposed upon more continuous data. My divisions I to V were rather like a sociologist's imposition of arbitrary dividing points on a continuous distribution of incomes.

2. The original stages were points on an MLU distribution, but in this work they have become intervals. Stage I, for instance, begins as soon as the MLU rises above 1.0, when multi-word utterances begin, and ends at 2.0. This is because our discussions are not limited to the data from Adam, Eve, and Sarah. Since we started in 1962, there have been numerous studies of the development of English and other languages which started when the child's MLU was less than 1.75 the target value for Stage I in the original analyses in our study. I have tried to put all this work together, and it is clear that construction begins before 1.75. Stage II extends from 2.0 to 2.50 because we found it possible to deal with all the data in this

period in a certain quantitative respect. Other considerations make intervals of all the later stages.

3. A stage is named (Semantic Roles and Syntactic Relations for Stage I; Grammatical Morphemes and the Modulation of Meaning for Stage II; Modalities of the Simple Sentence for Stage III; and so on, either for a process that is the major new development occurring in that interval or for an exceptionally elaborate development of a process at that stage. However, the whole development of any one of the major constructional processes is not contained within a given stage interval. Semantic roles go on developing after Stage I; the modulations of meaning extend from Stage II to beyond even Stage V. The germs of the major modalities of simple sentences (interrogation, negation, the imperative) are to be found even in Stage I in a syntactically rudimentary form, and there are combinations of the modalities, like the tag question, which do not appear until after Stage V. When we discuss embedding in Stage IV we shall have to go all the way back to Stage I to show why certain constructions (the possessive and the prenominal adjective) which appear in Stage I, and are analyzed by many linguists as embeddings, are not such in the child's speech. In general there is something of interest to say about all five major aspects of construction in all five stages. In general the stage discussion deals with the construction aspect for which it is named across the full range of data.

4. As mentioned in passing, not only the data of Adam, Eve, and Sarah but all the longitudinal and experimental data available to me on a given stage are discussed. There is far more information beyond our own, on Stage I, than on any other stage, including longitudinal studies of Finnish, Samoan, Swedish, Spanish, Luo, and German, as well as a number of studies of American English. The data thin out after Stage I simply because most of the investigators in question have not had time to carry their analyses beyond this point.

5. The stages are not simply descriptive but are organized as evidence and argument for and against certain generalizations. In Stage I, for example, the question is, on what evidence, if at all can the constructional meanings of the first sentences be inferred? There is one recurrent theme in all stages, that order of development, conceived in the right abstract terms is invariant across both children and languages and is primarily determined by the relative semantic and grammatical complexity of constructions.

Stage I

Semantic Roles and Grammatical Relations

First steps are difficult and important. In the days when speculation about the prehistoric origins of speech was an intellectually respectable activity almost all the speculation centered on the nature of the first words. Were they social signals, an overflow of emotion, a leap into symbolism, or just conditioned responses? A kind of play, a kind of tool, or a kind of magic? Once the nature of the first words had been established, interest in the evolution of language seemed to lapse; the assumption was, that the rest must simply be more of the same. Which means, I think, that arguments about the origin of language were not so much arguments about prehistory as they were arguments about the essential nature of man. Each theorist wanted language to begin with a step in the right direction, that direction being defined by the theorist's notion of what man had become. Since there were no data at all, theories of the first word were pure statements of faith. Nowadays speculation about the prehistoric beginnings of language is not a respectable activity, but speculation about the preliterate beginnings in childhood is. And, since interest has shifted from words to syntax, it is the nature of the child's first sentences that people speculate about and feel strongly about. There are some data, and that is limiting. Still, among sentences, it is just the first ones that offer the fewest clues to their underlying nature and which are, therefore, most susceptible of interpretation.

In this chapter I will review and criticize recent characterizations of the first sentences in order to arrive at a well-founded description of the semantic and grammatical knowledge that develops in Stage I; there will follow a description of questions about Stage I which are raised but not settled by available data. The chapter begins with a characterization of the data available concerning Stage I development in a variety of languages; a division is made between studies that can be ordered developmentally by MLU or some other simple index and those that cannot be ordered among themselves but which may be judged to contain information on Stage I. The listings of the data are followed by critical discussions of the most influential characterizations of such data. Each of these characterizations was originally developed out of some small part of the total data listed in Tables 9 and 10, and so various ones of these studies are introduced a second time as the data base of some characterization but the characterization is, in this chapter, tested against all the data. The movement of this long section, reviewing characterizations of Stage I speech, is slowed by the exploration of every ravine, rabbit hole, and cul de sac in its path but it does move, more like a sheet of lava, than an arrow, in the direction of the approach to Stage I speech I believe to be correct. It moves from the early, nonsemantic, "lean" characterizations, telegraphic speech and pivot grammar, to various semantic, "rich" characterizations in terms of relations, cases, operations, and the like. I think the discussions as a whole show that telegraphic speech and pivot grammar are characterizations which fit the data we now have only insofar as they correspond to semantic characterizations, and they do this quite imperfectly showing rather clearly that a semantic characterization or what I have called "rich interpretation" is the superior approach.

An important consideration causing us to settle on the method of rich interpretation is the evidence of word order. Lois Bloom (1970, based on her 1968 thesis) was the first to make explicit the point that, when a Stage I child speaking English uses two or three words in an utterance in just that serial order which is appropriate to the context of reference as an adult sees it, then the child has made a kind of discriminating response which may be taken as evidence that he intends the semantic relations the order implies and not just the meanings of the individual words. Word order suiting the nonverbal situation is a discriminating response just because other orders not suited to the situation are, after all, possible but not employed. The evidence of word order becomes a more complex story when languages other than English are considered, languages in which order is freer and less often contrastive than in English. The evidence is also more complicated when we consider performances other than spontaneous speech such as the ability to respond in a discriminating way to order in pairs of sentences which are otherwise identical and the ability to judge order in sentences as correct or not and, when incorrect, to set it right. This story to date is told in a section devoted to "The Role of Word Order." The conclusions are fairly complex but it does seem that for English, at least, Stage I children are able to use order appropriately in spontaneous speech and to make correct discriminating responses to contrasting orders, and so the method of rich interpretation is justified. However, judgments of correct and incorrect order as well as the ability to correct orders that are incorrect appear to be performances of which the child learning English is not capable until long after Stage I, indeed until Stage V or beyond.

The section called "The Major Meanings at Stage I" is the heart of the whole chapter. It reports new findings concerning Stage I which are made visible by following the method of "rich" interpretation. As far as possible the findings are quantitative and complete but for some studies they can only be fragmentary. It turns out that a rather short list of semantic propositions and relations (between 8 and 15) will encompass the nonlexical or compositional meanings of the majority of all multi-morpheme utterances produced by the Stage I children listed in Tables 9 and 10, and that these meanings seem to represent linguistically the sensori-motor intelligence which develops, according to Piaget's research, in the 18 months or so which normally precede Stage I. It further turns out that the expressive means common to all is the simple construction into single utterances of the relevant content words; for languages in which word order is rigid and contrastive there is the further expressive device of appropriate word order. Finally Stage I is not monolithic; development occurs as MLU increases. This development is always of the same two kinds. An increase in the number of relations expressed by: 1. concatenating, serially, more relations and omitting redundant terms; 2. unfolding of one term in a relation so that the term becomes itself a relation. In these data as a whole, as also in Stage II and in Brown and Hanlon's (1970) results with tag questions, there is evidence for what I have, not yet very seriously, called a law of cumulative complexity in language development. It is important to realize that as utterances get longer, and MLU increases, some sort of increase in complexity is bound to occur, but there is no a priori reason why the increase should take just the forms it does and, in particular, that these forms should be the same for all children studied, whatever the language in question.

A final section pushes hard at producing an actual grammar for Stage I speech, considering only the more promising semantically aware kinds of grammar (Schlesinger's, Fillmore's, and Bloom's) and ignoring the "lean" approaches of telegraphic speech and pivot grammar. Of course I do not succeed, in this section, in producing a fully satisfactory grammar. One never can when the only data are finite samples of performance and when the adult grammars themselves are not really complete. Nevertheless this slightly arid exercise proves worthwhile. Among other less important things, it made salient the fact that the Stage I child operates as if major constituents were optional even as from Stage II on he operates as if grammatical morphemes were optional. Furthermore, his constituent omissions do not correspond with the relatively lawful omissions practiced by his parents. He often leaves out what is linguistically obligatory. What this suggests to me is that the child expects to be understood if he speaks any appropriate words at all and, in fact, at home talking about present contexts, to family members, he usually is. What he is going to learn, of course, is to express always and, in some neurological sense automatically, certain meanings (agent, action, number, tense, etc.) whether that meaning happens to be redundant or not in a given situation. What he also learns, varyingly well, is not to say what is obvious in a given situation and to select his lexicon and syntax to fit his present addressee. In the degree that he does so his communication efforts move from being narrowly adapted — they work with his family and at home in concurrent situations — to being widely and flexibly adopted — they work with many addressees and with varying amounts of situational support. I speculate that it is necessary for any language to make obligatory and automatic certain meanings in order to leave central channeling capacity free to cope with the exigencies of each particular communication problem.

The Available Data

Adam, Eve, and Sarah at Stage I, when we first began transcribing their speech, were not at the very beginning of grammar. For the samples which define Stage I the mean-length-of-utterance (MLU) values were: 1.68 for Eve, 1.73 for Sarah, and 2.06 for Adam. Overt grammar or morpheme-combining begins really as soon as the MLU rises above 1.00. There are, in the literature or in progress, quite a few longitudinal grammatical studies which include reports for developmental stages lying between an MLU of 1.00 and the level at which our children were first studied. Combining these reports with ours we have information on an initial period which is bounded by an MLU of 1.0, the threshold of syntax, and an MLU of 2.0, the level of the most advanced child in the set — Adam.

Table 9.   Data that can be ordered Developmentally

Child[a]	Sex	MLU	Age at Data	Character of Data	Investigator	Language
Eric I	M	1.10	1;7	4 hours, taped	Bloom	American English
Kendall I	F	1.10	–	2 full days, transcribed on scene	Bowerman	American English
Gia I	F	1.12	1;7	7 hours, taped	Bloom	American English
Eric II	M	1.19	1;9	6 hours, taped	Bloom	American English
Gregory	M	–	1;7.5–1;11.5	Cumulative inventory	Braine	American English
Andrew	M	–	1;7.5–1;11.5	Cumulative inventory	Braine	American English
Steven	M	–	1;11.5–2;0.5	12 play sessions, taped	Braine	American English
Christy	F	–	2;0–2;3	Taped weekly, 45 minute sessions	Miller, Ervin	American English
Susan	F	–	1;8–2;0	Taped weekly, 45 minute sessions	Miller, Ervin	American English
Kathryn I	F	1.32	1;9	7½ hours, taped	Bloom	American English
Gia II	F	1.34	1;9	7½ hours, taped	Bloom	American English
Eric III	M	1.42	1;10	8½ hours, taped	Bloom	American English
Seppo I	M	1.42	1;11	2 hours, taped over 1 month	Bowerman	Finnish
Kendall II	F	1.48	1;11	1½ hours, taped over 2 days	Bowerman	American English
Viveka	F	1.50	1;11	4½ hours, taped over 1 month	Rydin	Swedish
Sipili	M	1.52	2;6	6½ hours, taped over 1 week	Kernan	Samoan
Tofi	M	1.60	2;2	2 hours, taped over 1 week	Kernan	Samoan
Eve I	F	1.68	1;6	3½ hours, taped over 6 weeks	Fraser, Brown	American English
Sarah I	F	1.73	2;3	3 hours, taped over 6 weeks	Cazden, Brown	American English
Seppo II	M	1.81	2;2	2 hours, taped over 1 month	Bowerman	Finnish
Rina I	F	1.83	2;1	2 hours, taped over 1 month	Bowerman	Finnish
Pepe	M	1.85	2;6	4 hours, taped in two consecutive days	Tolbert	Spanish (Mexico)
Kathryn II	F	1.92	1;11	9 hours, taped	Bloom	American English
Adam I	M	2.06	2;3	2 hours, taped over 1 month	Bellugi, Brown	American English

[a]Roman numerals after children's names were assigned by investigators and refer to specific ordered analyses; all children are in Stage I by our definition.

There are, to begin with, 19 reports on 13 children which are quite fully comparable with one another in that they use as primary data spontaneous conversation of and with the child at home, report MLU values (calculated by rules like those given in the Introduction and used by us), include in their reports all of their data or very substantial proportions of them, and address some or all of the theoretical questions that concern us. These include, to begin with, the three reports at Stage I for Adam, Eve, and Sarah based on 713 utterances of tape-recorded speech in each case and with known MLU values. In 1968 Lois Bloom completed a doctoral dissertation at Columbia (published as a book in 1970) based on a longitudinal study of three children (Kathryn, Gia, and Eric). Bloom used tape recorded spontaneous speech and reported MLU values but she placed her grammatical analyses at different points and worked from larger samples. For the period of interest, 1.0 to 2.0, we have two grammars written for Kathryn, three for Eric, and two for Gia. Melissa Bowerman, in her 1970 doctoral dissertation at Harvard, transcribed on the scene two full days of the speech of an American child, Kendall, when Kendall's MLU was 1.10, and again when it was 1.48. For American

English this gives us 12 grammatical analyses of 7 children, the analyses well scattered across the range of Stage I.

In 1969 Keith Kernan completed a doctoral dissertation at Berkeley (with Dan Slobin as one of his advisers) on two children: Sipili, a boy of 2;6 (two years, six months) and Tofi, a girl of 2;2 (two years, two months). Though Kernan has extensive data on these children and on 10 others, between two and five years of age, his grammar for Sipili is based on two visits in one week which yielded a total of 852 utterances, taped on the scene and transcribed by Kernan with the help of Sipili's aunt. The MLU was 1.52. The grammar for Tofi is based on three visits in one week when the MLU was 1.60. Both these children live in the village of Faleasa in American Samoa. Kernan's study raises our total to 14 analyses of nine children, all with known MLU's.

In 1970 Melissa Bowerman completed her dissertation (in press). The primary focus of the thesis was on two children learning Finnish (a Finno-Ugric language) as their first language though their families were living in the United States. Bowerman deliberately made her study directly comparable with ours in using MLU values and basing her grammatical analyses on just 713 utterances, though the analyses themselves do not fall at just the same points. For the period of interest we have two grammars from one boy (Seppo) and one from a girl (Rina). The scope of Bowerman's thesis (now in press, Cambridge University Press) is very broad including insightful comparisons with studies of American English as well as with Kernan's study of Samoan. Her descriptive study of Finnish brings our basic sample to 16 analyses of 11 children.

In 1971 two students in a seminar with me added Stage I studies of additional Indo-European languages. Ingegard Rydin (1971) whose native language is Swedish taped and transcribed 895 utterances, taken in three sessions in one month, from Viveka, whose father was a Visiting Professor from Sweden in Boston. The MLU was 1.50. Kay Tolbert (1972) made a trip to Mexico, and on two visits in one week taped 791 utterances of Pepe, whose MLU was 1.85. This is a particularly valuable study, since Pepe is the only child in the basic set who can be positively identified as a member of a lower-class family. Rydin and Tolbert bring our total to 19 analyses of 13 children.

For five more children we have data somewhat comparable with that for the first 13, but not entirely so. In 1963 Martin Braine published an analysis of the first phase of grammar in three boys: Gregory, Andrew, and Steven. The mothers of Gregory and Andrew kept seriatim records of all comprehensible utterances that were not imitative of immediately antecedent models. They began before their sons had produced any word combinations, at a time when the verbal repertoire consisted of 10–20 single words. The data Braine used were listings for each boy of all distinct combinations (types not tokens) produced in the first four months after the beginning of combinations; in short, a cumulative list of all sentences. The third boy, Steven, was to have been studied in the same way but, because there were questions about the intelligibility of his speech, the method of the seriatim record was abandoned. Steven's data were obtained from tape recordings of 12 play sessions that occurred over a four-week period in the fourth and fifth months after combinations began. Steven's data are probably quite similar to the data that a cumulative diary would have yielded. In addition to his analyses Braine has published the full data for Steven and Andrew and all but about 20 sentences for Gregory. Consequently it is possible in some degree to check his evidence and try alternative analyses. Unfortunately for me Braine did not take MLU values, and it is not possible to calculate them from the material published. In 1964 Wick Miller and Susan Ervin (now Susan Ervin-Tripp) described the early sentences of two children, Susan and Christy, whose speech they had been taping in weekly sessions of 45 minutes each. Susan's records begin at 1;8 and, according to her parents, Susan first began to make multi-word utterances at 1;7. Miller and Ervin discuss data for the period 1;8–2;0. Miller and Ervin discuss for their other child, Christy, data taken between 2;0 and 2;3. Miller and Ervin do not publish their complete data but for two-word utterances, the great majority of combinations in this period, they provide frequencies which permit certain kinds of analyses we shall be interested in making. Braine and Miller and Ervin bring our basic sample to a total of 24 grammatical analyses of 18 children.

I have attempted in Table 9 to place the 24 analyses in developmental order across the range of Stage I, which extends, in MLU terms, from 1.0 to 2.0. This is rather easily done for the 19 reports including MLU values and the order is that of the values, though it is worth mentioning that upper bounds (longest utterances) when given are consistent with the MLU values. Studies of highly inflected languages, like Finnish, Swedish, and Spanish, all report some difficulty in adapting our rules of calculation, invented for English, which is minimally inflected, to their languages. What I have used is, in each case, the author's choice of the linguistically most reasonable value. In Stage I the variation in values for highly inflected languages, dependent on decisions not covered by our rules is small about 0.10.

How can we order the remaining five children, those studied by Braine and by Miller and Ervin for whom no MLU values exist? It can be done, in a rough sort of way, building on the fact that as MLU goes up so does the variety of multi-word utterances. Eric I, for instance, yielded a total of only 19 different combinations at an MLU of 1.10; Kathryn I at MLU of 1.32 yielded 397 different combinations, and Kathryn II at MLU of 1.92 a total of 1,490 different utterances. These are all totals from Bloom's large samples, and are probably best interpreted as estimates of the total inventory. For samples using just 713 utterances, as some did, the increase in variety with MLU may be expressed as a kind of type/token ratio (TTR) where types are different multi-word utterances and tokens are *all* multi-word utterances including repetitions. The larger the value of the ratio the greater the variety of utterances. The range is from a TTR of .42 for Seppo I when his MLU was 1.42 to a TTR of .7 for Adam I at an MLU of 2.06.

For the children studied by Miller and Ervin and by Braine we shall want to work with estimates of complete inventories. Braine's records for Gregory and Andrew were, in fact, complete cumulative inventories of multi-word combinations and Steven's record, since it was based on 12 play sessions over a four-week period, probably comes close to being a complete inventory. The numbers of combinations are: Gregory, 89; Andrew, 102; Steven, 102. The samples for Christy and Susan were based on weekly 45-minute sessions over a period of three months, and so probably the number of combinations only slightly underestimates a full inventory. Miller and Ervin only give the figures for two-word utterances, but, since most combinations were of that length, we use them. They are: Christy, 210, Susan, 240.

For the four children in Table 9, having the lowest MLU values, it is possible to estimate the sizes of their complete inventories of multi-word utterances. Bloom's analyses were generally based on very large samples: Eric I, based on the smallest of Bloom's samples, four hours, produced only 19 combinations; Eric II, based on six hours, 87; and Gia I, based on seven hours, 141. Bowerman's Kendall I, based on two full days, produced a total of 102 different combinations. If we use these figures as (admittedly imperfect) estimates of cumulative inventories, their average is 87, which is also the value for Eric II, the most advanced of them. This value 87 is just below the 89 of Braine's Gregory and suggests that his children (Gregory, Andrew, and Steven) belong in that order after the four most primitive samples.

The next three samples are Bloom's. These are Kathryn I, Gia II, and Eric III, and their respective totals of different combinations are: 397, 141, and 243. The average of these values is 260, and that suggests that Christy and Susan with, respectfully, 210 and 240 different combinations, belong after Braine's children and before Kathryn I, and I have so placed them in Table 9.

What is the point of attempting a developmental ordering for as many samples as possible in spite of inescapable residual uncertainties of exact placement? We shall want to see not only what characterizes Stage I as a whole, in terms of presumed semantic and grammatical knowledge, but will wish to see how knowledge progresses in the course of this stage and whether there is anything like an invariant order of progression across children and languages. To that end we need to order on the basis of some sort of index external to the actual utterances in each sample. MLU and inventory size estimates are such external estimates. I know they are more meaningful than chronological age in the sense of predicting the character of sentences. But notice that there are a great many ways that sentences can increase in length — from the addition of inflections, the creation of new kinds of constituents, the appearance of embedding or coordination. Nothing about the character of the index, primarily an increase of utterance length, requires that that length should always be attained by the same internal means.

Table 10 sets forth the vital facts about a second sort of useful study. What all these studies lack is any good external basis for developmental ordering within Stage I. What they have in common is data or summary statements identifiably con-

Table 10.   Studies including information on Stage I but for which ordering within Stage I is not possible

Child[a]	Age Range	Character of Data	Investigator	Language
Hildegard	1;0–2;0	Parental diary, selectively recorded	Leopold	American English
Charles and Edmond	1;0–2;0	Parental diary, selectively recorded	Grégoire	French
Ulrike, Angela, and Georg	1;7–2;9, varying with the child	Taping and on-the-scene transcription of child with mother, 2 hours a month for 6–7 months	Park	German
Gil (M) and Gila (F)	From 1;0 for Gila and 1;2 for Gil, upper limit not stated	Transcriptions at home from first word until 6 years. Some utterances identified as among the first multi-word utterances. Otherwise details not given	Bar-Adon	Hebrew
Izanami (F)	About 2;0	Taping twice monthly in Tokyo of everything said to and by the child. Duration of visits not specified. Multi-word utterances ranged from 2–4 morphemes.	McNeill	Japanese
Susin (F)	2;2	Transcriptions on the scene by author-father. Three sessions of 4–6 hours each at ages 2;2 and 2;5 and 2;8. At 2;2 Susin had just started to make combinations.	Park	Korean
Othieno (M), Aoko (M), Ochieng (M), Risper (F), Rabuogi (M), and Akinyi (F)	1;7–2;7, varying with the child	Transcriptions on the scene with translators and reports of parents. Total corpus from all children: 191 utterances	Blount	Luo
Zhenya	?	In English only selective, interpretive comments	Gvozdev, Slobin	Russian

[a]M (male) and F (female) are used only for names which do not reveal sex to the speaker of English.

cerned with Stage I whether early or late, plus, generally, an interest in questions that will concern us. A very limiting consideration is that they are written in a language I can read. Most of the studies are recent, since recent studies are more likely to consider current issues, but there is also a sampling of older studies. The set as a whole is only a sample of the large literature on child speech, a sampling selected however for its relevance and accessibility, and not because it confirms any anticipated conclusions. The studies of Table 10 considerably expand the range of languages on which we can draw, and it is by language name that the entries in the table are alphabetized.

First comes Leopold's (1949) monumental description and discussion of the first two years in the grammatical development of his daughter Hildegard. Hildegard lived in a bilingual environment and was simultaneously acquiring both English and German. Next comes another classical older study, of the parental diary sort; the study Grégoire (1937) made of the first two years of his sons, Charles and Edmond. These boys grew up in Belgium and learned a French, somewhat affected by Walloonian dialect.

The third study, a study of German, is so contemporary as not yet to have been published. It was written by Tschang-Zin Park (1970a) of the University of Bern in Switzerland. Mr. Park had read an earlier draft of the present chapter, and he offers important observations and ideas on practically all the issues that concern us. Park started out to calculate MLU values but, running into the problems that inflectional languages raise, he gave up doing so. Park's method of collecting data was like ours: the children's conversation at home with mother, taped and also transcribed on the scene. The sampling schedule was two hours a month. Ulrike at the start of the study was 1;7, and at the end 2;2; for Angela the range was 2;1 to 2;6; and for Georg 2;4 to 2;9. Ulrike at the start was producing only one-word sentences but Park found that counting morphemes, her MLU was 1.24, and in only the second session, when she had begun to make two-word utterances it was 1.64. Park considered that these values must be "inflated" because of the inflectional character of German, and so he calculated no others.

Park's quandary may be illustrated with reference to German definite (*der, die, das,* etc.) and indefinite articles (*ein, eine, eines,* etc.). These forms vary by both gender and case as English articles do not. Careful linguistic method (Harris, 1951) requires a very elaborate pattern of evidence for the identification of segments including pairs of sentences partially the same and partially different plus a kind of relationship between tentative morphemes that is also found in other tentative morpheme pairs and more besides. Working from finite samples of child speech and unable to test pairs on the child, one can never meet these demanding criteria. What Park seems to have done is to count morphemes much as one would do if the full German grammar were present even though, as he says combinations were, generally, incongruent (e.g., *ein Häuser* rather than *ein Haus* and *Ursula trinken* rather than *Ursula trinkt*). Park's method of counting does seem to exaggerate the child's knowledge but we cannot afford to be critical of him because our own counting rules (in the Introduction) are not really very well rationalized. From the point of view of the full adult language they are quite inconsistent. We do not, for instance, count the "past" morpheme in irregular verbs like *got* and *did* because my preliminary once-through on the data showed that these were not used contrastively with *get* and *do* and the like in Stage I nor were they used consistently in a semantically appropriate way. We did, however, count such inflections as the plural and progressive because, while appropriately contrastive pairs were absent at I, they began to appear shortly thereafter. It would not be surprising if Park found our rules hard to generalize to German. In any case he seems to have "assumed the maximum" by way of contrast and so obtained large values.

What is the right way to count MLU in samples of child speech? I do not really know. Perhaps it would have been better if we had consistently assumed the minimum; it certainly would be impossible to wait for all the minimal contrasts. But then the index would not be as sensitive to real developments as it has proved. With inflected languages my own inclination would be to count as morphemes just those that were correctly used, which would bring values down a bit and be more likely to represent real development. Alternatively one might use other indices which also change with age (in our data) such as TTR for utterances or percentage of all utterances, imitated from a model not more than three utterances above. However, TTR soon approximates 1.0 (in our data) and percentage imitations soon approximate zero.

Happily, all these are only intended as interim external indices, known to be better than chronological age (the proof of this appears in "Stage II'). When we have found evidence of reliable internal semantic and grammatical change, and we will find it in both Stage I and Stage II, we can identify a child's construction level in these terms and ignore the various external indices.

Park's own judgment, based on internal structure compared with our reports on English, is that Ulrike's data were mostly from Stage I, whereas Angela and Georg spanned late Stage I and Stage II. Since he began transcribing Ulrike at the one-word stage and since the two MLU values he did calculate were below 2.0, it seems safe to agree with him about Ulrike. We shall also take his word on the levels of Angela and Georg.

Bar-Adon of the University of Texas has made a very detailed record of the speech of two children (Gil [m] and Gila [f], learning Hebrew as their first language. His records begin with the first word and extend until the age of six. He has published a report (1971) on a small sampling of this material, but the report does not include MLU's and so it is not possible to say whether all utterances in the report come within the interval we are calling Stage I. However, Bar-Adon sometimes tells us that he is talking about the first multi-word utterances the children produced (at 1;0 for Gila and 1;2 for Gil), and these are necessarily Stage I utterances. In addition, the report includes many general conclusions for these children learning Hebrew on questions that will concern us.

McNeill undertook the study of two little girls in Tokyo who were two years old in February 1966. They were visited and taped twice monthly. In his 1966a report on aspects of this work McNeill has nothing to say about one of the girls beyond the fact that she had so far produced only 17 word combinations. The other, given the pseudonym Izanami, a goddess of Japanese mythology who assisted at the Creation, produced a great many combinations. Since McNeill tells us that these were mostly 2–5 morphemes long we may assume that his selected observations about Izanami concern Stage I, which, in English, has an upper bound of seven morphemes.

Tschang-Zin Park has another report (1970b) as yet unpublished; a study of his own daughter Susin. At the time of the study the family was living in German-speaking Switzerland and, during her second year, Susin spent most of her afternoons with a Swiss family and started learning Swiss German, which her parents did not understand, before Korean. Just before 2;0, she made her first one-word utterances in Korean. At 2;3 two-word utterances began, and Park then started his study. He made on-the-scene transcriptions for 4 to 6 hours at each of three ages: 2;2, 2;5, and 2;8. He included only Korean speech. Park did not calculate MLU but the first session (the start of two-word sentences) clearly falls within Stage I. The second session, on the basis of internal evidence and assuming much cross-linguistic invariance, is either at the end of my Stage I or in Stage II. The third session at 2;8, when inflections and postpositions and even some embeddings and coordinations occurred, is far beyond Stage I. Korean belongs to the same language family as Japanese (the Ural-Altaic). It makes extensive use of inflections and employs postpositions as case markers. Except for a few minor restrictions, word order is entirely free.

Luo is a language of the Nilotic family spoken by about one million people in Nyanza Province in Kenya in east central Africa. Mr. Ben Blount, then a student at the University of California in Berkeley, went to Kenya in 1967 to make a study of the development of language in eight children encompassing the age range from 12 to 35 months. He intended to make his central procedure the collection on a regular schedule of large samples of spontaneous speech at home, usually with the mother as interpreter. In American and European families, at least of the middle class, it is usually possible to obtain a couple of hundred utterances in as little as half an hour, at least it is so, once any shyness has passed. Among the Luo, things proved more difficult. In 54 visits of half an hour or longer Mr. Blount was only able to obtain a *total* from all the children of 191 multi-word utterances. The problem was primarily one of Luo etiquette, which requires that small children be silent when adults come to visit, and the small children Mr. Blount visited could not throw off their etiquette even though their parents entreated them to speak for the visiting "European," as Mr. Blount was called.

Two of the Luo children were at the babbling or one-word stage, and so we may disregard them here. For the others, Othieno, Aoko, Ochieng, Risper, Rabuogi, and Akinyi, Blount (1969) has provided a list of all utterances together with English glosses. For a given child there are as few as two and never as many as 100 utterances, the number on which calculation of the MLU is ordinarily based, and so neither Mr. Blount nor we can order the children on this basis. He orders their speech, instead, in terms of the complexity of surface structure, which, of course, is related to both MLU and age. I have examined all the utterances and what Blount says about them and have concluded that his Stages 1 and 2 both fall within my Stage I, Blount's first early on in my Stage I, and his second stage near the end. Blount's Stage 1 consists simply of a small number of combinations of two nouns or one noun and one verb. In his Stage 2 he finds: "Noun phrases show considerable expansion over those in Stage 1 with adjectives, demonstratives, and nominals appearing as modifying elements" (p. 43). This is precisely the kind of internal change that one finds in the course of Stage I for children for whom we have MLU values. Blount's Stage 3, on the other hand, includes quite a few prepositional phrases, as well as a past tense, completed aspect inflection on the verb, as well as double verbals (e.g., *I want to go to speech*). Now all of these are among the changes that emerge in Stage II, in children for whom MLU values are known, and so I have concluded that just Blount's Stages 1 and 2 fall within my Stage I. Notice that I am here *assuming* an invariant relation between MLU and internal semantic and grammatical structure not demonstrating such a relation. The demonstration has to be made for the children whose MLU values are known as well as the internal character of their speech. Blount's data can only be used to point up interesting congruities or contrasts which exist if his data are selectively assigned to Stage I by the reasonable but not decisive procedure I have described.

A. N. Gvozdev has written a very detailed account of the linguistic development of his son Zhenya but the account has not been translated, and I cannot read Russian. Dan Slobin has extracted (1966, 1971b) from Gvozdev information on several important points.

Tables 9 and 10, especially 9, describe the primary data to which I shall make reference. They do not, of course, describe all the data that are useful and that I will have occasion to cite. There is, for instance, Chao's (1951) selective report of the early development of his grandson Canta, who was learning Mandarin. There is Rūke-Draviņa's (1963) account of the acquisition of Latvian by her son Dainis. There is Robbins Burling's (1959) account of his son Stephen's early learning of Garo, a Tibeto-Burman language of India. Indeed, Slobin (1971b), who is the leading American student of the older European diary literature as well as the leading "inspirer" of new studies of exotic languages, judges that there is at least scanty evidence on 30 languages from 10 or so major language families. The studies I have selected are those to which I can give the kind of close study in which I am interested.

Characterizations of the Data

Telegraphic Speech

Words in a telegram cost money, and so that is reason to be brief, to say nothing not essential. If the full message were: "My car has broken down and I have lost my wallet; send money to me at the American Express in Paris" the telegram would be: "Car broken down; wallet lost; send money American Express Paris." The telegram omits 10 words: *my, has, and, I, have, my, to, me, at, the, in.* These words are pronouns, prepositions, articles, conjunctions, and auxiliary verbs. The words retained are nouns and verbs. The adult user of English when he writes a telegram operates under a constraint on length and the child when he first begins to make sentences also operates under some kind of a constraint that limits length. The curious fact is that the sentences the child makes are like adult telegrams in that they are largely made up of nouns and verbs (with a few adjectives and adverbs) and in that they generally do not use prepositions, conjunctions, articles, or auxiliary verbs.

Early Characterizations

Brown and Fraser in 1963 described an experiment in which six children, between two and three years old, were asked to imitate 13 simple English sentences. The results appear in Table 11; the two youngest children were called Adam and Eve but they are not the children of our longitudinal study. Brown and Fraser point out that the younger children tended to preserve nouns, verbs, adjectives, and pronouns, and to omit articles, prepositions, copular *be,* and auxiliary verbs. They also omitted inflections: *showed* becomes *show, goes* becomes *go, books* becomes *book.* Adult telegrams, incidentally do not omit inflections, since these bound morphemes are not "charged" as words and are obligatory in English grammar. With increasing age the children in Table 11 retain more and more of the words that are at first omitted.

Brown and Fraser point out that the results may be rather effectively summarized in terms of the distinction some linguists make between "contentive" words and "functors." Contentives are the nouns, verbs, and adjectives and some, but not all, made concrete reference to persons, objects, actions, and qualities. The word classes, or "parts of speech" involved, have very many members and readily admit new members. Functors are forms that do not, in any simple way, make reference. They mark grammatical structures and carry subtle modulatory meanings. The word classes or parts of speech involved (inflections, auxiliary verbs, articles, prepositions, and conjunctions) all have few members and do not readily admit new members.

Table 12 from Brown and Fraser (1963) shows that, in the imitations of the six children studied, functors were more often omitted than contentives. Pronouns, it may be noticed, occupy a kind of intermediate position with respect to the proportion of the time they are omitted, and that is a fact to which we shall return.

The imitations of Table 12 have one further important property in common; they preserve the word order of the model. This is an aspect of the performance that is so familiar and somehow reasonable that one does not at once recognize it as an empirical outcome rather than as a natural necessity. But of course it is not a necessity, the outcome could have been otherwise. Words might, for example, have been said back in the reverse of their original order, the most recent first.

Finally, Brown and Fraser note that the telegraphic characterization fits the spontaneous sentences of the children they studied as well as it fits their imitations "For the striking fact about the utterances of the younger children, when they are approached from the vantage point of adult grammar, is that they are almost all classifiable as grammatical sentences from which certain morphemes have been

Table 11. Imitations of spoken sentences[a]

Model Sentence	Eve, 25½	Adam, 28½	Helen, 30	Ian, 31½	Jimmy, 32	June, 35½
1. I showed you the book.	I show book.	(I show) book.	C	I show you the book.	C	Show you the book.
2. I am very tall.	(My) tall.	I (very) tall.	I very tall.	I'm very tall.	Very tall.	I very tall.
3. It goes in a big box.	Big box.	Big box.	In big box.	It goes in the box.	C	C
4. Read the book.	Read book.	Read book.	-	Read (a) book.	Read a book.	C
5. I am drawing a dog.	Drawing dog.	I draw dog.	I drawing dog.	Dog.	C	C
6. I will read the book.	Read book.	I will read book.	I read the book.	I read the book.	C	C
7. I can see a cow.	See cow.	I want see cow.	C	Cow.	C	C
8. I will not do that again.	Do again.	I will that again.	I do that.	I again.	C	C
9. I do not want an apple.	I do apple.	I do a apple.	-	I do not want apple.	I don't want a apple.	I don't want apple.
10. Do I like to read books?	To read book?	I read books?	I read books?	I read book?	C	C
11. Is it a car?	't car?	Is it car?	Car?	That a car?	Is it car?	C
12. Where does it go?	Where go?	Go?	Does it go?	Where do it go?	C	C
13. Where shall I go?	Go?	-	-	C	C	C

Source: Brown and Fraser, 1963.

[a] ( ) indicates uncertain transcription;
  - indicates no intelligible imitation was obtained;
  C indicates imitation was correct.

Table 12.   Percentages correctly imitated of morphemes in various syntactic classes[a]

Syntactic Class	Correctly Imitated
Classes Having Few Members in English	
Inflections	44
Pronouns	72
Articles	39
Modal auxiliaries	56
Copular verbs	33
Classes Having Many Members in English	
Nouns	100
Adjectives	92
Main verbs	85

Source: Brown and Fraser, 1963.

[a]Using tests for differences between two percentages, the percentage correct in each of the classes with many members is significantly greater than the percentage correct in any of the classes with few members (p < .001, 2-tailed test).

omitted. You may have noticed that while Eve's sentences are not grammatically 'complete' they are somehow intelligible as abbreviated or telegraphic versions of familiar constructions. 'Mummy hair' and 'Daddy car' seem only to omit the possessive inflection. Both 'Chair broken' and 'That horsie' become acceptable copular sentences if we leave the word order intact and fill in *is* and *a* or *the*" (p. 188). It was even the case that the mean length-of-utterance (MLU) calculated for spontaneous sentences closely corresponded with the MLU calculated for sentences produced as imitations.

In 1964 Brown and Bellugi reported on the early sentences of two of the children in their longitudinal study: Adam and Eve. With respect to both imitations and spontaneous sentences they fully confirm the "telegraphic" characterization. There is a limit of length, contentives are produced and functors are not, normal word order is preserved. The authors speculate about possible reasons for these characteristics. The limit of length cannot be explained by immediate memory span, since it is the same for spontaneous sentences which have no antecedent models as it is for imitations. Neither is it a matter of the number of words in long-term memory since Adam and Eve at Stage I knew, at least, several hundred words. Presumably the real limitation involves the complexity, in grammatical or semantic terms, of the sentences that can be processed, a complexity reflected in sentence length.

The fact that the child's first sentences preserve normal word order partially accounts for the ability of an adult to "understand" these sentences and so to feel that he is in communication with the child. Brown and Bellugi note that: "It is conceivable that the child 'intends' the meanings coded by his word order and that,

when he preserves the order of an adult sentence, he does so because he wants
to say what the order says. It is also possible that he preserves word order just because
his brain works that way and that he has no comprehension of the semantic
contrasts involved" (p. 137). In English declarative sentences, order will distinguish
subject from object, modifier from head, subject from locative, possessor from
possessed even when such structure signs as the possessive inflection, the copular
verb, and prepositions are missing.

Brown and Fraser and also Brown and Bellugi opened their discussions of
telegraphic speech with reference to imitation and then went on to say that the child's
spontaneous sentences seemed to be telegraphic in just the same way as his
imitations. When there is a model sentence the retention of contentives and loss of
functors is established by comparison with the model. How can one demonstrate
that functors are "missing" from spontaneous sentences which have no models? In
certain contexts particular functors are obligatory. For example, when a transitive
verb is followed by a count noun *(see ball)* an article is obligatory, and if it is absent it
may be said to be missing. When a cardinal number greater than one modifies a count
noun (e.g. *two ball*) the noun requires a plural inflection. For 11 contexts of this
type I have calculated the percentages of functors missing in the sentences of Adam,
Eve, and Sarah at I and the results are: Adam, 94 percent, Eve, 87 percent, Sarah,
84 percent. So the tendency to omit functors is a strong one. At Level V for the three
children the percentages of obligatory functors missing are: Adam, 26 percent, Eve,
33 percent, and Sarah, 21 percent. Between I and V great progress occurs in the
direction of standard English with respect to obligatory functors though even at V the
children have some distance to go.

In terms of gross percentages functors seem to enter child speech by a long gradual
process. However, these gross percentages sum across a number of very different
grammatical features: definite and nondefinite articles, progressive aspect, past
tense, plural number, and so forth. Each of these has an individual course of
development, and at any given point of time there is great variation among them
in the levels attained. At V, for instance, locative prepositions are almost always
present in obligatory contexts whereas the auxiliary verb *be,* obligatory with
the progressive, is still usually missing. In short, the functors are not one story but
many. These stories are the focus of Stage II.

Confirming Evidence

Simply as a descriptive characterization of a fairly rough sort "telegraphic
speech" is apt for Stage I, and seems very generally to be so. It is confirmed repeatedly
by the data from the studies listed in Tables 9 and 10 as well as by general statements
the authors make. Leopold (1949), for instance, writes of Hildegard: "The
preposition was omitted from all adverbial phrases" (p. 59) and "Articles were
not used at all during the first two years" (p. 64). Miller and Ervin (1964) wrote of
their children: "It is often striking that one can provide a translation of children's

utterances into adult utterances by the addition of function words and inflectional affixes. It appears that the children select the stressed utterance segments, which usually carry the most information" (p. 13). Bloom (1970) writes to the same effect about all her children in Stage I. Braine (1963) does not call special attention to it but the data he has published for Gregory, Andrew, and Steven mostly lack articles, copulas, prepositions, plural and third-person inflections.

The aptness of the telegraphic characterization for Stage I speech goes far beyond English and, insofar as the topic is raised, seems to be universal for the studies we are considering. Bowerman (in press), for instance, has calculated the percentage of functors present in obligatory contexts for Seppo I, Seppo II, and Rina I, and they are 3.1 percent, 8.2 percent, and 9.5 percent. Rydin (1971) has done the same for Swedish and obtained the higher value 39 percent, but she reports that almost all of these are the definite article with other functors almost invariably absent. Concerning the early Hebrew of Gil and Gila. Bar-Adon (1971) writes: "Even our few examples show clearly that during his speech at this stage, the child employs only the principal elements: he retains the major part of the 'content words' or 'contentives' especially nouns and verbs and some adjectives, but tends to omit 'function words' or 'functors,' especially prepositions, adverbs, conjunctions, determiners, certain inflection suffixes, etc." (p. 47). Grégoire's summarizing is: "L'enfant choisissant les mots capitaux dans les phrases 'imitées' et faisant tomber les autres . . ." (1937, p. 84). Chao (1951) makes piecemeal observations which suggest the telegraphic quality: "Subordination is mostly in the same word order as in S.M. [Standard Mandarin] but the subordinative particle *de* is not used" (p. 36). Slobin (1966) after studying Gvozdev's data for Zhenya writes: "Child grammar begins with unmarked forms" (p. 134). Korean has no articles, copula, or number inflection but its case-marking postpositions were almost all absent from Susin's speech until well after Stage I. Blount's Stage I Luo children lacked the plural inflection on nouns and had no tense or aspect auxiliaries with their verbs. Kernan's Samoan children used nouns without articles and formed the possessive without an obligatory particle (rather like the English preposition *of*).

Contradiction

Park, in his study (1970a) of the acquisition of German, finds contradictory results. He did a small imitation experiment with Ulrike at her one-word stage presenting two-or-three-word models like *Mein Teddy, Ein Brötchen,* and *Heike ist da.* He found, contrary to the findings of Brown and Bellugi (1964) and Ervin (1964), that functors like *mein* and *ein* and *da* were just as likely to be imitated as were contentives like *Teddy, Brötchen,* and *Heike.* Furthermore, in Park's tabulated two-word utterances from his children, one finds numerous occurrences of such functors as *das, ein, hier, mehr, ander,* and *da.* Park also calls attention to the fact that the sometimes separable verb prefixes like *ab, an, auf, mit, um, weg,* and *zu* were often used in Stage I speech apparently as the names of actions in place of full verbs. Park's own conclusion about telegraphic speech is: "Apparently, functors do not operate in the same manner in American and German children" (p. 6).

At first sight Park's paper suggests the breakdown, just in the case of German, of a description of Stage I speech, otherwise universally apt. In fact, however, his data are not so very different from data reported by other investigators. After all, no one found functors invariably absent from Stage I, only usually so. What is different about the German study is the stance Park takes up. Most of us, especially students of English, have taken the position that Stage I speech is, in the main, telegraphic and have tried to explain away the exceptions in one way or another. Park, in not committing himself to the maintenance of the generalization, turns us back to the data of the other studies to see what the *exceptions* to the rule have been like.

In the Brown and Fraser imitation data of Table 12, you may remember, that pronouns were correctly imitated 72 percent of the time, which made them quite different from inflection, articles, and the like. In fact, just about all studies of Stage I American English do find frequent occurrence of the personal pronouns *I, you, me,* and *my* as well as the demonstrative pronouns *this* and *that*. What is special about pronouns among English functors? All kinds of things. They can, for instance, function in what we have called in the Introduction major semantic roles as agent, patient, benefactor, and so forth. In syntactic terms they function in major syntactic relations as subject, object, and modifier. They do not express what the Introduction calls modulations of meaning as do English articles and inflections for plurality and person. In addition the pronouns are full syllables as the inflections are not, and they may receive one of the heavier stresses as the inflections may not. Which is to say there is more "phonetic substance" to the pronouns than to the inflections and so perhaps greater perceptual salience. That is not the end of the special qualities of the pronouns but it is enough for the moment. The way in which they are not peculiar among functors is that pronouns, like other kinds of functors, are small, closed grammatical classes.

The child Susan, studied by Miller and Ervin, made such heavy use of the words *off* and *on* that Miller and Ervin classified these terms as, what Braine (1963) called, "terminal pivots." They seemed privileged to follow any noun or verb in a two-word utterance. Braine's child, Andrew, also used *off* as a terminal pivot. Now, if these words *off* and *on* derive from the adult prepositions of the same form then it is odd that the children should use them in terminal position. Adults use the prepositions in prepositional phrases like *on the floor* and *off the table*. The likelihood is that Susan's and Andrew's *off* and *on* were derived from particles which belong to certain verbs. Forms like *take off* and *put on* as in *take it off* and *put it on* are to be regarded as separable verbs, as verbs in two physically discontinuous parts. They are, in fact, just like such separable German verbs as *aufmachen, mitnehmen, anfassen, anziehen,* and very many others. And Park's observation that particles like *ab, an, auf, mit,* and so on, occur in Stage I speech is not really at variance with the American studies. Examples like *Boat off* and *Water off* (Braine, 1963) in the American studies suggest that English particles sometimes function as Park suggests that German particles do in Stage I children; as the names of actions, replacing the full verbs to which they belong. As such, particles figure in basic semantic and syntactic relations. What else is special about them? Like pronouns they probably have more perceptual salience than do inflections and articles. They are full syllables, and they can take heavy stress as in *Take that off!* They can also occur in terminal position which may be perceptually favored.

What of Park's *mehr, ander, hier,* and *da?* They all have parallels in American studies. In fact *more, 'nother, here,* and *there* are among the words most reliably found in Stage I English. *Here* and *there* have two functions: they may operate like demonstrative pronouns in naming utterances (e.g., *Here book*) or as "pro-locatives," which can stand in for "understood" locative nouns much as pronouns can stand in for understood noun subjects and objects. In either case *here* and *there* play major semantic roles (for example, locative) and enter into major syntactic relations. They are also, of course, full syllables which can be stressed and can occur either initially or finally. *More* and *'nother* do not play any of the semantic roles listed in the Introduction but they do play an additional role we shall find universal in Stage I speech. They comment on or request the *recurrence* of a referent. In this role they are, from the syntactic point-of-view, modifiers in the basic relation "modifier-noun." And once again these forms are at least one syllable long and can be stressed.

This review of the major "exceptions" to the telegraphic characterization of Stage I English, exceptions which have been on record from the beginning of the contemporary interest in child speech, shows that Park's data for German are not really out of line with the data for English. There are also "exceptions" in all the studies of other languages but we are not able to describe all their properties in the language in question and so cannot be sure that they are consistent with the German and American data. Still they seem to be so. Blount, for instance, notes that while his Stage I children failed to use inflections for plurality, tense, or aspect they did use inflections for subject, object, and possession. McNeill notes that Izanami used the Japanese subject postposition *ga* often and correctly. Kernan notes the frequent occurrence in Stage I Samoan of *itda,* which may be translated as *there is,* and of *manta,* close to *more,* and of *upda,* close to *no* or *no more.*

From Categorical Description to Functional Relations

Let me say what I think Park's stance and the reexamination of familiar exceptions do to the characterization of Stage I speech as "telegraphic." They move us from a rather sterile description in terms of the linguistic category functor to the study of functional relations between variables characterizing functors and several kinds of Stage I performance. The outcome of this kind of functional examination will be a more complicated and refined sense of the "telegraphic" character of Stage I speech. What has become evident is that the category of functors or, as I shall call them in Stage II, "grammatical morphemes," is a category which in American English is defined by the partial convergence of a large number of characteristics or variables. Some, at least, of these variables affect the probability that a given form will occur in Stage I speech. The "exceptions" are simply those words that do not have enough of the determinants working against them. For a time developmental psycholinguists have tried to treat functors as a category defined by the nearly perfect conjunction of a set of variables and to make the functor-less, telegraphic description stick by selectively attending now to one and now to another of these variables. It has not been difficult for me, for instance, to forget the fact that pronouns and prolocatives are small closed classes just as surely as inflections, articles, and auxiliary verbs.

What must happen is that the category "functor" must undergo fission into a set of variables having different values for different forms and different values in different languages for comparable forms. What the study of languages other than English does, of course, is to change the correlations among variables and so help to force us to think not in terms of a class but of variables. Thus, Luo uses verb inflections where English uses prepositions and word order. German *ein* is not only an article like English *a* but also a pronoun cognate with *one*.

What are some of the properties or attributes which converge imperfectly on the category "functor" in American English? For Hockett (1958) who actually used the term and Gleason (1961) whose term, "function word" seems to mean the same thing, the core characteristics are: 1. the relatively small size of classes like articles, prepositions, pronouns, and the like, compared to nouns, verbs, and adjectives; 2. their relatively fixed membership. English does not readily admit new functors as it does nouns or verbs, and the native speaker commonly learns all the functors in his preschool years but learns new nouns, verbs, and adjectives throughout his lifetime. These two are the invariable characteristics. There are also characteristics applicable to some but not all. I will not attempt to exhaust these here, since Stage II is entirely focused on the acquisition of the English functors or grammatical morphemes but simply try to show that one functor is by no means the same as another.

Consider frequency first. It is obvious that most functors are more frequent than most individual nouns and verbs. Their frequencies are also more stable from sample to sample than are the frequencies of content words, since they are more independent of the topic of conversation. It is, perhaps, an indication of the minor role that frequency plays as a determinant of order of acquisition that it is just these high-frequency forms that are largely missing from Stage I speech. Still some lower limit of frequency is obviously essential to enable the form to be stored in long-term memory, its semantic ascertained, and the rules of its usage discovered. Table 52 gives frequencies for some of the major functors in samples of 713 utterances each from the parents of Adam, Eve, and Sarah. While the forms almost all have reasonably high frequency there is enormous variation among them in actual level. There are, for example, between 150 and 200 articles in each sample but 25 or fewer instances of the regular third person present indicative inflection and none at all of the functors that enter into the formation of the full passive in English. Here, then, is ample variation on one independent variable within the class of functors to help account for the variations one finds in their appearance in Stage I speech.

Consider next perceptual salience, which like high frequency should favor acquisition. Probably salience involves several things; perhaps amount of phonetic substance, susceptibility to heavy stress and high pitch, and the possibility of occurring in utterance-final position, which there is some indication (Blasdell and Jensen, 1970) that children favor in imitation. Inflections like the plural and possessive on the noun and the regular past on the verb are not even full syllables in English. In German, on the other hand, some of these are syllabic as in the -en of *Sie haben das Buch.* Words like *here, there, this, that, I, you,* and *more* are all full syllables as are the German equivalents. On this variable also, then, there is ample variation within the class of functors to account for the variation in performance from form to form within Stage I children, and on equivalent forms between children learning different languages.

Consider the semantics of the functors. There is, in the first place, the distinction between forms which can function in major semantic roles or relations like the personal and demonstrative pronouns and the prolocatives *here* and *there,* and forms like articles, inflection for number and tense and aspect, which only modulate basic meanings. In English these modulating forms, whether bound, like the inflections, or free, like the articles, never occur as total utterances, and it is inconceivable that they should, since their meanings are not separable from the major semantic relations. Then there is the matter of redundancy as opposed to informativeness. The third person present indicative inflection in English is perfectly redundant or predictable if the subject is expressed. The copula, before it is inflected for tense, and the possessive inflection {-s}, between a proper noun and the name of some possession (as in *Adam's chair*) are almost perfectly predictable. Probably redundancy militates against acquisition of a functor, and the information-redundancy variable need not come out the same, even for cognate forms in closely related languages like German and English let alone in somewhat analogous forms in unrelated languages.

Then there is the variable: conditioning of the functors by verbal context. Except for the progressive -*ing* English regular inflections have three phonetic shapes (allomorphs) which vary with the phonological properties of the stem. That should make them harder to learn. There is also conditioning by the class membership of the noun or verb stem and, in English as in German and other languages, there are numerous "irregular" classes. It is obviously hard to get these straight since children learning English say things like *digged* and *swimmed* well into their school years. There is even lexical conditioning in which the inflection is peculiar to just one stem *(ox — oxen)*. There is conditioning by semantic role or case; *I* is nominative, *me* is accusative, *my* is possessive. Some or all of these varieties of verbal context conditioning probably affect ease of acquisition of a functor. English functors are obviously greatly different from one another on this variable, and so are cognate forms between related languages.

In Table 13 I have taken some of the variables described above, treated them as binary rather than continuous, and assigned plus to the value assumed to facilitate acquisition and minus to the value assumed to operate against acquisition. This is a very rough, impressionistic table, and its only point is to show that words like *I, me, my, this, that, here, there,* and so forth, which are regularly found in Stage I speech in both German and English, constitute a very different class from inflections, articles, the copula, and so on, which are seldom found in Stage I.

Guesses about the effects of independent variables are only guesses but fortunately we are beginning to get experimental studies. One of these (Blaisdell and Jensen, 1970) is concerned with two aspects of perceptual salience: stress and word position.

Table 13.   Some properties of functors (small closed grammatical classes) with examples from English

Functor	Freq. High +[a] Low −	Syllabic + Not −	Semantic (Syntactic) Role + Modulation −	Info. + Red. −	Not Phon. Cond. + Cond. −	Not Gramm. Cond. + Cond. −
Pl. *-s*	+	−	−	±	−	−
Poss. *-s*	−	−	+	−	−	+
-ing	+	+	−	+	+	−
-ed	−	−	−	±	−	−
Past irreg.	+	+	−	±	+	−
-s pres. ind.	−	−	−	±	−	−
Copula	+	±	−	±	−	−
Articles	+	+	−	±	−	−
Here, there	+	+	+	+	+	+
This, that	+	+	+	+	+	+
I, me, my	+	+	+	+	+	+
More, 'nother	+	+	+	+	+	−
Particles	+	+	+	+	+	−

[a]Plus indicates value of the variable presumed to facilitate acquisition; minus the value presumed to operate against acquisition.

Abbreviations:

Freq. High — Frequency over 50 tokens in 713 utterances.

Info. — Information. Not guessable from verbal context.

Red. — Redundant. Guessable from verbal context.

Phon. Cond. — Phonetically conditioned as the several allomorphs of plurality are by the terminal sound on the stem.

Gramm. Cond. — Grammatically conditioned as in the case of *I, me, my.*

In English sentences these are hard to separate, and so the study employs strings of nonsense syllables such as:

tud	*gop*	*nʌk*	*pim**
mʌp	*kit*	*pod**	*tok*

The asterisk indicates the syllable receiving primary stress. Across the full set of 12 four-syllable strings primary and intermediate stress were equally distributed in all possible combinations with respect to serial position. The two variables were thus independent. Stress was defined as it is normally in English by increases of both pitch and intensity. The subjects were children between the ages of 28 and 39 months (probably well beyond Stage I), and what they were asked to do was to imitate each string as fully as possible. It was first established in a screening procedure that all the children taking part would have their imitative capacities overloaded by the model strings. Four nonsense syllables, though all were well-formed in terms of English phonology, are of course much more difficult than four words. The authors found, in this experiment, that both primary stress and terminal position favored reproduction of the syllable by the children, and so these variables have the effect they seem to have in naturalistic samples where imitations also often occur.

Two experiments by Scholes (1969, 1970) make it clear that, while stress and terminal position evidently favor immediate reproduction of nonsense words in strings which children may or may not process as sentences, perceptual salience is certainly not the only class of variable likely to be important in producing telegraphic speech. Scholes used real English words, contentives as well as functors, in some of his experimental conditions. The importance of stress, among factors probably affecting perceptual salience, was minimized by making up strings and sentences by splicing tapes of "citation style" readings of individual words, functors being given as prominent a stress as contentives. Of course inflections would still have gone unstressed. Scholes' child subjects were probably all well beyond Stage I, since the age range was generally from three years to five years. It is worth recording, as a matter of incidental interest, that when the model sentences employed real English functors the errors of children even in this age range were primarily deletion errors and that functors were deleted about three times as often as contentives. This outcome is consistent with what we shall learn in Stage II about the long drawn out process of acquiring full control of English functors.

What is particularly interesting in the 1970 paper is the suggestion the data make that the semantic roles of the functors are important determinants of imitation. I cannot take this idea very far because I do not have the full lists of sentences or detailed data. However, Scholes included both well-formed meaningful sentences *(My cat liked his milk)* and anomolous sentences *(My cat drove his milk)* and ill-ordered sentences *(Cat milk his my liked)*. What is particularly interesting is that, across sentences generally, the differential deletion of functors and contentives only occurred in significant degree in the well-formed sentences. Furthermore, in sentences composed partially of nonsense words and partially of real words, the nonsense accompanied by real contentives was more likely to be deleted than the nonsense accompanied by real functors. Scholes asks: "Could the child be equating importance with some semantic notion like propositional nucleus? Perhaps he could. If the semantic cohesion of the string is destroyed, the differential relation also disappears" (p. 169). Scholes suggests of the child: "So long as he can assign a reading to the string, he will delete the functors" (p. 170). What all this suggests to me, though the data are not detailed enough to prove the point, is that contentives and *certain* functors (like *his* or *my*) will be preserved in imitation because of the semantic roles or relations they play so long as these roles or relations can be made out. When the contentives are nonsense or when all-English strings are anomolous or ill-ordered the semantic factor that distinguishes most contentives from most functors is neutralized.

The Blaisdell and Jensen and Scholes studies are important not only because they put some experimental force behind guesses about variables but also because, by using imitation, they point to a second necessary change in how we deal with the telegraphic aspect of Stage I speech; it is necessary to differentiate the dependent variable. The simple sounding of a functor, whether in imitation or in a spontaneous utterance, is a very different thing from full semantic and grammatical control. Practically all students of child speech have recognized the necessity of making some distinctions on the performance side.

Hildegard, Leopold's daughter, before she was 24 months old, said both *piece of toast* and *drink of water*. The author notes that these phrases contained the only preposition heard before 24 months and that the phrases were completely rigid in form; there were no such variants as *piece of your toast* or *drink of cold water*. Therefore, Leopold suggests, the phrases were probably simply long words for Hildegard, words having no internal structure.

Sarah at I and Kathryn at I both used *that's* in ostensive sentences, and Susan used *this-a* and *have-a,* and Adam used *get-a* and, just beyond I, Adam used *it's*. It is certain that some, at least, of these are simply segmentation errors such that the child has mistakenly incorporated into a word as a terminal phoneme some functor that very commonly follows it without pause or other juncture sign. So long as the child uses his "word" in contexts which require the two morphemes one cannot detect the segmentation error. Utterances like *its book* and *this a book* and *I go get it,* since they are well-formed are unrevealing. However, Susan said *this-a Bonnie pants* and *have-a pants,* and Adam in I said *Mommy get it ladder* and in later samples he said *it's go* and *it's went*. In all these cases the seeming functor is out of place. Such over-extensions are explained if we suppose that the seeming functors are simply incorporated into the antecedent words, that the functors are really word-final sounds. Near the end of Stage II this problem is discussed at length.

Grégoire describing the development of articles in Charles and Edmond notes that before 24 months they were usually absent but that an occasional noun seemed to be preceded by *un, une,* or *la*. He rejects the notion that these really are the articles in question, neither the masculine-feminine gender distinctions nor the definite-nondefinite distinction is consistently observed. Grégoire's (1937) judgment is that in this early phase "l'article semble appartenir au mot" (p. 194).

Eric in II used *blocks* and *hats* and five other nouns which seemed to be inflected for plural number. He apparently did not over-extend these forms to produce such utterances as *a blocks* or *this hats*. Nevertheless, Bloom judges that the nouns are not really inflected. For the reason that none of the "plural" nouns ever occured in the singular. In the absence of a singular-plural contrast the probability is that the seven nouns in question were simply learned as words in a form having terminal sibilants; possibly because parents happened usually to use these nouns in a plural sense.

A number of the children in Table 9 (e.g., Gia I, Eric I, Eve I) sometimes produced a mid-vowel sound (the schwa) that one might take for an article or a preposition if it occurred before a noun. However, both Bloom and I, looking at the detailed distributional evidence are of the opinion that these schwas are not functors at all but simply phonetic extensions of certain words.

What all these examples show is that on the performance side one has in addition to total absence and full control what might be called "prefabricated routines," which to the casual listener may seem to include one or another functor. On careful examination, however, they prove to be rigidly limited in distribution or semantically inappropriate and so distinguishable from full control. Full control has been given a reasonable operational definition in Stage II, and the story of its development for a set of English functors is told there.

In place, then, of the description of Stage I speech as "telegraphic" in lacking what linguists have called "functors" we now have a very large number of independent variables which assign quite different descriptions to different functors and also several dependent performance variables including, at least: 1. total absence; 2. occasional presence in routines; 3. full control. The functional relations between the two sets of variables are in process of being worked out.

Slobin (1971), drawing upon his considerable knowledge of the course of acquisition in different languages, has postulated some very likely "operating principles," which amount to postulations about the effects of various values of the independent variables. For example:

Operating Principle A: Pay attention to the ends of words (p. 335).
Operating Principle C: Pay attention to the order of words and
                  morphemes (p. 348).
Operating Principle E: Underlying semantic relations should be
                  marked overtly and clearly (p. 346).

And he offers many others, most of them plausible on his evidence. These are principles on which he suggests that children everywhere operate in processing adult language. Slobin goes on to develop their consequences in terms of features of child speech that should be universal.

I think the dependent variable Slobin has in mind is always full control. If we think of other performance outcomes and of combinations of values of the independent variables that apply to functors then we may guess at a new characterization of the telegraphic character of Stage I speech. It would go something like this:

1. If functor x has some minimal frequency, high perceptual salience, is unconditioned by verbal context, and expresses a basic semantic role rather than a modulation, then it will be fully controlled in Stage I (used freely and correctly).

2. If functor x has high frequency and high perceptual salience then whether conditioned or not, and whatever its semantic role, it will occur in Stage I but only in prefabricated routines.

3. If functor x has low frequency and low perceptual salience and is verbally conditioned and expressive of a semantic modulation then it will be completely absent from Stage I.

What has become of the characterization of Stage I speech as "telegraphic?" I think it remains valid if we understand "telegraphic" not as the total absence of words from small closed grammatical classes but rather in the sense of the three propositions above. What seems to be clearly lacking in Stage I in all the studies we have reviewed is full semantic and grammatical control of those functors that encode semantic modulations rather than basic semantic relations.

Competence and Performance

A team of investigators at the University of Pennsylvania, Shipley, Smith, and Gleitman (1969) has asked the interesting question: Is the Stage I child's "competence" as telegraphic as his performance? By competence they mean grammatical knowledge, and they quite correctly argue that samples of performance constitute only an imperfect set of clues to competence. The Pennsylvania team has thought of an experimental method for obtaining some clues that go beyond spontaneous speech production. It is a method that inquires into the child's response to utterances of various kinds. They worked with 11 children between 18 and 33 months old whom they divided into three groups in order of increasing grammatical maturity: holophrastic, telegraphic, and mature. The children were assigned to one group or another on the basis of median-length-of-utterance *(median,* not *mean).* The median is a measure of central tendency less sensitive to extreme values than the mean and, since distributions of utterance lengths are skewed to the right at this age, medians should run somewhat lower than means. The median values for the holophrastic group were 1.06–1.16; for the telegraphic group 1.40–1.85; the mature group 2.50–3.50. On the basis of these values we can identify the groups in our own terms: holophrastic as "early Stage I"; telegraphic as "later Stage I";

and mature as "beyond Stage I." We may disregard the last of these groups
and consider only the results for "early" and "late" Stage I.

The mothers of the children directed to them mild imperatives of three types:
well-formed or verb-functor-noun imperatives like *Give me the ball;* telegraphic or
verb-noun imperatives like *Give ball;* and holophrastic or noun imperatives like
Ball! The nouns in the commands were familiar terms like *horn, ball,* and *drum.* The
verbs were either ones normally associated with the nouns (*Throw ball, Blow horn,
Bang drum*) or else such general terms as *find, give,* and *show.* Obedience to any
of these commands, even to the noun alone, would seem to entail, at a minimum,
touching or looking at the object named. Of course, for some of the verbs, full
compliance would require more but as a common, minimally appropriate response to
the whole range of commands the Pennsylvania researchers decided to use touching
or looking. The question was whether the child would most often respond in this
minimally comprehending way to a command having the same form as his own
speech or to a command at another level. The result: early Stage I children responded
best to holophrastic or telegraphic commands, the kind they themselves most often
produced. However, later Stage I children responded best to the mature command
with functors included which would not have been their own most usual way of
speaking. Shipley, Smith, and Gleitman take this result to be evidence that telegraphic
(or later Stage I) children have a competence that extends beyond their performance,
and so the investigators judge that conclusions drawn from production data
alone must underestimate the real level of grammatical knowledge.

It is necessary to ask what kind of knowledge has been demonstrated. Knowledge
of the meanings of the functors or of their grammatical roles has not been demonstrated. The sentences did not include contrasts like *Give me the ball, Give him
the ball* or *Give me the ball, Give me a ball,* and so the sentences could not test for
understanding of the functors. The kind of knowledge the results suggest to me is
knowledge that the sentences with functors sound more "natural" or "usual" coming
from mother than does a telegraphic sentence. The only thing that need actually be
processed in the sentence in order to give rise to a response of touching or looking
is the object noun *ball* or *horn* or whatever. Probably the telegraphic or holophrastic
imperative from mother was sufficiently odd to give the child pause and interfere
with his response. It is not apparent that this is more competence or knowledge than
is manifested in the performance of the late Stage I child. As we have seen the child
at this time probably does control certain "functors" (e.g., *me, here, there*),
whereas others (e.g., articles, copula, inflections) are not controlled until long after
Stage I. These latter, however, do occasionally seem to be "heard" in Stage I
speech simply because they belong to the child's pronunciation of certain unanalyzed
and routine phrases. If we grant that the Stage I child may be aware of the usual
presence of "article-sounds" in the pronunciation of familiar nouns like *ball* and
horn even though, as Stage II shows, he is far from controlling the articles themselves,
then the data of Shipley and others are not surprising and do not demonstrate that

"competence" assessed by their method is greater than the competence attributed to the child on the basis of his own speech performance.

The discussions of Brown and Fraser (1963), and also of Brown and Bellugi (1964), because they started with the telegraphic properties of imitations, might seem to imply that child speech at I is no more than a repertoire of memorized sentences "cut down" from adult originals. The authors did not intend to suggest this, and both papers actually discuss the process of rule induction which makes the child's speech productive. Nevertheless, the characterization of speech as telegraphic, even in the much more complicated sense we have given it here, does not in its own right provide for productivity, for the construction of new sentences; it is a purely descriptive characterization. In 1963, the same year that Brown and Fraser published, Martin Braine characterized the beginnings of syntax in terms of a few simple productive rules, rules corresponding to none in the adult grammar.

Pivot and Open Classes

Braine's rules utilize just two word classes, classes which are now called "pivot" and "open," and the rules generate only two-word sentences. If one looks, in the Brown and Fraser and the Brown and Bellugi papers, at the sections discussing the child's induction of the latent structure of language one finds certain rules proposed for two-word sentences (e.g., "class 1 + class 2" and "modifier + noun") which resemble the rules in Braine's pivot grammar. In 1964 Miller and Ervin, reporting on the two-word sentences of Susan and Christy, utilized two word-classes, "operators" and "nonoperators," closely parallel to Braine's pivot and open classes, and wrote rules similar to Braine's. In a short while, this convergence of three independent and geographically well-separated studies on a pivot grammar description for the first sentences was widely accepted as a major datum of developmental psycholinguistics. Slobin (1969) found, in the international literature, reason for thinking that pivot and open classes might be a universal feature of early speech, and McNeill (1966b, 1970b) developed an argument relating these classes to putative universals of grammar and to adult competence as formalized by Chomsky (1965). Very recently, however, Melissa Bowerman (in press) has shown that the evidence for pivot and open classes was never very clear cut, has provided evidence from her own study of the acquisition of Finnish as a first language that the classes are not universal, and, for one child (Kendall I), evidence that the classes are not even invariably found for children learning English. Lois Bloom (1970), in her study of the acquisition of English by three children, has also shown that pivot and open classes are not always found with children learning English. Even more important, Bloom has shown that the pivot and open characterization of child speech is a superficial one which greatly underestimates the child's linguistic knowledge. Further evidence against even descriptive universality has come from

Blount (1969), for Luo; Kernan (1969) for Samoan; Park (1970a, 1970b) for German and Korean; and Rydin (1971) for Swedish. We had better go back to the beginning of the story.

Braine's Original Characterization

Braine studied three children, Gregory, Andrew, and Steven, using *seriatim* records of all comprehensible utterances that were not imitative of immediately antecedent models. The records covered the first four months following the start of multi-word utterances. What did Braine find? Most of the word combinations of all three boys were just two words long. There were many single-word utterances and a very few utterances three, four, and even five words long. The majority of the two-word sentences from all three boys manifested the following pattern. Initial words were few in number, not more than nine or ten different ones, whereas the final words were extremely various, with each one occurring infrequently. The initial words in these sentences always occurred in utterance-initial position. Braine christened them "pivots." The words in second position, because they, most of them, belong to the large open classes of English, the noun, verb, and adjective classes have come to be called "open" words. In addition to the $P + O$ construction Braine found a less frequent $O + P$ construction such that the diverse words in first position seemed to be drawn from the same population as the O words in $P + O$, while the words in second position, though they did not overlap at all with the P words of $P + O$, were like them in being few but frequent and in always occupying a given sequential position. Since the two pivot classes have nonoverlapping memberships the proper form for the construction rules is $P_1 + O$ and $O + P_2$. The two construction rules with pivots do not account for all the sentences produced by any of Braine's children. In each case there is a residual category, comprising something like 20–25 percent of the total utterances. The residual utterances are a varied lot including some longer than two words, but some, in each case, might be described by the rule $O + O$, since they combine two words of the kind that occur in O positions. Braine suggested that these utterances represented the major growing point in the child's grammar; in the fifth and sixth months following the first combinations they became numerous.

Table 14 sets down, from Braine's article, two examples of each $P_1 + O$ construction and of each $O + P_2$ construction. In addition, the table contains three examples from each child of the $O + O$ construction. In some cases two examples constitute a total inventory. In other cases there were many more than two in the total set. The two presented were selected to illustrate the variety, in terms of English parts-of-speech, within the O class. In some cases most O words in a construction belonged to a single part-of-speech. In Gregory's $O + P_2$ constructions, where P_2 is *it*, all O's were, in fact, transitive verbs.

In further characterizing the distinction between P and O words, Braine notes

Table 14.   Examples of three types of construction in the speech of Braine's children

Child	$P_1 + O$	$O + P_2$	$O + O$
Gregory	See boy See sock	Push it Move it	Mommy sleep Milk cup
	Pretty boat Pretty fan		Oh-my see
	My Mommy My milk		
	Night-night office Night-night boat		
	Bye-bye man Bye-bye hot		
	Hi, plane Hi, Mommy		
	More taxi More Melon		
Andrew	All broke All fix	Boot off Water off	Papa away Pants change
	I see I sit	Airplane by Siren by	Dry pants
	No bed No down	Mail come Mama come	
	More car More sing	Hot in there Milk in there	
	Hi, Calico Hi, Mama		
	Other bib Other milk		
Steven	Want baby Want get	Bunny do Want do	Candy say Find bear
	It ball It bang		Two checker
	Get ball Get Betty		
	See ball See Stevie		
	Whoa cards Whoa jeep		
	More ball More book		
	There ball There high		
	Beep-beep bang Beep-beep car		

That box
That Tommy
Here bed
Here truck

---

that *O* words seemed more likely to occur as single-word utterances than did *P* words. He did not say that *P* words *never* occurred as single-word utterances but explicitly called attention to the fact that some did, e.g., *more*.

In sum, there were a few frequent words which seldom occurred as single-word utterances and which, in two-word combinations, always occurred either in first position or in second position. These words were called pivots and subdivided into pivots 1 and pivots 2 according as they occupied either first or second position. There were many infrequent words which occurred both initially and finally in the position left open by pivots 2 or pivots 1 and which also occurred together. These words were likely to occur as single-word utterances. They were assigned to a category called open. Pivot and open are categorical notions — like noun and verb — but the categories do not correspond with any in the adult language. The categories are defined distributionally even as descriptive linguistics in a pretransformational period defined all word-classes distributionally. It does not seem possible to find any semantic common denominator in pivot words or in open words. Neither can one make distinctive semantic characterization of the three sentence types: $P_1 + O; O + P_2; O + O$. The only grammatical knowledge attributed to children by a pivot grammar is knowledge of "what words are permitted to go where."

The Convergence among Researchers on Pivot-Open Grammars

Miller and Ervin in 1964 described the early sentences of two children, Susan and Christy, whose speech they had been taping in weekly sessions of 45 minutes each. Distributional analysis of Susan's speech suggested the existence of three classes of pivot-like words; Miller and Ervin used the term "operators" rather than pivot. Two of the three pivot classes were first-position pivots; we will call them P_1 and P_1^1. Their memberships were as follows:

$$P_1 \rightarrow \textit{this, that, this one}$$
$$P_1^1 \rightarrow \textit{a, the, (an)other}$$

Miller and Ervin do not say exactly why they constituted these words as two pivot classes rather than as one, but the reason must have been distributional, and looking at their data one can see that there were systematic differences in the *O* words following the two. For example, P_1 sometimes were followed by *off* or *on* but P_1^1 never were. The third pivot class was:

$$P_2 \rightarrow \textit{off, on}$$

Open words before *off* and *on* were mostly nouns and verbs.

In Christy's speech, also there was evidence to suggest three pivot classes. They are:

$$P_1 \rightarrow \textit{this, this-a, that, etc.}$$
$$P_1{}^1 \rightarrow \textit{a, the}$$
$$P_2 \rightarrow \textit{here, there}$$

The initial pivot classes are about the same as Susan's; the P_2 class is a new one.

While there were utterances from both children characterizable in pivot and open terms the data do not justify characterizing the structure of Susan's and Christy's speech generally as a pivot grammar. Nor do Miller and Ervin do so. They point out that there are good distributional grounds for distinguishing nouns and verb classes in the speech of both Susan and Christy. And some ground for distinguishing such other classes as adjectives and particles. Possibly we should think of Susan and Christy as still having distinguishable pivot classes but as having moved beyond Braine's children in the direction of the word classes of standard English.

Something rather similar might be said of the children whose speech is described in Brown and Fraser (1963) and Brown and Bellugi (1964). The child Evie, whose speech is described in the first of these papers, is not the Eve who participated in the longitudinal study of Brown and his associates. Evie was visited just once for a 500-word sample. She was 25½ months old. Her mean utterance length was estimated at 2.6, and that would make her much more advanced than Braine's children.

Brown and Fraser begin by restricting their attention to the "simplest utterances in the record, those of just two words and among these, the utterances in which the initial word occurs at least twice" (p. 173). In this restricted sample they find evidence for a class C_1 which looks rather like an initial pivot. Its membership includes *a, the, that, there, two,* and *see.* Brown and Fraser also consider utterances with recurrent words in final position, and when they do so they find evidence of a C_2 class which includes *all gone, broken,* and *tired.* When the sample is enlarged to include three-word sentences the class of initial pivots C_1 must be subdivided with the articles going into a new class C_3. Classes C_1 and C_3 cannot simply be considered two classes of initial pivots, since members of C_3 also occur in medial position. Of course three-word sentences must in any case escape the rules proposed by Braine.

Brown and Bellugi, in their 1964 paper, were describing not total grammars but simply the evolution of the noun phrase in the speech of two children, Adam and Eve, whom they have studied longitudinally. At an early period, when the mean utterance length of the two children was close to 1.75, noun phrases generally consisted of just two words. The first word, called a modifier by Brown and Bellugi, would be drawn from the set: *a, big, dirty, little, more, my, poor, that, the,* and *two.* The second would be a noun drawn from a very large set. There is a certain similarity between the construction $M + N$ and Braine's $P_1 + O$, a similarity to which Brown and Bellugi call attention. However, there are also some differences. Members of the class *M* were all some sort of prenominal determiner whereas Braine had, in P_1 classes, not only determiners but verbs, interjections, adjectives, quantifiers, and pronouns. The members of class *N* were all nouns, whereas the *O* classes in Braine's data include verbs, adjectives, and locatives as well as nouns. In fact *M* and *N* are good standard English word classes on a very generic level. In the course of development the *M* class differentiated into such standard subclasses as articles, demonstratives, and adjectives. The total grammars for Adam and Eve at this time were far from being pivot grammars. There were utterances from both children that were three and four morphemes long, and something like a dozen word classes would be required to represent the structure of the full sets of sentences.

So, there is a modest amount of convergence in these studies. It does not, however, amount to a demonstration that Braine's three children in Maryland, Brown's three in Massachusetts, and Miller and Ervin's in California all began syntax with a pivot grammar. Only Braine's children seemed to have such grammars. The other children had certain constructions which looked like pivot-open constructions but they had other constructions beside these. However, as Table 9 indicates, only Braine's children, of those described in the early 1960's, were at the very beginning of syntax. The others were, in varying degrees, more advanced. Perhaps among them they represent later stages in which pivot and open classes, though still discernible, were beginning to break down into standard word classes. Interesting reports that a pivot-open distinction may be discerned in the early sentences of children learning Russian, Bulgarian, Croatian, French, and German as well as English deepens our interest in the distinction. Concerning Gvozdev's Zhenya, Slobin says: "There is clearly a small class of pivot words *(P)* and a large class of open words *(O)* which can be combined into three types of two-word sentences: $P + O, O + P,$ and $O + O$" (1966, p. 133). Perhaps the pivot-open classes are the universal primal word classes from which the standard classes of individual languages later derive.

A Universal Innate Hierarchy of Classes

One thing that has bothered many people about the pivot-open distinction is the fact that it seems to make no particular linguistic sense. If these are the primal classes why are they so? They have nothing obvious to do with the adult standard languages. In fact, pivot grammars look rather like a cul-de-sac. But does nature build a universal cul-de-sac?

McNeill has argued (1966b, 1970b) that pivot and open classes are evidence for the existence of a universal innate hierarchy of word classes. He develops his argument in connection with the Brown and Bellugi data on the differentiation of modifiers in Adam's noun phrases. McNeill points out that differentiation presupposes a generic classification in which there is a superordinate class embracing the full memberships of a set of subordinate classes. The members of a generic class must all manifest whatever characteristics define that class, and they must fail to manifest but potentially admit the characteristics that will eventually distinguish the subclass. Nouns are a class, in English, generic to such subclasses as count nouns and mass nouns, common nouns and proper nouns, abstract nouns and concrete nouns, and even generic to pronouns. It is not quite as clear but determiners seem to be a class generic to articles, quantifiers, adjectives, demonstratives, and others. In Adam's speech the subclasses do seem to differentiate out of the generic classes of the early noun phrase. The trouble is that these classes, modifier and noun as Brown and Bellugi called them, are not pivot and open classes at all, and McNeill's thesis concerns pivot and open classes.

McNeill suggests that the standard adult rules of a language like English are written in terms of very narrow categories of words (or morphemes) that embody such distinctions as animate and inanimate nouns, pure transitive and mixed transitive-intransitive verbs, and so on. Above this level is another that categorizes the same words more broadly. And above this another that catergorizes the same words still more broadly and so on, until, at the top, there is one class containing all the words of English. If we can suppose that there is a universal hierarchy of categories of this sort then perhaps the P-O distinction is one that is near the top of the hierarchy. For children to begin with this distinction means beginning with classes generic to all others from which the others can develop by differentiation. This is all very well for the classes of Adam's noun phrases, but how does it fit real pivot and open classes? We must go back to Braine's three boys.

Gregory's P_1 class included the verb *see,* the adjective *pretty,* the possessive pronoun *my,* the interjection *hi,* and the quantifier *more.* I have never heard of a grammatical theory that would assign these to the same generic class. In fact it is, in principle, impossible because, while the verb *see* was a P_1 for Gregory, the verbs *push* and *move* were assigned to the open class. And while the adjective *pretty* was a P_1, the adjective *hot* was in the open class. A class cannot be generic to a subclass unless it includes all the members of the subclass. McNeill writes in his 1970b statement of this argument: "Adam, for example, had the two articles in his Pivot class at Time 1; he did not have one in the Pivot class and one in the Open class. Similarly, every adjective then in Adam's vocabulary was in the Pivot class; there were none in the Open class. In fact, Adam's Pivot class contained every available member of several adult grammatical classes, even though none of these classes were themselves recognized in Adam's grammar" (p. 1086). All true enough of Adam's classes. But these were not pivot and open but rather noun, verb, modifier, and so on. Adam was well started on English. The real pivot and open classes, the only ones in the published literature are not generic at all.

In his more recent works (1970a, 1970b) McNeill, responding to data showing that so-called pivot classes are not reliably generic, including evidence from his Japanese subject Izanami (1970b, p. 1095), has abandoned the notion of an innate hierarchy of classes (1970a, p. 63). In these recent works McNeill redefines pivot and open classes in terms of grammatical relations and the cross-classification of words by syntactic features representing the relations. The general idea is that pivots are contextually "marked" forms limited to the expression of relations like modification, location, demonstration, and so on, while open words are nouns or noun phrases. This idea need not detain us, since it is clearly falsified by, among others, Bowerman's (in press) subject, Kendall I. Among the words Bowerman identified as pivots on the basis of frequency of combination and relative fixedness of position were *Kendall, Mommy,* and *Daddy* — all nouns. McNeill (1970a) ties his newest argument firmly to the statement: "With the exception of two English pronouns *(I* and *it)* the P class never contains N's or NP's" (p. 65).

Critique of the Pivot Grammar Characterization

This critique is aimed at three points: 1. the original distributional evidence; 2. the claim of universality; 3. the adequacy of the representation of grammatical knowledge. The first section is much indebted to Bowerman (1970), and the third section to Bloom (1970). The second section is based on data from Bowerman, Bloom, and many other sources as indicated.

1. *The Original Distributional Evidence.* A pivot grammar admits of the following constructions: $P_1 + O, O + P_2, O + O,$ and $O.$ It does not admit of: P or $P_1 + P_2$ or $P_2 + P_1.$ There are two important things to notice about these rules. The first is that they imply productivity along certain lines. No researcher has obtained all possible combinations of the kinds permitted by the rules but only some instances of each. The rules are generalized along lines suggested by performance but in a way that goes beyond performance in an effort to characterize competence or potential. The implication is that the child would find all the "permitted" combinations well formed. We shall consider whether this claim is justified.

The second important thing to notice about the rules is that the pivot grammar depends absolutely on the nonoccurrence of P and $P + P$ and on the restriction of certain pivots to initial position (P_1) and others to final position (P_2). If these restrictions were all removed we should have as possible combinations: $P, O, P + O,$ $O + P, P + P, O + O.$ What this reduces to is the following:

$$\text{Sentence} \rightarrow (W) + W$$

where W is any word. Which is no grammar at all. In short, the pivot structure does not exist unless the nonoccurrences implied by the rules are borne out by the facts. If the restrictions are not real then child speech has less structure than pivot grammars ascribe to it. On the other hand, if there are distinctions beyond those implied then child speech has more structure than pivot grammars recognize. If, for instance, all the O words following P_1 were nouns and all those preceding P_2 were verbs then the pivot grammar would be at fault in underdifferentiating the structure present.

a. *Productivity*. There is no doubt that at least some of the child's two-word utterances in the first few months after combinations begin to appear are original constructions. But not all the arguments that the child's utterances are constructions rather than memorized routines are really convincing. For example, I do not see that the numbers involved necessarily exclude memory.

McNeill (1966b) feels they do, and points out: "For the child in Braine's sample, for example, it would mean the memorization of at least 102 combinations — that being the size of his corpus — and surely this is an underestimate because these 102 sentences are only the ones that happened to turn up in Braine's sample" (p. 24). I do not know how McNeill arrives at an estimate of the child's memory capacity which renders the memorization of 102 sentences "implausible." I would point out, however, that the 713 utterances of Adam I contained 201 different words; Sarah I contained 234 different words, and Eve I, 187. Words certainly are memorized; there is no other way, since they are not constructed by rule. Eventually, of course, the numbers do exclude memorization but not in the beginning.

It is not the numbers that rule out a memorized repertoire but rather the inclusion in every corpus that has been studied of some utterances not likely to have been modeled by any adult, and so necessarily invented. Braine calls attention to such instances as: *See cold, Bye-bye dirty, All gone lettuce, No down, More high,* and so on. In acknowledging the occurrence of such utterances and agreeing that they establish productivity we must not forget that utterances of this kind are a small minority in child English. The overwhelming majority of utterances in any sample of child English I have ever seen are easily related to well-formed adult models. This is less true of some other languages. Slobin (1966) says: "Perhaps because the morphological system of Russian facilitates neologisms — which are a marked and delightful aspect of Russian child language. Soviet psychologists have not been attracted by mechanistic and imitation-based, passive models of language acquisition. They see first-language-learning as a highly active, creative process, rivaling the productions of the poet and artist in subtlety and originality" (pp. 131–132).

Park's (1970a) account of the development of German contains numerous examples of inflected forms which, because of errors in gender, person, number, and so on, would not have been modeled as whole utterances, by any adult. From Ulrike, for instance, we have:

> *Ein Haüser*   *(Haus)*
> *Ulrike trinken* *(trinkt)*
> *Auto fahre*   *(fährt)*

And many more, including word orders ungrammatical in German and never heard from adults. Bar-Adon (1971) supplies examples from child Hebrew, and Park (1970b) from child Korean. The evidence for early productivity is clear and, as Slobin

says, more obvious with languages having an elaborate morphology than it is
for English.

It is clear that some productivity exists even in the earliest English combinations,
but it is also clear that some memorization of combinations exists. It certainly
cannot be assumed that every seemingly multi-morphemic utterance the child
produces has that status for him. The general problem of the prefabricated routine,
not constructed from all its apparent elements, has been discussed and fully
exemplified in connection with the telegraphic characterization of Stage I speech.
A particularly clear example of such a routine from Adam I is the utterance
Put b'long, which has its origin in *Put it where it belongs* but which was used by
Adam in an inflexible and seemingly uncomprehending way. It was not until Stage IV
that Adam showed a general ability to construct locatives out of embedded
indirect questions.

Finally, the demonstration that productivity exists is not the same as a
demonstration that it follows just the lines laid down by the rules of a pivot
grammar. A grammar generalizes certain facts of performance in an effort to represent
competence or knowledge. There are always alternative generalizations that fit the
obtained performance equally well. How can one determine whether a particular
generalization is the correct one? With adults, the linguist can ask whether
particular strings are well formed or not. Everyone who has tried has found that
two-year-olds do not give sensible answers to questions about what one "can say"
and "cannot say." We have all tended to assume that the difficulty is the lack
of a technique for "engaging" this sort of competence. It is also possible, however,
that there is nothing to engage; nothing, at any rate, resembling the adult's feeling
for well-formedness. We shall return to this possibility in a later section discussing
experiments on the child's judgment of correct and incorrect word orders. Suffice
it to say that there have been no demonstrations that the Stage I child's sense of
well-formedness, if he has any, follows the lines of pivot grammar. We can hardly
hold this against pivot grammar, however, since it is so difficult to obtain judgements
from children so young.

Nevertheless — acknowledging that we have only obtained utterances to go on —
I think that the accumulation of data in the nearly 10 years since Braine first
proposed the pivot grammar has changed our expectations about what we are ever
likely to hear children say. The simple rules, $P_1 + O$ and $O + P_2$, which summarize
such obtained and interpretable utterances from Table 14 as *My Mommy
($P_1 + O$), I sit ($P_1 + O$), It ball ($P_1 + O$), Push it ($O + P_2$), Mail come ($O + P_2$),*
and *want do ($O + P_2$)* also predict a large number of others. Such others, for instance,
as *My hot ($P_1 + O$), I pants ($P_1 + O$), It two ($P_1 + O$), Hot it ($O + P_2$), Broke
come ($O + P_2$), I pants ($P_1 + O$), It two ($P_1 + O$), Broke come ($O + P_2$),* and
Get do ($O + P_2$). Perhaps, when Braine first wrote on pivot grammar
one could believe that utterances like these latter were only lacking because of

sampling limitations and would turn up in larger samples in which more of the potentialities of the grammar could be realized. In fact, however, sentences like these have been mighty slow turning up in the numerous and often large samples of Table 9. One must, after this decade of research, suspect that something besides the pivot grammar determines what children will and will not say.

b. *The reality of the restrictions.* Let us consider first the nonoccurrence of P and P + P. Braine pointed out that Andrew's pivot *more* did occur alone. McNeill, however, writes: "The most compelling argument in behalf of the pivot–open distinction is the fact that pivots *never* occur alone or in combination with each other" (1970b, p. 1078), italics mine). Miller and Ervin, and Brown and his associates did not say that the members of "operator" and C_1 classes (which resembled pivots) did not occur in isolation. Some of them certainly did occur alone: *all gone* and *broken* from Evie and adjectives from Adam's modifier class. It would certainly be very surprising if others of the words that have been included in pivot classes did not occur alone; for instance: *hi, bye-bye, more, here, there.* On the other hand, since pivots include *that* and *my* and *it* and *I* and *off* and *on* but open words are mostly nouns and verbs, we can be sure that, on the whole, pivots occur less often as single-word utterances. As to P + P combinations: Bowerman (1970) points out that Miller and Ervin's Susan had 10 combinations of class II + class I *(that off,* etc.) and that Braine's Steven had a few combinations *(want get, want more,* etc.) which combined pivots. In the earlier evidence the combinations seem to have occurred but to have been uncommon.

What of the claim that pivots have fixed positions? Braine, in his analysis of Gregory's speech, identifies *bye-bye* and *all gone* as P_1 words. He does not identify these words as pivots for Andrew, which must surprise the reader who looks at the "residual utterances" and finds four instances of "Bye-bye + O" and three of "All gone + O." It cannot be that the frequencies are too low, since there are words identified as pivots for Andrew which have frequencies equally low. The problem lies with other utterances in the residue: *Papa bye-bye* and *Airplane all gone.* Obviously the positions of *bye-bye* and *all gone* were not constant, and so the words which were otherwise qualified to count as pivots were not counted as such. In Miller and Ervin's data operator words could be said to "favor" one or another position, but they were certainly not invariably found there. Class II words, for instance, occurred 31 times initially and 9 times finally. As Bowerman (in press) points out, the problem is that the classes have been defined by multiple criteria which are correlated but not perfectly. When the usual correlation fails, the investigator decides which of the several criteria shall be decisive. This effort to make the generalization stick is surprisingly like that involved in supporting the characterization of Stage I speech as telegraphic in the sense of being devoid of linguistic functors. But Bowerman and Bloom took up the same skeptical stance toward pivot grammar that Park took toward the telegraphic characterization.

Is there any evidence that pivot grammars underdifferentiate early sentences? Braine had some evidence for Gregory of a substantive-verb distinction among *O* words; the P_2 *it* only occurred after verbs. Miller and Ervin make it perfectly clear that they did not feel justified in treating *O* words as an undifferentiated class. Nouns and verbs certainly could be distinguished and possibly also other classes. Brown and Bellugi only discussed the noun phrase in Adam I, but in the total sample nouns, verbs, adjectives, locatives, and several other classes had to be distinguished. An open class in Braine's original sense — "a part of speech mainly in a residual sense, and consists of the entire vocabulary except for some of the pivots" — can only be found in Braine's data and only in two of his three cases.

What does all this come to? It seems that only Braine's data, of the "classical" data on two-word sentences, satisfied at all well the defining properties of a pivot grammar. Susan and Christy, Evie, Adam and Eve all seem to have had grammars more complex than the pivot type. This is not to deny that there were some high frequency pivot-like constructions in all these children, but these constructions only approximated to the pivot model. Positions were not absolutely fixed; pivots did occur as one-word utterances and in combination with one another. Even Braine's data include a few departures from the ideal type of the pivot grammar. All this makes one suspect that none of the children of Table 9, not even Gregory, Andrew, and Steven, really had a pivot grammar. I mean to say that I do not believe they had *P* and *O* word-classes and intuitions about which combinations were well-formed and which were not. I believe instead that the "pivot look" of the earlier samples, especially of Braine's children, derives from the fact that certain semantic operations were understood and had a broad range of applicability and so were used a lot. We will return to this claim at the end of our discussion of pivot grammars.

2. *The Claim of Universality*. Bowerman (in press) having reviewed the original evidence, was somewhat skeptical about pivot and open classes by the time she was ready to analyze the early records of her children, Seppo and Rina, and so she cast her analysis into an explicit hypothesis-testing mode. Do the several criteria that are supposed to define pivots really converge on a single set of words in a sample, or do they not?

Seppo at I was 23 months old and had a mean utterance length of 1.4 which means he was probably more advanced than Braine's subjects but at about the same level as those of Miller and Ervin. From a corpus of 713 utterances Bowerman obtained 110 distinct combinations (types). Since one characteristic of pivots is supposed to be high frequency (in terms of types or different combinations), Bowerman selected all words occurring in five or more two-word utterances. Concerning these words she asked three simple questions: Did they occupy fixed positions in combinations? Did they occur as one-word utterances? Did they occur in combination with one another? With respect to position the results are as follows:

Word	Initial	Final	Total
pois, away, off	3	10	13
tipu, chick	8	1	9
bmbm, car	2	6	8
tuossa, there	4	2	6
täti, aunt, lady	4	2	6
pamma, closed	3	3	6
äita, mother	4	1	5

The simplest summary of this table is: no, they did not have fixed positions. In Bowerman's (in press) protocols, which preserve utterance sequence, Seppo sometimes produced an utterance in one order and then immediately switched position. For example:

poika tuossa boy there	*pois tipu* away chick
tuossa poika there boy	*tipu pois* chick away

Did the high-frequency, tentative pivots occur as one-word utterances? Yes, most of them did and were even among the most frequent one-word utterances. Did they occur in combination with one another? Yes, they did. In short, the criteria defining pivots do not converge in Seppo's data, and so he cannot be said to have had pivots at all. Seppo II, at MLU of 1.81, yielded the same result.

Rina at I was 25 months old and had a mean utterance-length of about 1.83. Her data at first did seem to yield pivots. The results for position for the four words of highest frequency are:

Word	Initial	Final	Total
tässä, here	36	2	38
Rina, Rina	26	2	28
täälä, here	13	7	20
ei, no, not	11	0	11

Three of these words show strong positional preference. However, all four occurred very frequently as one-word utterances, and three of them occurred in combination with one another. Which leaves the case doubtful. Analysis of the residual *O* class settles the doubt. Open words were certainly not undifferentiated. For distributional reasons it is necessary to distinguish nouns, verbs, modifiers, and locatives. It then turns out that each putative pivot has distinct privileges with respect to open words:

tässä before nouns
ei before nouns, verbs, or locatives
Rina before verbs

Since the supposed pivots do not have the same distribution before an undifferentiated open class, they are not characterizable as members of the same class at all. For Rina, too, then a pivot-open grammar simply does not fit the facts.

Bowerman's report on Finnish was one of the first and definitely the most detailed of what has become a flood of disconfirmation of pivot grammars in languages other than English. In all cases there seems to be the kind of frequency imbalance among words which is the starting point for the pivot-open distinction. A small number of words are used often in many different combinations, and a large number of words are used only very seldom. Then it turns out that the first set, the presumptive pivot class and the second set, the presumptive open class, fail to manifest one, some, or all of the distributional restrictions they are supposed to manifest. Thus Park (1970a) notes that his presumptive German pivots are not positionally specific but rather occur freely in either first or second position. They also occur in isolation and in combination with one another. With respect to Korean, Park (1970b) makes the same observations and, in addition, points out that both pivot and open classes are made up of the same sorts of words (nouns, verbs, adjectives, adverbs), and so McNeill's differentiation of a hierarchy of classes could not possibly apply. Kernan (1969) finds five high frequency forms of largely fixed position in Stage I Samoan, which positions, however, correspond with adult usage. However, he notes that one of these pivots, *le* the definite article, occurs only with common nouns while another, the nominative sign *ō,* occurs only with human names. Which means that the open class is not undifferentiated.

Reading Blount (1969) on Luo one has the impression that he is reluctant indeed to register an exception to what had been called a developmental universal — the pivot grammar. But his data are not very accommodating. "In terms of the original motivation for studying syntax, for investigating grammar, the present analysis can do no more than suggest that Luo children may have used such a grammar in the beginning stages of syntactic development. Unfortunately, the record is incomplete on the matter" (p. 93). And then, resignedly, "It may be concluded that pivot constructions do not occupy as important a position in the syntactic development of Luo children as in their American counterparts" (pp. 93–94).

Rydin (1971), familiar by this time with the criticisms made of pivot grammar, takes little time to say, for Viveka, that while Stage I Swedish shows the usual frequency imbalance, the high frequency forms occur both alone and with one another.

Clearly pivot grammars are not universal either cross-linguistically or within the American English community for the full period from MLU of 1.0 to MLU of 2.0. However, checking back to Table 9, we find that Braine's three boys were developmentally less advanced than any of the other children we have considered. It remains possible, then, that pivot grammars are universal just at the beginning of syntax, from an MLU of 1.0 to an MLU below 1.32. However, we have three analyses by Bloom which fall in the interval between an MLU of 1.10 and 1.19, and one by Bowerman for Kendall at 1.10.

Bloom explicitly entertained the pivot grammar hypothesis in connection with her early samples from Eric, Gia, and Kathryn. First let us consider the three most primitive: Eric I, Gia I, and Eric II. Only one of these, Eric II, seems to Bloom to look like a pivot grammar. Eric I contains too few multi-word utterances to make any sort of grammatical analysis possible. In Gia I, pivot-like constructions occur but do not predominate. Constructions combining two nouns $(N + N)$ and a subject noun and a verb $(N + V)$ are much more common. For good theoretical reasons which will shortly be described Bloom concludes that these constructions should not simply be generated by a rule $O + O$, and so the grammar is not, in her opinion, a pivot grammar.

That leaves Eric II, and it seems to Bloom that Eric II is a pivot grammar. The great majority of the constructions combine an initial "operator" or P_1 term (e.g., *hi, no, 'nother, here*) with a subsequent noun. There are a few constructions of other kinds but they seem marginal. It must be added that while P_1 words may be identified in two-word combinations the particular P_1 words that appear do not fail also to occur as single-word utterances. Some of them (e.g., *hi* and *here*) are among the most common single-word utterances. So the pivots found do not quite fit the full classical definition. Nevertheless, they are definable since they are restricted to initial position before nouns.

Bloom also entertains the pivot hypothesis in connection with her grammars for Kathryn I and Gia II which, in Table 9, lie just above the level of Braine's boys. She decides that neither of these is a pivot grammar though both contain some pivot-like constructions. In Kathryn I there is a small set of forms that occur frequently before a wide variety of nouns and verbs, and these frequent forms include such familiar pivots as: *hi, this, that's, more, 'nother,* and *no.* When all the distributional facts have been considered, however, Bloom finds that most of the pivot-like constructions are better generated, together with much else, by a rule: $S_1 \rightarrow$ Nom (Neg) $\begin{Bmatrix} NP \\ VP \end{Bmatrix}$. She also includes a rule for a second sentence type which is, in fact, a pivot sentence: $S_2 \rightarrow$ pivot $+ N$. This last rule, however, is required by just nine utterances, of which the majority begin with *hi.* So, pivot-like structures are distinctly marginal in Kathryn I. In Gia II, as in Gia I, pivot constructions are much outnumbered by $N + N$ and $N + V$ constructions.

In general, then, Bloom's results give some support to the notion that the "pivot look" in early sentences is more striking the nearer the child is to the beginnings of syntax, since Eric II was thought to be a pivot grammar though not quite of the "ideal" form. However, Eric I is matched developmentally (MLU = 1.10) by Kendall I. Of Kendall's eight most frequent words, only four were limited to one position, and they were all of them among Kendall's most frequent one-word utterances. Furthermore, six of the eight pivots were proper nouns, names of household members, and seemed clearly to be functioning in such semantic roles as agent and possessor. Bowerman erases any doubts we may have by printing all of Kendall's multi-word utterances together with glosses or situational notes on meaning in an appendix (in press).

3. *The Adequacy of the Representation to the Child's Grammatical Knowledge.*
The characterizations of child speech as "telegraphic" and as the output of a pivot
grammar have something in common: they stay close to the data, applying a
minimum of interpretation. In particular, they do not attempt to determine what
children *mean* by their first sentences. The first two characterizations blended the
values of methodological behaviorism with the methods of structural, pretransformational linguistics. From this point on we shall try the effect of a different
strategy, a strategy more richly interpretive and more concerned with meaning.

Parents, and adults generally, have always been willing to interpret child
sentences. Brown and Bellugi in their 1964 article discussed these interpretations
which they called "expansions." It quite often happened (about 30 percent of the time
for Adam and Eve at I) that a "telegraphic" sentence from the child was immediately followed by a parental interpretation or "gloss." These were intended as
confirmations of the truth of what the child was thought to have meant or, if
pronounced questioningly, as communication checks asking the child if he had meant
what the parent said. When Eve said: "Mommy eggnog," for instance, her mother
said: "Mommy had her eggnog" with a confirming "that's right" intonation, but
comparable utterances on other occasions received questioning "Is that right?"
intonations. Table 15 (from Brown and Bellugi, 1964) presents some examples
of expansion.

Table 15. Expansions of child speech produced by mothers

Child	Mother
Baby highchair	Baby is in the highchair.
Mommy eggnog	Mommy had her eggnog.
Eve lunch	Eve is having lunch.
Mommy sandwich	Mommy'll have a sandwich.
Sat wall	He sat on the wall.
Throw Daddy	Throw it to Daddy.
Pick glove	Pick the glove up.

Source: Brown and Bellugi, 1964.

Brown and Bellugi saw that adult glosses stood in a kind of reciprocal relation
to the child's imitations of adult sentences. Whereas the child "reduced" the model by
omitting functors, the adult "expanded" the child's sentence by adding functors.
The child's imitations usually preserved contentives in their original order and the
adults' expansions did the same. It was as if the adult took the child to mean at
least all that he said by means of contentives and word order. Using the ordered
contentives as "givens" or "constants" the adult built up the child's utterance into a
well-formed simple sentence by adding words, mostly but not exclusively functors.
Necessarily, however, any given telegraphic utterance out of context is susceptible of

a variety of interpretations; it can always be built up into any of a number of different sentences. However, the utterance never is out of context, and the adult uses context to decide on one out of the set of possible expansions. The adult glosses the child's utterance as just that simple sentence which, in view of all the circumstances, the child ought to have said and presumably did mean. When Eve said "Eve lunch" (Table 15) her mother might, on the basis of the words alone, have provided such expansions as "Eve has had lunch" or "Eve will have lunch," but on this occasion it was the noon hour and Eve was at the table eating, and so the expansion had to be: "Eve is having lunch."

Brown and Bellugi felt that they could not tell whether Adam and Eve really intended the meanings attributed to them by parental expansions, and so these authors were chiefly interested in "expansions" as a potentially valuable training technique. There were good reasons for thinking that expansions would be an especially valuable kind of feedback. The timing was optimal; they immediately followed the child's utterance. They confirmed everything he said that was appropriate to the circumstances and they set a learning target only slightly advanced beyond his performance, just advanced enough, one would think, to be interesting, but yet graspable. In 1965, however, Cazden reported an experimental study of the value of expansion training. She did not find any evidence that expansions were effective, and until the present no one has found such evidence. In Stage II an argument is made that Cazden's results leave open the possibility that expansions would be effective if they were timed to match the child's present capabilities with respect to particular functors.

There is another way of looking at expansions. Suppose we treat them as, in some degree, veridical, as accurate readings of the child's intended meanings. Suppose, in short, we take the parental rather than the behavioristic view of child speech. This, in effect, is what Bloom has done in her book (1970; based on her 1968 thesis).

It is not necessary to rely on parents to provide glosses; the researcher can do it himself. Indeed, researchers cannot help doing it. The adult mind receiving a telegraphic utterance in a given context quite automatically expands it into an appropriate sentence. To ensure that this would nearly always be possible Bloom included in her transcriptions helpful notes on the nonlinguistic setting. We, in our transcriptions, and Bowerman, in hers, did this only where it seemed vital. In fact, however, these occasional comments together with the surrounding speech context, from children and adults, are enough to make the sense of most telegraphic sentences clear.

If Bloom is correct, and the child at Stage I intends his multi-word utterances to express meanings something like those expanding adults attribute to him, then pivot grammars are inadequate as descriptions of the child's grammatical knowledge. The reason is as follows. In Kathryn I, Bloom obtained on two different occasions the utterance *Mommy sock*. On the two occasions Bloom's transcriptions describe the contexts in these terms:

Kathryn picked up her mother's sock.
Mother was putting Kathryn's sock on Kathryn.

In the first of these contexts an "expanding" adult would be likely to produce a genitive or possessive gloss; perhaps: "That's right, it's Mommy's sock." In the second context such an adult would be likely to produce a very different gloss: "That's right, Mommy is putting on your sock." In the second case the adult takes *Mommy sock* to be a subject-object relation rather than a possessor-possessed relation. Of course the investigator does not need the expanding adult to instruct him in the probable meanings of such utterances. He can be his own "expander" operating as the parent does from context and assigning the structural meanings, genitive (or possessive) and agent-object. In a pivot grammar both instances of *Mommy sock* would have the same structural representation: $O + O$. This representation does not distinguish the relation possessor-possessed from subject-object. The words themselves do not distinguish since they were the same on both occasions. If the distinction truly belongs to the child's competence or knowledge it must appear in the grammar. Lois Bloom concludes that this distinction and many others do belong to the child's competence and must appear in the grammar. A pivot-open characterization, she judges, is only a very superficial characterization. Beneath the surface of such utterances there is a more complex deep structure which must be included in the grammar.

Bloom's approach may be illustrated with reference to $N + N$ constructions. Kathryn used a great many of these as did Leopold's Hildegard and our Eve and Bowerman's Seppo and Rina and Gvozdev's Zhenya. One must begin by considering the possibility that no relation at all exists between the two conceptions named. Perhaps they simply co-occur in the child's mind as in the visual field. There seem to be a very few such cases. For instance:

Umbrella boot (Mother is bringing Kathryn's umbrella and
boots to where Kathryn is sitting).

One is at a loss to discover any semantic relation here. Now suppose that all $N + N$ combinations were also the simple co-occurrence of ideas and that relational interpretations were entirely in the adult's mind. One would expect order to be indifferent for the child; the two possible orders for any pair should be equally probable. That is what they are not. For example, when Kathryn pointed at her mother's socks she said, not *Sock Mommy* but *Mommy sock*. In general when the context suggested a possessor-possessed relation between the two nouns that Kathryn produced then the possessor noun came first and the possessed second. The same was true for subject and object.

For $N + N$ combinations Bloom finds two other relational interpretations frequently justified:

> Subject-locative
>> For example: *Sweater chair* (Kathryn puts
>> her sweater on the chair).
>
> Attributive
>> For example: *Party hat* (Kathryn is picking
>> up a hat for parties).

In all, then, there were four relational interpretations offered for Kathryn's $N + N$ combinations. A pivot grammar makes no distinction among the four and so underestimates the child's knowledge.

Bloom writes a grammar for Kathryn I which includes the following phrase structure rules.

$$1. \ S_1 \rightarrow Nom \ (Neg) \ \begin{Bmatrix} NP \\ VP \end{Bmatrix}$$

$$3. \ VP \rightarrow VB \begin{pmatrix} NP \\ Part \end{pmatrix}$$

$$4. \ NP \rightarrow (\textschwa) \ (Adj) \ N$$

$$5. \ Nom \rightarrow \begin{Bmatrix} N \\ Dem \end{Bmatrix}$$

With these rules it is possible to generate distinct underlying structures for the four relations. Figure 3 contains derivations and tree structures for an example of each kind.

Figure 3 cannot be understood without some additional information. The subject and object *Mommy* and *sock* are dominated, respectively, by *NP* and *S* and by *NP* under *VP*. This defines the relations as they will eventually be defined in adult English. The derivation will not work, however, with just the rules I have given, since Rule 3 would generate a verb *(V)* as well as an object noun, and there is no verb in the surface structure. In Bloom's full grammar there is a reduction transformation which operates when a sentence derivation includes three category symbols. Category symbols are those symbols in underlying strings from which lexical items are derived. The transformation deletes one, and in the example of Figure 3 it must be assumed to have deleted the verb. Bloom uses the reduction transformation to represent a limitation on sentence complexity; Kathryn only produced three subject-verb-object sentences, and Bloom elected not to represent these in her grammar.

The genitive derivation assigns *Mommy* and *sock* to *Nom* and *NP* nodes, which are both dominated by *S*. No rules beyond those given are needed. The attributive derivation puts both nouns under *NP* in the predicate and makes the first subordinate to the second, which is, therefore, the head noun. It is necessary to know that nouns used attributively were listed as *Adj* in the full grammar along with true adjectives which were also used attributively. Finally the locative requires phrase structure rules a bit different from those given. The constituent *VP* would have to rewrite as *V Prep P* as well as in the ways provided (hence Rule 3ᵃ in Figure 3, IV),

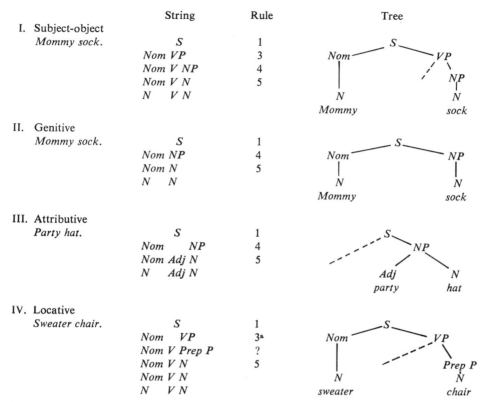

Figure 3.   Derivations and tree structures for $N + N$ constructions of four kinds (based on Bloom, 1970)

and the *Prep P* would have to rewrite as *N* (*?* in **Figure 3**, IV, indicates another rule needed here).

   Whether Bloom's derivations are the right ones need not concern us yet. The important point is that there are distinct grammatical relations (in terms of the phrase structure) for all the distinct semantic relations. Consequently it would be possible for a semantic component to provide correct "readings" for all four kinds of sentences, which is something that could not be done if the relations were defined in pivot and open terms. Finally one sees that there is a deep structure for each sentence that is more complex than the surface structure, and this deep structure is closer to adult English than the surface structure is. That makes some sense of the common observation that children at this stage seem able to comprehend grammatical relations that are more complex than any they explicitly express. The deep structure representation is also similar enough to English so that one can imagine it developing into English. It is hard to imagine that to be the case if one begins with pivot and open classes.

Bloom's criticism applies most tellingly to the rule $O + O$ within pivot grammars. This is because $O + O$ permits the generation of superficially identical strings with distinct interpretations; *Mommy sock* is one such. Since the words do not change, the change of meaning must be represented by distinct deep structures. Rules of the form $P_1 + O$ or $O + P_2$ are much less likely to generate superficially identical strings with more than one meaning. *More candy, Hi candy, All gone candy,* and so on, seem to have only one possible interpretation apiece. The differences in the relations expressed in the several cases are expressed by different pivot words, and so the deep structure need not be different. These pivots, and most pivots, have a quite constant meaning as words and a constant relational meaning in constructions. In this respect they are to be distinguished from sub-stantives like *Mommy,* which, while they have a constant semantic as words, have quite a variety of relational meanings. There is *Mommy* the agent of an action *(Mommy push), Mommy* the possessor *(Mommy sock), Mommy* the object of an action *(Kiss Mommy),* and so on. Bloom suggests that a child learning English must acquire both kinds of knowledge but that children may differ in the relative attention given in the beginning to the two kinds of knowledge. She suggests that there may be distinguishable strategies for beginning English, some children learning first a number of forms of fixed function (pivots) and others learning first forms of variable function.

Eric II, you remember, was characterized as a pivot grammar by Bloom. By this she meant that Eric's sentences were mostly of the $P + O$ type. The other two children, Gia and Kathryn, began with some $P + O$ contradictions but they also had many $O + O$ constructions which expressed such relations as possession, location, subject-object, verb object, and so on. Bloom suggests that it may be the strategies that are different. It is Bloom's suggestion that pivot grammars are not a universal first step in syntax but are one possible first strategy in English.

Summary

Pivot grammars do not correctly characterize the sentences of children at Stage I, not of children universally and not even of children learning American English. To begin with, the rules simply do not fit the evidence; pivot words do occur in isolation, pivots occur in combination with one another, sentences longer than two-words are fairly common in I, and there is distributional evidence which indicates that more than two word-classes exist. If, in addition, it is correct, that children at I intend such structural meanings as genitive, locative, agent-action, and agent-object then the $O + O$ rule of pivot grammars is inadequate because it fails to differentiate such structural meanings.

For children learning American English the pivot grammar tends to be more accurately descriptive the nearer the child is to the lower bound of Stage I (MLU of 1.0). If, however, the child at this lower level has many $O + O$ constructions (e.g., Kendall I, Gia I, and Kathryn I), and if it is correct to suppose that he uses them to express basic structural meanings then the pivot grammar is still inadequate as a description of his total competence because it fails to represent distinctions that belong to that competence. Bloom is perhaps correct in suggesting that in the early part of Stage I some children may adopt a pivot grammar as a strategy for beginning English while others do not. The claims of universality for the pivot grammar even for all children learning English at an early point in Stage I, let alone for all children anywhere in Stage I learning any language, seem to me completely discredited both by evidence and reasoning. The probability is, in my opinion, that the notion of pivot grammar should simply be jettisoned altogether. Slobin (1971a) in one of his most recent publications while, not going quite as far as I have, has responded to recent data and theory by granting that the classical pivot grammar "can no longer serve as a representation of the child's competence at the two-word stage" (p. 7).

Bloom has introduced into our discussion the suggestion that children intend to express structural meanings like locative, genitive, and agent-object, and the suggestion that an adequate grammar at I must have the means of representing such meanings. She has also shown one way that the job can be done. It is not the only possible way. We go on now to some other ideas about the meanings expressed in child sentences and the proper grammatical structures to represent them.

Concepts and Relations

I. M. Schlesinger (1971)[2] has come to the child's early sentences, not with a model of grammatical competence from linguistics but with a model of sentence production and sentence comprehension of his own devising. We will consider only the model of production. The psychological generation of a sentence does not, of course, begin with the symbol S in the manner of a generative grammar, since the speaker will not have undertaken to enumerate and describe all the sentences of his language but only to produce one that will express his present intention. The germ of the sentence is, in fact, said to be an intention; more exactly that part of the speaker's total intention which he means to embody in words. This intention is pre-verbal. It is composed of conceptions and relations, not of morphemes or words though we will have to use words to represent both conceptions and relations. Schlesinger refers to the preverbal representation of the meaning of a sentence as an "I-marker" (for "intention-marker") as contrasted with the "P-marker" (for "phrase-marker"), which some transformational linguists use to represent the deep structure, pretransformational, form of a sentence. I-markers become sentences in Schlesinger's model through the operation of "realization rules." Realization rules

2. Schlesinger's paper has been a long time getting into press. I first read it in 1968, and so Schlesinger was, along with Bloom, one of the first to apply the method of "rich interpretation" to child utterances as well as one of the first to propose replacement of the grammatical level of deep structure with semantic intentions.

accord each element in the *I*-marker a sequential position and determine its grammatical category. Schlesinger further suggests that hierarchical structure in sentences can be created by the ordered application of two or more position rules. And that such "transformations" of order as are involved in English negatives and interrogatives may be managed by making realization rules *conditional* so that one set of rules is applied when an *I*-marker contains a negation and another when it does not.

The above are only a set of loose suggestions for a model. For some of the simpler steps, however, Schlesinger offers a more formal treatment. Consider the sentence *John catches the red ball*. The *I*-marker for this sentence would include the following conceptions and relations:

red	is attribute of	*ball*
[*the* [*red ball*]]	is object of	*catches*
John	is agent of	[*catches* [*the* [*red ball*]]]

The *I*-marker is operated upon by the following realization rules:

$$R1 \; Att \; (a,b) \rightarrow N \; (Adj \; a + Nb)$$
$$R2 \; Ob \; (a,b) \rightarrow V \; (Vb + Na)$$
$$R3 \; Ag \; (a,b) \rightarrow S \; (Na + Vb)$$

Rule R1 may be expanded to read: When *a* is an attribute of *b* then *a* precedes *b* and *a* is an adjective, *b* a noun, and the combination is itself a noun. Rule R2 would read: When *a* is an object of *b* then *a* follows *b* and *a* is a noun, *b* a verb, and the resultant combination is itself a verb. Rule R3 reads: When *a* is an agent of *b* then *a* precedes *b* and *a* is a noun, *b* a verb, and the result is a sentence. Schlesinger points out that these rules could work either in the order given (from bottom to top of a derivational tree) or in the reverse of the order given (from top to bottom of a derivational tree). He judges that we do not now have enough knowledge of the production process to choose between these orders.

The "concepts" of *John catches the red ball* have here been represented by words, and so it must be unclear how the concepts differ from words. Schlesinger suggests that a single concept will usually have a whole set of words associated with it. For example, there might be a single concept "good" associated with such words as *good* (adjective), *well* (adverb), and *goodness* (noun). If now we have an *I*-marker for the sentence *John eats well* in which the concept "good" modifies the concept "eat" then the realization rule for modification will assign the grammatical category verb to "eat" and adverb to "good" and so the word selected for "good" will, in fact, be *well*. For some grammatical relations, and the attribute relation is one such, there must be a number of realization rules. Besides his R1: *Att (a,b) → N (Adj a + N b)* Schlesinger offers an R6: *Att (a,b) → N (V$_{ing}$ a + N b)*. In the production of *John catches the red ball* how does it happen that R1 is employed rather than R6? An alternative rule R6 might be blocked by the absence from the set of words associated with a concept of words belonging to the categories the rule employs. R6 requires a noun for the concept "ball" and that exists. R6 also requires a verb for "red." *Redden* would seem to be such a verb, though not a common one. Why should not the *I*-marker, therefore, yield *John catches the reddening ball?* Since this sentence would seem to have the same *I*-marker as the other, the two ought presumably to mean the same thing. In fact, they do not.[3]

If we were to follow out all the implications of the rules provided by Schlesinger we should probably find other problems. In addition, of course, the rules provided are only fragments of the total apparatus that would be required. Even in *John catches the red ball* the subject noun must be marked singular and third person, and the verb as present and the noun features must be "transported" to the verb to accomplish grammatical agreement. Schlesinger does not provide any rules for these purposes. We have not described the comprehension model sketched by Schlesinger for, as he says, it is not an algorithm, and so not yet a successful model. Finally Schlesinger offers no sort of general proof that his approach, if elaborated, would be adequate to the facts of adult linguistic performance. He claims only to offer steps toward a formalization of production and comprehension.

Schlesinger's Characterization of Child Speech

Schlesinger's "steps" acquire much of their interest from their aptness for the description of the child's first sentences. Schlesinger does not introduce new child-speech data but rather culls his examples from the papers of Braine (1963), Brown and Bellugi (1964), and Brown and Fraser (1963), and Miller and Ervin (1964).[4]

The *I*-markers of sentences, concepts, and relations, are said to be determined by the *cognitive* capacity of the child. They are presumed to be universal and innate, but not specifically linguistic, and not even peculiarly human. First-language learning is primarily, therefore, a matter of learning the realization rules in effect in that community into which a child is born. Realization rules, as Schlesinger has formulated them, order the conceptions in a relation and also assign them to grammatical categories. In two-word utterances, in the data he has examined, Schlesinger finds about eight different relations expressed. With respect to the order of the conceptions the expressions are generally in correct adult form. With respect to grammatical category, as judged in terms of adult speech, they are sometimes

3. In the 1971 published version of his paper Schlesinger responds to this objection (p. 89, n. 9) by saying that, since *reddening* has a different meaning than *red,* it would not belong to the same concept and so *reddening ball* could not be realized from the same *I*-marker as *red ball.* I agree, of course, that the meanings are different but confess that I do not know how to decide, in general, when different words belong to the same concept and when to different.

4. Kernan (1969) has explored Schlesinger's and related, semantically based grammars in connection with Stage I Samoan.

incorrect. Inflections, auxiliaries, and prepositions Schlesinger notes are largely absent. His suggestion is, then, that two-word sentences express concepts in certain relations. That the first aspect of adult grammar to come under control is conception order. Grammatical categorization comes later and, presumably, the functional morphemes still later.

The eight relations expressed in child speech, together with examples of each, now follow:

1. Agent and action: *Bambi go; Mail come; Airplane by.*
2. Action and object: *See sock; Want more; Pick glove.*
3. Agent and object: *Eve lunch* (Eve is having lunch);
                         Mommy sandwich (Mommy will have a sandwich);
                         Betty cinna toast (Betty is to have some cinnamon toast).
4. Modifier and head: *Pretty boat; More nut; Baby can.*
5. Negation and *X* (where *X* is any variable):
                         No wash;
                         No wet (= I am not wet);
                         No mama (= I don't want to go, Mama).
6. *X* and dative: *Throw Daddy* (= Throw it to Daddy).
7. Introducer and *X*, ostensive sentences: *See boy; There book;*
                         That blue.
8. *X* and locative: *Sat wall;*
                         Baby highchair (= Baby is in the highchair);
                         Baby room (= Baby is in the room).

Schlesinger Compared with Bloom

Schlesinger's characterization of child speech includes the telegraphic characteristics: inflections, prepositions, auxiliary verbs, and articles are not generated by his realization rules; contentives and certain functors (for example, *more, no*) are generated and in normal order. His analysis departs from the telegraphic description in that he attributes to the child certain relational semantic intentions. Like Bloom, Schlesinger makes a "rich" interpretation. He differs from Bloom first of all in that he offers a model of production rather than a grammar. This difference does not really go very deep. Schlesinger's model could be made into a grammar of sorts by expanding *S* as a set of alternative conceptions and relations. This would provide a "deep structure" for sentences that was directly semantic. In addition, a Schlesinger grammar would have a second component — the realization rules — for creating surface structures out of deep structures. Bloom's grammar is of the sort proposed by Chomsky in 1965, in which the deep structure of a sentence is generated by phrase structure rules, a lexicon, and certain rules of lexical selection. This type of deep structure provides all the information required by a semantic component of the Katz and Fodor (1963) type, but is not itself directly semantic. A grammar of the

Chomsky (1965) type, the type proposed by Bloom, also has a transformational component which transforms deep structures into surface structures. At the time when Schlesinger wrote his paper very few linguists had proposed that the Chomsky type of deep structure should be eliminated in favor of a directly semantic structure, but since then several have done so (for example, Fillmore, 1968; McCawley, 1968a, 1968b). These authors have shown that some decisions affecting the surface form of a sentence, for example, selection of reflexive forms, pronouns, definite and nondefinite articles, are based on meaning rather than grammatical deep structure, and so that there are reasons, beyond those raised by Schlesinger, for making meaning the only deep structure. As yet, however, no one has shown how to write anything approaching a complete grammar of this type.

Let us, then, think of Schlesinger's production model as a kind of sketch for a semantically based grammar. When his ideas are looked at in this way, how do they compare with Bloom's ideas? The important difference can be illustrated with reference to the utterance *Mommy sock* from Kathryn I, produced when mother was putting on Kathryn's sock. Schlesinger and Bloom would agree that Kathryn understood Mommy to be the agent of an action in which sock figured as an object. They would agree that this understanding belonged to the child's competence and had to be represented in her grammar. They would agree that *Mommy sock* produced when Kathryn was picking up her mother's sock had a different meaning and required a different representation. Where they would disagree is on the proper form of the representation.

As Figure 4 indicates, Schlesinger would begin with a semantic level involving agent and object relations and the concepts "Mommy" and "sock." He has not indicated how he would represent the action of "putting on" which does not appear in the surface sentence. He might attribute the concept to the child and assume that what was lacking was a word for the concept. However this problem would be handled, the important point is that Schlesinger's "realization rules" would directly translate the semantic representation into a surface form by selecting words belonging to appropriate parts-of-speech and assigning them the order normal in adult speech for the relations intended. Schlesinger's representation would entirely bypass the level of grammatical deep structure.

Bloom, by contrast, does not include the semantic level in her formal grammars, but she makes interpretations and uses them to shape the grammar. She takes the position that the deep structure representation of a sentence must include every-thing necessary for a semantic interpretation. Therefore, since *Mommy sock* has an agent-object interpretation on one occasion and a genitive interpretation on another this single surface sentence must at a minimum have two distinct deep structures upon which distinct interpretations can be based. What should the deep structures be like? For the agent-object sense, Bloom elects for a deep structure fundamentally the same as that provided for such an adult sentence in Chomsky (1965). Chomsky defines the sentence relations called subject and object in these

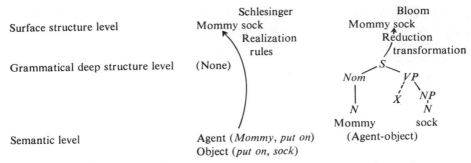

Figure 4. Comparison of Schlesinger's and Bloom's representations of a sentence

terms: the subject of a sentence is the *NP* directly dominated by *S;* the object of a predicate is a *NP* directly dominated by *VP*. And so, in Bloom's deep structure representation in Figure 4, *Mommy* is dominated by *S* and *sock* by *VP*. To account for the fact that there is no verb in the surface sentence though a *VP* is postulated in the deep structure Bloom proposes a "reduction transformation" which deletes the verb. She takes the position that the sentence has for Kathryn at I the same basic grammatical relations as for the adult but that the child operates under a complexity limitation that deletes the verb.

Without entering upon a discussion here of the comparative merits of the two representations in Figure 4, I should like to point out that in addition to the possibility that one is right and one wrong there is the possibility that both are correct but ordered developmentally. Bloom's grammars for child speech are closer than Schlesinger's to the serious grammars that have been written for adult speech. It is not impossible that the child starts Stage I with a grammar like Schlesinger's, and sometime before the end of I attains a grammar like Bloom's.

Having recognized the differences between Bloom and Schlesinger in formal apparatus and notation we must go on to their area of agreement. This goes beyond the adoption of the method of "rich interpretation" to the actual listing of major types of interpretation. Schlesinger's "relations" were induced from studies other than Bloom's but they fit Bloom's data extremely well and accord well with Bloom's own interpretation of her data. Almost all of Schlesinger's "relations" occur in Kathryn I, Gia I, and Gia II. Eric's earliest grammar we know was approximately pivotal, but in Eric III four of Schlesinger's relations occur. It is not just that the relations occur in Bloom's data; they are among the structural meanings that occur most frequently and are the meanings Bloom herself discusses.

The full story on frequencies for Bloom's data, and generally for the studies listed in Table 9, appears later in this chapter but we perhaps need here an indication of the degree of convergence between Bloom and Schlesinger. In Gia II, for instance, the frequencies were: agent-action, 15; action-object, 38; agent-object, 19; modifier-head, 84; negation-*X*, 0; *X*-dative, 0; introducer-*X*, 2; *X*-locative, 3. Most of the relations of low or zero frequency in Gia II were present in high frequency in Kathryn I; this is true of negation-*X,* introducer-*X,* and *X*-locative. Only the *X*-dative relation is missing or of vanishingly low frequency. This last fact is consistent with the other data for Stage I; the dative is extremely marginal at I.

There are some structural meanings common in Bloom's samples and discussed by her which Schlesinger does not list among his relations. One of these is the genitive or possessive. It is used to identify the person having special rights in a given thing or space (e.g., *Daddy chair* or *Daddy study*) and might be said to express a primitive sense of territoriality and property. It is also used for property of a more transitory sort: portions of food or drink assigned to someone for consumption *(Mommy coffee)* Schlesinger found genitives in the data he examined, but instead of listing them as such he included them under modifier-head relations.

Bloom also finds in high frequency a "quantifier $+ \left\{ \begin{array}{l} \text{Noun} \\ \text{Verb} \end{array} \right\}$" construction in which the quantifier is either *more* or *'nother.* The construction is used, Bloom says, to comment on or request "recurrence" of a thing or action. Looking at the sample utterances we notice that no distinction is made among reappearance of a particular instance, first appearance of a new instance of a familiar type, additional quantity of a mass, and new performance of a familiar action. All are expressed with *more* or *'nother.* Schlesinger also found these constructions in his data but he counted them as forms of modifier and head noun.

Where Schlesinger has a single "negative" relation Bloom identifies three distinct meanings. "Nonexistence": the referent is not manifest in the context and there is no expectation of its existence. Often the referent has been manifest in the recent past. Forms used to express this meaning include *no more* and *all gone* as in *All gone magazine* (Kathryn II) and *No more juice* (Eric II). "Rejection": the referent was present or imminent and was rejected or opposed by the child. For example, Kathryn in I said *No dirty soap* as she pushed away a sliver of worn soap. "Denial": the utterance denied that an actual (or supposed) assertion was the case. For instance, Kathryn's mother (in II) said: "Here it is. Here's the truck." And Kathryn responded: "No truck," denying her mother's assertion. Bloom found for her samples which fall in Stage I (below MLU of 2.0) *Nonexistence* was often expressed syntactically. Kathryn and Eric had begun to express *rejection* and *denial* in sentences but Gia had not. Indeed, Gia only very rarely used negative sentences in Stage I; the few she did use (mostly near the end of I) expressed nonexistence. Grégoire gives examples of the use of *non* by his two boys which suggest the meanings: rejection and nonexistence; Chao's examples for Canta's use of *buh (not)* all suggest rejection; Slobin's examples of Zhenya's early use of *nyet (no)* suggest nonexistence and rejection. Schlesinger's examples of negation seem to include all three meanings, but he does not explicitly distinguish them.

Finally Bloom found in high frequency the construction *Hi* + *N.* She noticed that it was not used as a greeting to persons arriving on the scene. It was not even limited to persons, but addressed to animals and even inanimate things. The child would suddenly "light up" and address some referent that had been present all

along. Bloom suggests that it is a "noticing reaction." Schlesinger failed to find
this construction in the data he examined perhaps because most investigators have
excluded greetings and rejoinders and exclamations from the data they have discussed
on the presumption that such forms are not grammatically revealing.

The fact that Bloom lists *more + N* and the genitive separately while Schlesinger
puts them together with attributive constructions into a modifier-head construction,
and that Schlesinger lists a single negative meaning where Bloom lists three,
introduces an important point about semantic relations or basic semantic roles. How
finely should they be sliced? Consider Schlesinger's "modifier and head" examples.
Pretty in *Pretty boat* might be said to add an attribute to a particular boat, to
further specify the referent of *boat*. *More nut* probably meaning *More nuts* refers
to additional instances of a class which is not the same as further specification of an
instance. *My stool* is a possessive and *my* names the person having property rights
in the stool. Among Schlesinger's negatives we find both *No wet* and *No, Mama*. The
former denies the truth of an assertion: *I am not wet*. The latter does also but,
rather more obviously, it represents rejection of or resistance to an interpersonal
force *(I don't want to go, Mama)*.

And so on. Each "relation" is cognitively heterogeneous — to some extent. It is
not clear why relations should not be more finely subdivided than they are by
Schlesinger so as to separate out, for instance, possessives from other relations of
modification and "resistances" from other sorts of negation. In pointing out certain
obvious subtypes within the relations we have not made the finest distinctions
it is possible to make. Ultimately *each* utterance expresses a distinct relation which
is the meaning of that utterance. Why should we not suppose that a child's
"intentions" are as varied as his utterances. On the other hand, Schlesinger has not
made his relations as generic as is possible. His modifiers might be combined with
his negations. Both occupy first position and both modify the sense of whatever
is in second position. Meanings of sentences may be described so generically as to
make no distinctions (a sentence expresses a complete thought) or so specifically
as to make as many distinctions as there are sentences or with any number of
distinctions in between these extremes. The question is, of course, which of the
possible distinctions is, in fact, functional or "psychologically real"? This is a
question to which we shall return.

Though we have not solved the problem of "psychological reality" for semantic
relations we shall begin to keep track of those that have been proposed. Bloom's list
includes Schlesinger's but is more finely differentiated. Table 16 represents the
relation between the two.

The Acquisition of Grammatical Class

Schlesinger's realization rules for adult speech may be said to combine rules
of order and rules of categorization. He contends that children learn rules of order
first and rules of categorization second. If this is true we should find that early in

Table 16. Major semantic relations in Stage I as described by Schlesinger (1971) and Bloom (1970)

Schlesinger	Bloom
Agent and action	Subject and predicate
Action and object	Verb and object
Agent and object	Subject and object
Modifier and head	Attributive
	Genitive
	Recurrence
Negation and x	Nonexistence
	Rejection
	Denial
x and dative	–
Introducer and x (ostensive sentences)	Demonstratives with predicate nominatives
x and locative	Subject and locative
	Verb and locative
–	Noticing reaction

Stage I conceptions are named in the order appropriate to the relation intended but that the words used sometimes belong to the wrong grammatical categories from the adult point of view. Later in Stage I category errors should diminish in frequency. In the examples from Schlesinger that I have listed there is only a single category error: the agent-action sentence *airplane by* does not employ a verb in second position which is what the realization rule requires. Martin Braine, whose example this is, says that an airplane was flying past when the sentence was uttered. The word *by* may derive from the preposition *by* or from the interjection *bye-bye*. Both may be among the set of words having to do with a concept of "going past or away" but neither is a verb. In his original article Schlesinger cites four other category errors, all of them from Braine: *more wet, all gone sticky, all gone outside* (the outside is all gone when the door is shut), *more outside* (meaning "I want to go outside again"). In the full evidence described by Table 9 there are additional examples of category errors but not a great many of them. In Gia I, Gia II, and Andrew we have examples of *more* used with verbs and adjectives as well as nouns; for instance, *more write* (Gia I), *more hat* (Andrew). Eric II uses *'nother* with an adjective: *'nother wet* for wetting his pants again. The most common category errors occur with *hi* or *hello*. In Hildegard, Kathryn I, Gia I, Eric II, Gregory, and Adam I, *hi* or *hello* are used to animals as well as humans and even to inanimate objects: *Hi Katz* (Hildegard), *Hi spoon* (Kathryn I), *Hi plane* (Gregory). Category errors, though never frequent, do seem to be more frequent early in Stage I than they are later in the stage.

Whether rules of order are learned before rules of categorization does not seem to be determinable from present data. The category errors to which Schlesinger gives attention are matched in the data of Table 9 by such order errors as *Nose blow*

(Hildegard) and *Balloon throw* (Gia I) and *Apple eat* (Christy) and *Suitcase go get it* (Adam I), and by quite a few examples in Kendall I and II. Both kinds of error occur; both are infrequent in English. And one sort of error does not seem to appear earlier in Stage I than the other. In short, the evidence does not support the theory that rules of order are learned before rules of adult categorization. Both are usually observed and occasionally violated in Stage I. For inflected languages in which word order is more flexible than it is in English and less important for signaling meanings (for example, in German, Finnish, Japanese, Korean, Russian) the data are complex and will be separately considered at a later point. What, in general, seems to happen is that some Stage I children learning such languages show considerable flexibility of word order whereas others are quite inflexible in using only certain orders.

Grammatical Relations, Predication, and Topic-Comment

David McNeill in his paper "Developmental Psycholinguistics" (1966b) and again in his chapter for *Carmichael's Manual of Child Psychology* (1970b) and his recent book *The Acquisition of Language* (1970a) has presented evidence that the two- and three-word sentences in early samples of Adam all express one or more of the basic "grammatical relations" as these relations were defined by Chomsky in 1965. McNeill's thesis is related to Schlesinger's, and is very similar to Bloom's but there are differences. These may be very generally expressed by saying that Schlesinger was chiefly concerned with semantic relations, Bloom with both semantic and formal relations, and McNeill only with formal relations. Some further explication is necessary.

Formal Definition of Grammatical Relations
In *Aspects of the Theory of Syntax* (1965) Chomsky showed that the grammatical relations (or functions) traditionally named subject of the sentence, predicate of the sentence, direct object of the predicate, and main verb of the predicate are all represented in the tree structure generated by the phrase structure rules of the base component of a grammar. Consider the simple tree structure of Figure 5. The relation: subject of the sentence is defined as follows. The subject is the *NP* which is directly dominated by *S* or "sentence." Therefore: *Adam*. The object of the predicate (or *VP*) is the *NP* directly dominated by *VP*. The main verb of the predicate is the *V* dominated by *VP*. Relations are more numerous than these. In general any phrase structure rewriting rule defines a set of grammatical relations but only certain ones, those involving the higher level, more abstract grammatical categories, have traditional names. The relation modifier of a noun phrase is another named relation. If the object *NP* in Figure 5 branched into *little* and *Eve* then *little* would be the modifier of that *NP*.

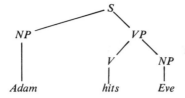

Figure 5.   Tree structure for a simple sentence

Grammatical Relations Distinguished from Semantic Relations

Knowledge of the grammatical relations in a sentence is essential to its interpretation. If we know only that *Adam, Eve, little,* and *hits* are somehow combined into a sentence we do not know who hits whom and who has the attribute little. The possibilities are separated out by assigning the words to the functions (or relations): subject, object, modifier, and head. Let us look at this matter more closely.

The English verb *hit* names an action in which there are two essential roles; there must be someone who initiates the action, someone who hits, and there must be someone (or something) who receives the force of the action. (A logician would say that *hit* is a predicate having two "terms" or "arguments." In order to make a sentence using the word *hit* one must specify the persons in the respective roles. How is this to be done? The person in the role of hitter is made the subject of the sentence and the person in the role of receiver of the force is made the object of the sentence. In a simple declarative sentence like *Adam hits Eve* the subject is in preverbal position and the object in postverbal position. However the functions, subject and object, are much more abstract than this example suggests. Across English sentences generally, subject and object cannot be coordinated with any particular sequential positions. We have, for instance, the passive-voice sentence *Eve was hit by Adam* in which the name of the one who hits is still the deep subject of the sentence but it is not in preverbal position.

The difficult thing to keep straight is the fact that subject and object are not semantic roles but are grammatical functions which are used to identify the occupants of semantic roles. Consider the verbs *give* and *receive* in the sentences:

> *John gave Jane a present.*
> *Jane received a present from John.*

Both verbs must have persons in the role of present-giver. For *give* the name of the person in this role *(John)* becomes the subject of the sentence, but for *receive* this is not the case. For *receive,* the present-giver (still *John*) becomes the object of a prepositional phrase. The subject with *receive (Jane)* is the name of the person in the role of gift-receiver. This semantic role when the verb is *give* is coordinated with the grammatical role of indirect object. *Give* and *receive* make an especially instructive pair, since they clearly separate grammatical function from semantic function or role.

If we examine many verbs we find that the semantic roles associated with them may be grouped into a smaller number of types. For example, the verbs *hit, push, pull, kiss, feed, dress,* and so on, all must have someone in the role of action-initiator usually called agent, as well as someone (or something) in the role of receiver of the force, suffering a change of state because of the force, usually called simply object or, as by Chafe (1970), patient. For all these verbs the semantic agent becomes the grammatical subject and the semantic object or patient becomes the grammatical object. The verb *receive* demonstrates that agents are not always coordinated with the grammatical subject; the agent in *Jane received a present from John* is *John,* not *Jane.* However, *receive* is unusual in this respect (see subsequent discussion under case grammar). In English, agents usually are subjects.

What must a child learn about verbs like *hit* and *push* and *kiss* in order to use them to make sentences which express propositions. He could simply learn for each verb, the grammatical functions associated with the two semantic roles. For *give* the initiator is the subject; for *receive* the initiator is object of the preposition *from.* The child need not form the abstraction agent at all since he does not necessarily have to use it. However, there is a potential economy or advantage in forming that abstraction. If he discovers (not consciously, of course) that some verbs have the type of semantic role called agent, and that this role is, for these verbs, always coordinated with sentence subject then when he learns new verbs that have agent roles he can generalize the regularity and guess that the agent with these verbs, as with the others, will be the grammatical subject. That generalization would usually be correct, though in the odd case of *receive* it would be incorrect.

It is by no means the case that all two-term or two-argument English verbs take a semantic agent and object. Consider the verbs *see* and *hear* in *Adam sees Eve* and *Adam hears Eve.* In these sentences Adam does not initiate any action and Eve does not receive any force. One would rather say that Adam is affected by stimulation of which Eve is the source. The Adam role, the person-affected role, with such verbs has been called a dative by Fillmore in his case grammar and an experiencer by Chafe (1970); the Eve role is difficult to characterize semantically. Fillmore, we shall later see, calls it objective but he uses this term with a very special sense. Chafe (1970) would consider the role a variety of patient. With *see* and *hear* and quite a few other verbs the experiencer or dative role is coordinated with the grammatical subject and the patient with the grammatical object.

Most of the verbs that children use in Stage I are agent-object verbs. It is for this reason that Schlesinger could say that sentences at Stage I express, among others, the semantic relations: agent-action; action-object; agent-object. He did not say subject-verb, verb-object, subject-object because he was talking about semantic relations rather than formal grammatical relations. Schlesinger also did not suggest that the semantic relations were coordinated with grammatical subject and object in Chomsky's sense. He suggested instead that the words in the agent and object roles were identifiable as such by simple word order. This is a possible alternative for the range of sentences in question just because they are all simple, active, declarative sentences in which semantic roles are consistently coordinated with sequential positions. Schlesinger's characterization of child sentences does include the claim that they operate with the abstractions agent and object, and not simply with the particular semantic roles associated with the many verbs they learn. It is not clear, however, that he was fully aware of the difference between semantic relations and grammatical relations since he includes, among agent-action relations, *Mail come,* and, among action-object relations *See sock. Mail* is not an agent though it is a subject and *see* is not an action though it is a verb.

Bloom used the terms agent and object for the corresponding semantic roles and subject and object for their grammatical coordinates. She holds that the child operates with grammatical relations in Chomsky's sense but she is also interested in the various semantic relations coordinated with these. Bloom's position is that the child operates with semantic abstractions like agent-object, notice, recurrence, nonexistence, rejection, denial, and so on. Some of these are coordinated with grammatical relations such as subject and object and modifier and some with particular lexical items like *more, all gone,* and *hi.* McNeill seems to have just the formal grammatical relations in mind since he uses Chomsky's configurational definitions. And yet, even in his recent book (1970a) he speaks of "combining words to *express the grammatical relations*" (p. 67) [italics mine]. Why would anyone want to express the configuration called subject? In his book McNeill also calls the grammatical relations "logical" (p. 67). I cannot see what Chomsky's formal configurations have to do with logic. My impression is that McNeill moves unwittingly from the formal grammatical relations to various semantic relations, perhaps assuming a perfect convergence between the two, a convergence that does not exist. Possibly, however, his position is that there are no abstractions of the agent-patient type operating in the child but that he simply marks the particular semantic roles associated with particular verb and noun combinations.

Evidence of Grammatical Relations in Early Adam

By grammatical relations McNeill (1966b) means: 1. subject of a sentence; 2. main verb of a predicate phrase; 3. object of a predicate phrase; 4. modifier of a noun phrase; 5. head noun of a noun phrase. McNeill takes his definitions of them from Chomsky. For data McNeill used some of the very early transcriptions of our subject, Adam; the analysis is limited to two-word and three-word utterances.

McNeill suggests that certain two-word and three-word combinations would be consistent with the expression of one or more grammatical relations while others would be consistent with none at all. His conclusion is that all Adam's sentences are expressive of grammatical relations; no others occur. A very impressive result, since there are more *possible* combinations inconsistent with the expression of relations than consistent with such expression.

How are inconsistency and consistency assessed? To begin with, the words in the utterances are assigned to morpheme classes, and consistency is reckoned with reference to class sequences rather than to sequences of particular words. Two of the classes correspond closely with classes in adult English grammar. The third, and only other, is a class that some, including McNeill, believe to exist in child speech: pivots. In early Adam, presumed members of the pivot class are *a, the, that, my,* and such descriptive adjectives as *big, green, poor,* and *pretty.* These pivots are all words that can precede nouns in an *NP;* they are all modifiers of some sort, and were so designated by Brown and Bellugi (1964).

With just three word classes there are 3^2 or nine possible two-word sequences and 3^3 or 27 possible three-word sequences. McNeill judges that only four of the two-word sequences and eight of the three-word sequences would be consistent with one or more grammatical relations. Five two-word sequences and 19 three-word sequences are left inconsistent. Only consistent sequences occur, and they occur with the frequencies presented in Table 17 (from McNeill, 1966b). Table 17 also lists the grammatical relations with which McNeill judges each sequence-type to be consistent.

To see how the judgments of consistency are made, let us look at just the two-word cases. *P + N* sequences include such instances (from Adam I) as: *Big drum; My pencil;* and *Two light.* That these express relations of modification seems fairly clear. *N + N* include such instances as: *Adam belt* and *Daddy chair,* which are reasonably interpreted as possessives, and possession is a kind of modification. There are also some *N + N* combinations which do not suggest relations of modification, but rather look like a subject and object without a verb. McNeill makes the assumption, also made by Bloom, that verbs can be omitted from predicate phrases,

Table 17.   Sentence patterns in children's speech that correspond to basic grammatical relations

Pattern	Frequency	Corresponding Grammatical Relations
P + N	23	Modifier, head noun
N + N	115	Modifier, head noun, subject, predicate
V + N	162	Main verb, object
N + V	49	Subject, predicate
Total	349	
P + N + N	3	Modifier, head noun
N + P + N	1	Subject, predicate, modifier, head noun
V + P + N	3	Main verb, object, modifier, head noun
V + N + N	29	Main verb, object, modifier, head noun
P + N + V	1	Subject, predicate, modifier, head noun
N + N + V	1	Subject, predicate, modifier, head noun
N + V + N	4	Main verb, object, subject, predicate
N + N + N	7	Subject, predicate, modifier, head noun
Total	49	

Source: McNeill, 1966 b.

and so treats such *N + N* combinations as consistent ones. *V + N* sequences include such instances as *Wash hand, Read book,* and *Hear tractor* which do strongly suggest the relation: object of a predicate phrase. Finally, *N + V* combinations include such instances as *Adam write, Mommy come,* and *Piggy squeak* which suggest the relation subject of a sentence. This is what the data are like and this is the way the judgments are made. There are, I think, three minor qualifications or questions to raise concerning McNeill's test of his hypothesis.

1. For Adam I it is not quite the case that all utterances express grammatical relations. There are a few utterances, very few, which are instances of McNeill's "inconsistent" sequences. For example:

N + P	*Pillow dirty* (and two others).
V + V	*Must go.*
N + V + V	*I can write and I take hit.*
V + V + N	*Must go Catherine.*
P + P + N	*Dirty my hands.*

There are a few other utterances which are instances of "consistent" sequences but which in fact do not seem to represent the usual relations associated with the sequence or indeed any other of the basic grammatical relations. For example:

Paper find.
Book boy.
Part trailer.
Car mosquito.
Pencil paper.
Paper pencil.
Pencil doggie.

Most of these defeated the efforts to provide interpretations of all the adults on the scene and are likely to embarrass *any* theory at all about the significance of early child sentences.

2. McNeill's assumption that verbs may be omitted from predicate phrases may be too strong to permit a completely fair test of the hypothesis that all utterances express grammatical relations. When an utterance like *Mommy sock* from Kathryn I is used in circumstances such that Mommy is putting on Kathryn's sock it seems clear that an agent-object semantic relation exists such that a person is acting, in some way, upon a thing but it is less clear that the grammatical relations subject and object exist since the formal definition of these requires a verb. At any rate some explanation is needed for the absence of the verb; Bloom's "reduction transformation" is one such explanation.

3. In Adam I some of the utterances that are instances of consistent sequences do not, in fact, seem to represent the usual relations associated with that sequence but

do seem to represent other sorts of grammatical relation. The other relation most clearly and frequently expressed is the locative. It is a proper grammatical relation since a grammar of the type of Chomsky, 1965, would include in its base component a rule rewriting predicate phrase, or possibly prepositional phrase, into a set of constituents including the locative. One may properly speak of the relation "locative of a predicate phrase" (or "of a prepositional phrase"). In Adam I some of the locatives have the form $V + N$, some $N + N$, some $N + V + N$, some $V + N + N$. For example:

$V + N$	$N + N$	$N + V + N$	$V + N + N$
Sit water?	Adam home.	Adam fall toy.	Sit Adam chair.
Write paper.	Jowha home.	Tractor go floor.	Put truck window.
Put floor.			
(and five others).			

Constructions like these were also frequent in Eve I and in Sarah I, in Kendall I, and in two of the children studied by Bloom as well as in Stage I children learning languages other than English. There seems to be no doubt that locative of a predicate is one of the grammatical relations frequently expressed in the first sentences, and that McNeill's classification of utterances like the above as modifier, subject, and the like is a mistake that results from dealing with word classes rather than with particular words in situational contexts. Fraser (1966) has raised the same point in a general form about McNeill's analysis.

The above qualifications and questions only blur the picture a little. McNeill's conclusion remains true in striking degree: most early sentences do seem to manifest one or more of the basic grammatical relations, and that is an important discovery. They may, in addition, manifest one or more abstract semantic relations, as Bloom and Schlesinger believe. However, an alternative clearly exists. Sentences like *Adam write* and *Mommy come* and *Wash hand* need not be said to identify persons in the abstract roles of agent and object but only to identify persons in such particular roles as: the one who writes, the one who comes, those that are washed. The words in these particular roles, are identifiable in the child's sentences because he has placed them in their appropriate grammatical roles.

Predication as the Primary Relation

In his chapter for *Carmichael's Manual of Child Psychology* (1970b), McNeill has added something to his thesis that the early sentences express basic grammatical relations. The relations expressed in the early Adam samples are usually, McNeill finds, relations involving the predicate of the sentences. Using the assumptions he employed to test the thesis that obtained word combinations are consistent with grammatical relations, McNeill finds, in addition, that a large majority of the combinations are consistent, specifically, with a relation involving the predicate.

There are, therefore, McNeill says, "predications." And so predication seems to be the primary function of early sentences. This is a thesis that appears to agree with one interpretation of the child's holophrastic or single-word utterances. Grace De Laguna in her book *Speech: Its Function and Development* (1927) argued that predication is the function of holophrastic speech. In addition, McNeill finds in the early Adam samples and in the early sentences of two Japanese children whom he has been studying that a subvariety of predication which he calls "intrinsic" precedes another subvariety which he calls "extrinsic."

1. *De Laguna's Thesis.* Let us start with De Laguna's discussion of holophrases and predication. She offers no explicit definition of predication but appears to regard the term as one having a single well-established meaning. In fact, of course, the term predicate, as opposed to subject, and the derivative term predication, are used in both grammar and logic, and, in neither discipline, with complete consistency (Chomsky, 1965; Copi, 1967; Long, 1961; Quine, 1960). So it is a bit difficult to figure out just what De Laguna means by predicate and predication. However, it is clear what McNeill means by them. He uses the terms in Chomsky's grammatical sense, according to which a predicate is a *VP* directly dominated by the node *S*. McNeill understands De Laguna to be saying that the child's single-word utterance always belongs to the grammatical predicate of that full sentence which expresses the full meaning that the child may be presumed to have in mind. I do not understand her in quite the same way.

"What the baby does from the beginning, when he is not indulging in pure vocal play, is to talk in complete, if rudimentary sentences" (De Laguna, p. 87). "The simple sentence-word is a complete proclamation or command or question, because the speech in which it occurs is so closely bound up with the attitude of response to his immediate surroundings" (De Laguna, p. 91). In these and other passages De Laguna gives it as her opinion that, though the child speaks in single words, each such single word has a meaning which requires a full sentence for its expression in the adult language. Such undifferentiated sentence-words are said by De Laguna to be "implicit predications." In this sort of context I believe that De Laguna means by predication the sorts of meanings — propositions, questions, and so on — which are ordinarily associated with full sentences. Predication means something like "propositionalizing" or "sentence-making." In such contexts De Laguna does not, I think, have reference to the predicate as a *part* of a sentence.

How do single words manage to suggest sentences? One case that De Laguna discusses extensively is the "predicate proclamation." Of this she says: "What is proclaimed in it always has reference to some object or event or general state of affairs whose existence is *presumed*. This presumption may take the form of pointing to the thing in question, or perhaps of intently regarding it. The predicate proclamation does not announce its presence or existence, but calls attention to some specific property having a bearing on the given situation. In such a case there is virtual or implicit predication; but the language form is rudimentary" (De Laguna, pp. 98–99). As an example she tells of a little French child who pointed to her brother's slippers and (the brother being named Raymond) said: "Mon-mon." As another example she tells of a child stretching out a dirty hand and saying: "Ca-ca" (which is a term of disgust). In this context I think that "predicate" carries its usual grammatical sense and also its usual logical sense. The French girl's "mon-mon" might reasonably be glossed as "These shoes are Raymond's" and the other child's "ca-ca" as "My hand is dirty." In both cases the subject goes unexpressed, since shoes and hand were already objects of shared attention and presumed existence. The word spoken, in each case, belongs to the grammatical predicate of the sentence expressing the full meaning. In logic, one usually means by *subject* that term in a proposition which refers to a thing or class of things endowed with indefinitely numerous attributes and by predicate a second term that modifies the subject by adding one or more fresh attributes. De Laguna's predicative proclamation would seem to define subject and predicate in terms consistent with this logical sense as well as with the usual grammatical sense. And in this context De Laguna is certainly saying what McNeill takes her to be saying: the child's single-word utterances belong to the predicates of the full sentences that would adequately express the child's meanings.

The implicit predication of the proclamation becomes explicit when the subject, whose existence is presumed, is named. Adding *Those shoes* and *My hand* to *Raymond's* and *dirty,* we have sentences which are complete but for the copula. By this account, then, speech begins with the use of terms drawn from predicates and advances by the addition of subjects. However, De Laguna goes on to say: "It is not to be supposed that the differentiation of structure occurred only in the proclamation of presence and the predication proclamation" (p. 104). And she describes a case in which the child's holophrase appeared to specify a subject. The little girl whose brother's name was Raymond came running to her father in tears one day when Raymond had been teasing her and said: "Mon-mon." For this De Laguna suggests the somewhat stilted gloss "Raymond has made me unhappy." In this case the word spoken is the subject of the intended sentence. And so it was in another example where a child having been put out of the kitchen by her mother complained to her father: "Maman." In cases like this it seems reasonable to think of the meaning carried by the predicate as that which is already in the focus of attention and need not be specified. Before the child speaks we have essentially the meanings "someone made me cry" and "Someone chased me out of the kitchen." What the holophrases do is specify the subject.[5]

I think De Laguna's position was essentially this: 1. All single-word utterances

5. William Labov (1970) in a private communication, has suggested that "subject" and "predicate" seem not to be the appropriate terms here but rather "topic" and "comment." "Everyone seems to agree that subject and predicate relate to the surface structure of more complex constructions, or at least can be confined to grammatical relations rather than the kind of intent or attention focusing considered here."

have sentence meanings; 2. Some single-word utterances belong to the predicate of the sentence that would express the full meaning and some belong to the subject; 3. In a variety of ways the originally unexpressed parts of sentences come to be made explicit.

2. *McNeill's Evidence.* McNeill, in any case, believes that holophrases are predicates, and that the child's early sentences are also primarily predicative. His evidence on this last point derives from an analysis of Adam's early transcriptions. The words used by Adam were, we know, classified as pivots *(P)*, nouns *(N)*, and verbs *(V)*, and utterances were then expressed as sequences of word classes. Certain ones of the possible sequences, you recall, are consistent with the expression of one or more grammatical relations, and others are not. Almost all *obtained* sequences turned out to belong to the types expressive of grammatical relations. Among the sequences expressive of grammatical relations some would express relations involving the predicate and some would not. Predicates would be expressed by the following types: *VN, NV, VNN, VPN, NVN, NNV,* and *NPN* (the last assuming an absent *V*). Between 70 and 90 percent of Adam's sentences were of these types, and so the majority of his sentences were predicative, though not only predicates, since *NV, NVN, NNV,* and *NPN* all presumably also have subjects. However, McNeill points out that the most frequent patterns were *VN* and *VNN,* from which subjects are missing. Which seems to McNeill to provide some support for De Laguna's contention that children first produce isolated predicates and then add subjects.

Adam was 28 months old, and the holophrastic stage for most children ends at about 18 months. What happens in between? In between, in McNeill's opinion, come the pivot grammars that Braine has described. The sentences of Braine's three boys analyzed in pivot terms were mostly either $P_1 + O$ or $O + P_2$. The open *(O)* class words were mostly nouns or verbs which means Braine's boys chiefly produced $P_1 + N, P_1 + V, N + P_2,$ and $V + P_2$. If we were to look at these sequences in the same way that McNeill looks at Adam's we should find exactly none of them consistent with predication, and three of them not consistent with the expression of any grammatical relation at all. McNeill (1966) says nothing of predication in connection with pivot grammars and so, in this presentation, pivot grammars appear as an unaccountable digression in the path from predicates to subject-and-predicates. In his more recent works (1970a, 1970b) McNeill has attempted to introduce more continuity by redefining pivot and open classes in terms of grammatical relations and syntactic markers, but we have already seen that this redefinition does not satisfy the evidence that seeming pivots are often (as in Kendall I) nouns.

How does it happen that Braine's boys produced combinations described as $P_1 + V, N + P_2,$ and $V + P_2$ whereas Adam did not? The explanation lies with the difference between the supposed *P* classes. Brown and Bellugi (1964) we recall called the class in question, in Adam's speech, *M* for modifier rather than *P*. The members of *M* were all prenominal modifiers or determiners: *a, the, my, that,* and so on. For just this reason the class *M* was generic to determiners, and on this

fact McNeill (1966b, 1970b) built his thesis that the child has innate knowledge
of a universal hierarchy of word classes. That thesis runs into trouble when we look at
the membership of the *P* classes in Braine's children. For these classes are not
generic in the way that Adam's *M* is. P_1 for Andrew has as members, *all, I, no, see,
more, hi,* and *other;* his P_2 were *off, by, come,* and *down there.* The P_1 classes
for the other boys are equally heterogeneous. Now we can see why Adam had no
$P_1 + V$ *(the want)* or $N + P_2$ *(book the)* or $V + P_2$ *(want my);* it is surely because
determiners do not occupy such positions in English. Andrew, on the other hand,
with very heterogeneous *P* classes could very well have $P_1 + V$ *(I see, I shut)*
and $N + P_2$ *(Plane by, Mail come)* and $V + P_2$ *(fall down there, sit down there).* In
fact, I would suggest both Braine's boys, and Adam, were expressing semantic
relations by means of grammatical relations but these relations were not exclusively
predicative. The mistake lies, I think, with the classification of words as pivots
and with the whole conception of pivot grammars.

3. *Intrinsic and Extrinsic Predication.* Finally, McNeill (1970b) has noticed that
the omitted but contextually implied subject of many of Adam's subjectless
predications is *I. Change diaper* meant that Adam wanted to change the diaper and
Hit my ball described what Adam was about to do. Adult speakers, we know, tend to
omit subjects when the subject is obvious. If two people have been waiting for an
elevator, which then arrives, and one boards but the other lingers the one who boards
may well say: "Coming?" rather than "Are you coming?" This fact about adults leads
McNeill to wonder whether Adam believed that sentences involving himself as
subject were clear in just this way, and so required no explicit subject. Which in its
turn leads to the consideration of a general distinction between intrinsic predicates
which seem to entail their subjects and extrinsic predicates which do not. The notion
is that the intrinsic predicate is so closely linked with its subject as to seem almost
a property of the subject. Habitual activities *(Daddy teaches),* class memberships
(A collie is a dog), and various truisms *(All men are mortal)* are all forms of intrinsic
predication. Temporary locations *(A dog is in the yard)* and short-lived activities
(I am reading) are forms of extrinsic predication. In Japanese a distinction of this
kind has certain grammatical reflexes, and McNeill's data on Japanese child speech
suggests that intrinsic predication precedes, developmentally, extrinsic predication.
McNeill believes that there is evidence to the same effect in the speech of Adam
and Eve, and that Adam's tendency to omit the first-person subject results from a
feeling, on Adam's part, that anything predicated about himself is intrinsic. We
will not follow McNeill into the details of his argument because the data from Adam
which are its starting point do not seem strong enough to carry the thesis.

In Adam I, while there are many subjectless sentences that seem to call for *I,* it is
not the case that this subject is always omitted. In fact, either *I* or *Adam* appears
as explicit subject in 23 sentences. Evidently, therefore, Adam did not feel that
everything predicated of himself was intrinsic. Is there, however, some difference of
intrinsicality between sentences with *I* and sentences without *I?* There is none that

I can see. As a matter of fact almost all the predications which either have or should have first-person subjects look extrinsic to me, and that is not as it should be if intrinsic predication is as prominent at this age as McNeill believes it is. Perhaps the trouble lies with my failure to grasp the slightly Japanese contrast between extrinsic and intrinsic. But that cannot be the whole trouble. Because there are some predications which appear both with *I* present and with *I* omitted, but called for, Adam I includes not only *Change diaper* but *I change diaper;* not only *Hit ball* but *My hit ball* (*My* is here a variant form of the first-person subject). I conclude that there is really nothing to support the notion, for children learning English, that intrinsic predication precedes extrinsic. There is, however, the empirical fact that Adam often omitted first-person subjects, and the fact needs an explanation.

A final point about the general thesis that early sentences manifest relations involving the predicate. Certainly many of them do, perhaps the majority for children at the level of Adam I. We must remember, however, that in many cases these predicative sentences can be more closely described as manifesting such relations as subject and predicate of a sentence, object of a predicate, subject and object, locative of a predicate, and so on. To characterize all these as predications is to prefer a more generic characterization to a more specific characterization. It is possible to do this but it is necessary to show why the generic characterization is preferable. One way of doing this would be to show that the generic characterization is genuinely functional for children; that they are, in some sense, predicating, in all the cases which may be described in alternative and more specific terms. That has not been done.

Topic and Comment
Jeffrey Gruber (1967) has found evidence in the spontaneous speech of one child that early sentences have as their immediate constituents a topic and comment rather than a subject and predicate. The child (Mackie) was one of the subjects studied by Margaret Bullowa. Weekly samples of one-half hour each were taken over a period of several years; the evidence for the topic-comment distinction appeared between 790 and 881 days, in the first half, therefore, of the third year.

Gruber offers as an example of topic-comment construction in adult speech the sentence: *Salt, I taste it in this food* or, alternatively: *I taste it in this food, salt.* His provisional definition holds that a topic is a *NP* cogenerated with a clause (or sentence), such that the referent of the *NP* is identical with some *NP* in the clause. The clause is the comment. By cogeneration Gruber means that both *NP* and clause are dominated by the same *S* node. In the end Gruber argues that child sentences must begin as pure comments (or predicates) to which topics are next added with subjects eventually emerging out of topics. This would mean that Mackie at 28 months was still in a presubject stage.

What Gruber has by way of clear evidence is a very few sentences from Mackie which do seem to have a *NP* either antecedent or subsequent to a clause which makes the same reference as a *NP* in the clause. For example: *It broken, wheels; Car, it broken; Those other, put them?* Besides these few sentences which fairly directly suggest the topic-comment form there are a great many which seem simply to be subject-predicate sentences, for example, *Girl go away, Me take the wheel, Where's the wheel.* Most of Gruber's paper is devoted to elaborate and ingenious arguments for supposing that sentences like these have underlying structures unlike their surfaces, structures such as *me, (I) take wheel* and *Where is (it), the wheel,* which would make them into topic-and-comment constructions.

Gruber's argument builds on certain well-established distributional peculiarities of child speech. For example: the fact that pronoun subjects are often omitted, that copulas are sometimes present and sometimes absent; that *wh-* questions at first fail to transpose the subject and the verbal auxiliary. The argument has, then, evidence to support it but this evidence is all open to interpretations other than those made by Gruber. Which means that the only very clear evidence consists of those few sentences which seem on the surface to be topic and comment sentences. They are few in Gruber's data, and in all the data described in Table 9 I can find fewer than a dozen instances. Two such are *Shadow; go get it* and *Daddy suitcase; go get it* from Adam I. On the other hand, there are thousands of sentences that seem to be subject and predicate constructions. It would be absurd to try to argue all these latter away in an effort to establish the topic-comment sentence as the norm.

The sentences from Mackie that are quoted by Gruber (especially *wh-* questions) indicate that Mackie in the first half of his third year was linguistically advanced beyond Stage I. Gruber has analyzed data that are more mature than any described in Table 9. If Mackie's sentences had a topic-comment structure and if pure predication (or comment) is supposed to precede topic-comment then one would expect to find in Stage I pure predication. Instead, what one finds is a lot of evidence for the subject-predicate distinction which, on Gruber's theory, ought only to appear at a more mature stage than Mackie had attained. So I conclude that there is nothing in the notion that topic and comment represents a sentence organization prior to organization into subject and predicate.

Case Grammar

No one so far has suggested in print that Charles Fillmore's (1968) case grammar provides a better framework for the description of children's early sentences than does any other grammar, but it is a good thought.[6] The study of case in linguistics has traditionally meant the study of these semantic relationships between nouns and other parts of sentences which are marked by affixes on the noun. Fillmore has

6. Bowerman (in press) in her dissertation has carefully explored the application of case grammar to Stage I Finnish, and Kernan (1969) has used a related, semantically based approach. Bowerman finds that case grammar has both advantages and disadvantages in comparison with a transformational grammar of the Chomsky (1965) type.

abstracted the semantic relations from the process of affixation and proposed that there is a universal set of "presumably innate" concepts which are expressed in all languages whether by affixation, suppletion, clitic particles, or word order. In English these case meanings are primarily expressed by prepositions and word order.

Fillmore's basic list of case concepts appears in Table 18. These are the ones, presumably, of whose universality he is most confident. He names several others as possible additions to the list: benefactive *(B)* as in "John did it for *Mary*"; comitative *(C)* as in "Adam walked home with *Mommy*"; temporal *(T)* as in "They arrived at noon." [7]

The possible relevance to child sentences is signaled by the very names of the cases: agentive, dative, locative, and objective sound like Schlesinger's semantic relations and also like Bloom's or McNeill's grammatical relations. But there is an important and clarifying difference between Fillmore's cases and either kind of relational concept. In the treatments of Schlesinger, Bloom, and McNeill there tends to be a one-to-one relation between semantic and formal relations with the result that one easily forgets that they are two things. Schlesinger can say that the agent-object relation is expressed by putting the agent noun first and the object

Table 18. Fillmore's case concepts defined and exemplified

Case Name	Definition	Example (italicized noun is in designated case)
Agentive (*A*)	The typically animate, perceived instigator of action	*John* opened the door. The door was opened by *John*.
Instrumental (*I*)	The inanimate force or object causally involved in the state or action named by the verb	The *key* opened the door. John opened the door with the *key*.
Dative (*D*)	The animate being affected by the state or action named by the verb	*Adam* sees Eve. John murdered *Bill*. John gave the book to *Bill*. *Daddy* has a study.
Factitive (*F*)	The object or being resulting from the state or action named by the verb	God created *woman*. John built a *table*.
Locative (*L*)	The location or spatial orientation of the state or action named by the verb	The sweater is on the *chair*. *Chicago* is windy. John walked to *school*.
Objective (*O*)	The semantically most neutral case: anything representable by a noun whose role in the state or action named by the verb depends on the meaning of the verb itself	Adam sees *Eve*. The *sweater* is on the chair. John opened the *door*.

Source: Adapted from Fillmore, 1968.

7. See Chafe (1970) for a semantically based theory of the structure of language that is closely related to Fillmore's, as Chafe repeatedly acknowledges, but which defines the basic "case meanings" somewhat differently. Table 1 in this book is primarily based on Chafe.

second. In Bloom's treatment the semantic notions are not coordinated with sequential positions but they are coordinated with grammatical subject and object. In Table 18 we see that the agentive case is not always the first word in the sentence and is not always the surface subject. And certainly subjects are not always agentives; in Table 18 instrumental, dative, locative, and objective case nouns all appear as surface subjects. Clearly Schlesinger is right when he says that consistent semantic characterization of the grammatical subject is impossible for English. The objective case in the examples of Table 18 is not always in final or postverbal or any other position. Neither is it always the grammatical object of the predicate; in *The sweater is on the table* the noun in the objective case is actually the grammatical subject of the sentence. Clearly, also the grammatical object is not always a noun in the objective case; in Table 18 dative and factitive case nouns both appear as grammatical objects.

In Fillmore's case grammar then the semantic concepts are distinct from any particular means of expression or any particular grammatical relation. Why should semantic relations and grammatical relations tend to collapse together for Schlesinger, Bloom, and McNeill, and not to do so for Fillmore? In part it is because Fillmore is not describing the child's early sentences but rather all sentences in English. Therefore, he includes the passive voice which is not used by children in the early stages of language acquisition but which separates agents from subjects and from preverbal position. Therefore, also, he includes a verb like *murder,* which seldom appears in child speech but which uses a dative case noun as grammatical object. In part, however, the difference must be attributed to the fact that Fillmore explicitly defines his cases in semantic terms, as Schlesinger, for instance, does not, and then tries to stick with the definitions. Fillmore would not classify *Mail come* as an agentive though Schlesinger does.

The objective case in Fillmore's set is unlike the others in that it is not given an independent semantic definition. It is a kind of residual case. Fillmore finds, as have other writers on case, that all cases but one can be given a clear semantic definition. The objective case is left to take its full sense from the verb.

The basic structure of a sentence is, in Fillmore's theory, the "proposition," a tenseless set of relationships involving nouns and verbs. Again we are immediately struck by the relevance to children's early sentences, for surely they are tenseless relations among nouns and verbs. Fillmore develops the deep structures of sentences with some such rules as appear in Figure 6. The immediate constituents of a sentence are not subject and predicate but modality and proposition. Modality includes tense, aspect, mood, negation, and much more. Fillmore does not develop this constituent in his 1968 paper. Proposition expands as a long list of sentence types, each one of which is defined as a verb *(V)* plus some combination of cases. Every case expands in the same way, as a case marker *(K)* which in English can be a preposition or an inflection, and a noun phrase *(NP)*. Noun phrases expand as determiner *(D)* and noun *(N)*.

Sentence → Modality + Proposition
Modality → Tense (*Neg*), etc.

$$\text{Proposition} \rightarrow \begin{cases} V + A \\ V + O \\ V + D \\ \text{etc.} \\ V + A + O \\ V + A + D \\ \text{etc.} \end{cases}$$

$$\left.\begin{matrix} A \\ I \\ D \\ F \\ L \\ O \end{matrix}\right\} \rightarrow K + NP$$

$$NP \rightarrow D + N$$

Figure 6.   Deep structure rules for case grammar[a]

[a]The form of the rules is based on Fillmore's discussion but he does not fully specify how they are to be written.

Agentive and dative cases require nouns that have animate referents. Therefore, in case grammar the lexical entries for nouns include features like "+ animate" (for *Adam, Daddy*) and "− animate" (for *ball, tree*). To ensure that appropriately marked nouns are selected for given case roles there would have to be, in a full grammar, obligatory rules saying, for example, that nouns in the agentive or dative case must carry the feature "+ animate."

Verb entries in the lexicon specify the case environments or case frames in which particular verbs can occur. The verb *open,* for example, can occur in the following four sentences:

The door opened.	*(V + O)*
John opened the door.	*(V + A + O)*
The wind opened the door.	*(V + I + O)*
John opened the door with a chisel.	*(V + A + I + O)*

The best way to represent this range of possibilities is to assign *open* the frame "+ [__*O(I)(A)*]," which says that the verb must occur with an objective case noun and may occur with an instrumental and/or an agentive.

The assignment of case frames to verbs effects a kind of classification into verb types, and it is just here that case grammar provides an especially felicitous notation. Consider the parallel sets of verbs listed below:

see	*look*
hear	*listen*
know	*learn*

The members of each pair are closely similar in meaning but not identical. In *Adam sees Eve* one has the sense that he is passively affected whereas in *Adam looks at Eve* one has the sense that he is initiating action, training his receptors on a given object. There is a similar contrast in the other pairs, and it is a contrast that seems to be rendered quite exactly by assigning the feature "+ [__A]," instigator of action, to the verbs on the right and "+ [__D]," person affected, to the verbs on the left. These case frames effect a subclassification of the verbs, and this sub-classification is one having extensive syntactic consequences. The verbs on the right, usually called "action" or "process" or "nonstative" verbs, may be used in the imperative *(Look at me),* may be replaced by *do so,* may be used in the benefactive *(Listen for your own good),* and may take progressive aspect *(be looking, be listening, be learning).* For the verbs on the left, the "statives," none of these possibilities exists. One does not order someone to *know* or say *I am knowing* or any of the rest.

Lexical entries for verbs may differ not only with respect to case frames but also with respect to rules specifying that nouns in particular cases are to become the surface subjects of sentences including certain verbs. This provision effects a very neat description of the difference between two verbs we have already had occasion to discuss: *give* and *receive.* The two verbs are essentially synonymous and also have the same case frames: "+ [__A,O(D)]." The difference between them is that the verb *give* makes a surface subject of the noun in the Agentive *(A)* case: *John gave a present to Mary,* whereas the verb *receive* makes a surface subject of the noun in the dative *(D)* case: *Mary received a present from John.* The pair *like* and *please* in English is susceptible of the same kind of analysis.

In Figure 7 we have deep structure representations (my own) of some sample English sentences. Each one is an array consisting of a verb *(V)* plus a number of noun phrases *(NP)* holding labeled case relations to the sentence. Deep structures are converted into surface structures by a variety of mechanisms. One of these involves the creation of a surface subject. Fillmore says that, in general, subject selection seems to follow the rule: "If there is an *A,* it becomes the subject; otherwise, if there is an *I,* it becomes the subject; otherwise, the subject is the *O*" (p. 33). In the top-left deep structure of Figure 7 there is an *A,* and so the constituent Ø + John" is moved to the front of the structure and directly attached to *S* so as to yield, ultimately, the sentence: *John opened the door.* In the structure on the right in Figure 7 there is no *A* but there is an *I,* and so this structure is forepositioned so as to yield *The chisel opened the door.* We can imagine a third case, for which no diagram is provided, which includes only an *O,* and after forepositioning of *O* yields *The door opened.* In the bottom diagram of Figure 7 there is both an *A* and an *I* and so it is the *A* that would be forepositioned. The general rule selecting the surface subject may be overridden by the special rules we have mentioned, requiring particular cases to function as subject of particular verbs (for example, *give, receive).*

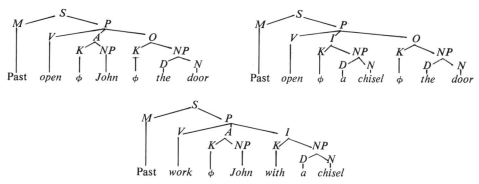

Figure 7.   Sample deep structures generated by case grammar

Another mechanism involved in the creation of surface structures is a rule which deletes the case marker *(K)* for grammatical subjects and objects. In English these grammatical roles are only marked by word order. When nouns are not functioning as subject or object their case relations are often marked by prepositions. Fillmore suggests that the rules may look something like this:

1. The *A* preposition is *by: The door was opened by John.*
2. The *I* preposition is *by* if there is no *A: The car was hit by a stone.* If there is an *A* the *I* preposition is *with: John hit the car with a stone.*
3. The *O* and *F* prepositions are typically zero.
4. The *B* preposition is *for: She did it for me.*
5. The *D* preposition is *to: He gave the present to Mary.*
6. The *L* prepositions are semantically nonempty and so are selected from the lexicon. Prepositions like *in, on, under, over* do more than mark the case as locative; they encode spatial relations.

In the bottom diagram of Figure 7 the instrumental case, being neither subject nor object, is marked by *with.*

Besides the transformation that accomplishes subject-fronting and case deletion for subjects and objects there are several special rules of interest to us because they operate in constructions that occur among the child's early sentences. There is, for instance, the locative sentence with *be,* which in the child's telegraphic version can come out: *Sweater chair.* The preposition *in* is developed as a case marker for the locative, the articles develop from *D,* and the grammatical subject *sweater* would be in the objective case. But where does *be* come from? In sentences of this type Fillmore has the verb rewrite as Ø and both tense and *be* are introduced from the modality constituent. How about a copular predicate adjective sentence which in the child's version may be *Hands dirty?* Fillmore, in agreement with

Paul Postal and George Lakoff, considers adjectives to be a subset of verbs. Therefore, *dirty* is dominated by *V*. The subject *hands* is in the neutral objective case and *be* in this case as when the verb is zero is introduced from the modality constituent.

What of the genitive, which in the possessive sense is so frequent in child speech? Fillmore offers distinct treatments for "alienable" and "inalienable" possessions. Inalienable possessions are body parts and kin: *John's face, John's son, John's wife*. Alienable possessions include clothing, toys, portions of food and drink: *John's hat, John's bicycle, John's coffee*. Most, though not quite all the genitive constructions of children, concern alienable possessions. These constructions are developed by Fillmore, as by many transformational grammarians, out of simple sentences with *have* as verb: *John has a hat; John has a bicycle, John has a cup of coffee*. The possessor (John) is in the dative case — as a person affected by the state named — and becomes subject of the sentence. The possessed object is in the neutral objective case. Fillmore takes the position on *have* that, in sentences such that *V* is $\varnothing$, *have* is obligatorily inserted just in case the subject is an *NP* that is not from the *O* case. Since the subject in *John has a hat* is from the dative case, *have* is an obligatory insertion. The *have* sentence, when it is embedded in another sentence, is transformed by additional rules into *John's hat*. In this construction the inflection *-s* functions as a dative case marker.

Adam I in Case Grammar Terms

For all the previous characterizations of early sentences we have had data to consider, data cited by the author of the characterization. Since case grammar has not been put forward as a framework for characterizing early sentences, we have no data to consider. Let us, therefore, use Adam I.[8]

In the 713 utterances of Adam I there are 202 which consist of two or more words. Of these 153 may be classified in case grammar terms if we ignore occasional vocatives, rejoinders, interrogative intonations, and negative words. The 49 utterances that cannot be so classified are mostly uninterpretable strings *(Car mosquito)*, rejoinders *(OK, kitty)*, greetings *(Hi, boot)*, and would be left over as a residual by most grammars. A few, utterances that cannot be analyzed in terms

8. I want to make explicit the particular stance I am taking with regard to Fillmore's case grammar lest I seem to do that author an injustice. I am, in the first place, considering only his 1968 paper, and this paper did not set out to create anything approaching a full grammar of adult English and makes no reference at all to child speech. I have undertaken only to expose the surprising aptness of the fundamental ideas in the paper for the description of child speech and also to point out some ways in which case grammar as presented in that first paper seemed inappropriate to represent child speech. Fillmore has written many papers since 1968, and if I were more ambitious I would undertake to evaluate the usefulness for representing child speech of case grammar as it now stands or even, if I were surer of myself in the role of linguist, try to reformulate it where it does not seem to work well for our purposes. But others will have to do these things, and there are many indications that they will do so.

of case grammar, could be analyzed in terms of grammars other than case grammar, for example, the *Wh-* questions that occur.

How should we judge whether a grammar of adult English provides a good framework for the analysis of Stage I speech? The first criterion should be completeness. Is it possible to analyze all the sentences in a corpus in terms of the grammar? Case grammar, as of 1968, does quite well as the figures in the previous paragraph show. Its chief shortcoming from the point of view of Stage I speech is the lack of any account of imperative, negative, and interrogative operations. For child speech beyond Stage I there will be many other shortcomings: no account of verbal auxiliaries or of inflection for number or of determiners and almost nothing on embedding and conjoining. One reason why case grammar seems so peculiarly well adapted to Stage I speech is the fact that the features of the grammar in Fillmore's 1968 paper mainly concern the deep structure of simple sentences, and that is almost all that is needed for Stage I speech. Of course, case grammar has continued to develop since 1968, and many constructions not described in the original paper may eventually be given fully satisfactory treatment.

Another criterion of adequacy must be the simplicity and interest of the generalizations that will serve to carve out Stage I speech from adult speech. The following generalizations characterize Adam I in case grammar terms.

1. All 6 case concepts posited as universal are to be found in Adam I though the instances of the factitive are a little doubtful.

2. There is a simply stated sentence complexity limit: Except for one sentence the limit is two cases to a sentence. Sentences using two cases vary in type. They include $V + A + L, V + A + O, V + A + C, V + D + O, V + L + O,$ and $V + A + I.$ The sentence that exceeds the limit is *I like pick dirt up firetruck,* which appears to involve embedding. In most child samples there is something like this to make the investigator wonder if he is hearing things. Very possibly sentences of this type represent the child's effort to say what he already knows how to conceive but has not yet learned how to say in a fully grammatical way. They may be evidence of cognitive development in advance of strictly linguistic development.

3. There is a simply stated constituent complexity limit: only $D + O,$ the genitive, occurs as an embedded constituent. It functions as $O, L,$ and $I.$

4. In general, Stage I speech represents a greater development of one major constituent of S than of the other. Stage I sentences are "propositions." There is no tense, aspect, mood, number, or the like. From the modality constituent only the simplest reflexes of the negative, imperative, and interrogative occur.

5. What is missing from the proposition? All case markings *(K)* are absent, whether prepositions or the possessive inflection. In addition, almost all determiners are missing. There is nothing in case grammar to suggest why just these two constituents should be missing.

6. Also missing are the irregular verbs *be* and *have. Be* is developed out of the modality constituent when the sentence has an adjective in verb position or when it is

verbless. *Have* is inserted under V when the subject is a *NP* not in the *O* case. Nothing in case grammar suggests why just these two omissions should occur.

7. What of the transformations that create surface structures from deep structures? The subject-fronting rule selects *A* if present, otherwise *I*, otherwise *O*. When there is an agent in a sentence it seems always to be in subject position so we should have to say that the rule is working for agents. However, there are a few sentences without an agent having a *NP* in the *I* case, and that noun is not in subject position; for instance, *sweep broom*. And there are many sentences, without an agent, having a *NP* in the *O*, and that noun is usually not in subject position, for instance, *Change diaper* and *Put truck window*. Of course it may be that there are "understood" agents in all such sentences which have been deleted, but that is a further assumption. On the face of it the subject-fronting rule works out oddly, as learned in part but not altogether. This leaves the transformations which delete case markers *(K)* for subjects and objects. Such markers are always missing, but since all case markers are missing — including those that would be obligatory in adult speech — there is no evidence relevant to these rules.

A third criterion of adequacy in a grammar as a framework for the analysis of child speech is the account it gives of errors, peculiarities of distribution, and surprising absences of errors. The grammar that succeeds here must be especially impressive since the grammarian will not usually have had knowledge of the data his theory explains. There is a surprising error absence in child speech at the next level above Stage I. The first of the verbal inflections to be used is the progressive *-ing*. This inflection is used in adult American English only with "process" verbs, never with "statives" such as *want, see, like,* and *know,* and that is the way Adam, Eve, and Sarah used it from the start. They never used the progressive with a stative verb. This is surprising because all the other inflections, the past and present indicative on the verb, the plural and possessive on the noun, were overgeneralized to unsuitable stems. What accounts for the strange invulnerability of statives?

In case grammar statives are marked $+ [\_\_D]$, and so distinguished from process verbs which are marked $+ [\_\_A]$. The case concepts themselves, since they are all expressed at Stage I, seem to be at least very early learned if not innate. Perhaps then verbs are also assigned their "case frames" very early, conceivably even before the child uses the verbs. If that were so then stative and process verbs would have been distinguished as subclasses long before the progressive inflection was ever used. Consequently the distributional break in the inflection following the lines of these covert classes would be easily learned and followed. We know that stative and process verbs are distinguished by several syntactic processes other than progressive inflection and, as it happens, one of these, the imperative, can be found in Stage I speech. In their use of the imperative children observe the subclass break as perfectly as they do in their use of the progressive. There are no imperative statives in the early sentences. So case grammar seems to give a good account of this surprising absence of error.

Table 19.   Multi-word utterances of Adam I classified in case grammar terms[a]

Declaratives or Imperatives with Verbs		Declaratives or Imperatives, Verbless	
$V + A$	Adam write (12)	$D + O$	(genitive) Adam hat (27)
$V + I$	Sweep broom (3)	$D + O$	embedded as O See Daddy car (4)
$V + D$	Give doggie (2)	$D + O$	embedded as L Sit Adam chair (2)
$V + F$	Play checkers (?) (3)	$D + O$	embedded as I Play Momma
			slipper (1)
$V + L$	Write paper (11)	$L + O$	Adam home (8)
$V + O$	Change diaper, Pillow dirty,		
	Hear horn (61)		
$V + A + L$	Adam fall toy (8)		
$V + A + O$	I beat drum (16)		
$V + A + C$	I sit you (with) 1		
$V + D + O$	Adam see that, Give		
	doggie paper (10)		
$V + L + O$	Put truck window (12)		
$V + A + I$	I play bulldozer (?) (1)		
$V + A + I + D + O$	I like pick dirt up fire-		
	truck (1)		

Interrogatives		Negatives	
$V + A$	Daddy go? (5)	$V + A$	I not fall (3)
$V + L$	Sit water? (2)	$O + L$	No pictures on there (1)
$V + O$	Remember Bozo?	$V + D + O$	No I see truck (1)
	Like it? (7)		
$V + A + L$	Kitty go home? (1)		
$L + O$	Pictures in there? (2)		

[a] *Unclassified residue:* Put b'long, Car mosquito, Hi, boot, No fall. (49)

However, if we follow out all the implications of the account it does not work so well. If case frames are learned very early should not verbs that have obligatory cases always appear with nouns in these cases? Unhappily they do not. The verb *put* has three obligatory cases: an agent, object, and locative. But in Adam I we have *Put floor,* which contains only a locative and *Put light,* which contains only an objective. There are quite a few such instances with *put* in I and long after. However, among verbs *put* is unusual in requiring three cases and, indeed, Adam's sentence complexity limit presumably prevents him from using more than two. However, *put* is not the only verb that occurs with obligatory cases missing. This also happens at I with *make, turn off, fix,* and eight others. The theory can be repaired by making additional assumptions but then it would lose the simplicity that originally made it impressive.

In samples after Stage I there are certain errors which it seemed reasonable to think that case grammar might explain. Adam, Eve, and Sarah all occasionally used "accusative" pronouns, the pronouns designed to serve as surface objects, as "nominative" pronouns or subjects. Sarah, for instance, said *Her curl my hair* and

Her crashed, and Adam said *Why me sitting on it?; Why not me careless?; What me do?; Where me sleep?* In case grammar terms surface subjects are sometimes agentives, sometimes datives, sometimes instrumentals, and sometimes objectives. Is it possible that the accusative pronoun occurs as subject only when the subject belongs to particular cases, perhaps to the objective? An interesting hypothesis but one that is not confirmed by the evidence. There are accusative subjects in the agentive and dative cases as in the objective case. Whatever the explanation of these errors it does not seem to be obtainable from case grammar.

After Stage I, for a very long time Adam used *it's* as if it were a single word, as *It's went.* At the same time he used *it.* What governed the choice between the two? Was it the deep structure case membership of the pronoun or its surface structure role as subject or object? It was definitely the latter. *It's,* if it was used at all, was always the surface subject and *it* the surface object pronoun, whatever their deep structure cases. Of course, this outcome and the one above may only mean that Adam quickly learned the general lesson for English that pronominal forms are determined by surface subject and object roles, and not by underlying cases. All that can be said is that there is nothing here that argues for the reality of case grammar.

Looking farther ahead one thinks of many hypotheses to test in connection with case grammar. When the children begin to fill in the prepositions, all of which are missing at Stage I, will the order of acquisition reflect underlying cases? The preposition *with,* for instance, marks both the instrumental *(sweep with a broom)* and comitative *(walk with Mommy)* cases. If the cases have psychological reality the two employments of *with* might develop at different times. If *with* is only a word in prepositional phrases there should be no difference in time of acquisition between phrases we would classify as instrumental and phrases we would classify as comitative. When the children begin to conjoin simple sentences to make compound sentences we shall again have something to look for. One of the most interesting claims Fillmore makes is the following: "Only noun phrases representing the same case may be conjoined" (p. 22). Other linguists have suggested that distinct noun phrases may be conjoined whenever they belong to otherwise identical sentences provided only that the *NP*'s fill the same surface grammatical roles. From *Jack went up the hill* and *Jill went up the hill* either theory would (daringly) predict *Jack and Jill went up the hill.* But from *John broke the window* and *A hammer broke the window,* case grammar would predict correctly that *John and a hammer broke the window* would be ill formed, whereas the other theory would not.[9] The question will be whether children ever make errors of this kind and so reveal more reliance on surface grammatical roles than on underlying cases.

I think we have been able to show that case grammar offers a framework for the

9. William Labov (private communication 1970) cites: "A strong arm and a heavy rock broke the window" as an example of a sentence conjoining an agent and an instrument. I have to admit that I feel unsure whether such a sentence is fully grammatical or not. In any case it is evident that Fillmore's (1968) claim about conjoining is far from having been established.

analysis of child speech that is at least promising. Whether it offers more than the other frameworks we have considered cannot yet be said.

Conclusions

This has been a critical review of the more influential characterizations, produced in the last decade, of Stage I speech. It has been a review with a direction to it, from the nonsemantic terms of telegraphic speech and pivot grammar to the highly semantic and fairly similar terms of Schlesinger, Bloom, and Fillmore. The description of the child's first multi-word utterances as telegraphic was of course only revived and not originated in this decade. In the 1963 formulation of Brown and Fraser telegraphic speech is speech entirely composed of contentive words, which are words belonging to the large open classes called noun, verb, and adjective, and entirely lacking functors or function words, which are words belonging to such small closed classes as inflections, prepositions, articles, auxiliary verbs, pronouns, prolocatives, and so on. Simply as an unexplained descriptive generalization the telegraphic characterization is roughly true for all the Stage I speech that has been studied. This only rough and never very revealing truth has now given way to a set of more interesting, not yet fully tested, functional hypotheses. It has given way because of Park's (1970a) German data and his lack of interest in accommodating them to the old characterization and because of "exceptions" that have always existed in the American English data, including many words cognate to Park's exceptions like *more, 'nother, here, there,* and because several experimental studies have pulled apart variables that tend to converge on English functors. The data at present suggest that those functors which have some minimal frequency and perceptual salience and which enter into the expression of such semantic relations as recurrence *(more, 'nother),* location *(here, there),* and possession *(my),* and agent-action *(I, you),* and action-object *(it),* and are not conditioned in a complex way by verbal context will attain full productivity in Stage I. Functors not having all these characteristics are likely either to be totally absent from Stage I speech or else present only in certain prefabricated routines. Thus the categorical telegraphic characterization when closely examined over a variety of languages dissolves in a way that points toward the importance of semantic variables as far as the child's intentions are concerned, and variables of frequency, salience, and complexity of verbal conditioning as far as the expressive medium is concerned.

In its 1963 version the telegraphic characterization of Stage I speech was much less suggestive than another that appeared in the same year: the pivot grammar. Pivot grammar was more interesting because it provided for the most salient and psychologically challenging feature of sentence construction: productivity. The fate in this decade of the pivot grammar characterization is remarkably similar to that of its age-mate: telegraphic speech. Pivot and open classes unlike functors and contentives, were not borrowed from linguistic theory but were abstracted from distributional characteristics of child speech. However, pivot and open classes resemble functors and contentives in another respect: they are defined by multiple criteria which were at first thought to be perfectly convergent but later proved not to be so. Pivots were defined as high frequency forms, having fixed positions in two-word utterances, never occurring as single-word utterances and never occurring together. For a few years investigators sought to preserve the generalization as a universal truth, and when the data were not perfectly accommodating, and they never were *perfectly* accommodating, the investigator preserved the generalization by, in effect, giving priority to one or another of the imperfectly convergent criteria. Then Bloom and Bowerman came along, like Park feeling no particular motivation to preserve received views but interested rather in testing them as hypotheses. And, I think it is fair to say that the pivot grammar collapsed at once when approached in this spirit. What Bloom found for a couple of children learning English, what Bowerman found for a child just beginning English syntax and for two Finnish children, Park found for Korean and German, Rydin found for Swedish, and so on. There is always, it seems, a fairly sharp frequency break with a few words used often and in many combinations, and a larger number of words used seldom and in fewer combinations. But these presumptive pivot and open words fail to manifest some or all of the other distributional characteristics they are supposed to have. Presumptive pivots do occur as single-word utterances, in two-word combinations their positions are not generally fixed, and they do combine with one another. Exactly as in the case of telegraphic speech the hypothesis-testing stance taken up with regard to new data led to a second look at all the sets of old data and the conclusion that they too had been full of exceptions, with only Braine's data coming close to satisfying the distributional claims. With this collapse of the empirical base for pivot grammar, and for other reasons besides, McNeill's ideas of an innate hierarchy of subclasses also, in my opinion, falls.

The discontinuity in most Stage I speech between words entering into many combinations and words entering into few combinations, which is what gives the "pivot look" to many samples of Stage I speech, is the single distributional characteristic that pretty well survives across all the studies of Tables 9 and 10. To anticipate a later discussion it is worth pointing out that among the common pivots one very often finds ostensive nominating forms like *it, this, that,* and *there;* forms expressing recurrence like *more* and *'nother* and *again;* and forms expressing nonexistence (or disappearance) like *all gone, no more, 'way* — and in languages other than English their approximate equivalents. I think that the "pivot look" results from two factors: 1. the child's understanding of an elementary closed semantic set comprising: referent existence (nomination), referent recurrence, and referent nonexistence; 2. existence, recurrence, and nonexistence may be predicated of just about any person, place, action, or quality, and so have a very broad combinatorial potential quite unlike that of such semantically limited terms as *swim, eat, hot, pencil*. These two together could account for the "pivot-look," which is by no means the same as a pivot grammar.

In addition to the collapse of empirical distributional support pivot grammar has suffered a second even more telling and also more fruitful attack on theoretical grounds. Lois Bloom proposed that the kinds of semantic relations which adults assign telegraphic combinations like *Mommy sock,* on the basis of attendant nonverbal context, do in fact belong to the child's intentions. Her important insight, which we shall examine at length, is that the child's speech contains a certain kind of evidence that the relations are in his mind, and not just in the mind of the adult interpreter: the evidence of word order. The child acquiring English in a huge majority of cases orders his words as they should be ordered if the semantic relations suggested by context to adults are what he intends.

Suppose we accept this evidence and the kind of rich interpretation of child utterances that it justifies, "rich" relative to the nonsemantic telegraphic and pivot grammar characterizations. It then becomes important to note that there are in child speech minimal pairs, like *Mommy sock,* which on one occasion seem to have one interpretation and on another occasion a different interpretation. In the case of *Mommy sock,* one context suggested agent-action and another context suggested possessor-possession. If these different interpretations belong to the child's intentions, hence to his knowledge or competence, then the pivot grammar description is inadequate because it does not provide distinct descriptions for such pairs. *Mommy sock,* for instance, would be an instance of $O + O$, whatever its meaning.

Bloom concludes that there must be something in the linguistic descriptions to carry the differences of meaning. She was writing in the tradition of a Chomsky *Aspects* (1965) grammar, later called by Chomsky (1969) the standard theory, in which the semantic component is entirely interpretive, and the deep structures of sentences are required to contain everything necessary to produce correct interpretations. Consequently Bloom assigns distinct grammatical deep structures corresponding to the sets of semantic relations she feels justified in attributing to the Stage I child. Figure 3 illustrates the way this can be done. In effect, *Mommy sock* with one sort of grammatical deep structure would receive an agent-action interpretation and with another sort of deep structure a possessor-possessed interpretation.

If one adopts the approach of "rich interpretation" to Stage I speech in the sense of believing that the child's semantic intentions include certain roles or relations, Bloom's formal representation is not the only possibility. In the same year that I read Bloom's dissertation (1968), which was published in 1970, I read Schlesinger's paper on semantic relations, which was published in 1971. Schlesinger completely bypasses the level of grammatical deep structure and moves directly from semantic intentions to surface structures somewhat in the manner of what has come to be called generative semantics (McCawley, 1968a, 1968b). His approach to word order is somewhat different from Bloom's. Instead of treating appropriate word order as evidence of the existence of certain semantic intentions, which I believe he considers more or less self-evident, he points up the fact that, in English at least, word order seems to be the first aspect of syntax the child controls. It is striking that the lists of semantic relations attributed to the Stage I child by Bloom and Schlesinger are closely similar (Table 16). They are not, however, identical. Bloom's list is longer; she differentiates certain relations that Schlesinger lumps together. This is a very important fact because it makes it clear that the relations or roles are abstract taxonomies applied to child utterances. That it is not known how finely the abstractions should be sliced and that no proof exists that the semantic levels hit on by any theorist, whether Bloom, Schlesinger, Fillmore, or whomever, are psychologically functional. Nor is this a nonsense question. It is an empirical question awaiting a technique of investigation.

McNeill (1966b and elsewhere), still taking a "rich interpretation" approach to Stage I multi-word sentences, proceeds in a fashion distinguishable from either Bloom or Schlesinger. He is (1966b) explicitly concerned with grammatical deep structure relations like subject, modifier, and object, which he defines, following Chomsky (1965), in completely formal configurational terms. In 1966 McNeill made a demonstration of considerable importance: Adam's early utterances were almost entirely limited to combinations exemplifying basic grammatical relations even though word combinations not exemplifying such relations constituted a larger potential (but unrealized) set. Where I become confused about McNeill's argument is when he speaks of the early utterances as "expressive" of the relations which by Chomsky's definition are purely formal, nonsemantic, highly abstract configurations. At times McNeill seems in his earlier writings to suppose that a formal notion like subject is always expressive of a semantic notion like agent. This is definitely not the case, as Fillmore (1968) has most conclusively demonstrated. It is possible, however, that McNeill intends rather to say that formal relations like subject and object serve to mark particular semantic roles associated with verbs as their various logical arguments. This is a highly defensible position and may be the level at which psychological reality exists. Intermediate semantic abstractions like agent, patient, beneficiary, and so on, may only be an imposed taxonomy. What the child may know is that for each particular transitive verb, like *hit, call, see,* the formal subject and object mark persons and objects in the respective quite specific semantic roles. Parenthetically, one should add that this semantically specific position need not be tied to formal relations as highly abstract as subject and object in Stage I speech. Bowerman (in press) has shown convincingly that most of the constructions motivating such abstract relations in the description of adult language are missing in Stage I speech. One stays closer to the data if one supposes that the expressive means are such less abstract characteristics as preverbal and postverbal position.

Chomsky (1969) and Katz (1967) have argued that many of the semantically based linguistic theories are merely "notational variants" of the standard theory and, from the linguistic point of view, I think they are right. From the psychological and developmental point of view, however, the new theories pose real empirical questions about the kinds of constructs that are, in fact, functional. Does a child, for example, generalize word position rules or grammatical relation rules across agents or must he learn such rules for each noun separately in the agent role as opposed to the patient or beneficiary role?

We may pass over the discussions of predication and topic-comment, since our conclusion was simply that these characterizations are either unclear or not well supported by the evidence, and move directly to Fillmore's (1968) paper on case grammar. This paper was not written as a contribution to the study of child speech but rather as a first step in a semantically based alternative to an *Aspects* (Chomsky, 1965) type standard linguistic theory. Struck by the fact that Fillmore's semantically defined "cases" (like Chafe's, 1970, semantic roles which appear in Table 1 of the Introduction) correspond very closely with the relational meanings of Schlesinger and Bloom, I have investigated the aptness of case grammar (as of 1968) for describing the utterances of Adam I. The upshot of this investigation is that case grammar captures quite a few revealing generalizations but is not strongly confirmed as psychologically functional by the few sample hypotheses I have loosely derived from it. Case grammar has, in fact, about the same set of virtues as the descriptions of Schlesinger and Bloom, though it is at points more clearly and explicitly developed. I have made no attempt to evaluate the usefulness of case grammar as it has developed since 1968.

In sum I think that both evidence and argument in the past decade have moved us and should move us from the earlier nonsemantic characterizations of Stage I speech as telegraphic or as governed by a pivot grammar. The direction of the movement is toward a richer interpretation assigning a limited set of semantic relations or roles to the Stage I child's intentions. In English, at least, the prevailing use of appropriate word order is interpretable as evidence that the child has such intentions and is describable as one of the first aspects of syntax that the child controls. While there is much in common among the characterizations of Stage I speech which have taken this direction, there are also important differences among them and several crucial questions for which no one has offered any significant evidence.

In the section that immediately follows we shall look more closely at the evidence of word order, extending our treatment beyond English to languages in which order is less important as a syntactic device. And for English itself we will go beyond the evidence of appropriate order in spontaneous utterances to consider experimental evidence of the child's ability to use contrastive order as a basis for discriminating response as well as his ability to make judgments of well formedness with respect to order.

The Role of Word Order

In the preceding review we have been interested in word order entirely as a kind of discriminating response, giving evidence, beyond the evidence of an interpreting adult, that the Stage I child when he produces multi-word utterances has in mind or "intends" certain semantic relationships. Bloom (1970), Leopold (1949), and others have noticed that shortly before the emergence of two-word utterances children often produce in succession two related single-word utterances. There is no problem ordinarily in distinguishing a two-word utterance from two single-word utterances because the child ordinarily controls prosodic features which make the difference obvious even to the phonetically untrained. Bloom finds in Gia I and Eric I (when MLU's were about 1.10) numerous examples of the successive naming of two or more aspects of a referent. For example, Gia picking up her mother's slippers said *Mommy,* and then being asked *What is that?* she said *Slipper.* And after a bit, once again *Mommy.* Eric, looking out the window at the streets below where cars were going by, said *Car.* And, after a bit, *See.* Then *Car* once again. Bloom generalizes about such cases: "The order in which the forms occurred when the child successively named aspects of the referent in this way was variable" (p. 11). Which is precisely not the case as soon as the child begins to produce two-word utterances. Then, as Bloom says, "The consistency with which the surface order corresponded to the inherent grammatical relation within the utterance was impressive" (p. 11). With two words, two orders are possible, with three words, six orders. The child's use of just that order which is appropriate in the model language for the relations existing in the situation, an order corresponding to the inclination of the interpreting adult, constitutes a kind of discriminating response on the child's part giving evidence that he and not only the observing adult has certain semantic relations in mind. That is the gist of Bloom's (1970) very important argument.

Some readers are likely to feel impatient with me for dwelling at such length on the evidence of word order. Does it not, after all, converge on another sort of perfectly familiar evidence, the evidence of the child's ongoing activity and of his immediate nonverbal environment, evidence that has always sufficed for parents and adults generally and has led them to interpret the child's multi-word utterances as meaningful propositions. Even as now, after much kicking and screaming, I propose to do? Not quite. The evidence of word order is not quite the same as the evidence of the contemporaneous situation, and there are problems with simply taking the interpretations of adults as a pipeline to the child's real intentions. Here, for instance, are three problems:

1. The method of rich interpretation is as applicable to single-word utterances as to multi-word utterances. The fact that parents regularly expand two-word utterances into complete simple sentences and that parents are confident that children "intend" the meanings of these sentences has been offered as an argument for rich interpretation. But parents do the same for one-word utterances and are as confident that children mean, what they, parents, say. Eve's mother, about to get lunch ready and hearing Eve say *Lunch,* would have been quite as likely to expand that word into "Yes, Mommy is going to fix Eve's lunch" as she would when Eve said *Eve lunch.* Possibly the method of rich interpretation should be applied to single-word utterances, and such utterances should be recognized as propositional in sense as

De Laguna (1927) and many others have said. If one thinks not, however, then it is necessary to say why not.

2. If the method of rich interpretation simply followed the lead of expanding parents it would credit children with semantic intentions involving much more than the basic semantic relations listed by Schlesinger and Bloom, and represented by Fillmore's cases. "Eve is eating lunch" attributes to Eve not only the agent-object meaning but also the meanings associated with the verbal auxiliary and verbal inflections: present tense and progressive aspect. Expansions regularly include all the obligatory little words that children omit: articles *(a, the),* prepositions *(in, on, over, under),* inflections (past, plural), auxiliaries *(will, can).* Associated with all such forms are subtle relational meanings. Perhaps it is correct to suppose that Stage I children have such meanings, but if not, then why not?

3. In principle it is not possible for the method of rich interpretation simply to follow the lead of parental expansions. It is not possible because parents, and adults generally, are not perfectly agreed about the expansions appropriate for given utterances in full context. They cannot be, because appropriate expansions are potentially of endless length. Every event occurs in a time and a place so why not say? "Yes, Eve is eating lunch in the kitchen at noon on October 8." And every such sentence can be embedded in another that begins "I think . . ." or "I know . . ." And so on, indefinitely.

The answer to all three problems is fundamentally the same: Stage I children in their two-word and three-word utterances give evidence of just the kinds of semantic intention listed by Schlesinger and Bloom, and represented by Fillmore's cases; the evidence that is most ubiquitous and useful is the preservation of normal word order. Therefore, the case for rich interpretation is better with two-word and three-word utterances than with one-word utterances because these latter do not manifest order. Therefore, also, present tense and progressive aspect and the definite-nondefinite distinction and temporal relations are not included in the child's presumed semantic intentions. There is no evidence that these meanings are understood in utterances consisting of content words, normally ordered. The method of rich interpretation applied to Stage I speech does not follow parental expansions insofar as these expansions build up single-word utterances and insofar as they add never-expressed functors but only insofar as they attribute to the child the basic semantic intentions suggested by the ordered forms he produces.

The absence of the evidence of word order for relational or propositional intentions in the period of single-word utterances that precedes Stage I is not of course the same as the absence of any evidence whatever for such intentions. The fact that contentive word order in Stage I provides no evidence that the child intends to express such meanings as plural and singular number, immediate past tense, progressive aspect and the like is also not the same as the total absence of evidence for such intentions. Quite a few investigators (especially Patricia Greenfield Marks, David McNeill, Dan Slobin, John Macnamara, and Lois Bloom) are exercising great ingenuity in looking for evidence of semantic (or cognitive) intentions in advance of anything to which the child currently gives adequate linguistic expression. Let us suppose that such efforts succeed, as I think in some measure they will, what then becomes of the role of word order in Stage I English?

If independent evidence is developed showing that single-word utterances have behind them the same range of relational meanings as do the multi-word utterances of Stage I then the important difference between two periods does not lie with semantic intentions but rather with expressive means. And the important thing to say about word order in Stage I is that the child shows control of a mechanism of expression lacking in the prior single-word period. The role of word order as a kind of discriminating response, as evidence of semantic intentions, becomes secondary.

In Stage II of this book I report that when the child is using only unmarked generic verbs his parents, responding to the reference situation, interpret these verbs in just four primary senses:

1. As expressing the occurrence, contemporaneous with the utterance, of some action or process of temporary duration; in short present progressive aspect.

2. As expressing the occurrence in the immediate temporal past of some process or action; in short past tense, limited to the immediate past.

3. As expressing the child's current intention or wish; the meanings carried by such semi-auxiliaries as *wanna, gonna, hafta.*

4. As imperatives.

I also report in Stage II that, as the child learns to inflect the verb and modify it with auxiliaries, it is just the above four senses that he first learns reliably to mark linguistically.

Suppose it proves to be the case, as Slobin (1971b) believes, that the child has the four semantic intentions when the full context, and adults responding to the context, suggest that he has them, well in advance, therefore, of the time when he reliably expresses the meanings in a linguistic way. In this case the difference between the period in which the child's verbs are unmarked and the period when they are appropriately marked will not lie with his semantic intentions but with his control of expressive means varying in grammatical complexity.

The general lesson is this. In the degree that we develop evidence of semantic intentions that is other than the evidence of normal adequate linguistic expression it will become possible to separate semantic development, which is no doubt related closely to general intellectual development, from development of the expressive mechanisms. Slobin in his important 1971b paper shows that this can be done to some extent now, especially when ingenious use is made of comparative evidence.

It is Slobin's contention that both cognitive or semantic and strictly linguistic abilities may be ranged along dimensions of complexity that will predict their respective order of acquisition. In general he thinks the evidence is that semantic development precedes the strictly linguistic development of expressive means, and that it will prove to be a general rule that old linguistic forms are used to express new ideas before adult forms for these ideas are controlled. I think Slobin's

conception, backed as it is with ingenious use of comparative evidence, is likely
to be the generally correct one, though of course it does not exclude the possibility
that some meanings are shaped or focussed by particular linguistic forms.

The discoveries about cognitive development of the Genevan psychologists, led
by Piaget, can certainly offer many valuable clues as to the sequential unfolding
of semantic intentions. As I will later argue in this chapter the intellectual achievements of the first 18 months of life, what Piaget calls the sensori-motor period,
seem to be just the necessary prerequisites for the semantic relations expressed by
word order in English in Stage I. In part, however, we cannot expect to rely on the
Genevan results because they have, naturally enough, not studied all the kinds of
meanings language expresses.

I would like to describe one example of Slobin's efforts to separate semantic
(or cognitive) development from development of the linguistic means of expression.
I select it because it shows so well that evidence making this separation can be
found, often in rather surprising places. He draws upon studies by Melanija Mikës
and Plamenka Vlahovíc of children in Yugoslavia who were bilingual in Hungarian
and in Serbo-Croatian (Mikës, 1967; Mikës and Vlahovíc, 1966). Before the age
of two years two bilingual girls were productively and appropriately using a set
of Hungarian locative case endings on nouns, forms expressing such locative notions
as in English are coded by "into," "onto," "out of," and so on. In Serbo-Croatian,
on the other hand, the same girls had barely begun to develop locative
expressions. The Serbo-Croatian forms seem, on the face of it, to be more complex
than the Hungarians, since they employ locative prepositions as well as a variety of
case endings. This discrepancy within the usage of the same children provides a means
of prying apart semantic development and strictly linguistic development. When
these children spoke Hungarian they correctly used forms expressive of several
locational notions, and one does not hesitate to credit them with the corresponding
semantic intentions. What are we to say of these children when, speaking Serbo-
Croatian, they failed to express locational intentions even though engaged in actions
calling for them such as putting a doll into a drawer. Though the child when speaking
Serbo-Croatian says the equivalent of *doll drawer* the fact that the same child,
if she were speaking Hungarian would say the case inflection equivalent of *doll into
drawer* constitutes a reason for supposing that the locative notion "into" is intended
semantically also in the Serbo-Croatian instance. Perhaps it is the unequal
complexity in the two languages of the expressive means that keeps the forms at
different levels when the semantic intentions are the same. Slobin's reasoning here
and throughout the 1971b paper seems imaginative and cogent to me.

The Period of Single-Word Utterances

Demonstrating semantic intentions that are in advance of their adequate linguistic
expression for the period of single-word utterances is an extremely difficult thing
to do. However, some very clever people are convinced that it can be done, even

that it has been done. I myself think that as of 1971 it still has not been done but there are some suggestive leads, and I do not feel at all sure what the outcome will be.

As a typical kind of case let us consider one mentioned by Bloom (in press) in a first-draft report of her study of the single-word period in the development of her daughter, Allison, a very protracted period in Allison's case, extending from 9 months to 21 months. Allison is putting juice into cups and giving the cups to Mommy. To this example let me add a second, one that I have observed at length: a child is trying to open a door; she pushes on the door and reaches up toward the key, but in vain. When mother gets up to lend a hand the child cooperatively steps aside. These two examples are complicated sensori-motor patterns involving interaction which, if they were to be described in well-formed sentences, would involve numerous semantic relationships and much besides. In the first case one might say: *Allison is putting juice into cups and giving them to her mother*. A compound sentence with subject deletion expressing at least the relations or roles agent, locative, object or patient, beneficiary or dative, as well as present tense and progressive aspect. The second situation might be rendered by an adult as: *I want to open the door with the key*. A complex sentence expressing intentionality, the roles agent, object or patient, and instrument, as well as specificity with regard to two referents.

So long as the data are limited to complex instrumental acts of the sort described, presumably no one would be inclined to attribute to the child all the semantic intentions involved in the adult descriptive sentences. To do so would be absurd. In the first place, animals at nearly all phyletic levels engage in such complex actions, and one does not want to attribute semantic intentions so generously. In the second place, adults who can make sentences of the kind illustrated are most of the time engaged in such action plans, but only from time to time, and when we have an auditor, do we have the corresponding semantic intentions. On the face of it, then, it seems necessary to distinguish at least three levels here:

1. The sensori-motor pattern itself as a form of action in the world.
2. The ability to represent or think about the pattern without necessarily intending to speak about it.
3. The semantic intention to make a sentence expressive of the pattern.

So long as the child simply pours and hands around cups of juice, and so long as the child simply tries to open a stubborn door there is presumably no temptation felt by any researcher to attribute any semantic intention whatever. Not just no temptation to attribute the full intentions behind the adult sentences but no temptation to attribute any intention at all. This is because the actions as described lack any component that might be described as purely communicative in intent. Every component in the action pattern has a noncommunicative role to play, and so there is nothing to suggest a semantic intention. But suppose the first child says some single-word, *juice* or *cup* or *give* or whatever, and suppose the second child says *Mommy* or *key* or *open*. Then at once the way is opened to interpretation. But the problem is how far to go.

To attribute the meaning of the full sentences, and both could be made still fuller, is absurd. But if not some relatively full intention then how much of an intention? The most serious possibilities are simply to name one or another aspect of a complex situation while engaged in a performance or the intention to name one or another relation in the performance even though by a single word. Parents will not hesitate to suppose that the child means some full sentence or other, but we cannot take them as our guide, since it is really quite indeterminate how complex a sentence they will offer as an interpretation of the child's single-word utterance.

In curbing the natural tendency toward over-interpretation it is useful to recall that not a few animal species have the ability to do as much as has been described. A pet cat that wants to be let out can jump up on a table, rattle a latch, and meow at anyone present. Washoe, the chimpanzee raised by the Gardners (1969, and diary reports), in her early months with them clearly *did* all the things corresponding to the roles, relations, or cases of Bloom, Schlesinger, Fillmore, and Chafe. Later on, and before she began to use signs, she would sometimes add a communicative element. In one case putting the human observer's foot on the lever of a garbage can she could not operate by herself, in another case putting the observer's hand on a weeding tool when she wanted help, and of course often pointing to indicate locations. In cases like these, too, the generous attributor of semantic intentions should consider how far he is prepared to go.

If single-word utterances at some point in development are to be established as responsive to semantic intentions more complex than they seem to express, then what is needed is evidence, evidence that goes beyond the conceivably too generous interpretations of adult onlookers. What would such evidence be like? I will describe several kinds of observations that have been made.

All observers agree that the single-word utterances used by children before Stage I vary in prosodic features in a way that makes some sound declarative, some interrogative, and some emphatic. The question is whether this prosodic variation is semantically contrastive or simply a kind of free variation or else a fixed characteristic of particular words. The evidence is at present mixed. Weir (1966), Miller and Ervin (1964), and Lahey (1971), all cited by Bloom (in press), report that, while particular prosodic patterns do not seem to be tied to particular words the variation that occurs does not seem to be used for semantic contrast prior to the onset of syntax. Menyuk and Bernholz (1969), on the other hand, report evidence of contrastive use. In the speech of a child 18–20 months old they identified five words each of which was judged, on independent contextual grounds, to be intended in three different semantic modalities: statement, question, and emphasis. When spectrograms were made of the five sets of word triplets, there proved to be distinct modality differences. If this result is confirmed, and I rather think it will be, then there will be evidence that single-word utterances are not always simply intended as names but are sometimes intended to express semantic modalities associated with distinct sentence types in the adult.

Some would probably take the results of Menyuk and Bernholz (1969) to mean that the single-word utterances are "holophrases" or one-word sentences. I myself would not, but rather agree with Lois Bloom that the term "sentence" had better be reserved for its usual sense — a structural specification of relationships among elements. In this sense single-words cannot, by definition, be sentences but they can be expressive of semantic intentions of greater complexity than the naming of referents.

Patricia Marks Greenfield, when at the Center for Cognitive Studies at Harvard, made systematic records and observations at one-month intervals of two children (Matthew and Nicky) throughout the single-word period of their development. Greenfield's own report of her evidence and conclusions was, in 1971, still in preparation. However, she tells me that she believes all the semantic relations we shall postulate as the major multi-word meanings of Stage I are already present in the single-word period and that they tend to appear in a fixed order. McNeill (1970b) working from personal communications with Greenfield about her data has published a presumptive order of semantic development in which reference and predication, for instance, appear early with attribution, location, object, and subject coming later. Smith (1970), also working from Greenfield's data, has in an under-graduate honors thesis at Harvard come to similar conclusions.

In order to establish a progression of relational meanings it is first necessary, of course, to establish the meanings themselves. In all I have heard and read about Greenfield's data the establishment of the meanings of the single-words is heavily dependent on the interpretations made by mothers or other observers. A progression based on interpretations, however, is itself subject to more than one interpretation. Obviously one possibility is that the interpreter correctly reads the child's semantic intentions, and so the progression is a progression of intentions in the child. Another is that what actually progresses in the child is the kinds of sensori-motor schemata he controls in which he embeds his single words never intending more than the naming of some aspect of the total situation. But the parent or observer being sensitive to the full nonlinguistic setting progresses in the interpretations he assigns these single words.

What kind of evidence would go beyond interpretations? I know of one good example, noted by Greenfield, and also by Bloom (in press). Suppose the child has names for a range of referent objects like *chair, hat, comb, toothbrush,* and that he begins by using these words for all instances of the classes in question. Suppose, at a later time, he stops calling a certain hat (or whatever) by its usual name and says instead when it is present *Daddy,* and suppose that the hat is, in fact, *Daddy's.* And that the child does the same for a variety of objects at about the same time calling them sometimes by class name but often by the names of their possessors. This kind of change in naming practice does seem to me to be a fairly clear sort of evidence for the emergence of the cognitive notions we call possession.

Bloom (in press) in her careful observations of Allison notes that at first Allison used names like *Mama* and *Dada* not only when the corresponding persons were present but also in pointing to objects belonging to or associated with the persons in question. In this early period, however, she did not yet know the class names of the objects themselves, and so no shift in naming had occurred. It was, rather, as if the child had a rather undifferentiated notion of object and associated persons. Later, at 16 months, Allison did know the class names. She then sometimes named the object and sometimes the possessor. At this point she may have had some conception of possession. However, even this relatively good evidence is not, as Bloom points out, a guarantee that the child intended when he spoke to express the relational concept. Simply having a concept in some form is obviously not the same thing as intending to express it on a given occasion.

Bloom (in press) offers several kinds of interesting evidence that in the single-word period the child does develop the cognitive prerequisites for the semantics of Stage I sentences. She does not see that this evidence offers any compelling reason for supposing that single-word utterances are sentences nor even that the child's developing knowledge is as yet linguistic in character. I agree with her. However, we have Greenfield's full report still to come, and the period of single-word utterances is clearly going to be the focus of much research activity in the immediate future, so it would be rash to guess what conclusion the data may eventually justify.

The preceding discussion is primarily intended to point up what might be called the dual role of word order in Stage I speech. On the one hand, it can be used as a variety of discriminating response giving evidence that the child intends to express relations in his first multi-word utterances and is not simply naming aspects of a situation in temporal succession. On the other hand, in the degree that evidence exists for relational intentions prior to Stage I, then word order in Stage I becomes an expressive device, an aspect of syntax making relational intentions clearer than they can be when speech is limited to single words. It is really in this latter role that word order (and, more generally, morpheme order) interests Slobin (1971b). He proposes that it is a universal of child speech to preserve for words and morphemes the standard order of the input language. From these putative universals, which Slobin (1971b) frankly grants research may eventually disconfirm, he infers that a basic expectation the child brings to the task of grammatical development is: "Operating Principle C: Pay attention to the order of words and morphemes" (p. 348). In the discussion that follows we shall consider word order from both points of view, as evidence of relational intentions and as an expressive device added on in Stage I which increases the precision of statement of semantic intentions present prior to Stage I.

There are now four major kinds of evidence with regard to word order: 1. its appropriateness in the child's spontaneous speech for a variety of languages including some where order is a major syntactic device like English and some for inflected languages where order is relatively free; 2. experimental evidence of the English-speaking child's ability to make discriminating comprehension responses to contrasts

of word order; 3. experimental evidence of the English-speaking child's ability to
judge whether sentences are well formed or not with respect to word order and
his inclination to make corrections when they are not; 4. preliminary evidence on the
impairment of word sequencing skills in receptive aphasics. Evidence of all kinds
is now accumulating at a great rate, and much that I will report is taken from reports
not yet published.

Word Order in Spontaneous Speech

In all the samples of Stage I English listed in Table 9 the violations of normal
order are triflingly few: *Nose blow* (Hildegard), *Slide go* (Gia I), *Apple more*
(Christy), *Paper write* (Adam), *Horse . . . see it* (Kendall I), *See Kendall* (when
Kendall sees, in Kendall II), and perhaps 100 or so others. Of utterances in normal
order there are many thousands. However, there is at least one exception to the
general rule for English-speaking children. Braine (1971) says that his subject,
Gregory, at the age of 24–25 months passed through a phase in which the order of
major constituents seemed to be free. There was no apparent semantic contrast
between pairs like: *Gregory fix it* and *Fix it Gregory; Fall down rabbit* and *Rabbit
fall down.*

Concerning French, in which order is a major syntactic device, Professor Hermina
Sinclair de-Zwart of the University of Geneva said in a lecture in Buffalo, in the
summer of 1971 that variations on normal order are not uncommon in the speech
of the Swiss children she has studied.

In German, which is more elaborately inflected than English, there is in adult
simple sentences a certain amount of variety of word order. Thus *Ulrike trinkt Kaffee*
would be the normal agent-action-object order but *Kaffee, trinkt Ulrike* is a not
uncommon comment-topic variant, and of course the interrogative, since it simply
interposes subject and verb, offers a third model: *Trinkt Ulrike Kaffee?* However,
Park (1970a) in his report on Ulrike, Angela, and Georg makes it very clear that he
found more variety of order in the children's speech than could be explained either
by the grammar of German simple sentences or by dominant orders in adult speech.
With regard to subject, verb, and object, for example, it appears from his tabulated
data that across all three children five of the six possible orders were at least
occasionally used, and of these only three could be considered grammatical. Furthermore, the interrogative order was sometimes used by the children with declarative
intonation, and so their use was not really grammatical. In fact, Park finds that
ungrammatical orders were actually *more* common than grammatical ones, though the
older children, Angela and George, who were probably beyond Stage I, showed
more variety than the youngest, Ulrike, who was clearly in Stage I.

Park's (1970b) report on his daughter Susin's acquisition of Korean offers the
sharpest possible contrast. In this language, order is about as free as it ever is. The
parents modeled all the following, for instance: *S-O-V (Susin cap look-at); O-S-V*

(Cap Susin look-at); O-V-S (Cap look-at Susin); S-V-O (Susin look-at cap).
And what did Susin do? Freely vary the possibilities or perhaps probability-match against parental practice? No, she used one order only: *S-V-O (Susin look-at cap).*

Slobin, reporting on Gvozdev's Zhenya, contributes another case in which the child showed less variety than did his models. In Russian, an inflected language, order is relatively free but the dominant adult practice is to use: *S-V-O.* Zhenya did not at first freely vary order but oddly enough he also did not limit himself to the most common order but rather used *S-O-V.* Later on, he switched to *S-V-O.* In 1966 Slobin was inclined to think this result meant that children always consistently marked underlying grammatical relations in terms of word order but that frequency in the model was not the major determinant of their practice.

Concerning Luo children, Blount tells us, "Several conclusions can be drawn from what information is available, the most important being that from the outset all of the utterances except one (number 2) followed the model of adult speech in terms of word order" (p. 94). Concerning Hebrew, Bar-Adon tells us, "First the word order is most often (although not always and not by all children) retained as in the model or target language" (p. 444). Concerning Viveka's Swedish, Rydin tells us, "Word order is inflexible and conforms with the most dominant adult word order" (p. 54). Concerning the Samoan of Sipili and Tofi, Kernan gives us only the odd note indicating that order matched the adult model.

In Finnish, adult order is grammatically free, but, as in the case of Russian, adults mainly use *S-V-O.* Bowerman studied not one but two children, Rina and Seppo, and the two behaved differently with respect to word order. Rina reflected the dominant adult *S-V-O* order in both two-word and three-word utterances, but Seppo used both *O-V* and *S-O-V* more often than the dominant orders.

I have deliberately let these outcomes "tumble out" in the order in which they came to hand because I think that mode of presentation best suggests the extravagant variation in the data. This is a set of outcomes that offers something to disconfirm almost any hypothesis. It is evidently not the case, for instance, that human children everywhere find some single order sensible for cognitive reasons having to do with the order in which attention might be captured by an agent, an action, and an object. It is evidently not the case that human children will limit themselves to the orders that are dominant in the speech they hear from parents. It is evidently not the case that children will always probability-match the orders they hear. It is evidently not the case that when order is free in the model language all children will select some single order with which to represent a particular semantic relation.

With what conceivable hypothesis could the results described be consistent? It remains possible that children start with Slobin's Operating Principle C and do "pay attention to the order of words and morphemes," perhaps even checking the possibility that there are correspondences between certain orders and the set of semantic relations they know. What happens next may depend, in the first place, on the degree of consistency in the model language and, in the second place, on all the variables that affect learning, including, besides frequency, at least attention, the spacing and array of instances, reinforcement, and so on. For model languages in which word order is highly consistent with respect to particular semantic relations (like English) it appears as if most, though not quite all, always will use the order that is appropriate to the relation. And in this case, at least, word order can also function in its role as evidence of semantic intentions. When there is more freedom or inconsistency in the model at least the following outcomes are possible: 1. selection of one order from among those heard and that one not necessarily the most frequent (Zhenya, Seppo, Susin); 2. variation in word order corresponding with the range of variation heard or even going beyond it (Ulrike, Angela, Georg). Presumably other outcomes are also possible, and presumably what happens for any one child depends upon learning variables operating at particular times and not assessed by any investigator as such thus far.

Discriminating Response to Contrastive Word Orders

This kind of experiment has thus far only been done with children learning English. The procedure requires pairs of sentences using just the same words but with differences of order that signal differences of semantic relation. Figure 8 pictures two referent situations which can be named by a minimal pair of sentences of the kind described. On the left *The dog is biting the cat* and on the right *The cat is biting the dog*. In both pictures just the same creatures and action are involved. The difference is that the arguments of the verb, the agent and patient (or object) roles, are assigned to different creatures and coordinated with different words in the two cases. It is the relations in the total situation that change, and the change is encoded in the English sentences by a change of word order. The child's ability to respond comprehendingly to the order contrast can be tested, as it was in the first study of this sort (Fraser, Bellugi, and Brown, 1963) by asking the child to point appropriately to the picture named by each sentence. In later studies action equivalents of this kind of problem have been created in which the child is given a car and a truck, for example, and told *Make the car hit the truck* or *Make the truck hit the car*. In either the pointing or the acting out procedure when the interest is in the child's ability to respond to word order alone it is necessary to make the two alternative situations about equally probable, which means the sentences must be credibly reversible. The empirical work done thus far has all focused on agent-patient (or object) relations though it is potentially extendable in English, at least, to prepositional phrases like *White on red* and *Red on white* and perhaps beyond.

In the Fraser, Bellugi, and Brown experiment (1963) the interest was not only in word order but on comprehension of a variety of grammatical contrasts. There were just four pairs of pictures which, like Figure 8, tested comprehension of the agent-patient contrast. Twelve children between the ages of 37 and 43 months were tested. They answered correctly 85 percent of the time.

Of course, the child of 37 months is well beyond Stage I, often by a year or more. However, Lovell and Dixon (1965) in Britain administered the same comprehension test to 20 two-year-olds (mean age: 2;6, two years, six months) as well as to children three, four, five, and six years old. The two-year-olds were correct 60 percent of the time. This figure is difficult to interpret because one cannot define an exact baseline of chance success. The baseline is not 50 percent as it would be for adults because children do not understand, as adults do, that on such a task the subject is to point just once at each picture. Children often pointed twice at the same picture, and on most problems in the test scored well below 50 percent. I suspect that most of the successes represented genuine comprehension; that there were few chance successes. And so that the two-year-olds showed significant ability to decode the contrast. The older age groups almost always solved the agent-object problems. Most of the other problems in the test involved functor contrasts: inflections for number, tense, and aspect; articles and auxiliary verbs. On all these, two-year-olds had scores below 50 percent, usually much below.

Bever, Mehler, and Valian (in press) have done a very large-scale study of sentence comprehension in children from two to eight years of age (263 of them). These investigators used both active and passive sentences and, for both types, reversible and irreversible sentences as well as sentences semantically "probable" in one form and improbable in the other. From all their data I wish to pick out only the results for the youngest children (2;0–3;0) with active sentences that are reversible like: *The horse kissed the cow* and *The cow kissed the horse*. The children were asked to act out the sentences in this experiment rather than point to pictures. When the child would not act out the sentences the experimenter did so himself and asked the child to indicate which alternative went with a given sentence. The authors report 95 percent correct responses for their youngest group on reversible active sentences. On the face of it this seems a very high level of success by comparison with results in other studies of comprehension or, indeed, by comparison with almost any linguistic result one attempts to obtain from two-year-olds.

The surprise at the result is mitigated when one considers what the authors chose to treat as data. They included only clearly correct or incorrect responses, whether these were cases in which the child acted out the sentences or cases in which he

The dog is biting the cat.   The cat is biting the dog.

Figure 8.   Pictures illustrating agent-object relations

chose between the experimenter's actions. They did not count as data cases of no response or of responses not clearly scorable for one reason or another. Their two-year-olds apparently reacted in ways not counted as data something like 15 percent of the time, which indicates that the percentage of correct responses on total trials for active reversible sentences was about 80 percent. Allowing for the fact that the paired-pictures form of the test is undoubtedly more difficult than the action form, the Bever et al. results seem to be roughly consistent with those of prior investigators.

A two-year-old group probably includes some subjects in Stage I and some beyond. Since none of the experimental studies so far described reported MLU's for their subjects, we are left somewhat uncertain about the ability of Stage I children to respond appropriately to contrasts of word order. Jill and Peter de Villiers (1971), graduate students in psychology at Harvard, carried out a small-scale study of comprehension, in the acting-out format, with children for whom they calculated MLU's in accordance with the rules presented in the Introduction to this book. Their study included several groups and investigated more problems than the response to word order in active reversible sentences. I will here describe only the most directly relevant outcome. For an early Stage I group, four subjects having MLU's of 1.21 or less, 37.5 percent of all trials were correct whereas 62.5 percent were incorrect or fell into one of the nondata categories of the Bever et al. study. When the results of these same children are limited to the data categories of clearly correct or clearly incorrect then 60 percent are correct and 40 percent incorrect. For a late Stage I group, having MLU's in the range 1.93–2.08, the results for all trials are 62.1 percent correct and 27.9 percent either incorrect or in a "nondata" class. Scoring the same group, in the manner of Bever et al., the outcome is 81 percent correct and 19 percent incorrect. This outcome is fully consistent with the large scale Bever et al. study, which, with a similar procedure and age group, found about 80 percent of clearly scorable responses correct.

From these several studies of the young child's ability to make appropriate comprehension responses to pairs of sentences matched in all but word order, I conclude that the probability is that the Stage I child learning English can do this and therefore that word order in its role as evidence of relational intentions and as the first aspect of the syntax of the expressive medium to be learned is confirmed. This becomes especially apparent if the evidence is considered in conjunction with the prevailingly appropriate order of the child's spontaneous utterances. There are numerous qualifications to be entered and hypotheses to be considered. Experimental work (though not the evidence of spontaneous speech) has been exclusively limited to agent-patient relations. There is in de Villiers' data a suspicion of evidence that appropriate discriminating responses to order increase in the course of Stage I, but the numbers of subjects are too small to draw conclusions. The major change that occurs in Stage I is in the percentage of trials that are either clearly correct or incorrect, and that change probably represents the child's increasing malleability as a subject.

Word order in its second role as an expressive syntactic device acquired in Stage I is more puzzling. There is much in the world-wide data of spontaneous speech to suggest that while the child may have relational intentions to communicate he shows little or no concern with the adequacy of their communication, often freely varying the order. It is as if the child expected to be understood — as indeed he will be by adults in the same situation and having memories in common with him. In all the discriminating response studies we have reviewed, the Stage I child learning English responds at an approximately chance level to passive voice reversible sentences. If he set great store by word order as a mechanism of communication one would expect him to be usually wrong, since the passive voice sentence reverses the order of the active voice sentence. But that he does not do. Which once again suggests a lack of concern with the adequacy of his communications. Further evidence to this effect now follows.

Word Order Judgments and Corrections

The linguistic scientist typically does not rely on some corpus of mere speech performance in constructing his grammatical descriptions. If he is himself a native speaker of the language he is likely to rely upon his own judgments of the grammaticality or not of various strings he thinks up in order to test his rules; if he is not himself a native speaker he will ask for judgments from people who are. It has been said of the study of child speech that it cannot really get very far in the study of grammar because such judgments have proved extremely difficult to elicit from children under four years or so. It was with great interest, therefore, that I read a recent paper by Gleitman and Shipley (in press) because they seemed to have found a way to elicit such judgments from children just over two years old.

The children, Sarah, Amy, and Allison are three of five that have been studied longitudinally by these investigators. The other two children would not cooperate. Gleitman and Shipley worked with sentences of four types: normal word order and complete *(Bring me the ball)*; normal word order and telegraphic *(Bring ball)*; reversed word order but complete *(Ball me the bring)*; reversed word order and telegraphic *(Ball bring)*. All sentences were simple imperatives. The procedure was as follows. At first the experimenter played the role of teacher and the children's mother the role of judge. The teacher would say a sentence of one of the types described. The mother was to judge it as "good" or "silly," and when the sentence was good she simply repeated it. When it was silly she made the requisite grammatical changes. Only sentences like *Bring me the ball,* which were both full and well ordered were called "good," and repeated as such. All others were judged "silly," and corrected with respect to word order, the provision of obligatory functors, or both. All this was preliminary to testing of the child. The idea was that she should learn the mother's role and, given her turn in that role, extend it appropriately to new instances. She was also given the chance to be teacher. More generally, when verbal instructions as such seem too complex for a child one can exemplify conformity to them as a role and then simply test the child's ability to extract the essentials of the role and extend it to new cases. It is a method for asking questions of children that cannot be directly put, and I have successfully used it, in slightly different form, for inquiring into the child's ability to construct English tag questions.

The major results for the three children's judgments in the test period, subsequent to the period of role exemplification, appear in Table 20. I must say that on first reading these results I was very excited about them, both because of the methodological advance involved and because they seemed roughly to confirm what I believe about Stage I. Comparing columns one with two and three with four, one sees that correct word orders were judged "good" rather than "silly" about two-thirds to twice as often as incorrect word orders. While we have no MLU's for Sarah, Amy, and Allison, the fact that they were just past 2;0 suggests that they were somewhere in Stage I. This outcome is especially interesting when compared with the absence and provision of functors (column one compared with three and two with four). Sarah and Amy show no signs of being sensitive to this feature, to which the spontaneous utterances of Stage I children suggest they should not be sensitive. Allison does show some sensitivity to functors but Gleitman and Shipley say that Allison was, in very many ways, more advanced than the other two little girls, and so it is not unreasonable to suppose that she was beyond Stage I.

Table 20.   Percentages of "good" judgments of three children on four kinds of sentence

Child	Well-formed		Telegraphic	
	Correct Word Order	Incorrect Word Order	Correct Word Order	Incorrect Word Order
Sarah	92	75	100	58
Amy	80	50	82	58
Allison	80	58	58	58

Source: Based on Gleitman and Shipley, in press.

Peter de Villiers, being less attached to my views than I am, pointed out to me that I was overlooking certain not so agreeable aspects of the data. In the first place, while incorrect word orders were called "good" less often than correct orders were, they were still called "good" somewhat more than 50 percent of the time, and that seems odd if word order is the major expressive device of Stage I English. De Villiers also pointed out something "odd" about the "corrections" the children made. To begin with, the children did not reliably play this part of the role, mostly limiting themselves to "good" or "silly" but occasionally they did make corrections. In a few cases incorrect word orders were set right syntactically; *Song me a sing* became *Sing me a song* and *Ball me the throw, Throw the ball.* But in a larger number of cases the corrections were not of word order at all but were semantic corrections or continuations; *Iron up the pick* to *Iron the clothes.* And in some cases already correct word orders were "corrected" in the same kinds of ways: *Bring book* to *Close book*. Finally the role of teacher or sentence creator was played fairly often only by Allison. She made up 20 sentences of which 18 were well-formed imperatives. The fact that she limited herself to imperatives indicates that the role was available to her in these terms. But of order reversals, which the model teachers frequently produced, she produced only one. Clearly then these results are not simply confirmatory of word order as the salient aspect of syntax controlled in Stage I.

Stimulated by these observations concerning the Gleitman and Shipley study, the de Villiers (1972) undertook a study of their own using a variant of the original method. They worked with eight children having MLU values in the range of 2.87–4.67; all were, therefore, well beyond Stage I. The sentences were all simple imperatives. Some had word order and semantics correct *(Drive your car)*; some had only word order reversed *(Cup the fill)*; some had word order correct but were semantically anomalous *(Drink the chair)*. The children were asked to judge each sentence "right" or "wrong" and, if "wrong" correct it. The results were that judgments of word-order incorrect sentences as "wrong" were not made over 50 percent of the time until MLU reached 4.16 (which falls after Stage V by my system). Above this value all subjects did judge word-order incorrect sentences as "wrong" better than 50 percent of the time though never always. With respect to active correction in terms of word order, only the most advanced subject (MLU = 4.67) reversed the word order over 50 percent of the time. Semantic "corrections" were, for all subjects, at a higher level than word-order corrections. They were often not corrections, strictly speaking, as when a child called *Man a draw* "wrong" and corrected it to *Keep the man out*.

This small study raises many questions which deserve to be studied on a larger scale. One extreme possibility is simply that children do not have a given syntactic feature on the level of judgment and correction until long after they have it on the levels of spontaneous speech and discriminating response. In fact, it has long proved difficult to get consistent judgments of grammaticality from adult speakers; see Gleitman and Gleitman (1970) for a review of the literature and some imaginative new data. I am indebted to Bever (1970) for making the point that judgments of grammaticality are not a pipeline to knowledge or competence but rather one sort of performance and a sort we know very little about. Performances on the level of spontaneous speech, comprehension of contrasting sentences, and judgment of grammaticality may develop at different points in the child, and not converge upon one another, even approximately until near the end of the preschool years. Genevan cognitive psychology has made us very familiar with the fact that knowledge present at one level (say the sensori-motor) may not become available at another level (say the representational) until a much later age. I realize that linguists at the Massachusetts Institute of Technology, subscribing to the standard theory of Chomsky or to its "extended" version (Chomsky, 1969), might wish to say that there is no grammar as such in the absence of a sense of well-formedness, but if "grammar" is to be restricted in this sense one can still speak of internalized implicit rules when conformity in performance is the only evidence. Obviously distinctions of level in rule-knowledge must be made, since there is one level — explicit formulation of rules — which only a small group of professionals ever attains, the linguists themselves and teachers of grammar.

Another possibility is that what the de Villiers (1972) have shown is that for children as for adults who are not linguists semantics is simply more salient in language than is syntax. The de Villiers sentences, all simple imperatives, were irreversible. *Fill the cup* is possible but *Cup the fill* is not. In these circumstances the meaning that *must* be intended is certain whatever the order. In these circumstances "right" and "wrong" may just be governed primarily by the possibility of the action. It would be a valuable variant to use both pictures or actions and reversible agent-action-patient constructions like *Truck hit car* and *Car hit truck*. The question then would be whether the structure of a sentence uttered for a given picture or action was "right" or "wrong" for just that referent situation. In these circumstances the problem parallels the paradigm for comprehension of word-order contrasts. However, the responses "right" or "wrong" and, in the latter case, active correction are different. They might or might not mature at about the same time as comprehension.

We shall have to wait for more research to settle these difficult questions, but one thing seems clear from the results of the de Villiers and of Gleitman and Shipley. The child does not show a steady concern with communicating. It is as if he rather took it for granted that he would be understood if he spoke at all.

Word Sequencing in Receptive Aphasics

If, as Slobin (1971b) has suggested, paying attention to the order of words and morphemes is a primary "operating principle" in the child's acquisition of language then it seems reasonable to expect an impairment of this principle specific to verbal materials in persons suffering from linguistic impairment produced by brain injury.

Martin Albert (in press) of the Aphasia Research Center of Boston Veterans Administration Hospital has developed, in collaboration with Frank Benson, an interesting verbal sequencing test and collected some highly suggestive data using it. The Verbal Sequencing Test works with 20 common objects, the names of which all subjects know. The tester does not point at the objects but rather names certain ones of them (starting with two and working up). The subject is not required to speak at all but simply to point at the objects the tester has named in just the sequence of the original naming. Thus there is no problem for the subject of speech production or of learning the names of certain objects. Rather, what is required is that he retain the sequence of the names and represent it by an order of pointing.

The Verbal Sequencing Test is contrasted with a Visual Sequencing Test. In this latter test the tester speaks no names but simply points to a certain number of objects in a certain order. The subject is also to point and to do so in the original sequencing order. Additional tests were used to control for one and another factor.

Subjects were of three kinds: two sorts of surgically verified brain-damaged patients and a group suffering from no brain damage but rather from spinal cord or peripheral-nerve diseases. All the brain-damaged subjects were right-handed, which would mean that linguistic functions were, but for rare exceptions, primarily located in their left cerebral hemispheres. In these circumstances, if there is a sequencing problem peculiar to verbal material, then the three groups should differ significantly on the Verbal Sequencing Test but not on the Visual Sequencing Test. And so they did. The left-brain-damaged subjects performed most poorly on the Verbal Sequencing Test. The right-brain-damaged subjects did significantly better but were still worse than the patients with diseases of the spinal cord or peripheral nerves. On the Visual Sequencing Test there were no significant differences at all among the groups. A further analysis was carried out, going beyond the locus of brain damage to the actual presence or absence of diagnosed aphasia. None of the right-brain-damaged subjects was aphasic; the majority of the left-brain-damaged subjects (29) were aphasic but 14 were not. The 29 actually aphasic subjects had much the worst average score on the Verbal Sequencing Test whereas the 14 left-brain-damaged, but not actually aphasic subjects, scored at almost the same level as the right-brain-damaged subjects, none of whom were aphasic.

While any sort of brain damage produces some degree of deficit in verbal sequencing ability the ability is most strongly associated with left-brain damage (in right-handed persons) and in particular with those who are aphasic. It seems possible to Albert, therefore, that there is a group of neurons in the left cerebral hemisphere organized to carry out the specific function of maintaining and utilizing the sequential aspects of verbal acoustic inputs. It is of particular interest to us that Goodglass, Gleason, and Hyde (1970) have used a Sequencing Test similar to Albert's both with aphasic patients of various types and with six-year-old children. They found that the best of the aphasic groups performed below the level of the six-year-olds. This is what we should expect if attention to the sequential order of words and morphemes is one of the earliest principles to operate in language acquisition.

Conclusions

It is abundantly clear that in view of the complexity of the results already obtained and the rate at which new results are appearing any conclusions about word order in Stage I must be very tentative. I think the following ideas are consistent with all that has been learned, though not strongly required by them.

In the first place, word order may be considered from two points of view: as a kind of discriminating response constituting evidence that the semantic intentions behind the child's early multi-word utterances consist of relations like recurrence, nonexistence, location, agent-action, action-patient, and so on. In the second place word order can be considered as an expressive device, an aspect of linguistic syntax, which helps to communicate semantic relations. Word order cannot be considered in the second fashion, as an expressive device, unless there is evidence other than the evidence of word order that the child intends to express semantic relations. This is a completely general point in that it states the circumstances in which we may hope to separate semantic development from grammatical development.

The work so far reported on the period in which the child produces only single-word utterances seems to me at this point to fall short of having demonstrated that the child intends his single-word utterances to express semantic relations. What seems very clear is that the relations exist in terms of practical action, of what Piaget calls sensori-motor intelligence. There is some evidence that the relations also exist on a representational, general cognitive level, and it is quite possible, especially just prior to Stage I that the child has relational meanings in mind when he speaks single-word utterances. It is very difficult to conceive of evidence that goes beyond the possibly too generous interpretations of observing adults, and I think the question is still open.

It seems reasonable to me to attribute to Stage I children Slobin's (1971b) operating principle: "Pay attention to the order of words and morphemes." The Albert data on aphasics at least weakly support the existence of such a principle. The principle alone, however, is not enough to cause Stage I children all over the world always to use the orders appropriate to the relations they intend, or to use contrastive order as a sure guide to comprehension, and certainly not to judge ungrammatical orders ill formed and in need of correction in just this respect. There are far too many factors operating besides Slobin's principle to produce so uniform a set of outcomes.

First there is the role of order in the model language. Is it relatively free or is it semantically constrained? And this is a matter not only of grammar, of what the language permits, but of probabilities, of what parents usually do. In the case of English, where order is not free but semantically constrained, it looks as if most children "paying attention to order" learn to use it in consistently appropriate fashion in their spontaneous speech and as a guide to comprehension at least in the agent-patient (or object) case. It is quite possible that the very earliest spontaneous multi-word utterances are properly ordered simply because the human mind tends to preserve order while looking for semantic correlates. The de Villiers' (1971) data suggest that there may be some increase in Stage I in the consistency with which agent-patient roles are based on order, the consistency is well short of perfection even at the end of Stage I. The results of Gleitman and Shipley (in press) and of the de Villiers (1972) suggest that basing sentence judgments and sentence corrections on order may be a higher level performance than using order in production and comprehension, probably becoming reliable long after Stage I.

Where the model language uses order in a relatively free way, the range of outcomes in the child's spontaneous speech is wide. We have no information for such languages on the use of order in comprehension and grammatical judgment but, by definition, it would not be important in these cases just because order is relatively free and case inflections and other devices serve to mark semantic relations. If we suppose that the human child has everywhere an initial tendency to pay attention to order he might be expected to come to a variety of conclusions about order when exposed to languages like Finnish, Korean, German, and so on. The particular implicit conclusion to which the individual child comes should depend on the values of variables affecting learning in his detailed life history. Evidently it is possible for him to conclude that particular orders are required, even when these are not the most frequent orders in parental speech. But, equally evidently, he can conclude that order is completely free, even freer than either the language's grammar or the practice of the child's parents indicates. But of course the child generalizes, and he may generalize too widely here as he often does in working out the references made by particular words.

What is clearly not the case is that the human child finds it necessary to settle on particular orders to be used consistently to express particular semantic relations. Nor, in fact, does the evidence suggest that Stage I children find it necessary to hit upon any sort of consistent expressive device, for example; inflections, to mark basic relations. To be sure, Blount (1969) suggests that subject and object inflections on the verb are among the first used in Luo, but across the full set of languages that have been studied such expressive devices cannot be uniformly found in Stage I.

For English there is a fair amount of evidence that word order can function in its role as discriminating response giving evidence of relational intentions. The evidence comes from spontaneous speech and from experiments on comprehension based on agent-patient order. My guess is that Stage I children everywhere have the same set of relational intentions, partly because of impressive uniformities to be described in the meanings assigned their utterances by observing adults and partly because of uniformities of developmental progression. In the Introduction, discussing the chimpanzee Washoe's multi-sign constructions, I have already indicated that when the evidence of order is absent or weak there are other considerations which may incline one toward the attribution of relational intentions. I do think, with Slobin (1971b), that semantic and grammatical development are two practically independent processes with different complexity orderings. My guess is that whether children grammatically mark their semantic intentions in Stage I depends on the complexity of the marking mechanism. Evidently word order is among the simpler mechanisms, perhaps the subject and object inflections in Luo are also fairly simple. Other sorts of device may be relatively complex.

Running through all the data is one theme of considerable interest: the child's lack of concern with making himself clear or perhaps we should think of it as his assumption that if he speaks at all he will be understood. We shall have still more evidence to this effect when we consider the Stage I child's apparently capricious deletion of constituents from sentences when, from a grammatical point of view, the presence of the constituents is obligatory. The child also varies order more than he ought to if he were worried about being misunderstood. A related theme of equal interest is the fact that the child's confidence is justified. At home, in an action situation, with behavioral evidence of intention generally attendant upon the linguistic, with parental interlocutors who know what his experience has been, the child's utterances are almost redundant. If something is missing it can be supplied, if order is wrong it can be set right. Suppose the child acquires most of his basic semantic ideas early and well in advance of the means of normative expression (see Slobin, 1971b and also Macnamara, 1972), language development from the first word to the compound sentence would then be largely a matter of learning how to put more of what is intended into adequate expressive form. With what useful result? Ultimately with the result of making the utterance more freely "exportable," making it intelligible in a wider variety of situations and to a wider community. In the end it can be written in isolation on a piece of paper and understood by all who speak the language. I do not, in suggesting this broad theme of linguistic development, mean to say either that the child has all his meanings from the start or even very early on, nor do I mean to imply that there are no meanings he might never acquire if it were not that his language expressed them.

If saying more of what has long been intended is a general trend in language development it is important to realize that there is also a cut-off problem. One can always say too much, and one sometimes does. It was Macnamara who first made this point clear to me in a talk he gave at Harvard in 1970–71. His example was the simple imperative "Put on your shoes." It is not necessary and would seem very odd to go on in some such vein as this: "On your feet that is, the left shoe on the left foot and the right on the right, by inserting the respective foot in the respective shoe, lacing them up," and so on. A sentence well adapted to its function is, like a piece in a jigsaw puzzle, just the right size and shape to fit the opening left for it by local conditions and community understandings. The child has to learn to adapt the size and complexity of his sentences to changing situations and interlocutors. In the beginning he is very narrowly adapted, linguistically and in all other ways, to a very particular kind of setting.

The Major Meanings at Stage I

The major meanings at Stage I are those that require at least two morphemes to express them; they are not, in short, word meanings but compositional meanings carried by the Stage I child's multi-word utterances. The meanings will not be new to the reader. They have all already been introduced — in the Introduction as Chafe's roles or relations and, in this chapter, in connection with the discussions of the work of Schlesinger and Bloom and of Fillmore's cases. The reader will already have the impression that these various discussions, both the strictly linguistic ones of

Chafe and Fillmore and those based on child speech data like Bloom's and Schlesinger's, seem to converge on substantially the same set of compositional meanings and that this set is not a large one. What I have not yet done is report the prevalence of these meanings across all the studies listed in Tables 9 and 10. I will begin with quantitative reports on certain highly prevalent operations of reference and offer these as an explanation of the "pivot look" in Stage I speech, which is ubiquitous, though the pivot grammar is, I think, not justified as an inference from this "look." Then we have quantitative data from the studies that supply it or from which it can be obtained on eight minimal two-term relations and all their combinations. Because there are studies running the MLU range from 1.10 to 2.06 we have an opportunity to describe the increases of complexity that occur in the course of Stage I. Following the quantitative data comes a section that attempts explicit definition of the most prevalent relations plus all that can be gleaned by way of fragmentary data from the remaining studies. Finally there is a short section relating the major meanings of Stage I to what Piaget calls "sensori-motor intelligence."

Causes of the "Pivot Look"

   In the discussion of pivot grammar I made the comment that the "pivot look," which Stage I speech usually has, is probably due to the fact that there are always a few words which have, for semantic reasons, an extremely wide compositional potential. The pivot look is not the same as the pivot grammar. The look derives primarily from an impression that there is a sharp discontinuity of combinatorial frequency in the child's words; some, the pivots occurring in numerous different combinations and others, the open words occurring in very few combinations. This is the one observation relevant to the pivot grammar that does meet the test of all the data. If, in addition, the pivot words in two-word combinations are at least usually found in just one position, first or second, then the pivot look is especially strong. Of course the pivot grammar predicts other distributional facts which are quite reliably not present: failure of pivots to occur in isolation or in combination with one another, nondifferentiation of the open class, and so forth. I want to offer here some data indicating that the pivot look defined simply in terms of combinational differentials and *relatively* fixed positions is mainly due to the very wide utility of certain words and the accessibility to the child of their meanings.
   For 22 of the 24 studies listed in Table 9 (all but Eric I and Tofi), I have been able to identify the four most frequent presumptive pivots. The four are defined simply as the four words occurring in the largest numbers of different two-word combinations ("types" not "tokens"). All other pivot criteria have been neglected. It is not even the case that these presumptive pivots occur *only* in one position; they practically never do. In some studies (those of Bowerman, Brown, Kernan, Rydin, and Tolbert) the determination of the four leading presumptive pivots is quite

straightforward because the authors give frequencies and position preferences for four or more possible pivots. For the studies of Bloom, Braine, and Miller and Ervin the required frequencies are not directly given, and I have had to operate by inference to identify four leading presumptive pivots and their meanings. The numerous notes to Table 21 make explicit some of my misgivings about this procedure though not all of them. So Table 21 should be taken as a very rough set of estimated data but good enough, perhaps, since the point it makes is both minor and obvious. I should only add that the number four was not picked to make the data work out as anticipated but was selected in advance of detailed tabulation as the largest number of presumptive pivots that could be identified in almost all the studies of Table 9.

Even a casual impression of Stage I speech suggests that a great many utterances are concerned with the expression of three operations of reference, a kind of closed semantic set. I will call these operations "nomination," "recurrence," and "nonexistence" and suppose, for the moment, that their senses are obvious enough to need no definition. These operations of reference should be accessible to the child of 18 months or so, since they are among the attainments of what Piaget calls sensori-motor intelligence, the intelligence that develops in the first 18 months. In addition, these operations tend to be linked with just a very few words: in the case of nomination, *this, that, see, there, here,* and their equivalents in Finnish, Swedish, and Spanish; in the case of recurrence, *more, another,* and their equivalents; in the case of nonexistence, *all gone, no more, no,* and their equivalents. The operations have a third interesting property. They have the widest possible range of application. Any thing, person, quality, or process can be named, can recur, and can disappear. In this respect words like *that, more,* and *all gone* are quite different from such narrow-range words as *green, sit, swim, slow,* and the like. The combination of cognitive accessibility to the child, expressibility by a small lexicon, and the widest compositional potential might be expected to make operations of reference very prevalent in Stage I speech and partly responsible for the pivot look of such speech.

Of course accessibility of meaning and compositional potential are only two of the factors likely to affect the prevalence of words in child speech. There is, in addition, at least the factor of what the child is interested in talking about. Since most of the studies of Table 9 were dialogues between mother and child, one might expect self-reference and references to Mommy to loom large in Stage I, especially since the meanings belong to sensori-motor intelligence, and their compositional range is quite large.

Table 21 lists just those of the four presumptive pivots for each child which seem to express either one of the three operations of reference or to be a reference either to self or mother. Since there are 22 studies and 4 pivots per study the initial population is 88 pivots. Of these, 45 or 51 percent seem to express one or another of the operations of reference. Another 21 refer to self or mother, and so 66 of

Table 21. Cases in which the four most frequent "pivots" expressed a basic operation of reference or referred to self or mother

Child	MLU	Nomination	Recurrence	Nonexistence	Self	Mother
Kendall I	1.10				Kendall	Mommy
Gia I	1.12	/ə/[1]	more			Mommy
Eric II	1.19	/ə/[2]	another	no more[7]		
Gregory		see		all gone		
Andrew			more, other	no[8]		
Steven		it, that, there				
Christy		this, that, a, the[3]				
Susan		this, that[4]				
Kathryn I	1.32	/ə/[5]	more	no[9]		Mommy
Gia II	1.34	/ə/[6]	more			Mommy
Eric III	1.42	/ə/	more	no more	I[12]	
Seppo I	1.42			pois (away)[10]		äiti (Mommy)
Kendall II	1.48	that			Kendall	Mommy
Viveka	1.50	titta (see) dár (there)				
Sipili	1.52	le (the), 'O (sign of nominative)			au (me, my, mine)	
Eve I	1.68	a			Eve	Mommy
Sarah I	1.73	a, there		gone[11]		
Seppo II	1.81	tuossa (there) siinä (there)				äiti (Mommy)
Rina I	1.83	tässä (here), täällä (here)			Rina	äiti (Mommy)
Pepe	1.85	mirale (look-at)	otro (other)		mio (mine)	
Kathryn II	1.92	this, that			Kathryn	Mommy
Adam I	2.06				Adam, my	Mommy

[1]Bloom treats this form as schwa, a phonetic extension, but it is usually used with single nouns to name things.

[2]Schwa before noun or verb is said by Bloom to be the most frequent construction; it often seems simply to name, but it is also used in other ways.

[3]These are the members of Christy's two P classes, and they seem to have the highest frequencies though it is not possible to be sure from the figures given; they were often used to nominate but had also other uses.

[4]These were often used to nominate but they also had other uses; exact frequencies not given.

[5]This form occurred before *Adj* + *N* as well as *N* alone, but it was extremely frequent in the latter use.

[6]Schwa before *N* or *V* is described as the most frequent construction; before verbs it suggests the pronoun *I* and before nouns an article.

[7]Mostly in the sense of nonexistence, but also once as rejection and once indeterminate.

[8]Braine's paraphrases indicate that at least some of these express rejection rather than nonexistence.

[9]Mostly in the sense of nonexistence but also twice as rejection and once as denial.

[10]*Pois* is a verb particle like *away* in *take away;* it is used both to comment on disappearance and to command it.

[11]*Gone* occurred in second position, after nouns.

[12]Schwa before verb occurred 64 times, and for this reason and because it sometimes sounded like *I* Bloom judges that it is.

the pivots, or 76 percent, are accounted for by these few meanings; all accessible to the child, tied to a small lexicon, and of wide compositional potential. Quite often the fifth or sixth ranking presumptive pivot would have made the list had we gone beyond four. When two or more words were tied in frequency for one of the top four ranks the selection was made by a random process.

The pivot look is not the same as the pivot grammar, and the point of the demonstration in Table 21 is to argue that the pivot look which is indeed prevalent in Stage I is an epiphenomenon of other, primarily semantic considerations. In what way is the pivot look different from the grammar? It is true that with words like *that, more,* and *all gone* the descriptions $P_1 + O$ and $O + P_2$ might be used without underrepresenting the child's knowledge, since the distinct lexical items are there to carry the distinct referential senses, and a deep structure is not clearly required. The problem with these cases is that the words are not strictly limited to one position; they do occur in isolation and some occur in combination with one another. So the full distributional pattern is not what the pivot grammar says it should be.

For self references and mother references the difference between the look and the grammar is even more profound. The child's name and his mother's name, even when limited to first position in two-word utterances, frequently play three quite distinct semantic roles: the agent; the possessor in genitive; the entity in entity-locative expressions. Since the words used remain the same across what appear to be quite distinct semantic intentions, representation of such constructions as $P_1 + O$ would seriously under-represent the child's knowledge. Some sort of deep structure to differentiate the constructions, whether grammatical in the manner of Bloom or directly semantic in the manner of Schlesinger and Fillmore is clearly called for.

Prevalent Relations and Development in Stage I

With this topic we move up one level of abstraction. The operations of reference (the simple semantic set of nomination, recurrence, and nonexistence) are coordinated with one or just a few recurrent words. Words like *that, more,* and *all gone* operate like frames or "slots" through which a variety of other forms rotate. Some of the resultant constructions, though not all, are what a logician (Reichenbach, 1947) would call propositional functions; they have the form: $f(x)$. The function (or predicate or property) has a fixed value, but the logical subject (or argument) is represented by a variable which can assume many values, thus: *All gone (ball), All gone (soup), All gone (kitty).* We could proceed in this way identifying particular predicates and expanding to two-place and three-place functions as sentences grow more complex. However, particular terms quickly grow very numerous, even in the course of Stage I, and no short list will account for the majority of sentences in this stage. However we can discern a fairly short list of *types* of semantic functions or relations, types like *agent-action, possessor-possession,* which will account for the majority of utterances in Stage I.

Description in terms of a set of prevalent semantic relations may be little more than a technique of data reduction, a way of describing the meanings of early sentences short of listing them all. Even as a reduction technique it has a certain value. It reveals the fact that Stage I utterances, in all the languages for which studies exist, concentrate on the same set of meanings, a set far short of the meanings that languages are able to express and, in adult usage, do express. It reveals the further fact that the increases of complexity occurring in the course of Stage I are the same for all the children and languages that have been studied and proceed in accordance with a principle of cumulative complexity. Besides serving to summarize data and to reveal uniformities it is possible, of course, that the semantic relations represent a psychological *functional* level in sentence comprehension and production but, of this, there is as yet no strong evidence. The types of relation I will describe are already familiar to the reader from the work we have surveyed of Chafe, Fillmore, Schlesinger, and Bloom. What we have to offer that is new is some rough quantitative data on a set of children representing four different languages.

The data are presented in Tables 22, 23, and 24. To understand what these tables do and do not show it is necessary to explain how they were compiled. First: the selection of children. Only studies from Table 9 for which MLU values are known were considered, since only these studies can be assigned a developmental order independent of the internal character of the data samples. From the studies of Table 9 it was only possible to use those which either: 1. classify all utterances in terms of the semantic types I am interested in and report numbers for each type or; 2. report, usually in an appendix, all the utterances in the sample together with probable semantic readings based on context and adult glosses. Studies of the first sort are Eve I, Sarah I, and Adam I as well as Viveka (Swedish) and Pepe (Mexican Spanish). Studies of the second sort are Kendall I, Kendall II, Seppo I, Seppo II, Rina I (all Finnish) and Sipili and Tofi (Samoan). Unless the author of the study reported the classification and count himself, I did it from his reported corpus and notes on the utterances. I have, of course, followed the author's judgment wherever possible but am myself responsible for the ultimate figures. The total set of samples yielding quantitative data numbers twelve.

Second, there is the determination of the set of semantic relations to be counted. Basic here is the set of minimal two-term relations. These are, as I have named them in the tables:

1. Agent and action
2. Action and object
3. Agent and object
4. Action and locative (or location)
5. Entity and locative (or location)
6. Possessor and possession
7. Entity and attributive
8. Demonstrative and entity

Table 22. Prevalent semantic relations of two, three, and four terms expressed as percentages of total multi-morpheme types

Construction	Kendall I	Seppo I	Kendall II	Viveka	Sipili	Tofi	Eve I	Sarah I	Seppo II	Rina I	Pepe	Adam I
MLU	1.10	1.42	1.48	1.50	1.52	1.60	1.68	1.73	1.81	1.83	1.85	2.06
Multi-Morpheme Types	100	111	152	112	112	75	146	183	272	203	242	229
Two-term Relations												
Agent and action	22	30	20	04	03	12	10	06	24	11	05	07
Action and object	07	04	10	22	08	17	10	04	03	02	08	16
Agent and object	05	03	03	00	00	00	09	00	01	01	01	00
Action and locative	03	01	03	04	01	07	01	01	06	00	09	05
Entity and locative	18	11	09	02	01	01	05	01	10	06	05	02
Possessor and possession	19	01	09	05	14	03	10	07	04	02	12	11
Entity and attribute	06	10	05	07	01	03	04	06	12	03	07	05
Demonstrative and entity	01	00	03	23	01	00	03	10	01	25	00	01
Three-term Relations												
Agent, action, and object	00	06	05	00	00	01	03	04	02	10	03	06
Agent, action, and locative	00	00	03	00	00	01	00	01	07	04	04	03
Agent, object, and locative	00	00	00	00	00	00	00	00	00	00	01	01
Action, object, and locative	00	00	01	00	00	04	00	00	00	01	03	00
Four-term Relations												
Agent, action, object and locative	00	00	00	00	00	00	00	00	00	00	01	01

Table 23. Prevalent semantic relations, with one term (*NP*) expanded, expressed as percentages of total multi-morpheme types

Construction	Kendall I	Seppo I	Kendall II	Viveka	Sipili	Tofi	Eve I	Sarah I	Seppo II	Rina I	Pepe	Adam I
MLU	1.10	1.42	1.48	1.50	1.52	1.60	1.68	1.73	1.81	1.83	1.85	2.06
Multi-Morpheme Types	100	111	152	112	112	75	146	183	272	203	242	229
Two Terms with *NP* Expanded												
Agent and action	00	01*A*	00	00	00	00	00	01*AP*	01*A*	01*A*	02*AN*	00
Action and *object*	00	00	00	01*A*	00	03*AN*	00	00	01*AN*	01*A*	02*PAN*	01*P*
Agent and *object*	00	00	00	00	00	00	00	00	00	00	00	00
Action and *locative*	00	00	00	00	00	00	00	00	00	00	01*P*	01*P*
Entity and locative	00	00	00	00	02*P*	00	00	00	01*P*	00	02*PAN*	01*P*
Possessor and *possession*	00	00	00	00	00	00	00	00	00	00	01*AN*	00
Entity and attribute	00	00	00	00	00	00	00	00	00	00	01*N*	01*P*
Demonstrative and *entity*	00	00	01*P*	01*A*	00	00	03*P*	03*AP*	01*A*	02*AP*	01*P*	00
Three Terms with *NP* Expanded												
Agent, action, and *object*	00	00	00	00	00	00	00	00	00	01*A*	01*P*	01*A*
Agent, action, and *locative*	00	00	00	00	00	00	00	00	00	00	01*P*	01*A*

A = attributive; *N* = nominative; *P* = possessive.

Table 24. Percentages of multi-morpheme types expressing prevalent relations and falling into other categories

Construction	Kendall I	Seppo I	Kendall II	Viveka	Sipili	Tofi	Eve I	Sarah I	Seppo II	Rina I	Pepe	Adam I
MLU	1.10	1.42	1.48	1.50	1.52	1.60	1.68	1.73	1.81	1.83	1.85	2.06
Multi-Morpheme Types	100	111	152	112	112	75	146	183	272	203	242	229
Prevalent Relations	81	67	72	69	30	51	58	44	74	70	70	64
Other Constructions	17	04	07	16	65	35	41	42	22	27	20	30
Uninterpretable	02	29	21	15	05	14	01	14	04	03	10	06
Total	100	100	100	100	100	100	100	100	100	100	100	100

These eight minimal relations determined the rest which simply consist of *all* combinations of the eight occurring in the twelve samples. As it turns out the existent combinations are of just two basic kinds: 1. the stringing together of two or more minimal relations with deletion of redundant terms to yield such three-term compositions as agent-action-object and such four-term compositions as agent-action-object and locative; 2. the expansion of one term, always as it happens a noun phrase of the nominative, attributive, or possessive sort, in what is otherwise a composition of either two terms or three terms (for example, not just *Eat lunch* but *Eat Eve lunch*). Minimal two-term relations and concatenations of them into three or four terms with redundant elements deleted appear in Table 22. Constructions including one "expanded" term, always a noun phrase, appear in Table 23. It is important to understand about this procedure that, although an element of arbitrariness entered into the selection of the initial set of minimal two-term relations, the tabulation of combinations of these is not arbitrary but complete. No other combinations occurred.

The relations are defined semantically rather than grammatically. Thus "agent and action," for instance, does not necessarily imply the serial order: agent(1) + action(2). No particular serial order was necessary to cause a construction to be classified in one way rather than another. Seppo, for example, used both possible orders for action and object but no order difference is represented in the table; only the semantic type. English-speaking children might say either *Big dog* or *Dog big* (omitting the copula); both were simply counted as entity and attribute. In short the list of relations says nothing about the order of the terms. Neither is it to be supposed that terms like "agent and action" were treated as equivalent to such grammatical notions as subject and predicate (or verb). If a grammatical subject and verb did not name the perceived initiator of an action and the action then the construction was not counted as agent and action. One fairly common kind of exception occurred with subjects and predicates like *Adam see* or *Hear horn* where there is clearly no agent taking an action but rather a person affected in a given way through his senses (Fillmore would say the subject was in the dative case; Chafe would say in the experiencer role). A grammatical object that was not the recipient of a force and so did not satisfy my semantic definition of object was not counted. The only exception at all common in these data is the grammatical object that is what Chafe calls a complement, as in *Eve sing song*. Such cases were not counted as prevalent relations for the present tabulations. It should finally be noted that the relations have been named in semantic terms rather than in grammatical terms, even when the terms have had to be a little clumsy precisely in order to set aside grammatical implications.

Where, if at all, do the operations of reference (nomination, recurrence, and nonexistence) appear in the figures of Tables 22 and 23? Whenever possible the operation was reclassified into some more generic type of which it constituted a high-frequency instance. Thus *"More + N,"* an expression of recurrence, was counted as a form of attributive. Some cases of *"That + N"* or *"This + N* could be identified as more than simple naming utterances and recognized as demonstratives with an omitted copula, and they were counted as "demonstrative and entity." Numerous other operations of reference, especially simple nominations and expressions of nonexistence, could not clearly be classified under any of the generic relations, and so do not appear in Tables 22 and 23.

The relations counted in Tables 22 and 23, which I have called the prevalent relations, are summed for each child in Table 24, and it can be seen that they account for about 70 percent of most samples. Two notably lower values were obtained for Sarah I and Sipili. The explanation of these lower values is the same in both cases; the mothers of these children did not, as they were asked to do, converse in a natural way with their children in the presence of the investigator but rather made a continuing determined effort to elicit speech from their children. The only way mothers in general can think of to do this is to ask the names of things, and that is just what the mothers of both Sipili and Sarah did in these first sessions. The resulting protocols for the children were, consequently, overloaded with the names of things, simple nominatives like *a book,* which were not counted among the prevalent relations. It is not certain what causes a mother to do this. Probably the child feels uneasy and so is quiet, and the mother is the sort to worry about wasting the investigator's time. "Eliciting" interactions of this kind did not dominate even the first sessions with the two other children in our study, Adam and Eve. Nor did they with Kernan's second Samoan child. He writes: "Tofi was at ease during these sessions, and contrary to the case with Sipili, most of her utterances were spontaneous rather than answers to questions" (1969, p. 93).

Even if we set aside Sipili and Sarah I and take 70 percent as the approximate proportions of a Stage I child's relaxed conversation that is concerned with expressing the prevalent semantic relations obviously the relations do not account for *all* of Stage I speech. What else goes on? As Table 24 indicates there are always some utterances that are simply semantically uninterpretable whether by the investigator, the mother, or whomever. For some of these one cannot offer any reasonable hypothesis whatever. For others one can offer two or more, often from the set of prevalent relations, but there is nothing that enables one to choose among them.

Finally in Table 24 there is the entry "other constructions" with values ranging as low as 4 percent and as high as 65 percent (Sipili, and mostly nominatives). If I am going to argue, as I wish to do, that learning to express a small set of semantic relations and their combination constitutes the principal work of Stage I then these "other constructions" have to be explained. They are, essentially, of three kinds: 1. additional semantic relations which could perfectly well be counted among those in Tables 22 and 23 but which are of lower frequency across the full set of data than any that have been counted; 2. very infrequent and apparently uncomprehending use of forms which will become fully productive in Stages II and III, such as the plural and progressive inflections in English, the semi-auxiliary *wanna,* and the preposition *in*; 3. idiosyncratic forms, used by only one or two children, usually infrequently and inflexibly. I will say a little about each of these.

The first category, semantic relations of low frequency, is probably the most interesting. It is entirely possible that all of them lie within the competence of Stage I children, and their omission from Tables 22 and 23 may be nothing more than an accident resulting from sampling limitations and the setting of an arbitrary cut-off point for Table 22. Clearly there is considerable variation in frequency among the eight two-term relations of Table 22, as they stand, from such highly frequent cases as agent and action, action and object, possessor and possession, to the distinctly marginal agent and object. A different cut-off point would have excluded this last, which does not occur at all in five of the twelve samples. Other two-term relations which occur with low frequency in at least some samples but are not entered in Tables 22 and 23 are:

1. instrumental *(Sweep broom)*
2. benefactive *(For Daddy)*
3. indirect object datives *(Give me book)*
4. experiencer or person affected datives *(Adam see)*
5. comitatives *(Go Mommy)*
6. conjunctions (in the sense of simply naming present objects as when Kendall said: *Kimmy Phil*)
7. classificatory *(Mommy lady)*

If these relations and the combinations into which they entered were added to Tables 22 and 23, the tables would become very much larger and spottier, spottier in the sense of having many more zero frequency entries. In Table 24 the percentages of total utterances accounted for by "relations" would, of course, come closer to 100 percent though they would still not quite reach that value in most cases.

The second category, infrequent and apparently uncomprehending use of forms which will reach a criterion of control in stages that lie just ahead, includes, for English, inflections like *-s, -ing,* the prepositions *in* and *on,* the semi-auxiliary *wanna,* the copula *is.* In the languages other than English, equivalents of these forms are quite often the ones found "sprinkled" in samples near the end of Stage I. As we shall see in Stage II these forms which seem to "modulate" the meanings of the basic relations are not, in English at least, acquired suddenly and completely but rather develop in a gradual way over rather long periods. Samples near the end of Stage I seem to pick up the very first occurrences of these forms, which, if they were used wherever adult English requires them, would have frequencies as high or higher than any of the two-term relations.

About the third category, idiosyncratic and inflexible terms, there is nothing new to say. Probably any form that is perceptually salient and highly frequent in the speech of a particular parent (*now* or *soon*) can become "lodged" in the speech of that parent's child though it will not be used in a full range of appropriate environments.

We have not quite come to the end of the qualifications that must be entered about Tables 22, 23, 24. In almost all the twelve samples there were instances of both vocative forms and greetings; often together as in *Hi, Mommy*. These have simply been counted among "other constructions" in Table 24. There is not, I think, any doubt that Stage I children control such forms but they have little grammatical or semantic interest.

Finally there is evidence in Stage I of the semantics, if little of the grammar, of the major simple sentence modalities other than the affirmative, declarative modality. There is evidence of some understanding of interrogative, negative, and imperative modalities. In the Introduction I have explained that the whole development of the major constructional processes (semantic relations, the grammatical morphemes, the modalities of the simple sentence, embedding, and coordination) is never contained entirely within one of the five stages in terms of which this work is organized. Quite typically there is something of interest to say about each process in each stage, but a stage derives its name from the process that seems to dominate it. Semantic relations dominate Stage I but the germs of the interrogative, negative, and imperative modalities also can be found there.

The development of the simple sentence modalities of interrogation, negation, and the imperative is the subject of Stage III, and so I will say here only enough to indicate that the semantic beginnings are in Stage I. With respect to *yes-no* questions, all the children except Seppo and Rina, the Finnish children, produced some utterances which adults interpreted in this fashion. In the adult grammar of all the languages except Finnish the *yes-no* question is marked by a distinctive rising intonation as well as by such other characteristics as transposition of subject and verbal elements *(Are you with me?)* In Finnish there is no distinctive intonation for *yes-no* questions; questions are marked by a particle which is attached to the word being questioned, typically the verb, and that word is brought to the front of the sentence. Seppo and Rina, unlike the other children produced no recognizable *yes-no* questions at I nor for long after. The *yes-no* questions produced by the other children were, however, recognizable as such by intonation alone. They did not, in Stage I, utilize the rearrangements of order belonging to the adult forms. Our children, Adam, Eve, and Sarah in fact did not produce well-formed *yes-no* questions until Stage III or later. Probably what these results mean is that the *yes-no* semantic is available to Stage I children but that there is a difference of difficulty in expressive means such that intonation is more easily grasped than rearrangements of order or the affixation of particles. Finnish children, because their language does not make available the easy expressive device, do not produce recognizable questions in Stage I.

Among *wh-* questions, or, to name them less parochially, questions requesting specification of a certain grammatical constituent or semantic role, only two kinds were at all common. A question asking the name of some referent; in English *What's that?* or some variant thereof, including *Who'at* and *'ts at.* A question requesting the locus of a referent; in English *Where N* or *Where N go* most commonly. The picture across all twelve children is a bit uneven with some children using both kinds of form (Adam, Eve, and Sarah) and some using only one or the other. What is common to all cases is the inflexibility of the forms. There are no such variants in English, for instance, as *What are these* or *Where did you put it* or the like. In Stage III English, one finds the full flowering of *wh-* questions in their many different forms, and I shall argue that the precursors that appear in Stage I must be generated by some simpler mechanism either as fixed routines or as simple frames in which a set of words could rotate.

There is no question, from behavioral and contextual evidence, that all the children at Stage I produced large numbers of utterances with the apparent intent of moving another to take an action. There are many sequences in which a child produced a series of varied utterances all having a single instrumental goal. Eve, on one occasion, trying to induce her mother to read to her, held her aim on this objective over some 48 exchanges. Although there is no question of the ubiquity of the semantic intention there is a problem of recognizing imperatives by form in Stage I English and many other languages. There is no really reliable intonational marking in English. The subjectless surface sentence, with *you* the understood subject, marks imperatives fairly clearly in adult English. Stage I children speaking English produce many such sentences but the difficulty is that they often omit the subject also from sentences clearly intended to be declarative, and so there is no unequivocal formal marking of their imperatives. Finnish children occasionally, though not at all frequently, used the verb in a form marked as imperative. Pepe did so quite often in Spanish. So these observations strengthen the conclusion that Stage I children often have the intentions most often expressed by the imperative, but actually their concomitant behavior could not leave one in any doubt about this. The same is true for the Gardners' chimpanzee Washoe, who, when her signs failed to have their effect, did not hesitate to pull into position the person she wanted to take action or to attempt to mold the other's hands or lift a foot.

In all the twelve children there is also evidence of negative intentions ordinarily expressed with some single negative word and never in the well-formed adult way. Most of the meanings seem to express nonexistence but there are also some that appear to signify refusal to comply and some that seem to express denial of an assertion. The evolution of the negative is a complex story. My account is reserved for Stage III but see Bloom (1970) and Bellugi (in press) for penetrating discussions of developments in English that are already available.

How do the modalities of interrogation, negation, and the imperative affect the frequencies of Tables 22, 23, and 24? Where the utterance is classifiable as one of the prevalent relations it is counted as such. This is the case, for instance, with such English interrogatives as *My ball?,* which would be classified as possessor-possession, disregarding the rising intonation or an imperative like *Hit ball,* which would be classified as action and object, though the context might make it clear that the intention was imperative. Utterances like *What that?* and *Where book?* and various negatives could not be classified as belonging to any of the prevalent relations, and so they are simply tallied in with the "other constructions" of Table 24.

We have, at last, finished recounting the many qualifications and arbitrary decisions that lie behind the data of Tables 22, 23, and 24 and may now consider what these, obviously rather rough, data do positively indicate. Because the data are rough I am not disposed to force them beyond the several things that appear very clearly from inspection alone.

It is in the first place of some interest that there exists a short list of semantic relations that will account for the majority of Stage I utterances produced by twelve unacquainted children learning four different languages. In the next section when we review the evidence available from the full set of studies described in Tables 9 and 10, we will see that the same relations appear to account for a majority of utterances in all Stage I studies on record. If the list of relations is made a bit longer the percentages of utterances accounted for goes up but the universality of appearance in samples of modest size goes down. The eight two-term relations listed in Table 22 mostly appear with some frequency in each sample. There are just 9 zero frequency entries out of 96 (8 x 12) total entries. It is not, I think, terribly important whether the list of relations numbers 8 or 12 or, including all that were found, 15. The point is that the number is still small and the result suggests that children, whatever the first language they learn, begin to talk about the same limited set of things. The question might be asked: what else is there to talk about? The answer is: very many things indeed. For instance aspects of time and manner, past and future events, conditional and hypothetical statements, causality, varieties of spatial relation, number, and so on. What the Stage I child talks about, I will shortly argue, is the sensori-motor world which he has organized in the first 18 months of his life.

What expressive means does the child employ in talking about the relations he understands? Most generally the simple concatenation under one utterance contour of the words which interact to create a compositional meaning that is different from the meanings of the two words in sequence. But also in languages with fixed and contrastive word order most children seem to employ appropriate word order as an expressive mechanism. Intonation, as in the interrogative, is also employed. Inflections and derivational affixes and permutations of order and numerous other expressive devices are not used.

In the second place Tables 22 and 23 show that as the MLU increases across Stage I the elementary two-term relations are combined in just the same two ways by all the children recorded. These two ways may be grasped most easily from a kind of "as if" description but it is important to remember that it is only an "as if" description, since the real nature of the psychological processes is unknown. In one sort of complex construction it is as if two or more of the elementary relations were concatenated with all repetitions of terms struck out or deleted. Thus a construction like *Adam hit ball* (agent, action, and object) seems to have as its components *Adam hit* (agent and action) and *Hit ball* (action and object) with the repeating action *hit* deleted once. One can think of similar "as if accounts" for the remaining three-term and four-term relations of Table 22.

In the second sort of complex construction, those of Table 23, it is not as if relations were simply concatenated with deletion. It is rather as if one term, an agent or object or locative or possession or entity but always a *NP,* itself "unfolds" as a two-term relation. For instance, in the action and object construction *Hit ball* the object is represented in a maximally simple way by one word. In *Hit Adam ball,* on the other hand, the object unfolds as itself a relation of possessor-possession. In Table 23 the nature of the unfolded relation(s) is indicated in parentheses as *A* (attributive), *N* (nominative), and *P* (possessive). These three exhaust the varieties that occur.

Table 25. Percentages of multi-morpheme utterances consisting of four varieties of relations of more than two simple terms

Sample	MLU	Three Terms	Two Terms with Expanded *NP*	Four Terms	Three Terms with Expanded *NP*
Kendall I	1.10	0	0	0	0
Seppo	1.42	6	1	0	0
Kendall II	1.48	9	1	0	0
Viveka	1.50	0	2	0	0
Sipili	1.52	0	2	0	0
Tofi	1.60	6	3	0	0
Eve I	1.68	3	3	0	0
Sarah I	1.73	5	5	0	0
Seppo II	1.81	9	4	0	0
Rina I	1.83	15	4	0	1
Pepe	1.85	11	10	1	2
Adam I	2.06	10	4	1	2

Table 25 makes a further point about the two varieties of construction which involve more than a single elementary relation. It is evident that three-term relations (like agent-action-object) are on about the same level of difficulty as two-term relations in which one term is expanded (like *Hit Adam ball*). Most of the children who have constructions of the one kind also have constructions of the other kind, and the percentages tend to rise together through the course of Stage I. It should be noted that both kinds of construction may be said to be composed of, or at any rate to express, just two elementary relations. This suggests that the effective complexity limit on the child's constructions may be stated in terms of the number of elementary relations he is able to program into a single sentence. This view is supported by the two rightmost columns of Table 25, from which it appears that four-term relations (like agent, action, object, and locative) are of the same degree of complexity as three-term relations in which one term is expanded. Only the three most advanced of the twelve children have any of either and, of these three, two have both. The two kinds of construction are describable as composed of or expressing the same number of elementary relations: four. This result again then suggests that sentence complexity limits in Stage I may be stated in terms of the number of elementary relations that may be programmed into a single sentence.

Is there not, however, an alternative and rather more obvious way of stating complexity limits in Stage I? The two kinds of sentences composed of two elementary relations *(Adam hit ball* and *Hit Adam ball)* are both always going to be made up of just three words whereas the two sorts of sentences composed of three elementary relations *(Adam hit ball there* and *Daddy sit Adam chair)* will, in all cases, consist of just four words. So, why not simply say that the complexity limit is set by the number of words, or morphemes. Put this way is it even clear that the figures in Table 25 represent an empirical discovery? After all, the children are ordered by MLU, and as the mean length of utterance gets longer so does the upper bound or longest utterance, and one may reasonably presume that three-word utterances will first become more common and then four-word utterances.

While the critical spirit is upon us let us take note of an even more devastating possibility revealed by Table 22. It may be seen that the number of multi-morpheme types (or distinct utterances as opposed to "tokens") in these child speech samples tends to get larger as the MLU rises. The total samples vary in size, though many consisted of approximately 700 distinct utterances. Obviously, then, the number of the total which were single-word utterances declined with increasing MLU, as one would expect. But perhaps longer utterances are always less frequent, and the differences are not really differences of ability but differences of sampling. If one had larger samples from the less mature children might they not have produced some composed of three and four minimal relations?

Table 26. Percentages of multi-morpheme utterances consisting of relations of more than two simple terms

Sample	MLU	Percentage	Language
Kendall I	1.10	0	English
Seppo I	1.42	7	Finnish
Kendall II	1.48	10	English
Viveka	1.50	2	Swedish
Sipili	1.52	2	Samoan
Tofi	1.60	9	Samoan
Eve I	1.68	6	English
Sarah I	1.73	9	English
Seppo II	1.81	13	Finnish
Rina I	1.83	19	Finnish
Pepe	1.85	24	Spanish
Adam I	2.06	17	English

There are answers to all these criticisms; such that it seems to me that real developmental differences of ability are demonstrated by the tables and also that these are not simply differences in the numbers of words in utterances. Perhaps the most important thing to point out is that the figures in the tables are not utterance *frequencies* but rather percentages. In Table 26, for instance, we see that in these samples of varying size there is a steady increase in the percentage of all multi-morpheme types composed of more than a single simple relation of two terms, an increase from 0 percent at Kendall I to between 17 and 24 percent for the three most advanced children. These are not increases that result from the fact that the total numbers of multi-morpheme types tend to increase, since they are not frequencies but percentages.

The other important point to realize is that though rising MLU values do necessarily entail increasing numbers of word or morphemes of some kind in utterances it is not at all a necessary result that these increases be increases of the kind reported, increases in the number of relations packed into each sentence. Increases of MLU could perfectly well be produced solely by increases in the number of functors or grammatical morphemes (like inflections, articles, prepositions, auxiliary verbs). Or they could be solely produced by embedding one simple sentence in another or by coordinating two or more simple sentences. And in fact, in later stages, the continued rise of MLU values is strongly affected by all these factors more or less in turn. That is why MLU is a good simple index of development from about 1.0 to about 4.0; it continues to be responsive to what the child is learning but it is primarily responsive to different kinds of knowledge at different times. The point about Stage I is that the compounding of relations is the major factor causing MLU to rise. The occasional grammatical morpheme, especially near the end of Stage I, has also some effect, but embedding and coordination do not affect the index at all in Stage I, since they do not occur.

There is a final conclusion to be drawn from the data we have seen, especially in Tables 22 and 23. It is a conclusion too obviously true to require an independent tabulation but it is an important conclusion because we shall find that it is a quite general rule in development appearing again and again in later stages. In an expansive mood we might even presume to call it a law. If we were to do so, it would be the law of cumulative complexity, a law describing many aspects of the child's development of language.

To illustrate cumulative complexity in its application to Stage I let us take a couple of particular examples. The three-term relation called agent, action, and locative is more complex, in the cumulative sense, than either of the individual relations called, respectively, "agent and action" and "action and locative." The three-term relation is more complex than either of the two-term relations because it involves all that either *one* of them involves plus something additional (in fact the other relation). Let us take a second example. The two-term relation action and object with the second term expanded as a possessive *(Hit Adam ball)* is more complex, cumulatively, than either of the individual simple relations called, respectively, "action and object" and "possessor and possession." The two-term relation with expanded object is more complex than either one of the other relations because it involves all the knowledge that either one of them involves plus something more (in fact the knowledge the other involves). In general, a relation of cumulative complexity exists in the following circumstances: $x + y$ is more complex than either x or y alone. The plus sign should not be understood to mean simple concatenation or serial ordering. In some cases it might seem to, but generally it simply means any means of combining the knowledge symbolized by x and y. It need not mean concatenation. In the present data the complexity increases are both semantic and grammatical, and we cannot separate the two. In other cases, as in Stage II, there is some possibility of separating the two.

What does the law of cumulative complexity predict? It predicts that any child able to construct $x + y$ will also be able to construct either x or y alone. It does not predict, as Brown and Hanlon (1970) first showed in connection with the development of tag questions in English that a child able to construct both x and y, severally, will be able to construct $x + y$. There is evidently, and this is simply an empirical discovery, some additional knowledge involved in putting the component items of knowledge together to make the more complex construction. Indeed in some cases, as shown in Stage II and also in the Brown and Hanlon paper, there may sometimes be quite long intervals, some months, between acquisition of the several component kinds of knowledge and their assemblage into the more complex construction. I have used the analogy already and it is not, I think, a misleading one, to conceive of x and y as knowledge componentry required for x and y so long as we do not think of the components as simply words or sequences of words.

How does the law of cumulative complexity manifest itself in Tables 22 and 23 for Stage I? We cannot in these samples, nor indeed ever in child speech, put together *specific* components, particular utterances like *Adam sit; Sit chair,* and *Adam sit chair*. One just does not get enough complete sets of such utterances from samples of spontaneous speech. It is necessary to think instead in terms of utterance types as I have done in all my tables. The general prediction then is that any child who produces some more complex construction will also produce the simpler component constructions into which it can be analyzed. Thus a child producing agent, action, and locative *(x + y)* constructions should also produce both agent and action and action and locative constructions. But the converse need not be the case; the components do not guarantee the composition. And this is overwhelmingly the case in Tables 22 and 23. The few exceptions one finds could easily result from sampling limitations.

Let us look at just two extreme examples. Kendall I (MLU of 1.10) produced some instances of all the elementary two-term relations, the components, but none at all of any of the more complex constructions that can be made up of these components. In her case, clearly the eight individual competencies are not sufficient to yield any of the complex competencies. Adam I (MLU 2.06) produces a large number and variety of complex constructions and, of course, he also produces all the elementary components (except the not strictly necessary "agent and object"). In short, Kendall shows that control of *a* and of *b* and of *c* and of *d* and of *e* and of *f* and of *g* and of *h* is not sufficient to produce control of any of their possible combinations, whereas Adam shows that control of combinations does indeed guarantee control of all components.

The critical spirit recovering, one might reasonably ask: how could it be otherwise? If $x + y$ entails more knowledge than either x or y alone it must entail x and y separately but not vice versa. There are two ways in which it could be otherwise. It could be otherwise if the analysis into components is not psychologically correct, if the true components have not been found. And so the law of cumulative complexity affords a kind of test of the psychological reality of various semantic and grammatical analyses. The results could be otherwise in another respect. There is no logical necessity in the fact that control of x knowledge separately and y knowledge separately are not together immediately sufficient conditions for $x + y$ knowledge. The fact that they never seem to be, that there is always some interval, is an empirical discovery not a logical necessity.

The principal conclusions suggested by the quantitative data available for twelve samples and four languages are as follows. A small set of simple semantic relations (between 8 and 15) will account for most of the utterances in all samples. The small set of simple relations combine in the same two ways, for short we may call them concatenation-with-deletion and expansion-of-one-term in all samples. The expansions, furthermore, are always of a NP classifiable as nominative, attributive, or possessive. It appears that the number of elementary relations entering into a complex construction effectively defines sentence complexity limits in all cases. Finally the development that appears in Stage I follows the law of cumulative complexity.

Definitions and Fragmentary Data

Lest we all lose our way I had better review what has been reported of the major meanings at Stage I and anticipate what is to be reported here. We began by trying to account for the pivot look that is ubiquitous in Stage I speech and which really reduces to the heavy use of a small number of terms in combination with a large variety of other terms. I think we succeeded in showing that this look is partially dependent on the ubiquity of just three operations of reference: nomination, recurrence, and nonexistence. The actual data reported are the cases in which words expressing these meanings appear among the four most common "seeming pivots" in the samples of Table 9. Occurrences of these meanings at a lower level of frequency was not reported, and so it remains to say what can be said on this level for the studies of Table 9 as well as the studies of Table 10.

Then, in Table 22, we reported percentages of total multi-word utterances accounted for by eight relational types for just the 12 studies for which complete data and interpretations are available as well as MLU values. These 12 all derive from Table 9. Some of the operations of reference, especially nomination and recurrence, were reclassified for this purpose under the respective relational types: "demonstrative and entity" and "attributive and entity." The nonexistence operations fall in Table 24 under "other constructions." It is necessary, therefore, to go back of the generic types in just these cases to check on the occurrence of the specific operations. Beyond that, it remains to say what can be said about the eight relations in the samples of Table 9, which were not included among the 12 samples for which we have complete quantitive data. As far as the 12 samples themselves are concerned, all eight relations were practically always present. In addition the fragmentary data on the eight relations from the samples of Table 10 remain to be reported.

Why are the data in this section fragmentary? For a variety of reasons. Not all investigations report on their complete samples; not all investigators report frequencies, and not all investigators have been interested in semantic operations and relations. In this section I will report only explicitly positive or negative data or statements. There is no point in remarking on all the cases in which no relevant information is presented and no point in putting the results in a table because the reports are just not sufficiently comparable. What then can one hope to do with such data? What is the point of reporting fragments? Certainly one cannot confirm or disconfirm the universality within these samples of the three operations and eight minimal relations, since they were not always looked for or reported on. The most one can do, if the data so work out, is suggest that they may be universal. This suggestion will be strong or weak in the degree that the same relations turn up in unacquainted children acquiring historically remote or unrelated languages. My impression is that the suggestion is fairly strong now and will grow stronger as studies accumulate.

Finally, we have the definitions of the operations and relations coming in this late section after their frequencies have already been counted. That seems almost wantonly irritating. But it must be remembered that the definitions are fairly obvious and have already appeared in our discussions of the work of Chafe, Fillmore, Schlesinger, and Bloom. I wanted to set down the main conclusions about the pivot look and the law of cumulative complexity before attempting sharp definitions and reporting fragmentary data.

I feel very apologetic for the confusion that all this classifying and reclassifying of rather messy data threatens to cause the reader. It results, not from a taste for confusion, but from a wish to make use of as many studies of as many languages as possible, and the studies available are not easily compared with one another. However, I think breadth has the highest premium at this point. Later on, students of child language will attempt to make their work comparable and cumulative by adopting similar procedural canons; indeed this has already started in the last few years.

1. *Nomination.* Bloom, summarizing the contexts in which 308 such utterances occurred in Kathryn II, says that the referent was always manifest; either pointed at, looked at, or picked up. The presence of the referent made manifest by some action calling attention to it for the members of the communicating group, usually a dyad, defines this operation. It is similar to what Braine (1963) calls ostensive sentences and Schlesinger (1971) introducer + *x*. There are really two prototypical situations in which nomination occurs, and they differ with respect to the member of the dyad producing the pointing reaction or its equivalent. In one situation an adult asks *what's that?* and points, often at a picture in a book, and the child replies with a name and some such introducer, as *a, the, schwa, that, it,* or their non-English equivalents. In a second sort of situation the child initiates the interaction and does the pointing himself saying in addition to the name something like *this, that,* or *see.* There is a common variant of this case in which the adult says *Where's x?* and the child, again pointing, and often at a picture in a book, gives the name *x,* and says in addition *this* or *that* or *here* or *there.* The words *here* and *there* and their equivalents in other languages can function as prolocatives, as forms replacing full locative phrases. In the case under consideration, however, it seems more sensible to think of them as a kind of demonstrative for, it is clear, the adult question *Where's x?* is not a true locative question at all. The adult in these circumstances knows perfectly well where, in the present setting, *x* is. His question is really a way of testing the child's ability to match name and referent, a language game alternative to the *What's that* game, which leaves the pointing to the child.

Until now I have distinguished the pure nomination operation in which the child only names (usually in response to the question *What's that?*) and does not point, from the demonstrative and entity relation where the child points as he names and uses a demonstrative form. But, as can now be seen, this is a rather artificial distinction, and I will combine here the several cases in which names and manifest referents are linked and nothing else is expressed.

Of the 24 samples listed in Table 9, nomination forms were so common as to appear among the "seeming pivots" in 18 cases, and there were at least some instances in another three; only Seppo I and Tofi lacked any. Concerning Hildegard, Leopold (1949) tells us that *This + N* and *Here + N* were very frequent from the age of 1;9. Grégoire (1937) tells us that his boys used /sa/ derived from the question *Qu'est-ce que c'est que ça?* in pointing at and naming things. In Park's (1970b) tables of two-word utterances for three German children nomination expressions, utilizing such words as *da, hier, das,* and *ein* plus a name, are among the most frequent constructions. For Gil and Gila, Bar-Adon (1971) includes nomination examples among the earliest constructions *(Ze buba* [*This doll*])*.* Concerning Susin's early Korean, Park (1970a) notes the occurrence of 28 different names together with *itda* which means, roughly, *there.* Blount (1969) had a total corpus of only 191 utterances from a collective total of six children of various ages. In the total corpus there are at least seven utterances that seem to express nomination (*Ma wendo* [*This visitor*]). Almost all the studies in Tables 9 and 10 reported some instances of nomination, often very many. Evidently the simple naming function is one of the most reliable in Stage I speech.

Since the word pairs *this-that* and *here-there* and their equivalents in other languages often appear in constructions expressing nomination, it should be possible to find out whether Stage I children used such forms with appropriate proximal-distal semantic contrast. The contrast itself is relative to the speaker, and so correct comprehension and production entails the overcoming of one variety of egocentrism. In addition, the actual distances involved in the proximal-distal contrast vary with referents and situations in adult usage in a complex way that, so far as I know, has never been described. For example: *Sign right here* might mean *just next to my index finger,* whereas *Here we have a superb example of Gothic architecture* might refer to a cathedral many yards away (examples from de Villiers, 1971).

As it happens none of the authors of the studies listed in Tables 9 and 10 seems to have thought to pay attention to the child's control of the proximal-distal contrast. Jill de Villiers (1971) has made a start on the controlled study of this contrast. She worked with 18 children 23–35 months in age, 9 boys and 9 girls, and worked with production only. An example of her methods may be given with respect to *here* and *there*. The experimenter placed a truck out of reach and asked *Where is the truck?* This was tried also with the truck near the child. As so often happens with well-devised tests of young children's linguistic knowledge some children found a way to evade the test. While they might point and say *here* when the truck was nearby, when the truck was farther away, instead of saying *there,* some children moved themselves to the vicinity of the truck and, once again, said *here.* In general, de Villiers feels that her initial results are inconclusive. Some children seemed to use the proximal-distal contrast correctly in production of *here-there* and *this-that,* and some did not. There was a slight tendency for control of the contrast to improve with linguistic maturity as assessed, very roughly, by the longest utterance heard from the child, but the tendency was not marked and the index of maturity was not based on large enough samples of speech. In any case de Villiers has shown the way to a more thorough study of the problem.

2. *Recurrence.* The term is Bloom's and she discusses its meaning in connection with the appearance in Gia II of 64 instances of *More + N* and 23 of *More + V.* The construction either comments on (declarative) or requests (imperative) "recurrence" of a thing, person, or process. Recurrence itself means different things in different cases. It may mean the reappearance of the same referent already seen; it may mean the appearance of a new instance of a referent class of which one instance has already been seen, and it may mean an additional quantity (or "helping") of some mass of which a first quantity has already been seen. In the less mature samples *more* is sometimes involved, simply as a request form. As the samples become more advanced this "incorrect" usage drops out. Bloom finds no semantic distinction between the child's use of *another* and *more,* though *another* is not used before verbs.

In adult English, of course, *more* would be limited to the modification of pluralized count nouns or mass nouns. Children at first use it with unmarked count nouns, mass nouns, proper nouns, verbs, and even adjectives. In the more mature samples of Table 9 the part-of-speech diversity of the head word shows some tendency to decline. Before Eric III (MLU $= 1.42$) three children are reported to use *more* before words that are not nouns; after Eric III, none.

In 7 of the 24 samples of Table 9 recurrence forms were frequent enough to count among the "seeming pivots." In another 13 samples some, often many, instances occurred. Only Eric I, Seppo I, and the two Samoan children lacked any.

What of the children listed in Table 10 who were learning various languages other than English? Leopold reports that Hildegard used the German word *mehr* as her first "attributive adjective" beginning at the age of 1;6. Grégoire's Edmond used *Encore;* as for Charles there is no report. Park's tables for his three children learning German include examples of *mehr, auch,* and *einmal* used with other words in a sense he identifies as recurrence. One cannot tell how frequent the expressions were or whether it was the case that some were obtained from all the children. For Izanami, Gil and Gila, Zhenya, and the Luo children no instances happen to be recorded in the published studies but this is very likely only because the authors were either not interested in the matter or were working from very small samples. The case for the "universality" of recurrence as one of the operations expressed by Stage I children is, on present evidence, less strong than that for nomination but still fairly strong.

In Eric III there is a sequence in which he alternated between *more* and *no-more.* For instance:

> *More noise* (turning a wheel to make a friction noise).
> *No more noise* (stopping the wheel).

More expressed recurrence and, for Eric, *No-more* expressed its opposite, "nonexistence," and this is the operation to be discussed next.

3. *Nonexistence.* The term once again is Bloom's. She found in her data that the syntactic expression of negation (as opposed to one-word expression) began with the meaning of nonexistence and then progressed to rejection and denial. In the Bloom samples contained in Stage I nonexistence was the predominant negative meaning though both rejection and denial also occurred. In two-word utterances nonexistence was typically expressed by a negative operator with a nominal or predicate form. For example: *No more noises* (Eric III); *No hat* (Kathryn II); *All gone egg* (Andrew); *Sun gone* (Sarah I); *Dog away* (Seppo I), *Any more play* (Seppo II).

The nonexistence expressed in the constructions in question is not intended to be absolute; Bloom does not mean to suggest that the child believes that when objects go out of the visual field they pass into the void. Piaget of course has argued that children very early in the sensori-motor period, before they have formed the concept of the enduring object, do believe something of this sort. However, the Stage I child has passed beyond sensori-motor intelligence. The use of question asking for the locations of absent objects *(Where N?)* late in Stage I suggests that the child conceives of objects when they are out of the visual field as existing in other locations. In any case Bloom means by nonexistence, nonexistence in the reference context of the utterance; whether the presently nonexistent is thought to be absolutely nonexistent or simply elsewhere located is left open.

In very many cases, as terms like *all gone* and *no more* would suggest, the present nonexistent was quite recently existent in the reference context. The word nonexistence does not suggest prior presence nearly as well as does a word like disappearance. Disappearance is exactly right for many cases, and it is the real opposite of recurrence, since both terms presuppose prior presence and then contrast by expressing, respectively, absence now or reappearance now. However, prior presence does not fit all cases. It seems rather to be one of many bases for something that is an essential ingredient of the nonexistence meaning. What is essential is an expectation of existence which the nonexistence sentence disappoints. Negatives of all kinds function only in contexts of expectation; they sometimes deny what someone anticipates or asserts, and they sometimes reject offerings or influence attempts that another expects to be accepted. Prior existence, then, is simply one basis for expecting present existence, one ground for the expectation that the nonexistence sentence strikes down. There are other grounds for such expectation, for instance, custom or habit, and so "nonexistence" really is a better term than "disappearance" for the meaning in question.

The nonexistence terms, like the recurrence terms, were used to command as well as to comment on. Seppo's word *Pois* (away) seemed to mean *Disappear!* as often as it meant *X has disappeared.*

In seven of the samples of Table 9 nonexistence terms were frequent enough to count among the first four seeming pivots. In addition, such terms occurred in Kendall I and II, Sipili, Eve I, and Adam I. In sum, in just 12 of the 24 studies is the nonexistence meaning reported.

The following are the reports of nonexistence meanings for the studies in Table 10. Grégoire writes of Edmond's *non encore:* " . . . marque, en général, la non-existence, l'absence, souvent la disparition" (1937, p. 57). You could not come closer than that. Park finds the meaning expressed by *kein* and *alle* in his German children. Park finds the word *upda* used eight times with other words in the sense of *there is no* in Susin's Korean. There seems to be just one example in all of Blount's Luo corpus. Slobin reports for Zhenya the form *nyet kavó,* which seems to mean nonexistence in some cases. The other authors of studies in Table 10 are simply silent on the subject. As with recurrence, then, the evidence for the linguistic universality of the nonexistence meaning in Stage I children is far from perfect, but one must note the limitations of the data and the reports and the fact that there are positive reports for a number of historically unrelated languages.

We proceed now, from the three basic operations of reference, to the various relation types. With these we are no longer concerned with particular words and so not with "seeming pivots." In addition Table 22 reports full quantitative data for 12 of the samples of Table 9, and so we need not repeat the information in that table; almost all these samples contained some instances of each relation type. It remains to report on the other 12 samples in Table 9 and on the samples of Table 10.

4. *Agent and Action*. Fillmore (1968) defines the agent as the typically animate instigator of action and Chafe (1970) as someone or something, usually but not necessarily animate, which is perceived to have its own motivating force and to cause an action or process. This latter is the definition we have used, not insisting on animacy. Most agents in all samples are animate *(Mommy, Adam, bear, I, you)* but a few are not, as in *Car go*. Actions involve perceived movements; terms like *come, go, pull, push, stand up, write*. However, several children in the judgment of the investigators who studied them, used particles from separable verbs as if they named actions (Susan's *off* and *on*, Seppo's *away*, Hildegard's *auf*, and others).

Of the 12 previously unreported studies in Table 9, all 12 (by my classification) include at least a few instances of agent and action, often many. Turning to the studies of Table 10 we find positive reports in all cases making any report. In sum, there are positive reports for French, German, Korean, and Luo. With respect to the universality of agent and action as a Stage I meaning the evidence in these data is very strong. Every study presenting relevant data or making any relevant comment finds the construction.

5. *Action and Object*. Fillmore used "object" as his residual case which he did not attempt to define in semantic terms. Chafe (1970) uses "patient" in a sense that is akin to mine in that it includes someone or something suffering a change of state as *wood* in *He cut the wood*. However, Chafe also uses patient for someone or something in a given state as in *The wood is dry,* and I prefer entity and attribute for such cases. Object, in my sense is not semantically neutral but is someone or something (usually something, or inanimate) either suffering a change of state or simply receiving the force of an action. The object may be the name of a person or thing or a pronoun like *it* or *that*.

Of the 12 previously unreported studies of Table 9 all but Eric I and possibly Gia I appear to include at least a few instances of action and object by my classification. I should note here that I am not holding to criteria of "productivity," such as Bloom uses, but reporting simply on occurrence as such and am doing so for all this section on fragmentary data. For the studies of Table 10 there are positive reports for French, German, Korean, and Luo; in fact for all the studies making a relevant report. The case for universality of action and object in Stage I is as strong as that for agent and action.

6. *Agent and Object*. Agent and object do not constitute a grammatical relation in Chomsky and McNeill's configurational sense because there is no overt verb phrase to dominate the object. They can be made into grammatical relations by positing the deletion of verbs present in the deep structure, which is what McNeill

proposes and what Bloom does with her "reduction transformation." We should, however, consider the possibility that agent and object may themselves constitute a semantic relation. Consider a child kicking a ball or turning a key. The agent and object seem to be in direct interaction; a person initiates movement in a thing. If one does not classify qualities of movement (turning or kicking) the relation seems to be a direct one.

In Table 22, reporting quantitative data, the agent-object relation was the most marginal in the set of elementary relations; it did not turn up at all in five samples. Of the previously unreported 12 studies the agent and object relation is clearly present in only four, all studies by Bloom. It is possible that such relations occurred in some of the studies by Braine and by Miller and Ervin but nothing they say justifies that inference. Of the studies in Table 10 there are positive reports only for Zhenya, Hildegard, and the German children studied by Park. Evidently, the agent and object relation is very unlikely to be universal on present evidence. It is, however, worth noting that investigators working before Bloom established this relation for her children, by taking careful account of context, would have been less likely to notice it than to notice agent and action, action and object just because agent and object is not on the face of it a grammatical relation, and is not found in adult speech.

7. *Action and Locative (or Location)*. Locatives hardly seem to need defining. As Chafe puts it, it is the place or locus of an action as in *Tom sat in the chair*. Fillmore adds a necessary further note; the locative may mark the spatial orientation of an action as in *John walked to school*. The interesting thing about Stage I locatives is that they practically always omit the preposition (or case ending or whatever), which is obligatory in the adult language and which provides a finer encoding of the spatial relation involved. In Adam, Eve, and Sarah the prepositions most often called for but practically always missing were *in* and *on*. In Eve's first six protocols, for instance, there were 44 locatives which clearly required *on* and 33 that required *in*. We shall see in Stage II that these are the first two prepositions to be reliably supplied, and it may be that children intended the meanings before they expressed them but there is no independent evidence of that. Another possibility is that the primordial locative (without preposition) expressed something like juxtaposition in space, a meaning that comes closer to *at* than to any other preposition. Herbert Clark (1971) has made an interesting argument that *at* in the juxtaposition sense is the simplest of all locational senses.

In adult English, as in German and French and Finnish, and perhaps all languages, there are "pro" forms which can replace locative constituents of any degree of complexity. These forms, *here* and *there* in English, have also a proximal-distal semantic. Stage I locatives are either simply the names of places or one of the pro forms.

In the 12 previously unreported studies of Table 9 there is very little clear evidence of the action and locative relation. Andrew has three or four. It is possible that some are included in more generic classes listed for Christy and Susan, but the break-down of data does not enable one to tell. Kathryn II probably had them but the report of her data in Bloom (1970) is incomplete. In general, then, there is an absence of evidence for the relation in these 12 studies, which is odd because the relation appears in 11 of the 12 studies reported in Table 22. Of the studies from Table 10 there are positive reports for Hildegard, for Park's German children, and for the Luo children. In the fragmentary data then the action-locative relation seems distinctly marginal, and yet in the complete quantitative data of Table 22 it is not.

8. *Entity and Locative.* An entity being any thing (or person) having a distinct separate existence it should be clear that I am using the word only to remain semantic and avoid such as yet unjustified alternatives as subject or nominal. In entity-locative relations one can sometimes tell from the context that the omitted verb is a copula *(Lady home* for *The lady is home).* Sometimes, however, the missing verb probably names an action *(Baby table* for *Baby is eating at the table),* and in such cases the entity is an agent really. Complicating the problem further is the fact that *here* and *there* can function, and in Stage I most often do, as demonstratives of a sort; that is, they function deictically to point out the locus of a referent. We shall just have to combine all these in dealing with the fragmentary data.

The evidence for entity and locative is somewhat stronger than for action and locative. Even excluding deictic or demonstrative forms five of the 12 studies from Table 9 report instances. The demonstrative cases add another two, and in so advanced a child as Kathryn II it seems likely that the forms were simply not remarked on. For the data from Table 10 there are positive reports for Hildegard, Park's German children, Bar-Adon's Hebrew children, and Blount's Luo children.

9. *Possessor and Possession.* Possession is, for one thing, a syntactic device for producing indefinitely many names. It is interesting to think of it in relation to unmarked common nouns and to nouns marked with the definite article. Thus *chair* is the name of any instance of a certain class; *the chair* is a name for a specific instance identified by uniqueness or prior attention or entailment or any of a number of devices described in Stage II. The definite article serves to create names more specific than the class name but it is what might be called a floating temporary specifier, since any chair whatever can become *the chair* for a time, reverting to its nonspecific status as *a chair* whenever attention shifts. Possessions like *Mommy chair* or *Daddy chair* are nonfloating, permanent specifiers which name an entity more specifically than its class name can do.

The high frequency and apparent productivity of the possessive construction in child speech suggests that children are required in their behavior to distinguish between objects belonging to one person or another and objects belonging to no one in particular. Much detailed interaction in our transcripts suggests that children have primitive local notions of property and territoriality which they express with the possessive. The idea seems to be that the possessor has prior rights of use or access to his possessions, rights that supersede those of any other member of the family. This appeared most dramatically in our materials when Adam warned Ursula Bellugi, who was about to sit in Daddy's chair: *No, no Daddy chair, home soon.*

What has been said above about the meaning of possession applies really to "alienable" possession. "Alienable" possessives are much more common in Stage I speech than "inalienable" possessives but some of the latter do occur *(Dog tail* and *Mommy nose).* To say that these express "prior rights of access" would be pretty strained. They are better described as a different semantic altogether, as a permanent part-whole relationship. No doubt there is similarity in the two meanings to account historically for the fact that both are expressed by the genitive constructions, either the *dog's tail* or *the tail of the dog.* However, property + territory and part-whole by no means exhaust the meanings carried by the genitive construction in English and many other languages. The extremely important fact is that of the various genitive meanings Stage I children seem only to express possession in either the property or part-whole sense. Park calls explicit attention to this fact with respect to German. His children did not use such genitives as *die Entdeckung Americas* or *die Haupstadt Deutschlands.* But exactly the same can be said of American children and the English genitive. We certainly do not find *the discovery of America* or *America's discovery* or *the capital of Germany* or *Germany's capital* or such others *as the ship's captain.* In all the languages studied, the genitive construction seems to be limited in use at Stage I to the possessive and part-whole senses.

The productive acquisition of a syntactic construction seldom at first entails using it over the full semantic range to which it applies, but this is a fact easily overlooked; it requires careful detailed observation for the adult speaker to notice it. In Stage II we shall see that, for instance, the first past-tense verbs are limited to the immediate past and future forms to present intentions and imminent actions. We shall find the prepositions *in* and *on* limited to their spatial senses, and not applied in such abstract senses as *an idea in the air* or *a train on time.* Indeed all prepositions are at first used in only a narrow part of their full semantic range, generally in their spatial relationship or part-whole senses. Adjectives like *big, little, warm, cool,* and the like are used in their physicalistic senses before they are applied to personalities. Evidently, then, semantic meanings are not all on an even keel in being available to a child when he uses an adequate expression or even before. This is a subject that will, I feel sure, reward careful investigation.

In Chomsky (1958, though not in Chomsky 1969), genitives *(Mother's chair)* are derived from simple sentences with the verb *have (Mother has a chair).* "Alienable" possessives are generated in much the same way in Fillmore's case grammar but "inalienable" genitives are generated differently. There is nothing in Stage I speech to suggest the "alienable-inalienable" distinction in Fillmore's grammar. There is also nothing to support the early Chomskyan derivation from *have* sentences. On the contrary genitives precede such sentences and, throughout Stage I, *have* sentences are infrequent. If the usual transformational derivations of attributives and genitives are assumed to hold for the *A* and *G* constituents in Stage I speech then the sentences containing these constituents are not "simple" sentences but are complex sentences, with one simple sentence being embedded in another. These would be the only "embeddings" in Stage I and almost the only embeddings until Stages IV and V. There is reason, therefore, to doubt that the derivations apply and to seek some other derivation that will leave intact the generalization that Stage I sentences are all simple sentences.

Of the 12 previously unreported studies of Table 9, ten contained at least one possessive, often many. Only Eric I and Eric III seemed to lack them, and the one recorded for Eric II belonged to a small residual set not generated by Bloom's proposed grammar for this sample. For the samples of Table 10, Leopold tells us that Hildegard used possessives from the age of 1;7, and there are attested examples for French, Park's study of German, for the Hebrew of Gil and Gila, for Susin's Korean, for Luo, and for Zhenya's Russian. In fact, for all studies making any relevant report. The case for the universal availability of the possessor and possession relation in Stage I is then among the strongest, ranking with agent and action, action and object, and nomination.

10. *Entity and Attribute.* This construction serves to specify some attribute of an entity which could not be known from the class characteristics of the entity alone: *little dog, hot pepper, yellow block.* In English and some other languages either order is likely to be heard, since the model language includes both the prenominal adjective *(Yellow block)* and the predicate adjective *(The block is yellow).* As with genitives there is a familiar transformational derivation (the prenominal from the predicate adjective) which would make the prenominal form an embedded sentence. As in the case of the genitive the child speech data do not support this derivation in any way, the prenominal position being generally the earlier and more common one. Attribution can also be expressed by two nouns in many languages. In English a construction like *Mommy doll,* meaning the doll that is a mommy, and not the doll that belongs to mommy, is a sort of attributive. Some authors call the attributive noun a noun adjunct. It is also worth noting that entity and attribute like possessor and possession may be viewed as a syntactically productive device for creating new names, more specific than the class name alone.

For the previously unreported studies of Table 9, ten of 12 include instances of entity and attribute. The exceptions are Eric I and Gia I and, in Eric II there is only a single instance. For the studies of Table 10 there are positive reports from Park's study of German children, for Bar-Adon's study of Hebrew children, for Park's study of Susin's Korean, for Blount's study of Luo children, and for Zhenya. The total picture is almost exactly the same as for possession, which is perhaps not surprising, since possession can be regarded as one variety of attribution, and so entity-and-attribute is among the most reliably reported meanings for Stage I children.

11. *Demonstrative and Entity.* The nature of this relationship has already been defined under nomination and the results presented there.

In connection with the report of full quantitative data in the previous section

I mentioned that there are another seven elementary relations (affected person as in *Adam see,* dative of indirect object as in *Gimme book,* complement as in *Sing song*) that appear in some Stage I samples but less reliably than any of the eight relations and three operations of reference. I shall make no attempt to define all these and trace their occasional occurrences in the fragmentary data. In the full quantitative data we have not only reported on the frequencies of the minimal relations but also on the frequencies of all the combinations in which they occur. For the fragmentary data, I shall not attempt this. There is one impression worth recording, however. Between Kendall I (MLU of 1.10) and Seppo I (MLU of 1.42) there is a considerable developmental jump. The second half of Stage I is much better represented in the quantitative data than the first half. From my study of the fragmentary data of children falling in this interval it is clear that expressions involving more than a minimal two-term relation increase very slowly from the 0 percent at Kendall I to the 7 percent at Seppo I and that the types are just those found in Tables 22 and 23.

In general conclusion the fragmentary data, poor as they are, support the notion that a rather small set of operations and relations describe all the meanings expressed in multi-morphemic utterances of Stage I children, whatever the language they are learning. It is not known whether these are the only compositional meanings children at this level of development are able to express or whether they are simply the meanings children are interested in. As a final note it is interesting to recall from the Introduction that when Beatrice and Allen Gardner (1971) analyzed the two-sign sequences of their chimpanzee, Washoe, in terms of the semantic intentions suggested by the situation a set of operations and relations almost identical with ours accounted for 78 percent of the total.

Sensori-motor Intelligence and the Meanings of Stage I

Linguists and psycholinguists when they discover facts that are at all general have, nowadays, a tendency to predict that they will prove to be universal and must, "therefore," be considered innate. The Stage I meanings have proved to have some generality in a sampling of child speech studies, and I do feel tempted to hypothesize universality. But not innateness. Not innateness because, though I have not worked out the relation in any detail, it is my impression that the first meanings are an extension of the kind of intelligence that Jean Piaget calls sensorimotor. And Piaget has shown that sensorimotor intelligence develops out of the infant's commerce with objects and persons during the first 18–24 months of life.

Piaget's research on the sensorimotor period, much of it involving observation of his own children, was done over 30 years ago. The greater part of it is reported in three books: *The Origins of Intelligence in Children* (1936); *The Construction of Reality in the Child* (1937); *Play, Dreams, and Imitation* (1945). *Origins* is concerned with very general characteristics of adaptive behavior, especially of the primary, secondary, and tertiary circular reflexes. It begins with the neonate's uncoordinated simple reflexes and ends, six stages later, with the advent of mental trial-and-error. *Construction* is a detailed account of the elaboration in infancy of the spatial and temporal fields, the first intuitions of causality, and the development of a conception of independent and enduring objects. The topics of the third book are given in the title. The three books together provide an immensely rich account of a development in many dimensions and across six stages of an essentially practical intelligence that is acted out rather than thought. The period ends (at 18 to 24 months) when the child becomes able mentally to represent reality, and so able to operate with symbols and commence the learning of language. Where should the meanings of the first linguistic constructions come from if not from the sensorimotor intelligence which directly precedes them?

Let us consider some of the intellectual prerequisites of Stage I meanings. Nomination and recurrence both presume the ability to recognize objects and actions. Nonexistence presumes the ability to anticipate objects and actions from various naturally occurring signs and also to notice when such anticipations of appearance or existence are not confirmed. The location question for objects nonexistent in the perceptual field, the question which in English takes the form *Where N?* or *Where N go?* seems to presuppose a world of enduring objects which are not "unmade" when they go out of sight but are simply displaced to new locations. Recognition, anticipation based on signs, the concept of the enduring object, awareness of a single space that contains the self as well as other objects, are all developed in the period of sensorimotor intelligence.

As acquisitions of the third stage, for instance, Piaget describes two processes which seem like primitive forms of nomination and recurrence. When the child, in the third stage (about 4 to 8 months), sees a familiar object, such as a rattle or a toy, he sometimes performs, in reduced and abbreviated form, the action schema most habitually associated with the recognized object. This "recognitory assimilation" or "motor recognition" is something like nomination which also evidences recognition by means of an action, an action of articulation, having no nonsocial instrumental utility. There is of course the large difference that names are associated with objects by social convention rather than by the accommodation of reflexes.

It is the third-stage infant, also, who develops what Piaget calls "procedures for making interesting sights last." The child of the second stage has developed the "primary circular reaction," which is a repetition of movements of his own body that were initially performed accidentally. Interest focuses on the movement rather than on its effects on the milieu. The third-stage child develops an interest in external effects and, when he accidentally produces an interesting one, he repeats the movement in an effort to cause the effect to recur. This procedure is tried even for spectacles at a distance over which the child's movements have no direct causal control. The recurrence construction, used to request rather than to comment, is a kind of generalized and socially efficacious "procedure for making interesting sights last." One notices also that the early linguistic expression of recurrence marks no distinction between successive appearances of one entity and successive appearances of several instances of one class. Piaget found the same difference disregarded by the sensori-motor child, for example, on an early-morning walk along a country road when the child said "There's the slug again" every time child and father came across another slug.

The productive, freely combinatorial, use of agent, action, and object constructions would seem, minimally, to presume the ability to distinguish an action from the object of the action and the self from other persons and objects. Piaget judges that mental life begins with an undifferentiated world in which none of these distinctions is made. The Stage I infant's reflexes are exercised on objects but not clearly distinguished from them. The object begins to emerge as an independent entity only when it becomes coordinated with multiple action schemas. Piaget's description of the time when each thing is conceived by the child in terms of the schemas into which it can enter — as "graspable," "suckable," "scratchable," and so on — is irresistibly suggestive of the development of lexical entries for nouns and verbs which describe the combinations into which they can enter. Which is not to say that the sensorimotor process is linguistic but rather that the linguistic process does not start from nothing and can build on data that are not linguistic. I remember in this connection the time when Eve said of herself *Eat sweater*. Certainly she had not heard sentences which would indicate that the word *sweater* should be marked "+ edible." But in her experience of sweaters she had undoubtedly discovered that they could be put in the mouth and chewed even if not ingested, and that is what she was doing when she spoke.

Agent, object, datives of indirect object, and person affected constructions if they are used in a freely combinatorial way, with the names of referents playing one role on one occasion and another on another, presuppose the knowledge that the self, other persons, and objects are all potentially "sources of causality" or initiators of forces and also, potentially, recipients of forces. Piaget judges this knowledge to be entirely lacking in the early sensori-motor stages. One can see that it has begun to evolve when the child tries to move the hand of an adult to set off some skilled action beyond his own agentive capacity. But a reasonably objective sense of causality does not evolve until the fifth stage.

In sum, I think that the first sentences express the construction of reality which is the terminal achievement of sensori-motor intelligence. What has been acquired on the plane of motor intelligence (the permanence of form and substance of immediate objects) and the structure of immediate space and time does not need to be formed all over again on the plane of representation. Representation starts with just those meanings that are most available to it, propositions about action schemas involving agents and objects, assertions of nonexistence, recurrence, location, and so on. But representation carries intelligence beyond the sensori-motor. Representation is a new level of operation which quickly moves to meanings that go beyond immediate space and practical action.

In suggesting that the meanings of the constructions of Stage I derive from sensorimotor intelligence, in Piaget's sense, I mean also to suggest that these meanings probably are universal in humankind but not that they are innate. I mean, in addition, to suggest the possibility that these meanings probably are not *exclusively* human even as sensorimotor intelligence is not. Both David Premack (1970) and the Gardners (1969) believe that the considerable success they have had in communicating with chimpanzees is dependent upon and starts with the fact that the chimpanzee as a species has a sensorimotor world much the same as man's.

Finally let me make it clear that this section concerns meanings, and not grammatical relations. The two are easily confused because terms like agent and object and locative and genitive have been used for both. I do not mean to say that such grammatical relations as subject of the sentence, object of the predicate, and so on, defined as Chomsky (1965) defines them, are a part of sensorimotor intelligence, and so learned rather than innate. The formal relations which express semantic relations are peculiarly linguistic, and I see nothing quite like them in sensori-motor intelligence. It is, however, beyond me, to figure out any way of testing whether the grammatical relations are innate or learned.

A Grammar for Late Stage I English

We are about to look at some of our data for the third time and to classify it in a way that is not quite the same as any used heretofore. This can hardly be welcome news to the reader, coming on so late a page, but there are new things to be learned from attempting to write a portion of a formal generative grammar. I began this chapter with the recent history of attempts to capture the linguistic knowledge of the Stage I child, and these attempts here progressed, for good reasons, from very "lean" nonsemantic interpretations to increasingly semantic ones. Portions of the data of one child or another were initially introduced to illustrate conceptions of telegraphic speech, pivot grammar, case grammar, and so on. The data were analyzed a second time, some quantitatively and the rest qualitatively, in purely semantic terms. And in these terms quite striking regularities of development became apparent. In arguing for the virtue of semantic analysis of multi-morphemic utterances it has never been my intention to deny the equal importance of analysis of form, of the means of expression. Indeed certain generalizations and problems emerge from this sort of analysis that the semantic analysis did not catch.

The plan is to present some of the major facts that would have to be represented in a generative grammar and to consider the advantages and disadvantages of representing them in terms of Schlesinger's kind of scheme, in terms of a Chomsky (1965) grammar such as Bloom (1970) has written and in terms of Fillmore's grammar as it stood in 1968. We shall only consider the data of Eve I, Sarah I, and Adam I, and will treat these three samples, which have many things in common, as a single corpus of 2,139 utterances. Since all three of these samples fall in the latter half of Stage I, we shall be concerned with selected problems in the grammar of late Stage I English. We know from Tables 22 and 23 that the late Stage I English samples have much in common semantically with those for Sipili and Tofi (Samoan), Seppo and Rina (Finnish), and Pepe (Spanish). In addition, Kernan (1969) has written case-type grammars for the Samoan children, and Bowerman (in press) has written both case-type and Bloom-type grammars for her Finnish children. The problems are remarkably similar to those that arise from English-speaking American children but we have not all chosen to focus our attention on just the same things.

My goal will not be a complete grammar because, having tried that years ago, I know it cannot be done from just a corpus of speech produced, however large the corpus. That effort takes one into endless distributional detail of doubtful generality, and never sufficiently complete. I will, however, give a couple of examples of this sort of detail, detail that would be considered in a full grammar if only so that you will be glad I do not propose to go further. What I have done is to distill out what seem to be the most reliable and potentially instructive facts about Stage I grammar and attempt several kinds of formalization of these. Attempting various sorts of generative grammar when we know in advance that none can be definitely established on present evidence is obviously not worthwhile because of any grammar that will be produced but rather because the degree of explicitness in generative grammar forces a kind of close analysis that exposes interesting and potentially answerable questions that are likely to go unexposed when a less demanding goal is set and a more casual analysis undertaken.

Facts to be Represented

How does one enable a reader to participate in the representation problem? It might appear that the problem — 2,139 utterances with contexts — should be set before him in raw unprocessed form. That would be maximally fair but totally useless because it would take many months to absorb the kinds of details a formal representation has to cope with. It follows that the utterances have to be reduced to some kind of graspable typological form. But to what form? We have typologized the facts, in purely semantic terms, in Tables 22, 23, and 24, and will need that information. But much more is needed to write even a part of a grammar, for instance, word order. Also since we are now limiting our problem to late Stage I English, we want to include semantic relations like the dative of indirect object *(Give doggie bone)* and the person affected and stimulus (as in *I hear horn*) as well as other constructions which appeared in the English samples but were not reliably found in all the other languages. Any useful typology must to some extent *impose* a grammatical description on the data but, since our purpose is to explore different possible descriptions, the one imposed should be as neutral and generally agreed upon as possible, and still it will be necessary to remember that the classification is only provisional and really requires to be proved appropriate to child speech.

Table 27.   The types of construction in late Stage I English[a]

General Type of Construction	Subtypes
Major modalities except declarative	*Yes-no* question as rising intonation on one or more words
	Imperative as subjectless verb or verb with *you*
	Negative as *no* or *not* alone or with other words
Main-verb sentences	Agent-action-dative-object-locative
	Person affected-state-stimulus
Missing copula sentences	Demonstrative-entity
	Entity-locative
	Entity-attributive
Noun phrases	Attributive-entity (includes Recurrence)
	Possessor-possessed
Information requests resembling *wh-* questions	*Who 'at?*
	Where entity (*go*)?

[a]Parentheses indicate optionality. They are not used wherever they apply but only on the last child sentence.

What I have decided to do is to recognize that whatever else one may say of child English it is moving toward the adult form of the language, and most child utterances are identifiable as imperfect versions of one or another type of adult English sentence or constituent. There are some sentence and constituent types that any grammar of adult English that I have ever read finds it necessary to take account of, and I consider classification on this level maximally "uncommitted" to any particular formalism. These, then, are the major types of construction listed in Table 27. To name the terms in these constructions I have used the semantic terms of Tables 22 and 23 even where these are clumsy ("entity" for what seem always to be nominals), and even where I have had to make up some clumsy terms like "person affected" and "stimulus" for sentences like *I hear horn* which *may* involve subjects and objects, grammatical concepts, but which certainly are not agents and objects in the semantic sense. In a few cases particular words could be used because the constructions in question were inflexible in always using just those words. Finally, it is essential to know that in Table 27, as was not the case in Tables 22 and 23, the order of the terms is as they appeared practically always in the samples. That is important because word order seems to be the major syntactic mechanism controlled in Stage I English.

   1. *The Principal Constructions.* These appear in Table 27, and only a few comments need be made. Sentences may be declarative, interrogative, imperative, or negative. In late Stage I there is reason to believe that children had at least rudimentary understanding of the differences among the four. They also controlled simple means of expressing the modalities, and these are described in Table 27.

   In the grammar of adult English there is a deep cut between main verb sentences and sentences with the copular verb *be.* The copula takes predicate adjectives *(John is happy),* while main verbs do not. Predicate nominals in copular sentences are made to agree in number with subject nominals; subject and object nominals in main verb sentences are not made to agree in number. Copular sentences have three sorts of predicate complement: nominals, adjectives, and locatives. The sentences are described by the following representation:

$$NP - Tn - be \quad \begin{Bmatrix} Adj \\ NP \\ Loc \end{Bmatrix}$$

The children in Stage I had the three kinds of copular sentences except that tense *(Tn)* and *be* were not expressed, and the only kind of subject *NP* occurring with predicate nominatives was the demonstrative pronoun.

The representation of agent-action main verb sentences in Table 27 does not correspond with any actually obtained sentences, since none contained five major constituents. What we have is a representation of all the major constituents that *ever* occurred in the order of their appearance in sentences; we will call this the agent-action implicit paradigm. The actual sentences typically contain only two or three major constituents. These pairs and triplets varied in the particular constituents they put together but all constituents were drawn from the set of five in Table 27 and preserved the order of Table 27. So the abstract description there represents a kind of pattern *implicit* in what was obtained but more complex than anything obtained. Constructions with a "person affected" subject and a "state" verb were much less numerous than agent-action constructions; the paradigm is simpler and was in fact concretely realized in quite a few sentences.

Besides the two main kinds of sentences there were constructions which, as they appeared, are not sentences at all but, from the adult point-of-view, only noun phrases *(NP)*. These encoded the meanings possessive, attributive, locative, and recurrence. In Table 27 recurrence expressions are included under attributives.

Finally, all three children had forms for asking the name of a referent, and these are represented by Adam's *Who 'at?* Adam and Sarah also had forms asking for the location of a referent which combined a *NP* naming an entity with *where;* the verb *go* being optional. Eve did not produce this kind of question until II.

2. *Sampling of the Main Verb Paradigm.* Table 28 breaks up the implicit paradigm of Table 27, agent-action-dative-object-locative, into just those different types of "fragments" that actually occurred. From five constituents with a fixed order it is possible to create ten different kinds of constituent pairs. Of these ten kinds we see, from Table 28, that six actually occurred. In judging whether this is a sufficiently complete sampling to justify the conclusion that the five-constituent pattern of Table 27 is, in some sense, the underlying reality it helps to know that "datives of indirect objects," had, in general, a very low frequency at Stage I. However, this need not mean that control of indirect objects was marginal at I for the reason that only a small subclass of verbs can take the indirect object (for example, *give* and *show*), and so the frequencies are always low, in adult speech as well

Table 28.   Constituent combinations that occur and constituents that are omitted from the main verb paradigm

Ordered Constituents Present	Constituents Omitted	Example
Agent-action-dative-object-locative	None	*Mother gave John lunch in the kitchen.* (non-occurring)
Agent-action	Object	*Mommy fix.* (Eve I)
Agent-object	Action	*Mommy pumpkin.* (Eve I; *is cutting a*)
Agent-locative	Action	*Baby table.* (Eve I; *is eating at a*)
Action-dative	Agent, object	*Give doggie.* (Adam I; *you give it to*)
Action-object	Agent	*Hit ball.* (Adam I; *I*)
	Agent, locative	*Put light.* (Adam I; *I, there*)
Action-locative	Agent-object	*Put floor.* (Adam I; *I, it*)
Agent-action-object	None	*I ride horsie.* (Sarah I)
Agent-action-locative	None	*Tractor go floor.* (Adam I)
Action-dative-object	Agent	*Give doggie paper.* (Adam I)
Action-object-locative	Agent	*Put truck window.* (Adam I)
Agent-action-object-locative	None	*Adam put it box.* (Adam I)

as child speech. The children's protocols are only samples, and sampling problems have to be considered. Since the base frequency of datives was low, the chances of obtaining the various possible constituent pairs which included the dative would be extremely low in any 2,139-utterance sample. There is, therefore, some reason to set aside those of the possible combinations that include a dative, and when that is done there are only seven possible pairs, and six of these occur.

There are ten possible constituent triplets if the dative is included, and of these four actually occurred. With the dative left out there are just six possible triplets and four occur, though one includes a dative. Of quadruplets there is only one (in Adam I), and the full set of five constituents never occurred. What these results suggest is that the five-constituent pattern of Table 27 is indeed implicit in the sentences at Stage I because these sentences are a very liberal sampling of the implied pairs and triplets. However, there may also be some kind of a complexity limitation which prevents the realization of the full pattern or even, except for one sentence, of four constituents from that pattern. Another possibility, one that would make a complexity limitation no problem, is that the world of the Stage I child at home with mother is such that the needs of communication seldom require as many as four or five constituents. The familiar setting, the shared memories, the tendency to be concerned only with the present go far toward making speech redundant.

There is, sometimes, reason to believe that a single-word utterance is functioning as a fragment of the agent-action paradigm, as, in short, an agent or an object or whatever. Assigning interpretations to single words is, we know, an even more uncertain undertaking than assigning them to short sequences, since there is no word order to offer guidance. However, reference context or a parental gloss or something about the sequence of the child's utterances does occasionally suggest an interpretation for the single-word utterance. For instance, Adam once said *Ball* and then *Hit ball,* and that suggests that the first utterance was an object. Another time Adam said *Kitty* and then *Ride bulldozer* and then *Get in kitty* which may mean that the initial *Kitty* was an agent. Using this kind of undeniably weak evidence I find instances of single words in every role except the dative. Assigning relational roles to single-word utterances that occur in late Stage I is not quite the same as doing so for one-word utterances that occur before Stage I at a time when no multi-word utterances occur at all. In this latter case there is less ground for assigning such meanings, but once multi-word utterances begin to occur and the ordering of words gives evidence of relational semantic intentions it seems reasonable to extend the method of "rich interpretation" to the single-word utterances that occur.

For main-verb sentences with person affected subjects and state verbs, the occurring types are: person affected–state; person affected–stimulus; state-stimulus; person affected–state–stimulus. In short all possible pairs and triplets fitting three constituents in a fixed order, including the full pattern which is explicit in this case rather than implicit. There are also single-word utterances which seem to play each of the sentence roles.

3. *What is Missing.* The fact that in agent-action there is some kind of control of five ordered constituents but that most obtained sentences contain only two or three suggests that one or more constituents must usually be omitted. It is not, of course, the case that every sentence the child produces could, from the point of view of adult grammar, contain all five constituents. Intransitive verbs *(walk* in *Adam walk)* may not take objects. Most verbs *(put, eat, fix,* and so on) may not take datives. Even where a child's sentence could take a given constituent which is not present in the surface form one must judge in certain cases that the constituent is not obligatory in adult speech. Imperatives, for instance, may have *you* as the subject of the surface form but *you* may be omitted. A sentence like *Mommy is cutting a pumpkin* could add a locative *(in the kitchen)* but need not. When all the above are set aside we still have certain sentences for which the adult grammar requires a constituent that the child fails to produce. Some transitive verbs obligatorily take objects, and so one may fairly judge that, in a sentence like *Mommy fix,* the object has been omitted. Nonimperative sentences must have subjects, and when there is none and the verb names an action requiring an agent, one may fairly judge that the agent has been omitted (as in *Hit ball* when Adam was in fact the agent). A few verbs (only *put* in the Stage I samples) obligatorily take locatives as well as agents, and so one may judge that in a sentence like *Put light* a locative has been omitted. Then there are sentences that lack obligatory constituents only on the assumption that the context-guided interpretation is the correct interpretation. When the child says *Mommy pumpkin* if the agent-object interpretation of Table 28 is correct then an obligatory verb is missing. When the child says *Baby table* if the agent-locative interpretation of Table 28 is correct, then once again an obligatory verb is missing.

If the interpretations of the foregoing $N + N$ utterances were incorrect, and the child intended them as, for instance, genitives, then the assumption that obligatory constituents were lacking would be a mistake.

The judgment that a given constituent is missing is partly guided by knowledge of what is obligatory in adult grammar and partly by interpretations of child utterances based on the reference context. There is one other kind of evidence: the "replacement sequence." Braine (1971), whose term this is, defines the replacement sequence as a set of child utterances such that: "(a) the utterances of the set occur during a fairly short time period during which there is no detectable change in the eliciting situation (i.e., nothing happens in the environment to indicate that the utterances are not equivalent in meaning), and (b) the longer utterances of the sequence contain the lexical morphemes of the shorter utterances". One of his examples is: *Stand up # Cat stand up # Cat stand up table.* From such a sequence one might judge that the initial and shortest utterance was an action with both agent and locative missing. Replacement sequences also occurred in Adam, Eve, and Sarah, at I. For example:

1. Eve. *Have it?*
   Eve. *Papa have it?*
2. Sarah. *Want potty.*
   Sarah. *Potty.*

The first set is evidence that an agent may be omitted and the second that a state verb may be omitted. Others will be cited where they are relevant. Braine called such sets "replacement sequences" because over longer time periods one always finds that the simpler version, the elliptical sentence, appears earlier in development than the longer version and that, after a period of coexistence, the longer generally *replaces* the shorter.

Table 28 lists all the different constituents that are sometimes missing in agent-action sentences; they are: agent, action, object, and locative. Indeed, *every* constituent, except the dative, is sometimes missing in contexts where it is obligatory. Probably the dative is only absent from this list for sampling reasons, and the correct generalization may be: any of the major constituents may be omitted. This is an important generalization to the interpretation of which we shall return near the end of the chapter.

Main verb sentences with person affected subjects operate just like those with agent subjects with respect to missing constituents. Every constituent is sometimes missing. The stimulus (though not obligatory) from *I see* in Eve I; the person affected from *Want bibby* (Eve I) and *Hear tractor* (Adam I) and many others; the state from *Mommy celery* (Eve I), which should have included *wants*.

Major constituents are not functors; they are all expressed in Stage I speech by nouns or verbs. So it is not the omission of major constituents that accounts for what has been called the telegraphic aspect of speech. The sentences of Table 28 all also omit functors. *Mommy fix* in adult speech would be *Mommy fixes* or *Mommy is fixing; Baby table* not only leaves out *eat* but *is eating at a; Give doggie* leaves out *to the* as well as an object. The functors missing from contexts in which they are obligatory include, at Stage I: inflections of the verb and noun, articles, prepositions, and auxiliary verbs.

4. *Constituents Present and Missing for Copular Sentences and Noun Phrases.* For copula-type sentences that are just two-words long, if a constituent is missing we have the one-word utterance, and that is always hard to interpret. On one occasion Eve said *Light* and then, immediately, *That light,* and so we might judge that the first *Light* was a fragment of a copula-type demonstrative-entity with the demonstrative pronoun missing. There are also instances of this sort in which an entity (or nominal subject) appears with an attributive adjective missing and in which a locative occurs without its nominal subject. With three kinds of two-word copula sentences there are six possible one-word fragments; of these three occur. With possessives and attributives the only clear one-word fragments are all possessors (without possesseds) found in Eve I. For instance:

> Mother.   *Eve's soup is cool.*
> Eve.   *Mommy cool.*
> Mother.   *No, Mommy's is hot.*

There is a model for this truncated possessive in adult speech and Eve, in her use of it, lacks only the inflection.

There is another question about attributives and possessives: whether they themselves are fragments of larger constructions. At the more mature end of Stage I those noun phrases which have occurred frequently as independent utterances begin to appear as agents, objects, locatives, entities, and so on. They are the elaborated noun phrases which constitute one of the major advances occurring in Stage I. Since they sometimes occur as constituents of larger constructions, we must ask whether in some of their occurrences as independent utterances they ought to be regarded as fragments of such larger constructions. And it does sometimes seem as if they should be. For instance:

> 1. Mother. *What's that?*   Adam. *Adam hat.*
> 2. Mother. *What is that?*   Adam. *Big house.*
> 3. Adam. *I sit chair.*   Adam. *Daddy chair.*
> 4. Eve.   *More cracker.*   Mother. *You want more cracker?*

In 1 and 2 above, the possessives standing alone might be analyzed as demonstrative-entity constructions with *that* missing. In 3 the possessive alone might be analyzed as a locative with agent and action missing, and in 4 the attributive alone as an object with person-affected and state missing.

Table 29.   Examples of elaborated noun phrases as constituents

Construction	Possessives		Attributive	
Agent in agent-action	Sarah.	*My tail all-gone.*[a]	Sarah.	*More tail gone.*
Object in action-object	Adam.	*Daddy suitcase go-get-it.*[a]		
Locative in action-locative	Adam.	*Sit Adam chair.*		
Stimulus in state-stimulus	Adam.	*See Daddy car.*	Eve.	*Want more grapejuice.*
Locative in state-locative	Adam.	*Like Adam bookshelf.*		
Entity in entity-attributive	Adam.	*Dirty my hands.*[b]		
Entity in demonstrative-entity	Eve.	*That Mommy soup.*	Sarah.	*More tree there.*
Object in agent-action-object				
Agent in agent-action-locative			Adam.	*There go 'nother one.*[b]

[a]Words connected by hyphens are to be regarded as a single word.
[b]Word order is other than the most usual.

Since attributives and possessives are sometimes explicitly constituents of larger constructions and since there is sometimes contextual evidence that they ought to be analyzed as constituent fragments, one must consider the possibility that all possessives and attributives standing alone should be regarded as constituent fragments even though there is usually no clear contextual evidence. And even a more general possibility — that all utterances which as surface forms are not complete sentences, just as possessives and attributives are not, should be regarded as constituent fragments of complete sentences from which other constituents are missing. We have seen that some $N + N$ utterances seem to be such fragments, and so do some single-word utterances. Perhaps all are really and so perhaps all utterances are derived from implicit complete sentences. This broaches one of the more difficult and fundamental of the problems presented by Stage I speech, and we will return to it in connection with the several possible forms of grammatical representation.

5. *The Elaborated Noun Phrase.* Table 29 provides examples of noun phrases in all the constituent roles they filled for Adam, Eve, and Sarah at I. Most of the noun phrases occur in what would be the predicates of the sentences if the sentences were in adult form; as object locatives or predicate nominatives. Of predicate noun phrase possibilities only the dative fails to be elaborated. There are just a few sentences in which the elaborated noun phrase appears as, what would be from the adult point of view, the subject, either agent or entity. Beyond Stage I there is much greater elaboration of noun phrases in the predicate than in the subject which is something Bloom also found in her children. The beginnings of that difference appear in Stage I.

The noun phrases themselves are almost all possessives or expressions of recurrence (usually with *more*). These latter are here called attributives. There were only two instances of attributives other than these expressing recurrence, and these were both marked for doubtful transcription.

Examples of Detail that will not be Represented

1. *Pronouns*. While there is some variation of detail across children in the use of pronouns, all three children employed *I, you, it* (or *that*), and *my* in the following ways: *I* and *you* as agent or person affected; *it* or *that* as object of action or as stimulus; *my* as possessor. All of these semantic roles are also noun or noun-phrase roles, and so it is clear that pronouns in child speech, as in adult speech, are a kind of noun. A complete Stage I grammar could not, however, simply enter *I, you, it,* and *my* into its lexicon as nouns. Pronouns would have to be marked as a subclass distinct from nouns for the reason that they may not become head words in either attributive or possessive *NP*'s; one may say *More juice* or *Daddy chair* but not *More I* or *Daddy it*. Among pronouns further differentiation would be necessary because *I* and *you* function as grammatical subjects (agent or person affected), while *it* is an object and *my* is a possessor. The distributional pattern here parallels the animate-inanimate pattern for *NP*'s in Stage I speech; animate *NP*'s function as agent, person affected, or possessor, and so are like *I, you,* and *my* whereas inanimate *NP*'s function as objects, and so are like *it* or *that*. If, in a Stage I grammar, nouns were to be marked as "+animate" or "−animate" the same marker might be used for pronouns. (See Bowerman, in press, and Bloom, 1970, for a discussion of animate-inanimate markers.)

Even subclassification into pronouns, animate and inanimate, would not be delicate enough to capture the distributional distinctions among *I, you, my,* and *it*. Among the animate pronouns *(I, you,* and *my)* only *my* may be a possessor. *I* and *you* differ in that *you*, but not *I*, sometimes functions as agent in sentences which are marked in our transcriptions as definitely "imperative." Then there are a few sentences which would motivate classifying *it* and *you* together; *it* is occasionally a grammatical subject though usually an object and *you* occasionally an object though usually a subject. The pronoun *my* is sometimes used by Adam (and by other children in Stage I) as a grammatical subject. And so on. Syntactic markers and selection rules which would capture just the distributional distinctions observed among pronouns in Stage I would be complex and inelegant, and one could not be sure how much of the complexity and inelegance was a result of sampling limitations.

The Stage I pronouns do not constitute any kind of a natural subclass (or sub-classes) of the class of English pronouns. The full set of English pronouns subdivides on such bases as the following: personal-impersonal *(he* and *it)*; singular-plural *(this* and *these, he* and *they)*; masculine-feminine *(he* and *she)*; first, second, and third person *(I, you,* and *he)*; nominative-accusative-genitive *(I, me, my)*. If we use just these features to subclassify *I, you, it,* and *my* we need the contrasts personal-impersonal; nominative-genitive; first, second, and third person. In short, more features than pronouns. Notice how radically wrong this outcome is for McNeill's theory that word classes develop by differentiation.

The Stage I pronouns do closely parallel Stage I nouns. As *I* and *you* are common pronoun subjects so are *Adam* (or *Eve* or *Sarah*) and *Mommy* common noun subjects, and the prominence of *my* among genitives is matched by *Adam* (or *Eve* or *Sarah*) though *your* does not appear as a match for *Mommy*(s). The prominence of *it* and *that* as objects is matched by inanimate *NP* objects. In the child's discourse one finds instances of pronoun substitution which show that the pronouns are linked to appropriate *NP* antecedents. For example:

> 1. *Adam write.*
>   *I write.*
> 2. *Hit ball.*
>   *Hit it.*
> 3. *Mommy read.*
>   *You read.*

It seems then that the selection of pronouns to be learned at I is governed by the selection of *NP's* at that stage rather than by the structure of pronominal paradigms in English grammar.

2. *Separable Verbs.* There are in English numerous verb + particle constructions such as *pick up, put on, bring in.* These constructions, usually called "separable verbs," accept *NP*'s after the particle *(He picks up his coat)* or between the verb and particle *(He picks his coat up).* They accept pronouns in internal position only; *he picks it up* but not *he picks up it.* Chomsky in 1957 proposed generating verb + particle constructions by a phrase structure rule, "$V \rightarrow V_1 + Prt$" along with supplementary rules indicating which V_1 can go with which *Prt.* Rules of this order would produce strings in which *NP* follows V_1 and *Prt.* To generate strings in which the *NP* occupies the internal position, between V_1 and *Prt,* Chomsky (1957) proposed an optional transformation interchanging *NP* and *Prt.* By this derivation sentences with *NP* in internal position are derivationally more "complex" than sentences with *NP* following the particle.

Separable verbs can be found in Stage I speech; there are four of them, for instance, in Adam's sample. In all instances the *NP* is in internal position. This means that the derivationally more complex sentence appears before the derivationally less complex sentence. Perhaps this should be interpreted as an exception to the law of cumulative complexity or perhaps it just indicates that the Chomsky 1957 derivation is not the correct one for separable verbs at Stage I. Since *NP* always follows *V* and precedes *Prt,* it would be possible to group *Prt* with locatives as a constituent following the object *NP* with certain verbs. On the other hand, it is possible to regard the absence of the derivationally simpler sentences, with *NP* following *Prt,* as a fact about performance rather than competence as a "sampling" phenomenon resulting from the higher frequency in performance of the more complex sentence.

3. *Schwa.* The unstressed mid-vowel occurs in pre-nominal position in both Sarah I and Eve I, and according to context variously suggests *a, the, that,* and *want.*

In Sarah there is phonetic variation between [ə] and [æ], and it appears to be conditioned by the form of the parental question eliciting a vowel + noun answer. The frequencies look like this:

	What's this?	*What's that?*
[æ] + noun	2	9
[ə] + noun	10	3

This conditioned variation appears to be a rule of discourse that cannot be included in a grammar, but the fact that it exists makes it very difficult to settle on the correct representation of the prenominal mid-vowel in the grammar.

4. *Animate and Inanimate.* There is a strong tendency in Stage I for agent or person affected nouns to be animate and for object nouns to be inanimate. Both Bloom and Bowerman include this tendency, which is not a rule of adult grammar and not invariably observed in child speech, in their Stage I grammars. They do it by assigning nouns the features "+animate" or "−animate" and blocking the appearance of "+animate" nouns in object positions and "−animate" nouns in subject positions. However, this representation runs into certain difficulties.

There are two kinds of sentences in child speech where the adult grammar calls for the observance of an animate-inanimate distinction. Vocatives ought always to be animate but in Stage I speech they are not; Adam says *Hi belt, Hi spoon,* and the like. Reponses to the question *Who is that?* ought always to be animate whereas responses to *What is that?* ought always to be inanimate. In Adam, Eve, and Sarah at I they were not. Sarah's mother, for instance, asked *Who's that?* pointing at a picture and having a person in mind but Sarah noticing just where her mother's finger pointed responded *A eye.* Another time the reverse misunderstanding occurred. Sarah's mother asked *What's that?* (meaning an article of apparel), and Sarah answered *A boy.* If animate-inanimate is a distinction which children observe where the adult model does not require it how is one to understand their failure to observe it where it is in fact required by the model?

5. *Summary.* The full distributional detail of Stage I speech, of which we have only given samples, poses some difficult problems of formal representation, problems which, in my opinion, cannot be "solved" by appeal to samples of natural speech alone. It seems likely to me that in Stage I speech there are a great many unanalyzed "chunks" as well as much that is produced by grammatical rule. However, spontaneous speech alone does not enable use to decide in every case which is which. If one tries to treat everything that occurs as the result of productive rules the rules must be very strangely discontinuous and inelegant.

A Schlesinger-type Grammar

While Schlesinger's (1971) own discussion of Stage I English focuses on two-word sentences, which he interprets as expressions of two-term semantic relations, he does also propose a mechanism for the generation of more complex sentences. One of his examples is: *John catches the red ball*. Schlesinger proposes that the production of this sentence begins with a complex *I*-marker (for semantic intentions), which is created out of elementary relations so bracketed as to yield a correct result. The *I*-marker for *John catches the red ball* looks like this:

Ag (John, [Ob ([Det (the, [Att (red, ball)])], catches)]) (1971, p. 88).

The italicized words should be understood to represent concepts while the terms *Ag, Ob, Det,* and *Att* name relations. The bracketing defines the conceptual units between which a given relation exists. Thus the relation of attribution exists between *red* and *ball* but the relation agent exists between *John* and, not *catches* alone, but *catches the red ball*. The utterance would be produced from the *I*-marker by successive application of four of the elementary "realization" rules: attribution, determiner, object, and agent. The order of application of the rules should, Schlesinger suggests, be determined by the bracketing of the *I*-marker. One possibility he suggests would be to start from the innermost brackets and work outwards which, for the present example, yields the order described above. The reverse order is also a possibility, in Schlesinger's opinion, and he judges that there is not enough knowledge of the process of production to make a choice between the possibilities.

Since late Stage I English includes sentences of three and four words as well as of two, a Schlesinger-type grammar for this stage must employ both elementary rules for two-term relations and certain sequential combinations of elementary rules. In Table 30, which offers a sketch of a Schlesinger-type grammar, the elementary rules appear first and then the required sequences, which, however, are not exhaustively listed. The elementary rules are set down in a notation employed by Schlesinger which collapses together position rules and rules of categorical assignment. Each rule names a semantic relation and uses the symbols *a* and *b* to stand for the concepts (not words) so related. The rule itself assigns an order to the concepts and assigns both concepts and their combination to a part-of-speech or category. Schlesinger has not written out rules for all the two-term relations appearing in Stage I, and so I have had to invent some, following his model as closely as possible. The rule combinations simply identify the elementary rules involved by number and list them in the order of their appearance in the inventory of elementary rules, an order that is not intended to represent sequence of application.

Table 30 is only concerned with the basic semantic relations and their expression by word order. Nothing is said about interrogative and imperative modes. The rules are not accurate on the level of detail that would distinguish separable verbs from verbs generally, pronouns from nouns, animate nouns from inanimate, and so on.

The representation of Table 30 meets one major requirement for this stage. For strings like *Mommy sock,* which can have more than one meaning if one follows the

Table 30.   A Schlesinger-type grammar for late Stage I English

Single Rules	
Main Verb Sentences (Two Terms)	**Missing Copula Sentences**
1. Agent-action(a, b) → $S(Na + Vb)$	8. Introducer-$X(a$, b) → S (*Dem a* + Nb)
2. Agent-object(a, b) → ?($Na + Nb$)	9. Nominal-locative(a, b) → $S(Na + Nb)$
3. Agent-locative(a, b) → $V(Na + Nb)$	10. Nominal-attributive(a, b) → $S(Na + Adj\ b)$
4. Action-dative(a, b) → $V(Va + Nb)$	
5. Action-object(a, b) → $V(Va + Nb)$	**Noun Phrases**
6. Action-locative(a, b) → $V(Va + Nb)$	11. Attributive-nominal(a, b) → $N(Adj\ a + Nb)$
7. Person affected-state(a, b) → $S(Na + Vb)$	12. Possessor-possessed(a, b) → $N(Na + Nb)$

Rules in Sequence	
Main Verb Sentences (Three Terms)	**Main Verb Sentences (Two Terms with NP)**
1,5 Agent-action-object	1,12 Agent (possessor-possessed)-action
1,6 Agent-action-locative	6,12 Action-locative (possessor-possessed)
	Missing Copula Sentences with NP
	8,12 Introducer-X(possessor-possessed)
Main Verb Sentences (Four Terms)	**Main Verb Sentences (Three Terms with NP)**
1,4,5 Agent-action-dative-object	1,5,12 Agent-action-object (possessor-possessed)
1,5,6 Agent-action-object-locative	1,6,12 Agent (possessor-possessed)-action-locative

method of rich interpretation, there are as many distinct deep structures as are needed. *Mommy sock* might have any of the senses: agent-object, entity-locative, or possessor-possessed. Rules 2, 9, and 12 provide the respectively appropriate deep structures. *Give doggie* might have the sense action-dative or the sense action-object, and rules 4 and 5 provide the appropriate deep structures. And so on for other such cases. The representation of Table 30, then, improves upon pivot grammars in one important respect.

The "deep structures" of Table 30 are directly semantic whereas the deep structures of a Bloom-type grammar are not. It is important to recognize, however, that Schlesinger's deep structures are only names for semantic relations. He does not even provide definitions for these names in the way that Fillmore does for some rather similar notions. Even definitions, of course, are far from providing an adequate semantic theory. An explicit generative semantics would provide rules for amalgamating the senses or semantic readings of individual words according to the relation into which the words enter. The senses of *Mommy* and *sock* would amalgamate in one way when the relation was that of agent-object and in another when it was possessor and possessed. While the semantic theory of Katz and Fodor (1963) provides explicit amalgamation rules, it does not provide distinct types of amalgamation for the various relations in question (though see Katz, 1967 on this point). Uriel Weinreich (1966) has distinguished two sorts of amalgamation: "linking" (or logical multiplication), which applies to attribution, and "nesting," which applies to the relation agent-object. However, Weinreich's theory is incomplete and contains many difficulties. In sum, there exists no explicitly generative semantic theory that is adequate to the task of sentence interpretation.

The Schlesinger-type elementary rules of Table 30 have the same form whether the utterance in question is a main-verb sentence (or sentence constituent), a missing-copula sentence, or simply a noun phrase. For Stage I speech this is an appealing feature, since the features of English grammar which make main-verb sentences, copula sentences, and *NP*'s profoundly different are, as yet, mostly unrealized. Looking ahead, however, we must wonder how Schlesinger's rules can grow into the English grammar which they so little resemble.

On the level of rule combinations a Schlesinger-type grammar does not distinguish between a three-term relation (like agent-action-object) and a two-term relation with elaborated *NP* (like agent [possessor-possessed]-action) nor between a four-term relation and a three-term with elaborated *NP*. The members of the simpler pair are both combinations of two rules and the members of the more complex pair are combinations of three rules. We have already seen (Tables 22 and 23) that the two members of the pairs described seem to be linked in development; just those children, for instance, who create four-term relations also create three terms with elaborated *NP*. There is, therefore, some reason for thinking that the two kinds of development represent the same increment of complexity and so for looking favorably upon a grammatical representation that equates them as Schlesinger's does. However, the equation seems to be too perfect.

Consider the sentences *Adam hit ball* and *Sit Adam chair*. The first is an agent-action-object which is presumably generated by rule 5, which orders the object *(ball)* after the action *(hit),* followed by rule 1, which orders the agent *(Adam)* before the action that must be supposed to be identified by appropriate bracketing as *hit ball.* The second sentence is presumably generated by rule 12, which orders the possessor *(Adam)* before the possessed *(chair),* followed by rule 6, which orders the action *(sit)* before the locative *(Adam chair).* But how is *Adam chair,* which is generated by rule 12, recognized as a locative? However it is supposed to be done, it seems as if the mechanism should be different from that which identifies *hit ball* as the action for which *Adam* is agent. *Hit ball* at least is an action, though not a maximally simple one, but the possessive *Adam chair* is not as it stands, identifiable as a locative. With no discernible difference between the mechanisms of combination there is no formal provision for a difference of semantic amalgamation. But surely we do not "add" meanings in just the same way in the two cases with one being (agent + action) + (action + object) and the other (possessor + possessed) + (action + locative).

The problems with Schlesinger's treatment of complex sentences (more complex than two-term relations) go beyond the one described above. Consider, for instance, such a sentence as *Give doggie bone* (an action-dative-object). This sentence is presumably generated by rule 4 (action-dative) and rule 5 (action-object). But the mechanism of combination cannot be the same as for an agent-action and action-object *(Adam hit ball),* where the action that combines with agent can be understood to be the total constituent yielded by action-object. The output of rule 4 cannot be a constituent of rule 5 and the output of 5 cannot be a constituent of 4. The sentence *Give doggie bone* also cannot be generated in the manner of *Sit Adam chair.* In the former case the actions of the two elementary rules, 4 and 5, are the same. In the latter case there is no such identity in the two elementary rules: action-locative and possessor-possessed.

Finally there is one completely general aspect of linguistic knowledge, which some grammars have explicitly represented, that is in Schlesinger's model simply taken for granted. The problem is illustrated in Schlesinger's (1971) Table 3 which is here produced as Table 31. He uses this table in explicating the generation of *John catches the red ball.* Notice that the variables *a* and *b,* which stand for concepts in the relational rules, can sometimes be represented by single words *(red* and *ball),* sometimes by two words *(red ball),* sometimes by three *(the red ball)* and more *(catches the red ball).* This is the "bracketing" operation which makes the result come out right. Without such brackets one can imagine *catches* alone functioning as the action that must follow the agent *John* or *ball* alone as the object that must follow *catches.* The right bracketing is essential if the right results are to be obtained. But how is the bracketing itself done? There are no rules that place the brackets and, in fact, this essential part of the operation is supplied by the implicit knowledge of the reader who knows English. In short, there is no algorithm for bracketing, and so the theory is not an explicit one in this respect. A Bloom-type grammar, following the Chomsky 1965 model, creates a bracketed deep structure by explicit algorithms, the phrase structure rules.

In summarizing the facts about late Stage I which require to be represented in a grammar, we found some reason to think that the child at this time operated with an implicit paradigm for main-verb sentences that was more complex than anything ever realized in performance. The paradigm was: agent-action-dative-object-locative, but no sentence containing as many as five constituents was realized in performance. The evidence for the paradigm consisted in the rather full "sampling" of the paradigm on the level of single, double, triple, and quadruple terms. Of course the paradigm generalizes beyond the "facts" in that it predicts combinations not included in the full sampling. Table 30 does not generalize in this way. Instead of describing an implicit paradigm to which obtained combinations

Table 31. The relations in an *I* marker

a	Relates to	*b*	Notation
red	is attribute of	*ball*	*Att (a,b)*
the	determines	*[red ball]*	*Det (a,b)*
[the [red ball]]	is object of	*catches*	*Obj (a,b)*
John	is agent of	*[catches [the [red ball]]]*	*Ag (a,b)*

Source: Schlesinger, 1971.

"point," it lists just the obtained combinations. Table 30 is, therefore, closer to the data than is the paradigm. It is also redundant in a way that the paradigm is not. Table 30 lists agent-action, action-object, agent-object, and so on, frequently repeating terms which have an invariant order more economically described as: agent-action-dative-object-locative.

In summarizing the facts of late Stage I we found that most constituents were sometimes omitted from contexts in which they are obligatory in adult English. From main-verb action sentences agent and action and dative and object and locative were all sometimes missing, as were person affected, state, and stimulus from main-verb state sentences. From copula-type sentences demonstratives were sometimes missing and so were entities and locatives. Noun phrases in isolation seemed sometimes to be derived from sentences lacking demonstratives or agents and actions or persons affected and states. These facts suggest a completely general "optionality" of constituents. It is as if an utterance can be created from any one or more of the terms in the rules of Table 30.

Notice that it is not generally the case that some terms are obligatory and some optional. Consider just agent, action, and object terms. There are obtained utterances consisting of all three in correct order, any two in correct order, and (using rich interpretation on rather thin evidence) any one standing alone. It follows that the implicit paradigm cannot be (agent) action-object or agent-action (object) or anything of the sort. It would have to be (agent) (action) (object) plus a convention that at least one must occur. What this means for Schlesinger's elementary rules is that each term in each relation must be marked optional. The possibility of "expressing" relations by single terms would somehow have to be added to the rules.

A Schlesinger-type representation is, in summary, superior to such purely formal representations as the pivot grammar in that it distinguishes among superficially identical but semantically distinct strings. It has also the good quality of enumerating the semantic relations which dominate late Stage I English, several other languages, and conceivably all languages at this stage. This semantic emphasis brings to light a generality that formal treatments overlooked. A Schlesinger-type representation has the further advantage of revealing the fact that sequential word order is the only expressive device employed at all consistently in Stage I English to mark major semantic relations. The deficiencies of the representation derive from the fact that the generative rules are not fully explicit and from the fact that the rules so far sketched could not be more than a tiny fragment of a complete grammar of adult English. Expressly tailored to the facts of early child speech it is unclear how these rules would develop into a grammar adequate even to Stage II speech let alone to adult speech.

A Case Grammar

Although there are, in the samples of Adam, Eve, and Sarah, a few instances of instrumental, benefactive, and factitive cases we shall, in the interest of simplicity, omit these and consider only the agent, dative, objective, and locative plus the "essive" case for predicate nominatives—Fillmore (1968) uses the term and makes the suggestion that it be used for predicate nominatives. Predicate nominatives are so frequent in Stage I that they must be somehow represented in a grammar for that stage. In this discussion, to reiterate what I have said in originally describing case grammar, I am not going beyond Fillmore's first paper on the subject (1968).

Fillmore uses agentive and locative concepts in the way that we have consistently used them in this chapter, but his use of dative and objective is broader than ours has been. The dative case in Fillmore's theory includes the person affected role *(Eve see* or *Eve want)* and the possessor role *(Adam hat)* as well as the indirect object role. The objective case is Fillmore's semantically uncharacterized case, his "wild card" as it were, and the uses he includes, besides that of direct object, are: subject of entity-locative sentences *(Sweater chair);* subject of attributive sentences *(Hand dirty);* possessed object in genitive constructions; presumably also as subject in such predicate nominative constructions as *That book.*

A case grammar (as of Fillmore, 1968) like a grammar of the Schlesinger-type does the minimal job of providing distinct deep structures for superficially identical strings, which we assigned distinct meanings by the method of rich interpretation. *Mommy sock* in a genitive reading would involve the dative and objective cases; in its other familiar reading it involves agentive and objective cases. A case grammar, unlike a Schlesinger-type grammar, represents the addition of a major constituent to a sentence in a manner quite different from the elaboration of one constituent into a *NP.* A three-term sentence like *Adam hit ball* is a simple sentence with two cases. A two-term sentence with an elaborated *NP* like *Sit Adam chair* would not be a simple sentence at all but a complex sentence with the genitive (dative and objective) being embedded. Fillmore's analysis affords no explanation for the apparent equivalence in complexity between sentences of *n* simple terms and sentences of *n*-1 terms in which one *NP* is elaborated.

Table 32 sets down some of the rules that would be needed for a case grammar of Stage I. Figures 9, 10, and 11 contain tree structures for all major construction types: main verb sentences; missing copula sentences, noun phrases.

Fillmore offers no rules for the generation of *wh-* questions. The *Who 'at* and *Where N (go)* forms could be added on to his grammar as an expansion of S_1, alternative to S_2. The modality constituent is intended by Fillmore to be the point of origin of such modalities of the sentence as a whole as interrogation, negation, and imperative. Since these modalities achieve some expression in Stage I speech, a rule has been added to Fillmore's general account which expands modality as Q (interrogation), *neg* (negative), and *imp* (imperative). The Q symbol could be rewritten by a morphophonemic rule as the rising interrogative intonation which is the only expression of interrogation at this stage. The *imp* symbol should only occur with *you* as subject or with no subject at all, but Fillmore offers no rules to achieve this kind of effect. There are not enough negatives at Stage I to guide a development of *neg.*

Table 32.   A case grammar for late Stage I English

Base Structure	
Phrase Structure Rules	**Case Frames for Verbs**

1. Sentence → modality + proposition	*fix* + [____ (A) (O)]
2. Modality → $\begin{Bmatrix} Q \\ imp \\ neg \\ \phi \end{Bmatrix}$	*put* + [____ (A) (L) (O)]
	see + [____ (D) (O)]
	want + [____ (D) (O)]
3. Proposition → $\begin{Bmatrix} (V)(A)(D)(L)(O) \\ VE\ (O) \\ V(L)\ (O) \end{Bmatrix}$	ϕ + [____ (L) (O)][a]
	+ [____ E (O)]
	+ [____ (D) (O)]
4. *A* or *D* or *E* or *L* or *O* → *K* + *NP*	*big* + [____ (O)]
5. *NP* → *N(S)*	

Transformations	
1. Subjectivalization	a. *M-V-A-X* ⇒ *A-M-V-X*[b]
	b. *M-want-D* (O) ⇒ *D-M-want-O*[c]
	c. *M-ϕ-L-O* ⇒ *O-M-ϕ-L*
	d. *M-ϕ-E-O* ⇒ *O-M-ϕ-E*
	e. *M-ϕ-D-O* ⇒ *D-M-ϕ-O*
2. Sequential Ordering	*X-V* (D) (L) (O) ⇒ *X-V-*(D) (O) (L)

[a] I am sure a proper linguist, certainly Fillmore, could devise something better than ϕ to enter in the lexicon.
[b] *X* is any variable.
[c] M is modality.

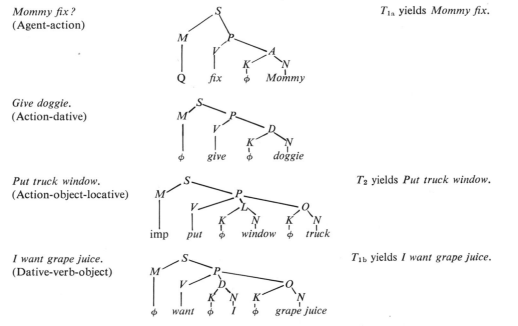

Mommy fix?
(Agent-action)

T_{1a} yields *Mommy fix.*

Give doggie.
(Action-dative)

Put truck window.
(Action-object-locative)

T_2 yields *Put truck window.*

I want grape juice.
(Dative-verb-object)

T_{1b} yields *I want grape juice.*

Figure 9.   Tree structures for main verb sentences generated by a case grammar

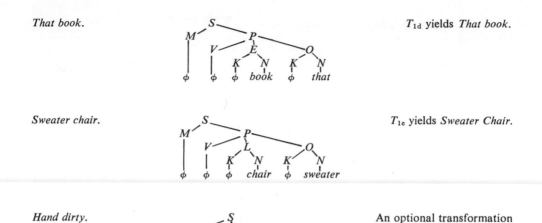

That book.

T_{1d} yields *That book.*

Sweater chair.

T_{1e} yields *Sweater Chair.*

Hand dirty.

An optional transformation subjectivalizing *O* would yield *Hand dirty.*

Figure 10.   Tree structures for missing copula sentences generated by a case grammar

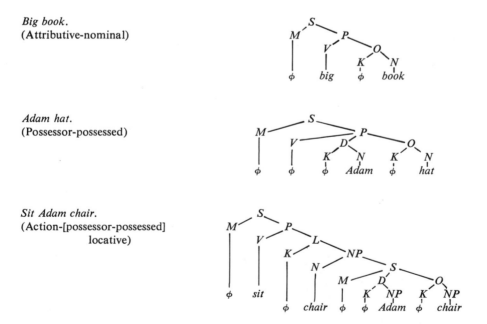

Big book.
(Attributive-nominal)

Adam hat.
(Possessor-possessed)

Sit Adam chair.
(Action-[possessor-possessed]
          locative)

Figure 11.   Tree structures for noun phrases generated by a case grammar

The base structure rule rewriting "proposition" poses two great problems: optionality of constituents and surface ordering of constituents. Let us first consider optionality. Fillmore suggests that the expansion of proposition be thought of as a list of formulas such as $V + A$, $V + O + A$, $V + D$, etc.; a list where at least one case category must be chosen and where no case category appears more than once in a given sentence. The list of multi-word sentence types at Stage I might start as: $V + A$; $V + D$; $V + L$; $V + O$; $V + A + L$; $V + A + O$; $V + D + O$; $V + L + O$; $V + F + O$; $V + A + L + O$. If we were to rewrite proposition as just this list certain inconsistencies and redundancies would arise. For example, the inclusion on the list of $V + A$, $V + O$, and also $V + A + O$ suggests a more economical representation as: $V(A)(O)$. However, this representation cannot be correct because it does not allow for agent-object sentences in which no verb is manifest. Which suggests: $(V) (A) (O)$. This representation permits the occurrence not only of all three constituents and of any two but also of any one: V or A or O. That is as it should be because we have found that single-word utterances occur in I which seem to be intended in an agentive or objective or action sense. Listing sentence types in the way that Fillmore suggests would not allow for single-word utterances unless both V and each case were enclosed in parentheses to indicate optionality. But then we should have a list that included: $(V) (A)$; $(V) (O)$; $(V) (A) (O)$. Clearly the first two terms are redundant and $(V) (A) (O)$ says everything there is to say. Similar considerations argue for $(V) (A) (L)$ and $(V (D) (O)$ and $(V) (L) (O)$, and ultimately for complete collapsing of the list into $(V) (A) (D) (L) (O)$.

The essive case (symbolized E) cannot be included in the general collapse because predicate nominatives in Stage I only combine with the objective case, and while the objective is optional the essive (or name) is not. There is, further, no reason to mark V for optionality because V for this copula-type sentence is never represented on the surface but is always ø. This state of affairs I have clumsily rendered by listing ø in the lexicon of verbs, providing it with the case frame $+[\_E(O)]$, and allowing for a rewriting of proposition as: VE(O). This solution leaves certain inconsistencies. Predicate nominatives are not the only "missing copula sentences"; there are also nominal-locative and nominal-attributive types. The nominal-locative never has a manifest verb, and this fact is best rendered by providing the lexical entry for ø with an appropriate case frame: $+[\_(L)(O)]$. The missing-copula sentence of the nominal-attributive type *(Hand dirty)* cannot, however, be handled in the same way. For in Fillmore's system adjectives are a subclass of verbs, and a sentence like *Hand dirty* is simply $V + O$, and V is not ø but *dirty*. Therefore, nominal-attributive sentences are not grouped with the other two missing-copula types but generated out of the $(V) (A) (D) (L) (O)$ structure.

The fully collapsed $(V) (A) (D) (L) (O)$ structure, with each constituent optional, cannot be quite right since it allows for the possibility of selecting no constituent at all. Fillmore suggests using linked parentheses ( ) to indicate that at least one of the elements so linked must be chosen. Therefore, linked parentheses are used

for the full set $ X V X A X D X L X O X $ because at least one member of this full set
is needed to make a sentence. This does not come to quite the same thing as Fillmore's
axiom that at least one case must be selected; it says, rather, at least one case or
the verb. There is a further problem with the fully collapsed formula. It permits the
selection of all the optional elements which would mean a more complex sentence,
five constituents, than any actually obtained. A "complexity limit" of not more than
four might somehow be added to the grammar (perhaps in Bloom's manner) or
one might permit the possibilities to exceed the complexity of anything obtained on
the assumption that the absence from the corpus of a five-constituent utterance
is simply a sampling phenomenon.

The markings for optionality in the base rule expanding proposition must be
matched by optionality in the case frames assigned to verbs in the lexicon. A verb like
put which in adult English must have agentive, objective, and locative cases, in
Stage I speech may have any one of these or none at all. By this form of representation
one aspect of grammatical development will be progressive elimination of optional
markings to represent the child's gradual realization that certain forms are obligatory.

It is important to realize that the optionality in the base structure of a case
grammar does not destroy its fundamental advantage over a pivot grammar of
providing distinct deep structures for superficially identical strings with different
meanings. When *Mommy sock* is an agent-object construction that fact is represented
in the deep structure even though no verb is present. This is because the object
meaning is not rendered in Chomsky's manner by a formal configuration relating a
NP to *V* but is represented by direct categorical labeling of *NP*'s as agentive and
objective. In this respect, case grammar is like a Schlesinger-type grammar and unlike
a Bloom-type grammar.

The second important problem posed by the rewriting of proposition is the
ordering of cases. In Table 32 the ordering is simply alphabetical: *A, D, L, O*. This
arbitrary ordering is intended to represent the cases as actually unordered in the
base; we use the alphabet because any left-to-right representation must include some
sort of ordering. In fact, we know that the cases or "relations" of Stage I do have a
definite surface order: agentives, those datives that name a person affected, and
certain objectives precede the verb and are subjects; datives, objectives, and locatives
when they follow the verb, follow it in this order.

Fillmore proposes to create surface orders out of deep structures by rules of
subjectivalization, objectivalization, and sequential ordering. His subjectivalization
rule does not simply move one case to a preverbal position, it moves one case
to a position in which it is directly dominated by *S* and so makes that case the subject
of the sentence in Chomsky's formal terms. Fillmore's rule is: if there is an agentive,
it becomes the subject; otherwise, if there is an instrumental, it becomes the
subject; otherwise the subject is the objective. This rule will not do because, for one
thing, sentences having an objective as the only case *(Hit ball)* often do not make

a subject of it. Fillmore does not write an explicit objectivalization rule, but the idea seems to be to move the case selected for direct object next to the verb and deprive it of its preposition, if any. For Stage I speech it is not possible simply to move the objective case to direct object position because this case sometimes serves as subject and because the dative must sometimes follow the verb. There are no examples of sequential ordering transformations in Fillmore's (1968) discussion.

In the rule of Table 32 that rewrites proposition it would have been possible to order the cases as they are ordered in the sentences of Stage I. In doing so, however, we should have assigned to the presumably universal deep structure certain facts about surface order in English. Therefore, we have not done so but have used an arbitrary order to represent cases in the deep structure. How might the obtained surface order be derived from such a deep structure? A subjectivalization transformation which applies only to the agentive (T_{1a}) seems appropriate, since the agentive if present is always the subject. The rule must be supplemented with others which subjectivalize particular cases when they occur in particular arrays and with particular verbs. Thus, in a sentence like *I want grape juice* it is the dative (person affected) that must become the subject. And in a sentence like *Sweater chair,* for which V is $\emptyset$, it is the objective *(sweater)* that would have to become subject. In Table 32 transformations 1b, 1c, 1d, and 1e exemplify subjectivalization rules specific to certain verbs and case frames. In the case frames for verbs, listed in Table 32, underlining has been used to identify the case that must be subjectivalized where this is not the agentive.

The problem remains of ordering correctly the various cases that may follow the verb. The second transformation of Table 32 provides that whenever there are at least two such cases they appear in the surface sentence in the order: *D-O-L.* Hence *Give doggie paper (D-O); Put truck window (O-L).* This sequential ordering rule must apply after all the subjectivalization rules and must apply only to cases following the verb so as not incorrectly to order *Sweater chair (O-V-L); Adam hat (D-V-O); I want grape juice (D-V-O).* With respect, then, to the general problem of the surface order of cases it is clear that the particular rules Fillmore (1968) has sketched for adult English will not serve for Stage I, but it appears to be possible to write other rules following the general lines of his description which will serve.

Table 32 omits certain rules that Fillmore includes for adult English. The modality constituent, for instance, would include an obligatory tense constituent, but because verbs at Stage I are unmarked for tense we have not included such a constituent. Fillmore would also have a rule developing *be* from modality in certain sentences where V is $\emptyset$: predicate nominatives *(E + O)*, nominal-locatives *(L + O)*. Table 32 does develop V as $\emptyset$ in such sentences but does not add *be,* since the copula is missing at Stage I. Where V is $\emptyset$ and the subject is not the objective, which in Table 32 is the genitive sentence $D + O$, Fillmore would obligatorily insert *have.* This word is not found in Stage I speech, and so the rule is not needed. Fillmore would develop *be* from modality in one last case: sentences where V is an adjective *(Hand dirty)*. He does not indicate how the rule would be written, but in any case it is not needed for Stage I. The symbol K, which appears in the rewriting of every case, is used by Fillmore as the source of case-marking prepositions, and also for the case-marking possessive inflection. In Stage I speech, K is not represented by any morphemes in the surface sentence, and would be rewritten as $\emptyset$. Alternatively, of course, K could simply be omitted from the rewriting of the cases in the way that *be* and *have* are omitted. However, K is a constituent of the base structure which Fillmore thinks of as developing in diverse ways to suit the surface structures of diverse languages. It is, for that reason, retained in the rules for Table 32 though it would eventually be realized as $\emptyset$. Because the only grammatical device marking case relations in Stage I speech is word order it would make sense to relate sequential order to K. However, I do not see how that can be done.

The derivation of genitive and attributive noun phrases and their utilization as *NP*'s in larger constructions poses difficult problems for a case grammar. Consider such "simple" genitives as *Adam hat* and *Eve lunch*. Following Fillmore's lead we should develop these out of $V + D + O$ with $\emptyset$ as verb. Rule T_{1e} would make D the subject. By this derivation *Adam hat* and *Eve lunch* are simple sentences in which *have* does not yet appear. A sentence like *Sit Adam chair* in which the genitive functions as the locative case would not, in Fillmore's view, be a simple sentence. Rather one simple sentence, the genitive, is embedded in the locative case of another. The derivation is accomplished by permitting *NP* (phrase structure rule 5) to expand as a noun and a sentence *(S)*. Since *NP* appears in the rewriting of every case, the recursive element S is embedded in every case. The N in the locative is, in the present case, *chair* and makes the same reference as the objective-case N in the embedded sentence. To obtain the surface sentence *Sit Adam chair* from the deep structure of Figure 11 we should need rules deleting the second occurrence of *chair* (dominated by O) and reattaching the dative constituent *Adam*) to the *NP* dominated by locative in a position before the noun *chair*.

Consider such a simple attributive as *Big ball*. Fillmore presumably would derive this construction out of $V + O$ with V being the adjective *big*. An attributive can also take the form of a missing copula sentence: *Ball big*. To generate this form (see *Hand dirty*) in Figure 10 an optional transformation subjectivalizing the objective would be needed. We should need to block this rule in cases where the attributive is a *NP* embedded in a larger construction as in the sentence *Hit big ball*. Fillmore does not illustrate the derivation of sentences of this kind, but we may suppose they would develop out of S embedded in *NP* in much the same way as the genitive. In effect *Hit big ball* would embed *Ball (is) big* in the objective constituent of *Hit ball*.

One of Fillmore's axioms really requires that sentences with genitive and attributive constituents be complex rather than simple sentences. It is the axiom that not more than a single instance of a given case may occur in a simple sentence. Consider a sentence like *That Mommy soup*. The matrix sentence is a predicate nominative or $V + O + E$ sentence. The objective element is *that,* the subject. The genitive also contains an objective case, since it is analyzed as $V + D + O$. Therefore, a predicate-nominative sentence that utilizes a genitive constituent such as *That Mommy soup* cannot be a simple sentence. The two objective cases must be analyzed as the only instances of this case in two distinct simple sentences. While we have this effect of the axiom in mind, we should note that it has other effects. The simple predicate nominative *That soup* contains two nominals which are not easily characterized semantically and so, since the objective case is the semantically neutral case, we must wonder why the sentence is not analyzed as $V + O + O$. Clearly the reason is that this analysis would violate the axiom that a particular case does not occur more than once in a single sentence. It is for this reason, really, that the essive case must be invented for the nominal *soup.* This is one of the points at which Fillmore's (1968) grammar seems rather arbitrary.

The analysis of constituent genitives and attributives as sentences embedded in the *NP* is not entirely satisfactory. For one thing nothing in the grammar prevents the embedding of every sort of sentence in the *NP,* since the embedded element *S* is free to expand in all its possible forms. In fact only genitives and attributives (in fact expressions of recurrence) are embedded in Stage I. So additional constraints are needed. Then there is the problem that most kinds of embedding do not occur until long after Stage I. However, Fillmore does not develop most other kinds of embedding (for example, predicate complements) out of *S* embedded in *NP,* and so it could be argued that recursion begins in late Stage I, but only in the *NP.* However, relative clauses in Fillmore's view develop out of *S* in *NP,* and they do not appear in child English until Stage V.

Because there are reasons to be dissatisfied with the analysis of constituent genitives and attributives as embedded sentences, one speculates about alternatives. It is appealing, for instance, to think of genitives *(G),* attributives *(A),* and expressions of recurrence *(R)* as a set of named cases and to suppose that just these cases are optional constituents of the regular cases. Thus the objective and locative and the others would rewrite as noun *(N)* or as *G, R,* or *A.* This treatment seems especially reasonable since the genitive, attributive, and recurrence meanings seem as clear and primitive as the meanings associated with the agentive, objective, and locative. Yet in Fillmore's treatment these latter are all treated as named categories whereas the genitive and attributive can only be characterized as amalgamations of cases, as, respectively, $D + O$ and $V + O$. A semantic interpretation component would have its operations governed by named categories when the operations involved the agentive and objective, but by combinations of such categories when the operations were genitive or attributive.

How would *G, A,* and *R* be expanded? This is where the troubles begin. For *G* one thinks of the possibility of a verbless case expanding as $N + N$ and for *A,* perhaps, a verbless case expanding as $Adj + N$. These would be radical departures from Fillmore's (1968) grammar, since he requires that cases be associated with verbs and he treats adjectives as a subclass of verbs. When this line of thought is followed we soon have something so radically unlike Fillmore's system as not to be a case grammar in the same sense at all.

We have seen that there are difficulties with the representation of Stage I speech as a case grammar, but these are less serious than the difficulties with a Schlesinger-type grammar. We have the impression that the job could be done. At some points the representation is apt and even revealing; at others it seems arbitrary or wrong. The case grammar has a further advantage over a Schlesinger-type grammar. It foreshadows certain future developments: the addition of tense to modality and of the rules supplying *be* and *have*. This, of course, is because Fillmore started with the adult language and indeed had no intention of describing child speech. Schlesinger started with certain facts of the simplest child speech and paid little attention to the relation between these and adult competence. While case grammar (1968) deals with more aspects of English than does Schlesinger's grammar of semantic relations it falls far short of Chomsky's (1965) grammar in this respect. In case grammar as of 1968 there is simply no account given of *wh-* questions, *yes-no* questions, the many kinds of negation, the details of conjoining and embedding. All of these things are treated by Chomsky, and so grammars following his lead, such as those Bloom has written, start with a great advantage: they lead toward a grammar that represents a large part of adult knowledge.

A Bloom-type Grammar

Bloom's grammars follow the general scheme described by Chomsky in *Aspects of Syntax* (1965). A grammar of this type has two major components: a base component and a transformational component. The base generates *deep structures* which are phrase markers containing all the information relevant to the semantic interpretation of a sentence; deep structures provide the *input* to a semantic component of the kind that has been outlined by Katz and Fodor (1963). The transformational component maps the deep or underlying phrase markers into *derived phrase markers,* the *surface structures,* which are the *input* to a phonological component. Bloom has not and we will not attempt to specify the semantic or the phonological components, but only the grammar that relates the two. For Stage I speech the transformational component is of slight importance. Stage I sentences are very nearly describable as deep structures serving as inputs to both the semantic and the phonological components. The distance between deep and surface structures which is introduced by transformational rules grows greater as language develops.

The base component gives formal representation to three kinds of knowledge concerning the structure of sentences:

1. *Knowledge of Constituent Structure.* This is the sense one has that a sentence breaks up into hierarchically ordered sub-wholes. Constituent structure is produced

by rewriting rules of the form $A \rightarrow X$ where A is a category symbol (for example, S or NP or N or V) and X is a string of category or terminal symbols. Each rule must rewrite only a single symbol. If V NP could be rewritten by a single rule *(V NP $\rightarrow$ Aux Vb Det N)* rather than separately *($V \rightarrow$ Aux Vb; NP $\rightarrow$ Det N)* we should fail to represent the fact that *Aux* and *Vb* are the natural parts of V while *Det* and N are the natural parts of *NP*. The rewriting rules have an implicit partial ordering that results from the way in which the symbols are utilized; a rule rewriting a symbol *($V \rightarrow$ Aux Vb)* must follow the rule introducing the symbol *(VP $\rightarrow$ V NP)*. The rewriting rules impose a structure on a string of symbols which may be represented either as a labeled bracketing or as a tree-diagram. The bracketing of a string into constituents is, we have seen, necessary for the correct operation of a Schlesinger-type grammar but that grammar provides no algorithms which will do the bracketing, and so leaves this aspect of our knowledge of the structure of sentences without formal representation.

2. *Knowledge of Grammatical Relations.* This is the sense we have that certain words function as the subject of a sentence, others as the predicate and others, within the predicate, as direct object. We have seen that knowledge of grammatical relations is essential to the semantic interpretation of a sentence *(The cat is biting the dog* versus *The dog is biting the cat)*. The rewriting rules, without supplementation of any kind, provide natural definitions of the basic grammatical relations. Each relation is represented by a distinctive formal configuration. Thus the subject of a sentence is the *NP* dominated by *S* and the direct object the *NP* dominated by *VP*, and so on. A Schlesinger-type grammar does not utilize the abstract formal relations subject and object, and so on, but rather maps such semantic roles as are termed agent or object or attribute directly into surface word order. Fillmore's case grammar does not assign the grammatical relations subject and object to the deep structure at all but creates surface subjects and objects by transformation.

3. *Knowledge of Subcategorization and Selection.* We know that words belonging to the same part-of-speech or category do not all have the same privileges of occurrence. Among nouns, some (proper nouns and pronouns) may not follow articles or adjectives, some (count nouns) may follow cardinal numbers and be pluralized while others (mass nouns) may not. Among verbs we know that some (transitives) may be followed by object *NP*'s while others (intransitives) may not. We know, furthermore, that certain verbs must have a subject that is animate *(see, hear, feel, want)* while others must have an object that is animate *(surprise, please)*. Knowledge of this kind is represented by Chomsky (1965) in two alternative ways. It may be best to describe these in connection with a specific base component and an illustrative sentence.

Table 33 presents an illustrative fragment of the base component taken from Chomsky (1965). In connection with this fragment Chomsky discusses the derivation of the sample sentence *Sincerity may frighten the boy,* and we shall do the same. Rules (i) through (v), plus (vii), (xvi), and (xvii), are rewriting rules (or branching

Table 33.   An illustrative fragment of the base component of adult grammar

---

(i)   S → NP   Predicate-Phrase

(ii)   Predicate-Phrase → Aux   VP (Place) (Time)

(iii)   VP → $\left\{ \begin{array}{l} \text{Copula} \quad \text{Predicate} \\ V \left\{ \begin{array}{l} \text{(NP) (Prep-Phrase) (Prep-Phrase) (Manner)} \\ S' \\ \text{Predicate} \end{array} \right\} \end{array} \right\}$

(iv)   Predicate → $\left\{ \begin{array}{l} \text{Adjective} \\ \text{(like) Predicate-Nominal} \end{array} \right\}$

(v)   Prep-Phrase → Direction, Duration, Place, Frequency, etc.

(vi)   V → CS

(vii)   NP → (Det) N (S′)

(viii)   N → CS

(ix)   [+Det—] → [±Count]

(x)   [+Count] → [± Animate]

(xi)   [+N, + —] → [± Animate]

(xii)   [+Animate] → [± Human]

(xiii)   [—Count] → [± Abstract]

(xiv)   [+V] → CS/α — Aux — (Det — β) $\left.\right\}$, where α is an N and β is an N

(xv)   Adjective → CS/α · · · —

(xvi)   Aux → Tense (M) (Aspect)

(xvii)   Det → (pre-Article — of) Article (post-article)

(xviii)   Article → [± Definite]

(sincerity, [+N, +Det — , —Count, +Abstract, · · ·])

(boy, [+N, +Det—, +Count, +Animate, +Human, · · ·])

(frighten, [+V, +—NP, +[+Abstract] Aux — Det
       [+Animate], +Object-deletion, · · ·])

(may, [+M, · · ·])

Source: Chomsky, 1965.

rules) which assign a constituent structure that cracks the sentence into *sincerity* and *may frighten the boy* at the deepest level, then into *may* and *frighten the boy* and then into *frighten* and *the boy,* and so on. The same rewriting rules represent *sincerity* as subject of the sentence, since it is the *NP* directly dominated by *S,* and *the boy* as object of the predicate, since it is the *NP* directly dominated by *VP,* and so on. With rule (vi) the processes of subcategorization and selection begin. In the base component of Table 33 these processes are accomplished by special kinds of rewriting rules, and this is one of two alternative representations.

     Rewriting rules like (i) through (v) introduce no lexical items into strings though they may introduce grammatical morphemes such as *past* or *be + ing.* Rewriting rules do introduce lexical category symbols such as noun and verb and adjective. The problem of subcategorization and selection is essentially one of replacing these category symbols with just those lexical items that are "appropriate" in the context of the string as a whole. It is the problem, for instance, of generating *Sincerity may frighten the boy* but not *A sincerity may frighten boy* or *The boy may frighten sincerity,* and so on. The method of Table 33 accomplishes appropriate substitution by assigning syntactic features to complex symbols *(CS),* which are developed out of each lexical category symbol, and adopting a convention that the only lexical items which may replace particular complex symbols are those which are marked in the lexicon with features matching the symbols in question. There are three distinct phases in the development or expansion of complex symbols.

Rule (vi) says that *V* is rewritten as *CS* (or complex symbol) rule (viii) says the same for *N.* By a convention which is not a rule of the grammar but simply an understanding of what this kind of rule does we must understand the rewriting of *CS* in the following way. In the first place the *CS* is assigned a feature that represents the lexical category symbol; thus $+V$ for rule (vi) and $+N$ for rule (viii). In the lexicon, words like *sincerity* and *boy* and, indeed, all nouns will have the feature $+N$ while *frighten* and all verbs will have the feature $+V$. It is going to be one aspect of the convention that substitutes lexical items for fully developed complex symbols that the item and the symbol must have the same lexical category symbol.

Rule (vi) does something else that is rather more complicated. It assigns to a complex symbol as a syntactic feature the categorical frame in which that symbol occurs. With the understanding that the frame is "local" in the sense of including the categorical context only to the limits of the immediately dominating phrase. Thus, since every *N* develops out of *NP,* the frame assigned a particular $+N$ complex symbol consists of just those other categories which in the derivation in question are dominated by *NP.* Since rule (vii) rewrites *NP* as *(Det) N (S'),* the possibilities are: $[+Det—S']$; $[+Det—]$; $[—]$; and so on. Notice that with the distinction $[+D—]$ and $[—]$ we have separated common nouns from proper nouns. The rewriting of *VP* (rule iii) is much more complex than the rewriting of *NP* (rule vii), and so the possible categorical frames are correspondingly more numerous. The verb *frighten* in *Sincerity may frighten the boy* will have the frame $[+—NP]$ which marks it as transitive and distinguishes it from an intransitive verb like *walk,* which would have the frame $[—]$. In the lexicon at the bottom of Table 33 we find that *sincerity* and *boy* both have the frame $[+Det—]$ and that *frighten* has $[+—NP]$. It will be part of our understanding of the convention of lexical substitution that lexical items must match the complex symbols for which they substitute with respect to syntactic frames representing local categorical frames. The assignment of local categorical frames is called by Chomsky *strict subcategorization.*

The rules that effect *strict subcategorization* are context-sensitive; the additions to the *CS* depend upon the context of the *CS.* Rules (ix) through (xiii) are context-free rules. They apply only to a *CS* developing out of the $+N$ lexical category. These rules assign to the *CS* certain *inherent* syntactic features. Rule (ix) says that nouns which take determiners may be either $[+count]$ or $[−count]$, and rule (x) says that nouns that are $[+count]$ may be $[+animate]$ or $[−animate]$. The *CS* that is to be replaced by *boy* will so select alternatives, from rules (ix)–(xiii), as to acquire the features: $[+count]$, $[+animate]$, and $[+human]$ whereas the *CS* that is to be replaced by *sincerity* must acquire the features [−count] and [+abstract]. In the lexicon of Table 33 we see that the lexical items *boy* and *sincerity* are marked correspondingly and the substitution convention requires this sort of match, with respect to inherent features between nouns in the lexicon and the complex symbols they are permitted to replace.

Inherent features, like [+animate] and [−animate], are needed because there are verbs that must have animate subjects *(see)* and verbs that must have animate objects *(surprise)* and adjectives that must modify animate head nouns *(intelligent)*. Chomsky has shown that there are reasons why selection of this kind should be represented by allowing nouns freely to acquire the features in question and then selecting verbs and adjectives for their appropriateness to such noun-defined contexts. This is to say that there are reasons why nouns should be represented as *selectionally dominant,* and Chomsky even proposes that selectional dominance may be an aspect of the universal (cross-linguistic) definition of nouns.

Rule (xiv) is again a context-sensitive rule. It assigns to the *CS* developing out of *V* a particular frame, and in this way is like rules (vi) and (viii), which also assign frames. The difference is that the frames of rules (vi) and (viii) are categorical and local whereas the frame of rule (xiv) is neither. The rule says, in effect, that the *CS* for *V* is to be assigned a frame consisting of all the syntactic features of the subject noun and all the syntactic features of the object noun (if any). The symbols α and β stand for variables ranging over features. In the case of our sample sentence *(Sincerity may frighten the boy)* the most important features of the framing nouns are [+abstract] for the subject and [+animate] for the object, and these are the only ones appearing in the "feature frame" assigned to *frighten* in the lexicon. As usual the substitution convention is that the lexical item must match the complex symbol it replaces, this time with respect to feature frames.

Now we are in a position to understand something about the ordering of the rules in Table 33. (Rules (ix) to (xiii) which assign inherent features to the noun complex symbol must precede rules (xiv) and (xv) because the inherent features must be available for inclusion in the feature frames of verb and adjective.

To summarize, the way is prepared for selection of lexical items appropriate to particular contexts by developing complex symbols which have all the features the item must have. Features are assigned in four ways: 1. the *CS* is marked positively for the lexical category that dominates it; 2. the *CS* acquires as a feature its local categorical frame (strict subcategorization); 3. a noun *CS* freely acquires inherent features; 4. verb and adjective *CS*'s acquire feature frames from the nouns with which they are in construction. The fully fashioned *CS* is a kind of fishhook designed to retrieve just those lexical items that match it.

As we have described it, subcategorization is effected by special sorts of rewriting rules, nonbranching rules which cross-classify the *CS*. There is an alternative, and it is the alternative which Bloom adopts. The alternative eliminates the sub-categorization rules from the set of rewriting rules. Lexical category symbols rewrite not as complex symbol *(CS)* but as Δ which is a fixed dummy symbol. And so the "vocabulary" of the preterminal strings generated by the rewriting rules consists of grammatical morphemes and Δ. Terminal strings are created by replacing each Δ with an appropriate lexical item. The subcategorization rules which bring this about are all assigned to the lexicon. This leaves a *categorical component* in the base which is entirely made up of context-free rewriting rules and which has as its role the assignment of constituent structure and the definition of grammatical relations. Chomsky (1965) speculates that it is this categorical component which is most likely to be, at least in part, universal and innate — representing not what is learned about a particular language but what the human mind brings to any language.

How are subcategorization and selection effected by the second method? The context-free rules that assign inherent features to nouns figure in the lexicon as rules of syntactic redundancy. Thus a rule like (xii) that rewrites [+animate] as [±human] says, in effect, that all human nouns will be animate but that animates are not all human. Nouns in the lexicon are marked, accordingly, and as far as inherent features are concerned may be freely substituted for Δ. But how does the grammar ensure that only appropriate substitutions will be made? Essentially by relying on exactly the kinds of contextual information already described but by utilizing it in a different way. The subcategorization rules we have described select certain frames in which a *CS* appears and assign corresponding syntactic features. The rule of lexical substitution provides that lexical items may be substituted just when their features match those of the symbol. This rule of lexical substitution is, as such, context-free. It makes no reference to context but simply works when symbol and item are matched with respect to features. Suppose, however, that the rule of lexical substitution is made context- sensitive. The verb *frighten* could then substitute for Δ only when Δ appeared in certain contexts. In which contexts? In a context where Δ was followed by an *NP* and where the subject noun was abstract and the object noun animate and so on. In fact in just those contexts which satisfy all the conditions specified by the syntactic features of *frighten*. In effect, then, the information in the *CS* is not developed as a *CS* which the item must match but is stated as the context in which the item may be substituted. This replaces the single context-free rule of lexical insertion with separate context-sensitive rules for various lexical items. In effect these rules are substitution transformations with the system of syntactic features stated as the *structural index* which permits a particular substitution transformation to operate. While this change may seem only notational Chomsky has shown that there are some substantive differences between the two representations that may ultimately establish one as preferable to the other. At present, as when Bloom wrote, there is no consensus on the best way to represent subcategorization and selection.

4. *The Child's Categorical Component.* Table 34 presents the portion of the adult categorical component presented by Chomsky (1965) and alongside it a version of the Stage I categorical component, a version that uses Chomsky's symbols ("Place" rather than "Loc") and notation so as to facilitate comparison of the two. The Stage I component is complete but the adult component is far from complete,

Table 34. A fragment of the adult categorical component and a Stage I categorical component

Adult	Stage I
(i) S → NP Predicate-Phrase	(i) S → Nominal VP
(ii) Predicate-Phrase → Aux VP (Place) (Time)	(ii) VP → $\left\{\begin{array}{l}\text{Predicate}\\ \text{V(N) (NP) (Place)}\end{array}\right\}$
(iii) VP → $\left\{\begin{array}{l}\text{Copula Predicate}\\ \text{V} \left\{\begin{array}{l}\text{(NP) (Prep-Phrase) (Prep-Phrase) (Manner)}\\ S'\\ \text{Predicate}\end{array}\right\}\end{array}\right\}$	(iii) Predicate → $\left\{\begin{array}{l}\text{Adjective}\\ \text{NP}\\ \text{Place}\end{array}\right\}$
(iv) Predicate → $\left\{\begin{array}{l}\text{Adjective}\\ \text{(like) Predicate-Nominal}\end{array}\right.$	(iv) Nominal → $\left\{\begin{array}{l}\text{N}\\ \text{Dem}\end{array}\right\}$
(v) Prep-Phrase → Direction, Duration, Place, Frequency, etc.	(v) Place → NP
	(vi) NP → (M) N
(vii) NP → (Det) N (S′)	(vii) M → $\left\{\begin{array}{l}\text{M}\\ \text{N}\end{array}\right\}$
(xvi) Aux → Tense (M) (Aspect)	
(xvii) Det → (pre-article of) Article (post-Article)	
Etc.	

for example, tense is not rewritten, prepositional phrases are not reduced to lexical category symbols, and so on. A complete adult component would contain many more rules.

Notice, first, that certain ones of the symbols are present in the adult component and missing from the Stage I component. Auxiliary, copula, and determiner are eventually represented by grammatical morphemes, by past and progressive inflections, the verb *be,* the articles *a* and *the,* and the absence of these symbols from the Stage I component reflects the absence from Stage I speech of most grammatical morphemes. Preposition and *like* are also missing, since prepositions are absent from Stage I speech.

Notice, next, that the symbol *S′* embedded in the verb phrase for the generation of predicate complements and in the *NP* for relative clauses is missing from the Stage I component. *S′* in the rewriting rules represents the recursive element in grammars of this type, and it is the presence of *S′* that makes it strictly true that the adult grammar will generate *infinitely* many well-formed sentences. In Stage I speech the only constructions that might be embedded sentences are the genitive noun phrases and attributive noun phrases. It is possible that these should be generated as embedded sentences, but the child's Stage I component of Table 34 reflects the view that they should not be so represented. It generates them out of *NP,* which may have a modifier *(M)* that is a noun *(Adam hat)* or an adjective *(dirty hand).*

Between the adult component and the Stage I component there are great differences in the complexity and variety of the sentences that may be generated. Chomsky's rule (ii) allows for place and time adverbials following the full *VP* and within the *VP* allows for prepositional phrases of various kinds as well as manner adverbials. In Stage I speech all this is reduced to the single place or locative, which may occur in missing-copula sentences or in main-verb sentences and which expands as a prepositionless *NP*. In the Stage I component, all missing-copula sentences develop out of the predicate; these include predicate-adjectives, predicate-nominals, and expressions of place. Chomsky develops only predicate-adjectives and predicate-nominals out of predicate, separating these from place. Chomsky's predicate constituent occurs after *V* as well as after copula. His predicate appears after *V* because in adult speech there are main verbs which take predicate-adjectives *(seems happy)* and also main verbs which take predicate-nominals *(became a general)*. Verbs belonging to these subclasses are entirely missing from our sample of Stage I speech.

In Chomsky's component there is only one *NP* whether as subject, predicate object, indirect object, prepositional object, or whatever. In Stage I speech, subject noun phrases are all only one word (except for a single exception) while object and locative noun phrases may be two-word genitives or attributives, and so "nominal" is distinguished from *NP*. In addition, there are the noun phrases which function as indirect objects; these appear in the Stage I component as *N* following *V*. They are always a single word but are not representable by nominal, since demonstratives may not function as indirect objects. In the adult categorical component indirect objects might be generated as one sort of prepositional phrase coming after the object *NP* in the manner of *Adam gave a bone to the doggie*. The prepositionless indirect object preceding the direct object *NP (Adam gave the doggie a bone)* would be derived by transformation from the propositional phrase. Stage I speech calls this derivation into question, since the prepositionless form which the derivation would represent as the grammatically "more complex" form precedes the "less complex" form developmentally.

While there are many differences between the adult and the Stage I categorical components there are also fundamental identities. These include the division of the sentence into constituents, the configural definition of such relations as subject, predicate, and direct object, and the deep cleavage between main verb sentences and copula-type sentences. In some of Bowerman's (in press) grammars for Finnish these identities in the categorical component are preserved though she develops an interesting argument questioning whether so "abstract" a concept as subject is really necessary. There is then some support for Chomsky's hypothesis that aspects of the categorical component are universal and, possibly, innate.

A Bloom-type grammar for Stage I is superior to a pivot grammar in the same basic ways as a Schlesinger-type grammar or a case grammar. Superficially identical strings like *Mommy sock* are assigned the distinctive deep structures that the method of rich interpretation requires them to have. However, the form given these deep structures depends upon the representation of complexity limits and the general optionality of major constituents, and so we must first discuss these matters.

In her corpus for Kathryn I, Bloom had only three strings in which there were terms representing three major category constituents:

Me show Mommy.
'chine make noise.
Man ride ə bus.

Except for these sentences two major categories seemed to be the limit of complexity. Bloom elected to write a grammar that did not generate the three sentences above, a grammar that includes an obligatory reduction transformation operating on any terminal strings that included three or more major terms.

Consider the example of *Mommy sock* in the agent-object sense. Bloom says that her categorical component will generate for this sentence such a deep structure as:

With this deep structure the noun *sock* is derived out of *VP* along with an unspecified verb. As a consequence the grammatical relation "object of the predicate" has its proper configurational definition; it is a *NP* directly dominated by *VP* and generated with *V* out of *VP*. This would mean that the semantic component could amalgamate the senses of *Mommy* and *sock* in the manner appropriate to subject and object. And Bloom judges that this is essential. However, if *Mommy soc*k has the deep

Table 35. Bloom's reduction transformation and sample strings resulting from its operation

Reduction (obligatory)			
Structural description: #-X-Y-Z		where X, Y, Z are category symbols such as NP, VP, N, and V	
Structural change: $\#\text{-}X_1\text{-}X_2\text{-}X_3 \Rightarrow \#\text{-}X_i\text{-}X_j$		where $o \leqslant i < j \leqslant 3$	
Examples: Mommy put sock			
$\qquad X_1 \quad X_2 \quad X_3$	X_i	$(<)$	X_j
Mommy	0		1
Put	0		2
Sock	0		3
Mommy put	1		2
Mommy sock	1		3
Put sock	2		3

structure described how does it come about that there is no actual verb in the sentence spoken? This is where the reduction transformation comes in.

The transformation appears in Table 35. It is obligatorily applied when a string includes three category symbols as would, for instance, *Mommy put sock.* Table 35, especially the notation: $o \ll i < j \ll 3$, needs some explication. The subscripts i and j, respectively, identify the first and second terms in the surface structure and the subscripts 1, 2, and 3 the first, second, and third category symbols in the deep structure. The statement $i < j$ says that the first surface term must represent a category symbol to the left of (a lower subscript than) the category symbol represented by the second surface term. Within these limits we are told that either i or j may be equal to 3 (represent the rightmost category symbol) or less than 3 (represent either the middle or leftmost symbol) including zero, which means no surface term at all. What then are the possibilities? If i is zero then there is only one term *(j)*, and it may represent the subject *(Mommy)*, the verb *(put)*, or the object *(sock)*. These are one-word utterances in relational roles, and we have seen that the method of rich interpretation suggests that such utterances occur at Stage I. The remaining possibilities are, as Table 35 indicates, the various two-term sentences which we have called agent-action, agent-object, and action-object. All these occur, we know, in Stage I speech. What cannot occur, with the reduction transformation in the grammar, is a three-term string like *Mommy put sock.* This is the essence of Bloom's analysis. The grammar generates deep structures complex enough to support the meanings required by rich interpretation, deep structures more complex than the surface structures obtained, because of the operation of a reduction transformation.

Bloom's essential analysis can be applied to our problem, late Stage I speech, by simply setting a higher complexity limit. The limit should not be two category symbols, since in Adam, Eve, and Sarah at I there were many sentences of the agent-action-locative and action-object-locative types. However, there was only one sentence representing four category symbols, and that suggests that the reduction transformation should be advanced one notch beyond Bloom's Kathryn I grammar so as to operate on four-term strings. Notice how exactly parallel the conditions are between Kathryn I and Adam I, Eve I, and Sarah I. Just as Bloom had three sentences which violated her complexity limit so we have one and would have another if Pepe I were considered.

There are some things about Bloom's formalization that are not clear to me. She writes as if the implicit verb *put* were simply never specified but represented by the dummy symbol Δ when the reduction transformation yields *Mommy sock.* However, I cannot see why the lexical substitution rule would not first replace Δ with *put* and then delete it. Furthermore, while the reduction transformation seems clearly to generate one-word sentences with relational interpretations, Bloom does not actually discuss this aspect of the rule.

Bloom gives serious consideration to an alternative to the reduction transformation: the representation of all categories in base strings as optional. One of her reasons for rejecting optionality and preferring a reduction transformation is the occasional occurrence of a series of two-word utterances all in the same situation; such as *Lois read, Read book,* and *Lois book.* Such sequences do indeed suggest a ceiling on complexity best represented by reduction. Another objection to optionality is that this notation implies the possibility of exercising all options and generating strings that exceed the complexity limit of three terms. The same problems exist for the use of optionality in our categorical component of Table 34. Adam, Eve, and Sarah, like Bloom's children, produce a small number of closely related three-constituent utterances in sequence. Furthermore, suppose the constituents nominal and *V* were placed in parentheses (to indicate optionality) in addition to those constituents already in parentheses: indirect object *(N);* direct object *(NP);* locative (Place), and modifier *(M).* The fuller optionality is suggested by the fact that both subjectless and verbless sentences occur along with sentences requiring but lacking indirect objects, direct objects, and locatives. If all options were exercised how long a sentence might we have? As long as: nominal-*V*-*N*-$\widehat{MN}$-$\widehat{MN}$. This is a total of seven terms when, in fact, the longest utterances obtained had only four terms. The limit would be nine were it not for the fact that subjects and indirect objects have been labeled nominal and *N,* and so distinguished from *NP,* which can expand as $\widehat{MN}$ in the direct object and locative roles. So, Bloom's objections to optionality apply to our problem even more forcefully than to hers.

Bloom has a third objection to optionality. She feels that the semantic interpretation of a string like *Mommy sock* as agent-object requires the postulation of a dummy element linking the two manifest categories in the underlying representation. The relational nature of the grammatical function direct object depends on the existence of another constituent also dominated by the same syntactic node. This is a debatable point. Suppose *V* were optional, and in the generation of *Mommy sock* the *V* option were not taken. It would still be the case that *sock* would be dominated by *VP* and so distinguished in this deep structure from *sock* in a possessive *Mommy sock,* which the categorical component of Table 34 (though not Bloom's grammar) would generate as a simple *NP.* The question is whether it is enough that superficially identical strings have distinct deep structures when they have distinct interpretations or whether it is necessary that these deep structures have certain definite forms.

Bloom's position seems to be that the deep structures must have the formal configurational properties which Chomsky uses to define such sentence relations as subject, predicate, object, locative, and so on. It is perhaps first necessary to remember that if the deep structures do satisfy the formal definitions of grammatical relations this is essentially the same thing, within a Chomsky-type grammar, as assigning appropriate semantic relations in a Schlesinger-type grammar or appropriate case concepts in a grammar like Fillmore's. A categorical component like either of those of Table 34 does not explicitly contain terms like agent, object, dative, and so on. However it implicitly contains configurations which define subject, direct object, indirect object, and so on. And since the categorical component delivers these relations to a hypothetical semantic component which is presumed to take account of the relations in assigning interpretations to sentences, the deep structures of a Chomsky-type grammar do the same job as Schlesinger's relations or Fillmore's cases. It is true that the semantic relations are more salient, more visible, in Schlesinger's and Fillmore's representations, and it is very possible that the great semantic uniformities of Stage I speech would not have been noticed without the Schlesinger and Fillmore approaches. However, Schlesinger's relations are only named and Fillmore's cases are only named and roughly defined; neither theory offers a truly generative semantic component, and so they are not fundamentally an advance over a Chomsky- or Bloom-type representation. The Katz-Fodor semantic component (which Bloom assumes) is generative but still deficient, since it does not have distinct amalgamation rules for relations like genitive, attributive, agentive, objective, and so on.

I do not mean to suggest that the grammatical concepts, subject and object, for instance, are fully equivalent to semantic concepts like agentive and objective. In late Stage I, for instance, grammatical subjects are of two types in semantic terms. With verbs like *hit* and *put* the subject is an agent, and instigator of action. With verbs like *see, hear, want,* and *like* the subject is a person affected; Fillmore would say a kind of dative. How can this semantic difference be captured by a grammar that represents both agents and persons affected as subjects? It can do it if we assume that the semantic component operates differently with verbs like *hit* and *put* than with verbs like *see, hear, want,* and *like.* For the action verbs the subject role identifies that argument of the verb that is to be given an agentive interpretation and distinguishes it from the argument of the verb that is to be interpreted as the recipient of action, the grammatical object. For state verbs the grammatical subject identifies the argument of the verb that is to be given a person-affected interpretation. Every kind of verb has arguments in distinct semantic roles and the grammatical relations subject, direct object and indirect object can serve to distinguish all such semantic roles even though the relations themselves have no consistent semantic interpretation. As we have seen the verbs *give* and *receive* entail the same three roles, giver, gift, and recipient, but the roles are assigned to distinct grammatical relations. We have also seen that grammatical relations like subject and object though they serve to distinguish semantic roles, as surface order also does, are more abstract notions than surface order. A Bloom-type grammar assumes that the abstract grammatical relations as they are formally defined by the rewriting rules function, even in Stage I, to distinguish the semantic roles associated with various verbs.

Since a semantic component which amalgamates meanings in distinctive ways for the various grammatical relations has not thus far been described, it is not clear what forms deep structures must assume in order to yield appropriately distinct interpretations for superficially identical sentences. It is possible that for an agent-object interpretation of *Mommy sock* the deep structure must include a dummy symbol for the *V*, nothing more specific than that and nothing less so. This is Bloom's assumption. However, we cannot rule out the possibility that it would be sufficient for *sock* to derive from *VP* with the *V* not present at all in the deep structure and simply an unselected option in the rewrite rules. We also cannot rule out the possibility that the *V* must actually be specified in the deep structure (for example, *put on*) and deleted after specification. This latter possibility would suggest that children intend specific meanings for unrepresented constituents and so, perhaps, they would reject interpretations that preserve the relational meanings (agent-object) but propose incorrect verbs *(Mommy is mending the sock)*. It seems likely, in fact, that they would reject such interpretations.

Perhaps neither the reduction transformation nor general optionality is correct. To optionality there are the objections Bloom makes: the grammatical relations are not always represented in the usual ways; the exercise of all options predicts sentences more complex than any that occur. To the reduction transformation there are other objections. It makes of the complexity limit an absolute ceiling, but three sentences in Kathryn I broke through that ceiling and so had to be excluded from the compass of the grammar. In late Stage I speech several sentences break through the higher ceiling of three terms. In general, in all samples, it is clear that frequencies fall as sentences grow more complex. Is it not possible, then, that the complexity limits assigned both Kathryn I and late Stage I are a function of the sizes of the samples? Might not larger samples at either point include a sentence or two still further beyond the limits than those obtained? One cannot rule out the possibility that the exercise of all options lies within the child's competence at both points. Perhaps the real ceiling at late Stage I is seven terms.

There is a second objection to the reduction transformation, an objection that stems from a critical difference between the situation at late Stage I and the situation at Kathryn I. Strong motivation for the reduction transformation stemmed in Kathryn I from the occurrence of three kinds of two-term construction, agent-action, action-object, and agent-object, together with the nearly total absence of con-structions combining the three terms. As Bloom points out, the two-term relations strongly suggest that Kathryn had knowledge of the underlying agent-action-object (or subject-verb-object) sentence pattern, but something or other seemed to require that one term be missing from the surface structure. The fact that agent-object constructions occurred was especially striking, since there are no models at all for these in adult speech whereas there are models for agent-action *(I see)* and action-object (imperative *Hit the ball*). It did indeed look as if one term had to be deleted even when the result was seriously ungrammatical from the adult point-of-view. In late Stage I agent-object constructions are still to be found along with the two other kinds of two-term relations. But the impact of the facts has changed. Now agent-object constructions, and the other two-term constructions, occur in the same samples with full three-term constructions. Why should that be so? It cannot be a complexity limit that knocks the third obligatory term out of these constructions. Would we not have guessed from Bloom's formulation of Kathryn I that when the complexity ceiling went up to three terms that the two-term relations which are, from the adult point-of-view, ungrammatical, would have ceased to appear. The facts are otherwise and so do not really suggest reduction for reasons of complexity, at all, but suggest rather that the child does not understand how much it is necessary to say to make well-formed sentences.

There is, finally, the objection to the reduction transformation that it makes a later stage grammatically simpler than an earlier stage. The sentence *Mommy sock* has the same derivation as the sentence *Mommy put on sock* except that the derivation of *Mommy sock* includes one more step, the reduction transformation, and so is the more complex of the two. The notion that development proceeds from the more complex to the less complex, that rules are dropped as the child develops, is not in accord with our expectations in these matters.

Perhaps the mistake lies with our failure to put into the child's grammar, besides the rules for fully grammatical complete sentences, certain rules of ellipsis which operate also in adult speech and seem to be quite lawful though they are not all fully understood. The parental performance in our samples after all includes a good many sentence fragments in addition to the full sentences, but Chomsky does not make the category symbols of the adult categorical component optional and does not use a reduction transformation. He does not do so presumably because he has limited his description to fully grammatical and complete sentences. Adult speech has frequently been described as a severely degenerate sampling of completely grammatical speech, full of false starts, mistakes, and so on. In fact, our parental speech to Stage I children is not degenerate in this way at all. There are few false starts and mistakes perhaps because the parent tailors his intentions to his listener, a small child, and so undertakes only rather simple sentences. Still the parental speech does include numerous nonsentence fragments. What are these fragments like?

For the most part the fragments that occur in parental speech are well-formed constituents of sentences and sometimes conform to quite clear principles that might be incorporated in a grammar though these principles transcend the bounds of the single sentence and prescribe certain kinds of sentence exchange. Not many such principles have actually been formulated even roughly but one that has is the rule which provides that an answer to a *wh-* question may consist of just the constituent which the question requests the respondent to specify. For example:

Who hit the ball?	*Adam.*
What did he do?	*Hit the ball.*
What did he hit?	*The ball.*
Where did he hit it?	*Over the fence.*
Etc.	

Here, then, are circumstances in which an adult may (not must) quite properly and grammatically produce constituent fragments. And among those that parents produced in these circumstances in the samples at Stage I, I find:

> *Right here.*   (locative)
> *The spoon.*   (object)
> *Mommy's soup.*   (genitive)
> *Fix Lassie.*   (action object)

Here, then, are models for utterances the child produces which seem to omit certain obligatory constituents.

There seem to be other rules permitting nonsentence fragments. For instance, an adult may produce a full sentence with final declarative juncture and then, as an afterthought, add a constituent which would come later in the sentence than the constituent produced. For example:

> *That's the boy swimming.*
> *At the beach.* (locative)

Or an adult may repeat a final constituent. For example:

> *That's a shoe.*
> *A shoe.*

Then there are rules which cannot be formulated entirely within linguistic terms, rules that allow fragments to be produced in reference situations which make unexpressed constituents obvious to both speaker and listener. Thus, when one or another child was eating lunch, one or another mother said all of the following:

> *Little bites, baby.*   (*You take* assumed)
> *Good?*   (*Is it* assumed)
> *More?*   (*Do you want* assumed)
> Etc.

In addition there are mild departures from grammaticality which are acceptable in colloquial speech. *Yes-no* questions are not always formed with the first member of the auxiliary and the subject interchanged. In fact, both subject and auxiliary or auxiliary alone may be omitted:

> *Do you want your lunch?*
> *You want your lunch?*
> *Want your lunch?*

If we add to the interrogatives of the last type the many imperatives parents produced *(Eat your lunch)* it is clear that there were many subjectless sentences in parental speech to serve as models for the subjectless sentences of the children.

The speech of Stage I children includes sentence fragments as does the speech of their parents. This could mean that the children have learned the categorial component of Table 34 and, in addition, have learned rules of repetition, ellipsis, colloquialism, and the like which would enable them to produce an adult-style performance. It is clear that this is not the case. For the fragments produced by children are not limited to just the discourse and reference situations in which adults produce them and are not limited to just the types that adults produce. Children use constituents rather than sentences when they are not responding to *wh-* questions and when the unexpressed elements are not obvious. They produce subjectless sentences which are intended neither as imperatives nor interrogatives. They omit obligatory verbs *(Mommy sock)* and objects *(Put floor)* and locatives *(Put book)* to produce fragments such as adults never produce.

Suppose Stage I children were unable to learn the rules of discourse, ellipsis, and so on which govern adult performance. What kind of impression would they develop of performance? Would they not overgeneralize the facts and overlook the governing contingencies and develop an impression that in speaking one is free to produce a full sentence or any natural part of it? Agent + action + object, or any one alone, or any two in proper sequence. It is my guess that this is approximately what happens, that Stage I children have the grammatical knowledge represented by Table 34 but utilize that knowledge in the very free way described. Since many of the semantic intentions children have are, in reference context, redundant, their performances communicate well enough. What they will have to learn is that in order to communicate some things it is necessary to say more and, in addition, that it is obligatory by convention to express certain things even when communication would not be impaired if one did not.

In Stage II, which is concerned with grammatical morphemes, we shall find that the oscillating optionality of major constituents like subjects, objects, and verbs which appears in Stage I is matched by a more frequent and long-term optionality of noun and verb inflections, and of such little words as articles, prepositions, and the copula. The grammatical morphemes of Stage II all express meanings; they modulate the semantics of the basic relations, but they are very often redundant. So often, in fact, that one can identify, from text alone, numerous contexts in which particular morphemes are obligatory and score such contexts for presence or absence of the morphemes. What this suggests to me is that a major relatively slow aspect of language learning involves learning to express always, whether redundant or not, certain forms: subject, verb, and object, of course, but also number, tense, definiteness of referent, precise character of spatial relations, and so on. Eventually the child learns to omit forms, only where adults do so; he learns the rules of discourse and ellipsis.

It is important to realize that the speech of the Stage I and Stage II child *works* very well within the range of situations he normally encounters in spite of its oscillating, apparently lawless optionality. He is normally talking about present or clearly impending circumstances or about desires he has which may be inferred from cues other than his speech. And he is normally talking to someone, a member of his family, whose memory encompasses most of the child's memory. He need not in fact say everything that the grammar books consider obligatory. Indeed he often need say only a word or two or nothing at all in order to be understood. His speech then may be described as well-adapted but *narrowly* adapted. If he is going to communicate about the past and future and about what is potential, and to do so with others who do not know the contents of his memory then he must learn to *say more*. Ultimately, if he is going to write, he must learn to express everything that might be needed by persons unknown. He must, in fact, become *widely* and *flexibly* adapted.

What shall we make of the fact that any language has some set of meanings which it is obligatory always to express (except in defined discourse cases) even though these meanings, whether subject or object or location or number or tense or definiteness, must often in context and with a given addressee be redundant? Perhaps it is economical to learn to express some things always, to automatize them, so that the speaker's or writer's central processing capacity, which we know to be sharply limited, may be deployed in solving the particular communications problem of the moment. After all any sentence is potentially endless, there is always a time, a place, and a manner to be specified, logical and causal relations that might be expressed, and so on. These things which are nonobligatory but optional depending on the larger communicative intent may be what we reserve our central processing capacity for — along with assessment of the informational requirements of the addressee. Perhaps it is economical to build up neural networks, and the evidence of Stage II suggests that some of these take a long time to build, which will guarantee the invariant expression of certain meanings so that central processing capacity can be left free to deal with the communicational exigencies of each individual situation — the selection of words and constructions likely to be familiar to the addressee and adequate to the message, the omission from the expressive medium of many expressions which, in context, can be taken for granted.

Summary of Grammar Types

This, at least, can be said briefly. All three types we have pursued have the advantage over either telegraphic speech or pivot grammar of being able to take account of, though not fully represent, the semantics of Stage I utterances. This means that the "rich" grammars unlike the "lean" ones are able to expose what appear to be the major uniformities characterizing Stage I speech both in its total course and with respect to the developments occurring in that course. In the late 1960's a Chomsky-type grammar of the sort Bloom used was more elaborately developed than the newer semantically based approaches of Fillmore and Schlesinger. This means that a Chomsky-type grammar of this date provides formal representational apparatus for many more aspects of adult English than do the recent semantically based approaches, for example, selection and subcategorization. On the other hand, the semantic approaches have made salient the continuities of development which the Chomsky approach made it easy for all of us (except Lois Bloom) to overlook. And it cannot be assumed that the more semantic grammars will continue to lag behind the Chomsky grammar, because work on the semantic grammars started some ten years later than work on the Chomsky grammar.

In General Summary

I began the section on Stage I by describing the data now available for the study of Stage I speech and proceeded to review and criticize the most influential characterizations of such speech offered in the last decade. The characterizations are taken up in approximate historical order but this order happens to correspond with a movement from nonsemantic "lean" characterizations to semantic or "rich" characterizations.

The characterization of Stage I speech as telegraphic in the sense that it is composed of content words and lacks functors is accurately descriptive in a rough sort of way of all speech studied in this period. However, when the characterization is taken very seriously and approached as a challenging hypothesis (as by Park, 1970a) it is clear that it needs to be reformulated from a rather sterile conception in terms of word classes borrowed from linguistics (content words and functors) into a set of functional hypotheses relating certain characteristics of words (the kind of meanings they code, their perceptual salience, the degree to which their forms are linguistically contingent) to several different levels of linguistic control. Looked at this way the comparatively functor-free character of Stage I speech is exposed as an incidental consequence of the fact that genuinely determinative variables tend to break on the content-functor line, but do not always do so.

The pivot grammar, which at least provides for productivity as telegraphic speech does not, clearly fails to be adequate in two major respects. Its distributional claims are now shown to be false for most Stage I studies, whether early or late in the stage. The pivot grammar under-represents the child's knowledge, since it provides the same sort of description for utterances which in context seem clearly to have very different meanings. Whatever representational conventions one adopts, the differences of meaning must be represented, since they evidently belong to the knowledge of the Stage I child. Even insofar as the distributional characters of pivot grammar are supported by data (there are, in fact, usually a few words of high frequency and many of low frequency) this fact seems to be correctly explained on semantic grounds.

So the chapter progresses to semantic characterizations including relations, operations, cases, grammatical deep structures which are to be interpreted by a semantic component, and so on. The differences are essentially differences of formal representation. The discussion is technical and on most points cannot really be conclusive. However, all the "rich" characterizations have a great deal in common though they do not perfectly agree on the set of compositional meanings the Stage I child expresses.

A critical argument causing us to favor some sort of "rich" characterization is Lois Bloom's (1970) observation that the child who uses two or three or more words in just that order which forms an appropriate expression for the semantic intentions the situation suggests may be said to make a discriminating response, since other orders are possible. The evidence of word order is less clear for languages which, unlike English, employ freer and noncontrastive orders. For these cases no simple conclusion is possible; children may settle on particular orders for particular meanings; they may vary order as freely as it is varied in the adult speech they hear; they may generalize beyond what they hear and vary order even more freely than the model language. The best guess is that what any child does is determined by specific and not-yet-studied learning variables that have operated in his history. What all do is concatenate *in some order* the words relevant to the semantic intentions they seem to have. In English, in addition, the order is in the vast majority of cases, appropriate. The role of order is further complicated by the fact, so far studied only with respect to English, that while Stage I children are able to use appropriate order in their spontaneous utterances and also usually to respond appropriately to contrasts of order, it is not until much later (Stage V or beyond) that they *judge* orders correctly and set them right when they are incorrect. All of which suggests that this aspect of English syntax is not a single competence emerging all at once in Stage I but rather a series of performances maturing at different times.

Perhaps the most significant conclusion of the chapter appears in the section called The Major Meanings at Stage I. It is here shown that a surprisingly short list of operations and relations (between 8 and 15) embraces the nonlexical, compositional meanings of all Stage I children whatever their first language may be. It is further argued that meanings seem to correspond on the level of linguistic propositions with the kinds of ideas that develop on an action level in the first 18 months of life, the period Piaget calls "sensori-motor" intelligence. It is further shown that the development that occurs in the course of Stage I is always the same. Two things happen: 1. concatenating serially more relations with redundant terms omitted; 2. unfolding of simple relations such that one term becomes itself a relation, always either possession, attribution, or recurrence. In these outcomes as again in Stage II, and in Brown and Hanlon's (1970) results with tag questions there is evidence for a law of cumulative complexity in language development, a law probably having both semantic and grammatical forms. While it is evident that utterances must get longer as MLU increases, no a priori reason requires them to get longer in just the particular ways they do.

A final section explores the problems encountered in writing fully explicit grammars for Stage I speech in the cases of the more promising semantically aware grammars of Schlesinger, Bloom, and Fillmore. No full explicit grammar proves to be possible but the attempt exposes one of the major findings of the chapter. The Stage I child operates as if all major sentence constituents were optional, and this does not seem to be because of some absolute ceiling on sentence complexity. In Stage II and after we shall see that he operates, often for long periods, as if grammatical morphemes were optional. Furthermore, the child's omissions are by no means limited to the relatively lawful omissions which also often occur in adult speech. He often leaves out what is linguistically obligatory. This suggests to me that the child expects always to be understood if he produces any appropriate words at all. And in fact we find that he would usually be right in this expectation as long as he speaks at home, in familiar surroundings, and to family members who know his history and inclinations. Stage I speech may then be said to be well *adapted* to its communicative purpose, well adapted but *narrowly* adapted. In new surroundings and with less familiar addressees it would often fail. This suggests that a major dimension of linguistic development is learning to express always and automatically certain things (agent, action, number, tense, and so on) even though these meanings may be in many particular contexts quite redundant. The child who is going to move out into the world, as children do, must learn to make his speech broadly and flexibly adaptive. It may be that automatizing a certain number of meanings leaves the human's limited central channel capacity free to cope with the exigencies of particular communication problems, which require that one say what is necessary, omit what is not, and use a lexicon and syntax familiar to the particular audience. It seems to be some kind of extreme end state which we achieve with varying success to put the message in writing to a readership that is unknown except on a gross categorical level.

Stage II

Grammatical Morphemes and the Modulation of Meaning

The critical samples for Stage II center on a mean length of utterance (MLU) value of 2.25 morphemes and an upper bound of 7 morphemes. As an interval we will define it as extending from an MLU of 2.00 (the upper limit of Stage I) until an MLU of 2.50. In this period, in Adam, Eve, and Sarah, a set of little words and inflections begins to appear: a few prepositions, especially *in* and *on,* an occasional article, an occasional copular *am, is,* or *are,* the plural and possessive inflections on the noun, the progressive, past, and third person present indicative inflections on the verb. All these, like an intricate sort of ivy, begin to grow up between and upon the major construction blocks, the nouns and verbs, to which Stage I is largely limited. However, in the course of Stage II we have only the first sprouting of the grammatical morphemes. Their development is not completed within the stage but extends, for lengths of time varying with the morpheme, beyond II and in some cases even beyond Stage V. The whole course of development of grammatical morphemes is the topic of this chapter. I have chosen to link this discussion with Stage II because the beginnings are here and are the most interesting new thing at II.

The most direct point of departure in Stage I for the argument and evidence of Stage II is the discussion, in I, of "telegraphic speech." The characterization of Stage I speech as, in the main, telegraphic was at first stated in terms of two rough linguistic categories: "contentives" and "functors" (or "function words"). The former (chiefly nouns, verbs, and adjectives) are always used frequently in Stage I speech while the latter (chiefly inflections, auxiliaries, prepositions, articles, and the copula) are used seldom or not at all. Linguists (for example, Gleason, 1961; Hockett, 1958) who have used the categories in question have, in defining them, tended to stress the fact that contentive word classes include numerous members and have a relatively "open" membership whereas the converse is the case for functors. Using only these criteria one would have to include among functors certain word classes, such as pronouns, demonstratives, and prolocatives, which are, in fact, regularly found in Stage I speech and so, to that extent, the original telegraphic characterization breaks down.

Close examination of contentive classes and functor classes (which are called "grammatical morphemes" in Stage II) shows that they are not precisely definable categories but rather represent the partial but imperfect convergence of a very large number of characteristics or variables, both formal and semantic. Without attempting an exhaustive list of the formal variables it is worth recalling that these include factors of perceptual salience, like amount of phonetic substance, usual stress levels, and serial position in utterances as well as differentially high and stable frequency levels as well as such grammatical complexity factors as conditioning by the phonological properties of the stem, the class membership of the stem, conditioning by case or semantic role in the sentence, number of allomorphs, and so on. Close examination of the notion of linguistic control of contentives and functors indicates that one must at least distinguish among: total absence from the child's speech;

occasional presence in fixed routines; and full control. In sum, the early characterization of Stage I speech as telegraphic, though roughly correct in crude categorical terms, must clearly give way to a set of more refined functional relations between forms having various values of the formal and semantic independent variables and the several levels of control that may be manifest in child speech. The present chapter, Stage II, is concerned with the order of acquisition of full control (as defined by a particular precise criterion) of certain grammatical morphemes, and with the relations between order of acquisition and the various formal and semantic characteristics of the morphemes.

Stage II is concerned with only *certain* English forms that might be considered grammatical morphemes, a set of 14. As is explained in a later section these 14 were not chosen either arbitrarily or with knowledge that they would yield the lawful results we shall find but simply because they were the only ones to which our criterion of acquisition was applicable. Stage II is also limited, unlike Stage I, almost entirely to the data of the children in our longitudinal study: Adam, Eve, and Sarah. This is the case simply because no other investigator has as yet applied the criterion of acquisition I shall employ. Indeed most of the studies that have gone beyond Stage I do not work with any sort of explicit criteria of morpheme control.

Stage II includes very detailed discussions of both the formal, especially grammatical, and also the semantic properties of each of the 14 morphemes studied, and I will not attempt here to preview these. There is one point, however, which badly needs some justification, and I will say here all that I have to say on it. How does one justify characterizing the semantics of all of the morphemes as "modulations" of meaning. To say this is to suggest some sort of distinction between the meanings the grammatical morphemes carry and the more "basic" relational meanings of Stage I such as agent-action, attribution, recurrence, and so on. To say "modulation" is to suggest a class of meaning somehow subordinate, less than essential. I think speakers of English probably share an intuition that there is this sort of difference between the constructional meanings of Stage I and those of Stage II but it is difficult to get beyond intuition to an explicit statement.

Gleason (1961) suggests that function words "contribute little or nothing to meaning but function as pure structural signals" (p. 156). Articles like *the, a,* and *some* strike him as the clearest example. The appearance of an article, any article, quite generally marks the leftmost boundary of a noun phrase *(NP)*. The newspaper headline *Beethoven Works on Hess Program,* for example, is subject to a misinterpretation because *Works* can be a verb, and there is no article to mark *Beethoven Works* as the noun phrase (NP) it is intended to be. An initial *the* or *some* or *several* would effectively mark the structure, and Gleason suggests that this structure-marking function which any article performs in virtue of the fact that it is an article is more important than the transmission of the lexical meaning associated with the choice of one article rather than another. Gleason adds that for different kinds of function word the importance of the structure-marking function does vary. In the case of prepositions he feels that lexical contrasts (as between *in* and *on*) are more important than they are in the case of articles, and he is not sure that, in this respect, prepositions are clearly different from nouns. Among function words Gleason holds that: "There is a complete intergradation from items which are almost purely structural markers, to ones which have considerable lexical meaning and for which the function of marking structure is incidental. A function word is any word near one end of this continuum" (p. 156).

Gleason does not, of course, deny that there are lexical meanings associated with the selection of one article rather than another as indeed there are lexical meanings associated with every grammatical morpheme. The contrast between the articles *the* and *a,* for instance, signals the distinction between specific and nonspecific reference. One of our children, playing with pencil and paper, announced her intention of drawing *a moon,* and *a* was correct because she had reference to a nonspecific instance of a given shape. Subsequently, however, she said: *You take the moon,* and this time *the* was correct because a specific moon had been created and already introduced into the conversation. On other occasions when this child spoke of *the moon* she meant the one up in the sky and, since this is a unique referent, it is always specific. Playing with a doll family the same child pointed to one and said *This is the mommy.* Why *the mommy* rather than *a mommy?* Because a family is a unit entailing just one mommy, and so the reference is specific. From the point of view of the listener, the child's mother, the child's selection of *a* or *the* was not very important because, in context, the specificity or nonspecificity of a given reference was ordinarily perfectly clear without the aid of the article. And so is it usually in English. Even an English lacking all articles, an article-free English, such as might be spoken by one whose native language is Japanese, is usually intelligible. However, if one considers not the listener's requirements but the speaker's accomplishment, the lexical meanings associated with articles and other grammatical morphemes seem very important. Articles are obligatory in many contexts, and the speaker must not only produce some article but just the right one, whether the listener needs it or not, and in order to produce the right one he must control the very delicate distinction between specific and nonspecific reference. I mean to suggest, then, that Gleason's sense of the relative insignificance of lexical meanings of function words is associated with the listener's role rather than the speaker's. For the English language in general it is a distinction that can be made, but it is not clear that the distinction has any relevance for our problem which is the acquisition of grammatical knowledge as revealed especially in sentence *production.*

Granting that grammatical morphemes have meanings, even as do "contentive" words, one nevertheless feels that there is some difference in the kind or quality of the meaning. Though, possibly, not just one difference distinguishing all grammatical morphemes from all contentives. It is sometimes said that contentives like *tree* and *hit* make reference whereas grammatical forms like the preposition *in* or the definite article *the* or the possessive inflection *-s* do not. But is that really true? To be sure there are reference-making situations which arise with contentives that do not arise with grammatical morphemes. One can point and say *That's a book* or even *Book*. One can respond to pointing and the question *What's that?* with the utterance *A book* and also to pointing and the question *What did John do?* with *Hit the ball* if not *Hit* alone. One cannot point and say *That's in,* let alone *That's the* or *That's -s.* Nor can one respond to questions and pointings with any of the grammatical morphemes for the reason that there are no *wh-* words in English which request the specification of particular grammatical morphemes though there are such words *(who, what, where, when)* for every sort of contentive word or construction. English includes no such word as **whel* which would enable one to request specification of a locative preposition with a question like **Whel is the penny the cup?* to which *In* would be a well-formed answer. Neither can one query articles only or inflections or the copula. There are clear differences of this sort between content words and our grammatical morphemes, but is the difference purely grammatical or does the grammar reflect a difference of meaning-type?

Some will feel that the grammatical differences are not the essence of the distinction. Behind the grammar, they may feel, and ultimately responsible for the grammar lies a difference in the possibility of reference itself. What sort of a difference? Is it that one can point at a book or at hitting and be confident that the other person will attend to the intended referent attributes whereas one cannot do this for the relation named *in* or to specificity of reference? This is not the case, or at least not obviously the case. For as philosophers and psychologists have long contended, any single pointing ought to be ambiguous. Is it the qualities defining books, whatever they are, that the pointer intends, or is it some accidental property of the particular book pointed at: the red color of the cover, the thickness of it, the size of it? It would seem as though the intended properties of books as such could only be abstracted from many pointings. But isn't it just this that is true of the relation called *in* and nonspecificity of reference and possession and so on? One can imagine possible pointings and namings which, though individually ambiguous, should converge on the intended sense. Thus: "That's a penny *in* the cup" and "That's a penny *on* the cup"; "That's *a* moon" and "That's *the* moon"; "That's *Daddy's* nose" and "That's *Mommy's* nose." The problem of the ungrammaticality of *That's in* or *That's the* is, incidentally, solved by constructing utterance pairs which highlight the grammatical morpheme by making it the only distinction between the members of a pair — and, optionally, by the use of heavy stress.

One might argue that the difference of reference lies elsewhere. At least a book may be pointed at without pointing at anything other than a book. And reference-making nouns generally do not necessarily entail anything other than their own reference. But what of verbs? The verb *hit* entails two arguments: an agent and an object. And in this respect it seems to be exactly like the preposition *in,* which also has two arguments, or the relation of possession, which again has two. Just as one cannot point at a hitting that includes no hitter and nothing hit so one cannot point at a relation "in" that involves no container and nothing contained or the relation "possession" without a possessor and a possessed. So there does not seem to be any consistent difference of this sort.

Still I and others[10] feel that there is some difference in the meanings of reference-making contentives and most grammatical morphemes. Some of the latter seem to "tune" or "modulate" the meanings associated with the contentives in the sense that the modulation is inconceivable without the more basic meanings. Thus *a* and *the* make the thing referred to by a noun specific or nonspecific. The present progressive *-ing* indicates that a process named by a verb is in progress at the time of speaking, but temporarily so. The past inflection indicates that a process named by a verb began and ended before the time of speaking. The plural inflection indicates that the thing referred to by a noun exists in more than one instance. It does not seem possible to think of these tunings or modulations without the things and processes they tune whereas it does seem to be possible to conceive of the latter without the former. Which is perhaps why the names alone are learned before the tunings.

But what shall we say of the possessive inflection, the prepositions *in* and *on,* the copular *be,* and the third person present *-s?* None of these seems to modulate the sense of a thing or a process. Three of them encode relations: the possessive, the prepositions, and the copula. What is the connection between these three relations and those expressed in Stage I by means of word order? The possessive inflection adds a usually redundant marker to such $N + N$ constructions as *Adam chair* and does not modulate the sense at all. The copular *be* appears in sentences with locatives, descriptive adjectives, and predicate nominatives. In the first two cases it adds a usually redundant marker to the expression of locative and attributive relations familiar in Stage I *(Sweater chair,* or *Ball big).* The third case, not often found in Stage I, includes sentences like *Daddy is a man* which seem to express an operation of classification. The present tense copula adds nothing to the meaning of the relation, but when the past tense copula appears — much later than II — it does modulate the relation. The *be* forms are used in English as auxiliaries with the progressive *-ing* in addition to being used as copulas. We shall see that in all the children the progressive is at first expressed by *-ing* alone and, in fact, this form reaches a criterion of 90 percent production in obligatory contexts before a single auxiliary *be* is spoken. The auxiliary *be* is completely redundant, being perfectly predictable from *-ing,* and it adds nothing to the meaning until, as with the copula, there is a past tense. The prepositions *in* and *on* seem clearly to modulate the simple locative expressed by nouns naming a movable object and a locus, in that order. *Sweater on chair* is a more exact expression than *Sweater chair.* Finally there is the *-s* inflection

10. Labov (private communication 1971) writes: "I think that the communicative content of most function words will eventually be seen as produced by discourse rules which orient the listener to one's point of view." I can certainly see how this applies to articles and tenses and aspect but not clearly that it applies to all the morphemes I have selected for study. But it is a most interesting idea.

put on the verb when the subject is third person singular and the tense is present. This is a form with rather complex grammatical determinants (number, person, and tense) which is, however, usually redundant. The person and number of the noun subject will normally be marked on the noun. The verb without the inflection *(She sing a song)* carries no contrastive meaning but simply registers as ungrammatical in a trifling sort of way.

In general summary, then, the grammatical morphemes we shall consider have the following kinds of semantic roles: 1. The progressive, past, and plural inflections, as well as the articles, seem to modulate the references made, in Stage I, by nouns and verbs in the sense that the modulations are inconceivable in isolation. 2. The locative prepositions seem to modulate, in the sense of specifying more exactly, the locative relation expressed by word order. 3. The present-tense copula and the possessive inflection seem to add redundant markers to relations of attribution, location, and possession expressed by word order in Stage I. 4. The present-tense auxiliary *be* seems to add a redundant marker to the progressive modulation. 5. The past-tense copula and auxiliary *be* when they appear seem to modulate further the meanings in question.

I am very sensible of the fact that these remarks do not constitute a satisfactory explicit definition of the kinds of meanings carried by our 14 morphemes. Indeed it looks as if they may not constitute a single class semantically except in the sense of being less essential than naming and the basic relations, either because they are inconceivable in isolation or because they render a meaning more precise or because they are usually redundant.

What follows next is the order of acquisition for Adam, Eve, and Sarah together with the sparse information available from the literature on other children learning English and other languages. Then comes a rather full discussion of the grammar, semantics, and frequency of the forms in question. This is succeeded by an effort to explain the approximately invariant order of acquisition in terms of the variables: semantic complexity and grammatical complexity. There follows a discussion of the important problem of "variability" in the use of the morphemes. And, finally, evidence that before the morphemes attain criterion they sometimes do not have separate morphemic status at all but are lumped together through errors of segmentation. An attempt is made to account for the fact that children usually segment correctly as well as for the occasional errors of segmentation.

The Order of Acquisition

We are interested in the acquisition of knowledge, both grammatical and semantic. At what point does the child know how to use a given form and when to use it? The data we have are data of spontaneous performance, and there are many difficulties in the way of defining a criterion of knowledge-acquisition in terms of performance data. For many sorts of construction, for example locative questions with *where,* one could consult the following: 1. the frequency with which the child uses the construction compared with the parental frequency, if the latter is fairly stable across samples; 2. the representativeness of the child's usage, the degree to which he exploits all the possibilities of the English *where* construction; 3. the grammatical and semantic appropriateness of the child's answers to the *where* questions of others. For many constructions, for example, noun phrases with two-or-more determiners or modifiers, only (1) and (2) are possible because there is no sort of parental utterance that tests the child's comprehension. So it is really frequency and variety of production that are the most generally available aspects of performance. The trouble with defining an acquisition criterion in terms of spontaneous frequency and variety, even when this is done in the light of parental frequencies, is that the numbers are bound to be responsive to the topic of conversation or the character of the interaction, in effect to what it is the child *undertakes* to say as well as what he is able to say. With grammatical morphemes we are in a somewhat better position. This is because the grammatical morphemes are *obligatory* in certain contexts, and so one can set an acquisition criterion not simply in terms of output but in terms of output-where-required. Each obligatory context can be regarded as a kind of test item which the child passes by supplying the required morpheme or fails by supplying none or one that is not correct. This performance measure, the percentage of morphemes supplied in obligatory contexts, should not be dependent on the topic of conversation or the character of the interaction.

How do contexts define "obligations"? Generally constraints are of four kinds:

1. Linguistic context, the child's own utterance. Thus *That book* pronounced with an intonation that makes *that* a demonstrative pronoun calls for a third person copula and an article.

2. Nonlinguistic context. If the child points as he speaks then the copula should be in the present tense rather than the past or future, and if he points at a single book the copula should be singular rather than plural. In the sentence in question it could be either uncontracted *(That is)* or contracted *(That's).*

3. Linguistic prior context, from child or others. If this is the first mention anyone has made of the book then the article ought to be the indefinite *a.* Had the noun been one that began with a vowel, such as *eraser,* then the obligatory indefinite would be *an.*

4. Linguistic subsequent context. The mother may confirm and expand the child's utterance as: *Yes, that's a book.* Occasionally the child himself expands his own utterance in this way. Coding for obligatory morphemes is a good deal easier than it is likely to seem when constraints are considered in the abstract. For the most part the several constraints converge on a single form, and the adult native speaker can tell at a glance what that form is.

How does the supplying of morphemes in obligatory contexts change with time? The gross change between I and V may be described as follows. As mentioned in Stage I, across all sorts of grammatical morphemes and contexts Adam, at I, produced only 6 percent of the required forms; Eve 13 percent; Sarah 16 percent. At V Adam produced 80 percent; Eve 57 percent; Sarah 85 percent. In the critical samples for Stage II we find that gross performance is better than at I, but much nearer I than V; for Adam 17 percent; for Eve 19 percent; and for Sarah 26 percent. Several not-surprising points are made by these figures. There is variation among children though all improve with time, and none is performing perfectly at V. The figures also suggest one rather surprising thing. It looks as if performance improves gradually and rather slowly rather than abruptly. However, the percentages quoted sum across all morphemes and a gradual rise in these percentages is not inconsistent with an ordered series of abrupt changes in the many particular morphemes.

Figure 12 presents individual acquisition curves for two grammatical morphemes, the progressive -*ing* and the plural -*s,* for Sarah over the whole course of her

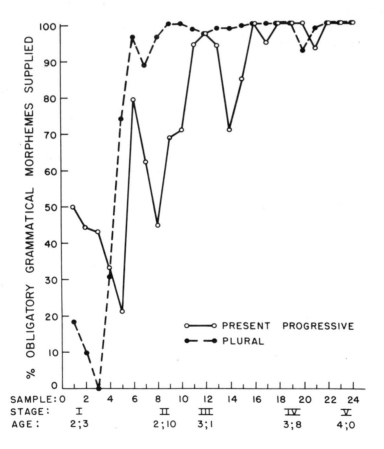

Figure 12. The development of progressive and plural inflections in Sarah

development from I to V. Each point, each sample number, represents four consecutive half-hour weekly samples. Sarah's samples were grouped in this way to make the sample size comparable to the samples for Adam and Eve which consist of two hours every other week. Plotted on the ordinate of Figure 12 is the percentage of each morpheme supplied in contexts where the morpheme is obligatory. The tremendous job of coding all these data was carried out by Courtney Cazden (1968). She coded all sentences in all samples from I to V not only for these two inflections but also for the other three English inflections: the past, the possessive, and the third person singular present indicative. The curves of Figure 12 are representative of the curves for the other inflections and also of the curves for certain additional morphemes to be discussed in this chapter.

There are several important things to notice in Figure 12. In the first place a considerable period of time elapses between the first appearances of a morpheme and the point where it is almost always supplied where required. The progressive ending, for example, is first supplied 100 percent of the time in obligatory contexts in sample 16. This comes 16 months later than sample 1 when -ing was supplied 50 percent of the time. We can be sure that there were some progressives and some plurals in Sarah's speech before we began to transcribe it, so that the time elapsing between first occurrences and a perfect performance is even longer than Figure 12 shows. It is true of all the grammatical morphemes in all three children that performance does not abruptly pass from total absence to reliable presence. There is always a considerable period, varying in length with the particular morpheme, in which production-where-required is probabilistic. This is a fact that does not accord well with the notion that the acquisition of grammar is a matter of the acquisition of rules, since the rules in a generative grammar either apply or do not apply. One would expect rule acquisition to be sudden.

In the early samples the curves describe some wild swoops up and down. This is again a general property of the curves of performance with grammatical morphemes, and I think it is explained by two considerations. The number of clearly obligatory contexts is smaller in the early samples than in the later because, in general, the constraints that define obligation are themselves acquired over time. Therefore the number of instances determining each data point is smaller in the earlier samples than in the later. The first point for the progressives, sample 1, was based on only four instances; the second point on 11. The sixteenth point was based on 26 sentences. To this we must add the fact that in summing across performances with a single grammatical morpheme we are, in varying degree, summing across performances requiring distinguishable bits of knowledge. In the case of the progressive, for instance, one obligatory context might include the question, said while pointing at a picture in a book, "What's the boy doing?" The child might know that such questions call for a progressive inflection on the responsive verb and yet not control that inflection when the speech cue was missing. Plural constraints include pure reference situations in which more than one instance is manifest (therefore *pencils* rather than *pencil*) as well as situations in which there is a plural determiner *(Two ___)* as well as situations in which the number of the subject constrains the number of the predicate nominal *(They are ___).* Obviously a child might know one of these things and not know another. Given that performance on even a single grammatical morpheme sums across various distinguishable kinds of knowledge and given that the number of instances in early samples is small the way is open for the wild swoops we see on the left in Figure 12. One small sample might primarily represent one kind of knowledge and another small sample a different kind of knowledge, and so the level of performance could careen wildly up and down.

At what point in an initially erratic, but gradually rising curve of performance, can "acquisition" be said to have taken place? In part, obviously, the answer must be arbitrary. However, we notice in Figure 12 that once a curve has passed above the 90 percent line for several consecutive samples it levels off within a range between 90 and 100 percent. This again is a fairly general property of the curves for inflections and other morphemes. Guided by this property of her data, Cazden defined the point of acquisition as "the first speech sample of three, such that in all three the inflection is supplied in at least 90 percent of the contexts in which it is clearly required" (p. 435). I have adopted the same criterion with the single difference that I have defined "sample" for Sarah in such a way as to make it comparable in size to the two-hour samples of Adam and Eve. One sample for Sarah consists of four consecutive half-hour samples. This difference between Cazden's definition and mine results in several small differences in points of acquisition for Sarah. In general, wherever special decisions about scoring had to be made I have simply adhered to those made by Cazden.

For the five English inflections we have complete data from Stage I to Stage V. For a set of additional morphemes only enough data were coded to locate the points of acquisition. The additional morphemes are the articles *a* and *the,* the prepositions *in* and *on,* the contractible copula and auxiliary, and the uncontractible copula and auxiliary. I did this coding and scoring after I had written the 15 complete grammars referred to in the Introduction. From the analyses done for the grammars the approximate locations of the acquisition points were known, and it was possible to find the exact points, in terms of three out of four samples at the 90 percent level, by coding between six and twelve samples in each case.

Not every morpheme scored attained criterion by Stage V in all three children. It would have been possible to consider all morphemes not at criterion by Stage V as unordered among themselves but all ordered after the morphemes that had attained criterion. However, this treatment would not have used all the information in the data. Some of the morphemes that fell short of the criterion at V were very close to it, and some were far from it. Therefore, for morphemes not at criterion by Stage V, I scored the last six hours of data in the set (three samples each for Adam and Eve, and twelve for Sarah) and obtained the mean percentage score. These morphemes were then ordered after V and, among themselves, in order of mean score without regard for the size of the differences between the means. For example, Adam at V had not reached criterion on the articles *a* and *the,* the uncontractible auxiliary, the contractible copula, and the contractible auxiliary. They were ordered as listed on the basis of the following mean percentage: 89 percent (articles); 68 percent (uncontractible auxiliaries); 61 percent (contractible copulas); 21 percent (contractible auxiliaries).

The Morphemes Scored

In this section we review scoring criteria, the nature of the obligatory contexts, and various ad hoc decisions made in connection with each morpheme. The end result of it all is 14 rank order scores for each child.

Cazden's Scoring of Inflections
1. *Present Progressive.* Adults form this construction with an auxiliary *be,* the form varying with the number and person of the subject, together with the inflection *-ing* on the main verb. All the children started out using the inflection without the auxiliary and attained criterion on the inflection long before they did on the auxiliary. For this reason Cazden separated the two components of the construction and tallied them separately. Several years later, for reasons to be described, I wanted to make a distinction among the auxiliaries which Cazden had disregarded: contractibility versus uncontractibility. And so I had to rescore the auxiliaries. It is my scoring that we shall use for the auxiliaries. From Cazden we take the complete scoring for the inflection.

Cazden did not include gerundives *(Stop crying)* or present participles used as modifiers *(Camping trip)* but only the *-ing* form when it was attached to the main finite verb. She kept separate tallies for different kinds of obligatory context. A nonverbal obligation exists when the transcription includes a note that the child is in fact *performing* the action he names as he names. An antecedent verbal obligation exists when the form of the mother's question requires the child to use the present progressive in his answer; for example, *What are you doing?* Another sort of antecedent verbal obligation exists when the child clearly means to imitate another's utterance, and that utterance is in the present progressive. A subsequent verbal obligation exists when another person "interprets" the child's utterance and, in doing so, uses a present progressive. A "routine" obligation exists when the child is reciting some familiar form that is ordinarily in the present progressive; for example, Eve's father when not at home was usually said to be at Emerson Hall (Harvard) "making pennies." Cazden also used a "miscellaneous category" for various kinds of rare and hard-to-characterize obligations. In determining the point of acquisition for *-ing* Cazden, and we here, simply sum across all these different kinds of obligations.

The *-ing* inflection has two allomorphs in adult English: /Iŋ/ and /In/. Fischer (1958), Labov (1966), and Anshen (1969) have shown that the two forms vary with the socio-economic class of the speaker ("lower class," "working class," "lower middle class," and so on) and with the style of the speech ("casual," "careful," and so on). The two allomorphs could not be separately tallied is the present case because only Sarah's data were transcribed with sufficient phonetic precision. And so the first of our fourteen grammatical morphemes is a progressive -ing, without auxiliary and undifferentiated by allomorph.

2. *Past*. In English there are both "regular" and "irregular" past forms. The regular past, which we shall symbolize as -*ed* certainly includes three phonologically conditioned allomorphs: $/\text{-d} \sim \text{-t} \sim \text{-id}/$. Because only Sarah's data were transcribed with the requisite precision the allomorphs were not separately tallied.

There are many forms of irregular past. Gleason (1961), not pretending to be exhaustive, lists 13 subclasses having three or more members each, another six subclasses containing two verbs each, and 34 subclasses containing a single verb each. Some of those that occur early in child speech are *came, fell, broke, sat,* and *went.* Irregular past forms were present, even at Stage I, in all three children and were *always* more frequent as a total set than the regular past, as they are also in adult speech. Clearly the regular and irregular past constitute partially distinct learning problems, and so there was reason to tally them separately. Ultimately, of course, each irregular subclass is a distinct problem, but if they are tallied separately the frequencies are too low to yield continuous data. So Cazden kept just two tallies, one for all regular pasts and one for all irregular pasts, and these constitute the second and third of our fourteen morphemes.

The contextual obligations are of the same general types as in the case of the present progressive. For example, a nonlinguistic obligation existed when the transcription included a note saying that the action the child named had occurred in the past. Several special decisions had to be made. The form *got* was excluded because it seemed to be used like a synonym for *have* though its form suggested a present perfect *(I've got)* with a missing auxiliary. When I studied tag questions in samples well after Stage V, I obtained clear evidence that *got* was simply an unmarked verb and not a past participle. The tag was formed with *do,* not *have*; *I got one, don't I?* And so Cazden's decision to omit *got* from a tally of past forms was correct. She also had to omit irregular verbs like *cut, hit,* and *hurt,* which in the past have the same form as in the present. She chose finally to omit the very infrequent forms that might have been perfectives or passives without auxiliary such as *I seen* and *It broken.*

3. *Third Person Singular Present Indicative*. This form, which is "governed" by the subject, has both regular and irregular variants in English. The regular, which we shall symbolize -*s*, has three allomorphs $/\text{-s} \sim \text{-z} \sim \text{-iz}/$ but for the usual reason, the allomorphs were not separately tallied. The irregular exists in only a few types (for example, *does, has*) but these have fairly high token frequencies, and, since the regular and irregular do constitute partially distinct learning problems, Cazden tallied them separately. They constitute the fourth and fifth of our 14 morphemes.

For the third person singular inflection it is peculiarly difficult to define obligatory contexts. For example, Eve, in sample 10, said: *Mommy use it*. The subject is third person singular clearly enough, but is it the inflection that is missing or a modal like *can* or possibly a present progressive? With the inflection we have: *Mommy uses it* which, for an adult, would mean that "using it" was something Mommy customarily did. The context in this case does not clearly indicate what Eve intended. Neither does it when Eve said *Cromer come on Wednesday* because, while Cromer (Richard Cromer, then a research assistant with the project) regularly visited on Wednesdays it is perfectly possible that Eve, thinking ahead to next Wednesday, intended: *Cromer will come on Wednesday*. Sometimes one can be more confident that a third person singular subject requires the *-s* inflection. For instance, when Eve, in sample 13, said of the baby *He want some milk out his cup*. The nonlinguistic context makes it clear that the reference was to the present time, and so *will* is ruled out. In addition, *want* is a state verb which does not take the present progressive *(He is wanting his milk)* in American English, and the children did not ever use such verbs in the progressive. *Want* as a stative also does not readily take *can,* so this seems to be a clear case in which *-s* is required but omitted. Cazden decided to include as obligatory contexts for *-s* only those cases in which a third person singular subject is combined with some other indication, such as a parental expansion or imitation model, which indicates that *-s* is the proper form.

It is, finally, important to note that the frequencies for *-s* when it was being reliably supplied were generally lower than for *-ing* and *-ed*. The figures vary with the character of the interaction but *-s* often occurs in 10–20 tokens per sample when *-ing* is occurring 30–70 times and *-ed* 20–40 times. The obligatory contexts occur with roughly proportionate frequencies prior to the point of acquisition. The data points for *-s* are, therefore, based on smaller frequencies than are those for the other two verbal inflections, and it is likely that the points of acquisition are somewhat less accurately placed.

4. *Plural*. Inflection for plural number exists in both regular and irregular forms in adult English. The regular form which we shall symbolize *-s* includes three familiar allomorphs, /–s ~ –z ~ –ɨz/, but these were not separately tallied for the usual reason. Among irregular forms there are a few words of fairly high frequency *(men, children, women),* but the overwhelming majority of noun stems in English follows the regular paradigm. Cazden found that irregulars were too few and infrequent to yield continuous data and so, while she took note of how they were handled, the only tally is of regular forms. And the regular plural is the sixth of our 14 morphemes.

The several forms of plural obligation have already been described. It may, however, be worthwhile to stress the fact that several partially distinct grammatical processes are lumped together under plurals: simple plural reference in naming, agreement with a plural determiner like *two, some,* or *many,* and predicate nominatives governed by a plural subject. We should also notice, because of its significance for certain analyses, that Cazden's plural tally does not include every grammatical form affected by number. The inflection for third person *singular* is governed by the number of the subject in conjunction with other features of the subject and verb. In addition, pronouns in English are selected in terms of the number of the referent *(him* in contrast to *them)* as well as in terms of person and gender. We have not included pronouns among the grammatical morphemes tallied in obligatory contexts.

5. *Possessive.* The morpheme marking possession in English has the same phonologically conditioned allomorphs as the plural, and these were not tallied separately for the usual reason. There are difficulties with treating the possessive genitive morpheme as a noun inflection comparable to the plural inflection. In adult English the possessive inflection is very rare with some nouns, and it is sometimes added to words that are not clearly nouns or which seem not to be the right nouns: *that man over there's hat* or the *mayor of Boston's reputation.* In Stages I to V such noun phrases as the above do not appear with the possessive morpheme; the morpheme is limited to single nouns and, usually, to animate single nouns. Cazden has treated it as a noun inflection, and we are counting it as our seventh morpheme.

The identification of obligatory contexts begins with $N + N$ constructions like *Fraser coffee* but not all such contexts require possessive inflection. They do if there is an expansion like *Yes, that's Fraser's coffee* or if the $N + N$ appears in a sentence like *That Fraser coffee* and so on. By contrast when Eve said *Fraser pencil* the expansion was *Fraser needs his pencil* and this $N + N$ was not counted as a context requiring the possessive. Many $N + N$ utterances must be interpreted as sentences lacking a copula; when Eve said *Eve horsie* she pranced around like a horse, and her mother took her to mean *Eve's a horsie.*

In addition to the $N + N$ construction in which the possessed object is named there is also, in English, an elliptical possessive which names only the possessor. For instance, in response to the question: *Whose little girl are you?* the response *Mommy* would be counted as an obligatory context for the elliptical possessive *Mommy's.* When Eve was going round the family group saying *That Mommy nose, That Eve nose,* and so on, the sentence, with appropriate pointing, *That Daddy* would be a context for elliptical possessive. Cazden adds to these examples the occasion when Sarah, telling how she had dropped her ice cream cone said: *And I shared Daddy's.* Cazden tallied the elliptical possessives in with the full possessives, but she kept track of the distinction, and we shall comment on it later. The grammar of the elliptical possessive is partially distinct from that of the grammar of the full possessive even as the grammar of the plural predicate nominative is distinct from that of simple plural reference.

Brown's Scoring of Prepositions, Articles, Copula, and Auxiliary

1. *Prepositions.* Several years ago I studied all of Eve's prepositional phrases in her first 12 samples (I to III) in conjunction with all the prepositional phrases spoken to her by adults in those same 12 samples. In the first six of these samples, Eve omitted prepositions more often than she supplied them. I found that it was almost

always possible to judge which preposition ought to have been supplied when none was. *Sitting chair* called for *in*; *Fall down floor* for *on*; *Piece celery* for *of*; *One Mommy* for *for*; *Play toys* for *with*. The judgments were based on the meanings of the words present, familiarity with certain routine phrases, and linguistic and nonlinguistic context. Only *in* and *on* were frequent enough to yield fairly continuous data. For most samples there were a dozen or more instances each of *in* and *on* supplied or of obligatory contexts requiring them. With the exception that samples 1 and 3 yielded no instances for *on*. Curves of the percentages of obligatory morphemes supplied for *in* and *on* (Figure 13) look somewhat like the corresponding curves for inflection. In early samples the curve moves erratically up and down but then it levels off between 90 and 100 percent. Analyses made at IV and V show that the performance stays at the 90 percent level or above. The acquisition curve for the prepositions differs from the curves for the inflections, copula, and articles in that one can, in the case of the prepositions, identify (between samples 6 and 7)

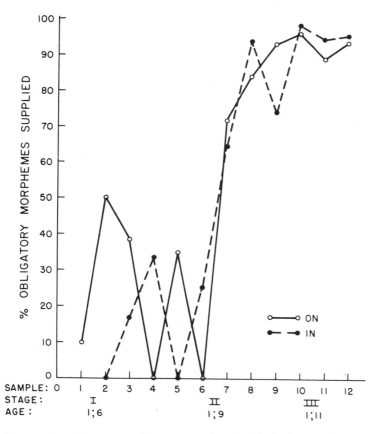

Figure 13.   The prepositions *in* and *on* in Eve's first twelve samples

a quite abrupt and continuous rise to criterion. Probably this is because the curves for *in* and *on* sum across much less varied semantic and grammatical subrules than do the curves for the other forms.

The grammars written for Sarah and Adam showed that prepositions developed in these children much as they did in Eve and that, as with Eve, *in* and *on* occurred frequently enough to yield continuous data. I located the acquisition points for Adam's *in* and *on* by scoring nine samples, and the points for Sarah by scoring 16 of her half-hour samples. The two prepositions *in* and *on* then, constitute our eighth and ninth morphemes.

2. *Articles.* I limited article coding to *a* and *the,* and did not attempt separate tallies of allomorphs though I kept track of contexts requiring *an* and of occurrences of *an.* As we have seen, *a* is used for nonspecific reference and *the* for specific reference. Furthermore, nonspecific reference may be subdivided into several types (introduction of a referent; reference to any instance of a class; idiom), and specific reference also may be divided into numerous types (unique referent, entailment, idiom). I attempted to tally all these separately but found, at once, that it was necessary to establish various "doubtful" categories. In the end the number of tallies in doubtful categories was so large that it was necessary to collapse all these distinctions and even that between *a* and *the* and settle for a single acquisition point for articles in general. There were simply too many contexts of which one could only say that an article was required, and not whether the reference was specific or nonspecific, let alone whether it was one variety of specificity rather than another. Consequently the articles *a* and *the* add only a single morpheme to our list, the tenth of fourteen.

In general, an article is obligatory in English wherever a common noun (not a proper noun like *Adam*) occurs in a sentence. Thus: *Man need it for house* called for articles before both *man* and *house.* In this case both articles should have been *the* because both *the man* and *the house* had been made specific by prior reference. In such other cases as *That train* the article *a* was required, since this was the first reference to the train. And in such other cases as *It's on couch* one could not tell which article was required but only that an article was required. It should be noted that while specific and nonspecific reference, and their varieties, often could not be coded there was a large number of perfectly clear instances, and we shall return to these when we discuss the semantic aspect of articles.

3. *Copula and Auxiliary* be. The verb *be* has three present tense forms: *am* (first person singular), *is* (third person singular), and *are* (second person singular and all plurals). These, together with the infinitive *be,* are the allomorphs of *be.* The selection of allomorphs is governed by grammar rather than phonology. The *be* forms are used as main verbs (the so-called copula) and also as auxiliaries of the progressive.

In doing the grammatical analyses for Stages I through V, I found the behavior of *be* particularly puzzling. For my analyses I separated out the several allomorphs and distinguished copulas from auxiliaries. It was clear fairly early that the copula-auxiliary distinction was a functional one and that auxiliary use in obligatory contexts developed more slowly than copula use. There was also a great deal of variation by allomorph and even by particular pronominal subjects, but this variation was very irregular from time to time and from child to child. The most puzzling thing was that, even with the data broken down by allomorph and in terms of copula and auxiliary, performance did not improve at all steadily, and was not close to criterion even by Stage V in Adam and Eve. Since the first copulas and auxiliaries appeared in Stage II, it looked as if the form must oscillate between presence and absence in obligatory contexts for something like two years, which seemed a very long time. And in this time progress was not at all continuous. Yet there were certain uses of *be* which were perfect or nearly so from quite an early point. For example, between II and III Adam almost always said *it's* where appropriate, whereas he said *this is* and *that's* only about 30 percent of the time where appropriate, usually saying *This dog* or *That kitty*. Between III and IV Adam used the following questions 36 times and never omitted a copula:

> *What is it?*
> *Who is it?*
> *Where is it?*

In the same samples there were 34 sentences of a set of closely related questions, but for this set the copula was omitted 17 times:

> *What's that?* or *What that?*
> *What's this?* or *What this?*
> *Who's that?* or *Who that?*

These and other unaccountable variations argued that we had not identified all the controlling variables for *be*.

The first clarification came when we noticed that Adam said such things as *It's went* and *It's will go* as well as *It's truck*. These overgeneralizations were the start of a trail of evidence which, in the end, showed that *it's* had not been analyzed by Adam into the pronoun and the copula but was rather organized in his grammar as the nominative or subject form of *it*. This discovery opened our eyes to a learning problem we had overlooked, the problem of segmentation, the breaking up of the essentially continuous stream of speech into morphemes and words. We shall come to the problem in this chapter but all that matters for the moment is that we had an explanation for the precocity of Adam's *it's* and a reason for separating *it's* from other uses of *be*. This was in Adam only, not in Eve and Sarah.

The most important illumination we owe to William Labov's (1969) paper "Contraction, Deletion, and Inherent Variability of the English Copula." At the very start of the article, which concerns nonstandard Negro English (NNE), now called "Black English" (BE), Labov writes: "However, whenever a subordinate (non-standard) dialect is in contact with a superordinate (standard) dialect it is not possible to investigate the grammar by eliciting intuitive judgments of grammaticality from native speakers. Data gathered by such a method will reflect the superordinate dialect more than the one studied" (p. 715). This statement suggests that Labov is in the same epistemological spot as the student of child speech, who also cannot draw upon judgments of grammaticality. And he has done what we have done, studied linguistic behavior. Labov's data in the present case derive from long-term studies of six adolescent and preadolescent peer groups in South Central Harlem and a subsample of 20 working-class adults from the same area. In addition, he worked with two white peer groups from the Inwood section of upper Manhattan, to obtain, as a basis for comparison, a picture of white nonstandard English (WNE).

The fundamental identity between Black English (BE) use of *be* and the child's use of *be* is its variable or probabilistic character. In BE, *be* forms are often omitted (Labov's analysis leads him to say "deleted") in contexts where they would be obligatory in standard English (SE). In this important respect BE resembles the speech of the child between Stage II and on beyond Stage V. With the difference that for the children we have studied, whose parents speak SE, the percentage of omissions declines with age and this, of course, is not true of the adult nonstandard dialect.[11] This is the beginning of a problem having a significance far beyond the copula *be,* and we postpone its discussion now in order to bring forward a more particular similarity between the BE use of *be* and child use, the similarity that brought order into our data.

Labov discovered that the variability of *be* forms in BE was a function of certain contingencies. The probability of omission varied with contingencies of several kinds, phonological, grammatical, and also situational. It was the grammatical contingencies that made the difference for us. In certain linguistic environments *be* forms were regularly supplied in BE. For example (from Labov):

> *Be cool, brothers.*
> *I don't care what you are.*
> *(You ain't the best sounder, Eddie!) I ain't! He is.*
> *Here I am.*
> *Who is it?*
> *What is it?*

The last two, the *wh-* questions, were among those from which Adam never omitted the copula between III and IV. And sentences like *I be quiet* and *I be good* and *Here*

11. Labov (1971) points out two qualifications that should be made in this statement. "Our main finding is that the rules are quite stable from 9–10 to 17–18 years. But then the percentage of deletion declines, even in casual speech." And, in addition: "We also have some evidence from Jane Torrey's work with younger children that the number of full forms of *is* is higher with 6–7 year olds, and deletion is learned, along with some other rules of the adolescent vernacular, as the child intensifies contact with the peer groups."

I am and *There it is* were also among those from which children almost never omitted the copula.

How do contexts like the above differ from contexts in which omission of *be* forms is frequent in BE? From Labov, here are some contexts of the second type:

> *Means he a faggot or sump'm like that.*
> *He fast in everything he do.*
> *You out the game.*
> *He just feel like he gettin' cripple up from arthritis.*

The difference in standard English is one of contractibility. Labov holds that the following general principle holds without exception: "Wherever SE can contract, NNE can delete *is* and *are,* and vice versa; wherever SE cannot contract, NNE cannot delete *is* and *are,* and vice versa" (p. 722). From memory of the data above and before I checked anything, I suspected that Adam, Eve, and Sarah at least in their later samples were following a more general version of this same rule: "Wherever SE can contract, child English can delete (whether *is, are,* or *am*) and vice versa; wherever SE cannot contract child English cannot delete and vice versa." This has proved to be the case.

Rules governing the possibility of contraction in SE have been formulated by Labov and will be discussed at a later point. What matters here is that contractibility has

Table 36. Performance with *be* forms classified by allomorphs, contractibility, and copula-auxiliary status (in percentages)

	Contractible				Uncontractible	
	Copula	Auxiliary			Copula	Auxiliary
-m	0.60	0.05	Adam, samples	am	1.00	–
-s	0.76	0.67	30–32	is	0.89	0.50
-z	0.44	0.15		are	1.00	0 60
-r	0.41	0.08		be	1.00	–
			Sarah ,samples			
			85–94			
-m	0.78	0.75		am	1.00	–
-s	0.96	0.91		is	0.94	0.92
-z	0.90	0.67		are	0.93	0.00
-r	0.58	0.62		be	1.00	–
			Eve, samples			
			17–19			
-m	0.29	0.08		am	1.00	–
-s	0.37	0.32		is	0.81	0.00
-z	0.38	0.00		are	0.60	0.50
-r	0.20	0.18		be	1.00	–

turned out to be the variable which, in conjunction with allomorphic status and the copula-auxiliary distinction, brings order into our data.

Table 36 presents the percentages of *be* forms supplied in various obligatory contexts in the last six hours of data, including Stage V, from Adam, Eve, and Sarah. It is not possible to use analysis of variance with data like these which include null entries, asymmetries, and wide variation in the numbers of instances entering into individual percentages. However, I think the picture is clear enough to enable us to determine by inspection that two variables strongly affect the percentages while a third has a marginal effect:

a. *Contractibility*. The relevant comparisons are between contractible and uncontractible copula allomorphs and contractible and uncontractible auxiliary allomorphs. Note, however, that the uncontractible *be* has no contractible counterpart and so cannot be included and that uncontractible *is* should be compared with both the -*s* and -*z* contractible allomorphs because it replaces both. With respect to the copula, all of Adam's and all of Eve's uncontractible forms are at a higher level than the contractible forms. For Sarah, three uncontractibles are higher than contractibles but *is* at 94 percent is lower than -*s* at 96 percent. However, both of these contractibles are above the criterion of acquisition whereas, in general, the differences favoring the uncontractible forms are differences between above- criterion levels and levels well below criterion. Supporting the conclusion that uncontractible copulas are advanced in performance beyond the contractible copulas is the result for uncontractible *be:* supplied where required 100 percent of the time by all three children. With respect to the auxiliary the results are almost even: five of nine possible comparisons yield a higher score for the uncontractibles. On the face of it this result should weaken our confidence in the conclusion, but in fact it ought not to do so because the number of instances of uncontractible auxiliaries (sometimes only one or two for a particular percentage) is too small to yield meaningful results. They were included for completeness.

b. *Copula-Auxiliary*. The relevant comparisons in Table 36 are the side-by-side columns under, respectively, "contractible" and "uncontractible." Of the 12 pairs

Table 37.   Performance rank orders for the allomorphs of *be*

Morpheme	Copula			Auxiliary		
	Adam	Sarah	Eve	Adam	Sarah	Eve
Contractible						
-s	1	1	2	1	1	1
-z	3	2	1	2	3	4
-m	2	3	3	4	2	3
-r	4	4	4	3	4	2
Uncontractible						
is	1.5	2	1	1	1	2
am	3	1	3	–	–	–
are	1.5	3	2	2	2	1

under "contractible" all but one has the copula at the higher level. Of the six pairs under "uncontractible" all show the copula form at a higher level. There is no doubt that the copula-auxiliary distinction is a significant one.

c. *The Allomorphs.* Table 37 presents the performance orders for the various morphemes, contractible and uncontractible, copula and auxiliary. With respect to the uncontractible morphemes there seems to be no regularity at all.[12] This, I think, may be because the copulas are almost all above the acquisition criterion level and, above that level, variation seems to be uninterpretable while the auxiliary percentages are based on so few instances as to be unreliable. With respect to the contractible morphemes, especially the copulas, there is some order, with -*m* and -*r* generally at a lower level than -*s* and -*z*. These may be reliable effects but it is not possible to be sure. Partly because the data are somewhat irregular and cases are few. In addition, there is the problem that the scores for some morphemes range over a greater variety of subjects than do others. For example, the morpheme -*m* has only *I* for subject, while -*r* has *we, you,* and *they* as well as plural noun phrases. Finally, some percentages are heavily weighted with a few very frequent utterances *(-s* with *What's that),* while for others almost every utterance is unique.

In scoring data for acquisition thresholds I have preserved the clearly significant distinctions (contractible-uncontractible); (copula-auxiliary) but have collapsed together all the allomorphs of *be.* I disregarded the allomorphs because the significance of this dimension of variation is marginal and, more important, because some of the allomorphs are too infrequent to yield continuous data, especially the uncontractible auxiliaries. What we have then are four morphemes: contractible copula, contractible auxiliary, uncontractible copula, and uncontractible auxiliary. These complete the set of 14 with which we are concerned. Points of acquisition were determinable from six samples for Eve, nine for Adam, and eight sets of four half-hour samples for Sarah.

Grammatical Morphemes Not Scored

Not all verbal inflections and auxiliaries have been included in the scoring. The perfective (represented by Chomsky (1957) as *have + en*), the passive (representable

12. Labov (1971) points out that uncontractible copula *am* is third ranking for both Adam and Eve. Labov adds that he and Jane Torrey have evidence indicating that the segmentation of *am* is the hardest of any of the allomorphs, and this factor may help explain the results. Labov suggests another factor that may have helped produce the results of Table 37: the consonant of contracted copula *are* is a liquid, the most difficult final consonant for children to produce, but in uncontracted form *are* is preceded by a clear vowel, which makes the morpheme easy for children to hear. Perhaps this is why the contractible copula -*r* ranks last for all children, whereas uncontractible *are* has a higher rank for Adam and Eve, though not for Sarah. I think these proposals of Labov's are very plausible but the data do not bear them out with perfect consistency, and they are not sufficient to explain all the entries in Table 37. So I continue to believe that the results in Table 37 are, as they stand, too inconsistent and fragmentary to be interpreted with confidence, but more research of another sort might very well demonstrate that Labov's suggestions are correct.

as *be* + *en* but better treated as a syntactic transformation) were omitted because they are almost totally absent through Stage V. The data we have beyond V for Adam and Sarah show that both constructions were late acquisitions.[13] Had they been included they would have *increased* the correlations among orders of acquisition of the three children, since they were well beyond V for all three. The modal auxiliaries *will* and *can* were not included because they are best discussed in connection with major sentence modalities in Stage III. The semi-auxiliaries *wanna, gonna, hafta, liketa,* and *tryna* are fairly frequent from Stage II on, and we shall have something to say about them in connection with the semantics of the progressive and past. However, it is not possible to identify obligatory contexts for these with any reliability and, in addition, they raise questions of sentence embedding, which are best discussed in connection with Stage IV.

In the sections describing the scoring of prepositions and articles I have pointed out that only *in* and *on* and *a* and *the* yielded sufficiently continuous data to be tallied for acquisition thresholds. Other prepositions were occasionally present from III on, including *of, for, with, by,* and *like,* and also other articles, including *another* and *some.* Indeed, *another* (or *'nother*) was used even in Stage I to express recurrence. Conjunctions have not been tallied because they were largely absent until IV and V and are best discussed in connection with the process of sentence coordination. Pronouns have not been included because they do not seem to be grammatical morphemes in quite the same sense as the others. They do not tune or modulate the meanings of nouns and verbs but rather stand in place of noun phrases. Some of them are present even in Stage I.

What we have then is a "selection" of 14 grammatical morphemes selected primarily because obligatory contexts can be identified for them and because they are frequent enough to yield continuous data. None of them, it should be remembered, has been conceived as narrowly as possible, all sum across more than one allomorph or more than one kind of grammatical structure. This kind of summing was dictated by the need to hit a level general enough to yield continuous data. It is reasonable to suppose that conceiving them more narrowly if the data would permit ought to increase the constancy of the order of acquisition across children because it would increase the constancy of what is being counted from sample to sample.

The Order of Acquisition

The order of the fourteen morphemes for Adam, Sarah, and Eve is pictured in Figure 14. The names of the morphemes are written from top to bottom to represent early to late. The spacing of the names relative to the stages (I to V) and to one another represents the spacing in time of the points of acquisition. The stages have,

13. Labov (1971) points out that perfectives and passives seem also to be late in the process of historical development in the Creole continuum.

you will recall, constant central mean-length-of-utterance (MLU) values for all the children: Stage I, MLU = 1.75; Stage II, MLU = 2.25; Stage III, MLU = 2.75; Stage IV, MLU = 3.50; Stage V, MLU = 4.00. The ages of the children at each stage vary, and they appear in Figure 14. Through Stage V the criterion of acquisition is three successive samples in which the morpheme appears 90 percent of the time, or more, in obligatory contexts. For all children three successive samples constitute approximately six hours of transcription.

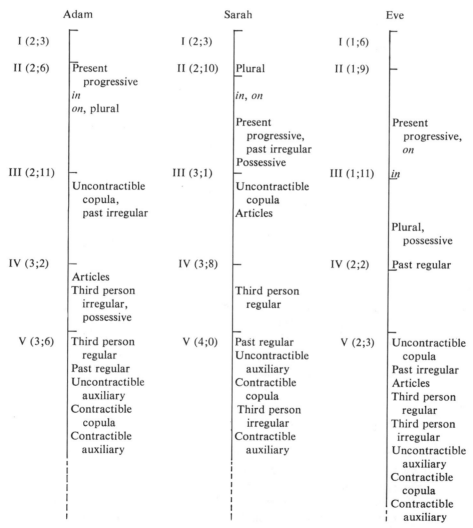

Figure 14.   The order of acquisition of 14 grammatical morphemes in three children

The morphemes listed below Stage V had not attained the 90 percent criterion at this point. They are ordered in terms of the percentages of the morphemes supplied in obligatory contexts in the last six hours of the records including Stage V. While this is actually an order of level of performance at V it probably corresponds quite closely with the order of ultimate acquisition. Consider, for example, the eight morphemes which in Eve, the youngest of the three children, had not attained criterion by V. The top three were all at average levels of 80 percent or more in the final six hours. These three morphemes, the uncontractible copula, the past irregular, and articles had all attained acquisition criterion before V in both Adam and Sarah. On the other hand, Eve's last three morphemes (uncontractible auxiliary, contractible copula, and contractible auxiliary), which were at levels 56 percent or below, had none of them attained criterion in Adam or Sarah by V. In further illustration, notice that the first of Adam's morphemes below V had attained criterion before V in Sarah.

While the morphemes below V are ordered with respect to one another in the particular child's performance it is not the case that a given ordinal position represents the same level of performance across children. For example, Sarah's tenth morpheme and the first below V, the past regular, was present an average of 95 percent of the time in the last six hours though not yet at a consistent level across samples of 90 percent or better. Eve's tenth morpheme, on the other hand, which was the fourth below V, the third person regular, was at a 77 percent level.

There are three important conclusions to be drawn from Figure 14. The most important is this: the developmental order of the fourteen morphemes is quite amazingly constant across these three unacquainted American children. The constancy may be expressed in terms of Spearman rank-order correlation coefficients (rhos). The rhos, corrected for ties are as follows: Adam and Sarah, 0.88; Adam and Eve, 0.86; Sarah and Eve, 0.87. The reasons why this degree of constancy should amaze are, I am sure, quite evident. The basic data consist of uncontrolled spontaneous speech. Performance levels are not simple frequencies which might be expected to be fairly stable in conversational English for morphemes of this kind but are a genuine quality of performance or competence measure: percentages supplied in obligatory contexts. For none of the morphemes can it be said that the instances counted are entirely homogeneous. For example, there are several allomorphs of the regular plural and several kinds of grammatical agreement are involved, and so the instances entering into one sample might represent quite a different range from the instances entering into another. Nevertheless the constancy is there. Some factor or some set of factors caused these grammatical morphemes to evolve in an approximately consistent order in these children. Of course I have known for years that this was true of grammatical devices generally because I could see it in the grammars that I wrote. But I had no idea in advance just how true it would prove to be for this set of morphemes when all were carefully scored and ordered in terms of the same criteria.

The second conclusion is that while order of development approaches invariance, rate of development varies widely. Compare Eve at age 2;3 (her Stage V) with Adam and Sarah at age 2;3 (their Stage I). Eve had attained criterion on six morphemes and was close to it on three others; all were present to some extent. Adam and Sarah had attained criterion on no morphemes at all, and most were completely absent from their speech.

The third conclusion is that MLU, or our Stages I to V, which are defined in terms of MLU, is a fairly good index of the level of development of grammatical morphemes at least through Stage V when MLU = 4.00. Adam, Eve, and Sarah at V had all attained criterion on five morphemes (present progressive, *on, in,* plural and possessive) and had either attained criterion or were very close to it (80 percent or better) on another four (uncontractible copula, past irregular, articles, past regular).

The third conclusion is that, while chronological age alone is a poor index of level of development, age in conjunction with MLU is a better predictor than MLU alone. Another way of putting this is that if two children at the same stage or MLU value are also at the same age they are more alike in their control of our grammatical morphemes than if they are at the same stage and the ages are quite far apart. Adam and Sarah are more like one another in terms of how much they have acquired at a given stage than either is like Eve, and Adam and Sarah are closer in age to one another than to Eve.

Acquisition Order in Other Studies of Spontaneous Speech

Until the spring of 1972 no one but Cazden and I had coded data in terms of presence in, or absence from, obligatory contexts but then Jill and Peter de Villiers (in press) did the job on a fairly large scale. They made a cross-sectional study from speech samples of 21 English-speaking children aged between 16 and 40 months. The speech samples ranged in size from 200 to 900 utterances. The de Villiers scored the 14 morphemes we have scored; they used our coding rules to identify obligatory contexts and calculated the children's individual MLU values according to our rules. Because their speech samples were much smaller than ours the problem of variability with certain morphemes was more severe and the de Villiers adopted the practice of including in the scoring of a given morpheme only transcripts which included at least five obligatory contexts for that morpheme.

Two different criteria of morpheme acquisition were used in the analyses of data. By method I, the morphemes were ranked in terms of the order of the lowest MLU sample at which each reached the 90 percent criterion; when more than one morpheme attained criterion at the same MLU the ranks were counted as tied. This is a kind of cross-sectional adaptation of our primary criterion. The second (II) way of calculating acquisition order is the same essentially as the method I used for morphemes that had not attained the 90 percent criterion by Stage V. The percentages supplied in obligatory contexts for each child were averaged across

Table 38.　Mean order of acquisition of 14 morphemes across three children

Morpheme	Average Rank
1. Present progressive	2.33
2–3. *in, on*	2.50
4. Plural	3.00
5. Past irregular	6.00
6. Possessive	6.33
7. Uncontractible copula	6.50
8. Articles	7.00
9. Past regular	9.00
10. Third person regular	9.66
11. Third person irregular	10.83
12. Uncontractible auxiliary	11.66
13. Contractible copula	12.66
14. Contractible auxiliary	14.00

all children and the morphemes were ranked for order of acquisition. The study then yielded two morpheme acquisition rank orders: I (utilizing a 90 percent criterion); II (utilizing percentages supplied). To compare with the de Villiers' two orders it was necessary to have a single rank order for the three children: Adam, Eve, and Sarah. This I obtained by averaging the orders appearing in Figure 14 across the three children. This procedure yields Table 38 in which the average of the three ranks follows the name of each morpheme.

We have then three rank orders for the same 14 morphemes scored in the same way and using closely similar criteria of acquisition. We will call the two orders of the de Villiers', I and II, and mine, III. The degree of invariance is, even to one who expected a substantial similarity, amazing. The rank order correlations are: between I and II, .84; between II and III, .78; between I and III, .87. These relations are only very slightly below those among Adam, Eve, and Sarah themselves. Thanks to the de Villiers it has been made clear that we have a developmental phenomenon of substantial generality.

There are numerous other interesting outcomes in the de Villiers' study. The rank order correlation between age and order II is .68, while that between MLU and the same order is .92, very close to perfect. So MLU is a better predictor than age in their study as in ours of morpheme acquisition. In fact with age partialed out, using a Kendall partial correlation procedure, the original figure of .92 is only reduced to .85, suggesting that age adds little or nothing to the predictive power of MLU.

One result reverses mine: the de Villiers generally found that the contractible copula and auxiliary *be* forms attained criterion before the uncontractible forms. Neither they nor I have a really persuasive explanation of this reversal. There are many possibilities and as yet no strong evidence for any one of them.

Except for the de Villiers' study (in press), reports in the literature all concern one or another subset of the full set of 14 morphemes, and so the best we can do is check the full ordering on our explicit criterion against various partial orderings on criteria that are either not explicit or explicit but different from our own. It is, however, of some interest to know how general the order seems to be and how free it is of any single acquisition criterion.

Besides the ordering of the 14 morphemes we know that they are almost totally absent in Stage I for Adam, Eve, and Sarah. The generality of this, roughly the "telegraphic" quality of child speech, was documented for English and all languages so far studied in our Stage I, and so I shall not cite data or statements to this effect here. The inherent variability of the morphemes, being sometimes present in and sometimes absent from, obligatory contexts, during the early course of development does still need the support of other data, and so I will include some of that here. We proceed study-by-study.

Menyuk's Work.

Paula Menyuk, in four research papers (1963a, 1963b, 1964a, 1964b), has presented cross sectional (one-time) data on several hundred children between the ages of three and seven years and longitudinal data on a very few children younger than three. In her book, *Sentences Children Use* (1969), Menyuk reviews and integrates this work and adds some new analyses and, apparently, some new data. I say "apparently," because in the book it is difficult to determine the exact data base of certain statements. As I make it out, however, the monthly longitudinal samples for two children from 2;0 to 2;9 are new data not described in the research papers. Presumably it is these data, plus the year-long study of a single normal child between the ages of two and three reported in 1964b, which Menyuk draws upon in describing the earliest stages of syntax. A sample of three seems quite large enough to me, if not to anyone else.

Menyuk's large cross-sectional samples are typically grouped as "nursery school," "kindergarten," and "first grade." They are high IQ samples (with means between 120 and 130) and high socio-economic status samples (the fathers typically being professionals). They are usually evenly balanced between males and females. The situational sampling for spontaneous speech is admirably broad: 1. children's responses to pictures of the "Blacky Test," a projective for young ones; 2. children's remarks in conversation with the researcher, who draws upon a standard set of inquiries; 3. children's talk among themselves, playing "family" in groups of three. Often, too, Menyuk made transcriptions of interaction in the school, whatever the character of the interaction. Besides spontaneous speech Menyuk has frequently used the method of imitation, either of well-formed adult sentences or of deviant child sentences. I include these results here rather than under "experimental data" because the imitation situation is a familiar and easy one for children and does not create the special problems of experimental testing. With so much fine data it is bad luck for me that Menyuk reports most of it in ways I cannot use.

I think Menyuk's way of presenting data is consistent with her choice of a title for the book: *Sentences Children Use*. This is a very cautious, close-to-the-data title, only one degree more general than: *Sentences Children Used*. There is none of your overambitious *The Acquisition of Language* claims here.[14] The title seems to reflect the view held by linguists at the Massachusetts Institute of Technology that one cannot learn about "competence" from mere "performance." In reporting the data, frequencies of constructions are never given. Instead Menyuk usually reports the number of children in a given group who used a certain kind of construction at all, whether once or many times. This decision may reflect another common M.I.T. position: how often a person uses a certain sort of construction reflects his motivation, the character of the interaction, and other such variables, all of which have to do with performance rather than competence. This is right, of course, and frequency as such is not a very useful variable. But frequency generally goes with diversity of type. And if one believes, as I do, and Bloom and Leopold and Grégoire and many others do, that a given utterance token can be produced without full knowledge of all the grammar that is in it, from the adult point-of-view, and even, at an extreme, as an unanalyzed routine, then diversity of type is important. For only if closely related variants occur is it likely that performance of a certain construction represents full grammatical understanding. And diversity is generally associated with high frequency.

Even with these differences of approach between us there are some things in Menyuk's work that bear on our question of the generality of the acquisition order. For example, in her (1969) book, she writes: "However, it should be stated now that the progression in this limited data seems to be from Verb to Verb + present progressive to Verb + past to Aux be/Modal + Verb. Although there are utterances at the early period which indicate the presence of an auxiliary ('Mommy's shaking pencil') the more frequent occurrence during the early months of this period, and somewhat later are utterances such as 'Marie writing name' and 'I making cake too' " (p. 37). Two important things are here. The second sentence reports that the auxiliary for the progressive was, early on, usually absent but occasionally present. That corresponds with our data. The first sentence says that, in acquisition, the unmarked verb precedes the progressive *-ing,* which precedes the past, which precedes the auxiliary *be*. All that is exactly as in Table 38. Menyuk also refers to modals, which we did not code for the present analysis.

On page 81 of *Sentences Children* Use we have a comment which is related to those above but which adds something significant. "Alternation between the use of the contracted form of the auxiliary 'be' and omission of the contracted form also occurs with preschoolers under the age of 3;6." What is new here is the specific limitation of alternation to *contracted* forms. Menyuk seems nowhere to say that, when

14. In 1971, P. Menyuk published *The Acquisition and Development of Language* (Englewood Cliffs, N.J.: Prentice-Hall). Which should teach me not to make wisecracks.

contracted copular and auxiliary *be* were alternating with omission, the uncontracted forms were almost invariably present. That this was the case with Adam, Eve, and Sarah can be seen in the data of Table 36 and in the rank order of Table 38 where we find that the uncontractible copula is rank 7, the contractible, 13, and the uncontractible auxiliary is rank 12, the contractible, 14.

Another comparison involving auxiliary *be* is of interest. In Menyuk (1963b), it is noted that of 48 nursery school children whose mean age was 3;8 all 48 made at least *some* use of auxiliary *be.* (This does not, of course, say that they were using it usually). Of the same 48 children only eight made any use of the perfective auxiliary *have,* and fewer than half of a first-grade group (mean age = 6;5) used the form. It seems clear that auxiliary *have* was acquired later than auxiliary *be,* and so it was by Adam, Eve, and Sarah. We did not tally this morpheme because there were almost no uses all the way through Stage V.

Concerning the development of noun and verb inflections Menyuk notes in her 1963b article that they are all at first sometimes present and sometimes absent. In Table 3, p. 415, she gives the number of children (out of 48) in nursery school who show at least *some* omission of certain morphemes and corresponding numbers (also out of 48) for first graders. The following entries have a rough sort of relevance to our problem (N = 48).

	Nursery School Omissions	First Grade Omissions
Possessive	7	0
Noun form (plurals)	10	6
Articles	16	2
Verb form *(-s* or *-ed)*	29	20

If we take the number of children showing *some* omissions to be a rough index of order of acquisition then the listing above is the order, from early to late, imposed by the nursery school data. For the first graders all but the verb form omissions were almost entirely absent. The order above corresponds with the order of these morphemes in Table 38 except for a single reversal of one position, the plural should precede the possessive.

This is all that I have been able to find in Menyuk's published work (through 1969) that is directly relevant to the generality of the order of acquisition. I have not, of course, searched only for supportive evidence but for all relevant evidence. However, the relevant evidence has all turned out to be supportive, specifically of the following: inherent variability of production of the morphemes, the appearance of the progressive *-ing* before the auxiliary *be* with the auxiliary oscillating between presence and absence at least until 3;6 in *contractible* contexts, and the auxiliary *have* coming well after the auxiliary *be.* In addition, there is confirmation of the ordering of two subsets of morphemes from Table 3: 1. generic verb, progressive *-ing,* past *-ed,* auxiliary *be;* 2. possessive and plural, articles, third person *-s* and *-ed.*

Leopold's Work

Werner Leopold's (1949) study of the development of speech in his daughter Hildegard deals in detail with only the first two years, and in that time none of the 14 grammatical morphemes attained our criterion. Nevertheless his book contains some observations relevant to our discussion. On the most general level there is the following: "The child, whose attention is at first drawn only to the major elements of the mechanism of communication neglects the morphological devices for a considerable length of time. The elements affected by this neglect are not only morphological endings and other modifications of the word-stem, but also form-words, that is, small words like prepositions and auxiliary verbs used for the same purposes" (p. 76). I include this quotation not because it attests to the telegraphic quality of early speech, for which we already have sufficient testimony, but because it makes a point of the fact that "little words" like prepositions and auxiliary verbs are treated in the same way as inflections. On the inherent variability of performance with the grammatical morphemes there are many attestations in Leopold. One will suffice: "The use of nouns without a plural ending continued along with the sporadic use of nouns with a plural ending (even beyond the two-year limit)" (p. 80).

From Menyuk I worked out the ordering of acquisition for two subsets of morphemes using a criterion available in her reports but quite different from my own 90 percent criterion. It is interesting to do the same with Leopold. The only basis for an ordering, offered by his report, is whether a given form occurred at all by the

Table 39. The 14 morphemes in order of acquisition for Adam, Eve, and Sarah; together with paraphrases of Leopold's comments on each morpheme for Hildegard's first two years

Morpheme	Comment
1. Present progressive	Two forms by 2;0. Not so numerous as plural.
2–3. *in, on*	"The preposition was omitted from all adverbial phrases."
4. Plural	First one at 1;10. A small number from 1;11.
5. Past irregular	Only *forgot* and *got* by 2;0. Latter seems synonymous with *have*.
6. Possessive	Concept expressed from 1;6 as $N + N$. First -*s* at 1;10. Not numerous.
7. Uncontractible copula	Dissyllabic *this* (as in *This 's mine* seems based on *this is*.
8. Articles	Not used at all in first two years.
9. Past regular	None at all through 2;0.
10. Third person regular	None at all through 2;0.
11. Third person irregular	None at all through 2;0.
12. Uncontractible auxiliary	No auxiliary with progressives through 2;0.
13. Contractible copula	Copula always missing until 2;0.
14. Contractible auxiliary	No auxiliary with progressives through 2;0.

Source: Based on Leopold, 1949.

age of two years. Table 39 summarizes Leopold's observations about each morpheme. Except for *in* and *on,* all the forms above the double line in Table 39, that is, ranks 1, 4, 5, and 6, are mentioned by Leopold as having occurred by the age of two years. All the forms below the line, ranks 7–14, are said not to have occurred at all. Except that the first of these, the uncontractible copula, rank 7, sounds as if it were present, since *this* in subject position is pronounced as a disyllable. Leopold's comments afford no basis for a ranking among forms that never occurred or among forms that did occur with the possible exception of plurals, which seem to deserve rank 1. I find it quite striking that these "first-occurrence" comments on a bilingual child studied more than 20 years ago should rather neatly divide the 14 morphemes into two sets such that there is only one cross-over with respect to the rank order we obtained from other children, using a different criterion, in the 1960's.

The Work of Ervin and Miller

Wick Miller and Susan Ervin (now Ervin-Tripp) in their 1964 paper describe the development of certain grammatical morphemes in three children: Harlan, Susan, and Christy. Most of the detail concerns Harlan, who seems to have entered Stage II at about 2;2, the most common noun markers were *the, a,* and the plural suffix *-s.* The markers were sometimes omitted in contexts where they should have been used: *I want the duck, I want the duck, I want duck* (p. 27). And, the following (p. 26) on verb markers: "The markers were not always used, however:

Inv:	*It popped.*
Harlan:	(To his mother) *My balloon pop.*
Mother:	*You popped it.*
Harlan:	*I pop it.*"

Miller and Ervin collected controlled, semi-experimental data which give evidence of inflection order, and we shall discuss that at a later point. Concerning morpheme order in spontaneous speech I find only the following. At 2;2 the progressive was simple *-ing* with no form of the auxiliary *be.* At 2;3 the auxiliary was used sporadically. It was not used consistently until 2;8. Since Harlan at 2;2 was using, sporadically, *-ed* and articles as well as *-ing,* we can infer that auxiliary *be* was acquired later than all these by Harlan, as by Adam, Eve, and Sarah.

Brown and Fraser's Imitation Data

In 1963 Brown and Fraser reported a small experiment on the imitation of sentences by six children, not including Adam, Eve, and Sarah, who came later. The sentences were simple and short. They included single instances of the following morphemes from the set that concerns us: progressive, plural, *in,* past regular, third person irregular, third person regular, contractible copula and contractible auxiliary. In addition there were eight instances of articles *a* and *the.* The children ranged in age from 25½ months (2;1.5) through 35½ months (2;11.5), and imitation performance showed considerable general improvement with age. The youngest child did not accurately reproduce even one sentence whereas the oldest accurately reproduced 10 out of 13.

Brown and Fraser demonstrated that the grammatical morphemes in the model sentences were much more likely to be omitted in the children's imitations than were the nouns, verbs, and adjectives. It is reasonable to suppose that a grammatical morpheme has a better chance of being retained and reproduced by a child when the child has acquired knowledge of the use of the morpheme than when he has not, and so, that retention compared to omission in imitation is a rough index of level of grammatical control. It is also reasonable to suppose that chronological age provides a rough ordering of grammatical maturity for these six children, who had similar middle-class white backgrounds. Building on these assumptions we may use the retention/omission results for the various morphemes as an independent test of the order of development in Table 38. If chronological age predicts grammatical maturity then preservation scores across all morphemes will be positively correlated with age, and they are so. If the morphemes were being learned by the Brown and Fraser children in the order of Table 38 then preservation scores for individual morphemes across all subjects should be negatively correlated with lateness in the order of Table 38.

The results are pictured in Table 40. The children are ranged in order of age and, as one sees in the last column, total preservation scores rise with age. The morphemes are ranged from left to right in acquisition order from early to late. The totals in the bottom row do fall as predicted from left to right though not with perfect consistency. The extremes nicely confirm the order of Table 38, since the three morphemes with the highest preservation scores are the three that come earliest in the acquisition order, and the two morphemes that come last in the acquisition order have the lowest and second-lowest preservation scores. The middle four are not ordered as the hypothesis predicts.

Table 40.   Preservation of morphemes in imitation data of Brown and Fraser[a]

Age	Present Progressive	in	Plural	Articles	Past Regular	Third Person Regular	Third Person Irregular	Contractible Copula	Contractible Auxiliary	Totals Correct
2;1.5	+	−	−	−	−	−	−	−	−	1
2;4.5	−	−	+	⅛	−	−	−	−	−	1⅛
2;6	+	+	+	⅜	+	−	+	−	−	3⅜
2;7	−	+	−	⅝	−	+	−	+	−	3⅝
2;8	+	+	+	⅞	+	+	+	−	+	7⅞
2;11.5	+	+	+	⅞	−	+	+	−	+	6⅞
Totals Correct	4	4	4	2⅞	2	3	3	1	2	

[a]Left to right order represents order of acquisition from Table 38.

Table 41.   Brown's acquisition order for the 14 morphemes and the partial rank orders of acquisition of other investigators

	Brown	Menyuk[a]		Leopold	Ervin-Miller	Brown-Fraser
1. Present progressive	1			1	1	1
2–3. *in, on*				2	—	1
4. Plural			2	1	—	1
5. Past irregular				1	—	—
6. Possessive			1	1	—	—
7. Uncontractible copula				1.5(?)	—	—
8. Articles			3	2	1	3
9. Past regular	2		4	2	1	4
10. Third person regular			4	2	—	2
11. Third person irregular				2	—	2
12. Uncontractible auxiliary	3	1		2	2	—
13. Contractible copula				2	—	5
14. Contractible auxiliary	3	1		2	2	4
(Perfective)		2				

[a]There are three columns for Menyuk because in her rules she provides evidence relating three different small sets of morphemes with respect to one another in terms of acquisition order but does not provide evidence relating morphemes from different sets.

Conclusions

There are many studies of the spontaneous speech of children learning English that include some reference to the 14 grammatical morphemes, but it is probably not worthwhile to extend the somewhat forced and partial analyses that are possible beyond those reported above. From the de Villiers (in press), after all, we have a quite general and exact replication of the order obtained for Adam, Eve, and Sarah.

How much "generality" for the order of Table 38 is suggested by the partial orderings of investigations using criteria other than our own? Table 41 summarizes all that we have gleaned. In a given column numbers appear opposite just those morphemes which are developmentally ordered with respect to one another by the data or summary statements of an investigator or pair of investigators. No column in Table 41 offers a complete ranking, most have gaps in them and most have ties. Still there is at least one observation relating each morpheme to each other morpheme though the relation is sometimes simply equivalence. For the most part the results support the ranking we have obtained from Adam, Eve, and Sarah. The three Menyuk columns, for instance, are exactly as they should be, except for the single reversal in the top two ranks of the third column. The Leopold column is exactly as it should be except for the rank assigned *in-on*. The Ervin-Miller column is perfect. The Brown-Fraser column is more mixed with the first three being fine and the last two correct except for a reversal of one position, but the middle rather mixed. Considering the fact that in all these studies criteria for order of development were used which are entirely different from the 90 percent criterion used with

Adam, Eve, and Sarah, and different also one from another, these results suggest that the order we obtained is fairly independent of criterion of acquisition, children studied, and investigator. With a full ordering, using criteria much like our own, we obtain the really astonishing confirmation the de Villiers (in press) have provided.

Acquisition Order in Controlled Studies

It was Jean Berko (1958), now Jean Berko Gleason, who invented the basic method used in these studies. The investigator will, for instance, point at a picture of a dog and say: "Here's a dog." And then at a second picture in which there are two dogs and say: "Now there are two of them. There are two ____?" The child subject is to supply the answer *dogs,* and in doing so he pluralizes the noun *dog.* Berko devised similar "eliciting techniques" for the progressive inflection, and for the past tense, possessive, and third person singular inflections. For the progressive she used a lead like the following. "This is a man who knows how to drive. What is he doing?" (A picture shows him driving.) "He is _____." In a similar way, eliciting contexts were set up for all the other inflections. This testing technique is possible just because there are obligatory contexts for certain grammatical morphemes, contexts created by denoting a referent and using critical words like *two* for the plural, the auxiliary *is* for the progressive, *yesterday* for the past, *every day* for the habitual action of the third person present, and *whose* for the possessive. The difference between Berko's test and our scoring of Adam, Eve, and Sarah is that, in the former case, the investigator supplies the obligatory contexts rather than the child. Furthermore, the investigator supplies a standard set of contexts whereas children spontaneously creating their own seldom hit upon the same one twice. The standard set does not usually provide a very representative sample of the whole range of usage. Performance on Berko's test, for instance, is dependent on knowledge of certain words (for

THIS IS A WUG.

NOW THERE IS ANOTHER ONE.
THERE ARE TWO OF THEM.
THERE ARE TWO_____.

Figure 15.   Method of eliciting the voiced plural allomorph

example, *whose* and *yesterday*) and on the ability to "read" correctly particular pictured reference situations. A large sample of spontaneous speech is likely to be more representative of the full range of usage.

There is a further difference. Berko was not primarily interested in the inflection of real English words but in the inflection of invented English syllables. It was not a *dog* that she showed her subjects but a *wug* and a *gutch* and a *niz* and a man *zibbing,* as well as a man who *ricked* yesterday and a man who *loodges* every day, and other wonderful creatures and actions. Berko used invented words because she wanted to test the "productivity" of the inflections, and with real words the possibility always exists that the inflected form has been memorized.

Berko's subjects were preschoolers and first graders, 32 of the former and 61 of the latter. The children at the preschool ranged in age between 4 and 5 years; the first graders between 5;6 and 7;0. This was not a longitudinal study, and so it could not provide points of acquisition for the inflections but only percentages of correct answers at two age levels. However, it is reasonable to suppose that the morphemes that proved more difficult at a given level would have reached a 90 percent criterion in spontaneous speech at a later time than the forms that proved less difficult. Table 42 presents the five noun and verb inflections in rank order of acquisition by Adam, Eve, and Sarah together with a substantial part of Berko's total data, enough to represent all the main effects. Looking in this table for smoothly falling percentages from the morphemes our children found more difficult to those

Table 42.   Berko's results for five morphemes arranged in Brown's order of acquisition

Morpheme	Instance	Percent Correct Preschool	Percent Correct First Grade
1. Present progressive	*zibbing*	72	97
4. Plural	*glasses*	75	99
	wugs	76	97
	luns	68	92
	cras	58	86
	tasses	28	39
	gutches	28	38
6. Possessive	*wug's*	68	81
	bik's	68	95
	niz's	58	46
9. Past regular	*melted*	72	74
	binged	63	80
	ricked	73	73
	spowed	36	59
	motted	32	33
10. Third person regular	*loodges*	57	56
	nazzes	47	49

Source: Based on Berko, 1958.

they found easier we experience a shock. There is no such smooth decline in percentages and, indeed, there is actually more variation among instances of the plural and past morphemes than there is between the morphemes themselves. More startling, the Berko results seem to represent much too low a level of success. Adam, Eve, and Sarah all attained the 90 percent criterion of acquisition for the progressive, possessive, and plural inflections before their fourth birthdays (Eve by about her second birthday), and the regular past and third person inflections were not far behind. But in Table 42 we find no scores of 90 percent for an inflection for the preschoolers, and these preschoolers were between four and five years old, and were from highly educated families. It will be the task of this section to account for these sharp divergences between the controlled and the naturalistic data.

Variation among Instances of a Morpheme

The plural, possessive, third person regular, and past regular inflections in English all have three phonological realizations, realizations that are phonologically conditioned, and so qualify as allomorphs (or predictable variant forms) of one morpheme. Berko's controlled tests focused on this allomorphic variation, whereas in our naturalistic study of the acquisition of the inflections we have not attempted to distinguish allomorphs, and that is one cause of the apparent inconsistency in the results obtained by the two methods.

By way of illustration consider the inflection for plurality. This inflection is not always /-s/ but is sometimes /-z/ and sometimes /-ɨz/. The only difference between /s/ and /z/ is that /z/ is voiced while /s/ is voiceless. In the pluralization of English nouns the voiceless allomorph is used when the noun stem ends in a voiceless consonant *(packs, pits)* and the voiced allomorph when the stem ends in a voiced consonant *(pads, pigs)* or a vowel *(foes, pleas)*. Since vowels are always voiced, the description can be simplified by saying that the voiceless allomorph is appended to a stem with a voiceless terminal and the voiced allomorph to a stem with a voiced terminal. This rule of "voicing assimilation" is not limited to the plural inflection but applies also to the possessive (compare *Jack's, Brad's, Joe's*) and the third person (compare *cheats, pads, sighs*) and, using another pair of consonants that contrast in voicing, to the regular past (compare *clipped, snagged, sowed*). In fact, voicing assimilation is so general as to be best described as a phonological, rather than an inflectional, rule (compare *Jack's sad, Brad's sad, Joe's sad* and most final consonant clusters, as in *pitch* and *fudge,* which are either consistently voiced or voiceless). So one might say that the rule of regular pluralization in English (and also of possessive inflection and third person inflection) is to append /s/ or /z/ in accordance with the phonological rule of voicing assimilation. However, there are certain cases not covered by this single rule.

Stems ending in /l/, /m/, /n/, or /r/, or in any vowel, all require the /z/ allomorph of plurality, possession, and the third person, but it cannot be said that this is a phonological necessity. For there are English words in which /l/, /m/, /n/, /r/, or some vowel, enter into a terminal consonant cluster with voiceless /s/: *pulse, dunce, hearse, dose, dice.* The necessity to use /z/ in *pulls, dons, hears, hoes, dies* seems then to be specifically inflectional. Finally, there is the case of the stem which itself ends in /s/ or /z/ or in the similar consonants /š/, /ž/, /č/, and /ǰ/. In all these cases the vowel /ɨ/ is suffixed before the voiced allomorph of plurality, yielding *kisses, roses, rushes, judges.*

All the descriptive generalizations made above, for the plural inflection are true also for the possessive and third person inflections. Regular past inflection, which employs the allomorphs /-t/, /-d/, and /-ɨd/, follows almost exactly the same rules. The only difference, beyond the fact that the rules employ a pair of stop consonants which contrast in voicing instead of /s/ and /z/, is in the contingency requiring suffixation of /ɨz/. For plural, possessive, and third person inflections this is necessary when a stem ends either in one of the consonants regularly employed as an inflection or in a set of closely similar consonants (š,ž,č,ǰ). For the regular past, /ɨ/ and the voiced allomorph are used only when a stem ends in one of the consonants regularly employed as an inflection, that is /t/ or /d/.

The contingencies governing the inflectional allomorphs can be stated in more than one way. Writing the rules in terms of distinctive features (Chomsky and Halle, 1968), one obtains something like the following (Anisfeld and Gordon, 1968) for the plural. Nouns are pluralized by appending a consonant having the complex of features: —grave, +diffuse, +strident, —nasal, and +continuant. These are just the features that /s/ and /z/ have in common. Stems ending in —grave and +strident sounds, which include /š/, /ž/, /č/, and /ǰ/), as well as /s/ and /z/, append /ɨ/ before undergoing pluralization. There is a general rule of voicing assimilation which assigns the same sign (+ or —) on voicing to the terminal sound as to the sound preceding it, and this rule includes plural inflection within its scope. Comparable "distinctive feature" statements are possible for all the regular inflections. The form in which a rule is stated is not a psychologically indifferent matter. We shall see that distinct statements make distinct psychological claims and that it is possible to devise experiments to choose between statements.

Looking back now at Table 42 we see that Berko selected nonsense stems that would enable her to sample the range of allomorphs, and it is the allomorphs that account for the large variation of performance within a single morpheme. Berko did not evenly sample the full range for all morphemes; the plural was quite fully sampled, the others very selectively. We must first set aside *glasses* and *melted* which are real words, and so not comparable with the nonsense syllable results. Among the nonsense syllables there are five which can be correctly inflected using only knowledge of the plural inflection and the general phonological rule of voicing assimilation. These are: *wugs* (plural, voiced); *wug's* (possessive, voiced); *bik's* (possessive, unvoiced); *binged* (past, voiced); *ricked* (past, unvoiced). Performance on

Table 43. Berko's data summarized in terms of the type of allomorphic rule (in mean percentages)

Morpheme	General Phonological Rule Only		Voicing Rule Specific to Inflections		Rule Specific to Each Inflection	
	Preschool	First Grade	Preschool	First Grade	Preschool	First Grade
1. Progressive	72 (1)[a]	97 (1)	–	–	–	–
4. Plural	76 (1)	97 (1)	66.7 (3)	89.3 (3)	23.7 (4)	36.5 (4)
6. Possessive	68 (2)	88 (2)	–	–	58 (1)	46 (1)
9. Past, Regular	65.3 (3)	78.7 (3)	36 (1)	59 (1)	23 (2)	32 (2)
10. 3rd Person, Regular	–	–	–	–	52 (2)	52.5 (2)

[a]Numbers in parentheses refer to the number of different nonsense stems of the type indicated by the column heading which entered into the calculation of the percentage.

Source: Based on Berko, 1958.

these five is quite reliably better for both preschoolers and first graders than is performance on comparable allomorphs; it ranges from 63 to 76 percent correct for preschoolers, and from 73 to 97 percent correct for first graders.

There is a second category of nonsense syllable such that English phonology does not serve to select the allomorph but such that a rule general across inflections does serve to select the allomorph. Stems ending in vowels or in consonants /n/, /m/, /r/, or /l/ must have the voiced allomorph in the plural possessive, regular past, and regular third person but not, we know, for phonological reasons. In Table 42 there are three stems which require their allomorphs as inflections rather than as phonological clusters, *(luns, cras, spowed)*. Preschool success on these ranges from 36 to 68 percent and first-grade success from 59 to 92 percent. They seem to pose a problem of greater difficulty than the stems that have phonologically constrained allomorphs.

Finally there is the class of cases in which the correct allomorph is not selected phonologically and is not completely general across inflections but is specific to particular inflections or classes of inflection. The past /ɨd/ is required just after stem-final /t/ or /d/. The plural, possessive, or third person /ɨz/ is required after stems ending in a consonant which is both —grave and +strident. In the data of Table 42 there are six stems in this category *(tasses, gutches, niz's, motted, loodges, nazzes)*. Preschool success on these ranges from 28 to 57 percent and first-grade success from 33 to 56 percent. This seems to represent a third level of difficulty.

Table 43 summarizes *all* of Berko's relevant data in a way that reveals the effects of the three categories of allomorphic determination as well as the effects of age and of the morpheme itself. Age is the most obviously important variable; with only one exception, first-grade results are higher than preschool results. Determination of the significance of the three categories of allomorphic variation is plagued by the numerous empty cells in the data matrix. However, all the data obtained are consistent with the following order of difficulty.

Table 44. Percentages correct for kindergarten children of three kinds of allomorphs

Kind of Allomorph	No Feedback	Feedback
1. Phonologically constrained		
/s/	61	88
/z/	63	85
2. General inflectional constraints		
/z/	56	76
vowel	52	70
3. Specific inflectional constraints		
/ɨz/	29	65

Source: Based on Table 1 of Bryant and Anisfeld, 1969.

1. Allomorphs selected by a general phonological rule *(wugs, biks).*
2. Allomorphs selected by a rule specific to inflections *(cras, tors, spowed).*
3. Allomorphs selected by rules specific to particular inflections or sets of inflections *(gutches, niz's, loodges).*

   Bryant and Anisfeld (1969) in a study primarily concerned with the effect of "feedback" on the ability of children to pluralize synthetic words, have incidentally confirmed the order of difficulty among allomorph types described above. Their subjects were 72 kindergarten pupils of mean age 5;11. They pluralized invented nouns like *tib,* for which the form is phonologically constrained, and nouns like *til,* for which it is constrained only as an inflection, and nouns like *tiz,* for which it is constrained as a plural inflection. I have converted their findings into "percentages correct" to make them comparable with Berko's results and, in Table 44, present overall means correct for the various kinds of allomorph in two feedback conditions. While feedback elevates the level of performance, in both conditions the order of difficulty among the allomorphs is as it is in Berko's study. The general level of performance of the children in the Bryant and Anisfeld study is somewhat below that of the children in the Berko study, probably because they were not so uniformly drawn from families of high educational and occupational status.

   In other experiments Anisfeld and his associates (Anisfeld, Barlow, and Frail, 1968; Anisfeld and Gordon, 1968) have advanced our knowledge of the form in which the plural inflection is actually stored by children. Consider those singular nouns that end in /l/, /m/, /n/, or /r/. These are nouns to which /z/ must be appended as plural inflection though not, as we have seen, because of the general phonological rule of voice assimilation. One might formulate the pluralization rule by saying that such singulars take /z/. Alternatively one might say that such singulars take a consonant with the features: +diffuse, −grave, +voiced, +continuant, −nasal, and +strident, the features that constitute /z/. If the rule is stored in the form of a complex of features then it should follow that if a speaker of English were required to choose between two proposed new plural inflections, neither of them /z/, he should prefer the one that more closely resembles /z/ as a complex of features.

The essential experimental procedure was to introduce a child to a new animal and a new name (for example, *nar*) and then, showing him two animals of the same type, ask which of two plurals he liked better for these animals (for example, *narv* and *narb*). The most important result was that, of the features constituting the proper plural /z/, only two constituted a reliable basis for preference as a new plural. These were the features +strident and +continuant. The feature of stridency is a kind of articulatory noisiness that results from forcing the air stream through a complex impediment, and the +continuant feature refers to a relatively continuous expiration of the air stream. The plural allomorphs /s/ and /z/ share these features with such other consonants as /f/, /v/, /š/, and /ž/, and these latter were the preferred new plurals.

Of the various features common to both /s/ and /z/, why should it be just +strident and +continuant that have a "plural sound" to subjects? The answer seems to be that these two are the "most characteristic" features of the plural allomorphs and "most characteristic" has here a quite exact sense. The continuant and strident features differentiate /s/ and /z/ from more other consonants than does any other pair of their common features. The set of consonants defined by the conjunction of +continuant and +strident is a smaller set than any other that can be defined by two features shared by /s/ and /z/.

It is of particular interest that the feature +voiced which distinguishes the allomorphs /s/ and /z/ did not constitute a basis for preference as a new plural. Thus, *narg* seemed no better than *nark* as a plural of *nar*. Anisfeld suggests that this means that the plural inflection is stored as a single archi-segment /sz/, unspecified with respect to voicing. The presence or absence of voicing in the plural case is, he suggests, organized as a phonological rule for the reason that it has a generality extending far beyond the plural. Psychologically, Anisfeld argues, there is only one marker of plurality in English. However, I would note that the phonological rule does not dictate the choice of /z/ with *nar* and *nil* and the like and so, even if voicing does not belong to the English speaker's conception of plural sounds, he must have knowledge that goes beyond the phonological of the role of voicing in inflection.

In Table 43 it is possible to examine the order of difficulty of the five inflections Jean Berko studied, with allomorphic variation held constant. Remember that the vertical order of the morphemes in Table 43 reflects the order of acquisition for Adam, Eve, and Sarah. In the first column, cases solvable by knowledge of the plural inflection and a general phonological rule, the quality of performance for both groups of children does generally decline from "earlier acquired" to "later acquired" morphemes. This is also true of the few data in the second column. It is not true of the data in the third column. The sampling of stems here is small and varies from morpheme to morpheme, and the explanation of the confusing order in the third column may lie with the sampling, but I have no more definite hypothesis to offer.

There is, then, only limited support for the order of acquisition in Berko's controlled data, but we do understand the reason for the wide variation in her data among instances of a morpheme.

The Low Level of Success

In Table 42, the preschool group, which was slightly older than Adam or Sarah and much older than Eve at Stage V, does not attain a level of 90 percent success on any allomorph of any morpheme. Yet our children attained that level for all the morphemes by V or shortly beyond. The kindergarten data of Bryant and Anisfeld, in Table 44, is even more startlingly below the level of Adam, Eve, and Sarah. What can account for this difference? The possibilities are all too numerous.

The "percentages" in the two kinds of studies are very different things. Berko's percentages are percentages of subjects succeeding on particular inflectional problems. Our percentages are percentages of obligatory contexts (representing a wide variety of particular inflectional problems) correctly filled by one subject. Berko's percentages would be responsive to individual differences, and if there were only a few preschool children who had not learned an inflectional rule or who did not understand the experimental task or who did not attend to it, then the group might never attain 90 percent. Our percentages sum across all allomorphs. In spontaneous speech it is clear that the various allomorph cases vary greatly in frequency with the simplest case — those solvable by knowledge of the inflection and a general phonological rule — being much the most common. A child might attain our 90 percent criterion for plural inflection and yet fail always with the stems that end in /s/ or /z/ or a similar consonant; these latter constitute less than 10 percent of any sample. The same sort of argument applies for stems ending in /l/, /m/, /n/, and /r/. I have examined the individual allomorphs in Eve's samples 10–17 and found that in samples 12 and 13 there is clear evidence of a special difficulty with stems ending in /s/ or /z/, and still some signs of such difficulty in sample 17 though the number of instances is too small to be sure. These considerations and others related to the difference in the data summarized as percentages could easily account for the discrepancy in general level of performance.

If our percentages are primarily based on allomorphs of the easiest sort then we might expect Berko's percentages for problems of this kind to be at about the 90 percent level. In fact, as Table 43 shows, they are nearer the 90 percent level than the results for the other kinds of allomorphs but they are still short of it, lying between 65 and 76 percent. This may be because they are percentages of subjects rather than of problems. But it could also be because they report on the inflection of synthetic words, nonsense syllables, rather than real words whereas our data being derived from spontaneous English necessarily involve real words only. Does this factor make a difference?

Jean Berko did, in her full test, include a few real words, and performance on two of these can be compared for the preschool group with nicely matched synthetic stems.

glasses	75% correct	*melted*	72% correct
tasses	28% correct	*motted*	32% correct

Obviously it makes a very great difference. It is, incidentally, worth noting that even on the real words Berko's subjects did not attain a 90 percent success level. However, *glasses* and *melted* both belong to the most difficult class of morphemes. Judging from the extent to which performance with this class of synthetic forms is depressed below the level of the easier classes, it seems reasonable to suppose that had Berko asked preschoolers to pluralize real words belonging to the easiest class of allomorph she would have obtained results at the 90 percent level. In other words, had she asked for the plural of *pig* rather than *wug*, the possessive of *Dick* rather than *bik*, the past of *click* rather than *rick*, her results would probably have looked like ours. This is to suggest, then, that if differences in allomorph sampling and the difference between real and synthetic words were removed, the levels of success shown by our children and by Berko's (presumably also Bryant and Anisfeld's) would have been about the same.

Miller and Ervin (1964; also Ervin, 1964) have provided information on the relation between the ability to inflect real words and the ability to inflect synthetic words, with the abilities being determined longitudinally in the same children. While the Miller-Ervin project involved intensive text collection from only five children, there was monthly controlled testing of an additional 19. This testing included plural inflection and even a set of phonetically matched real word-synthetic word pairs: *boy-kie*; *block-bik*; *bed-pud*; *horse-tass*; *orange-bunge*. Ervin (1964) summarizes the results as follows: "For nearly all the children, there was a time gap between the time when a familiar plural was used and the time when an analogous new word was given a plural. Thus, between the time when the child contrasted *block* and *blocks* and the time when he said two things called *bik* were *biks* there was a small but reliable gap of about two weeks. For *car* and *boy* and the analogous *kie*, the gap was about six weeks. For other words the gap was greater. In all cases — *pud*, *bik*, *kie*, *tass*, and *bunge* — the new contrast appeared later than the contrasts the children had heard" (pp. 174–75).

The Miller-Ervin result confirms the hypothesis that inflection of synthetic forms (as in Berko's test) is somewhat more difficult than inflection of familiar words and so helps explain the difference in success level between the naturalistic study and the controlled studies. We do not, however, know why the nonsense forms pose a more difficult task. It is possible, of course, that general rules of pluralization only operate when the stem is synthetic and that, in all other cases, the plural variant has been stored as such and only requires a plural reference to engage it.[15] This seems unlikely, however, for children begin to *overgeneralize* inflections adding them to

15. As Labov (1971) has pointed out to me these results and many others raise a question of great general importance: "One of the most pressing problems is to discover under what conditions speakers use general rules, and under what conditions they learn lists."

English word stems to which they are not properly added even before they attain our 90 percent criterion. There are other possible reasons for the difference in difficulty between real and synthetic stems. *Some* real-stem plurals may be stored as such even though others are created by rule. *No* synthetic word plurals can be stored as such, and so there would be two possible routes to success with a real stem, and only one with a synthetic, which might account for the general difference in difficulty. It is also possible that the synthetic stem poses a problem in its own right, since it is a novel phonetic sequence which the child must integrate whereas real stems would already exist as integrated units. That could mean an increment of difficulty in the case of pluralization of synthetic stems just sufficient to make failure more common than with familiar stems.

Ervin makes two other points of interest to us. She and Wick Miller found that allomorphs of the third class, stems ending in /s/, /z/, and the like for the plural, were learned quite a bit after other allomorphs, and this confirms the results of Berko and of Bryant and Anisfeld. In addition, Ervin reports of the analogical creation of new plurals: "We found that children formed new plurals in this way when they were between 2 and 3 years old" (p. 174). This is a particularly important point. Adam, Eve, and Sarah all attained our 90 percent criterion for plurals before they were three years old. The Ervin-Miller finding suggests that this criterion was not attained simply by the memorization of familiar plural forms. A possibility that would exist if we had only the experimental results of Berko and of Bryant and Anisfeld, since these investigators found that children, four years old or older, did not all always correctly inflect synthetic stems. One might have been left wondering whether still younger children were using inflections productively at all. Clearly they are.

There is one additional set of experimental data which should be described if only to illustrate how many things there are that can affect the competence a child manifests in a given situation. In 1963, Fraser, Bellugi, and Brown reported an experiment on the three-year-old child's ability to utilize certain grammatical contrasts in imitation, comprehension, and production. The experiment has been repeated on a much larger scale and with a greater age range by Lovell and Dixon (1965) in England. Of the contrasts studied, only two are at all relevant to the fourteen morphemes for which we have an order of acquisition: 1. singular/plural marked by inflections; 2. singlar/plural marked by *is* and *are*. The first of these contrasted such sentence pairs as: *The boy draws*; *The boys draw,* and the second such pairs as *The sheep is jumping*; *The sheep are jumping*. In the imitation task the child simply had to reproduce the contrasting morphemes correctly in the sentences. In the comprehension task he had to identify each sentence in a pair with an appropriate reference picture, and in the production task to speak the right sentence while identifying the appropriate reference picture. On all three tasks the problem that hinged on the auxiliaries *is* and *are* proved somewhat easier than the problem that hinged on the inflections, and that reverses the order in which the auxiliaries and inflections are acquired in terms of our 90 percent criterion. Furthermore, the general level of performance of these three-year-olds with the inflection problem was much lower than the results with spontaneous speech would suggest. But, in fact, there is no real conflict here. The results are simply not comparable.

In devising a good experimental test of the child's ability to extract from *is* and *are* the information about number implicit in these forms, one naturally follows the "rule of one variable" and composes sentences which contrast in only this one respect. Rather unnatural sentences. They must be so because the contrast of number with any regular noun subject must necessarily be doubly marked: *The boys are jumping.* Both noun and auxiliary carry the number contrast. If sentences like these were used, however, how should we know which contrast governed the child's response? There exist in English a few nouns *(sheep, deer)* not distinctively marked for plurality, and so it is possible to create pairs that differ in the auxiliary alone, and we did so. All very well as far as experimental design is concerned. But is this a performance task that can accurately assess the child's knowledge of the number marking of auxiliaries? Surely his perceptual routines are set for sentences in which number is doubly marked. Life does not confront him with many minimal contrasts. May he not have been seriously thrown off by the unrepresentativeness of the task? I am sure he was and that that is why he did so poorly. A related problem arises with the inflectional contrast in *The boy draws* and *The boys draw.* Each sentence alone is ordinary enough, and should be processed in a routine way. But the experimental design required the two sentences to be presented, one immediately after the other, and with pictures presenting a parallel minimal contrast. Even adults experience a kind of confusion at first. The movement of that useful *-s* inflection between noun and verb with opposite effects in the two cases is not something most people have noticed. Once noticed it seems confusing. How do we ever manage to understand sentences? I am afraid the answer is that in this kind of nicely controlled study one does not understand sentences in quite the usual way — and so the results are not necessarily a very clear indication of what is known grammatically.

Summary

Among controlled and experimental studies only Jean Berko's offers any independent evidence on the order of acquisition of grammatical morphemes, and her study does so only for the five regular inflections. When the effects of allomorphic variation are partialed out, Berko's data support the order we found except in the case of the third class of allomorph.

Experimental studies add something to our knowledge of the acquisition of inflections, something not available in the naturalistic data because of imprecision of transcription in some cases and insufficient frequencies of certain inflectional forms. What is added is the information that the regular allomorphs are ordered with respect to difficulty as follows:

1. Allomorphs selected by a general phonological rule *(wugs, biks)*.
2. Allomorphs selected by a rule specific to inflections *(cras, tors, spowed)*.
3. Allomorphs selected by rules specific to particular inflections or sets of inflections *(gutches, niz's, loodges)*.

This finding means that in counting the occurrences of the regular inflections we were not counting optimally homogeneous events. If the quality of transcription and the frequencies natural to spontaneous speech had permitted us to count occurrences of allomorphs, the likelihood is that the order of acquisition would have been even more stable across children than it was with morphemes being counted.

Experimental studies generally "date" the acquisition of inflections at much later chronological ages than does our naturalistic study. This seems to be not a fundamental disagreement on the facts but a seeming disagreement arising from such factors as the following:

1. Differences in the criterion of acquisition including percentages of children as opposed to percentages of contexts for one child.
2. The use of invented or synthetic stems as opposed to real stems.
3. The creation, in the interests of experimental design of quite unusual problems in sentence processing which probably throw off habitual routines.

To these, which have been rather clearly established, I would add the general problem of the experimental method which requires us to direct and hold the child's attention as one need not in the naturalistic study of spontaneous speech. It is, I have found, a very general fact extending far beyond the study of the grammatical morphemes that assessments of particular kinds of linguistic competence based on experimental findings "date" the competencies in question later than do assessments based on naturalistic data. The performance on which the estimates are based are always different especially with regard to the need to direct and hold attention. I think the naturalistic data can yield a truer estimate in the sense of an estimate that is less dependent on performance skills not routinely developed in the child. But the experimental data, needless to say, can often be complete, where the naturalistic data are seriously fragmentary. The two methods together give us the best chance of discovering the truth.

Acquisition Order for Grammatical Morphemes in Languages Other Than English

Ultimately, data in this category will be crucial. Crucial for working out the *determinants* of acquisition order. Because in one language, such as English, a given semantic, such as plural number, is linked with a very particular grammatical apparatus — noun inflection with three regular, phonologically conditioned, allomorphs and a certain number and variety of irregular forms, plus determiner agreement, and predicate nominative agreement, and verb inflection, when the subject is third person singular and the tense is present. The semantic and the apparatus are, furthermore, linked with a certain frequency level in parental speech. Obviously it is going to be difficult to learn anything at all about which one (or ones) of these confounded factors is responsible for the position in the acquisition order of the English plural. But other languages make different combinations of semantic, grammatical apparatus, and frequency, and so offer the possibility of separating variables that are confounded in English. This is the way it will be ultimately, but it is not the way things stand now. Not much information is now available on order in other languages, and what there is seldom utilizes an explicit criterion of acquisition, and never uses my criterion. In addition, it is difficult to use the reports for working out determinants because the authors have not supplied very detailed descriptions of the grammar and semantics of the morphemes, and I do not have a native speaker's grasp of any of the languages. We shall see in the next main section, how difficult it is, even for English and for an educated native speaker utilizing the large literature describing English, to get an accurate and detailed explicit knowledge of the fourteen grammatical morphemes.

Bowerman (in press), in her study of Finnish, has not yet analyzed the development of grammatical morphemes. Kernan's (1969) study of the two Samoan children, Sipili and Tofi, is limited to periods when the MLU was between 1.50 and 1.65, and so is essentially a description of Stage I. There is much valuable information on semantic and grammatical relations, but there is almost nothing on grammatical morphemes, since these were largely absent in Stage I. Blount's study of the development of Luo (spoken in Nyanza Province of Kenya) is based on observations of eight children ranging in age from 12–35 months, and the older children had MLU's as high as 4.24 (just beyond our Stage V). Consequently, Blount obtained some information on the order of development of grammatical morphemes in Luo which is a language having an elaborate productive morphology.

Blount tells us the following: "Almost all studies of child language have noted that inflections emerge suddenly, generally a few months after the beginning of two-word sentences. The emergence of inflections in Luo does not seem to be sudden, but they do appear after the two-word sentences" (p. 69). His observation agrees with our own, and I suspect that the impression of suddenness some investigators have had is with reference to first occurrences rather than reliable use wherever required. On the order of morphemes in Luo, Blount's summary may be paraphrased in this way:

1. The earliest productive morphology was the inflection of the verb for pronominal subject and object, which occurred at 20–21 months.
2. From two to six months later came the noun inflection for the possessive.
3. Verb inflections for tense came after noun inflections, and the first verb

inflection seems to have been the one that marks the event named as completed in the immediate past. Certain prepositions appeared at the same time, including *è* which means *in* or *on* or *to*. There were others at the same time which translate, roughly, as *toward, with, up to,* and *for.*

These results are somewhat suggestive. The first inflections code semantic relations and, except for their inflectional status, are like the child's *I, me, you* and *it,* which appear in Stage I and precede the inflections of English. The early appearance of the possessive reminds us that this form is also fairly early in English. The fact that the first of the verb inflections is the one that signifies an immediately past event reminds us that the American child's use of the past inflection, though it is in principle applicable to past times of whatever remoteness, is in fact used by him at first exclusively for the immediate past. In Luo there are a number of different past inflections for times varyingly remote. These few observations rather suggest that it is the semantic of the grammatical morpheme that determines its position in the acquisition order. Unfortunately we are not really in a position to conclude anything of the sort. For many reasons, but one that would alone suffice is the very small size of the speech corpus Blount utilized.

It was not lack of effort that made the corpus small. As mentioned in Stage I, Blount made something like 54 visits of half-an-hour or longer. But in all this time he obtained just under 200 multi-word utterances. Two hundred utterances distributed across eight children ranging in age from 12 to 35 months are simply not enough to establish an order of emergence for grammatical morphemes. A certain amount can be learned, as Blount has shown, about sentence types at various ages even from 200 utterances. But grammatical morphemes are sure to vary widely in frequency, and so a very small sample will be likely to pick up only those morphemes that are most frequent when others of lower frequency may, in fact be used but not represented in the sample.

On the development of Russian morphology, Slobin (1966) has given us valuable summaries of Russian studies and also has brought to our attention principles proposed in the Russian literature to explain orders of acquisition.[16] It is my own shortcoming that I cannot make a great deal of this material; I do not know any Russian, and a really delicate knowledge is required. First we have Slobin's report on Gvozdev's Zhenya. "Morphological markers enter when sentences increase from two to three or four words in length" (p. 136). The same is true of English; Stage I ends with an MLU of 2.0, and inflections, as well as function words, only begin to be common in Stage II. But Slobin goes on: "All words are unmarked in Zhenya's speech until about 1;10 and then, in one month between 1;11 and 2;0 there is a

16. In his fine paper (1971b) Slobin works from a broad comparative data base to propose numerous principles of his own which may govern order of acquisition. I decided that consideration of this paper would seriously throw off the structure of "Stage II" without materially affecting the research results which are the core of the chapter.

sudden emergence of contrasting morphological elements in various categories. In this one month previously unmarked nouns are marked for (1) number, (2) nominative, accusative, and genitive cases, and (3) diminutive; verbs are marked for (1) imperative, (2) infinitive, (3) past tense, and (4) present tense" (p. 136). How does this compare with American English?

In English, nouns are marked for number and possession (a genitive) but not for nominative and accusative cases. Some children use a diminutive /iy/ as in *doggie* and *kitty*, but it is not used in all households. For Adam, Eve, and Sarah we find *some* use of number and possessive inflection in Stage II but not that degree of reliable use which we have adopted as a criterion of acquisition. There is also some use of the diminutive by Sarah though we have not included this form in our set of fourteen. Certain pronouns are marked for nominative, accusative, and genitive; especially *I, me my,* though nouns do not take such markers.

The English verb has no special imperative marker but, in the imperative, is simply an unmarked generic form. The preposition *to* marks infinitives, and in constructions like *I wanna eat* and *I gonna go* there is a bit of phonetic substance that could be considered *to,* but when embeddings are discussed (in Stage IV) we shall see that this is probably not the correct construction to make of such forms. The past, both of irregular and regular, does begin to be marked in Stage II and the present, in progressive form, and in agreement with a third person singular subject also occasionally appears.

Superficially, at least, there is a good agreement in the Stage II morphemes between Russian and English, providing that these morphemes are characterized *semantically* rather than grammatically. There is agreement, that is, if Slobin's "emergence" refers to *some* instances and not to reliable control. If he intends the latter then there is a sharp disagreement, since these various forms in English do not all attain criterion in a single month or indeed at all suddenly. Rather they attain criterion over generally rather long though widely varying (between morphemes) periods of time.

Slobin's summary of later developments in Zhenya does not admit of exact comparison with English for familiar reasons: my ignorance of the grammatical details of the Russian forms and the lack of an explicit criterion for their acquisition. Dative and instrumental case markers (a function served by prepositions *to* and *with* in English) are said to "emerge" between 2;0 and 2;3. Eight different Russian prepositions (which control case selection) emerge between 2;4 and 2;6.

Certain general morphological phenomena and principles of acquisition described by Slobin can be checked against our data. He notes, for example, that the child must learn an instrumental case ending for each masculine, feminine, and neuter singular and plural noun and adjective and, within each subcategory, several different phonologically conditioned allomorphs. What the child at first does, however, is seize upon one suffix — "probably the most frequent and/or clearly marked acoustically" — and use it for every instance of that particular grammatical category. For example, Zhenya used the suffix *-om* for all singular noun instrumental endings although it ought to have been restricted to masculine and neuter singular nouns only. This suffix has only one other use whereas the dominant feminine singular instrumental ending (—oĭ) serves a variety of functions. Zakhorova (1958), in an experiment with 200 children, found that the youngest all used -om as a universal instrumental. Slobin notes that it has high frequency, is acoustically well-marked, and is limited in the functions it serves, and he suggests that some or all of these characteristics account for its choice.

Popova (1958) investigated gender agreement between nouns and verbs in very young children and found that the youngest overgeneralized the feminine ending —a. In older children the masculine ending tended to predominate and, in children still older, the two occurred together. Slobin suggests that there is an ontogenetic series with the later overgeneralized form tending to "drive out" the earlier before the mature period of coexistence.

The Russian child in overgeneralizing inflections also frequently disregards subcategory boundaries. He pluralizes mass nouns as well as count nouns and invents singulars for count nouns that have no singulars (like *scissors* in English). "In most of these cases it is of interest to note once again that full mastery of the morphological system comes relatively late in Russian-speaking children" (p. 140). And Slobin gives some very late ages: three years for gender agreement between nouns and verbs in the past; six or seven years for the declension of masculine and feminine nouns ending in palatalized consonants; eight years for the distinction between count and mass nouns. Of course, Russian has a much more complex morphology than English, and the overgeneralizations in child speech are correspondingly more exuberant.

Soviet psycholinguists, Slobin tells us, believe that the order of acquisition of morphological classes is largely due to their relative semantic or conceptual difficulty. There seems to be no explicit general definition of what it is that constitutes semantic difficulty, but Slobin extracts the following suggestions. Forms or classes making "concrete" reference emerge first, and these are said to include number, the diminutive, and prepositions of spatial relation (as opposed to time relation or relations of purpose). Classes based on a "relational" semantic seem to be more difficult. Here I am surprised to find cases and tenses (which seemed to be early acquisitions for Zhenya) along with persons of the verb. "Abstract" categories come later, we are told, but no definition is given of "abstract." Finally, gender is very late, and the reason seems to be the lack of a consistent semantic correlate.

From Slobin's interesting discussion I should like to single out for eventual consideration the following:

1. Where grammatically and phonologically conditioned variant forms exist, one is likely to be learned and overgeneralized, and the factors determining that one seem to be: frequency, clarity of acoustical marking, and consistency of function.
2. Prior to the mature period in which conditioned variants co-exist there is

likely to be a succession of overgeneralized forms with the later "driving out" the earlier.

3. The primary determinant of the order in which mature forms are acquired is semantic complexity, forms making "concrete" reference being less complex than forms making abstract reference. Most difficult of all are the forms lacking any consistent semantic correlate.

There are numerous well-known studies of the development of French and German, but there is no point in reviewing them here. The difficulties are always the same: no explicit criterion of acquisition and insufficient information about the semantic and grammatical character of the morpheme.

The Grammar of the Fourteen Morphemes

We should like to be able to order the morphemes with respect to grammatical complexity and so learn whether complexity is a determinant of order of acquisition. The grammatical knowledge entailed in productive control of a morpheme may be distinguished from any particular formal representation of that knowledge. The inflection of the verb in *he walks* and *she runs,* and the like, entails knowledge of the number and person of the subject noun phrase as well as the tense of the verb as well as knowledge of three forms of the inflection which covary with phonological characteristics of the verb stem as well as knowledge that certain stems are irregular, and so on. Formal representation of this knowledge in a generative grammar is likely to make some use of deep structures (whether grammatical or directly semantic) and syntactic features and subcategorization rules and transformations and allomorphic rules and so on. Such representations have changed many times in recent years and, for the most part, there is no clear consensus on the right representations today. And yet our informal conception of the knowledge to be represented has not changed very much. The informal conception is more stable than its representation but, unfortunately, an informal conception does not yield an order of complexity. Only a formal representation can do that, and the formal representations change. However, complexity orderings are not necessarily changed by every change in formal representation and seem, indeed, to be almost as stable as the informal conception of the knowledge. Necessarily we shall have to select one set of formal representations, but there is good reason to think that the complexity relations derived from it will have a general validity going beyond the particular representation.

The representations I have selected are those offered by Jacobs and Rosenbaum in their 1968 book, *English Transformational Grammar.* I chose to use the Jacobs-Rosenbaum system for two reasons: it was, at my time of writing, fairly up-to-date in

its use of linguistic research; it is fairly inclusive, offering treatments of almost
all of the 14 morphemes. The Jacobs-Rosenbaum representation has one deficiency:
it is not always fully explicit and not always fully detailed. The book is intended
to be a text rather than a treatise, and so the authors have allowed themselves to be a
bit sketchy about matters that are not central to their instructional purpose.

In basic design the Jacobs-Rosenbaum grammar follows Katz and Postal (1964)
and Chomsky (1965). A distinction is made between deep and surface structures.
Deep structures are intended to include all the information needed for a semantic
interpretation and surface structures the information needed by the phonological
component. Deep structures are mapped into surface structures by meaning-
preserving transformations. The deep structures of questions and negatives include
the respective morphemes QUESTION and NEG, which trigger obligatory
transformations.

The phrase structure rules (omitting QUESTION and NEG, since these are not
germane to our topic) are extremely simple:

$$1. \ S \to NP \ Aux \ VP$$
$$2. \ NP \to \begin{Bmatrix} (ART) \ N \ (S) \\ NP \quad S \end{Bmatrix}$$
$$3. \ VP \to VB \ (NP) \quad \begin{Bmatrix} (NP) \\ (S) \end{Bmatrix}$$

Entries in the lexicon consist of paired elements such that the first element is a
representation of the sound of the word and the second of its meaning. The meaning
is represented in part as a set of features, the presence of a feature being marked
by a plus sign and the absence by a minus sign. The lexical entry for the proper noun
Rome takes the following form:

$$Rome$$
$$<+N>$$
$$<-common>$$
$$<+concrete>$$
$$<-animate>$$
$$<+count>$$

These features, which Jacobs and Rosenbaum call "a representation of meaning,"
correspond to Chomsky's syntactic features and, in particular, to "inherent" syntactic
features. They categorize Rome as a noun $<+N>$ and subcategorize it as "proper"
$<-common>$, concrete $<+concrete>$, inanimate $<-animate>$, and count
$<+count>$. The lexicon also contains redundancy rules which express such
generalizations as: "all nouns with the feature $<+human>$ are to be interpreted

as containing the feature $<$ +animate$>$." Redundancy rules make it possible to write shorter lexical entries, since the generalizations they express substitute for many individual feature entries.

Jacobs and Rosenbaum follow Lakoff (1966), Fillmore (1968), and others in treating verbs and adjectives as the same sort of constituent in deep structures; both are verbals ($< + VB >$). The difference between them is represented in the lexicon with the feature $< +V >$ for verbs and $<-V >$ for adjectives. This treatment of verbs and adjectives is justified by an appeal to certain similarities between the two: there are process and state verbs and there are process and state adjectives; there are transitive and intransitive verbs and there are transitive and intransitive adjectives.

The features that appear in lexical entries are those which a word always has, such as $< +$common$>$, $< +$concrete$>$, $< +$count$>$. There are also other features which a word sometimes has and sometimes does not have such as, in the case of nouns, $< +$singular$>$ and $<-$singular$>$. Features of this latter kind are introduced by Jacobs and Rosenbaum with "segment structure rules." A segment is a cluster of features. Segment structure rules apply before lexical items are introduced into deep structures. An example of a segment structure rule is the following:

$$N \rightarrow \quad \begin{array}{c} < +N> \\ < \pm \text{singular}> \end{array}$$

This rule states that a noun dominates a segment which is either singular (if the $< +$singular$>$ option is taken) or plural (if the $<-$singular$>$ option is taken). Particular nouns in the lexicon do not have either the feature $< +$singular$>$ or the feature $<-$singular$>$ but when a noun is introduced into a deep structure the features it has are combined with those generated by the segment structure rules, and so the noun acquires number. Another pair of features introduced into noun segments by segment structure rules is $< +$definite$>$; $<-$definite$>$. Features introduced into verb segments in this manner include: $< +$progressive$>$; $<-$progressive$>$ and $< +$present$>$; $<-$present$>$. Just as it is not a stable property of particular nouns to be either singular or plural, definite or nondefinite, so it is not a property of particular verbs to have progressive aspect or not to have it, to be in the present tense or in the past tense.

In the Jacobs-Rosenbaum grammar there are only two lexical classes that appear in deep structures: nouns and verbals. Adjectives are a variety of verbal. Articles which do appear in the phrase structure rules offered in the first section of *English Transformational Grammar* are, after some discussion, dropped from deep structures by Jacobs and Rosenbaum. From nouns and verbals, segments, or bundles of features, are created by segment structure rules. These rules introduce just those features which are not invariable features of particular nouns and verbals but rather occasional features: $< \pm$singular$>$, $< \pm$definite$>$, $< \pm$progressive$>$,

$<\pm$present$>$, and so on. The feature content of segments is further specified by
the introduction from the lexicon of items whose features are added to those
generated by the segment structure rules. Where in this scheme do prepositions,
articles, and copulas come from? Where do the inflections for plurality, possession,
progressive aspect, past tense, and third person singular come from? The very
interesting thing about the Jacobs and Rosenbaum grammar, from our point of view,
is that all these forms, inflections as well as "little words," are derived in the same
general fashion. Segments representing them are introduced by transformations
which are triggered by the presence in noun and verbal segments of particular
semantic features.

Which features are they that trigger the introduction of segments for prepositions,
articles, copulas, and the inflections? Nouns and verbals have some features which
have no surface representation, such features as $<+$animate$>$, $<-$animate$>$,
$<+$concrete$>$, and $<-$concrete$>$. Presumably this is because these features are
unchanging in a noun from one use to the next. But other features, those that are not
unchanging in the noun, do have surface representation. These are the features
introduced by segment structure rules: $<\pm$singular$>$ affect the inflection of the
noun; $<\pm$definite$>$ affect the selection of articles; $<\pm$progressive$>$ and
$<\pm$present$>$ affect the inflection of verbals. And still other features, less familiar
than those above, affect the introduction of prepositions and copulas and of the other
inflections. In the Jacobs-Rosenbaum grammar the 14 morphemes are introduced
transformationally when nouns and verbals have their meanings modulated by
the presence or absence of particular features.

In the Jacobs-Rosenbaum grammar lexical items are introduced at two points in a
derivation rather than at one point as in most transformational grammars. The first
"lexical pass" occurs after the operation of segment structure rules but prior to
the operation of any transformations. This is where lexical substitution usually occurs
in a transformational grammar, but, since Jacobs and Rosenbaum use transformations to introduce all the segments (or feature-sets) underlying grammatical
morphemes, it is necessary to provide for the substitution of words and affixes
for these segments. And so there is a second lexical pass which follows after the
operation of transformations and which primarily adds grammatical morphemes.
While Jacobs and Rosenbaum have written a grammar rather than a program
simulating the psychological process of sentence construction it is possible that the
two lexical passes belong in such a program and it is also possible that the second
lexical pass is developmentally a later acquisition than the first. The first lexical pass
would produce strings of nouns and verbals, the kind of string that would underlie
Stage I telegraphic speech. The second lexical pass would introduce the grammatical
morphemes which develop at various times after Stage I.

In describing the grammar of the 14 morphemes our starting point is the
developmental order of Figure 14, but we shall depart from this order where
exposition is made easier by bringing together related constructions not contiguous in

the developmental order. For instance, the present progressive without its auxiliary is the first morpheme in the developmental order but the twelfth and fourteenth morphemes in that order, which are respectively the uncontractible and contractible progressive auxiliaries, are so closely related grammatically to the progressive without auxiliary that it is desirable to discuss all three together. Table 45 summarizes the grammatical knowledge, in Jacobs-Rosenbaum notation, entailed by each of the 14 morphemes.

The Progressive

Progressive aspect is not treated by Jacobs and Rosenbaum as a deep structure constituent in the manner of Chomsky (1957), where it enters into the rewriting of auxiliary as a constituent *(be + ing)*. Jacobs and Rosenbaum tied the progressive as a feature $<+$progressive$>$ added to verbals having the feature $<+V>$. Jacobs and Rosenbaum acknowledge that it is still debatable whether such a treatment is correct and that they have simply made one choice where other choices are also defensible. Presumably $<+$progressive$>$ is added by a segment structure rule, since it is not a stable property of particular verbs to have progressive aspect. For the sentence *Adam is eating,* we should have, after the application of segment structure rules and the first lexical pass, the following (simplified) representation:

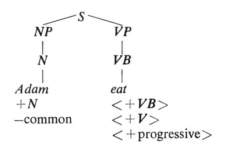

Jacobs and Rosenbaum point out that not all verbs may take progressive aspect but rather only those that are "action" verbs. One may say *Adam is eating* or *walking* or *talking,* since these are all actions, but not *Adam is liking ice cream* or *Adam is needing new shoes* or *Adam is resembling his mother.* Jacobs and Rosenbaum propose to represent these facts by marking the lexical entries for action verbs with the feature $<+$action$>$ and marking others $<-$action$>$.

What Jacobs and Rosenbaum call action verbs and nonaction verbs have been more commonly called "process" and "state" verbs. Lakoff (1966) has shown that the covert categories of process and state verbs govern a number of grammatical processes. Besides progressive aspect there is the imperative mode. One may say *Please eat your lunch* or *Please walk to school* but not *Please like your lunch* or *Please need new shoes.* Benefactive expressions are also used with process verbs *(He is singing for her)* but not state verbs *(He is liking his lunch for her).* And there are still other grammatical processes that break on the process-state line but only the imperative and progressive are relevant to early child speech. In such speech there are very many process verbs and only a few state verbs. The chief state verbs are *want, like, need,* and *know.* The important fact is that our three children never used their state verbs in either the imperative or the progressive, though they did often use process verbs in these forms. It is possible, then, that they had subcategorized verbs on process-state lines. We shall see, in discussing problems of segmentation, that it is not certain that they had done so, but for the present we shall assume they had, and represent this knowledge (see Table 45) as lexical subcategorization by the Jacobs-Rosenbaum features $<+$action$>$ and $<-$action$>$.

Jacobs and Rosenbaum, following Lakoff (1966), point out that adjectives are also subcategorized on process-state lines, and that this is a major argument in favor of deriving adjectives and verbs from the same sort of deep structure constituent, namely verbals. *Honest* and *patient,* for instance, are process adjectives, and one may say *He is being honest* and *Be patient, please* whereas *short* and *thin* are state adjectives, and one may not say, *Be short* or *He is being thin.* In our data there are almost no utterances relevant to the process-state distinction in adjectives. There are several imperatives in *be (Be quiet, Becky),* and these use process adjectives as they should. There are no uses at all of *be* in the progressive and that, we shall see, affects the representation of the progressive.

What is the nature of the semantic distinction we have called "process" and "state"? That is a question which we shall defer for the next major section in which the semantics of the 14 morphemes are discussed.

It is to be presumed that when a verb ($<+$V$>$) segment has acquired the feature $<+$progressive$>$ then only those verbs may be substituted for it in the first lexical pass that are marked $<+$action$>$. In fact, Jacobs and Rosenbaum do not provide an explicit mechanism for accomplishing this effect, and this is one point in which their representation of progressive aspect is sketchy.

The deep structure following the first lexical pass does not yet include either the auxiliary copula or the progressive inflection *-ing.* Both of these are introduced transformationally by Jacobs and Rosenbaum. It is an advantage of their representation from the developmental point of view that the two forms are introduced by two distinct rules and so it is easy to represent the child's immature auxiliary-free progressive by simply omitting one rule. The 1957 Chomsky representation which treated *(be + ing)* as a single constituent offered no natural way of representing the primitive form.

The transformation which introduces the copula segment is called the progressive segment transformation. It introduces to the left of the verbal a segment containing the features $<+$progressive$>$ and $<+$copula$>$. The transformation that introduces the progressive inflection *(-ing)* is called the progressive affix transformation. It introduces a segment with the features $<+$affix$>$ and $<+$progressive$>$ in the following position: to the right of that segment which follows the copular auxiliary segment. In the case of *Adam is eating* the segment following the copula is the verb *(eat)* but we shall see that it need not always be so. The two transformations yield the following structure.

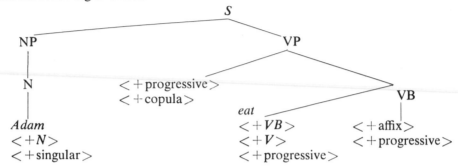

The copula segment would ultimately be replaced by the appropriate form of *be (is)*, the verbal by *eat*, and the affix by *-ing*.

Jacobs and Rosenbaum point out that their transformations will also work for sentences with $<+$action$>$ adjectives plus *be* in the progressive, such as *Souza is being honest*. An additional transformation is needed, one that introduces the copula when the verbal is an adjective, and it is necessary that the three transformations be applied in a certain order. It is this case that motivates the definition of the position for the inflection as: "to the right of the segment which follows the copular auxiliary segment." With predicate adjectives this will serve to place *-ing* after *be*, which is where it belongs rather than after the verbal. However, sentences like *Souza is being honest* do not occur anywhere in our transcriptions, and so it is not necessary to formulate the rules in such a way as to provide for them. The position of the inflection may be defined as: to the right of the verb segment.

For the progressive without auxiliary, the primitive progressive, which is the first grammatical morpheme to attain criterion, only one transformation is needed: the progressive affix transformation. For progressives with auxiliary (whether contractible or uncontractible) two additional transformations are needed. One is the progressive segment transformation, which introduces the auxiliary copula. The other, the auxiliary incorporation transformation, we have not yet described. What it does is copy the features of the first segment of the *VP* (here the auxiliary with features $<+$progressive$>$ and $<+$copula$>$) if this segment is not a verb (which it is not in the present case) onto the *AUX* segment. The transformation then deletes the first segment of the *VP* (here the auxiliary copula). In effect this rule puts the copula under the *AUX* and combines its features with tense ($<+$present$>$ or $<-$present$>$). In short, the full auxiliaries (ranks 12 and 14 in the developmental order) are more complex than the primitive auxiliary by two transformational rules. They are, furthermore, more complex by virtue of the tense feature introduced by segment structure rules ($<+$present$>$ or $<-$present$>$), since the full auxiliaries in Adam, Eve, and Sarah were not always in the present tense but were often past tense.

We have not yet described all the differences of complexity between the primitive and the full progressives. It must be remembered that when the auxiliary copula is present it appears in three forms in the present tense (*am, is, are* uncontracted) and two in the past *(was, were),* and these forms are selected by the person and number of the subject *NP* (as well as by tense). Jacobs and Rosenbaum propose an auxiliary agreement transformation to accomplish these effects. It copies the number and person features from the noun subject onto the auxiliary. The person features ($<+$I$>$, $<+$II$>$, $<+$III$>$) would presumably appear in lexical entries with all nouns and pronouns being $<+$III$>$ except *I,* which is $<+$I$>$, and *you,* which is $<+$II$>$. *Adam* in *Adam is eating* would be in the third person ($<+$III$>$). The number features ($<+$singular$>$ and $<-$singular$>$) will have been introduced by segment structure rules. The tense features would already be in the *AUX* segment having been introduced by segment structure rules, and in the case of our sample sentence the combination of third person, singular, present tense would serve to select *is* as the appropriate form of the auxiliary.

Finally, then, we find that the full auxiliaries (ranks 12 and 14) are more complex than the primitive auxiliary (rank 1) by virtue of three transformations, one lexical feature, two segment structure features, and one feature introduced transformationally. This is, we may already judge, a very large difference of grammatical complexity, a difference of the right order to account for the fact that the primitive and full auxiliaries are at opposite ends of our developmental order. This is a strictly cumulative difference of complexity, since the full auxiliary involves all the grammatical knowledge of the primitive auxiliary plus much other knowledge.

The difference between the contractible and uncontractible auxiliaries remains to be explained. Labov (1969) offers some phonological rules (pp. 722–728) to represent contraction. These rules employ the "nuclear stress" rule and the "vowel reduction" rule from Chomsky and Halle (1968), to which Labov adds his own "weak word" rule and a specification that the contracted form must carry tense. Without going into the details it may be said that the uncontracted forms are, in general, *phonologically* simpler than the contracted in that they involve fewer phonological rules. The uncontractible forms reach criterion before the contractible, and so the order of acquisition is consistent with the order of phonological complexity.

The Prepositions "in" and "on"

Concerning prepositions, Jacobs and Rosenbaum write: "To grammarians there seem to be almost as many unanswered questions about prepositions as there are about any other single topic in English syntax" (p. 136). And: "As to the origin of prepositions, the tentative position taken here is that they originate as features in deep structures — in particular, as features of noun segments" (p. 138). The authors are not entirely explicit about the rules to be used for introducing prepositions. What follows is my interpretation and expansion of their rather sketchy remarks.

Jacobs and Rosenbaum judge that all noun phrases have prepositions associated with them in their deep structures but that these prepositions are, in many cases, transformationally deleted. The reasons for making this assumption are quite persuasive. While there are no prepositions in a sentence like *The army destroyed the fortress,* prepositions appear in such transforms as *The fortress was destroyed by the army* and *The army's destruction of the fortress.* If transformational rules for sentences like these are to be written in maximally general form it is necessary to eliminate particular prepositions from the statement of the rules and to associate them, instead, with nouns. A single nominalization rule, for instance, might then be written for constructions having different prepositions such as *The mathematician's concentration on the problem* and *The army's destruction of the fortress.*

It is clear that the selection of particular prepositions is in part dependent on the particular noun as in the sentences:

> *The party was on Monday.*
> *The party was at noon.*
> *The party was in May.*

It is equally clear that the selection of prepositions is in part dependent on verbals as in the sentences:

> *He flew to Bombay.*
> *He approved of Bombay.*

Jacobs and Rosenbaum suggest that prepositions are generated on noun segments and that verb selection is partially governed by the prepositions associated with the nouns with which they are in construction. But how exactly is this to be represented?

Consider the child's sentence: *Eve sit on couch.* Presumably the second noun segment acquires the feature $<+on>$ by a segment structure rule. In the first lexical pass it must be necessary to substitute only the sort of noun that can be the object of *on,* and so it seems necessary to suppose that a noun like *couch* is marked in the lexicon with a feature $<\pm on>$. This feature takes its plus or minus value from the noun segment. The lexical feature must be $<\pm on>$ rather than $<+on>$ because *couch,* and nouns generally, may be the object of more than one preposition. Presumably a verb like *put* is marked with a contextual feature indicating that it may have, as direct object, a noun that takes *on*; perhaps such a feature as

$<\pm$ _____ $N^{+on}>$. These notational suggestions seem to be consistent with what Jacobs and Rosenbaum say, but I cannot be sure that they are exactly what the authors intend. There are unsolved problems with this notation and with any explicit version I can imagine of the Jacobs-Rosenbaum proposal.

The introduction of the preposition itself would apparently begin with a preposition segment transformation placing a segment to the left of the noun marked $<+on>$ and copying that feature onto the new segment. On the second lexical pass the segment would be replaced by *on* from the lexicon.

In Table 45 the grammar of *in* and *on* is summarized. It involves one transformation and three features. The prepositions *in* and *on* are tied at rank 2.5 in the acquisition order whereas the progressive without auxiliary holds rank 1 in that order. The grammatical complexity of the prepositions and the progressive is not strictly comparable, since they employ different features and transformations, but it is worth noting that, in terms simply of the number of features and transformations, they are equal; both involve one transformation and three features. This seems to accord with the fact that they occupy adjacent ranks in the order of acquisition.

Plural and Singular Number

Number affects a great many different constructions in English. The plurals that figure as rank 4 in the acquisition order all include a noun marked for plural number. The vast majority of these nouns were inflected with three regular allomorphs ($/-s \sim -z \sim -iz/$) but there were a few instances of such irregular forms as *men, children,* and *women.* In the simplest case we simply have plural reference in naming with the plural number judged to be necessary because more than one instance of the referent is manifest. Often, however, the plural noun was accompanied by some sort of article or determiner, such as *two, some,* or *more.* In these cases the grammar is more complex because there is the problem of agreement in number for the determiner and the noun. In a third set of cases the plural noun was a predicate nominative, as in *They are men,* and then there is the complication of agreement in number with the subject. All these cases were counted together as plurals, and so there is considerable variation of grammatical complexity within the category which, as a whole, holds rank 4. In summarizing the grammar of plurals for Table 45 I have marked with the letter *b* those features and rules which, because they represent determiner agreement or predicate nominative agreement, were not invariably involved. The remaining unmarked features and rules are the irreducible core involved in every sort of plural. Finally, we shall want also to consider the regular and irregular third person singular verb inflections (ranks 10 and 11), since these involve the grammar of number.

We have already seen that number begins as a feature, either $<+singular>$ or $<-singular>$ entered on noun segments by a segment structure rule. Not every sort

Table 45. Summary of the grammar of each of the 14 morphemes in Jacobs-Rosenbaum notation[a]

Morpheme	Lexical Features	Segment Structure Features	Transformations
1. Present progressive	+ action − action	+ progressive	Progressive affix T
2. 3. *in-on*	± *on* —N ± *on* ± *in* —N ± *in*	+ *on* + *in*	Preposition segment T
4. Plural	+ common + count − common − count	+ singular − singular	Noun suffix T
5. Past irregular	+ irregular	+ present − present	Verbal agreement T
6. Possessive	−	−	−
7. Uncontractible copula	+ V + I + II − V + III	+ singular + present − singular − present	Copula T
8. Articles	+ common + count − common − count	+ definite + singular − definite − singular	Article T
9. Past regular		+ present − present	Verbal agreement T
10. Third person regular	+ III	+ singular + present − singular − present	Auxiliary agreement T
11. Third person irregular	+ III + irregular	+ singular − singular	Auxiliary agreement T
12. Uncontractible auxiliary	+ action + I + II − action + III	+ progressive + singular + present − singular − present	Progressive affix T
13. Contractible copula	+ V + I + II − V + III	+ singular + present − singular − present	Copula T
14. Contractible auxiliary	+ action + I + II − action + III	+ progressive + singular + present − singular − present	Progressive affix T

[a]Jacobs and Rosenbaum are not responsible for this version. It represents my interpretation of what they say together with my notion of what they might say where their descriptions are incomplete. In addition, as the text indicates, it has not been possible to invent a notation for all aspects of the usage of these forms.

of noun may be pluralized. Common nouns (<+common>) like *table* may be, but proper nouns (<−common>) like *Adam* may not be; count nouns (<+count>) like *table* may be, but mass nouns (<−count>) like *sand,* except in special uses absent from early child speech, may not be. Jacobs and Rosenbaum do not say how this effect is to be accomplished but however it is done, it will be necessary to use the features "common" and "count" to subcategorize nouns in the lexicon. These features create covert subcategories comparable to the process and state categories within the verbal category.

When a noun segment carries the feature <−singular> an additional segment is introduced by a noun suffix transformation. However, this transformation must only

Transformations			Features Introduced by Transformation	Regular Allomorphs	Irregular Allomorphs
			+ affix		
Article T[b]	Nominal agreement T[b]		+ affix + article[b]	/-s~-z~-ɨz/	A few (*men, women*, etc.)
					Many (*came, went*, etc.)
–	–		–		–
Auxiliary incorporation T	Auxiliary agreement T		+ copula		6 (*am, is*, etc.)
			+ article		1 (*an*)
Verb suffix T			+ affix	/-t~d~-ɨd/	
Verbal agreement T	Verb suffix T		+ affix	/-s~-z~-ɨz/	
Verbal agreement T					A few (*does, has*, etc.)
Progressive segment T	Auxiliary incorporation T	Auxiliary agreement T	+ affix + copula		6 (*am, is*, etc.)
Auxiliary incorporation T	Auxiliary agreement T		+ copula	/-s~-z~-ɨz/	2 (*–m~–r*)
Progressive segment T	Auxiliary incorporation T	Auxiliary agreement T	+ affix + copula	/-s~-z~-ɨz/	2 (*–m~–r*)

[b]Not involved in all plurals.

operate with regular nouns which take one of the -*s* allomorphs, and so not with *man* or *woman* or *foot*. Jacobs and Rosenbaum note the necessity of blocking the transformation in these cases but do not provide a mechanism for doing so. The noun suffix transformation introduces a segment to the right of the noun, and this segment carries the features $<+affix>$ and $<-singular>$. On the second lexical pass it becomes -*s* with the correct allomorph being contingent on phonological properties of the stem, presumably selected on the phonological level. The minimal grammar of plural inflection, then, involves the features "common," "count," "singular," and "affix" as well as the noun suffix transformation and rules to select the regular allomorphs and the several irregular forms. In grammatical complexity it is not strictly comparable with either the progressive or the prepositions *in* and *on* but, simply in terms of number of rules and features, it involves one more feature than the constructions that precede it in the acquisition order, the same number of transformations (one), and an allomorphic apparatus not involved in the "simpler" constructions.

Plural constructions often involve additional complexity. Determiners, or as Jacobs and Rosenbaum prefer, articles, if present in an *NP* must agree in number with the noun. Articles like *two, some, these,* and *those* go with plural nouns whereas articles like *a, another, this,* and *that* go with singular nouns. Articles are not selected by number only but also by such features as "definite" (for *the* rather than *a*) and "near" (for *this* rather than *that*). We shall disregard these at present, since these aspects of selection did not have to be correct for a construction to count as plural in our research. Jacobs and Rosenbaum introduce segments underlying articles with an article transformation. It adjoins to the left of the noun, and under *NP,* a segment with the feature $< +\text{article}>$ plus all the features on the nouns except $+N$. The segment would then be appropriately marked to be replaced by articles from the lexicon agreeing with the noun in number. Plurals with articles then are more complex than plural names by virtue of one feature ($< +\text{article}>$) and one transformation.

Jacobs and Rosenbaum do not present a treatment of agreement in the predicate nominative but we can guess how it might go. What is needed is a nominal agreement transformation that copies the number feature from the subject noun onto the predicate noun. There is, however, the problem of preventing the predicate noun from acquiring a number feature independently of the subject noun as a result of the operation of the segment structure rules. To my knowledge this problem has not been solved in any formal representation of the predicate nominal.

So the rank 4 plural category includes constructions at three levels of complexity: plural names, articles and plurals, predicate nominals. These three are strictly ordered by cumulative complexity, since each more complex form includes everything in the less complex forms plus something additional. It would be valuable to have separate acquisition order data from the three, but the problem is that some forms are not frequent enough to yield continuous data. We shall see, however, that Cazden found a way to compare predicate nominals, the most complex of the three, with the other two lumped together, and that she found the predicate nominals developing later as they should if grammatical complexity is a determinant of order of acquisition.

Because the third person present tense form of the verb is contingent on the singular or plural number of the subject, among other things, it is convenient to discuss its grammar here. The third person singular present tense verb is regularly inflected with /–s ~ –ʒ ~ –ɨʒ/ and has such irregular forms as *does* and *has.* While there are only a few different irregular forms they are among the most frequently used verbs in English, and so the data were continuous enough to make possible the identification of a point of acquisition for irregular forms distinct from the point for regular forms. In the order of Table 38 the third person regular holds rank 10 and irregular rank 11. The grammar of a sentence like *Sarah walks* begins with the noun segment that is to become the subject. This segment acquires the feature $<+$ singular$>$ from the segment structure and the lexical entry, *Sarah,* adds the person feature $<+$ III$>$. The *AUX* constituent acquires the tense feature $<+$ present$>$ from the segment structure rules. The first transformation needed is the auxiliary agreement transformation, which copies the number and person features from the subject noun onto the auxiliary segment. This segment being marked for tense, person, and number carries the necessary information to produce the inflection, but in a sentence like *Sarah walks* there is no auxiliary verb, and it is the main verb that requires to be inflected. Therefore a second transformation is needed, the verbal agreement transformation, which deletes the auxiliary when it does not carry a $<+$ copula$>$ feature as is the case here, copying its number, person, and tense features onto the verbal. For regular verbals the remaining necessity is a verb suffix transformation, which introduces an affix segment (marked $<+$ affix$>$) to the right of the verbal and copies onto this segment the number person and tense features of the verbal. The lexicon then supplies the inflection *-s,* which presumably becomes the appropriate regular allomorph on the phonological level.

Jacobs and Rosenbaum note that for irregular verbs like *has* and *does* the verb suffix transformation must be blocked. Their discussion concerns the past tense but the problem is the same for irregular verbs in the present indicative. Jacobs and Rosenbaum write: "Possibly these verbs show their idiosyncrasy in the lexicon. Such a feature would block the application of the verb suffix transformation and the appropriate past tense form would be drawn from the lexicon to replace the verbal segment. It is not yet understood exactly how to incorporate exceptions into a grammar" (p. 134). In Table 45 I have used the lexical feature $<+$ irregular$>$ to mark the existence of the problem, but it must be understood that the representation of irregulars is not complete.

The third person inflections involve either three or four features and two or three transformations and some allomorphic apparatus. In the order of acquisition they precede the progressive with auxiliary, which involves six features and four transformations. The third person inflections follow long after the primitive progressive and the prepositions *in* and *on,* which involve three features and one transformation. The third person inflections also fall well after the plurals, but since the plurals range in complexity from four features and one transformation to four features and three transformations, this ordering is hard to interpret. Generally, the constructions we have considered follow an order of acquisition that corresponds with a rough order of grammatical complexity. But complexity defined in terms of the numbers of features and rules, regardless of the character of the features and rules, may be meaningless.

Past Tense

The regularly inflected form holds rank 9 in the order of acquisition and the irregular form rank 5. Verbs that form the past in an irregular way are extremely numerous and varied: *came, went, did, made, saw, ate, ran, held, hit, rode,* and so on. The regular inflection *-d* has three allomorphs: /–t ∼ d ∼ –id/.

Tense is represented in deep structures by the features $<+$present$>$ and $<-$present$>$, which are generated by the segment structure rules on the auxiliary segment. When the auxiliary is not a modal and does not have the feature $<+$copula$>$, as in a sentence like *Eve walked home,* the verbal agreement transformation deletes the auxiliary and copies its features (for example $<-$present$>$ onto the verbal segment. When a verbal segment is marked $<-$present$>$ the verb suffix transformation introduces a segment to the right of the verb with the features $<+$affix$>$ and $<-$present$>$. This affix is replaced by the lexicon with *-d,* which the phonological component changes into the appropriate allomorph. For irregular verbs the verb suffix transformation must be blocked (perhaps by a feature $<+$irregular$>$), and there must be as many particular allomorphic rules as there are distinct types of irregular formation.

The positions of the past tense forms in the order of acquisition do not seem to be explained by their grammatical complexity. The irregular form, which involves one less transformation than the regular, precedes the regular. And the order irregular-regular for the past tense reverses the third person inflection order which is regular-irregular. And the irregular past tense, since it involves only two features and one transformation, seems to be even simpler than the primitive progressive which holds rank 1 in the order of acquisition. Of course the grammar of the irregular past has not been made fully explicit. In particular some number of very particular allomorphic rules is involved. So this is to say that rough calculations of grammatical complexity fail to predict the developmental order when we arrive at the past tense.

The Possessive

The possessive is a problem. Jacobs and Rosenbaum do not offer a derivation but only point the direction they would take, which is the direction all other transformational grammarians have taken with this construction. They point to the following parallels:

> *Eric's dictionary.*
> *Eric has a dictionary.*
> *The dictionary which Eric has.*

Every possessive phrase can similarly be matched by a simple sentence with *have* and a relative clause constructed from the same simple sentence. These facts suggest that the deep structure of a genitive should be like the deep structure for a relative clause. For *I sit Adam's chair* roughly the following:

```
                    S
         NP                VP
         |         VB           NP
         N         |        N        S
         |         V        |    NP        VP
         I         |      chair  |      V      NP
                  sit           N     |      |
                               Adam  has     N
                                             |
                                           chair
```

Jacobs and Rosenbaum suggest that a genitive transformation could easily be written to generate the likes of *Adam's chair* from the relative clause structure.

The objections to this derivation and others like it for child speech are as follows. The first genitives, those in early Stage I, occur independently as if they were complete sentences in themselves. Neither at that time nor when they first appear as constituents in sentences does one find that corresponding simple sentences with *have* occur at all frequently. And the relative clause sentences which are by this derivation most closely similar to the genitive do not occur at all until much later: Stage V or beyond. So the parallels that motivate the derivation for adult speech are simply not present in child speech. For that reason I think the derivation is wrong for child speech and possibly also for adult speech.

Unfortunately this leaves us without a Jacobs-Rosenbaum representation of the possessive. I have written a very inelegant derivation within the general framework of a Chomsky-style grammar but it will not fit the phrase structure of Jacobs and Rosenbaum. So I just have to omit the possessive from Table 45, as well as from the discussion which is to come of the relation between grammatical complexity and order of acquisition.

The Copula

The uncontractible copula holds rank 7 and the contractible rank 13. Jacobs and Rosenbaum confine their discussion of the copula to the case in which it is followed by a predicate adjective as in *Cowboy is big.* In fact in child speech, as well as in adult speech, the copula also occurs with predicate nominatives *(Eve is girl)* and with locatives *(Sweater is on chair).* The derivation in these latter cases could, in part, be the same as it is in the predicate adjective case but, in part, it would have to be different. The predicate adjective derivation is all we have, and that is what has been summarized in Table 45.

Adjectives you recall are treated as a variety of verbal. They have in common with verbs the feature $<+VB>$ but are distinguished from verbs by the feature $<-V>$. This feature would presumably be entered by a segment structure rule. When a verbal is marked $<-V>$ the copula transformation introduces a segment to the left of the verbal with the feature $<+$copula$>$. The auxiliary incorporation transformation then incorporates the copula segment into the auxiliary. Copulas must agree in person and number with the subject noun — exactly as auxiliary copulas do. Consequently, person features ($<+$I$>$ or $<+$II$>$ or $<+$III$>$) and number features ($<+$singular$>$ or $<-$singular$>$) must be copied onto the auxiliary segment by the auxiliary agreement transformation. A tense feature will already have been added to the auxiliary by the segment structure rules. The copula segment will then be so marked as to select the proper form of the copula: *am, is, are, was,* or *were.*

Contractibility for the copula works as it does for the auxiliary copula. The uncontracted form is phonologically simpler than the contractible, and it is also earlier in the order of acquisition.

Articles

The articles we counted were *a* and *the,* and we were not able to establish separate acquisition points for the two but only one point for the two combined. However, when the judgment could be made whether context called specifically for *a* or for *the* it proved to be the case that the correct form was usually supplied. And so there is reason to attribute to the children knowledge of the distinction between definite and nondefinite reference, and it is with the features $<+$definite$>$ or $<-$definite$>$ that the generation of articles begins.

Noun segments are assigned the feature $<+$definite$>$ or $<-$definite$>$ by segment structure rules, which also assign them the number features $<+$singular$>$ or $<-$singular$>$. Nouns themselves are subcategorized in the lexicon into common nouns ($<+$common$>$) and proper nouns ($<-$common$>$), count nouns ($<+$count$>$) and mass nouns ($<-$count$>$). These four sets of features are not free to occur in all possible combinations. Proper nouns must be definite and may not be plural. Mass nouns may not be plural. Jacobs and Rosenbaum do not explicitly represent these facts, and so their representation is incomplete. We can only list the features involved as we have done in Table 45.

The article transformation introduces a segment to the left of the noun and copies onto it all the features of the noun. When the features are $<+$common$>$, $<+$count$>$, $<+$singular$>$, and $<-$definite$>$ the lexicon will supply the article *a.*

The article *an* is an allomorph of *a* supplied when the noun begins with a vowel. Instances of *an* were too few to yield continuous data and so were excluded from the count. When the noun features are <+common>, <+count>, and <−singular> or <+common>, <+count>, <+singular>, and <+definite> and in certain other cases the lexicon will supply *the*.

If we think of grammatical complexity as determining order of acquisition then articles seem to be seriously misplaced, more seriously than any other of the 14 morphemes. In Table 45 articles are represented as involving five features but only one transformation. It is worth remembering, however, that the Jacobs-Rosenbaum representation is quite seriously incomplete in this case in particular. It does not represent the constraints on combination of the various noun features.

Before attempting a general assessment of the importance of grammatical complexity in determining order of acquisition we need to set down the facts about two other classes of variable which seem likely to play a determining role: semantics and frequency.

The Semantics of the Fourteen Morphemes

No author seems to have characterized all the meanings that concern us, and so I shall draw upon several and sometimes will have to fill in with ideas of my own. Most students of language seem to assume that there must be a single meaning associated with each inflection and function word, one meaning for progressive aspect, one for perfective aspect, one for past tense, one for plural number, and so forth. It often turns out that the single meaning that will fit all instances must be a very rarefied conception. I think it is a mistake to suppose that a grammatical operation must always express a single meaning. Since many "content" words have, in the course of time, come to stand for a chain complex of related but distinguishable meanings, I do not see why grammatical morphemes, most of which have a very long history, should not do the same.

The Progressive

There are two meanings to be described, that of the progressive inflection itself and that of the process-state covert subcategorization (<+action> and <−action>), which divides verbs into those that take the progressive and those that do not. First, the inflection. Ralph B. Long in *The Sentence and Its Parts* (1961) writes: "Progressive-aspect forms are normal when predications tell of actions, events, or states of affairs that are in process at the time of writing or speaking, and are thought of as begun but not ended, with beginnings and/or ends felt as relatively close to the time of writing or speaking" (p. 125). Martin Joos, in *The English Verb* (1964) takes much the same position; he refers to the meaning of the progressive as "temporary aspect" or "limited duration." The action or state named is said to be completely "valid" or true at the time of the utterance but the probability of its being true at times prior to and subsequent to the time of the utterance is said to fall off symmetrically. W. F. Twaddell (1963) and numerous other authors agree that the progressive expresses a temporary duration including the time of the utterance.

The word "progressive" tends to suggest some goal-directed action which is making "progress," that is, advancing toward a goal, at the moment of utterance. In fact, however, the verb need not name a goal-directed action or indeed any sort of action. We can say *He is standing immobile* or *He is sleeping peacefully,* and the absence of a goal or of any "kinetic" quality does not block the use of the progressive. So the verb may name a state of affairs as well as an action.

When we say that the action or state named by the verb with progressive aspect is true at the time of the utterance it must be added that the exact sense in which this is so varies with the meaning of the individual verb. If someone asks: *What are you doing now?* and the answer given is *Talking to you,* that concrete action is, in fact, true as one answers. But one might alternatively, and more reasonably, give such an answer as *Teaching at Harvard.* This is "true" at the time of utterance only if we understand teaching at Harvard to be a professional affiliation that does not lapse in the interstices between lectures.

When a verb names an action, modulating it for temporary aspect does not necessarily carry the sense that a single natural unit of the action is in progress as one speaks. If one says *I was killing flies when the phone rang,* the sense is that the call came in the course of a set of repetitions of a very brief action of a certain type. On the other hand it is possible to stretch out the action by saying: *I was killing a fly when the phone rang.* The process becomes rather nastily deliberate.

There are past progressives and future progressives as well as present progressives with the difference being marked by the auxiliary copula. Only actions and states named by verbs in the *present* progressive are true at the time of the utterance. For progressives, generally, we need a more abstract notion: they are true at some time of reference. Thus: *I will be driving home when your plane takes off* or *I was eating dinner when you left. Driving home* is true at a future time indicated and *eating dinner* was true at a past time indicated. In both cases the probability that the action is true falls off on one or both sides of the point of reference. Moving the point of reference from the moment of utterance to other times in the past and future is a kind of cognitive "decentering." By the time Adam, Eve, and Sarah attained criterion on the full progressive, the progressive with auxiliary copula, they used some past auxiliaries as well as present auxiliaries though not yet future auxiliaries. With the primitive progressive one cannot tell whether it is a present, past, or future form, since the auxiliary that carries this information is absent. However, the primitive progressives almost always seem to have a present sense, since one can usually see that the action or state named was true as the child spoke. The auxiliary, if it had been present, would have been redundant at this time but when the possibility developed of marking the auxiliary for past or future time it ceased to be redundant.

Did the children use the progressive to express the notion of limited duration? In the early samples, of course, before the progressive reached criterion it was often omitted where the context suggests that it ought to have been used. Once criterion had been attained, however, the signal was seldom omitted where called for. In Eve's records, for instance, there are just two such omissions after criterion (between Stage II and III). But was the child's use of the progressive restricted to cases of temporary duration or was it often used where it was semantically inappropriate? I have looked at all of Eve's progressives from this point of view. Quite often, of course, one cannot be sure whether limited duration should be signaled or not. But where I could be sure I found that Eve used the progressive inappropriately in only seven instances involving five different verbs. So it does seem that temporary duration as well as present time were intended by the child when the progressive was used.

The child's referential consistency suggests that temporary duration including the present, the time of the utterance, was the sense of the primitive progressive; temporary duration including some reference time in the past was added when the full progressive developed. But referential consistency is not enough. Present temporary duration is a characterization which implies the possibility of expressing certain contrasting meanings, a possibility that clearly exists for adult speakers. Whether the child intends temporary duration must depend not only on his referential consistency but on whether he has the possibility of expressing anything other than temporary duration. Whether the child intends a reference to the "present" must depend on whether he has the possibility of referring to anything other than the present. What was the sense of the progressive in the children's own terms, in terms, that is, of the other modulations of the verb that they were able to express? I have studied all of Eve's verbs in all her samples and have studied substantial numbers of the verbs in the samples of the other children at all five stages in an effort to answer this question.

For all three children, and for all children thus far described, the verb is initially in generic unmarked form. At Stage I this generic verb is usually understood by the parents in one of four senses:

As as imperative: *Get book.*
As a past: *Book drop (dropped).*
As expressive of an intention or prediction: *Mommy read (gonna read* or *will read).*
As a progressive expressive of present temporary duration: *Fish swim (is swimming).*

The parents do, in fact, "expand" or "gloss" the child's generic forms in this way. Once in a while also they may expand a generic form with *can* or a past progressive or something else, but the four types listed above account for most cases. Furthermore

I, as a student of the transcript and not a parent, find that the context of the child's utterance usually suggests one of the four modulations described.

After Stage I the children gradually learn to modify the generic verb in three ways:

1. As a primitive progressive, with *-ing* but no auxiliary, and almost always naming an action or state in fact of temporary duration and true at the time of utterance.

2. As past, with *-d* or an irregular allomorph but with the time range at first limited to the immediate past: *It dropped* or *broke* or *spilled* or *fell*. The range expands to include several hours or a full day and eventually longer periods. In sample 14 (about Stage IV) Eve said: *Remember we went to Rhode Island,* and her mother responded: *Goodness, yes, that's a month ago!* The exclamation indicates how unusual it was for Eve to make reference to so remote a time.

3. As a generic verb with such semi-auxiliaries or "catenatives" as *gonna, wanna,* and *hafta.* These forms have not been included in our list of grammatical morphemes because it is impossible to code contexts as requiring one or another of them. Typically when one of these seems possible so do the others and also often, such modal auxiliaries as *will, can,* and *must.* It is not clear that the children use the several catenative verbs in a semantically distinct way. My judgment is that Eve did not even as late as Stage IV. There was often no discernible obligation or compulsion in her *hafta,* for instance. She would say *I hafta eat my ice cream* though one might have thought *wanna* or *gonna* more apt. The children showed individual partialities for particular catenatives. *Hafta* was Eve's favorite, and her heavy use of it made her sound for a time like a harried executive. It also resulted in the creation, when she was learning a certain well-known song, of the following gem: *I hafta pee-pee just to pass the time away.* The best semantic characterization I can hit on for the child's catenatives is "intentionality" or "imminence." They were used to name actions just about to occur, a kind of immediate future which was often also a statement of the child's wish or intention.

These three operations on the verb correspond with three out of four semantic intentions most commonly attributed to the child before he expressed them, when all his verbs were still in generic form.[17] The fourth intention, the imperative, has no reliable grammatical marker, though *please* is an occasional marker. *Please* was, in fact, added along with the other three markers, but generally the development of the imperative in this period is simply a matter of the increasingly exclusive use of the generic verb for just this purpose. In Stage I the generic verb serves all purposes, but as the child begins to express the progressive, the past, and the intentional overtly, the use of the generic verb is very gradually restricted to the imperative only, which is a proper adult use.

17. Slobin (1971b) has taken these results to mean that the child had the semantic intentions in question before he expressed them, and that may well be correct. What is lacking, of course, is evidence beyond context and other than mature expression which nevertheless demonstrates that the child had the intentions.

The primitive progressive attained criterion before the past but not very long before the irregular past. We had no criterion for intentional-imminent catenatives but they became frequent in Stage II at the same time as the primitive progressive. It seems correct, therefore, to say that the progressive carried a meaning of present time in the child's terms, since it contrasted with an immediate past and an intentional-imminent future. These contrasts were not at first quite like the adult contrasts in that the total time span was narrower. The children did not attain criterion on the full progressive until long after Stage V, and by then the children could speak of remote past and future times, could use modal auxiliaries as well as catenatives, and could move the temporal reference point into the past.

Does the primitive progressive carry the sense of temporary duration in the child's terms? In adult English the temporary duration of the present progressive arises out of contrasts with certain nontemporary senses of the simple present tense form, the unmarked generic verb. An adult would say *We are living in Cambridge* to suggest that Cambridge is probably a temporary place of residence and would use *We live in Cambridge* when there was no reason to suppose the residence temporary. An adult would say *I am driving a bus* to name an ongoing temporary activity and *I drive a bus* to say what he does for a living, to characterize himself vocationally. An adult has such generic forms as *I pronounce you man and wife* to name instantaneous action of no duration. And *The milkman comes on Mondays* to name recurrent, habitual actions. And *Two and two make four* for timeless relations. *France borders on Spain* for comparatively permanent relations. All these are uses of the generic verb to express actions and events and states without any implication of temporary duration. The child, we know, starts out using nothing but generic verbs, and he still uses very many of them after he has acquired the primitive progressive, the immediate past, and the intentional-imminent future. But are his generic verbs used to express characteristic activities, instantaneous activities, recurrent activities, timeless relations, and permanent relations?

The generic verbs of Stage I are, we have seen, usually expanded into imperatives, past, progressive, and future forms. Only very rarely does a parent gloss a child's generic verb with a present tense form having no implication of temporary duration. The major exception is the use of *have* as in *I have bike* to express what seems to be permanent ownership. Present tense forms clearly implying permanent and instantaneous and recurrent actions and relations did not become common in Eve's speech until sample 15, which is between Stages III and IV. Then we find *Fraser comes on Saturday* (recurrent action); *Cromer wears glasses* and *The train goes on it* (permanent relations); *I say "bike"* (instantaneous action). It seems then that the implication of temporary duration is not at first a part of the meaning of the present progressive because there are almost no expressions of nontemporary durations. Another way of putting it is: all present forms refer to action and events of temporary duration, but since these do not contrast with permanent, instantaneous and timeless actions and events, it is not clear that "temporary duration" is a part of what the child intends to express. From about Stage IV it does seem to be a part of the child's intention.

Contractions and, especially, expansions of semantic range with no change of formal expressive means is a general feature of language development, which has not begun to receive the study it deserves. The use of generic verbs to express recurrent actions, permanent relations, instantaneous actions but not acts of temporary duration described here is one example. One might add the example of the genitive, which is, at first, used only for possession and part-whole relations but which has, in most languages, many other uses involving no important changes of grammar. The use of terms like *smooth, rough, warm, cold, sharp, dull* is at first limited to tactile and thermal experiences and only much later to personalities. Just about every "abstract" term in a language has historically a set of earlier more concrete uses, and there is some reason to suppose that the child's usage roughly recapitulates these historical progressions. Indeed, it is an interesting empirical question whether the abstract sense of a term, for instance, *adhere* as in *Spain adheres to the Catholic faith,* could ever be grasped without a prior apprenticeship with more concrete senses *(The cloth adheres to your hand).*

We come now to the semantic characterization of process and state verbs. The former are said freely to take the progressive though they need not necessarily be in the progressive. The latter are said to resist the progressive. If the progressive signals temporary duration then it is reasonable to expect that process verbs would carry meanings easily conceived as of temporary duration and state verbs meanings not easily so conceived. What do dictionaries say about these words "process" and "state," and what have the words to do with duration? A *process* is said to involve gradual change moving toward an end or a result whereas a *state* is said to be an unchanging mode or condition. The fact that process implies an end or result would seem to predispose processes to temporary duration, and the fact that states are unchanging would seem to predispose them to permanent duration or to timelessness. As clear instances of process verb sentences we might think of the following:

> *They are smelting iron.*
> *The sugar is dissolving.*
> *I am learning the words to the song.*
> *I am thinking about the third problem.*
> *I am digesting my meal.*

As clear instances of state verb sentences we might think of these:

> *Two and two equal four.* (Not *are equaling.*)
> *France borders on Spain.* (Not *is bordering.*)
> *The key fits the lock.* (Not *is fitting.*)
> *I know the words to the Star Spangled Banner.* (Not *am knowing.*)
> *I believe in the Immaculate Conception.* (Not *am believing.*)

It appears that when a state is likely to be temporary it may take the progressive even though the state is internally homogeneous and moves toward no end. Thus all the following are perfectly acceptable sentences:

> *This pillar is holding up the whole building.*
> *The clothes are hanging on the line.*
> *I am standing immobile beneath your window.*
> *He is sleeping peacefully.*

The evidence thus far suggests that when a verb names a process ($<+$ process$>$ semantically) it may always take the progressive. When a verb names a state ($<-$ process$>$ semantically) it may or may not take the progressive. Whether it does or not depends on the likelihood of the state being temporary. Perhaps $<-$ process$>$ or state verbs should be further subcategorized as $<+$ temporary$>$ like *hold, hang, stand,* and *sleep* or $<-$ temporary$>$ like *equal, border, know, fit,* and *believe* according to the likelihood of the state's being temporary.

By the above criteria the verbs *want, like,* and *need* would all seem to be $<+$ state$>$ and $<+$ temporary$>$. But the difficulty is that when these verbs are used with a clearly temporary sense they are not put in the progressive. As witness the following:

> *I want my lunch.* (Not *am wanting.*)
> *I need something to drink.* (Not *am needing.*)
> *I like this dessert.* (Not *am liking.*)

Sentences like these suggest that in the case of human and animal psychic states or processes we may need to draw a different distinction. What one notices about all the above is that they are involuntary. So also are the states in two sentences cited earlier as clear cases of state verbs:

> *I know the words to "The Star Spangled Banner."*
> *I believe in the Immaculate Conception.*

And of the sentences cited earlier as instances of process verbs, those that are human psychic processes are also voluntary.

> *I am learning the words to the song.*
> *I am thinking about the third problem.*

The possibility exists then that when a voluntary-involuntary distinction can be made, as it can for human and animal psychic states or processes, it is the distinction with respect to volition that better separates out verbs that may take the progressive from those that may not. Volition would be the better criterion because in addition to categorizing correctly *know, believe, learn,* and *think* it categorizes correctly *want, need,* and *like* as the process-state distinction does not. Allen (1956) has in fact suggested that state verbs are "mainly verbs of condition or behavior not strictly under human control" and Joos (1964) seems to agree.

The voluntary-involuntary distinction fits many facts. Lakoff (1966) has argued that the process-state distinction governs the applicability of the imperative and benefactive modes as well as of the progressive. It surely makes sense to command someone to perform what is voluntary (to *walk* or *talk* or *learn* or *think*) but not what is involuntary (to *like* or *need* or *believe* or *know*). It makes sense to say of a voluntary action that it was done for someone or other (benefactive), but it does not make sense to speak so of an involuntary action *(He eats spinach for his mother's sake* but not *He likes spinach for his mother's sake).* The fact that the science of psychology is not entirely clear which human and animal psychic processes are voluntary and which involuntary does not discredit the notion that such a distinction affects grammar. The distinction is older than the science of psychology, and it may be presumed to operate with a "perceived" or common-sense notion of volition and its limits.

What other facts does the voluntary-involuntary distinction fit? We have in English the following pairs of closely similar verbs:

see	*look at*
hear	*listen*
feel	*touch*

Those on the left do not freely take the progressive, imperative, and benefactive whereas those on the right do. Presumably then those on the left are state verbs and those on the right process verbs. What is the semantic difference between *see* and *look at?* Surely the former names an involuntary passive visual registration whereas the latter names a purposive training of the visual receptors (by voluntary musculature) on certain objects. What is the difference between *hear* and *listen?* Hearing is involuntary auditory registration whereas listening is, usually, a tuning of attention to certain sound sources, a tuning that is voluntary. One says: *I am listening to the music* or *Please listen to the music* or *I will listen to the music for your sake,* but *hear* may not readily be substituted for *listen* in these sentences. *Feel* and *touch* are also, respectively, involuntary and voluntary. *Feeling* is something that happens to certain receptors, willy nilly, whereas *touching* is palpation with the finger tips.

There are certain English verbs which, used in one sense, may take the progressive and in another sense may not. *Hear* is such a verb. In the sense of simple auditory registration it is involuntary and does not take the progressive. But *The judge was hearing the case* is perfectly acceptable English. Judicial "hearing" is a voluntary process involving auditory registration but going well beyond it. The imperative and benefactive modes may also be used with judicial hearing. The link between volition and the progressive is further suggested by the fact that one can sometimes use a state verb in the progressive and thereby suggest a slightly unusual, more voluntary sense. Thus: *Adele has one of her headaches* seems involuntary but *Adele is having one of her headaches* suggests voluntary histrionics.

While the voluntary-involuntary distinction fits the facts of *see, hear, feel, listen, look at, touch,* and *have,* it is necessary to point out that the distinction between process as "change moving toward an end" and state as "an unchanging condition" also fits these facts. If there is a voluntary purposive connotation to *look at* as opposed to *see* and to *listen* as opposed to *hear* and to *touch* as opposed to *feel* then there is also a connotation of movement toward a result, even a goal. If *Adele is having one of her headaches* is more voluntary than *Adele has one of her headaches* it is also more "kinetic" and purposive, more suggestive of change and of an end. What all this suggests is that there is a kind of natural correlation between voluntary and process, involuntary and state. All that is voluntary like everything that is a process readily takes on temporary duration, since volition is not likely to be exerted permanently. The involuntary, on the other hand, is more likely to be an enduring, relatively permanent, disposition in the organism. When, however, states are of temporary duration the verb takes the progressive aspect *(is holding, is standing)* unless the state is an involuntary psychic one *(want, need, know),* in which case the generic present is used even for temporary duration.

Even the elaborate statement above does not quite fit all the facts. What shall we say of the sentence *I am digesting my meal?* It seems to be involuntary but a process and of temporary duration. In this kind of case it is not volition that is determinative but rather the fact that the verb names a process of temporary duration. Perhaps volition, in common sense psychology, is only applicable to psychic events, and physiological events like digestion, salivation, perspiration, and the like are treated like physical processes, such as dissolving or melting or fracturing. If the voluntary-involuntary distinction is treated as inapplicable then the applicability of the progressive should depend on whether the verb names a process or a state, and so it does with physiological verbs. It is consistent with classification of physiological events as physical rather than psychic that the imperative and benefactive modes are excluded in both cases. It is scarcely more reasonable to command another to digest or perspire than to command him to decay or to crumble. It should be noted, however, that all these are processes and may take the progressive, and so it is not the case that the three grammatical operations — progressive, imperative, and benefactive — always cohere as a single set governed by process-state subcategorization.

Finally there is a problem with the set of verbs that started our inquiry into volition, with *want, like,* and *need.* It is too absolute to say that these involuntary states may not take the progressive. In certain cases they do. Once upon a time when I was on a plane landing in Austin, Texas, I was thinking about these very verbs and the fact that they could not take the progressive when a gentleman standing in the aisle said to the girl next to me: "Are you wanting your suitcase down?" What will account for this case? The wanting was as involuntary as it is in *I want my lunch* and yet the progressive was used. In circumstances, however, where the states had a definite duration that was clearly temporary. The girl would shortly leave the plane. What seems to have happened is that the exceptionally clear applicability of the meaning "temporary duration" overrode all else. What it means more generally I think is that actual usage will not quite stay within the confines of any rule. As Labov has written to me (February 12, 1971): "Mild, penumbrous disjunction is just the price of living." I am inclined to think that disjunction is more typical of unself-conscious human cognition than the conjunctive classes we attribute to ourselves when we undertake to represent our cognition.

Does it make sense to attribute a distinction we can scarcely define to children when they start to use the progressive? One might think not but there is a difficulty. The children do use a small number of state and involuntary verbs rather often, especially *want, like, need, know, see,* and *hear,* and they never put these verbs in the progressive form. They use a great variety of process verbs, and these are often in the progressive form. What makes this fact impressive is a comparison with the children's use of other inflections: the regular past, the regular third person singular, the regular plural, and the regular possessive. All these inflections are sometimes overgeneralized morphologically in the sense of being added to stems to which they should not have been added. The children created such errors as *comed* and *drinked,* and *doos* (*do* + *-s* for third person subject) and *stand ups* and *mans* (plural) and *sheeps* (plural) and *mines* (possessive). Table 46 lists all the overgeneralizations that ever occurred in the records from Stage I through Stage V with different subvarieties of overgeneralization separated by lines. What concerns us here is the single stark fact that the progressive in our data is unique among inflections; the progressive in our data alone is not overgeneralized. And the opportunity for overgeneralization was there. The children need only have ignored the involuntary nature of the states and said *wanting, liking, needing,* or the like. Why should no errors occur with the progressive inflection when they do occur with all other inflections?

The answer at first seems obvious. The subclassification of verbs which governs the progressive is a principled one whereas the subclassifications governing the applicability of regular past, third person, plural, and possessive inflections are all unprincipled. In all these latter cases the grammarian simply speaks of regular (or rule-governed verbs) and irregular verbs. There is no semantic distinction between verbs like *walk, talk, want, like,* and *try,* which take the regular past, and verbs like *come, go, fly, see,* and *hear,* which take one or another irregular form in the past. And there is no semantic distinction between *boy, girl, dog, horse,* and *tree,* which take the regular plural, and *man, woman, sheep,* and *foot,* which form their plurals irregularly. The case is the same for third person and possessive inflections. When subcategories are unprincipled the child has no choice but to learn by rote for each verb and noun which class it belongs to. In his reasonable expectation that such unprincipled learning will not be required of him he applies a general rule, and so makes mistakes. The slowness of the rote learning process may be judged from the fact that errors of overgeneralized regular inflection persist well beyond the preschool years. The verbs *want, like, need, know, see,* and *hear,* which may not ordinarily take the progressive inflection in American English can be semantically distinguished from the many verbs that may take the progressive inflection; the former are all involuntary states. Surely the child learns the principle, subcategorizes the verbs accordingly, and so makes no mistakes. What is more the subcategorization has a usefulness that goes beyond the progressive. The involuntary state verbs are also excluded from occurring in the imperative mode, and the child makes no mistakes here either; he never orders someone to want something or to know something. The benefactive mode does not often appear in early child speech, but when it does the child seems never to use it with involuntary state verbs.

Table 46. Morphological overgeneralizations of the five inflections from Stages I through V

Inflection	Eve	Adam	Sarah
Verb *-ing*	(none)	(none)	(none)
Verb *-ed*	comed (4)	falled (2)	goed (2)
	doed	feeled	growed
	drinked	growed	heared
	falled (8)	maked	hurted
	goed (5)	throwed (2)	maked
	seed	waked up	runned
	throwed	—ᵃ	swimmed
	weared	broked	waked up
	—ᵃ	felled	winned (2)
	tored		—ᵃ
			caughted
			flewed
Verb *-s*	none	doos	stand ups
		—ᵃ	
		fells	
		gots	
		wents	
Noun *-s*	mans	deers (2)	childs
(plural)	peoples	firemans (3)	fishes (2)
	sheeps	mans	knifes
	snowmans	milkmans	knittings
	—ᵃ	peoples (2)	pantses
	mens (2)	auntses	toothes
	—ᵃ	—ᵃ	—ᵃ
	somes (2)	feets	deers
	twos	firemens	feets
	manys	mens	reindeers
	[bok-box]	reindeers	teeths
		schoolses	—ᵃ

Inflection	Eve	Adam	Sarah
		streets lights	milks
		—[a]	thems
		coffees	pinks
		dirts (2)	
		honeys	
		ketchups	
		milks	
		moneys	
		sugars (2)	
		—[a]	
		somes	
		threes (3)	
		twos	
		—[a]	
		greens	
		slipperys	
Noun -s (possessive)	mines (5)	mines (36)	mines hims

[a]Separate subvarieties of overgeneralization

But is it reasonable to suppose that our three children were all able to learn a concept like involuntary state before they were three years old, and Eve before she was two? Maybe not. What other possibility is there? They might learn of each verb individually whether it is "*ing*able" or not and refrain from using -*ing* with a verb until they have learned that it is permissible. There is weak support for this hypothesis in certain facts about Eve's progressives.

I looked at all Eve's verbs in all samples to determine how frequently each one was used in the progressive and how frequently each was used in generic form. The involuntary state verbs were never in the progressive. Certain process verbs *(do, eat, make, go)* were in the progressive as often or even more often than in generic form. The surprise was that there were other process verbs, in fact 19 of them, which were never in the progressive and so, as far as Eve's usage was concerned, they might have been state verbs.

I next looked at the speech of Eve's mother in samples 4–6, which precede the frequent use of the progressive by Eve, to see what opportunities Eve had had to learn of each verb that it was "-*ing*able." The opportunity was expressed as a ratio between progressive uses and unmarked generic uses. For the involuntary state verbs the ratio was always zero; there were no progressives for these. For the five process verbs which Eve most often used in the progressive the mean opportunity ratio was exactly 1.0; they were in the progressive precisely as often as they were in the generic form. What of the 19 process verbs which in Eve's samples looked like state verbs since they were never in the progressive. The opportunity ratio was .13; they were in generic form about 7 times as often as in the progressive form. This opportunity ratio is much nearer that for involuntary state verbs than it is for the process verbs, which Eve most often put in the progressive. These facts show that it is possible that Eve was not really operating with the process-state subcategorization at all but simply with information that a verb was *"ingable"* or not, based upon her mother's practice. The facts do not, of course, prove that Eve had missed the process-state distinction. She may have had a categorical grammatical imperative forbidding the use of the progressive with involuntary state verbs and no such imperative for the 19 process verbs not used in the progressive but simply no occasion in these samples to express temporary duration in connection with them.

If the child simply marks each verb as able to take the progressive when he notices it being used in the progressive and does not apply the progressive to any verb until it is so marked then he will make no overgeneralization errors. But the same procedure would produce an errorless performance with the other inflections and performance with these inflections is not errorless; it is so with the progressive alone. There must be some critical characteristic that is peculiar to the progressive. It is, of course, the first inflection, and it is possible that the learning strategy applied to the first is not applied to those that come later, but there is no independent evidence of this nor any argument for it. The subcategorization governing the progressive is peculiar in that it governs other grammatical operations, and one of these, the imperative, is developmentally antecedent to the progressive. Imperative constructions are already common in Stage I. If we suppose that the child learns to subcategorize verbs into those that may be in the imperative and those that may not then he will come to the progressive with just the subcategories he needs. That would explain the absence of errors in his use of the progressive. But what about error in his use of the imperatives? If it is absent there, why is it so? In fact, one cannot tell whether errors are absent from imperatives in Stage I. Sentences like *Want lunch* do occur but at this stage subjects seem to be quite freely omitted when the intention is declarative, and so we would hesitate to call *Want lunch* an imperative which uses an involuntary state verb.

The absence of error with the progressive may suggest to some that the underlying subcategories are part of the innate knowledge that the human species brings to the language acquisition task. McNeill, for instance, has argued (1966b) that whichever grammatical subcategories are universal in the world's languages must be innate and that a child uses the distributional evidence of the language to which he is exposed simply to discover which categories are used locally and what grammatical features they govern. Making certain assumptions we can imagine the process as follows. Before he uses the progressive inflection at all the child uses individual state and process verbs with apparent semantic appropriateness. As each verb is learned it may be that the semantic entry includes not only elements of meaning peculiar to the particular verb but also the semantic aspects of all applicable innate subcategorizations, including perhaps, state and process meanings. This would mean, in effect, that *like* is tagged as an "involuntary state" and *walk* as a "voluntary process." When the child, later on, begins to attend to the fact that some verbs take -*ing* and some do not he will have ready a set of subcategorization hypotheses to account for the cleavage. He will check the distributional data against the various pre-established subcategorizations to see which of the latter is determinative. In the case of -*ing*, the process-state subcategorization defines the proper dotted line. No errors at all need appear in performance.

There are fatal difficulties with this sort of argument. One is that children do not operate with the "unprincipled" subcategories governing the past, third person, plural, and possessive inflections as the theory suggests they should. They ought to attempt to order regular and irregular inflections in terms of one or another of the innate subcategories. They should test the hypothesis that the verbs that take -*d* in the past are all transitives and the others intransitives or that those that take -*d* are "animate" actions and the others not, or something of this kind. In our data there is no suggestion of anything of the sort. More seriously the process-state distinction seems a poor candidate for innateness because its use is apparently very far from being universal in the world's languages. One clue to this is the fact that errors of the type *I am liking her very much* are very commonly made by persons learning English as a second language, and I have not found them limited to speakers of any particular first language or even language family. It seems as though most people learning English as a second language encounter the process-state distinction for the first time. There are even some differences between British English and American English. Joos (1964) has even suggested that process-state is "a split unique or almost unique among the languages of the world" (p. 102).

And we must leave here the problem of the error-free progressive. No explanation has been established. Ideas have been put forward but for none is there any strong evidence.

The Prepositions "in" and "on"

The Jacobs-Rosenbaum representation of the grammar of prepositions treats them as features on nouns. In Table 47 I have listed the nouns that occurred with *on* and also those that occurred with *in* in Eve's samples 10–12. A comparison of the two lists reveals the semantic principle distinguishing them. Nouns with *in* generally name objects having cavities or internal spaces which can contain other objects: *bag, box, cupboard, pocket, mouth, basement, bathroom.* Nouns with *on* generally name objects having flat surfaces which can support other objects: *floor, page, paper, table, tray.* And containment-support seems to be the distinction between spatial *in* and *on.* There are, of course, objects which may either contain or support; the flat palm of the hand offers support but, as the fingers curl, it offers containment. A wastebasket typically functions as a container but turned over, its bottom surface offers support. *Cromer's coffee* listed with *on* seems out of place until you know that the rest of the sentence was *Don't sit on*; the cup of coffee could not very well contain the object offered.

Table 47. Nouns in prepositional phrases with *in* and nouns with *on* for Eve's samples 9–12

With *in* (containment)	With *in* (intermingling)	With *on* (support)
bag	fingers	calendar
basement	hair	couch
bathroom	snow	Cromer's coffee
bed		dollie
box		floor
briefcase		head
carriage		leotards
chair		paddle
cupboard		page
desk		paper
envelope		pillow
hand		plate
highchair		porch
kitchen		shelf
living room		stool
mailbox		table
mouth		tray
pants		
pocket		
study		
truck		
wastebasket		

The fact that some nouns may take either *in* or *on* indicates that the selection of the prepositions is not controlled by the noun alone. Jacobs and Rosenbaum point out that the verb may also help to select (or be selected by) the preposition, but in cases like *Put it on your hand* and *Put it in your hand* this is not the case. The fact is that *in* and *on* code the semantic features containment/support, and it is not clear how Jacobs and Rosenbaum would represent this fact.

In Eve's prepositional phrases a second sense of *in* is discernible in such instances as *in my hair* and *in the snow*. I have called this sense "intermingling." It is clearly related to containment in that an object is surrounded and not just supported, but the object does not occupy a cavity as it does in containment. Eve's phrase *Pencil is in my fingers* seemed to be her own creation, and it looks like an extension of the meaning "intermingling" to a new instance.

In early child speech the containment and support expressed by *in* and *on* seem always to be spatial, but in adult speech both meanings exist also in abstract nonspatial forms. A phrase such as *in adult speech,* from the previous sentence does not name an object with a cavity, or even an object, and yet there is an abstract kind of containment involved.

In adult speech there are also uses of *in* and *on* which seem to be idiomatic rather than semantically principled. *We say in a minute* and *in a little while* and *in July* but *on Wednesday* and both *on time* and *in time*. I can see no contrast here, however abstract, between containment and support. Some of these idiomatic phrases turn up in early child speech. Eve, for instance, in samples 9–12 used *in a minute* and *in a little while* as well as *talk on telephone* and *show on TV*. These unprincipled uses seemed to offer her no more difficulty than the principled uses. It is in idiomatic phrases that the role of the noun as selector of the preposition is likely to be clearest.

Is there reason to attribute to the children the semantic distinctions: containment-intermingling/support? Almost all uses of *in* and *on* in the samples seem to be correct. However, almost all these correct uses could be learned as so many individual phrases: *on floor, in bag, in bathroom, on table*. Eve's *pencil in my fingers* is a rare case of apparent extension of a concept to a new instance. We carried out a series of simple controlled inquiries to see whether the children understood the spatial distinctions coded by the prepositions or had simply memorized phrases.

Using a cup and a toy dog, for instance, the experimenter said, first: *Put the dog in the cup* and then: *Put the dog on the cup*. In the first case the cup was to function in its usual role as container, and a phrase like *in the cup* might easily have been memorized. In the second case the child was to invert the cup and put it to an unaccustomed use as a flat surface supporting an object. Other pairs of sentences all followed this same principle. We found an initial tendency in the children to persist in using an object according to its customary use, and so to put things in cups, ashtrays, boxes, and the like even where the experimenter said *on*. However, this was a very transient rigidity, and after a few trials the children all responded appropriately to the contrast between *in* and *on*. Therefore, I conclude that they understood the semantic distinction but were briefly thrown off by requests to use an object of fixed function in an unaccustomed way.

With *in* and *on*, always the first prepositions learned and always learned together, the primitive sense of location which seems simply to involve a movable object and a locus becomes differentiated into locational containment and locational support. One has the impression that a pair of distinctive features has emerged. The essential difference being that between a flat or convex surface beneath an object and a concave surface which, in some degree, encircles the object. If you place a pencil on the flat palm of your hand then very gradually curl the fingers you will see that there is something like an *on-in* threshold.

Plural and Singular Number

The semantic distinction is between one instance of a type named and more than one. Children seem to have some grasp of it even in Stage I, since the reference operation called "recurrence" and expressed by *more* or *'nother* usually refers to additional instances of a type already present or recently present. What remained to be learned after Stage I were the many grammatical reflexes of singular and plural number. Our category "plurals," which occupied rank 4 in the order of acquisition, included the use of plural nouns as names in reference situations, the use of such nouns in agreement with determiners like *a, the, these,* and *those,* and the use of predicate nominatives agreeing in number with subjects. By the time this omnibus category attained the 90 percent criterion, the plural-singular contrast was also being marked with other forms. The numeral *two* was used by all the children to refer to more than one instance though not always to just two. The pronouns *some, they,* and *them* contrast in number with *one, it, he,* and *she.* By the time the noun inflected for plurality attained criterion the children also almost always used pronouns with singular or plural number correct according to the reference situation or to the *NP* antecedent. Thus, Adam, at IV said: *They hanging* of several socks and *This can't hang* of one. And Sarah, at III, responded to her mother's *I think you need new slippers* with *Them dirty.* It seems clear that the children are to be credited with a distinction between one and more than one.

There is no possibility that the children had simply learned that certain nouns *(shoes, pants)* were ordinarily plural and others ordinarily singular. The same nouns were sometimes assigned singular number and sometimes plural number according to the intended meaning. Morphological overgeneralizations of the plural inflection in semantically appropriate circumstances were plentiful in all children even before the criterion was attained: *feets, mans, sugars.* There were also back formations creating nonexistent singular stems in semantically appropriate circumstances: *one bok* from *box* and *one pant* from *pants.*

On the receptive side, however, there was an unexplained lag. We did controlled tests with pairs of utterances like *Give me the pencil* and *Give me the pencils* where the child had equal opportunity to present one or more than one pencil. A correct response in these circumstances was contingent on the child's ability to use the presence and absence of the inflection as the signal of intended number. Well after they had attained criterion in spontaneous speech the children had failed to respond in a consistently correct way to the controlled inquiry.

In fact we never did get consistently correct performance on this receptive task because both we and they grew tired of trying it. Why there should have been this lag on the receptive side we do not know. It cannot be because the children lacked knowledge of the semantic distinction and of its grammatical expression because they gave copious evidence of it in production. It may be, as I have suggested previously, that the creation of good experimental materials, sentences varying in a single feature, throws off the child's usual comprehension processing routines. Perhaps he is more accustomed to having the plural marked twice in a sentence as in: *Give me some pencils* (or *those,* or *two,* or *all the*).

Past Tense

Long (1961) and Twaddell (1963) and Joos (1964) all recognize that the past tense modification of the English verb signals two distinguishable meanings. One of these is "earlierness," the occurrence of an action or state at a time anterior to the time of the utterance. For example:

> *We lived in Cambridge.*
> *Columbus discovered America.*
> *Man evolved from an ape-like ancestor.*

As the examples indicate the past modification may be used for events of any degree of remoteness from the present. The verb form as such does not specify the extent of earlierness though other forms such as *until recently* or *in 1492* or *millions of years ago* may do so. The statement that the past tense signals earlierness should not be taken to mean that the absence of the past necessarily denies earlierness for it does not. In a narrative one might begin in the past and then as one gets caught up in the account shift to the more vivid present although everything described in fact occurred at an earlier time.

The second use of the past is to posit a substitute for reality as in:

> *If I were in your place I would go.*
> *I wish I shared your opinion.*
> *George might help if you asked him.*

The main verbs are all in the past and so also are the modals. But these modifications do not signal a shift on the time scale; they mark the entertainment of a possibility. Such forms are usually called the conditional or subjunctive.

Joos and Twaddell both point out that the two distinguishable senses of the past can be collapsed into a single more abstract meaning. For the meaning Twaddell coins the term "unactual." The idea is that events named in the past tense never exist in fact as one speaks here and now. Either they existed at an earlier time or they are simply posited as alternatives to what exists.

One of the most delicate contrasts in adult English is that between the past in the sense of earlierness and the so-called present perfect (*have + -en*), which also usually refers to earlier events but adds an explicit signal of "current relevance." The term is Twaddell's, and it is as good as any, though no term seems to me to quite capture all possible contrasts. Consider the following two sentences: *We lived in Cambridge for ten years*; *We have lived in Cambridge for ten years.* In the former case it would be reasonable to suppose that "we" do not now live in Cambridge, that some interval has elapsed between the time when we lived in Cambridge and the time of the utterance. In the latter case it would be reasonable to suppose that "we" live in Cambridge still, that the condition named continues into the present. If the elapsing of an interval is explicitly noted in a sentence then it seems that the present perfect may not apply. Thus *We lived in Cambridge some time ago* but not *We have lived in Cambridge some time ago.*

However, the present perfect is sometimes used for events or states clearly completed in the past. A judge might say to a defendant: *The jury has heard the evidence and has found you guilty.* It would also, of course, be possible for a judge to say: *The jury heard the evidence and found you guilty.* What is the semantic difference in such a case as this? The judge who spoke the first sentence would be about to develop its consequences for the defendant, about to sentence him perhaps. The judge who spoke the second sentence would not be about to act on the basis of the jury's decision. That decision would have less current relevance. We might imagine him talking to the one-time defendant, some years after the defendant had suffered his punishment, the judge recounting what happened and justifying his own action. *The jury heard the evidence and found you guilty.*

While the present perfect signals current relevance the absence of the present perfect does not deny current relevance. A simple past may have this property as when a child says: *Sharon hit me,* and it is intended to explain her present tears.

The rank of the irregular past in the order of acquisition is 5 and the rank of the regular past is 9. Of the various meanings that past forms can signal, what meanings are signaled by the children? The meaning "earlierness" seems to be the only one intended. Until the child attains criterion he, of course, often fails to use the past form when the context suggests that he ought to use it. When the form is used both before criterion and afterwards it is most often coded as semantically appropriate, in Cazden's complete coding though it is quite often coded as only "questionably appropriate." Many uses are questionable because the context does not always clearly define the intended time reference. How often is the past used in clearly inappropriate circumstances? In all the records of all the children Cazden's coding identifies only 22 instances of the use of past forms where no past form should be used. Incorrect uses of the past are few, and even these few do not suggest a failure of time sense. For example, Eve in sample 16 (Stage IV, which is before she attained criterion), was speaking of something her father had been going to do, and the dialogue went as follows:

> Eve: *He goed to make another one.*
> Eve: *He went to make another one.*
> Mother: *He was going to make another one.*

Eve's mother understood Eve's inappropriate uses of past forms of *go* as attempts at the past progressive, and that may be what they were. Eve was not wrong in assigning the event to an earlier time but only wrong in her notion of how to do this. In sample 17 Eve twice said: *What did you doed?* She was actually correct in signaling earlierness but mistaken in signaling it twice. Sarah made some similar errors: *Did you bought this?* and *I didn't did nothing.* None of these suggests a failure to understand the meaning "earlierness." There are only seven uses of the past which seem to me to be clearly semantically inappropriate. For instance: *Because*

I will break them apart and stepped on them (Adam in sample 26); *Don't take cookies till we ate dinner* (Sarah in sample 66).

Appropriate uses of the past begin with a small set of verbs which name events of such brief duration that the event is almost certain to have ended before one can speak. These are: *fell, dropped, slipped, crashed, broke.* It is reasonable to guess that these forms may have been always or almost always in the past in mother's speech. Very soon, however, and long before criterion was attained, each child began to use past forms in a variety of appropriate circumstances. Sometimes in response to a question like *What happened?* Sometimes in a sentence with forms like *yesterday* or *already.* Sometimes in recounting events known to have occurred earlier as when Sarah said: *I slept over Nana's*; *I was good girl.* It seems clear that all three children by the time they attained criterion with the irregular and regular past were using these forms to signal "earlierness." The degree of earlierness was at first very small but it expanded with increasing age.

Cromer (1968) searched 12 one-hour samples from Adam and 12 from Sarah for expressions of the hypothetical sense of the unactual. Cromer did not require that the form of expression include a past tense verb, since his focus was on meaning rather than grammar. However, his search would have retrieved any uses of the past in the hypothetical sense. Through Stage V Cromer found no hypotheticals at all, whether expressed with a past tense verb or not. I also found none in the samples from all three children taken at I, II, III, IV, and V. Cromer found the first true hypotheticals in Adam at 4;6 and in Sarah at 4;10 when both children were well beyond Stage V. Of the hypotheticals found from this age on, not all by any means were expressed with the aid of a past tense verb. It may safely be concluded that neither the regular nor the irregular past was used in the hypothetical sense when it attained criterion, and it was only rarely used in this way even by the age of six years.

Cromer shows that there are several varieties of hypothetical meaning. There is the child's statement of a convention of make believe as when Sarah says of a scarf: *Mommy, this will be the baby's blanket, okay?* There is the statement of untested "possibility" as in Adam's: *Something might come out my pocket.* There is the proposition marked for "uncertainty" such as Adam's: *Maybe she left it for me.* And there is the positing of conditions contingent on other conditions: *And I'm gonna turn into a knight if you do that.* Cromer also shows that although all these meanings may be expressed with the aid of a past tense verb none of them requires such a verb. What is important for us at this point is the fact that the use of the past tense verb did not include the expression of any of the hypothetical senses at the time when the grammatical form attained criterion.

The present perfect form of the verb created with an auxiliary *have* and the past participle of the verb seems to be entirely missing through Stage V. I found none in the samples at I, II, III, IV, and V. Cromer found none at all for Sarah and none for Adam until after Stage V, and only a very few then. Before concluding that the children had no marker for current relevance, however, we must consider the possibility that there were perfective markers present in some less than complete form.

The progressive, which is grammatically very similar to the perfective, at first appears without its auxiliary. What is the possibility that the perfective starts the same way? A perfective without its auxiliary would simply be the past participle of the verb. For the majority of English verbs the past participle and the simple past are identical in form: *walk, walked, have walked*; *hit, hit, have hit*; *dig, dug, have dug*. For these verbs we have no way of distinguishing a simple past from a past participle without auxiliary, and it is possible that some we have counted as simple pasts ought to have been counted as perfectives. Fortunately there is a minority of verbs for which the forms are distinct: *see, saw, have seen*; *am, was, have been*; *write, wrote, written*; *fall, fell, have fallen, break, broke, broken,* and others. If the past participles of any of these verbs occur they can be recognized. A very few of them do occur.

Sarah used *done* and *seen* several times; Adam and Eve used *been*. The total number of cases is very small, and for all of them the possibility is open that the child intended a simple past and simply selected the wrong form even as he occasionally said *goed, tored, broked, felled,* and the like.

Is there, then, no way to tell whether the child through Stage V used the perfective? The progressive though it begins without an auxiliary does, from Stage III, quite often have an auxiliary in the case of all three children. Such auxiliaries appear in all samples after III except two of Adam's and one of Eve's. This is not the case for the present perfect auxiliary, and there is no reason why that auxiliary should be more difficult than the progressive. The words themselves, *have, has,* and *had* all appear as main verbs though not as auxiliaries. It seems safe to conclude on the basis of the absence of the auxiliary and the rarity of distinct past participles that the present perfect form was not used through Stage V, and must have attained criterion later than any of the 14 morphemes we have considered.

The Possessive

Many languages, perhaps all, make some grammatical distinction between two kinds of possession: inalienable and alienable (Fillmore, 1968). In the case of inalienable possession, objects are obligatorily possessed. The features of a face and parts of a body are good examples. Everything that is a nose at all is somebody's nose and everything that is a hand is somebody's hand. Kin terms like *son, nephew,* and *brother* similarly always presuppose a possessor; one is always a son, brother, or nephew of someone. In the case of alienable possessions objects are optionally possessed. Articles of clothing, furniture, and so on, are all alienable possessions. It is not the case that whatever is a hat is somebody's hat, and even when it is possessed, the possibility exists that it will change owners.

Alienable possessions include spaces as well as objects. An assigned parking space in the garage of a large apartment building is a good example. Possession of the space does not involve its perpetual occupancy any more than possession of a hat involves always wearing it. A possessed space must be available whenever its availability is tested. There may also be an expectation (as there is with ownership of a house) that unauthorized persons will not use it even when its owner has no need of it.

Among alienable possessions relatively lasting assignments may be distinguished from short-term assignments, especially the assignment of consumables. A serving of food or drink is an assignment of a portion that is not expected to last but to be consumed. Reserved seats at the theater are strictly timed assignments; they must be available to their owners for certain hours on a given date but not beyond. Subscription seats, of course, operate on a kind of periodical basis. Books "signed out" of a library are dated assignments covering days or weeks.

In adult English alienable and inalienable possession may both be expressed in a range of forms. For instance:

	Alienable	Inalienable
	Adam chair	*Adam tooth*
	my chair	*my tooth*
	I have a chair	*I have a tooth*

One sort of context distinguishing between the two is the following: *Adam has a missing tooth* but not *Adam has a missing chair*. Constructions of this type are too few to permit us to say anything about the children's knowledge of a grammatical distinction between alienable and inalienable possession.

In Stage I, Adam, Eve, and Sarah and all the children so far studied, whatever the language, produced some constructions which seemed in context to be possessives. Our children used an $N + N$ construction in the order possessor-possessed, with the inflection missing. In Stage I all but one of the examples in our data are examples of alienable possession. These included long-term assignments of objects and spaces *(Mommy umbrella, Daddy chair, Daddy study)* as well as short-term assignments of consumables and nonconsumables *(Fraser coffee, Eve seat)*. Eve produced one spontaneous, nonimitative example of inalienable possession: *Horsie eye,* as she pointed. After Stage I there are plenty of examples of inalienable possession, and there is no evidence really that these posed any greater difficulty than the more frequently occurring alienable possessives.

The possessive construction in English provides an opportunity for the creation of specific referent names as opposed to nonspecific categorical terms: *Daddy chair* is a certain chair, whereas *chair* or *a chair* is any instance of a given type. Definite articles *(the chair* or *this chair)* and definite pronouns *(this* or *it)* also create specific referent names and in this respect resemble the possessive. The difference is that the possessive creates names having a longer lifetime than do definite articles and pronouns. The pronoun *it* can only stand for a certain chair as long as that chair is the most salient named inanimate singular object. *The chair* as a name for a certain chair can last for the life of a continuous discourse. *Daddy chair* can be a permanent name functioning as long as the chair is an object of common knowledge for a speaker and listener. Perhaps in the beginning children learn a limited list of possessives as simply names of a sort without discovering the generative rule that makes it possible to create any number of names on the same principle. Even in Stage I, however, there are indications that the possessive is more than a memorized list of names. The children produced some that in context seemed to be novel: Eve said: *Rangy coat,* which seemed not to have been named before, and *Fraser coffee* for the very first of the hundreds of cups of coffee Colin Fraser was to be served.

The possessive inflection did not reach the 90 percent criterion until Stage III or after in the three children. Long before that there was plenty of evidence in conversation that they fully understood the conception involved. In the sample for grammar II, for instance, Eve went round the family circle pointing and saying (always appropriately): *That Eve nose*; *That Mommy nose right there*; *That Papa nose right there.* Sarah, in II was asked by her mother: *Whats my Mummy's name?* and Sarah answered correctly: *Nana.* In Adam II we have the following exchange which shows that he understood that the reference made by possessive pronouns is relative to the speaker.

> Adam: *Doggie bit me mine boot.*
> Mother: *A doggie bit you in your boot.*
> Adam: *Yeah.*

An effort to deceive Sarah in III failed as follows:

> Mother: *Your name is Courtney.*
> Sarah: *No.*
> Mother: *What's your name?*
> Sarah: *Sarah. I told you before.*

The correct conclusion seems to be that children understood the semantics of possession well before the attainment of criterion on the inflection.

The Copula

The copula in English *(am, is, are, was, were, be)* encodes several kinds of meaning. Sometimes it is identity *(I am Adam)*, sometimes membership in a set *(Socrates is a man)*, sometimes possession of an attribute *(The horse is grey)*, sometimes a state of location *(Mary is at home)*. The copula is associated with all these meanings but is it really needed to express them? Would not the subject together with the predicate nominative, predicate adjective, and predicate locative — the content words being in that order — carry the full sense without the copula?

Many languages manage without a present tense copula (Russian, Hungarian, Hebrew), and English could really do so also. If one omits present tense copulas from the sentences in which they are obligatory these sentences seem to be easily intelligible and not subject to confusion with any others. For example:

> *Adam boy* (predicate nominative)
> *Adam in chair* (predicate locative)
> *Adam little* (predicate adjective)

The only case I can think of in which confusion could occur is that which uses a demonstrative pronoun as subject together with a predicative nominative. Thus *That book,* even with pointing might mean either *That is a book* (an assertion) or *That book over there* (a kind of name). In the former case *that* is a demonstrative pronoun and in the second case a demonstrative article (or determiner). Even this confusion would disappear when articles are introduced, since the article is used only in the predicate nominative of the association *(That a book* or *That book).*

Using sentences containing articles and other known cases I compared the assertion and name forms of Sarah with respect to stress and pitch to see whether there were distinctive intonation patterns that could be used to sort out more primitive strings lacking articles for which the interpretation was indeterminate. Such patterns were found. With predicate nominative assertions in which *that* was a pronoun there was usually primary stress and pitch level 3 on both *that* and the predicate noun (roughly: *Thát bóok*). On the other hand, nominative utterances in which *that* was a determiner usually had primary stress and pitch 3 on *that* but lower levels of stress and pitch on the head noun (roughly: *Thát book*). There is more to the full story than this but the point is that the copula is not strictly needed even for those strings which are the same on the segmental level — for the reason that they are super-segmentally distinct.

There are three allomorphs of the present tense copula *(am, is, are),* and these are governed by the number and person of the subject. Does it not follow that the form of the copula communicates the number and person of the subject and so carries a meaning? It may do so but because the subject will always also be present the meanings carried by the copula are redundant.

When past tense is added to a grammar the copula, in the form of *was* or *were,* carries the tense and begins to convey a nonredundant meaning. When modal auxiliaries are added to the grammar the meaning carried by the copula, now in infinitive form, becomes more complex. If the modals were always present the meaning of the infinitive *be* would be less precise than the modal itself and redundant with it. What happens in fact, however, is that the most common modal to be used with *be* is *will,* but this modal is often omitted, leaving sentences like: *I be right back* and *Cromer be right down.* These are easily read as future tenses with *will* omitted and *be* carrying the communication load.

Adam and Sarah both attained the 90 percent criterion on the uncontractible copula midway between III and IV whereas Eve seems to have done so just beyond V. By the time they attained criterion all three children were using both past tense forms (usually *was* but occasionally *were*) and infinitive forms with an implied *will.* It may be said, then, that the copula had ceased to be totally redundant semantically by the time it attained threshold.

The contractible copula attained threshold much later than the uncontractible in all three children; indeed it was always among the last three morphemes to be acquired. Is there some semantic difference between the contractible and the uncontractible that might account for the large distance between them in the acquisition order? I think there is not. In simple declaratives, pronoun subjects that take the contractible copula are: *I, you, he, she, it, we, they,* and *that.* Contraction is not possible for *this, these,* and *those (this is a book, those are soldiers).* In *wh-* questions with *who, what, where,* and the like, the form of the copula varies with the subject but because the copula directly follows the *wh-* word the possibility of contraction does not vary with pronouns as it does in declarative sentences. For *I, he, she, this,* and *that* contraction is possible *(Who's he, Who's this).* For *you, we, they, these, those,* and *it* contraction is not possible *(Who are you, Who is it).* With the pointer words *here* and *there* contraction is possible in the order: *Here's a book* and *there's a book* but not in the order: *Here it is, There it is.* In general both contractibles and uncontractibles code redundantly person, number, animacy, and nearness. There is no difference in the semantics of contractible and uncontractible forms that could account for the difference in acquisition time.

The Third Person

The third person regular inflection /-s/ is selected just in case the subject is third person and singular and the verb is present tense. The few third person irregular inflections *(does, has)* are governed by the same features. Can we, therefore, say that the third person communicates person and number? It may do so but its work is always redundant, since the subject and verb will always be there to convey the same information. In this respect it closely resembles the copula.

When past tense and modals are added the copula is sometimes not redundant. However, the third person inflection is usually redundant even in these situations. The past tense takes the verb into another form (/-ed/ or some irregular form). The modal, if it is present, carries the message. If it should be missing then the absence of an inflection on the verb might be said to carry the message. *He walk* might be said to imply *will* or *can* or *must,* once these are usually present, for the reason that the verb inflection for a third person present singular should be /-s/ unless some kind of auxiliary is implicit. This is, obviously, a rare and marginal sort of case.

There are in English a few nouns that do not change form for plural number (*sheep* and *deer*). With either of these nouns as subject the contrast between a marked and an unmarked verb (*The sheep graze* or *The sheep grazes*) is potentially informative about the number of the subject. Again, however, the case is rare, and there is some doubt that children would be able to take advantage of this potential information. There is then no semantic exclusively associated with the third person, and the information that is associated with it is almost always redundant.

Articles

The English article *the* is said to be definite and the article *a* nondefinite or indefinite. There are other definite and nondefinite forms in English: the article *an* is an allomorph of *a*, the article *some* is a nondefinite plural; the pronouns *he, she, it,* and *them* are definite and the pronouns *one, ones,* and *some* are all nondefinite. I have counted occurrences in obligatory contexts only of *a* and *the,* and my discussion of the semantics of definite and nondefinite forms will be limited to these two. The discussion is much indebted to searching articles by Karttunen (1968a, 1968b) and to conversations for several years with Michael Maratsos. Maratsos' thesis was completed in 1971. In citing it I have limited myself to noting points where his conceptualization differs from mine and to several of his main results which are directly related to my findings with the naturalistic data. There is very much more in the thesis itself, including important results which one could never glean from naturalistic data, but that is Maratsos' story to tell.

The terms definite and nondefinite sound semantic but we shall not use them so. For the semantic distinction governing the use of *a* and *the* we shall use the terms specific and nonspecific. Definite and nondefinite will be used as names for the grammatical forms *a* and *the* (and by extension *an, some, one* and *he, she, it, them*). It is necessary to distinguish between forms and semantic because definite and nondefinite forms do not stand in a simple one-to-one relation with specific and nonspecific meanings.

When a speaker intends a specific reference or when a listener understands a reference to be specific he has in mind not just any instance of the class or set named by a noun but some unique instance or individual of that class or set. Suppose a young man asks his father: "Can I have the car Saturday night?" Both son and father understand that the reference is not to just any car but rather to a particular car, the family car, a 1967 Mercedes, beige in color, slightly dented on one door, and with various other familiar properties. Suppose, on the other hand, a young man says to his father: "If it is okay with you I am going to use my savings to buy a car." Suppose, further, that the young man has not yet looked at any cars and has no idea what car he would buy. In these circumstances both son and father would understand that the reference is to no particular car but to some unidentified instance of the class in question of which nothing further can as yet be said.

To what cognitive processes do specific and nonspecific reference correspond? [18] The kind of metaphor I have in mind is a memory system in which items are represented as file cards. A specific reference such as that to the family car is a unique entry, a particular card distinct from all others on which is entered all the information about the family car, a set of properties possessed by no other entry. A nonspecific entry such as that to a *car* is a card on which are listed only the properties of the class of things called *cars*. The entry becomes specific as soon as it includes any properties which make it distinctive or unique in the memory store, and this includes the information: "one the son will buy with his savings." The introductory sentence: "If it is okay with you I am going to use my savings to buy a car" is therefore enough to transform a nonspecific entry into a specific entry. The use of *a* and *the* reflects the speaker's sense of the entries to which he is alluding, the stored information which may appropriately be brought to bear in understanding his sentences and the proper locations or memory addresses to which the new information he introduces should be assigned. Underlying definite and nondefinite reference are cognitive processes of some delicacy and importance.

The articles *a* and *the* are discourse forms, and the semantic rules governing their use can only be stated in dyadic terms, the dyad being that of the speaker and listener. The listener may be an actual person, a large audience, or simply a "readership." Of course the choice of the form is always made by the speaker, and so it is not the actual facts about a dyad that govern usage but rather the facts as represented in the mind of the speaker. It is the speaker's *conception* of speaker and listener that governs definite and nondefinite reference. Whenever there is an actual listener present, such as a parent attending to a child, the opportunity exists for the listener to correct the speaker's conception of him and of his state of knowledge. When Sarah said to her mother, in sample 64, *Where's the black tape?* her mother responded: *What black tape?* This is as if mother were to say: "Evidently you think I know *which* black tape you have in mind but in fact I do not."

With our preliminary remarks in mind the relation between the use of the definite and nondefinite forms and specific and nonspecific forms is as represented in Table 48.

Before entering into the interpretation of Table 48 it is worthwhile noticing why forms and meaning must be distinguished. The definite form *the* applies if, and only if, the reference is specific for both speaker and listener. And nonspecific reference for both speaker and listener implies the nondefinite *a* but the converse is not the case. When the points of view of speaker and listener diverge, either in the manner of the upper right quadrant or the lower left quadrant the speaker uses *a*. This means that specific reference does not, in all cases, entail the definite *the* and the nondefinite *a* does not, in all cases, entail nonspecific reference. Only a rule that

---

18. Maratsos' (1971) discussion of this subject has caused me to sharpen my phrasing in this paragraph so as to make it clear that the specific entry must not only include information but information making it unique within the memory store. Maratsos adds the important point that uniqueness can be lost with time as new entries are added to memory.

distinguishes the speaker and listener roles can make sense of the semantics of definite and nondefinite forms.

I originally thought that the upper right quadrant of Table 48 was "null," with "null" meaning a case that does not arise. I could not think of any examples in which reference for the speaker would be nonspecific while reference for the listener would be specific. Since both speaker and listener are conceptions in the mind of the speaker, it seemed to me impossible for the listener to know something the speaker would not. But I was wrong. The speaker may be unable to give the specifics and yet know that the listener must be able to do so. I am grateful to my colleague Douwe Yntema for pointing this out to me and coming up with the "spy" example, in which the speaker may be presumed to know that the listener could, in fact, supply a lot of specifics about this spy even though the speaker himself cannot. Still there is something distinctive about this quadrant. Labov writes me (1971) that statements of this kind are heard as requests for confirmation, and that does seem to be the case for all the examples I have thought of. Presumably it is so because the speaker, who can only guess that there are specifics in the mind of the listener, is subject to correction.

When the reference is specific for both speaker and listener the article used is *the,* the definite. Thus a son, speaking to his father, intends to refer to a particular car and knows that his father will understand this intention when he says *Can I have the car? The* car is *that* car which is most salient in the household to which both son and father belong, the family car. For two persons having a large fund of common experience there will be many such specific referents salient enough for both so that either person in the speaker's role can count on being able to evoke in the other

Table 48.   The relation between definite and nondefinite forms and specific and nonspecific reference in speaker and listener

Listener (as conceived by speaker)	Speaker	
	Specific	Nonspecific
Specific	Definite: *the* [Karttunen's "discourse referent"] Examples: *Can I have the car? Let's move the desk.*	Nondefinite: *a* Examples: *There is a spy hiding in your cellar. You once wrote an article on superstition.*
Nonspecific	Nondefinite: *a* Examples: *I saw a funny-looking dog today. John tried to lift a piano yesterday.*	Nondefinite: *a* Examples: *I don't have a car. I need a new belt. I want to catch a fish. I talked with a logician. I am looking for a book.*

the reference he intends with no characterization beyond the definite article and the class name.

In what other circumstances can a speaker be sure that a specific reference will be correctly understood? There are a number of cases. When a reference has been introduced with a sentence that asserts its existence, such as *I saw a beautiful car today,* the speaker can be sure that a subsequent reference to *it* or *the car* will be understood by the listener to refer to that car which is beautiful and which was seen today. However, neither linguistic introduction nor long-accustomed salience is necessary to ensure that a specific reference will be understood. If two people are rearranging furniture in a room that contains just one desk, a sentence *Let's move the desk* will be understood to apply to the only desk present; a desk that will have such other properties as may be known by looking at it. And there are other cases in which the speaker may count on the listener understanding a specific reference. We will have a full discussion of them, which will be a kind of extended definition of the upper left quadrant of Table 48, as soon as we have characterized the other quadrants.

In the case of the lower left quadrant the speaker has a specific instance or individual in mind but he knows that the listener cannot as yet have that specific instance or individual in mind. If a speaker says *I saw a funny-looking dog today* he does not have just any canine in mind but a very definite dog about whom he has quite a lot of distinctive information. However, the listener was not there when the speaker met the dog and so, for the listener, no specific entry exists as yet. In what might be considered deference to the listener's point of view the speaker uses the nondefinite *a.* The speaker judges, however, that his first sentence has caused the listener to start a separate new entry in memory labeled: "dog; funny-looking, seen by speaker." And so the speaker in a follow-up sentence refers to *the dog* or *it* intending with this definite reference to activate the specific new entry. If the speaker adds *The dog bared his fangs at me* he intends the information to be added to the store that includes "funny-looking." In other words the follow-up sentence belongs in the upper left quadrant where references are specific for both speaker and listener. And, in fact, the introductory sentence *I saw a funny-looking dog* is assumed to establish a specific referent which will last as long as the discourse and which may be referred to with pronouns immediately after introduction and with *the dog* or a characterizing phrase *the dog I saw* for the life of the discourse and beyond. *John tried to lift a piano yesterday* does the same for a certain piano, which becomes *it* or *the piano* or *the piano John tried to lift.* Notice that with increase of time and the accumulation of potentially confusable entries in long-term memory the "addressing" of the reference would have to become more detailed: *the piano John tried to lift when we were living on Concord Avenue.*

Maratsos (1971) has pointed out that in colloquial speech one often uses *this* rather than *a* to identify a referent specific for the speaker but not for the listener. Thus: *I saw this funny-looking dog today* or *John tried to lift this piano yesterday. This* as a demonstrative article signaling a near object is not literally applicable because no visible referent is present. It seems rather as if English may be evolving a distinct article for the lower left quadrant, an article identifying a reference that is specific for the speaker and nonspecific for the listener. The usage seems still to be colloquial and possibly dialectal but it probably has a future, since it serves to resolve a potential ambiguity, that involving sentences which may belong in either the lower left quadrant or the lower right. If one said: *I was looking for a house yesterday,* either a specific address might be intended (lower left quadrant) or some nonspecific instance as in house-hunting (lower right quadrant). If *this* were reserved for the former case the ambiguity would be resolved. *This* seems to function at present rather like *you-all* as a potentially informative signal, resolving ambiguities in the speech of some speakers which are left unresolved in the speech of other speakers.

The lower right quadrant remains. This is the case in which the reference is nonspecific for both speaker and listener. When one says: *I don't have a car,* it is not some specific car that is intended but rather any car at all. And similarly with *I need a new belt* and *I want to catch a fish.* In none of these cases does the speaker intend a specific instance and in none of these cases does the listener think that the reference is specific. Furthermore, the introductory sentence does not serve to set up a new entry, a specific reference, to which new information may be added. At least not in the ordinary way of a sentence like *I saw a funny-looking dog today.* One does not follow up *I don't have a car* with *The car is a Mustang* or *I need a belt* with *It is black* or *I want to catch a fish* with *There it is!* Such discourse would clearly be very strange. The strangeness seems to derive from the fact that one is giving information which presupposes existence about a car whose nonexistence has just been asserted and about a belt and a fish whose existence is on a kind of fictional or hypothetical plane.

Karttunen (1968a) points out that, although noun phrases that fall within the scope of negation as does *car* in *I don't have a car* do not introduce any referents at all, noun phrases dominated by verbs like *want* and *need* do in a way introduce referents. One can keep referring to them provided the discourse stays in the fictitious or hypothetical mode of their introduction. Thus: *I need a belt*; *it must be black* or *I want to catch a fish and eat it for dinner.* The follow-up references are definite because the information is intended to be added to the specific entries established in the opening sentences. Fictitious or hypothetical referents seem to have a short life span; they cannot easily be discussed outside the sequence of fictitious clauses introducing them. One does not, later in a discourse, refer to *the belt I need* or *the fish I wanted to catch.* All this is a little bit imprecise; Karttunen (1968a) discusses some of the difficulties which impede a more precise formulation.[19]

19. Maratsos (1971) considers "existence," either actual or hypothetical, to be implied along with uniqueness by specificity. My feeling is that it is existence of unique memory entries, some of them marked perhaps as "hypothetical," rather than existence of referents that matters.

Besides nondefinites under the scope of negation, which have no referents, and nondefinites commanded by "fictitious" verbs (like *want* and *need*), which establish short-term fictitious referents, there are nondefinites like the last two in the lower right quadrant of Table 48: *I talked with a logician*; *I am looking for a book.* In cases like this the speaker may genuinely intend some nonspecific instance of a class and the listener may so understand him. However, such noun phrases out of context are, as we have seen, actually ambiguous as far as the speaker's intention is concerned. He could mean just any instance and he could mean a specific instance. He might, for example, be looking for any book at all to weight down some flying papers or he might be looking for *Anna Karenina.* Certain follow-up sentences would disambiguate the first sentences. If he exclaims *Here's one* then the original reference was nonspecific, but if he exclaims *Here it is* the original was specific. Only when the intention is nonspecific does the sentence belong in the lower right quadrant; when it is specific the sentence belongs in the lower left quadrant. The setting, together with accompanying actions and utterances, will usually indicate which sort of sentence it is. And some speakers, sometimes, will use *this* as in *I talked with this logician* or *I am looking for this book* to signal a lower left quadrant case.[20]

Table 49 provides the promised expansion of the upper left quadrant of Table 48; it is a listing of the kinds of circumstances in which the speaker assumes that the listener will be able to retrieve an intended specific reference. The list is probably not exhaustive and examples do not necessarily fit into only one category. In speaking of *the moon, the earth,* and *the sky* one speaks of referents that are unique in almost everyone's experience, and so a definite reference will always retrieve the appropriate

Table 49. Circumstances in which a speaker having a specific referent in mind may assume that a definite reference on his part will retrieve the same specific referent in the listener

Reference	Example
1. Unique for all	the moon, the earth, the sky
2. Unique in a given setting	the desk, the ceiling, the floor
3. Uniquely salient for a given social group	the car, the dog, the boss, the Pledge, the Constitution
4. Made salient by pointing, nodding, spotlighting	the chair, the singer
5. Made salient by stimulus characteristics that capture attention	the dog, the explosion, the motor
6. Specified by entailment	the engine, the head, the captain
7. Specific by definition	the last sentence, the first of the month
8. Specified by a prior utterance	the funny-looking dog

20. See Maratsos (1971) for an extended discussion of the nonspecific generic intention.

referent. In unusual circumstances the referents may not be unique, and then the form becomes nondefinite: Adam in sample 32, when he was only three and one half years old, was cutting out shapes from paper one day and said, correctly, *That look like a moon.*

In physical settings containing only a single instance of a class, definite reference will mean the same thing to speaker and listener. In any room one can say *the ceiling* and *the floor*. In a room containing just one desk one can say *Let's move the desk* and be understood. For given social groups, a family, a class, a pair of lovers, a work group, an organization, a nationality, there may be specific references which are the only instances of a set that are common to the experience of all group members or else, if not the only instances, are uniquely salient instances. Running over the examples of Table 49 you will sense the groups in which these definite references would work. For *the car* and *the dog*, a family; *for the boss,* a work group; for *the Pledge,* Temperance workers; and for *the Constitution,* Americans. Situationally specific references may not be freely exported to other physical settings, and references specific in one group may not be effectively used in all others. *The dog* is unequivocal at home but it is not unequivocal abroad.

Where neither physical setting nor social group membership makes a referent unique it can be made salient by pointing or nodding or spotlighting. In a room of many chairs one can intend one and use the definite and be understood if the speaking is accompanied by pointing. In this case specificity is guaranteed by acting to direct the listener's attention, but it is not always necessary to direct attention; sometimes one can count on attention having been "captured" because of the stimulus characteristics of the referent; its intensity, its movement, any abrupt change, including cessation. If a dog charges into a lecture hall a speaker can say *Get him out, please* or *Get the dog out, please* and need not first say *Behold, a dog.* If a bomb goes off one can say *What was it?* and not get the response *What was what?* If the sound of the motor of the car which is always of a certain quality suddenly changes quality or simply fails one can refer to it in the definite and be understood. In all these cases the speaker's use of definite reference reflects his sense of where the listener's attention is. The definite and nondefinite are forms which reflect the tuning of two consciousnesses and help keep them in tune.

Consider the following sentence *I was driving down the freeway when the engine started to miss.* Why is *engine* definite? Which engine is it? Clearly the engine of the car the speaker was driving down the freeway. But that engine is not unique in the experience of the dyad and it has not been pointed at and its sound cannot now be heard. A certain engine is, however, "entailed" (to use Karttunen's, 1968b, term) by the rest of the sentence. Driving entails a car and each car entails just one engine. Notice that one would not, in such circumstances, speak of *the headlight* or *the tire* because a car entails more than one of each. Adam, in sample 32, said to his little brother, Paul: *Let me bash you on the head.* Why *the head?* Because the rule is one to a person. Or consider the sentence: *When I sailed on the Nieuw Amsterdam*

I got to know the captain. A ship has only one captain. Specificity by entailment depends upon knowledge of the parts making up all kinds of wholes. This is knowledge that can continue to grow through a lifetime though, no doubt, at some point at a decelerating rate. To speak of *the tenor soloist in Verdi's Requiem* is to invoke a moderately esoteric sort of knowledge.

The case of *the tenor soloist* brings out an interesting point. Suppose the speaker could be sure that the listener would not know that there is always only a single tenor soloist in Verdi's Requiem. Would the speaker out of deference to the listener's point of view speak of *a tenor soloist* in his introductory sentence? I think probably not. It seems as if the speaker when he knows more about a given stable part-whole relation than his listener sometimes speaks from his own information letting his choice of article instruct the listener.

All the circumstances thus far discussed (1–6 in Table 49) are not strictly linguistic, so that there is no possibility of writing adequate rules for the use of *a* and *the* which stay within the bounds of linguistic science. The rules are psychological, and to some extent social. However, circumstances 7 and 8 in Table 49 do involve linguistic rules. There are, in the first place, certain terms, such as *first* and *last,* which by definition take the definite. Finally, there is the rule that a referent introduced by a nondefinite becomes specific in the act of introduction and may thereafter be referred to by definite forms. It is essential to recognize that it is not the repetition of a word that justifies the definite form but the repetition of a reference. Thus *I hit a man$_1$* may be followed by *A man$_2$ called the police* if the second man is, as the subscripts indicate, a different man from the first. Chomsky (1965) suggested that referential indices (like the subscripts) might be used in writing linguistic rules to represent the definite and nondefinite. Karttunen (1968a, 1968b) has shown that there are many difficulties with this proposal.[21] Finally, in connection with the lower right quadrant of Table 48 there are special limitations on the rule that an introductory nondefinite sets up a discourse referent which is specific. It does not apply for noun phrases which are within the scope of negation, and it applies only in a special way to noun phrases in a "fictitious" mode. It is far from clear how to write linguistic rules that would distinguish fact from fiction.

All this discussion leaves one puzzling case. When pointing and naming something new, a thing both parents and children often do, one says *That's a train* or *That's a bear.* Why does the introductory sentence use a nondefinite form? Nominatives of this sort are used in situations in which both speaker and listener are attending to the same specific referent and, in addition, the speaker is likely to be pointing at it. This should be an upper left quadrant situation, a combination of circumstances 4 and 5 in Table 49. Consider a closely related set of sentences: *Look at the train* or

---

21. Maratsos (1971) has clearly demonstrated that what he calls the "most recent referent theory" will not account for the process by which a listener assigns the correct antecedent reference to a definite form.

Look at the bear. These, too, are often spoken when the referent is the object of attention and are often accompanied by pointing. But, with *Look at,* the noun takes the definite article. What is the difference in the two cases? When a referent is nominated the thing itself is specific enough but it does not yet exist *by name* for the listener. He must be presumed not to have a specific entry marked *train* or *bear,* since the speaker judges it necessary to name them for him. In this sense they do not yet exist as what Karttunen calls "discourse referents" though the objects themselves, without names, are specific for the listener. Sentences using *Look at* are exactly the same except that they presuppose knowledge of the name in the listener and so specific named entries, and that may be the critical consideration. Maratsos (1971) is inclined to think that the more important consideration is the speaker's intention simply to assign a class membership; the speaker has no intention of causing the listener to create a new unique reference for the particular bear or train. Maratsos convincingly shows that one can speak in this generic mode when not naming *(I took out a girl from Vassar last night)*. If the follow-up were something like *I really prefer Radcliffe girls,* then the original statement was intended to be understood generically. If it is something like *What a prude she turned out to be,* the intention was specific. It's the follow-up that tells.

Some languages, Japanese is one, do not habitually mark nouns as definite or nondefinite, and this must now strike us as very strange. Because the difference between specificity and nonspecificity seems an essential one which we can hardly imagine a language managing without. *Give me a book* is very different from *Give me the book,* and *The dog is dead* could be devastatingly different from *A dog is dead.* Yet speakers of Japanese seem not to miss the definite-nondefinite distinction at all. This makes me wonder whether the forms are really needed for communication, are needed, that is, by the listener if he is to understand the speaker.

Listed below are various kinds of sentences we have considered with the articles omitted from all of them.

> *Can I have car?* (Son to father.)
> *Let's move desk.* (In room with one desk.)
> *I saw funny-looking dog today.*
> *John tried to lift piano yesterday.*
> *I don't have car.*
> *I need new belt.*
> *I am looking for book.*
> *Sky is beautiful today.*
> *Look out, boss coming!* (Two workers in an office.)
> *I was driving on freeway when engine began to miss.*
> *Last sentence is good.*

It is amusing to notice that the simple deletion is enough to make these sentences sound like the English of a native-speaking Japanese. By what means could a listener process each sentence and correctly determine whether the references were specific or nonspecific? Perhaps with the following rule: "Search first for a specific reference salient in your own mind and likely to be salient for the speaker and, if you find one, assume that that reference is the one intended. If you do not find a specific reference assume that the reference is nonspecific." This would yield the correct interpretation in most cases. For the first sentence, a specific car would be retrieved and for the second a specific desk, but no specific dog for the third. And so on. With negatives the listener would not even have to search for specific referents. In the case of *I am looking for book* the listener could go wrong but so could the native speaker of English if the sentence were *I am looking for a book*. Suppose that there were many books lying about which did not seem to meet the searcher's requirements. This fact would make it clear that *a book* was intended specifically, but it would do the same if the sentence were simply *I am looking for book*.

The listener would, of course, sometimes go wrong with sentences such as we have listed. When the son says *Can I have car?* and means not the use of the family car but the money to buy a new car the listener who followed my rule would go wrong. So he would if the speaker of *I was driving on freeway when engine began to miss* meant not the engine of his own car but the engine of another car. In cases like this an uncommonly heavy communication burden would fall upon the article. My guess is that such cases are actually rare, and that most speakers would avoid placing such reliance on the articles as is involved in *Can I have a car?* or *I was driving on the freeway when an engine began to miss*. They would be likely, I think, to reformulate these in such terms as *Can I buy a car?* and *I was driving on the freeway when somebody's engine began to miss*. In Japanese, too, of course, one can when reference specificity is in doubt, resolve the ambiguity by recourse to forms other than articles. I have no data at all on this but it looks to me as if listeners to English would not usually need to rely on definite and nondefinite forms to indicate specificity of reference though of course the presence of the forms means that they *may* do so.

Can the speaker of English do his job without calling upon the semantic knowledge summarized in Tables 48 and 49? Is there an easy route to productive control of definite and nondefinite articles? I think not, except within a very restricted discourse. For nouns like *moon, earth,* and *sky* one could fairly safely follow the rule of always using *the,* making the article a part of the name as it is with *the Hague,* since *moon, earth,* and *sky* are going to be definite in almost any circumstances and in any company. However, most nouns, nouns like *car, dog, book,* and *engine* cannot be assigned either *the* or *a* as a part of their names. Can one perhaps follow the rule that *the car* and *the dog* are, at any rate, the invariable names of the specific car and dog that belong to one's family. Yes, as long as you speak only to the family but not if you speak to others; the names must then become *our car* and *our dog* or something of the sort. Can one, perhaps, follow the simplifying rule of attending only to the specificity of the referent in one's own mind, disregarding the problem of its specificity for the listener. The case for *car* already indicates that some distinctions must be made among listeners, but perhaps these can be limited to fixed categorizations like "family" and "outsider." But, then, we would not know what to do with the distinction between *I saw a really nice car today,* which the listener, whether family member or outsider, has not seen, and *Lets move the car* when speaker and listener, family or not, are trying to solve the problem of an obstructed driveway. Can one manage without part-whole entailment? Definitely not. For example, it is *the horn* that is a part of some specific car but *a horn* that one goes to an automotive parts dealer to buy. In general it seems to me that the semantic rules we have described are the rules a speaker must operate with if he is to deploy the definite and nondefinite articles across the full range of situations that can arise in our linguistic community.

To say that the speaker of English needs the semantic knowledge summarized in our Tables 48 and 49 if he is correctly to deploy definite and nondefinite forms in a wide range of situations and for a wide range of listeners is not, of course, to say anything about the form in which such knowledge must be stored. Our discussion, like linguistic discussion in general, strives to find the maximally simple and general rules that will account for usage. But, as Maratsos (1971) quite tellingly argues, this knowledge might actually be stored by language users in less elegant form, as a very large set of subrules applying to particular kinds of situations. He has some evidence that this is the case in the variation he finds across problems that are, potentially, subsumable under a single general rule; variation in the performance of young children and also, surprisingly, of some adults. The problem of the level of generality at which both semantic and grammatical rules are in fact stored by language users is of course a profound and completely general one.

To summarize the preceding discussion, one can learn from a speaker's performance with articles much about his knowledge of the semantic and grammatical rules governing them, but from the listener's response one can learn little about his knowledge of the rules in question. This conclusion directs us to study the child's use of articles rather than his response to the usage of others. As our discussion suggests, not all uses are equally informative. In restricted situations it is possible for articles to be used correctly in the absence of full command of the relevant semantics.

In counting the occurrences and nonoccurrences of *a* and *the* in obligatory contexts I attempted to distinguish the various circumstances of Tables 48 and 49 and so to determine whether the required form was *a* or *the*. This proved to be not possible. For instance, one cannot always tell from the transcriptions whether a specific object not previously referred to in speech was in the focus of attention for speaker and listener and so whether the child should use *a* or *the* in mentioning it. One cannot always tell whether a part-whole context is implied: thus when Eve said *I'm a Mommy* was she simply placing herself in a set in which case she spoke correctly or was she assigning herself a role in a pretend-family in which case she ought to have said *the.* Because there were many doubtful cases I lumped together all contexts requiring either *a* or *the* and established a single acquisition point for articles. It is, however, worth reporting that when the doubtful cases are excluded and separate acquisition points tentatively identified for *a* and *the* these are within a sample or so of one another, and so it seems that the definite-nondefinite articles are acquired as a system. For Adam the acquisition point for articles was just past IV (when his age was about 3;3); for Sarah the point was shortly before IV (when her age was about 3;5). Eve had not attained threshold by V (when her age was 2;3) but she was then supplying articles in 80 percent of obligatory contexts, so probably she attained threshold soon after V, perhaps at about three years.

How much did Adam, Eve, and Sarah understand of the semantics of definite and nondefinite reference by the time they attained threshold for obligatory articles? The relevant samples are those used for Grammars IV and V, and the samples between them for which occurrences were counted. From these data Tables 50 and 51 are derived. In form the two tables are based on Tables 48 and 49. Table 48 labeled four quadrants in terms of the possible conjunctions of specific and nonspecific, for speaker and listener. Of these four quadrants, one — speaker nonspecific, listener specific — proved to contain no cases, to be null for the children and, by my observation, such cases are also very rare for adults. That leaves three major cells, and these are the three entries in the left margins of Tables 50 and 51. From Table 49 we take the eight kinds of circumstances in which a referent is specific for both speaker and listener, and these appear in the top third of the left margins of both Tables 50 and 51. The three subvarieties of the case in which a referent is nonspecific for both speaker and listener are derived from our discussion of the examples in Table 48. They are any instance of a class; negatives; "fictitious" referents.

Table 50 simply lists some correct examples of every sort of definite and nondefinite usage in the three children, and there are nonimitated examples of all forms. No significance at all is to be attached to the number of examples of each type in Table 50; I have simply selected enough in each case to suggest the kinds of things the children could do. In Table 51, on the other hand, the number of examples has some significance for this is a complete list of errors of definite and nondefinite usage classified by type. I have listed only those that I thought were, judging by the context, most clearly erroneous. There were a good many doubtful cases, with the degree of doubt varying widely, and so unfortunately one cannot be sure that the errors in Table 51 correctly represent the relative frequency of errors of each type. Still it is likely that they do.

In Table 50 the first three categories of definite reference are all cases in which some referent is unique or uniquely salient for both members of the dyad. Here we have *the sky, the floor, the mailman,* and *the TV*. In the fourth case a referent is made salient by looking at it or pointing at it as in: *Look at the trailer*. Referents of the fifth type are salient because they capture the attention of both members of the dyad. There are in the samples no instances of this sort which resulted in the use of the definite articles, but there were some which resulted in the use of a definite pronoun.

Table 50.   Examples of correct instances of definite and non-definite reference from Adam, Eve, and Sarah from Stages IV to V

	Semantic Class	Example
	Reference	
	1. Unique for all	1. *the sky* (Sarah), *the ground* (Eve)
	2. Unique in a given setting	2. *the floor* (Adam), *the couch* (Eve), *the ceiling* (Sarah)
Speaker Specific and Listener Specific	3. Salient for a social group	3. *the mailman, the TV* (Sarah), *the subway* (Adam)
	4. Made salient by action	4. *Look at the trailer* (Adam)
	5. Made salient by stim. characteristics	5. *It fall down* (Eve), *Who's she?* (Eve, as girl enters)
	6. Specified by entailment	6. a. Parts of a car: *the driver's wheel* (Adam)
		b. Parts of a boat: *the motor* (Adam)
		c. Parts of a train: *the caboose* (Adam)
		d. Parts of a face: *the nose* (Adam)
		e. Parts of a doctor's office interaction: *the nurse* (Sarah)
		f. Parts of a family: *the grandma* (Eve)
		g. Parts of a bandage: *the sticky of the bandage* (Eve)
	7. Specific by definition	7. *That's the middle* (Sarah), *The next page* (Eve)
	8. Specific by prior utterance	8. *That a jeep. I put some in the jeep.* (Adam) *This was a big rabbit. And scared the rabbit* (Sarah)
Speaker Specific and Listener Nonspecific		*He's a witch* (Adam) *That a bunny rabbit* (Adam) *I made mine a garage* (Adam) *It's a gun* (Eve)
Speaker Nonspecific and Listener Nonspecific	1. Any instance of a class	1. *Put a band-aid on it* (Eve) *A wheel looks like a Q* (Adam)
	2. Negatives	2. *This don't have a wheel on it* (Adam)
	3. "Fictitious" referents	3. *I need a clothespin* (Adam) *Make a B* (Sarah)

Thus, when a girl walked into the room Eve promptly said: *Who's she?* Not *There's a girl. Who's she?* The sixth case is entailment, and I thought it worthwhile to make a complete (or nearly so) list of the kinds of part-whole relations of which the children evidenced knowledge. In all these cases the child was speaking without a model to imitate. Speaking of the parts of a boat Adam said *the motor* and Eve, speaking of the members of a family, said *the grandma.* Eve even said: *The sticky of the bandage,* which is something she may never have heard an adult say. The seventh case consists of forms that are specific by definition: *the middle, the next page,* and others. In the eighth case a child makes a referent definite in a sentence that follows upon a nondefinite introduction. These were present in very great number, and there is no way the performance could be generated except by knowledge of the rule that when a reference is made a second time it becomes specific. Cases in which a reference was specific for the child but nonspecific for the listener and in which the child used the nondefinite suiting the listener's point of view appear next. One class of these was very common: nominative sentences such as *That a bunny rabbit.*[22] Except for these naming statements, instances were few. But there were a few.

There were numerous instances of all subvarieties of the case in which a referent was nonspecific for both child and listener. Any instance of a class: *A wheel looks like a Q*; negatives: *This don't have a wheel on it*; fictitious referents: *I need a clothespin.*

Consider now the errors in Table 51. The result I think most significant is the large number of errors in the category: speaker specific and listener nonspecific. This is the case in which the points of view of the speaker and listener diverge. In all these cases the English rule is to use the nondefinite suitable to the other's point of view. What all three children often did was to speak from their own point of view, "egocentrically" in Piaget's sense. I feel particularly confident that the sentences listed were errors because the listener often responded uncomprehendingly. Sarah said *I want to open the door* and her mother responded *What door?* Which is to say "You speak as if I should have some specific door in mind but in fact I do not." Eve said *Where's the stool?* and her mother said *There's one over here*; the response uses a nondefinite pronoun as if to say, "I do not know which specific stool you are thinking of." There were not only many errors in this category, there were also few correct instances except for the special class of naming statements like *That a bunny rabbit.* It seems quite likely, therefore, that the children had not learned to "decenter," to use Piaget's term, from their own point of view to that of the listener when the two diverged. They had, however, learned to use the nondefinite *a* in naming things.

There were fairly numerous errors in two subclasses of the category in which discourse referents exist for both speaker and listener: entailment and reference specified by a prior utterance. All these should have been *the* but were *a.* It sems to me that there are far too many correct and unimitated instances of both to suppose that the children did not know that when a whole entailed one of a certain part the article

22. Maratsos (1971) questions whether these naming statements are correctly listed as speaker specific, since the intention may simply have been to classify. Judging from conversational follow-up he is right about some of these but others seem to have been intended specifically.

Table 51. Full list of errors in definite and non-definite reference for Adam, Eve, and Sarah from Stages IV to V

Semantic Class		Error and Correction
	Reference	
	1. Unique for all	1. —
	2. Unique in a given setting	2. *It's something a man have* (Eve) *Let me see you ride a bike* (Adam)
Speaker Specific and Listener Specific	3. Salient for a social group	3. *He been on a couch* (Sarah) *We saw them in a zoo* (Sarah)
	4. Made salient by action	4. —
	5. Made salient by stim. characteristics	5. —
	6. Specified by entailment	6. *I don't like a crust* (Eve Mother: *I know you don't like the crust.* *I'm a Mummy* (Eve) Mother: *Are you the Mummy?* *That a kitchen* (Adam) *Where there's a heel* (Eve, of a sock) *A chin* (Eve, naming features of a face)
	7. Specific by definition	7. —
	8. Specified by prior utterance	8. *A lady named Gloria* (Eve) *He on a fox's nose* (Eve) *I never drop a watch* (Adam) *I lost a train* (Adam) *A jeep is coming* (Adam)
Speaker Specific and Listener Nonspecific		*The father* (Sarah) Mother: *What father?* *Where's the black tape?* (Sarah) Mother: *What black tape?* *That's the good pencil* (Sarah) Mother: *What?* *I want to open the door* (Sarah) Mother: *What door?* *I'm trying to find the record* (Sarah) *The cat's dead* (Sarah) Mother: *What cat?* *And the monkey hit the leopard* (Adam) *And that the bowl* (Adam) Mother: *What bowl?* *And the baby sleeps in the bed* (Adam) *"Put it up" the man says* (Adam) Mother: *Who's the man?* *I gonna have bite of the seed* (Eve) *Where's the stool?* (Eve) Mother: *There's one over here.* *We going in the house* (Eve)
Speaker Nonspecific and Listener Nonspecific	1. Any instance of a class	1. —
	2. Negatives	2. —
	3. "Fictitious" referents	3. —

should be *the* and that when a reference is repeated the article should be *the*. We know that each part-whole assemblage has to be learned as such, and so probably the entailment errors that occurred simply resulted from the fact that particular assemblages had not yet been learned. The occasional failure to make a second reference definite probably is a performance error resulting from occasional failure to keep track of prior references rather than from ignorance of the rule. There were no errors at all in the last category in which the reference is nonspecific for both child and listener. I do not know why this should be so.

In general our study of spontaneous speech suggests that children somewhere between the ages of 32 months and 41 months, roughly three years, do control the specific-nonspecific distinction as coded by articles. With the qualification that they are not likely to "decenter" to the listener's point of view when that point of view is different from their own; in this respect they seem egocentric. The children are also likely to make occasional performance errors of other kinds.

We shall shortly see that Maratsos' (1971) experimental results corroborate these most general findings. Before the attainment of the 90 percent criterion I have found that the child's use of articles cannot support any inferences about his control of semantic and grammatical rules. This is partly because certain seeming articles in earlier samples probably are not organized as separate morphemes at all but are rather features of the pronunciation of particular words. This segmentation problem is discussed at a later point. Even the inferences we have made from performance at criterion are very weak, and concerning many points naturalistic data permit no conclusions at all. For additional knowledge then we must rely on experimental work with problems carefully devised to reveal underlying knowledge. Maratsos (1971) has invented many ingenious problems of this kind and has used them with children between two years, eight months, and four years, seven months, in age.

Maratsos (1971) has devised tests of both production and comprehension. For example, a test of productive control of the eighth subcategory of Table 49 goes roughly like this. The experimenter begins: "Once there was a man who went out into the jungle. Now the man was very lonely. He saw two animals, a monkey, and a pig. 'Maybe one of those animals will come out and be my friend,' he said. And one of them did. Who went out to the man?" (Answer: either *the monkey* or *the pig* but not *a monkey* or *a pig*.) In a contrasting version the story speaks of *some* monkeys and *some* pigs and, then, of course, the answers should be nondefinite, either *a monkey* or *a pig*.

Maratsos (1971) constructed eight such story pairs in order to test systematically children's productive control of the definite-nondefinite contrast. His younger group (roughly three-year-olds) was accurate 73 percent of the time, and his older group 85 percent; both groups displayed well over chance accuracy. There is a great deal more to the results than this, and Maratsos (1971) should be read for the full story.

To test comprehension Maratsos (1971) used toys and asked the child to act out what was said. In one case there were four dogs, four cars, four boys, and a hill. The child was to act out the story the experimenter told. The experimenter would say: "This little boy named Tommy came along. He went up and started talking to one of the dogs." (Experimenter manipulates Tommy.) "See them talking? Well, they talked and talked and now, while they are talking, suddenly (a, the) dog drove away." The child in acting this out should put dog_1 (the one talking to Tommy) into a car if *the* is the option taken and any dog rather than dog_1 if *a* is used. In devising a test like this one puts a somewhat unusual communication burden on *a*; in real circumstances the speaker would be likely to say *another*. The contrast, nevertheless, seemed to work.

Maratsos devised a variety of such tests of comprehension, and the main result is that both his younger and older groups showed competence well beyond chance. Their scores averaged about 85 percent correct, and there were no significant age or sex differences. Concerning his overall experimental results Maratsos concludes that they are corroborative of our naturalistic data in indicating that children as young as three years control the factor of specificity-nonspecificity of reference insofar as this involved only their own knowledge. His results also confirm the naturalistic data in showing that children made many mistakes when it was necessary for them to consider the point of view of the listener; like Adam, Eve, and Sarah they were often egocentric. Maratsos' (1971) full report includes a large number of other results of great interest not revealed by our naturalistic analyses.

We have now completed our survey of the semantics of the fourteen morphemes. Speaking in a purely impressionistic way I would say the following. The definite and nondefinite articles seem to involve the greatest semantic complexity of the lot. The progressive, the past, and the plural all involve semantic conceptions of a slightly lower complexity. The possessive involves a conception that seems already to be well started at Stage I. The copula and the progressive auxiliary represent information that is usually, though not always, redundant. The third person inflection carries information that is almost always redundant.

The Frequency of the Fourteen Morphemes in Parental Speech

We wanted to be able to test the hypothesis that the frequencies with which particular morphemes are modeled for a child by his parents affects the order in which the child acquires those morphemes. Since frequency generally facilitates learning, the hypothesis is that the more frequently a morpheme is modeled the earlier it is acquired. We wanted to know how the parents' speech habits might affect the child, independently of the possible shaping of these habits to fit the child's own inclinations and preferences in the use of the morphemes. Therefore we decided to base our estimates on samples prior to II, II being the stage in which the child begins to use some of the fourteen morphemes. We decided to use samples immediately, rather than remotely, prior because we did not want to move into the period where a parent might judge a child incapable of benefiting from the use of the morpheme.

Using the samples immediately prior to II we hit a point at which the parent's speech was evidently complicated enough for the child to learn the fourteen morphemes from it. For each parental pair we began with the sample immediately previous to the first sample of II and drew 713 utterances moving backward from the end of that sample which was the point nearest II. For Adam this meant samples 5 and 4 (II being based on sample 6) and for Eve it meant samples 5 and 4 (II being based on 6 and 7). Sarah's II was based on samples 31–34. Sample 30 happened to have poor recording fidelity, and so the parental utterances were drawn from 29, 28, 27, and 26. The number 713 is the number of utterances on which each child grammar was based, and so the size of the parental samples is the same as the size of the child samples used for grammars.

Within the selected samples only parental utterances were used. This meant the exclusion primarily of utterances from the adult investigators present at the session. We excluded their utterances because they were only occasionally present. It was the parents who were usually with the child, and so their frequencies that were most likely to influence the child's learning. In fact most of the utterances were from mothers; there were only a few from fathers. There is no reason to think that the habits of the parents differed with respect to the frequencies involved.

Among parental utterances in the selected samples certain ones were omitted: those that exactly imitated an immediately antecedent utterance of the child and those that "expanded" an immediately antecedent utterance of the child by preserving his content words in the order he used and filling in obligatory functors. Imitations and expansions were excluded in order to minimize the child's influence on the utterances in question.

The tally was extremely detailed. Each allomorph, regular or irregular, of each morpheme was separately counted. In addition, each semantic subtype of the definite and nondefinite article was separately tallied. The rules used in determining what to count were for all morphemes the same as the rules we used in tallying morphemes supplied and omitted by the child in obligatory contexts. We counted omissions by parents also though these were very few.

The number of obligatory morphemes omitted was 19 for Sarah's parents, nine for Adam's parents, and only three for Eve's parents. In general omissions are rather evenly spread across morphemes and subvarieties. For Sarah's parents one omission was, however, somewhat more frequent than any other: the initial auxiliary *are* in a question before *gonna*. Thus *You gonna sing your song?* rather than *Are you gonna sing your song?* This is, of course, a familiar informal variant. A few of the omissions seemed to result from the parent's intention to imitate the "baby talk" of the child, but none of the parents did this very often. The omissions were never numerous enough to bring a set of obligatory contexts below the 90 percent point, which was our criterion of acquisition for the children. So it is not the case that any of the children was hearing a dialect in which any of the morphemes was absent more than 10 percent of the time. In this respect the models were uniform.

Table 52 lists the 14 morphemes in the order of acquisition of Table 38, which is the mean order across the three children, and presents the frequency of each morpheme for each pair of parents. In Table 52 we also have the frequencies for full passives and present perfectives because there has been some discussion of the apparent absence of these constructions from the children's speech. The absolute frequencies of Adam's parents are higher than those for the other two sets of parents.

Table 52. Acquisition order (children's) and frequencies for the 14 morphemes plus passives and perfectives in the three sets of parents

Morpheme	Adam's Parents	Sarah's Parents	Eve's Parents
1. Present progressive	65	28	67
2.5. *in*	37	20	40
2.5. *on*	20	16	32
4. Plural	57	57	33
5. Past irregular	71	45	25
6. Possessive	25	16	30
7. Uncontractible copula	57	65	53
8. Articles	233	157	162
9. Past regular	28	9	7
10. Third person regular	25	19	7
11. Third person irregular	25	7	6
12. Uncontractible auxiliary	35	5	16
13. Contractible copula	164	100	126
14. Contractible auxiliary	30	13	52
Full passive	0	0	0
Present perfect	3	13	2

Table 53. Acquisition order (children's) and frequency rank orders for the 14 morphemes in the three sets of parents

Morpheme	Adam's Parents	Sarah's Parents	Eve's Parents
1. Present progressive	4	6	3
2.5. *in*	7	7	6
2.5. *on*	14	9.5	7
4. Plural	5.5	4	8
5. Past irregular	3	5	10
6. Possessive	13	9.5	9
7. Uncontractible copula	5.5	3	4
8. Articles	1	1	1
9. Past regular	10	12	12.5
10. Third person regular	11.5	8	12.5
11. Third person irregular	11.5	13	14
12. Uncontractible auxiliary	8	14	11
13. Contractible copula	2	2	2
14. Contractible auxiliary	9	11	5

This was because Adam's parents tended to use longer sentences, which, of course, allow for more functors.

Table 53 presents the rank orders of the frequencies for the 14 morphemes. The rank order for each parent shows significant positive correlation with the rank order of each other parent. The Spearman rank order coefficients (rhos) are: for Eve's parents and Adam's, .63 ($p < .05$); for Eve's parents and Sarah's .73 ($p < .01$); for Adam's parents and Sarah's .77 ($p < .01$). These correlations are somewhat lower than those for acquisition order among the children (which were: Eve and Adam .86; Eve and Sarah .87; Adam and Sarah .88) but they are still very substantial. It looks as if there were a rather stable frequency profile for the 14 morphemes in parental speech. We shall see in the next section whether or not these frequencies predict the order of acquisition.

Even on the allomorphic level of detail there is stability of frequency order. Frequencies for five sets of regular, phonologically conditioned, allomorphs appear in Table 54. Among plurals, possessives, and contractible copulas the frequency orders for the three sets of parents are almost exactly the same. Frequencies for the past regular and the contractible auxiliary are more evenly distributed among the allomorphs, and order is less stable across parents. When it comes to the irregular allomorphs of the past and third person (presented in Table 55) frequency order is definitely not stable. Past forms are very numerous in English, and there is only partial overlap in these samples on the forms included. The overlap is greatest, of course, for the high frequency auxiliary verbs.

There is a rather interesting footnote to Table 54. All three sets of parents sometimes failed to contract a copula or auxiliary *be* which was, nevertheless, susceptible of contraction. The effect, of course, is one of more "careful" speech; for example: *What is that?* rather than *What's that?* Adam's parents used the "careful" uncontracted *is,* rather than /-s/ or /-z/ where these could have been used, 25 percent of the time; Eve's parents did it 15 percent of the time, and Sarah's parents only 2 percent of the time. The pattern is the reverse of what we found for omissions. The parents of Adam and Eve seem to use slightly more "formal" or "careful" speech though all parents use the same range of forms.

Table 56 reports the frequencies for the various semantic classes of definite and nondefinite articles. The classes are the same as those of Table 50 and 51 except that the second and third subvarieties of specific reference had to be combined. When mother said something like *the kitchen* or *the floor* it was specific both for the given physical setting (the house or a room) and for a given group (the family) and so one could not distinguish between the two. This was usually the case for these subcategories, and for that reason the categories were combined. A glance at Table 56 shows that the frequency order is very stable across parents. In the parents' samples, as in the children's, there were no instances at all of the upper right quadrant of Table 48 in which the reference would be nonspecific for the speaker but specific for the listener. All three children lived in a speech environment in which reference

Table 54.   Frequencies of regular allomorphs in the three sets of parents

Morpheme	Allomorph	Adam's Parents	Sarah's Parents	Eve's Parents
Plural	-z	48	32	23
	-s	7	17	8
	-iz	2	8	2
Possessive	-z	23	14	32
	-s	2	1	0
	-iz	0	1	0
Past regular	-d	15	5	1
	-t	12	4	3
	-id	1	0	2
Contractible copula	-s	103 (plus 26 *is*)	55 (plus 1 *is*)	76 (plus 9 *is*)
	-z	12 (plus 14 *is*)	36 (plus 1 *is*)	24 (plus 8 *is*)
	-r	7	7	16
	-m	1	2	10
Contractible auxiliary	-s	5 (plus 1 *is*)	2	6 (plus 2 *is*)
	-z	5	3	16
	-r	16	8	17
	-m	5	0	11

Table 55.   Frequencies of irregular allomorphs in the three sets of parents

Morpheme	Allomorph	Adam's Parents	Sarah's Parents	Eve's Parents
Third person irregular	does	14	1	10
	doesn't	7	4 (I *don't*)	5
	has	4	2	1
Past irregular	did	39	21	9
	didn't	11	7	3
	would	6	2	5
	could	1	1	–
	should	0	2	–
	ate	1	–	–
	brought	–	–	1
	came	1	–	–
	fell	1	–	–
	forgot	–	–	1
	found	–	–	1
	froze	–	1	–
	lost	2	–	–
	made	–	1	–
	ran	2	–	–
	said	2	–	–
	saw	2	1	–
	thought	2	–	–
	threw	–	1	–
	told	–	1	–
	took	–	1	–
	tore	–	–	1
	went	–	3	2

was often specific for a setting or a group, fairly often so because of a prior introductory reference or because of entailment. Reference was rarely specific because it was unique for everyone or because either action or stimulus characteristics made it salient. Nonspecific references were most commonly nominalizations (naming statements) and simply references where any instance of a class was intended. Even the irregular allomorph *an* has the same relatively low frequency level in all parents. A certain number of articles used by each parent could not be classified in terms of these categories.

The general conclusion to be drawn about the frequencies of the 14 morphemes and their subvarieties in parental speech is that they present a profile quite remarkably stable across three unacquainted households. Adam, Eve, and Sarah were immersed in an ocean of English that contained the same set of ingredients in about the same proportions. There is enough constancy here to account for the constancy we have found in acquisition order if in fact it is the case that frequency facilitates acquisition.

Determinants of the Order of Acquisition

We are at last in a position to think about determinants. We have the facts about frequency and we have learned what we can about semantic and grammatical complexity.

Table 56.   Frequencies of the various semantic subvarieties of definite and nondefinite articles in the three sets of parents

	Semantic Class	Adam's Parents	Sarah's Parents	Eve's Parents
	Reference			
Speaker Specific	1. Unique for all	1	1	0
and	2+3. Unique in setting or for group	70	44	97
Listener Specific				
	4. Made salient by action	0	0	3
	5. Made salient by stimulus characteristics	0	0	0
	6. Specified by entailment	9	2	3
	7. Specific by definition	3	0	12
	8. Specified by prior utterance	22	8	5
Speaker Specific	Nominalizations	34 (2 *an*)	17 (2 *an*)	22 (1 *an*)
and	Others	2	6	3
Listener Nonspecific				
Speaker Nonspecific	1. Any instance of class	25	39 (2 *an*)	9
and	2. Negatives	11	5	1
Listener Nonspecific	3. "Fictitious" referents	23	14 (1 *an*)	3

Frequency

The three pairs of parents have, we know, a rather stable profile of frequencies for the morphemes. The question is whether that profile is related to the child's acquisition order, and there is a quite simple way of obtaining a general answer to the question. Which is to calculate the Spearman rank order correlation (rho) between two rank orders: one representing the order of acquisition averaged across children and the other the order of frequency averaged across parental pairs. The essential data have already been presented in Table 53.

Rho for the two average orders is $+.26$. With only 14 cases rho would need to be as large as .456 to justify us in rejecting the hypothesis that no relation exists (with $p \leqslant .05$). So we are not able to reject the hypothesis but must conclude that no relation has been demonstrated to exist between parental frequencies and child's order of acquisition. If a relation had been demonstrated to exist, it would still have been necessary to make a case for causality or determination.

If grammatical morphemes as a set are compared with nouns, verbs, and adjectives the grammatical morphemes are of course all rather high frequency forms. The early absence and long delayed acquisition of these more frequent forms has always thrown up a challenge to the notion that frequency is a major variable in language learning. But of course the grammatical morphemes tend to be unstressed forms of little phonetic substance and considerable grammatical and semantic complexity. So it has seemed unfair to compare them with nouns, verbs, and adjectives and necessary to keep open the possibility that acquisition order among grammatical morphemes may be influenced by frequency even though the morphemes as a total set are not acquired as easily as their frequency suggests they should be. Now, however, it seems that frequency is not a significant variable even within the set.

In correlating mean rank orders we have tested the effects of frequency in general parent-to-child English on the average acquisition order of individual morphemes. While there is much stability in frequency across parents and in order across children there are also residual individual differences. The test we have made says nothing of the role of differential frequencies across parents on differential points of acquisition across children. Test of this latter kind can, however, be made: two kinds of tests.

Suppose we express the points of acquisition for each child in terms of Stages I–V. If you look back at Figure 14 you will see that these points can easily be differentiated by eye in the following way. Acquisition may occur just in the sample(s) on which a particular stage grammar was based; thus *in* for Eve reaches criterion at III. It can occur between such a sample and the midpoint of the interval between two adjacent samples; thus articles reached criterion for Adam at a point we will designate IV. A morpheme can reach criterion just at the midpoint between two samples; Adam's uncontractible copula does so, and the point is designated III–IV. A morpheme can reach criterion between a midpoint and the next higher stage, as does Sarah's present progressive. We will designate the point in this case as III–. In short for any two samples one can, by inspection, establish five ordered points of acquisition; for example: II; II+; II–III; III–; and III. The morphemes reaching criterion beyond V pose a special problem, since no stages beyond V have been identified. As a quite arbitrary convention we will consider any of the first three morphemes beyond V to be acquired at V+ and any beyond that is acquired at V++. In this way I have determined the acquisition point of each morpheme for a given child in terms of his own stages, which stages have a constant meaning in terms of MLU.

If the frequencies of a given morpheme in individual sets of parents affect the acquisition points of individual children how could this effect be detected? Consider any two of the children, for instance Adam and Sarah. When Adam's acquisition point for a given morpheme precedes that of Sarah in terms of Stages I–V then the absolute frequency of that morpheme in the speech of Adam's parents should exceed its frequency in the speech of Sarah's parents. Thus, for Adam, the present progressive reaches criterion at II+, whereas for Sarah the same morpheme does not reach criterion until III–. It ought then to be the case that the frequency of the present progressive in the speech of Adam's parents should be greater than it is in the speech of Sarah's parents.   And this proves to be the case; the former frequency is 65 and the latter 28. Such a result confirms the effect of individual frequencies on individual points of acquisition.

Tests of the kind described can be performed for all three possible pairs of children. Only morphemes for which neither frequencies nor points of acquisition are the same for the members of a pair can enter into the test. Part *a* of Table 57 shows the outcomes with those confirming the frequency hypothesis marked plus and those disconfirming it marked minus. The null hypothesis we have considered is the possibility that the probabilities of plus and minus outcomes are both .5; that there is no significant difference favoring the frequency hypothesis. Tested against

Table 57.   Relations between individual parental frequencies and individual points of acquisition for the three pairs of children.[a]

a. Points of acquisition expressed in stages and frequencies as absolute numbers

               Adam-Sarah: 2+, 7–
               Eve-Sarah: 8+, 4–
               Adam-Eve: 4+, 7–

b. Points of acquisition and parental frequencies both expressed in rank order terms

               Adam-Sarah: 6+, 4–
               Eve-Sarah: 6+, 4–
               Adam-Eve: 5+, 4–

[a]Plus outcomes confirm the hypothesis that frequency affects order of acquisition. Minus outcomes disconfirm the hypothesis that frequency affects order of acquisition.

the expansion of the binomial, none of the outcomes in part *a* of Table 57 justifies rejection of the null hypothesis and, in fact, two of them are in the wrong direction.

There is another way of testing the effect of individual parental frequencies on individual points of acquisition. Both can be expressed in rank order terms. The acquisition points as positions between 1 and 14 in the child's rank order and the frequencies as positions between 1 and 14 in the parental frequency order. If frequency is a significant variable, when one child has a lower rank order score (earlier) for a morpheme than does another child then the first child's parents should have a lower rank order score (higher frequency) for the same morpheme than do the parents of the second child. Part *b* of Table 57 reports the outcomes for the three pairs of children. In direction all of the outcomes favor the frequency hypothesis, but tested against the binomial, none even approaches significance. We cannot reject the hypothesis that plus outcomes and minus outcomes are equally probable.

Thus far we have no evidence whatever that parental frequency of usage is a determinant of acquisition order, neither frequencies in general parent-to-child English nor the individual frequencies found in samples of individual households. Where else can we look for an effect? The first requirement is information on order of acquisition. We have some information of this kind for passives and present perfectives and also for the several allomorphs of the contractible copula.

Neither the passive nor the perfective seemed even to start toward criterion in the period between I and V. What were their frequencies like in parental speech? Table 52 contains the information. There were no passives at all in the samples from any of the parents. This surely is a limiting condition in which frequency has an effect. If a construction is not heard at all, it is not learned. No doubt one should really say if a construction is heard almost not at all, since larger samples from the parents would probably include a few passives. By passives I mean full passives, like *The radio was dropped by Joan,* passives with object and explicit subject. There were occasional instances of the truncated passive lacking a subject, *It was broken,* and of the truncated colloquial passive with *got, He got hurt.*

The present perfect has a lower frequency than any of the critical 14 morphemes in the speech of Eve's parents (2) and Adam's parents (3), but Sarah's parents produced 13 of them, which is a higher frequency than three of the 14 critical morphemes registered in their speech. If frequency were an important determinant of acquisition should not Sarah have shown some progress with the present progressive by V? Perhaps, but the actual list of perfectives produced by her parents exposes a problem.

The different perfectives are: *have got, have had, has heard, has come, has gone* with all but *have got* occurring just once. The past participles *got, had,* and *heard* are all the same as simple past forms, and the past participle *come* is the same as the simple present. Only *gone* is a distinctive form, *goes* being the present and *went* the past. If then Sarah actually had made a start on the perfective producing the same set of verbs as her parents, all at low frequency, and with the auxiliary still omitted, we would not have been able to identify the perfectives as such, except in the case of *gone*.

So the possibility exists that Sarah, and perhaps also Adam and Eve, had made some start on the perfectives. Nevertheless these forms were certainly not as well developed as the full progressive because the auxiliaries for this latter construction were often present at V. The full progressive and the full perfective are very similar in grammatical complexity so perhaps their differential development at V is one fact about acquisition order that can be attributed to differential frequency. The frequencies are, in fact, very different. However, we have seen that the perfective has a particularly rarefied meaning — earlierness in time but with current relevance — and it could be that it is this difficulty of the meaning that delayed acquisition of the form.

Finally we have some consistent acquisition order data on one set of allomorphs: the /-m/, /-s/, /-z/, and /-r/ of the contractible copula. In Table 36 we saw that, in samples at V, /-s/ and /-z/ were better developed than /-r/ and /-m/. Table 58 repeats these results alongside the relevant parental frequencies. Certainly the two allomorphs better developed at V were used very much more often than the two less developed allomorphs. And the frequency differential may have been the cause of the developmental differential. Unfortunately there is another possibility, and it is a possibility having some independent support. The better developed allomorphs, /-s/ and /-z/, were sometimes produced by the parents in "careful" uncontracted form whereas the less developed allomorphs, in the samples we have tallied were not. It is very clear that uncontractible copulas, copulas always produced in uncontracted form by parents, and also uncontracted auxiliaries attained criterion in all children in advance of their contractible counterparts. May not the occasional "careful" pronunciation of /-s/ and /-z/ as *is* be the factor causing these allomorphs to develop more rapidly than /-r/ and /-m/? This explanation seems more probable to me, but of course the evidence will not support a definite conclusion.

Perhaps in looking for the effects of frequency we are mistaken to count general

Table 58.   Development at Stage V of the regular allomorphs of the contractible copula and parental frequencies for the same allomorphs

Allomorph of the Contract-ible Copula	Percentage Present in Obligatory Contexts at V			Frequency in Parental Speech		
	Sarah	Adam	Eve	Sarah	Adam	Eve
-m	78	60	29	2	7	10
-r	58	41	20	7	1	16
-s	96	76	37	55	103	76
				(plus 1 *is*)	(plus 26 *is*)	(plus 9 *is*)
-z	90	44	38	36	12	24
				(plus 1 *is*)	(plus 4 *is*)	(plus 8 *is*)

construction types, morphemes or allomorphs and ought instead to compare the frequencies of *specific utterances* in parental speech with the acquisition of these same utterances by children. Of course we have counted constructions because I believe for many reasons — including the variety of instances and the overgeneralizations that occur — that the learning going on is rule learning rather than specific response learning. But I could be wrong for at least the earlier periods when the number of different utterances seems not yet to be astronomically large. Therefore, I have made one test of the role of frequency for specific utterances.

The number of different prepositional phrases employing *in* or *on* is small enough to make the tabulation of specific phrase frequencies practicable. To start with,

Table 59a. Eve's performance with particular phrases requiring the preposition *in* and the frequencies of those phrases in Eve's parents' speech; phrases occurring one or more times in parental speech from samples 1–6.

Head Word of the Phrase	Parent Frequency Samples 1–6	Child's C/I,[a] Samples 1–6	Child's C/I,[a] Samples 7–12
bathtub	3	0/6	0/0
bed	3	0/3	6/0
bowl	2	0/0	1/0
box	1	0/0	3/0
car	1	0/0	1/0
chair	6	0/2	4/4
coffee	4	0/1	0/0
corner	2	0/0	1/2
cup	3	0/0	1/0
cupboard	1	0/0	2/0
drain	2	0/2	0/0
fire	2	1/1	0/0
hall	1	0/1	0/0
highchair	4	0/1	6/0
holes	2	0/1	0/0
house	3	0/2	0/0
it	4	0/0	10/0
kitchen	6	0/2	2/0
living room	6	0/5	2/0
minute	9	0/1	18/0
picture	1	0/1	0/0
pocket	3	0/0	18/0
sandbox	1	0/1	0/0
study	3	0/2	5/1
there	10	5/0	20/0
toybox	1	0/0	2/1
week	2	0/1	0/0
while	1	0/0	0/3

[a]C/I signifies correct (the preposition *in* supplied) over incorrect (the preposition *in* missing).

Table 59b.   Eve's performance with particular phrases requiring the preposition *in* and the frequencies of those phrases in Eve's parents' speech; phrases having zero frequency in parental speech from samples 1–6.

Head Word of the Phrase	Parent Frequency Samples 1–6	Child's C/I,[a] Samples 1–6	Child's C/I,[a] Samples 7–12
bag	0	0/0	1/1
bedroom	0	0/0	1/0
briefcase	0	0/0	3/0
carriage	0	0/0	1/0
desk	0	0/0	1/0
envelope	0	0/0	1/0
finger	0	0/0	1/0
floor	0	0/0	1/0
hand	0	0/0	1/0
juice	0	0/0	1/0
mailbox	0	0/0	4/0
mouth	0	0/0	2/0
pants	0	0/0	1/0
sandwich	0	0/0	1/0
snow	0	0/0	3/0
treetop	0	0/0	1/0
truck	0	0/0	3/0
wastebasket	0	0/0	17/0
yours	0	0/0	1/0

[a]C/I signifies correct (the preposition *in* supplied) over incorrect (the preposition *in* missing).

I listed all the different prepositional phrases either containing *in* or lacking *in,* but clearly requiring it, in Eve's speech for samples 1–12, which start before the attainment of criterion and end after it. For each phrase, identified by its head noun, I calculated the ratio of "correct" performances, with *in* supplied, to "incorrect" performances with *in* omitted. This is the C/I ratio of Tables 59a and 59b.

The question was whether the specific phrases on which Eve had a better C/I index had been more frequent in the speech of Eve's parents than those on which Eve had a poorer C/I index. I next tabulated the frequencies of all the different phrases appearing in the speech of her parents for samples 1–6, whether or not Eve herself ever used the phrase. Samples 1–6 are the samples in which Eve was learning about *in,* and parental practice was little affected by Eve's practice. The phrases that occurred one or more times in parental speech are listed in Table 59a. The phrases used by Eve but having zero frequency in adult speech appear in Table 59b.

Parental frequencies for individual phrases range from 0 to 10. Eve's C/I indices are separately listed for samples 1–6 (before criterion) and samples 7–12 (including attainment of criterion). Because data on this level of detail seem never to have been reported I have presented the full picture in Tables 59a and 59b.

The results are simple but dramatic. There is no relation at all between the quality of Eve's performance with particular phrases and the frequency with which parents modeled those particular phrases. Essentially *in* is absent from Eve's speech in samples 1–6 (prior to Stage II) and *in* is always present where required in samples 7–12. This is as true of the phrases that had zero frequency in our sampling of parental speech as of those that had fairly high frequency. Clearly individual *in* phrases are not being learned piecemeal. They do not attain criterion one after the other in an order reflecting parental modeling. It is rather the case that the morpheme *in* is learned as a unit and appears in all phrases at about the same time regardless of modeling frequency. This same sort of analysis was made for *on* phrases, and the result was the same. So frequency is not a significant variable even on the level of particular phrases.

In sum, there is no clear evidence at all that parental frequencies influence the order of development of the forms we have studied. I am prepared to conclude that frequency is not a significant variable.

Semantic Complexity

Among the 14 morphemes there are four pairs such that the members of a pair are semantically identical: past regular and irregular; third person regular and irregular; contractible and uncontractible copula; contractible and uncontractible auxiliary. The fact that the members of each of these pairs are not acquired at just the same time indicates that semantic complexity is not, at any rate, the sole determinant of acquisition order. Since we are now concerned with the degree to which semantic complexity is a determinant at all, I wish to represent each semantically distinct form just once in the acquisition order. The first to be acquired of the two members of each pair seems to be the correct one to represent the semantic they share because it marks the point at which the semantic was first well controlled. In the mean acquisition order of Table 38 the first members of the critical pairs are: past irregular; third person regular; uncontractible copula; uncontractible auxiliary. Eliminating the second members of the pairs we have just ten morphemes in the new rank order of Table 60.

Table 60 also names the meanings expressed or presupposed by each morpheme. The simple progressive *-ing* without auxiliary expresses temporary duration including the time of the utterance, and it may presuppose the semantic distinction we have called "process" and "state." I say *may* because we found our evidence inconclusive as to whether the children were operating with this covert principle of verb categorization or had simply learned a list of verbs that could not take *-ing*. The parentheses around "process-state" are to suggest the uncertainty of its status. Containment and support are, respectively, the meanings encoded by *in* and *on*. Number, or the singular-plural distinction, is the meaning carried by the plural inflection and earlierness the only sense of the past at this time.

Table 60.   Mean acquisition order for ten morphemes and the meanings they express or presuppose

Morpheme	Meaning
1. Present progressive	Temporary duration; (process-state)
2.5 *in*	Containment
2.5 *on*	Support
4. Plural	Number
5. Past irregular	Earlierness
6. Possessive	Possession
7. Uncontractible copula	Number; earlierness
8. Articles	Specific-nonspecific
9. Third Person regular	Number; earlierness
10. Uncontractible auxiliary	Temporary duration; number; earlierness; (process-state)

Possession might have been subdivided into alienable and inalienable or into property and spaces but I have not done so. This sort of subcategorization is possible with all the meanings but there seems to be no principle by which one has to decide how finely the subcategorization should be cut. So I have decided not to subcategorize at all but simply to list each major meaning.

The last of the unitary morphemes is that carried by the definite-nondefinite article contrast, a meaning called specific-nonspecific. As our detailed discussion shows, this meaning entails a distinction between the points of view of the speaker and listener and subdivides into a large number of distinguishable cases. Nevertheless it is simply represented as specific-nonspecific and it occupies rank 8.

The morphemes occupying ranks 1–6 and also rank 8 are all distinct one from another, and may be thought of as unitary meanings. The morphemes occupying ranks 7, 9, and 10 combine two or more of the unitary meanings. The copula varies in form with the number of the subject (singular or plural) and also with the tense of the verb (hence earlierness). The third person inflection entails the same two, number and earlierness, since the inflection is only used with third person singular (not plural) subjects and *present* (not past) tense. Finally the uncontractible auxiliary, which is always also accompanied by *-ing,* combines number, earlierness, temporary duration, and possibly process-state.

There is no general theory of semantic complexity that makes it possible to assign complexity values to the seven independent unitary meanings. It is my impression that specific-nonspecific is the most complex of these, in some sense or other, and so perhaps the fact that it is the last of the meanings to be acquired is an indication that semantic complexity is a determinant of acquisition order. Without a theory of complexity, however, which predicts the difficulty of the specific-nonspecific meaning, no real importance attaches to this result.

There is a straightforward sense of semantic complexity, however, which predicts the ordering of those morphemes that depend upon compound meanings relative to just those unitary meanings of which they are compounds. This is the notion of comulative complexity introduced in Stage I. While the relative complexity of elements x, y, and z is unknown it may be said that $x + y$ is more complex than either x or y, and that $x + y + z$ is more complex than any of them. In short a morpheme that entails knowledge of any element x is less complex than a morpheme that entails knowledge of x plus something else. We have this sort of partial ordering in the cases portrayed in Table 61.

The ordering of Table 61 breaks down into the 9 specific predictions of Table 62; of these nine predictions, seven are independent of one another. When these predictions are checked against the mean acquisition order of Table 60 they are, without exception, confirmed for all the children. In order to check the predictions against the individual rank orders of the three children it is necessary to make one small change of procedure. While the third person regular precedes the third person irregular for Eve and Sarah the order of these two is reversed for Adam. It is the first form of the third person that is always relevant so, for Adam only, the predictions involving the third person are understood to mean the third person irregular. Similarly, while the past irregular precedes the past regular for Adam and Sarah, for Eve the order of these two are reversed, and so it is the past regular that is meant by past in her case. The uncontractible forms of the copula and auxiliary precede the contractible forms in all three children, and so it is the uncontractible forms against which the predictions are tested. The outcomes appear in Table 62: all predictions are confirmed except one, and that one (Adam's irregular past and uncontractible copula reached criterion in the same sample) is indeterminate. Restricting our test of significance to the independent predictions and counting the equal sign as an error $p < .0001$ by Sign Test. Therefore it appears possible that semantic complexity is a determinant of order of acquisition and a further demonstration of the law of cumulative complexity described in Stage I.

The nine predictions of Table 62 are also made by the Jacobs and Rosenbaum grammatical derivations of the constructions in question if we restrict our attention to one aspect of these derivations, one column of Table 45. For each unitary meaning there is a corresponding feature introduced into deep structure by the so-called segment structure rules. These are rules which assign to nouns and verbs features that are not invariable features of the nouns and verbs but possible features. The features are: $<+\text{progressive}>$; $<+\text{singular}>$, $<-\text{singular}>$; $<+\text{present}>$,

Table 61.   A partial ordering in terms of cumulative semantic complexity

$$
\left.\begin{array}{l}\text{Plural } (x) \\ \text{Past irregular } (y)\end{array}\right\} < \left.\begin{array}{l}\text{Uncontractible copula } (x + y) \\ \text{Third person regular } (x + y)\end{array}\right\} < \text{Uncontractible auxiliary } (x + y + z)
$$

$$
\text{Progressive } (z) < \text{Uncontractible auxiliary } (x + y + z)
$$

Table 62.   Outcomes of the predictions based on cumulative semantic complexity for Adam, Eve, and Sarah

Prediction	Sarah	Adam	Eve
Plural < uncontractible copula	+	+	+
Past, irregular[a] < uncontractible copula	+	=	+
Plural < third person regular[b]	+	+	+
Past irregular[a] < third person regular[b]	+	+	+
Plural < uncontractible auxiliary	+	+	+
Past irregular[a] < uncontractible auxiliary	+	+	+
Progressive < uncontractible auxiliary	+	+	+
Uncontractible copula < uncontractible auxiliary	+	+	+
Third person regular[b] < uncontractible auxiliary	+	+	+

Symbols:

< Construction on left acquired before construction on right.
+ Prediction confirmed.
= Prediction neither confirmed nor disconfirmed.
− Prediction disconfirmed.

[a]For Eve read past regular rather than past irregular.

[b]For Adam read third person irregular rather than third person regular.

<−present>. They compound exactly as do our unitary meanings. The process-state distinction is somewhat differently represented. As supposedly inherent features of particular verbs the entries <+action> and <−action> appear in the lexicon.

The features introduced by segment structure rules in the Jacobs and Rosenbaum notation belong to the deep structures of the sentences in which they appear. In this theory the deep structure of a sentence must include everything necessary for a semantic interpretation of the sentence, but the deep structure is distinguished from the interpretation. Another sort of linguistic theory would eliminate the grammatical deep structure and simply assign the features to the meanings of the sentences, a set of modulations of the meanings of nouns and verbs. Whether we regard the germs of progressive aspect, of tense and number as meanings or as deep structure features they are clearly distinct from the transformations which are the undeniably grammatical aspect of the derivations. In the Jacobs-Rosenbaum system the segment structure features trigger the transformations that produce surface structures. In another sort of theory one might say that the meanings trigger the transformations. The transformations themselves do not make the predictions of Table 62. I think it reasonable to treat the predictions from segment structure features as essentially semantic, and their confirmation as evidence that semantic complexity affects order of acquisition.

Grammatical Complexity

Before making a general test of the relation between grammatical complexity and order of acquisition there are several well-matched pairs to be examined. First among these are the regular and irregular forms of the third person and past marking of the verb. Within a pair the semantic is the same, and so whatever differences exist in order of acquisition may well be a function of grammatical complexity.

In the mean order of acquisition averaged across children (Table 38) the irregular past precedes the regular by four ranks whereas the regular third person precedes the irregular by one rank. The fact that the regular-irregular order is not the same in the two cases immediately disappoints the simple expectation that regular forms, being learnable by rule, must always precede irregular forms, which have to be learned individually.

Moving from the mean order of Table 38 to the individual orders of the three children (Figure 14) we find that for both past and third person one child out of three has an order reversing the mean order. For Eve it is the regular past that precedes the irregular and for Adam the irregular third person precedes the regular.

There are two questions then which the data pose: 1. Why should the dominant order be irregular-regular for the past with the gap being fairly large whereas the dominant order is regular-irregular for the third person with the gap being minimal? 2. Why should one child be unlike the other two in each case? In seeking an answer to the first question we must look at the differences between the regular-irregular contrast as it appears in connection with the past morpheme and the same contrast as it appears in connection with the third person morpheme.

The regular allomorphs of the past $/-d \sim -t \sim \text{id}/$ and those of the third person $/-z \sim -s \sim \text{iz}/$ are conditioned by the same phonological features of the stem and so seem to be closely comparable. The irregular allomorphs, on the other hand, differ greatly in number in the two cases. From Table 55 it can be seen that in the speech of the three parents there were just three irregular third person allomorphs and this is, in fact, the full set in English and is the set the children used. From the same table we see that the three parents used a total of 23 irregular allomorphs of the past and, though the children tended to use these same allomorphs, the list is far from being complete for English, which includes a very large number of distinct irregular past forms. In terms of variety alone, then, there just seems to be much more to learn in the case of the irregular past than there is in the case of the irregular third person, and yet it is past irregular that precedes the regular whereas the irregular precedes the regular for the third person.

Variety of types is not, however, the only dimension of regular-irregular contrast; there is the question of token frequency. Suppose we compare the frequencies in parental speech of just the three most often used past irregular allomorphs with the frequencies of the three third person irregulars, which, in this case, constitute the full set. The total frequencies across the three parents are as follows:

does	25	*did*	69
doesn't	16	*didn't*	21
has	7	*would*	13

The past forms have the higher frequencies.

The acquisition criterion for past irregular and third person irregular, as for all morphemes, was 90 percent appearance in obligatory contexts. In the speech of the parents of the three children the three most common allomorphs of the past account for 70–80 percent of all past irregulars, and the frequencies of the children closely match those of the parents. It follows (from the data of Table 55) that a child could attain "criterion" on the past irregular if he had knowledge of only the three most common allomorphs plus another two to four of the more common ones. This line of reasoning suggests that the past irregular may have enjoyed a token frequency advantage over the third person irregular. However, we have found that morpheme frequency has no significant general relationship to order of acquisition though the absolute relation found was positive. It seems reasonable to suppose that in just the case of *irregular* allomorphs frequency would be a significant determinant of acquisition. Because irregular morphemes cannot be learned by general rule but must be individually memorized and in memory tasks, generally, frequency is a very significant variable. This argument is quite speculative of course, since the naturalistic data are so fragmentary, but it does make sense and may explain the regular-irregular switch between third person and past.

We come now to the individual difference problem. Why should Eve had differed from Adam and Sarah in learning the past regular before the past irregular and Adam have differed from Eve and Sarah in learning the third person irregular before the third person regular? Only one possibility can be checked in our data, and that one not at all well. It might be the case that the parents of the "deviant" child in each case make greater relative use of the set of forms the child learns earlier. It is, of course, very unlikely that the frequencies in Tables 52 and 55 are reliable at this level of individual differences in certain morphemes. Table 63 reports the most relevant ratios, and a glance suffices to show that they do not fall as they should if the hypothesis were correct. So there is really nothing we can offer, even tentatively, by way of explanation of the individual differences among the children.

Cazden in her analysis (1968) of the development of noun and verb inflections in our three children has made two matched comparisons that are relevant

Table 63. Ratios of irregular and regular allomorph frequencies for three sets of parents (for the three most frequent allomorphs)

Morpheme	Sarah's Parents Irreg./Reg.	Adam's Parents Irreg./Reg.	Eve's Parents Irreg./Reg.
Third person	7/19	25/25[a]	16/7
Past	30/9	56/28	17/7[b]

[a]Learned irregular before regular unlike the other two children.
[b]Learned regular before irregular unlike the other two children.

to the role of grammatical complexity in acquisition. The first of these concerns the plural inflection.

Our plural morpheme (rank 4) is, we have seen, a collection of varyingly complex constructions. There are simple plural names (as in pointing, and saying *Blocks*) and there are plural nouns with plural determiners *(Two blocks)* and there are plural predicate nominatives *(They blocks).* The last of these is the most complex of the set. Though no entirely satisfactory representation of number agreement in predicate nominatives exists thus far, it is clear that such a derivation must involve a nominal agreement transformation (see Table 45), which is not required for the simpler sorts of plurals. Cazden has compared the children's performances on the simpler plurals with their performances on predicate nominatives.

Cazden could not compare the simpler and more complex plurals in terms of acquisition thresholds because predicate nominatives are too infrequent to yield stable threshold values. Therefore she simply calculated present/absent ratios for each of the two kinds of plurals across the whole range from I to V in all three children. The results appear in Table 64. Performance with the simpler plurals is about twice as good for all three children as it is for predicate nominative plurals. This appears to be an instance in which grammatical complexity is related to acquisition difficulty.

There is no semantic difference between the simple and the complex plurals. It is, to be sure, true that the plural inflection on the predicate nominative is always redundant with the pluralization of the subject *(They blocks; Those men are soldiers)* and with the verb *be* when it is present. However, one cannot attribute the differential omission of plural inflection in simple and complex cases to redundancy because the simple uses, too, are often redundant; for example: *Two blocks* or *Some soldiers.*

Which aspect of grammatical complexity is it that is related to performance with plurals? The syntactic features are all the same and so are the regular allomorphs. And so are all the transformations except one. There is an additional transformation in the case of the predicate nominative. This suggests that, of the various rules and features in a Jacobs-Rosenbaum grammar, it may be the transformations that are related to order of acquisition.

Cazden (1968) made a second matched comparison; this time involving the possessive. There are in child speech full $N + N$ possessives like *Adam's hat* and also

Table 64. Present/absent ratios for simple plurals and predicate nominative plurals in three children

Child	Simple Plurals	Predicate Nominatives
Sarah	.83 (67/81)	.54 (12/22)
Adam	.77 (124/162)	.43 (26/61)
Eve	.89 (48/54)	.30 (3/10)

Source: Based on Cazden, 1968

elliptical possessives which omit the possessed object, like *That's Daddy's* where *hat* is understood. We have no even approximately adequate derivations for these two constructions. Nevertheless it can safely be said that in a Jacobs-Rosenbaum grammar, or any other transformational grammar of the 1960's, the elliptical possessive would be the more complex of the two. In general it would be derived from the full possessive by a deletion transformation which in carefully defined circumstances would optionally permit the deletion of the possessed object.

In this case, as with plurals, Cazden found it impracticable to compare acquisition thresholds for all and elliptical possessives. What she did was to calculate present/absent ratios for the two sorts of construction in all samples up to the attainment of the 90 percent criterion threshold. The results appear in Table 65. Performance with elliptical possessives is about 6 to 10 times as good as with full possessives. In this case the grammatically more complex construction is handled *better* than the less complex constructions.

The result with possessives, then, reverses that with plurals. However, the match on conceivably relevant variables other than grammatical complexity is less good with possessives than with plurals. To be sure the semantic is the same. Parental frequencies are different but in such a way as strongly to favor the full possessive, these being, by Cazden's count, 7 to 20 times as common in parental speech as the elliptical forms. Two additional differences remain, and both of these favor the more complex elliptical form.

The inflection in the case of the full or attributive possessive is usually redundant *(Mummy's girl)* and it is not so with the elliptical possessive. Cazden illustrates the point with a remark made by Sarah after a trip to get an ice cream cone. "She told her mother, 'I shared Daddy's.' Only the inflection signified that it was the ice cream cone and not Daddy that was divided up" (p. 439).

Finally there is a difference of "perceptibility." It is easier to hear the inflection in the elliptical case where it is commonly the last sound in the sentence than in the full case where the inflection is likely to be very lightly touched in moving from one word to another *(Mummy's girl)*. The problem with differences of perceptibility is that, even if they are effective, it is difficult to be sure at which point in the total process their effect is exerted. Possibly the effect occurs in the child's perception of the parent's speech, and if that is the case then perceptibility is a factor affecting acquisition. It is conceivable, however, that the effect operates in the investigator's

Table 65. Present/absent ratios for full and elliptical possessives

Child	Full Possessives	Elliptical Possessives
Sarah	.06 (2/33)	.69 (11/16)
Adam	.16 (21/130)	.86 (37/43)
Eve	.07 (9/138)	1.00 (8/8)

Source: Based on Cazden, 1968

perception of the child's speech, in which case it is a kind of error in the recording of the data. We think, however, that the latter is not the case because all Sarah's data were transcribed phonetically and with great care exercised to make sure that nothing was missed. The difference between the full and elliptical forms is nevertheless as clear in Sarah's data as in the data of Adam and Eve.

What, then, are the possibilities? The superior performance with the elliptical possessive may simply show that an increment to grammatical complexity, when it is a matter of a deletion transformation, does not increase learning difficulty. Or it may mean that grammatical complexity alone does increase difficulty but that the increase is overridden by facilitation stemming from superior perceptibility or the fact of nonredundancy.

Two sets of matched pairs remain, and these have in common with the full and elliptical possessive a difference of perceptibility, but in the present case the difference of perceptibility runs in the same direction as the difference of grammatical complexity. The contractible and uncontractible auxiliary are, within each pair, matched except for the rules involved in contraction and a difference of perceptibility. The acquisition orders are perfectly consistent and clear (see Figure 14). In both cases, for three children, the uncontractible form is in advance of the contractible.

In the next major section we shall see that the order uncontractible-contractible poses a problem of high importance and considerable difficulty. Here, we shall be satisfied to point out that the order is that predicted by grammatical complexity (using Labov's 1969 rules for contraction) but is also that predicted by perceptibility. The phonetic substance representing the contracted copula and auxiliary is really minimal: *Here's a book* or *He's going* or *What's that?* The uncontracted forms, on the other hand, are represented by syllabic pulses: *Here it is* or *He is* (in response to *Who's going?*) or *What is it?*

Thus far we have considered construction pairs, the members of which have been matched semantically but not grammatically: regular and irregular past; regular and irregular third person; simple plurals and predicate nominative plurals; full and elliptical possessives; contractible and uncontractible copula; contractible and uncontractible auxiliary. The results with the regular and irregular forms seem to be related to the variety and token frequencies of the irregular forms. In all the remaining cases, except the possessive, the form having greater cumulative grammatical complexity was the later to be learned. The contrast between full and elliptical possessives suggests the operation of a perceptibility factor. This factor, if it is significant, provides an explanation of the priority of uncontractible over contractible forms alternative to the explanation in terms of grammatical complexity. This leaves only the difference between simple plurals and predicate nominative plurals as evidence of the role of grammatical complexity independent of all other factors. The grammatical complexity difference for the plurals is specifically a transformational complexity. It remains to make a general test of the relation between transformational complexity and order of acquisition without attempting to match semantics, regularity or irregularity, perceptibility and the like.

The most general sort of test of transformational complexity will simply order the 14 constructions in terms of the number of transformations involved in each according to the Jacobs and Rosenbaum derivations (see Table 45) and correlate this order with the rank order of acquisition averaged across the three children. In fact, however, the number of constructions must be 13 rather than 14 for the reason that we have no Jacobs-Rosenbaum derivation for the possessive. Table 66 provides the acquisition order and also the transformational complexity order for the 13 constructions. The Spearman rho for the two orders, corrected for the numerous ties, is .80, and this relationship is significant with $p < .01$.

Assessing transformational complexity in terms simply of the number of transformations in each derivation is a somewhat dubious procedure. In general it is probably the case that a construction involving more transformations involves more grammatical knowledge than one involving fewer transformations, but it need not always be so. Transformation rules vary in internal complexity, in terms, for instance, of the number of elementary transformations involved. It is certainly not safe to assume that all transformations involve a constant increment of complexity.[23] As explained in Stage I, a better rationalized index of complexity would be the cumulative number of transformations. In these terms a construction y is more complex transformationally than a construction x only if y involves all the transformations involved in x plus one or more others. Cumulative transformational complexity does not assume that transformations all add a constant increment of complexity. In assessing the role of semantic complexity we used a "cumulative" index; in fact no other was available. Can one similarly work with cumulative transformational complexity finding a partial order among the constructions and relating this to acquistion?

Table 66.   Acquisition order and transformational complexity order for 13 morphemes

Morpheme	Number of Transformations	Complexity Order
1. Present progressive	1	3
2.5 *in*	1	3
2.5 *on*	1	3
4. Plural	2 (1–3)	7
5. Past irregular	1	3
6. Uncontractible copula	3	10
7. Articles	1	3
8. Past regular	2	7
9. Third person regular	3	10
10. Third person irregular	2	7
11. Uncontractible auxiliary	4	12.5
12. Contractible copula	3	10
13. Contractible auxiliary	4	12.5

23. See Brown and Hanlon (1970) for a discussion of this point.

Table 67 shows just those partial orderings in cumulative terms that exist among the Jacobs and Rosenbaum derivations. The simple progressive, for instance, is cumulatively less complex than the full progressive with either contractible or uncontractible auxiliary because the simple progressive involves just one transformation (the progressive affix T) whereas the full progressives involve this one plus three others (auxiliary incorporation T, auxiliary agreement T, and progressive segment T). The partial ordering of the regular and irregular past and third person forms in Table 67 does follow from the Jacobs and Rosenbaum derivations we have used, but for two reasons it does not seem possible to use this ordering.

In the first place Jacobs and Rosenbaum note that for the irregular cases it would be necessary to "block" the operation of the verb suffix T utilized in the regular cases. The authors do not provide an explicit "blocking" mechanism but only identify the need for one. It cannot be right, however, simply to represent the irregular as simpler than the regular because the verb suffix T is not utilized in their derivation. In the second place there is the matter, already somewhat explored, of the variety of irregular allomorphs. These should contribute to the overall complexity of the irregular forms but cumulative transformational complexity takes no account of this dimension. For these two reasons I think one cannot use the partial ordering of the regular and irregular forms as a test of the significance of cumulative transformational complexity.

The order of acquisition predictions made by the ordering of simple and full progressives in terms of cumulative transformational complexity are clearly confirmed for all three children. For all of them the simple progressive is among the earliest constructions acquired, and the full progressives among the last. The difficulty is, however, that this same set of predictions was made on the basis of cumulative semantic complexity. Therefore, one cannot tell which set of predictions has been confirmed.

It is important to be quite clear about the situation at this point because it is near the heart of our entire discussion. Semantic complexity and transformational complexity have been calculated on the basis of distinct aspects of the constructions in question. The semantic complexity of the progressives has to do with the meanings: limited duration, singular and plural number, present and past times. In the Jacobs-Rosenbaum derivation these meanings are represented by segment structure

Table 67.   A partial ordering in terms of cumulative transformational complexity

Present progressive $<$ $\begin{cases} \text{Uncontractible auxiliary} \\ \text{Contractible auxiliary} \end{cases}$

Past irregular $<$ $\begin{cases} \text{Past regular} \\ \text{Third person irregular } < \text{ Third person regular} \\ \text{Third person regular} \end{cases}$

features. The transformational complexity of the progressives has to do with four transformations which map deep structures into surface structures: progressive affix *T*, progressive segment *T*, auxiliary incorporation *T*, auxiliary agreement *T*. It is not the case then that semantic complexity and grammatical complexity are assessed from the same features of the constructions. The problem is that the distinct assessments are, in fact, correlated in the constructions in question, and so one cannot tell whether the reliable acquisition ordering among progressives constitutes evidence for the role of semantic complexity or for transformational complexity or for both as determinants of acquisition.

The problem is not limited to the progressives but is, unfortunately, a general one for our data. Thus the third person regular and the uncontractible copula and the plural and the past irregular are all less complex, in a cumulative semantic sense, than the full progressives (see Table 61). But all these orderings are the same in terms of transformational complexity indexed, not cumulatively, but by the simple number of transformations (see Table 66) because the full progressives involve more transformations than does any other of the constructions.

Our conclusion must be that there is evidence that transformational complexity is a determinant of the order of acquisition but that, except for the simple plurals and the predicate nominative plurals, this evidence can be alternatively interpreted as demonstrating that semantic complexity is a determinant of the order of acquisition. Whether it will some day be possible to separate the two kinds of complexity remains to be seen. Advances in semantic theory yielding a general definition of complexity that could be applied to the elementary meanings in our set of morphemes may be made. More refined notions of grammatical complexity may eventually re-order some constructions or order some that are presently unordered. The study of languages not historically related to English may break down the semantic-grammatical confounding found in the one language and show where the real determinants lie. There is an approximately invariant order of acquisition for the 14 morphemes we have studied, and behind this invariance lies not modeling frequency but semantic and grammatical complexity.

The Problem of Variability

For the student of child speech there is fascination in the fact that certain of the morpheme omissions characteristic of the child learning standard American English are characteristic also of adult speech in various nonstandard or non-American dialects of English. Labov (1969) has shown that in Black English (BE), finite forms of the copula and auxiliary *be* are, in contexts permitting contraction often omitted (or "deleted"). Thus: *She the first one started us off* and *We on tape* and *Boot always comin' over my house to eat, to ax for food*. In addition, Labov has found that the regular past tense marker is often omitted in BE, yielding *pass* for *passed* and *roll* for *rolled*. He has furthermore, found that the regular third singular -*s* is often absent, yielding, for instance, *He work* rather than *He works.* Wolfram (1969) has confirmed Labov's findings for the BE of Detroit, and Claudia Mitchell Kernan (1969) has confirmed them in the BE of West Oakland. Bailey (1966) finds the contractible copula often absent in the English Creole of Jamaica, for instance, before predicate adjectives and predicate nominatives. In Trinidad English, Solomon (1966) notes that the uninflected generic verb is used for the simple past, whether the verb is regular or irregular.

The parallels between, specifically, BE and child speech extend to certain matters of detail. With respect to copula and auxiliary finite forms of *be,* the regular past *-ed* and the third singular *-s* both the adult dialect and the immature speech of the child learning standard English are characterized by what Labov calls "inherent variation," that is variation that cannot be reduced to certainty by the specification of any sort of contingency. In contexts in which deletion sometimes occurs Labov repeatedly stresses that no speaker always deletes and no speaker never deletes; all delete some proportion of the time. In child speech we continually find utterances produced within a few second of one another which are identical except that one lacks some obligatory inflection or other grammatical morpheme which the other possesses. This is inherent variation, a variation in performance that cannot be accounted for by any sort of contextual factor.

In BE there is, in addition to a basic inherent variability, a contingent variability, in fact many sorts of contingent variability. Two contingencies operating on the finite forms of *be* work in the same direction for BE and child speech. In the BE of Harlem, Detroit, and West Oakland *is* and *are* are often deleted in contractible contexts such as *He wild* or *They calling* but are almost always present in contexts which, in Standard English (SE), do not permit contraction. These latter include elliptical sentences in which the *be* forms are final *(He is!),* past tense forms *(She was likin' me),* imperative and infinite forms *(Be cool, brothers; You got to be good, Rednall!),* forms with certain pronouns *(What is it?),* and others. We have seen (Figure 14) that in the development of all three of our children the uncontractible forms of *be* attain the 90 percent acquisition criterion ahead of the contractible forms. In fact it is the case that at any point before the attainment of criterion uncontractible *be* forms are present a greater proportion of the time than are contractible forms (see, for example, Table 36).

In BE the proportion of the time that *is* and *are* are deleted is contingent on subsequent grammatical context. In particular deletion is more probable for *is* and *are* preceding either a progressive verb *(V + ing)* or the semi-auxiliary *gonna* (actually the progressive *be going to)* than it is before predicate nominatives, predicate adjectives, or predicate locatives. Precisely that is the case for child speech. We have seen, in Figure 14, that the copulas reach criterion before the auxiliaries, in both contractible and uncontractible cases and, in fact, prior to criterion it is very generally the case that copulas are present in a greater proportion of all possible cases than are auxiliaries. To summarize: two major contingencies affecting the probability that *be* forms will be absent operate in the same way in child speech and in BE: contractible-uncontractible; copula-auxiliary.

What can be the meaning of the several parallels between child speech and adult nonstandard dialects? It should, first of all, be said that they do not occur because the parents of Adam, Eve, and Sarah were modeling BE for the children. Although, as a matter of fact, one of the families, Adam's, is a Black family. This is a fact we have never, until this point, seen any reason to disclose, since it has not seemed to be relevant. However, it might be thought so if we did not make an explanation. Adam's parents are both college-educated, and they do not speak BE. Their speech does not include such BE forms as the use of *done* in place of perfective *have (I think he done gave her the rest)* or the so-called "habitual" *be (So it be easy for him to just pour the milk)* or, what Labov (1970) calls, "negative concord" *(There wasn't no trick couldn't shun her)*. Most directly to the point our frequency tabulations have shown that Adam's parents almost never omitted inflections or other obligatory functors. That also was the case for the parents of Eve and Sarah, except that Sarah's mother fairly often omitted *be* forms with *gonna*. Furthermore the omission of obligatory functors is a characteristic of the early speech of all the children learning English who have thus far been described, and they have practically all been white middle-class children. So the parallels between child speech and BE must have some explanation more interesting than the suggestion that the children had BE as their model language.

It is probably worthwhile to make explicit the untenability of an explanation related to that above. Children do not omit morphemes because *all* adults, whatever their dialect, also often omit morphemes. One might think that the omissions have been noticed in child speech because that speech has been more carefully transcribed than the parental speech and perhaps because the transcriber of child speech is less likely to "supply" everything represented in the written form of English than is the transcriber of adult speech. We are sure that that was not the case in our materials because selected samples of adult speech were very carefully checked by a skilled phonetician for just this possibility. In addition, however, Labov's research included a study of two white groups speaking a white nonstandard English (WNS). In this speech deletion of *be* forms practically never occurred.

The thought that comes next to mind is more interesting to entertain and more difficult to dismiss. It involves three propositions. 1. Perhaps child speech is, with respect to the treatment of grammatical morphemes, the same as BE or even the same as all the nonstandard dialects mentioned. 2. Perhaps child speech and nonstandard English constitute a less "complex" linguistic system than standard, adult American English. 3. Perhaps the less complex system has approximately the same communicative power as the more complex system for the reason that the forms omitted are either redundant or unimportant. The second and third propositions, if true, would account for the existence of a standard "reduction" of English, uniform across child speech and adult dialects.

The first proposition is certainly false in the most general form, since the several nonstandard adult dialects we have mentioned — BE, Jamaican Creole English, and Trinidad English — are not, as far as grammatical morphemes are concerned, the same dialect. Jamaican Creole English does not delete the copula in all the contexts in which BE does but only in some. The several adult dialects, in short, are quite distinct in their treatment of the grammatical morphemes in SE.

What about BE alone? Is it perhaps the same as child speech in its treatment of grammatical morphemes? Definitely not. Variable presence and absence characterizes, in child speech, all the 14 morphemes we have studied from their first occurrences in Stage II until the varyingly remote times, some of them beyond Stage V, when the 90 percent criterion is reached. For BE, variability has been reported only for contractible *is* and *are,* regular past *-ed,* third singular *-s,* and the perfective auxiliary *have.* It has not been reported for articles, the prepositions *in* and *on,* the plural, and so forth.[24] In fact, Labov (1970) explicitly says, while discussing the third person singular, "There is no general phonological process operating on clusters ending in -s and -z, for the plural is almost completely intact in NNE" (p. 56).

Let us narrow the comparison to the case for which we have the most detailed information: copula and auxiliary forms of *be* in BE and child speech. These are the same with respect to inherent variation and with respect to the direction of the effect of two major contingencies: contractibility-uncontractibility and copula or auxiliary status. Are they alike in all other respects? They are not. Labov describes certain significant contingencies in the BE use of *be* forms, which we either cannot investigate in our data or have not investigated. There is, for instance, stylistic contingency, a variation with the quality of social interaction. In excited groups more deletion occurs than in calm face-to-face interviews. There are phonological contingencies; for example, deletion practically always occurs after a sibilant. There are other contingencies described by Labov which we have studied and which do not operate in child speech as they do in BE.

While the contractibility variable operates in a roughly parallel way in child speech and in BE, it does not operate in *exactly* the same way. In BE Labov says that uncontractible forms are almost never deleted. In child speech, uncontractible *be* forms are, at any given point, deleted in a lower proportion of all possible cases than are contractible forms. However, the general developmental course of the uncontractible forms is like that of all the other grammatical morphemes. In particular, when uncontractibles first occur at all they are more often absent than present. This condition does not last very long but, while it lasts, child speech is, in this respect, quite unlike BE.

Among contractible forms in BE there are certain exceptions to the rule that forms contractible in SE may be deleted in BE. The form used with the first person

24. Labov (1971) writes that while his research has not focused on the point, he has seen some results suggesting that, in Southern syntax generally and in certain other dialects of English, articles and the prepositions *in* and *on* are quite often dropped.

singular subject *I*, which is *am* or more often the contracted *'m*, is not deleted in BE but it is deleted in child speech and not less frequently on the whole than is *is* or *are*. In BE with initial *it, that,* and *what, is* is regularly present in the form *i's* [Is], *tha's* [ðæs] and *wha's* [wʌs]. Labov sees these forms as resulting from some low-level process of assimilation which transforms them in such a way as to offer protection from the deletion rule. From which he reasons that the deletion rule must be ordered after the processes changing *it is* to *i's* and *that is* to *tha's*. In the speech of Adam, Eve, and Sarah the forms *it, that,* and *what* were, with only one exception, often used initially with no marking for *is*. The single exception was Adam's use of *it's* (in fact often pronounced *i's*). We shall see, in the next and final section of the chapter, that it was a monomorphemic form, resulting from a failure of segmentation. Claudia Mitchell Kernan(1969) explicitly rejects this possibility in the case of BE *i's,* and gives good reasons for doing so.

In BE the deletion of *be* forms is affected by antecedent as well as subsequent context. In particular, pronoun subjects are more likely to be followed by deletion than are noun phrase subjects. In child speech, also, the pronoun-*NP* status of the subject exerts a clearly significant effect on the proportion of deletions, but the direction of the effect is the reverse of that for BE. In early samples pronouns more often had *be* forms present than did *NP*'s. For instance, in Adam's samples 1–20, roughly Stages I to III +, there were no auxiliary *be* forms at all with *NP* subjects though there were 61 opportunities. In the same samples, out of 243 opportunities with pronoun subjects there were 58 *be* forms. Table 68 gives a representative set of results for copula *be* forms; the difference between the proportions present with the two kinds of subject is large enough to exclude the need for significance tests. It is my guess that these differences, like Adam's *it's*, result from segmentation failures. The frequently occurring combinations of pronoun + *be* form probably were monomorphemic forms for a time; the more varied and individually less frequent *NP* subjects would have had no opportunity to coalesce with *be* forms, and so no *be* forms appeared until this verb was organized as a separate morpheme. These segmentation errors would not be likely to appear in an adult dialect, and so the contingency is free to go in the reverse direction.

In general summary, child speech and BE are alike in just the following ways: copula and auxiliary *be* forms, regular past inflection, and third person inflection manifest both inherent and contingent variation; *is* and *are,* in contexts where SE

Table 68. Presence and absence of copula *be* forms with noun phrase and pronoun subjects in samples 15–17 for Adam and Eve

| | Subject Noun Phrase | | Pronoun Subject | |
Child	Present	Absent	Present	Absent
Adam	0	20	52	43
Eve	3	15	38	56

permits contraction, are more likely to be missing than in contexts where SE does not permit contraction; auxiliary *is* and *are* are more likely to be missing, other things equal, than are copula *is* and *are*. With respect to the additional contingencies affecting deletion found in BE we must say either that it is not known whether child speech shows the effect or that the effect is known to be different. So child speech is definitely not identical to BE in its treatment of *be* forms, and other grammatical morphemes, but there are certain similarities and these challenge interpretation.

What of the second proposition, the notion that BE and child speech forms are less "complex" than the forms of SE? We shall only consider this possibility for the *be* forms, since these are the most alike in BE and child speech and also the ones most intensively analyzed by Labov. In order to arrive at explicit rules for contraction and deletion Labov investigates in detail the variation of these two and of full uncontracted *be* forms with every sort of significant contingency. The argument and evidence are too complicated to review here; the conclusion is as follows: contraction and deletion seem to be both phonological processes involving, respectively, four and five basic rules not used with full forms, and so both would appear to be *more* complex phonologically than are full forms. The rule of deletion is distinct from the rule of contraction and ordered after it; the two rules are similar in the way they are affected by various contingencies but the effects on deletion are the more intense. The rules for BE, then, are not less complex than the rules for SE but slightly more complex.[25]

The first rule leading to contraction or deletion is the nuclear stress rule. This is a cyclical rule, taken from Chomsky and Halle (1968), which reassigns primary stress to the last lexical item within each phrase marker, reducing the stress assignment of all other items by one unit. The second rule, Labov's own contribution, is the weak word rule, and it operates to reduce "weak words," words which can occur with schwa as their only vowel, from [3 stress] to [-stress]. The next, the vowel reduction rule, again from Chomsky and Halle (1968), makes a schwa of the [-stress] rule. The contraction rule follows, and it removes the schwa occurring initially in a word before a lone consonant. The deletion rule, finally, removes even the consonant. This description leaves out rules for the assibilation of -t, for voicing assimilation, and numerous others, some of them needed for child speech and some not, but none affecting the complexity order which is: full forms $<$ contractions $<$ deletions.

The complexity order given above fits the fact that contractible *be* forms reach criterion after full or uncontracted forms in the development of all three of our children. The complexity in question is primarily phonological, however, rather than grammatical. And it may not be responsible for the delayed acquisition of the contractible forms, since some of the phonological rules involved are not specific to contraction of *be* forms but are needed also for other forms.

25. Highly relevant to this point is the following quotation from Labov (1971): "We also have some evidence from Jane Torrey's work with younger children that the number of full forms of *is* is higher with 6–7 year olds, and deletion is learned along with some other rules of the adolescent vernacular, as the child intensifies contact with the peer groups."

Our second proposition, that deletion is somehow less complex than the production of full or contracted forms, is directly contradicted by Labov's analysis. Deleted forms are, by that analysis, the most complex of the lot. And, indeed, a simple ordering by number of phonological rules does not describe all the complexity Labov packs into deletion.

The fact of variation, both inherent and contingent, in the use of grammatical morphemes, has puzzled me since I first detected it in child speech quite a few years ago. It was clear to me that variation challenged something taken for granted in generative grammar: the categorical nature of linguistic rules. But I could not see what to do about that. It was also clear to me that the slow rise in the probability of providing a morpheme in its obligatory contexts challenged the notion that language learning was primarily rule learning, since a categorical rule ought to be quite abruptly and generally manifest in performance. Now Labov has followed out the implications of variation in BE and argued that it is necessary to enlarge our conception of linguistic rules to include the variable rule as well as the categorical. His innovation has implications for the acquisition process.

Labov develops his argument using the context-dependent rewrite rule as an example, but in principle the argument applies to every sort of generative rule. Consider the following rule:

$$X \rightarrow Y/A\_\!\_B$$

It is read as: "X is always rewritten as Y in the environment $A\_\!\_B$ but never otherwise." The instruction is categorical. When faced with the fact of variation the writer of a generative rule can use an optionality symbol. Thus:

$$X \rightarrow (Y) / A\_\!\_B$$

Which is read: "X may be, but need not be, rewritten as Y in the environment $A\_\!\_B$." Two classes of outcome are provided for, but nothing is said about the frequencies of the two outcomes. Why should nothing be said? Labov has been able to show that, within limits, the proportions of cases, out of all possible cases, in which contraction occurs and in which deletion occurs and in which full forms are used are stable and characteristic of the BE dialect. He proposes that a specific quantity ϕ be added to the rule to denote the proportion of cases in which the rule applies. This proportion is the ratio of cases in which the rule actually does apply to the total population of cases to which the rule can apply and so it ranges between 0 and 1. For the familiar categorical rule, without optionality, $\phi = 1$. Labov defines ϕ as $1 - k_0$ where k_0 is the variable input, the factor limiting the application of the rule.

Labov has shown that in addition to variation in the application of a rule of contraction or deletion, as such, there are relatively stable contingent variations. Deletion and contraction, for instance, occur more often in BE in an environment characterized by a pronoun subject than in one characterized by a noun phrase subject. Why should there not be proportions associated with these individual constraints as well as with the basic rule? Labov judges that there should be and assigns to constraints the variables α, β, and so on. For a rule having two constraints, ϕ would be defined as follows: $\phi = 1 - (k_0 - \alpha \, k_1 - \beta k_2)$ where k_0, k_1, and k_2 are constants to be determined by empirical research. Labov goes on to develop actual rules for contraction and deletion which reflect the stable results of his research on BE.

The form of the variable rule is, of course, a reflection of certain linguistic performances, but is it a matter of "performance" alone, as Chomsky and others use the term, and not of "competence" or implicit knowledge? Performance factors are supposed to be strictly nonlinguistic influences on speech, such things as memory limitations and motivation. It does not seem to Labov that his "variables" are of this kind, and it does not seem so to me either. After all, the constraints are, many of them, grammatical and phonological and so surely linguistic. The variable rules must belong to the implicit knowledge of the speaker of BE, since his behavior conforms to them even though he cannot formulate them and is, in fact, "unaware" of them. Claudia Mitchell Kernan points out, "At no time during any field work was the deletion of finite forms of *be* ever mentioned by members of the community as one of the 'mistakes' made by Black speakers" (1969, p. 35). But explicit awareness and explicit norms of "correct" usage are lacking for most of the information represented by categorical rules also and this information has always been confidently assigned by generative linguists to the competence of the native speaker.

There is, to be sure, one difference between the variable rules of BE and the categorical rules of SE. The linguist who is a native speaker of SE can obtain extremely valuable information about categorical rules by making judgments of grammaticality concerning presumptive sentences he presents to himself. Or — much less reliably — he can obtain such judgments from other native speakers (see Gleitman and Gleitman, 1970, for a review of work with native speakers). Labov finds that this method cannot be used for the study of BE: "Whenever a subordinate (non-standard) dialect is in contact with a superordinate (standard) dialect, it is not possible to investigate the grammar by eliciting intuitive judgments of grammaticality from native speakers. Data gathered by such a method will reflect the superordinate dialect more than the one being studied" (1969, p. 715). From this fact Labov draws the refreshing conclusion: "Therefore it is necessary to study the subordinate dialect by more sophisticated methods, observing the use of this dialect in its normal social setting" (p. 715). This necessity operates for the rules of a subordinate dialect whether these rules be categorical or variable. For variable rules it probably operates whether the rules belong to a subordinate dialect or to the standard dialect, since it is unlikely that anyone can make accurate judgments about the proportion of cases in which he follows one contingent option rather than another. And of course the necessity of studying the use of speech as, at the least, an addition to judgments about it has been made clear by the work on word order of de Villiers and de Villiers (1972), which was discussed in Stage I.

Labov too argues that the study of speech in use has a role to play even for cases in which judgments are available and the study of speech in use may, perhaps, point the way to solution of many disputes. I am so strongly in agreement with what he says on this matter that I will quote him at some length. "When Chomsky first made the explicit proposal that the subject matter of linguistics be confined to the intuitive judgments of native speakers, he hoped that the great majority of these would be clear judgments (1957, p. 14). It was expected that the marginal cases, which were doubtful in the mind of the theorist and/or the native speaker, would be few in number and their grammatical status would be decided by rules formed from the clear cases. The situation has not worked out in this way, for it is difficult to find doubtful cases which have *not* remained problematical for the theory. It is not the number of doubtful cases which is at issue here: it is their location at points which are crucial in arguing cases of grammatical theory. One can see examples of this problem at any linguistic meeting, where paper after paper will cite crucial data as acceptable or unacceptable without obtaining agreement from the audience" (1970, pp. 36–37).

The study of speech in use does, of course, have some serious shortcomings as evidence of linguistic structure, but these have always seemed to me less devastating than they seem to the many linguists and psycholinguists who have never seriously tried to base inferences on performance. One shortcoming that has been for many an unexamined article of faith is the supposed ungrammaticality of everyday speech. Let me quote Labov again. *"The ungrammaticality of everyday speech appears to be a myth with no basis in actual fact. In the various empirical studies that we have conducted, the great majority of utterances — about 75 percent — are well-formed sentences by any criterion. When rules of ellipsis are applied, and certain universal editing rules to take care of stammering and false starts, the proportion of truly ungrammatical and ill-formed sentences falls to less than two percent"* (1970, p. 42). Precisely so, for the speech of parents in our samples. Brown and Bellugi in 1964 wrote: "Perhaps because they are short, the sentences of the mother are perfectly grammatical" (p. 135).

I believe, also, that the sentences of the children are grammatical in terms of their implicit knowledge of the structure of English (on the level of usage though not of judgment and correction), since generalizations based on performance have generally been confirmed by imitation tests and tests of comprehension. Probably the very young child's speech offers a more complete picture of his grammar than any sample of adult speech can offer for adult grammar because, in the child's case, the possibilities are much more limited. The work of Gleitman and Shipley (in press) and of de Villiers and de Villiers (1972) on judgments of grammaticality and the ability to make corrections as well as our own informal efforts on these lines suggest to me that judgment and correction are not a royal road to the child's grammatical knowledge. Like spontaneous usage, imitation, and discrimination of minimal sentence pairs, judgment and correction are performances. As performances they seem to be more difficult than the others mentioned, probably not always possible at all, and this suggests that we should conceive of grammatical knowledge as existing at multiple levels some earlier and more complete, others later and less complete.

Labov presents his stimulating ideas about variable rules and the study of speech in use not as replacements for categorical rules (which are probably much more numerous) and the method of grammatical judgment, which has yielded a large amount of knowledge, but as modest additions. In his writing there is none of that spirit of "total revolution and demolition of the past" which is so self-serving and unbecoming in a science.

If we were to write explicit rules capturing all the "knowledge" of grammatical morphemes manifest in the child's use of these morphemes at any point between Stage II and attainment of the acquisition criterion these rules would have to be variable rules. Inherent variability characterizes each of the morphemes and contingent variability operates in some cases, perhaps in all. These variable rules would have a different status, however, from those Labov has written for BE. In this latter case the values of the constants are presumably relatively stable for a speaker, and indeed for his dialect, over time. The child's speech, on the other hand, is in transition. His variable rules are eventually going to become the categorical rules of the SE spoken by his parents.

From our data, taken every week or every two weeks and analyzed in terms of certain contingencies but by no means as finely as possible, we can see that the values of the constraints generally fall over time and that ϕ slowly approaches 1. This is by no means a perfectly regular progression in our data; there are unaccountable regressions and unexplained abrupt advances. These might yield to more regular data if sampling were more frequent and data subcategories more numerous. We are not prepared to offer what we have as a set of accurate learning curves for a set of detailed subrules. But we are prepared to propose that the learning involved must be conceived as generally gradual change in a set of probabilities rather than as the sudden acquisition of quite general rules.

If our conception is correct it means that the learning of the intricate network of rules governing the 14 grammatical morphemes is more like habit formation and operant conditioning than anyone has supposed. Skinner's definition of operant strength in terms of response probability is surprisingly apt. "If a given sample of behavior existed in only two states, in one of which it always occurred and in the other never, we should be almost helpless in following a program of functional analysis. An all-or-none subject matter lends itself only to primitive forms of description. It is a great advantage to suppose instead that the *probability* that a response will occur ranges continuously between these all-or-none extremes. We can then deal with variables which, unlike the eliciting stimulus, do not 'cause a given bit of behavior to occur' but simply make the occurrence more probable" (1953,

p. 62). Most mathematical learning theories also conceive of habit strength in terms of the probability of a response in given circumstances. What we have not discovered, of course, is the circumstances which "reinforce" the grammatical morphemes, circumstances consequent upon their production which increase the probability of their production. It is not even known that any such consequent circumstances exist.

The variable character of the grammatical morphemes suggests a kind of rule learning that proceeds on a rather molecular level and gradually rather than abruptly. In certain respects, then, it is like operant conditioning or habit acquisition, and yet there is no doubt that what is learned is a set of rules, since the responses generalize in just the ways that the rules describe. Very likely this is only one of several, or even of many, kinds of learning involved in the total process of acquiring a first language.[26]

We have found that child speech in its variable treatment of certain grammatical morphemes somewhat resembles but is not identical to BE and other dialects of English. And we have found that variable rules allowing for the deletion of copula and auxiliary *be* are not less complex than the categorical rules of SE but somewhat more so. The third proposition remains to be considered: that the variable treatment of certain grammatical morphemes in child speech and various adult dialects of English has approximately the same communicative power as the categorical treatment of SE for the reason that the forms omitted are either redundant or unimportant. I think there is something in this third proposition. The very fact that we were able to identify large numbers of "obligatory contexts" and score for the presence or absence of required morphemes means that these morphemes when present were often redundant. In the $N + N$ construction the possessive inflection is usually redundant; with plural determiners like *some* or *two* the plural inflection on the head noun is redundant; with a plural subject and the copula *be* the plural inflection on a predicate nominative is redundant; when a main verb has the inflection *-ing* the auxiliary *be* form is redundant unless it is a past tense form; with past-time adverbials like *yesterday* or when the listener is familiar with the time of an event past tense markers are redundant; with a third person singular subject the *-s* inflection on the verb is redundant; for locative phrases using nouns like *floor, study,* and the like, prepositions *in* or *on* are redundant; for a listener well tuned to a speaker it will usually be clear whether a noun is intended specifically or nonspecifically even without *the* or *a*. The grammatical morphemes are especially likely to be redundant in face-to-face conversation between persons having a large fund of common experience, which is the situation for child and parent and for nonliterary adult dialects. It does seem likely to me, therefore, that grammatical morphemes are especially vulnerable to deletion because they are often redundant, and their omission will not result in serious misunderstanding. Le Page (private communication 1970)

---

26. Labov (1971) has also called my attention to the learning problem of the listener posed by variable rules. Does he need anything other than an optional rule? Is he sensitive to probabilities? And so on.

writes: "Loss of inflexion is the most commonly observed feature of Creole and contact languages" (p. 289).

Possibly the vulnerability of grammatical morphemes is enhanced by other factors. They are generally represented by minimal amounts of phonetic substance which are not stressed, and so there may be a perceptibility factor working against them. The meanings they convey are generally only "modulations" of the meanings carried by content words and by content word order, and those modulations may be less important than names and semantic relations. In sum, it seems probable to me that grammatical morphemes constitute an aspect of English grammar particularly susceptible to misconstruction both in adult dialects and in child speech. We have seen, however, that there is no evidence that the stable misconstructions of particular dialects are "simpler" than the standard construction; as far as is known they are just different.[27]

The Problem of Segmentation

In order to learn grammar, a child must segment the speech he hears into morphemes because morphemes are the ultimate units of grammatical rules. There are short-run regularities that can be formulated in smaller units, the segmental phonemes, but the long-run regularities that render an infinite number of meanings constructable and interpretable cannot be formulated in terms of phonemes.

It may be useful to imagine an erroneous segmentation into morphemes and what its consequences would be. Consider the following set of utterances that a child might easily hear: *my book, your book*; *my bike, your bike*; *my birthday, your birthday*. If we let a slash mark represent a morpheme cut, then the following segmentation is erroneous: *myb/ook, yourb/ook*; *myb/ike, yourb/ike*; *myb/irthday, yourb/irthday*. These morphemes look odd in print, but they represent sound combinations that are, in English phonology, easily pronounceable — think of *scribe* and *orb, Ike* and *oops.*

Suppose the child who has segmented in the above fashion goes on to store the contexts of each morpheme to the (unintentional and unconscious) end of discovering general and meaningful construction rules. The result may be represented in part as:

$$myb,[\underline{\quad}ook, \underline{\quad}ike, \underline{\quad}irthday]$$
$$yourb,[\underline{\quad}ook, \underline{\quad}ike, \underline{\quad}irthday]$$
$$ook,[myb\underline{\quad}, yourb\underline{\quad}]$$
$$ike,[myb\underline{\quad}, yourb\underline{\quad}]$$

Myb and *yourb* have identical context entries distinct from the entries for *ook* and *ike*, the latter two being themselves identical. In these circumstances it would be

27. Labov (1971) writes: "Our own data suggests that grammatical rules insert particles into a string of lexical items — some obligatory, some optional." There is a slight similarity here to Skinner's discussion of "autoclitics" in *Verbal Behavior* (1957) but it is slight.

reasonable to infer the existence of two morpheme classes ($C_1 \rightarrow$ *myb, yourb*; $C_2 \rightarrow$ *ook, ike, irthday*) and of a construction signifying possession which is created by selecting class members in proper sequence (C_1–C_2). These inferences founded on a mistaken segmentation do not lead anywhere. For the small set of utterances that preserve the artificial co-occurrence of certain morphemes and a subsequent /b/ phoneme, the segmentation would appear to work. Given *my b/rake* and *my b/and,* the child could construct *your b/rake* and *your b/and* with approximately correct meaning. However, outside this artificial range his false morphemes would not work. He would not hear *the ook, the ike, the irthday* or *myb pencil, myb doggie, yourb Mommy.* And he would find unanalyzable such new possessives as *my pencil, my doggie, my Mommy, your pencil,* and *your doggie.*

Compare the results of a correct segmentation. The context entries would look like this:

my, [__ *book,* __ *bike,* __ *birthday*]
your, [__ *book,* __ *bike,* __ *birthday*]
book, [*my* __, *your* __]
bike, [*my* __, *your* __]

One morpheme class would represent a start on possessive pronouns, and the other a start on count nouns. A construction rule written in terms of these classes correctly anticipates *your brake* from the occurrence of *my brake, my band* from *your band,* and so on, in an indefinite number of cases. Furthermore, the tentative morphemes *book, bike, birthday, my,* and *your* will recur with approximately the same meaning in such new constructions as *the book, my old hat,* and *your good friend.* A correct segmentation is repeatedly confirmed by its continuing ability to unlock regularities and structural meanings. An erroneous segmentation is a false trail winding off into the desert.[28]

In our materials there is no evidence of such errors as *myb/ook* and *yourb/ike.* There is, however, a small amount of evidence suggesting that certain ones of the grammatical morphemes, in the samples before they attained acquisition criterion, were organized erroneously into other words which they frequently followed. The two clearest cases are Adam's *it's* and Adam's *that-a.* Both seem to have been monomorphemes for a time.

What is the evidence that *it's* was a single morpheme? Until Stage II Adam produced no *be* forms at all. From II on, *be* forms were occasionally to be heard. The form *it's,* which seems to contain the contracted copula or auxiliary *'s,* was heard between II and III in 89 percent of all obligatory copula contexts and in 100 percent

28. The material on segmentation until this point is quoted from pp. 47–48 of: Roger Brown, Courtney Cazden, and Ursula Bellugi. "The Child's Grammar from I to III." In John P. Hill, ed., *Minnesota Symposia on Child Psychology,* Volume 2. University of Minnesota Press, Mpls. c. 1969 U. of M. By permission of the University of Minnesota Press.

of all obligatory progressive auxiliary contexts. Among pronoun subjects *that* had the next best record. It was, however, a record far poorer than *it's*; *that's* was present in 37 percent of obligatory contexts. All other pronoun subjects had still poorer records. This is to say that the development of *it's* was discontinuous with and much more rapid than all other pronoun + copula combinations; for example: *that's, he's, she's, I'm, you're.* From the start there was something special about *it's*.

The second item of evidence is the most important. When *it's* became frequent in appropriate contexts *(It's hot; It's dog; It's here)* it promptly overgeneralized to certain inappropriate contexts. The following are representative: *It's fell* (sample 14); *It's has wheels* (sample 21); *There it's goes* (sample 22). These forms, and there were many of them, suggest that *it's* was not organized as the pronoun *it* with the contracted copula *'s* but simply as one morpheme.

A third item of evidence suggests that *it's*, though monomorphemic, was not simply a pronunciational variant of the word *it*. When *it* was in the grammatical role of verb object, as it was hundreds of times, the overgeneralization *it's* never occurred. This is, in the first place, striking evidence that Adam had knowledge of grammatical relations. As such it confirms our judgment that these relations are known from Stage I on. In the second place the failure to overgeneralize *it's* to the object role indicates that the form was an allomorph of *it*, conditioned by grammatical role. In effect the nominative form of *it* and not just a free variant in the pronunciation of a word.

Further data complicate the picture. As we learned in the previous section, all seeming forms of *be* heard in Adam's first 20 samples (until just beyond Stage III) were heard with pronoun subjects. With *NP* subjects, like *Adam* or *Pop*, where *is* or *'s* was obligatory it was never heard at all until after sample 20. This may mean that, at first, all the allomorphs of *be* were organized with their respective pronouns as so many monomorphemes: *I'm, that's, you're.* However, there is still something special about *it's*, for *it's* occurred much more reliably than the others in obligatory contexts and *it's* overgeneralized frequently whereas the others overgeneralized rather seldom (*I'm turn over*, sample 15; *She's wear that hat*, sample 17).

There is one final puzzling discontinuity. When the uncontractible copula reached criterion about halfway between III and IV the overgeneralizations of *it's* did not immediately cease but were to be heard well beyond IV. This, in spite of the fact that there could be no doubt that the *be* verb forms had been correctly organized as such. Infinitive and imperative *be* occurred as well as ellipses like *Here we are* and *There it is* and the past tense forms *was* and *were* and interrogative sentences with *be* forms in initial position. All overgeneralizations of a pronoun plus a *be* allomorph ceased except for *it's*. So the monomorpheme *it's*, perhaps because it developed so early, was peculiarly resistant to reorganization. It is not possible to be sure about the correct explanation of the full pattern of evidence but it does seem clear that *it's* was a monomorpheme resulting from a segmentation mistake.

What is the evidence that *that-a* was monomorphemic? Until Stage II, articles were almost totally absent. Just after II (sample 8) the article *a* becomes frequent in sentences in which the demonstrative pronoun *that* is subject and the copula is called for but omitted, such sentences as: *That a dog*; *That a book*. As soon as this happens, however, *that-a* overgeneralizes to other contexts in which *that* is subject, but the form of the predicate nominative should preclude *a*. The following are illustrative: *That a my book* (sample 7); *That a Uncle Clyde* (sample 8); *That a screws* (sample 10). Table 69 tabulates the presence and absence of *a* with *that* for samples 5–13. The overgeneralizations are the uses of *That-a* in contexts requiring *That,* and Table 69 shows 27 of them between samples 7 and 11. They did not occur at all after sample 11. In this period it looks as if *that-a* was a monomorphemic form.

When *that-a* was monomorphemic it was not simply a pronunciational variant of the word *that*. The evidence parallels the evidence in the case of *it's*. *That* (like *it*) was often used as the direct object of a transitive verb, and in this grammatical role it was never replaced by *that-a* (see the last column of Table 69). Here once more is evidence that the child had knowledge of grammatical relations. The evidence goes a bit further than it did in the case of *it* because *that* was also sometimes used as a modifier, a demonstrative determiner, as in: *I want that book*. In this role also *that* was never replaced by *that-a*. It seems, then, as if *that-a* was, like *it's,* a nominative form.

In the samples between Stage II and III, the seeming article *a* was not restricted to occurrence after nominative *that*. In samples 9 and 10 it occurred 100 times following an uninflected transitive verb; for instance: *I got a ball*; *You lost a cup*. At the same time, however, it generalized to occurrence following a transitive verb where the form of the direct object ought to have precluded *a*. The following are illustrative: *Have a two minute*; *Firetruck want a this*; *You took a mine*. There were 18 such overgeneralizations in samples 9 and 10. They all occurred with nine strictly transitive verbs, verbs that must take an object, such as *get, got, have, put*. These verbs, since they were always followed by an object in parent speech, most usually have been followed by an article. Adam seems to have organized the usual article in with the verb to make such monomorphemic forms as *get-a, got-a,*

Table 69.   Correct and overgeneralized uses of *That-a* in Adam

Sample	Requiring *That-a*		Requiring *That*		As Noun Object	
	That	*That-a*	*That*	*That-a*	*That*	*That-a*
5 and 6	4	–	8	–	7	–
7	–	1	–	4	14	–
8	6	14	5	14	7	–
9	1	9	1	3	5	–
10	–	2	3	4	–	–
11	2	1	10	2	–	–
12	–	2	17	–	3	–
13	1	7	5	–	12	–

have-a, put-a and used these even when the direct object took a form (for example, pronoun) which would preclude an article in adult speech.

Table 70 tabulates the occurrences of articles in the different kinds of context where they were required for three points in Adam's development, all three points being prior to the attainment of criterion for articles which did not occur until sample 27. The 18 overgeneralizations of samples 9 and 10, the earliest point, are marked as "occurring and not required" (ONR) before certain objects of a verb. At this point there were 100 "occurring and required" (OR) instances after a transitive verb. For the most part articles were missing from all the other environments where they ought to have occurred. These nonoccurrences in contexts lacking an uninflected transitive verb support the conclusion that *get-a, put-a, have-a,* and the like were monomorphemic forms, even as *that-a* was.

Where, it may be asked, was *the* at this time? Most of the seeming articles, about 90 percent, sounded like *a.* However, after a verb ending in /t/ or /d/ the sound sometimes sounded like *the.* Probably *the* is best construed as a phonologically conditioned allomorph of *a* in these early samples, with no connection having been made to the specific-nonspecific semantic rule.

In samples 12 and 13 we find the total number of seeming articles tremendously reduced (from 123 to 26) and they stay at about this level until samples 20 and 21. At this point the seeming articles once again appear in abundance (172) and their status seems to have changed. There are now only two overgeneralizations and there are occurrences in the full range of appropriate environments. They have filled out their proper ecological niche as it were and have withdrawn from those places where they did not belong. My guess is that articles were at first (samples 9 and 10) organized into monomorphemic forms with *that* and certain transitive verbs. That

Table 70.   Articles at three points in time for Adam[a]

Context		Samples 9 and 10	Samples 12 and 13	Samples 20 and 21
Before object of a verb	OR[b]	100	17	96
	ONR[c]	18	5	2
Before noun standing alone	OR	5	4	51
	ONR	0	0	0
Before subject of a verb	OR	0	0	14
	ONR	0	0	0
Before object of a verb + *-ing*	OR	0	0	7
	ONR	0	0	0
Before noun in *Where N (go)*?	OR	0	1	2 (15 in sample 22)
	ONR	0	0	0
Total articles		123	26	172

[a]*a* and *the* combined; about 90 percent seem to be *a,* and *the* seems to be an allomorph of *a* occurring after terminal /t/ or /d/.

[b]Occurring and required.

[c]Occurring and not required.

they next (samples 12 and 13) went into a period of reorganization when they were seldom used and finally emerged (samples 20 and 21) properly organized as the distinct article morphemes. Some samples later, they reached criterion and were by then following the semantic rule of specificity-nonspecificity.

Adam's *it's* and *that-a* are the two clearest cases of morpheme segmentation errors in our data. There is also quite a bit of evidence for the existence of amalgams of pronouns and *be* forms like *I'm* and *he's* and amalgams of transitive verbs with articles like *get-a, pat-a,* and *drop-a.* There is some evidence from one or more of the children of such other amalgams as *want-to, have-to, going-to, another-one, what-that,* and *let-me.* The general impression we have is that morpheme segmentation is a real learning problem but one for which excellent solution procedures must exist, since it rarely goes wrong. What could these procedures be like?

In printed English the segments we call "words" are marked off from one another by spaces. Words are often monomorphemic though not always; *it's* and *dogs* are single words though they are not single morphemes. Is there in the stream of speech also a kind of spacing or pausing which segments the stream into words or morphemes? If there is, that could be the basis for the child's discovery of meaningful units. In fact, however, no such reliable pauses exist.

Many but not all morphemes are separated by what the linguist calls "open juncture," symbolized $/+/$. When detectable pauses do occur in speech they generally fall between morphemes, and pause is one phonetic manifestation of $/+/$. However pause is only an intermittent feature. How is $/+/$ identified more generally?

Consider the pairs *nitrate* and *night-rate, slyness* and *minus, mark it* and *market.* There need be no actual pause in either member of a pair, but still there is an audible difference in the amount of aspiration on the /t/, in the duration of the vowel /ay/, and in the release of /k/. For each pair there is a phoneme that takes two somewhat different forms. In order to be able to classify the related but different sounds as single phonemes and so to simplify description, the linguist creates the junctural phoneme $/+/$ and assigns to it the phonetic features distinguishing a pair (Harris, 1951). The phonemic transcriptions will then look like this: /nayt+reyt/, /slay+nɨs/, /mark+ət/, /naytreyt/, /maynɨs/, /markət/. It follows that the phonetic values of $/+/$ are a disjunctive set and elaborately so. It follows also that $/+/$ is not itself a segment at all, since aspiration, duration, and the like have no existence apart from particular vowels and consonants. The open juncture, in short, is an invention of linguistic science designed to simplify language description. How could a child possibly learn to recognize $/+/$ and use it to segment the speech he hears?

The /t/ one hears in *night rate* occurs also at the ends of words (e.g., *night* or *right*) and so can occur terminally in complete utterances, whereas the /t/ of *nitrate* is never terminal. Similarly, the /ay/ of *slyness* can be terminal (as in *sly* or *die*), but the /ay/ of *minus* cannot. And, in general, that form of a phoneme which is found within utterances at morpheme boundaries is found also in final position in total utterances, but the form found within utterances internal to a morpheme is never final in a total utterance. A child might learn that. He might learn also to give special status to utterance-internal consonants or vowels that assumed the forms they ordinarily assumed in utterance-final position. In fact, he might learn to make morpheme cuts at just these points and to make contextual entries in terms of the resultant units. He might do so but it seems a complicated and unlikely process.

The morpheme pairs for which errors of segmentation occur, *its, that-a, I'm, want-to,* and so on, are all pairs which in adult speech are usually *not* marked by any manifestation of open juncture. The fact that errors in our data are limited to such cases may mean that the perception of open juncture, where it does occur, is in fact an aid to the discovery of morpheme boundaries. However, it is by no means the case that every such unmarked boundary gives rise to an error of segmentation. Adults will run together *Pop's here* or *Adam's here* as well as *It's here* or *I'm here.* But only in the latter two cases is there any evidence of a tendency to collapse the two morphemes into one. The pairs which are mistakenly organized as morphemes have one characteristic in common that distinguishes them from other pairs which also lack open juncture but which are not organized together. The pairs that become monomorphemes have as pairs very high frequency in parental speech. The transition probability from the first member to the second has a relatively high value.

Nouns like *Pop* or *Adam* sometimes appeared as subjects of equational sentences, sentences with copula *is,* but they also often appeared as subjects of main verbs — too often, apparently, for Adam to make the mistake of thinking *is* belonged to the noun. *It,* on the other hand, appeared hundreds of times a day as the subject of equational sentences but seldom, surprisingly seldom, as the subject of any other verb. The high transitions in these pairs have nothing to do with grammar, of course, but are simply accidental statistical features of mother-child interaction. They suggest that statistical bias in the language sample to which a child is exposed can, in an extreme case, result in a partly erroneous formulation of the underlying grammar.

Olivier (1968) has devised an explicit discovery procedure for a simple and testable prototype of the child's segmentation problem. Olivier's procedure, programmed for the IBM 7094, did a remarkably good job of solving its problem and also made some mistakes which are like the segmentation mistakes children make. The program works on a corpus of English text which has been "collapsed" into an unbroken string of letters by removing all spaces and punctuation. The program is aimed at the "discovery" of the English words which have entered into the generation of the text but which are not marked in any direct and simple way in the data provided.

Olivier's procedure is not intended actually to simulate any part of the language acquisition process. Unbroken text, though like the stream of speech in lacking simple word boundary markers is, in many other ways, unlike the stream of speech. The problem set was word discovery rather than morpheme discovery. The text provided was not parental speech but the United States presidential nomination acceptance speeches by all candidates of the two major parties from Al Smith in 1928 to Richard Nixon in 1960. Olivier's procedures lead toward a better understanding of the child's problem of segmentation and perhaps more generally of grammar discovery even though they do not directly simulate these problems.

Olivier uses a stochastic mechanism, a frequency model but not a Markov process. What happens essentially is as follows. The model begins with a "dictionary" which is arbitrary in form and remote from the dictionary of English words into which it will ultimately develop. The starting dictionary has as its provisional "words" simply the 26 letters of the English alphabet, and each of these words is assigned the same probability. The program then receives successive "stretches" of text set arbitrarily at 480 letters, and finds for each stretch a maximum likelihood parsing into words. For this task certain "shortest path" algorithms from operations research are employed. On the basis of each parsing the dictionary is revised.

Revision involves adjustment of the probabilities of each "word" currently in the dictionary. The probability of each word after a parsing equals the number of appearances of the word in all parsings (or segmentations), up to and including the present, divided by the total number of appearances of words up to that point. There is also a procedure for adding words to the dictionary. After parsing a section each pair of consecutive words in the segmentation is lumped together and added to the dictionary. Thus, if *it* and *is* occurred in that order in a given parsing the provisional word *itis* would be added to the dictionary. There is, finally, a procedure for discarding "words" that have not worked out well. After every fiftieth section parsing, or whenever the dictionary contains more than 7,500 words, all "words" are discarded that have appeared only once.

Olivier evaluated the performance of his discovery procedure in terms of the convergence of the dictionary on a listing of actual English words and the convergence of successive segmentations on the word segmentations in the original uncollapsed printing. In terms of every sort of index the procedure did extremely well. After 550 sections, which represented just under 30 minutes of running time on the IBM 7094, the results went like this. Between 40 and 45 percent of text was segmented in a way that exactly reproduced the original printing. If you count the cases in which segments were either actual words or clumps of words like *ihave* or *allofus* or *ofthe* the results go up to about 75 percent. Taking a 4 percent sample of the entries in the dictionary at about this same point Olivier found that about 25 percent of the *types* were words. On the average, English words in the dictionary were occurring more frequently than nonword entries in maximum-likelihood segmentations. English words in the dictionary made up about 42 percent of the *tokens* in Sections 548–552.

Perhaps the quality of the program's performance is best conveyed by an actual parsing. Table 71 consists of the maximum-likelihood segmentation of Section 551. It is quite intelligible. There are many words. Among the word clumps one finds,

Table 71.   Maximum-likelihood parse of section 551

'l sof ourparty for ever as oneofthe fin est wehave ever held have you ever st opp edto
think ofthe me mor ies youwill take away fromthe convention the things that r un
through my mind are these that first day withits magn ificent spee ch es mr ho over
with his great less on sfor theamerican people mr w al ter jud d with oneofthe most
out standing ke y not e ad dr esse sin either party inhistory ourplatform and its
magn ificent present ationby ch uc k per c ythe chairman and last n ight our be lo ved
fighting president making thegreatest spee chi ever heard him make all of thisis part ofour'

Source: Olivier, 1968.

in the last four lines, both *its* and *thisis*. Discussing our evidence of segmentation errors in connection with his program Olivier writes: "Both phenomena suggest that the language processor, child or adult, is responsive to the same kind of statistical features of English that lead to the inclusion of word clumps in the dictionary generated by the word-grammar discovery device. In fact, *itis, iam, haveto, goingto,* and *letme* are all clumps in the dictionary produced on the test run, and it seems plausible that the rest of the clumps Brown *et al.* observed might have been included also if the input corpus had been more similar to mother's speech to children" (p. 107). It seems so to me too and I think it is quite likely that Olivier's program captures the essentials of the procedures children actually use. Of course parents who have the time and interest to do a lot of "naming" for a child before Stage I and also later on, for instance, many middle-class American parents, probably greatly aid the segmentation process by producing content words in isolation as full utterances. But children seem to learn their first languages well enough in circumstances where such "luxuries" are not available, and so it is necessary to think about more general procedures such as the one Olivier has simulated.

Summary

In Stage II we find the first appearances of noun and verb inflections and of such little words as articles, spatial prepositions, copula and auxiliary *be* forms. None of these "grammatical morphemes" is acquired suddenly and completely. Each of them is for a considerable period of time sometimes present and sometimes absent in obligatory contexts. The proportion of times a form is present gradually rises with time. We have taken, as a criterion of acquisition, presence in 90 percent of all obligatory contexts for three successive two-hour samples. When acquisition points were determined for 14 morphemes in our three unacquainted children it turned out that the order of acquisition was approximately invariant. A detailed study of the grammar and semantics of the 14 morphemes suggests that the order of acquisition is dependent upon relative complexity, grammatical or semantic. The order of acquisition is not significantly related to the frequency order of the morphemes in parental speech even though that order is quite stable across parents.

The 14 morphemes are governed by a set of categorical rules in the speech of the children's parents but they seem to be governed by variable rules in the children's speech before the acquisition criterion is attained. In this respect the child's speech resembles the speech of several nonstandard adult dialects of English. It is especially close to Black English (BE) with respect to the treatment of copula and auxiliary *be*. Both child speech and BE manifest inherent variability as well as grammatically contingent variability. Contingencies of contractibility and copula-auxiliary status exert similar effects in child speech and BE; other contingencies operate differently in the two. The fundamental difference is that BE as an adult dialect has variable rules containing a set of stable constants whereas in the variable rules of child speech the constants change with age until the rules become categorical.

In early samples following Stage II there is some evidence of segmentation errors involving such grammatical morphemes as the copula and auxiliary *be* and articles. The evidence is distributional rather than phonetic. Certain morpheme-pairs which constitute high frequency pairs seem to get lumped together as monomorphemic forms and so are overgeneralized to contexts in which they do not belong. Olivier's stochastic-process word-discovery procedures operate on English text which has been "collapsed" into an unbroken sequence of letters with considerable efficiency and success and make "lumping errors" like those children make. It seems likely that Olivier's procedures are similar to those children actually use in discovering the morphemes of their first language.

In semantic terms the grammatical morphemes appear to modulate the meanings of naming words, like nouns and verbs, and of the relations expressed by combining and ordering naming words. The grammatical morphemes add number, tense, aspect, specificity or nonspecificity, containment or support. These modulations are inconceivable without the major meanings they modify and for this reason alone grammatical morphemes could not be acquired before content words and rules of combination and order. In a face-to-face conversation between well-acquainted persons the meanings signaled by grammatical morphemes are largely redundant, they are largely guessable from linguistic and nonlinguistic context. And so they are dispensable in child speech and in nonliterate adult dialects in a way that content words and word order are not.

Conclusions

Sitting down to write a set of conclusions to this long book puts me in mind of the narrative problems Richard Wagner had with his *Ring des Nibelungen.* How could he cause his audience to keep in mind the extraordinarily complex story across four long evenings? Wagner's answer was to have some one or other — Wotan, Erda, and your odd Norn, dwarf, or forest bird — recapitulate substantial chunks every now and again. The audience, ever in a hurry, feels that the difficulty with Wagner's solution is that his retellings threaten to consume nearly as much time as the original enactments. While I personally do not begrudge him a note I wonder what the *Ring* would have been like if Wagner had guessed that it would so often be played a century later to audiences that understood no German.

I too have made use of the *langweilig* recapitulation — often to remind myself as well as the reader — what we have recently passed through. The dull tones of Erda are not, I am afraid, missing from this book. However, a chapter of conclusions will not yield to the simple recapitulation solution. If I say that the whole book is the conclusions, that is true, but disappointing. True, because practically everything written here is likely to be corrected or improved upon, and so all the arguments and complications of evidence are properly part of the only justified conclusions. But, obviously, one hopes that there is a little science as well as much myth in this work, and science ought to yield a modest number of general statements which are likely to stand up against new evidence and which are more worth keeping in memory than the twists and turns of the full plot. So I will take some risks and guess at what some of these generalizations with their implicit prophecies should be.[1]

1. Neither telegraphic speech nor pivot grammar affords a satisfactory account of Stage I constructions. I include this negative conclusion mainly because I think it is time both descriptions were dropped from introductory textbooks. Telegraphic speech is the more accurate of the two but that is chiefly because it is also the less ambitious. Roughly speaking, Stage I speech is, indeed, made up of content words and does lack functors. But there are exceptions, and these are such as to indicate that the rough categorical description is going to give way to a more interesting set of functional relations between a large set of variables characterizing constructions and several levels of linguistic control. Pivot grammar fails on all counts. Most of the evidence now contradicts the distributional claims made by pivot grammar, and in addition the formal notation the grammar makes available is inadequate to the representation of semantic differences which seem to belong to the child's knowledge.

2. The order of progression in knowledge of the first language, both semantic and grammatical, will prove to be approximately invariant across children learning the same language and, at a higher level of abstraction, across children learning

1. The discussion in this section is very similar to a portion of: Brown, Roger. "The Development of the First Language in the Human Species." *American Psychologist* (1972) 27. With permission of The American Psychological Association.

any language. There is at present evidence for just three major progressions. Two are described in this book: the evolution of the basic semantic and grammatical relations across many languages in Stage I; the acquisition of 14 English grammatical morphemes and the modulations of meaning they express in Stage II. The evidence for the third appears in Brown and Hanlon (1970), and it concerns tag questions like *doesn't it?* or *can't I?* and the fact that they appear later in the speech of Adam, Eve, and Sarah than all the component kinds of knowledge they involve such as negation, interrogation, and predicate ellipsis. Of the three major progressions for which evidence of invariance exists, only that occurring in Stage I, basic semantic and grammatical relations, has been demonstrated across some variety of historically unrelated languages. The evidence for the other two is thus far limited to American English and, in fact, largely to the development of Adam, Eve, and Sarah. This is primarily because data analysis in most studies has not yet moved beyond Stage I.

3. The primary determinants of acquisition order will prove to be cumulative complexity, both semantic and grammatical. This is a large claim summarizing many analyses both in this book and in Brown and Hanlon (1970). It needs some further justification and qualification here.

Recourse to grammatical complexity as a determining variable requires defense today because of its unhappy recent history in another domain of psycholinguistics: the experimental study of sentence processing by adults. Chomsky's *Syntactic Structures* (1957) inspired five years or so of highly ingenious work on what was called the "psychological reality" of transformational grammar. I agree with the retrospective analysis of this research by Fodor and Garrett (1966) that the chief proposition implicitly under test in this research is the idea that the psychological complexity of a sentence, as indexed by speed of comprehension, ability to recall, and so on, would be predictable from the grammatical complexity of the sentence in terms of the number of optional transformations involved in its derivation in Chomsky's *Syntactic Structures*. Thus passives and interrogatives and negatives were grammatically more complex than simple-active-affirmative-declarative sentences and might, therefore, be expected to be harder to process psychologically. For a number of years, five or so, most experimental results, and there were many of them, more or less confirmed this expectation. Then, almost at the same time, three things went wrong, as I see it, and conclusively disappointed the hope that grammatical complexity would predict psychological processing complexity:

As transformational linguistics extended the scope of its description of English it became increasingly apparent that the "transformed sentences" psychologists had actually studied were a small and rather special subset of the total. They were, naturally enough, just the types of sentences derived in *Syntactic Structures:* interrogatives, passives, negatives, and so on. In all these cases the grammar differs from that of the simple-active-affirmative-declarative sentence and so, apparently, does the meaning. Even in *Syntactic Structures*, however, there was another derivation that no psychologist studied experimentally: the simple sentence with a verb in two parts. As analyzed in *Syntactic Structures* a sentence like *John took his coat off,* with the noun phrase between the verb and its particle, is derived by optional transformation from the abstract string underlying *John took off his coat* in which the noun phrase is in its more usual position after the full transitive verb. The first form of the sentence is grammatically more complex than the second (it entails an extra optional transformation) but there is no discernible change of meaning. Is it nevertheless the case that *John took his coat off* is harder to process than *John took off his coat*? One hardly need do an experiment; one feels no difference of difficulty. And as Fodor and Garrett (1966) point out when experiments were done, with sentences differing in transformational complexity but not in meaning, differences of psychological complexity failed to appear. The difficulty at this point lay in the fact that the basic hypothesis held that psychological complexity should rise with transformational complexity, without regard for semantics, but it looked as if the hypothesis were only true for a subset of sentences which involved semantic change as well as transformational change and was actually false for sentences involving transformational change only.

While these things were happening in psychology, linguists at the Massachusetts Institute of Technology made some changes of their own in the derivation of certain sentences, not as a response to "mere psychological research," of course, but in the interests of the formal consistency and simplicity of their system. In effect, for reasons best described in Katz and Postal (1964), they decided that all transformations should be so written as to leave meaning invariant. They were all to be like the separable verb transformation of 1957, and not like the interrogatives, negatives, and passives of that period. To accomplish this effect it was, among other things, necessary to work out new derivations of the interrogatives, negatives, and passives such that they carried abstract morphemes in their deep structures standing in for the meanings in question, which morphemes would obligatorily trigger the necessary transformations. This derivational change meant that the "more complex" sentences with which psychologists had worked were formally recognized as different from simple-active-affirmative-declarative sentences not in the number of optional transformations but in their deep structures, which were intended to be the inputs to a semantic-interpretation component, as well as in the obligatory transformations producing the surface structure.

The first two changes come together in a maximally unfortunate way for the claim that psychological complexity is a function of the number of optional transformations in a derivation. The positive experimental results accumulated over some years can no longer be taken as a proper test of the original hypothesis for the reason that the sentences studied do not differ exclusively, or necessarily at all, in the number of optional transformations entering into their respective derivations. The small number of negative results, reported by Fodor and Garrett (1966) and involving besides the separable verb case the movement of sentence adverbials and the optional deletion of redundant predicate elements, are the only proper tests of the hypothesis. And so the general hypothesis has come tumbling down though, of course, the experimental results themselves have other interesting aspects.

How can we, in developmental psycholinguistics, pin any hopes on a variable like grammatical complexity, which has so ill rewarded those who used it in another area of psycholinguistics? Partly we can do so because our problem is a bit different and partly because we are not tying ourselves so closely to particular systems of linguistic notation (and so are somewhat less precise) and perhaps because we are not so optimistic about how near we are to solving our problems.

Our problem is different in that we are not concerned with the efficiency of sentence processing, in the sense of speed or accuracy or recall, but rather with the acquisition of construction types, with their first utilization at all in what may be considered a productive and comprehending way. Though no generative grammar can reasonably be considered a model of the process of sentence production or comprehension (it is much more like a set of axioms for testing whether a given string is or is not a sentence), generative grammars have, as their ultimate point, a distinctly psychological goal. They are intended to represent formally the knowledge that the native speaker must *somehow* utilize in producing and understanding sentences. Insofar as a grammar has correctly captured this knowledge it does not seem unreasonable that the relative complexity derivations will be a determinant of the order of their acquisition. But, what of the fact that linguistic theory is, today, in one of its unsettled disputatious phases, and that there is no real consensus on the correct form of representation of English or any language? The way we live with this situation is by noticing that there is a good deal of the substance of English grammar that seems to endure through all these disputes, and indeed was partly known before the invention of generative transformational grammars. But, of course, grammar that is not formally represented cannot yield a clear complexity order. So we play our game by settling on a particular grammar, for example, the Jacobs-Rosenbaum grammar in Stage II, which is reasonably up-to-date and inclusive of the constructions that concern us, and let it generate its predictions before we know the outcomes of our acquisition research.

Sometimes, as in Stage I, we play a different game, letting acquisition outcomes which are quite well established appear first and then looking at a variety of grammars comparing their respective abilities to represent the facts. We do not suppose that the study of language acquisition can build on a "finished" linguistic science but rather think of our work as one of several kinds that may help with the general understanding of language and even contribute to the solution of strictly linguistic problems, which are so often hung up nowadays on conflicting trained intuitions.

Our definition of grammatical complexity (semantic complexity, too) is limited in a way that has not been true of all conceptions of complexity utilized in psycho-linguistic research. In brief it is limited to the "cumulative" sense, defined and exemplified, in both Stage I and Stage II. We do not, for example, simply count the number of optional transformations in a derivation, or any other feature of a derivation, since this procedure involves the generally unwarranted assumption that any one transformation, or some other feature, involves the same increment to complexity of knowledge as any other. In our *cumulative* sense of complexity a construction $x + y$ may be regarded as more complex than either x or y because it involves everything involved in either of the constructions alone plus something more. The construction $x + y$ cannot be ordered with respect to a construction z even though $x + y$ might contain one more of some unit or other than does z. This is because we are not prepared to assume equality of units. As a result our several acquisition series can typically be only *partially* ordered rather than fully ordered.

The notion of cumulative complexity has the advantage of being applicable, as in Stage II, in a rough sort of way, to semantics as well as grammar even in the absence of a developed formal notation in semantics. So long as one can say that a given meaning x, however described, is involved in $x + y$ along with some additional meaning y an ordering is possible. Of course one hopes for the advent of more general and well-motivated definitions of both grammatical and semantic complexity that will make full orderings possible, where only partial orderings are now possible and will perhaps make the predictions to acquisition even stronger than they now are. The study of language acquisition is likely to contribute to these goals as well as to profit from their attainment.

Limiting our work to cumulative complexity might seem to make our acquisition orders necessary outcomes and not empirical discoveries at all. One might quite reasonably ask: "If $x + y$ involves all the knowledge of x and y, each taken alone, how could it fail to be the case that $x + y$ will be acquired later than its components?" The answer is that the prediction can fail if the analysis of requisite knowledge, grammatical and semantic, is faulty or if the evidence used to indicate constructional acquisition is insufficient. To cite an extreme example: if each sentence a child spoke over a period of time had been learned as an unanalyzed, unconstructed routine, not involving elaborate grammatical and semantic knowledge, then the law of cumulative complexity would fail to predict order of acquisition.

There is admittedly a kind of mutual dependence among all the factors involved, and one might reasonably say that I am taking the law of cumulative complexity as necessarily true and using it to validate sets of grammatical and semantic analyses and the utilization of certain empirical indices of acquisition. Beyond this level, however, starting with cumulative complexity opens the way to unquestionably empirical discoveries, such as the fact that for all three progressions so far studied the acquisition of the several components x and y alone does not promptly, or even very soon, lead to the acquisition of the construction $x + y$ that in some fashion, not necessarily linear as the notation might suggest, combines the two.

I am guessing that both semantic and grammatical cumulative complexity are important determinants of acquisition order but the two are often confounded. In Stage II semantic complexity seems to do a better job of predicting order of acquisition than does grammatical complexity but, because there is considerable confounding of the two for the 14 English morphemes and the Jacobs-Rosenbaum grammar is incomplete at several important points, the outcome must be considered indeterminate. All one can say is that semantic and grammatical complexity does a good job of predicting order of acquisition. In Stage I the problem is a bit different but at best is vexing. The difficulty here is that a single grammatical or expressive device, word order, is the clearest evidence that the child has the semantic intentions with which we are concerned. In languages not making much significant use of word order one must rely on the weaker evidence of contextual appropriateness as a basis for attributing certain semantic relations. For the investigator who is willing to lean on this evidence, as I and a number of others are, it is cumulative semantic complexity that predicts and, perhaps, determines order of acquisition in Stage I. The clearest evidence for the importance of grammatical complexity in its own right appears in the Brown and Hanlon (1970) study of English tag questions. The peculiar beauty of the English tag question is that it is semantically rather trifling, a request for confirmation, and it has such simple equivalents as *huh?* and *right?* Grammatically, however, well-formed tag questions are at a high level of cumulative complexity. The facts are that the grammatically simple tags like *right?* appear as early as Stage I, whereas the grammatically complex tags like *can't I?* do not appear until well after Stage V and, more to the point, well after the acquisition of the grammatical componentry that includes interrogation, negation, pronominalization, and predicate ellipsis. It seems, then, that in this case the long-deferred appearance of well-formed tags must be attributed to grammatical complexity in its own right. Besides these major tests of the possible roles of the two kinds of complexity there are many minor tests scattered through Stage I and Stage II.

4. Though the order of acquisition of linguistic knowledge will prove to be approximately invariant across children learning one language and, at a higher level of abstraction, across children learning any language, the rate of progression will vary radically among children. We have already seen that it does so, even among Adam, Eve, and Sarah. What will the determinants of rate prove to be? No one can know at present. No doubt there are family interaction variables that will account for some of the variance but I will go out on a limb and predict that, within some as yet unknown limits of interaction variation, the rate will also prove to be dependent on what the intelligence testers call *g* or general intelligence. Indeed I think it possible that studies of acquisition like that reported in Stage II will yield scores for children that will be able to predict with substantial success IQ scores on standard tests administered in the school years. At present IQ estimates in the first four or five years do not predict very well IQ scores based on tests taken during the school years (see Tyler, 1965, Chapter 4 for a summary). The above is really just a guess on my part and may prove quite wrong. I am inclined to make it partly because I think a reasonable conceptual definition of comparative intelligence is the rate at which individuals build general rule systems or theories comprehending sets of data to

which they are exposed. This is a notion that would fit Piaget's approach to intelligence as well as the study of language development, and it is already clear from several studies that intelligence is not a matter of the simple rapidity of improvement with practice on a motor or perceptual skill (see Tyler, 1965, for a summary).

Studying the early IQ test items, of Binet and Simon and Terman (see Terman, 1916) I have been fascinated by several linguistic subsets but especially by one that involves imitating sentences, with more and more syllables as chronological age advances. The authors of these items thought in terms of syllables but as I look at them I see also an order of increasing cumulative complexity. For instance, Terman (1916) lists as a three-year-old sentence, "I have a little dog;" as a four-year-old, "We are going to have a good time in the country;" and as a sentence the average adult can imitate: "Walter likes very much to go on visits to his grandmother, because she always tells him many funny stories." My guess is that it is the complexity and not the number of syllables that chiefly matters. It must be remembered that these IQ items were selected by a process of trial and error. The testers wanted sentences with a certain "operating characteristic": they should be failed by practically all children below a given chronological age, passed by 50 to 75 percent of the children at a given age, and passed by almost all children above that age. It does not seem unlikely to me that many sentences of 7 syllables or 13 or whatever were tried before sentences were found with the desired operating characteristics, and that these were the ones with the right complexity ordering, syllables being more or less beside the point. Or, alternatively, the test constructors may have hit intuitively on sentences at the right levels of complexity, because more complex sentences often do just feel more difficult to process, and yet the investigators would have thought only in terms of syllables because these are salient countable units, that require no technical linguistic knowledge to make them so. All this is just speculation but at least it is speculation that can easily be checked by research.

5. Frequency and perceptual salience will be minor determinants of order of acquisition. The possibility that the frequencies with which either specific utterances or construction types are modeled for small children affects order of acquisition has been exhaustively probed in Stage II. The upshot of the several kinds of test made is that, for the 14 English grammatical morphemes, there is no evidence whatever that frequency of any sort is a significant determinant of order of acquisition. Still some marginal role for frequency is really guaranteed; children will not learn constructions they never hear. What the minimal essential values may be is unknown but it is certainly possible that the very low frequencies, in adult speech to young children, of full passives and perfectives is a factor in the usually late acquisition of these constructions. The possibility also exists that frequency is important for irregular forms which must be memorized as such.

Perceptual salience, broken down into such variables as amount of phonetic substance, stress level, usual serial position in a sentence, and so on, is probably a more important variable. Experiments by Scholes (1969, 1970) and by Blasdell and Jensen (1970), for instance, described in Stage I, suggest that "salience" may have a role in producing the telegraphic quality of early English speech. In the naturalistic data there are numerous points at which one suspects that "salience" is a significant factor though this is never quite provable because of a natural confounding in the language with other variables. One thinks of the acquisition of uncontractible copulas and auxiliaries before their contractible equivalents, of the acquisition of utterance-final elliptical possessives before the possessive inflection in attributive position, of the seemingly earlier control of German *ein* than English *a,* and so on. As in the case of frequency *some* role for salience is guaranteed; the child will not learn what he cannot hear.

6. What impels the child to "improve" his speech at all remains something of a mystery. We can take "improve" simply to mean "bring into closer approximation to the speech of older persons around the child." It is surprising that there should be any mystery about the forces impelling improvement because it is just this aspect of the process that most people imagine that they understand. Surely the improvement is a response to selection pressures of various kinds; ill-formed or incomplete utterances must be less effective than well-formed and complete utterances in accomplishing the child's intent; parents probably approve of well-formed utterances and disapprove or correct the ill-formed. These ideas sound sensible and may be correct but the still scant evidence available does not support them.

At the end of Stage I the point was made that the child's constructions at this time were characterized by a seemingly lawless optional omission of every sort of major constituent including subjects, objects, verbs, locatives, and so on. The point was also made that omission seldom seemed to impede communication; the other person, usually the mother, being in the same situation and familiar with the child's stock of knowledge, understood correctly so far as one could tell, even the incomplete utterance. The suggestion was made that the Stage I child's speech was well adapted to his purposes, but that, as a speaker, he was very narrowly adapted. Speaking to strangers or of new experiences we guessed that he would have to learn to express obligatory constituents if he wanted to get his message across. And that may be the answer: the selection pressures to communicate may operate chiefly outside our sampling situation, which is typically the child at home with family members.

In Stage II we found that all the 14 grammatical morphemes were at first missing, then occasionally present in obligatory contexts, and after varying and often long periods of time, reliably present in such contexts. What makes the probability of supplying the requisite morpheme rise with time? It is surprisingly difficult to find cases in which omission resulted in incomprehension or misunderstanding. With respect to the definite and nondefinite articles it even looks as if listeners almost never really need them, and yet child speakers learn to operate with the exceedingly intricate rules governing their production. Adult Japanese, speaking English, do not seem to learn how to operate with the articles as we might expect they would if listeners needed them. Perhaps it is the case that the child automatically does this kind of learning but that adults do not.

Consider the Stage I child's unmarked generic verbs. In Stage II we made the point that parents regularly "glossed" these in one of four ways: as imperatives, past tense forms, present progressives, or imminent-intentional futures. It is an interesting fact of course that these are just the four modulations of the verb that the child then goes on first to learn to express. We have for years thought it possible that glosses or expansions of this type might be a major force impelling the child to improve his speech. However, all the evidence available, both naturalistic and experimental (it is summarized in Brown, Cazden, and Bellugi, 1969), offers no support at all for this notion. Cazden, for instance, carried out an experiment (1965) testing for the effect on young children's speech of deliberately interpolated expansions, introduced for a period on every preschool day for three months. She obtained no significant effect whatever. It is possible, I think, that such an experiment done now, with the information Stage II makes available, and expanding only by providing morphemes of a complexity for which the child was "ready," rather than as in Cazden's original experiment expanding in all possible ways, would show an effect. But no such experiment has been done, and so no impelling effect of expansion has been demonstrated.

Suppose we look at the facts of the parental glossing of Stage I generic verbs not as a possible tutorial device but rather as Slobin (1971b) has done; as evidence that the children already intended the meanings their parents attributed to them. In short, think of the parental glosses as veridical readings of the child's thought. From this point of view he has been correctly understood even though his utterances are incomplete. In that case there is no selection pressure. Why say more if what is being said works quite well?

To these observations of the seeming efficacy of the child's incomplete utterances, at least at home with the family, we should add the results of a study reported in Brown and Hanlon (1970). Here it was not primarily a question of the omission of obligatory forms but of the contrast between ill-formed primitive constructions and well-formed mature versions. For certain constructions, *yes-no* questions, tag questions, negatives, and *wh-* questions, Brown and Hanlon (1970) identified periods when Adam, Eve, and Sarah were producing both primitive and mature versions, sometimes the one, sometimes the other. The question was: did the mature version communicate more successfully than the primitive version? They first identified all instances of primitive and mature versions and then coded the adult responses for comprehending follow-up, calling comprehending responses "sequiturs" and uncomprehending or irrelevant responses "nonsequiturs." They found no evidence whatever of a difference in communicative efficacy and so once again no selection pressure. Why, one asks oneself, should the child learn the complex apparatus of tag questions when *right?* or *huh?* seem to do just the same job? Again one notes that adults learning English often do not learn tag questions, and the possibility again comes to mind that children operate on language in a way that adults do not.

Brown and Hanlon (1970) have done one other study that bears on the search for selection pressures. Once again it was syntactic well-formedness in contrast to ill-formedness that was in question rather than completeness or incompleteness. This time Brown and Hanlon started with two kinds of adult responses to child utterances: "approval" directed at an antecedent child utterance and "disapproval" directed at such an antecedent. The question then was: did the two sets of antecedents differ in syntactic correctness? Approving and disapproving responses are, certainly, very reasonable candidates for the respective roles, "positive reinforcer" and "punishment." They do not, of course, necessarily qualify as such because reinforcers and punishments are defined by their effects on performance (Skinner, 1953); they have no necessary, independent, nonfunctional properties. Still, of course, they are often put forward as plausible determinants of performance and are thought, generally, to function as such. In order to affect the child's syntax differentially, approval and disapproval must at a minimum be selectively governed by correct and incorrect syntax. If they should be so governed, further data would still be needed to show that they affect performance. If they are not so governed they cannot be a selection pressure working for correct speech. And Brown and Hanlon found that they are not. In general the parents seemed to pay no attention to bad syntax nor did they even seem to be aware of it. They approved or disapproved an utterance usually on the grounds of the truth value of the proposition which the parents supposed the child intended to assert. This is a surprising outcome to most middle-class parents, since they are generally under the impression that they correct the child's speech. From inquiry and observation I find that what parents generally correct is pronunciation, "naughty" words, and regularized irregular allomorphs liked *digged* or *goed*. These facts of the child's speech seem to penetrate parental awareness. But syntax — the child saying, for instance, "Why the dog won't eat?" instead of "Why won't the dog eat?" seems to be automatically set right in the parent's mind, with the mistake never registering as such.

In sum, then, we do not presently have evidence that there are selection pressures of any kind operating on children to impel them to bring their speech into line with adult models. It is, however, entirely possible that such pressures do operate in situations unlike the situations we have sampled, for instance, away from home or with strangers. It is also possible that one should look more closely at the small number of child utterances which turn up in most samples where the adult just does not seem to be able to make out what the child means. Perhaps these are the leading edge where the pressures operate. A radically different possibility is that children work out rules for the speech they hear, passing from levels of lesser to greater complexity, simply because the human species is programmed at a certain period in its life to operate in this fashion on linguistic input. Linguistic input would be defined by the universal properties of language. And the period of progressive rule extraction would correspond to Lenneberg's (1967) proposed "critical period." It may be chiefly adults who learn a new language in terms of selection pressures. Comparison of the kinds of errors made by adult second-language learners of English with the kinds made by child first-language learners of English should be enlightening.

7. Finally, I should like to predict that what de Villiers and de Villiers (1972) have discovered about "competence" and "performance" with respect to English word order in a small number of children will prove to be a general truth. Judgments of syntactic correctness and the setting right of incorrect sentences will not, I think, prove to be a royal road to the child's knowledge (or linguistic competence) but simply another performance. A performance which will generally, as in the case of word order, reflect knowledge of the structure of the language at a much later point than such other performances as spontaneous speech and discriminating response to minimally contrasting sentences. We shall find, I think, that there are multiple "levels" of knowledge of structure, as revealed by various kinds of performance, and that there is no clear reason to enthrone any one of these as the child's true competence. Some aspects of linguistic knowledge, as revealed in regularities of spontaneous speech, will not, I suspect, ever attain the judgmental level in the naive speaker. Prominent among these, perhaps, are the kinds of probabilities that Labov has found it necessary to enter into the rules describing Black English and other dialects. Beyond the level of judgment and correction is the level of rule formulation, and this is a level attained only by people who study linguistics.

References

Albert, Martin L. "Auditory Sequencing and Left Cerebral Dominance for Language." *Neuropsychologia,* in press.

Allen, William S. *Living English Structure.* London: Longmans Green, 1956.

Altmann, Stuart A. "The Structure of Primate Social Communication." In Stuart A. Altmann, ed., *Social Communication among Primates.* Chicago: University of Chicago Press, 1967, pp. 325–362.

Anisfeld, Moshe, Judith Barlow, and Catherine M. Frail. "Distinctive Features in the Pluralization Rules of English Speakers." *Language and Speech* (1968), *11*:31–37.

Anisfeld, Moshe, and Malcolm Gordon. "On the Psychophonological Structure of English Inflectional Rules." *Journal of Verbal Learning and Verbal Behavior* (1968), 7:973–979.

Anshen, Frank. "Speech Variation among Negroes in a Small Southern Community." Ph.D. diss. New York University, 1969.

Bailey, Beryl. *Jamaican Creole Syntax.* Cambridge, England: Cambridge University Press, 1966.

Bar-Adon, Aaron. "Primary Syntactic Structures in Hebrew Child Language." In Aaron Bar-Adon and Werner F. Leopold, eds., *Child Language: A Book of Readings.* Englewood Cliffs, N.J.: Prentice-Hall, 1971, pp. 433–472.

Bellugi, Ursula. *How Children Say No.* Cambridge, Mass.: M.I.T. Press, in press.

Berko, Jean. "The Child's Learning of English Morphology." *Word* (1958), *14*:150–177.

Bever, Thomas G. "The Cognitive Basis for Linguistic Structures." In John R. Hayes, ed., *Cognition and the Development of Language.* New York: Wiley, 1970, pp. 279–352.

————Jacques R. Mehler, and Virginia V. Valian. "Linguistic Capacity of Very Young Children." In Thomas G. Bever and William Weksel, eds., *The Acquisition of Structure.* New York: Holt, Rinehart, Winston, in press.

Blasdell, Richard, and Paul Jensen. "Stress and Word Position as Determinants of Imitation in First-Language Learners." *Journal of Speech and Hearing Research* (1970), 13:193–202.

Bloom, Lois. *Language Development: Form and Function in Emerging Grammars.* Cambridge, Mass.: M.I.T. Press, 1970.

————*One Word at a Time: The Use of Single Word Utterances before Syntax.* The Hague: Mouton, in press.

Blount, Ben G. "Acquisition of Language by Luo Children." Ph.D. diss. University of California, Berkeley, 1969.

Blumenthal, Arthur L. "Observations with Self-embedded Sentences." *Psychonomic Science* (1966), 6:453–454.

Bowerman, Melissa. *Early Syntactic Development: A Cross-linguistic Study with Special Reference to Finnish.* Cambridge, England: Cambridge University Press, in press.

Braine, Martin D. S. "The Ontogeny of English Phrase Structure: The First Phase." *Language* (1963), 39:1–14.

————"The Acquisition of Language in Infant and Child." In Carroll Reed, ed., *The Learning of Language.* New York: Appleton, 1971.

Brown, Roger. *Words and Things.* Glencoe, Ill.: Free Press, 1957.

————*Social Psychology.* New York: Free Press, 1965.

————"The First Sentences of Child and Chimpanzee." In Roger Brown, *Psycholinguistics*. New York: The Free Press, 1970, pp. 208–231.

Brown, Roger, and Ursula Bellugi. "Three Processes in the Acquisition of Syntax." *Harvard Educational Review* (1964), *34*:133–151.

Brown, Roger, and Colin Fraser. "The Acquisition of Syntax." In Charles N. Cofer and Barbara Musgrave, eds., *Verbal Behavior and Learning: Problems and Processes*. New York: McGraw-Hill, 1963, pp. 158–201.

Brown, Roger, Courtney Cazden, and Ursula Bellugi. "The Child's Grammar from I to III." In John P. Hill, ed., *Minnesota Symposia on Child Psychology,* Vol. II. Minneapolis: University of Minnesota Press, 1969, pp. 28–73.

Brown, Roger, Colin Fraser, and Ursula Bellugi. "Explorations in Grammar Evaluation." In Ursula Bellugi and Roger Brown, eds., *The Acquisition of Language* Monographs of the Society for Research in Child Development (1964), *29*. 92:79–92.

Brown, Roger, and Camille Hanlon. "Derivational Complexity and Order of Acquisition in Child Speech." In John R. Hayes, ed., *Cognition and the Development of Language*. New York: Wiley, 1970, pp. 155–207.

Bryant, Brenda, and Moshe Anisfeld. "Feedback Versus No-Feedback in Testing Children's Knowledge of English Pluralization Rules." *Journal of Experimental Child Psychology* (1969), *8*:250–255.

Burling, Robbins. "Language Development of a Garo and English Speaking Child." *Word* (1959), *15*:45–68.

Cazden, Courtney, B. Environmental Assistance to the Child's Acquisition of Grammar. Ph.D. diss. Harvard University, 1965.

————"The Acquisition of Noun and Verb Inflections." *Child Development* (1968), *39*:433–448.

Chafe, Wallace L. *Meaning and the Structure of Language*. Chicago: The University of Chicago Press, 1970.

Chao, Yuen R. "The Cantian Idiolect: An Analysis of the Chinese Spoken by a Twenty-Eight-Months-Old Child." In W. J. Fishel, ed., *Semitic and Oriental Studies*. University of California Publications in Semitic Philology, XI. Berkeley and Los Angeles: University of California Press, 1951.

Chomsky, Noam. *Syntactic Structures*. The Hague: Mouton, 1957.

————"Formal Discussion." In Ursula Bellugi and Roger Brown, eds., *The Acquisition of Language*. Monographs of the Society for Research in Child Development (1964), *29*. 92:35–39.

————*Aspects of the Theory of Syntax*. Cambridge, Mass.: M.I.T. Press, 1965.

————"The General Properties of Language." In Clark H. Millikan and Frederic L. Darley, eds., *Brain Mechanisms Underlying Speech and Language*. New York: Grune & Stratton, 1967, pp. 73–88.

————*Language and Mind*. New York: Harcourt, Brace & World, 1968.

————"Deep Structure, Surface Structure, and Semantic Interpretation." Bloomington, Indiana: Reproduced by the Indiana University Linguistics Club, January 1969.

————and Morris Halle. *The Sound Pattern of English*. New York: Harper and Row, 1968.

Clark, Herbert H. "Space, Time, Semantics and the Child." Paper presented at the Conference on Developmental Psycholinguistics at the University of New York, Buffalo, August 1971.

Copi, Irving M. *Symbolic Logic*. 3rd ed. New York: Macmillan, 1967.

Cromer, Richard F. The Development of Temporal Reference during the Acquisition of Language. Ph.D. diss. Harvard University, 1968.

De Laguna, Grace. *Speech: Its Function and Development*. New Haven: Yale University Press, 1927.

De Villiers, Jill G. "A Preliminary Investigation of Spatially Contrasting Terms in the Speech of the Two-Year-Old Child." Unpublished paper, Harvard University Psychology Department, Cambridge, Mass., 1971.

————and Peter A. de Villiers. "Development of the Use of the Word Order in Comprehension." Unpublished paper, Harvard University Psychology Department, Cambridge, Mass., 1971.

————"A Cross Sectional Study of the Development of Grammatical Morphemes in Child Speech." *Journal of Psycholinguistic Research,* in press.

De Villiers, Peter A., and Jill G. de Villiers. "Early Judgments of Semantic and Syntactic Acceptability by Children." *Journal of Psycholinguistic Research* (1972), 1:299–310.

Ervin, Susan M. "Imitation and Structural Change in Children's Language." In Eric H. Lenneberg, ed., *New Directions in the Study of Language*. Cambridge, Mass.: M.I.T. Press, 1964, pp. 163–189.

Feofanov, M. P. "Ob Uptreblenii Predlogóv v Detksoi Rechi" (On the use of prepositions in child speech). *Voprosy Psikhol.* (1958), No. 3, pp. 118–124.

Fillmore, Charles, J. "The Case for Case." In Emmon Bach and Robert T. Harms, eds., *Universals in Linguistic Theory*. New York: Holt, Rinehart, and Winston, 1968, pp. 1–87.

Fischer, John L. "Social Influences on the Choice of a Linguistic Variant." *Word* (1958), 14:47–56.

Flavell, John H. "Developmental Studies of Mediated Memory." In Hayne W. Reese and Lewis P. Lipsitt, eds., *Advances in Child Development and Behavior*. Vol. V. New York: Academic Press, 1970, pp. 181–211.

Fodor, Jerry, and Merrill Garrett. "Some Reflections on Competence and Performance." In John Lyons and Roger J. Wales, eds., *Psycholinguistics Papers*. Edinburgh: University of Edinburg Press, 1966, pp. 135–162.

Fraser, Colin. "Discussion of 'The Creation of Language.' " In John Lyons and Roger J. Wales, eds., *Psycholinguistics Papers*. Edinburgh: University of Edinburgh Press, 1966, pp. 115–120.

————Ursula Bellugi, and Roger Brown. "Control of Grammar in Imitation, Comprehension, and Production." *Journal of Verbal Learning and Verbal Behavior* (1963), 2:121–135.

Gardner, Beatrice T., and R. Allen Gardner. "Two-way Communication with an Infant Chimpanzee." In Allan Schrier and Fred Stollnitz, eds., *Behavior of Nonhuman Primates,* Vol. IV. New York: Academic Press, 1971, pp. 117–184.

Gardner, R. Allen and Beatrice T. Gardner. "Teaching Sign Language to a Chimpanzee." *Science* (1969), *165*:664–672.

Gleason, Henry A., Jr. *An Introduction to Descriptive Linguistics*. Rev. ed. New York: Holt, Rinehart, and Winston, 1961.

Gleitman, Lila R., and Henry Gleitman. *Phrase and Paraphrase*. New York: Norton, 1970.

Gleitman, Lila R., and Elizabeth F. Shipley. "The Emergence of the Child as

Grammarian." *Cognition: International Journal of Cognitive Psychology,* in press.

Goodglass, Harold, Jean Gleason, and Mary H. Hyde. "Some Dimensions of Auditory Language Comprehension." *Journal of Speech and Hearing Disorders* (1970), *13*:585–606.

Greenberg, Joseph H. "Some Universals of Grammar with Particular Reference to the Order of Meaningful Elements." In Joseph H. Greenberg, ed., *Universals of Language.* Cambridge, Mass.: M.I.T. Press, 1963, pp. 58–90.

Grégoire, Antoine, *L'Apprentissage du Langage: Les Deux Premières Années.* Paris: Librairie E. Droz, 1937.

Gruber, Jeffrey S. "Topicalization in Child Language." *Foundations of Language* (1967), *3, no.* 1:37–65.

Harris, Zellig S. *Methods in Structural Linguistics.* Chicago: University of Chicago Press, 1951.

Hayes, Keith J., and Catherine Hayes. "Intellectual Development of a Home-Raised Chimpanzee." *Proceedings of the American Philosophical Society* (1951), *95*:105–109.

Hockett, Charles F. *A Course in Modern Linguistics.* New York: Macmillan, 1958.

———"Logical Considerations in the Study of Animal Communication." In Wesley E. Lanyon and William N. Tavolga, eds., *Animal Sounds and Animal Communication.* Washington, D.C.: American Institute of Biological Sciences, 1960, pp. 392–430.

Inoue, Kazouko. *A Study of Japanese Syntax.* The Hague: Mouton, 1969.

Jacobs, Roderick A., and Peter S. Rosenbaum. *English Transformational Grammar.* Waltham, Mass.: Blaisdell, 1968.

Jakobson, Roman. *Kindersprache, Aphasie, und allgemeine Lautgesetze.* Upsala: Almqvist and Wiksell, 1941. English translation by Allan R. Keiler, *Child Language, Aphasia and General Sound Laws.* The Hague: Mouton, 1968.

Joos, Martin. *The English Verb: Form and Meanings.* Madison: University of Wisconsin Press, 1964.

Jorden, Eleanor H. *Beginning Japanese,* Parts 1 and 2. New Haven: Yale University Press, 1963.

Karttunen, Lauri. "What do Referential Indices Refer to?" Paper prepared for Linguistics Colloquium, University of California, Los Angeles, April 26, 1968a.

———"What makes Definite Noun Phrases Definite?" Rand Corporation, June, 1968b.

Katz, Jerrold J. "Recent Issues in Semantic Theory." *Foundations of Language* (1967), 3:124–194.

———and Jerry A. Fodor. "The Structure of a Semantic Theory." *Language* (1963), *39*:170–210.

Katz, Jerrold J., and Paul M. Postal. *An Integrated Theory of Linguistic Descriptions.* Cambridge, Mass.: M.I.T. Press, 1964.

Kean, John M., and Kaoru Yamamoto. "Grammar Signals and Assignment of Words to Parts of Speech among Young Children: An Exploration." *Journal of Verbal Learning and Verbal Behavior* (1965), 4:323–326.

Kellogg, Winthrop N. "Communication and Language in the Home-Raised Chimpanzee." *Science* (1968), 162:423–427.

———and Louise A. Kellogg. *The Ape and the Child.* New York: McGraw-Hill, 1933.

Kernan, Claudia Mitchell. "Language Behavior in a Black Urban Community." Ph.D. diss. University of California, Berkeley, 1969.

Kernan, Keith T. "The Acquisition of Language by Samoan Children." Ph.D. diss. University of California, Berkeley, 1969.

Klima, Edward. "Negation in English." In Jerry A. Fodor and Jerrold J. Katz, eds., *The Structure of Language: Readings in the Philosophy of Language.* Englewood Cliffs, N.J.: Prentice-Hall, 1964, pp. 246–323.

Labov, William. *The Social Stratification of English in New York City.* Washington, D.C.: Center for Applied Linguistics, 1966.

————"Contraction, Deletion, and Inherent Variability of the English Copula." *Language* (1969), *45*:715–762.

————"The Study of Language in Its Social Context." *Studium Generale* (1970), *23*:30–87.

Lahey, Margaret. "The Role of Prosody and Syntactic Markers in Children's Comprehension of Spoken Sentences." Dissertation prospectus. Teachers College, Columbia University, New York, 1971.

Lakoff, George. "Stative Adjectives and Verbs in English." The Computation Laboratory of Harvard University Mathematical Linguistics and Automatic Translation, Report No. NSF–17, 1966, pp. I–1, I–16.

Lenneberg, Eric H. "A Biological Perspective of Language." In Eric H. Lenneberg, ed., *New Directions in the Study of Language.* Cambridge, Mass.: M.I.T. Press, 1964, pp. 65–88.

————*Biological Foundations of Language.* New York: Wiley, 1967.

Leopold, Werner F. *Speech Development of a Bilingual Child: A Linguist's Record,* Vol. III, *Grammar and General Problems in the First Two Years.* Evanston, Ill.: Northwestern University Press, 1949.

Long, Ralph B. *The Sentence and Its Parts: A Grammar of Contemporary English.* Chicago: University of Chicago Press, 1961.

Lovell, Kenneth, and E. M. Dixon. "The Growth of the Control of Grammar in Imitation, Comprehension, and Production." *Journal of Child Psychology and Psychiatry* (1965), *5*:1–9.

Macnamara, John. "Cognitive Basis of Language Learning in Infants." *Psychological Review* (1972), *79*:1–14.

Maratsos, Michael P. "The Use of Definite and Indefinite Reference in Young Children." Ph.D. diss. Harvard University, 1971.

McCall, Elizabeth A. "A Generative Grammar of Sign." M.A. diss. University of Iowa, 1965.

McCawley, James. "Concerning the Base Component of a Transformational Grammar." *Foundations of Language* (1968a), *4*:243–269.

————"The Role of Semantics in Grammar." In Emmon Bach and Robert Harms, eds., *Universals in Linguistic Theory.* New York: Holt, Rinehart, and Winston, 1968b, pp. 124–169.

McNeill, David. "The Creation of Language by Children." In John Lyons and Roger J. Wales, eds., *Psycholinguistics Papers.* Edinburgh: University of Edinburgh Press, 1966a, pp. 99–132.

————"Developmental Psycholinguistics." In Frank Smith and George Miller, eds., *The Genesis of Language: A Psycholinguistic Approach.* Cambridge, Mass.: M.I.T. Press, 1966b, pp. 15–84.

————*The Acquisition of Language: The Study of Developmental Psycholinguistics.* New York: Harper and Row, 1970a.

————"The Development of Language." In Paul Mussen, ed., *Carmichael's Manual of Child Psychology,* Vol. I. New York: Wiley, 1970b, pp. 1061–1161.

————and Nobuko B. McNeill. "What Does a Child Mean When He Says 'No'?" In E. M. Zale, ed., *Language and Language Behavior.* New York: Appleton-Century-Crofts, 1968, pp. 51–62.

Menyuk, Paula. "A Preliminary Evaluation of Grammatical Capacity in Children." *Journal of Verbal Learning and Verbal Behavior* (1963a), 2:429–439.

————"Syntactic Structures in the Language of Children." *Child Development* (1963b), 34:407–422.

————"Alternation of Rules in Children's Grammar." *Journal of Verbal Learning and Verbal Behavior* (1964a), 3:408–488.

————"Comparison of Grammar of Children with Functionally Deviant and Normal Speech." *Journal of Speech and Hearing Research.* (1964b), 7:109–121.

————*Sentences Children Use.* Cambridge, Mass.: M.I.T. Press, 1969.

————*The Acquisition and Development of Language.* Englewood Cliffs, N.J.: Prentice-Hall, 1971.

————and Nancy Bernholz. "Prosodic Features and Children's Language Productions." *Quarterly Progress Report* No. 93, M.I.T. Research Laboratory of Electronics. Cambridge, Mass., 1969, pp. 216–219.

Mikeš Melanija. Acquisition des Catégories Grammaticales dans le Langage de l'Enfant." *Enfance* (1967), 20:289–298.

————and Plemenka Vlahović. "Razvoy Gramatickih Kategorija u Dečjem Govoru" (The development of grammatical categories in child speech). *Prilozi Proučavanju Jezika, II.* Novi Sad, Yugoslavia, 1966.

Miller, George A., and David McNeill. "Psycholinguistics." In Gardner Lindzey and Elliott Aronson, eds., *The Handbook of Social Psychology,* Vol. III, 2nd ed. Reading, Mass.: Addison-Wesley, 1969, pp. 666–794.

Miller, Wick, and Susan Ervin. "The Development of Grammar in Child Language." In Ursula Bellugi and Roger Brown, eds., *The Acquisition of Language.* Monographs of the Society for Research in Child Development (1964), 29. 92⟨9–34.

Niwa Tamako, and Matsuda Mayako. *Basic Japanese for College Students.* Seattle, Washington: University of Washington Press, 1969.

Olivier, Donald C. "Stochastic Grammars and Language Acquisition Devices." Ph.D. diss. Harvard University, 1968.

Park, Tschang-Zin. "The Acquisition of German Syntax." Unpublished paper. University of Bern, Switzerland, Psychological Institute, 1970a.

————"Language Acquisition in a Korean Child." Unpublished paper. University of Bern, Switzerland, Psychological Institute, 1970b.

Pfungst, Oskar. *Clever Hans (The Horse of Mr. Von Osten).* First English edition, 1911. New York: Holt, Rinehart, Winston, 1965.

Piaget, Jean. *The Origins of Intelligence in Children.* (1st ed., 1936.) New York: International Universities Press, 1952.

——*The Construction of Reality in the Child.* (1st ed., 1937.) New York: Basic
Books, 1954.

——*Play, Dreams, and Imitation in Childhood.* (1st ed., 1945.) New York:
Norton, 1962.

Ploog, Detlev, and Theodore Melnechuk. "Are Apes Capable of Language?" *Neurosciences
Research Program Bulletin* (1971), Vol. *9*, No. 5.

Popova, M. I. "Grammaticheskie Elementy Yazyka v Rechi Detei Preddoshkol 'nogo
Vozrasta" (Grammatical elements of language in the speech of pre-school children).
Voprosy Psikhol. (1958), No. 3:106–117.

Premack, David. "The Education of Sarah." *Psychology Today* (September 1970a)
4:54–58.

——"A Functional Analysis of Language." *Journal of the Experimental Analysis of
Behavior* (1970b), *14*:107–125.

——"Language in Chimpanzee?" *Science* (1971), 172:808–822.

Preston, M. S., Grace Yeni-Komshian, and Rachel E. Stark. "Voicing in Initial Stop
Consonants Produced by Children in the Prelinguistic Period from Different
Language Communities." *Annual Report Neuro Communications Laboratory.*
Baltimore, Md.: The Johns Hopkins Hospital, 1967.

Quine, Willard V. O. *Word and Object.* Cambridge, Mass.: M.I.T. Press, 1960.

Reichenbach, Hans. *Elements of Symbolic Logic.* New York: Macmillan, 1947.

Rosenbaum, Peter S. *The Grammar of English Predicate Complement Constructions.*
Cambridge, Mass.: M.I.T. Press, 1967.

Rūke-Dravina, V. *Zur Sprachentwicklung bei Kleinkindern: I. Syntax.* Lund: Häkan
Ohlssons Boktrycheri, 1963.

Rydin, Ingegard. "A Swedish Child in the Beginning of Syntactic Development and Some
Cross-Linguistic Comparisons." Unpublished paper, 1971. On file with Roger
Brown, Harvard University, Cambridge, Mass.

Schlesinger, I. M. "Production of Utterances and Language Acquisition." In Dan I. Slobin,
ed., *The Ontogenesis of Grammar.* New York: Academic Press, 1971, pp. 63–101.

Scholes, Robert J. "The Role of Grammaticality in the Imitation of Word Strings by
Children and Adults." *Journal of Verbal Learning and Verbal Behavior* (1969),
8:225–228.

——"On Functors and Contentives in Children's Imitations of Word Strings." *Journal
of Verbal Learning and Verbal Behavior* (1970), *9*:167–170.

Shipley, Elizabeth F., Carlota S. Smith, and Lila R. Gleitman. "A Study of the Acquisition
of Language: Free Responses to Commands." *Language* (1969), *45*:322–342.

Shirato, Ichiro. *Conversation Manual; Japanese.* New York: Crown, 1962.

Sinclair-de-Zwart, Hermina. "Developmental Psycholinguistics." In David Elkind and
John H. Flavell, eds., *Studies in Cognitive Development: Essays in Honor of
Jean Piaget.* New York: Oxford University Press, 1969, pp. 315–336.

Skinner, B. F. *Science and Human Behavior.* New York: Macmillan, 1953.

——*Verbal Behavior.* New York: Appleton-Century-Crofts, 1957.

——"Two 'Synthetic Social Relations.' " *Journal of the Experimental Analysis of
Behavior* (1962), *5*:531–533.

Slobin, Dan I. "The Acquisition of Russian as a Native Language." In Frank Smith and
George A. Miller, eds., *The Genesis of Language.* Cambridge, Mass.: M.I.T. Press,
1966, pp. 129–148.

————*A Field Manual for Cross-Cultural Study of the Acquisition of Communicator Competence.* Berkeley: University of California Press, 1967.

————"Universals of Grammatical Development in Children." Working paper No. 22. Language Research Laboratory, University of California, Berkeley, 1969.

————"Data for the Symposium." In Dan I. Slobin, ed., *The Ontogenesis of Grammar.* New York: Academic Press, 1971a, pp. 3–14.

————"Developmental Psycholinguistics." In William Orr Dingwall, ed., *A Survey of Linguistic Science.* College Park, Maryland: William Orr Dingwall, Linguistics Program, University of Maryland, 1971b, pp. 279–410.

Smith, Joshua. "The Development and Structure of Holophrases." Unpublished honors thesis. Department of Linguistics, Harvard University, 1970.

Solomon, D. "The Sytem of Predication in the Speech of Trinidad." M.A. thesis. Columbia University, 1966.

Stokoe, Jr., William C., Dorothy C. Casterline, and Carl G. Croneberg. *A Dictionary of American Sign Language on Linguistic Principles.* Washington, D.C.: Gallandet College Press, 1965.

Stolz, Walter S. "A Study of the Ability to Decode Grammatically Novel Sentences." *Journal of Verbal Learning and Verbal Behavior* (1967), 6:867–873.

Strawson, P. F. *Introduction to Logical Theory.* London: Methuen, 1952.

Terman, Lewis. *The Measurement of Intelligence.* Cambridge, Mass.: Riverside, 1916.

Tolbert, Kathryn. "Pepe Joy: Learning to Talk in Mexico." Unpublished paper, 1971. On file with Roger Brown, Harvard University, Cambridge, Mass.

Twaddell, William F. *The English Verb Auxiliaries.* Providence: Brown University Press, 1963.

Tyler, Leona E. *The Psychology of Human Differences.* 3rd ed. New York: Appleton-Century-Crofts, 1965.

Vygotsky, Lev S. *Thought and Language.* (1st ed., 1934.) Cambridge, Mass.: M.I.T. Press, 1962.

Weinreich, Uriel. "Explorations in Semantic Theory." In Thomas A. Sebeok, ed., *Current Trends in Linguistics,* Vol. III, *Theoretical Foundations.* The Hague: Mouton, 1966, pp. 395–477.

Weir, Ruth. "Some Questions on the Child's Learning of Phonology." In Frank Smith and George A. Miller, eds., *The Genesis of Language.* Cambridge, Mass.: M.I.T. Press, 1966, pp. 153–168.

Wolfram, Walter. *A Sociolinguistic Description of Detroit Negro Speech.* Urban language series, 5. Washington, D.C.: Center for Applied Linguistics, 1969.

Yamagiwa, Joseph K. *Modern Conversational Japanese.* New York: McGraw-Hill, 1942.

Zakharova, A. V. "Usvoenie doshkol'nikami padeshnykh form" (Mastery by preschoolers of forms of grammatical case). *Doklady Akad. Pedag. Nauk* RSFSR (1958), No. 3:81–84.

Index

A. *See* Articles *a* and *the*

Accusative: pronouns in relation to case grammar, 141–142

Action-locative: in Stage I, 173–187; definition and children manifesting, 194–195; facts to be in Stage I grammar, 202–209

Action-object, 114, 119; in Stage I, 173–187; definition and children manifesting, 193; facts to be in Stage I grammar, 202–209

Adam, an American child: basic statistics, 66, 86, 99, 106, 120; grammatical relations in early samples, 123–126; and holophrases, 129; his use of *its,* 142, 265, 391–392, 395; spontaneous word order, 156; and cumulative complexity, 186–187; on nonexistence, 192; and separable verbs, 211; his parents not modeling Black English, 381; his use of *that-a,* 392–394, 395

Adam, Eve, and Sarah, American children: design of the study, 51–59; MLU's at start, 65; basic statistics, 66; and telegraphic speech, 78; and pivot grammar, 94–95, 100–101; prevalent relations, 173–187; and *yes-no* questions in Stage I, 180; and *wh-* questions in Stage I, 181; on action-locative, 194–195; combined as corpus for late Stage I grammar, 201–202; and complexity limits, 236; grammatical morphemes starting in Stage II, 249; gross change over time in use of grammatical morphemes, 255–256; acquisition criterion for grammatical morphemes, 258; order of acquisition for 14 morphemes, 270–271; semantics of progressive, 316–318, 324; correct examples of articles, 351–352; errors with articles, 353–355; contractible copulas, 365. *See also* Adam; Eve; Sarah

Adaptation, linguistic, of child, 167–168; 241–242; conclusions, 410

Adjectives: as verbs, 138

Agent: defined, 8, 112, 122–123; defined in case grammar, 133; employed in case grammar 134–143; and sensorimotor intelligence, 200; facts to be in Stage I grammar, 202–209; in Stage I case grammar, 218–226

Agent-action, 110, 114, 116, 119; in Stage I, 173–187; in combinations, 177; high frequency in Stage I, 179; and sensorimotor

intelligence, 200; facts to be in Stage I grammar, 202–209. *See also* Subject of a sentence; Subject-object

Agent-object, 110, 114, 115, 116; discriminating contrast, 158–161; definition and children manifesting, 193–194; and sensorimotor intelligence, 200; facts to be in Stage I grammar, 202–209. *See also* Subject of a sentence; Subject-object

Akinyi, a Luo child: basic statistics, 70, 73; and telegraphic speech, 79

Albert, Martin L., 164–165, 166

Allen, William S., 322

Allomorphs, irregular: past, 260; third person singular present indicative, 260; plural, 261; copula and auxiliary *be,* 267–269; parent frequencies, 359–361

Allomorphs, regular: progressive, 259–260; past, 260; third person singular present indicative, 260; plural, 261; possessive, 262; productive elicitation of, 282–288; voicing rules, phonological, inflectional, for individual inflections, 285–289, 293; parent frequencies, 359–361; parent frequencies and children's acquisition order, 365

Altmann, Stuart, L., 35

American Sign Language: and Washoe, 33, 39–43

Anderson, Samuel, 52

Andrew, an American child: basic statistics, 66–69; and telegraphic speech, 79; and pivot grammar, 91–92, 95–96, 100–101, 119; on nonexistence, 191

Angela, a German child: basic statistics, 70–71; and productivity, 98; spontaneous word order, 156, 158

Animate: in case grammar, 135–136; not represented in Stage I grammar, 212

Anisfeld, Moshe, 285, 287, 290, 291. *See also* Productive elicitation of morphemes

Anshen, Frank, 259

Aoko, a Luo child: basic statistics, 70, 73; and telegraphic speech, 79

Apes, linguistic capacity of. *See* Chimpanzees, linguistic capacity of

Aphasic word sequencing, 164–165

Archisegment of plural morpheme, 287–288

Articles *a* and *the,* 13, 80, 195; specific-nonspecific, 251, 264; scoring for acquistion,